A+ GUIDE TO PC OPERATING SYSTEMS

Michael W. Graves

THOMSON

DELMAR LEARNING

Australia • Canada • Mexico • Singapore • Spain • United Kingdom • United States

THOMSON

DELMAR LEARNING

A+ Guide to PC Operating Systems

by Michael W. Graves

Vice President, Technology and Trades SBU:
Alar Elken

Editorial Director:
Sandy Clark

Senior Acquistions Editor:
Stephen Helba

Senior Channel Manager:
Dennis Williams

Senior Development Editor:
Michelle Ruelos Cannistraci

Marketing Director:
Dave Garza

Marketing Coordinator:
Casey Bruno

Production Director:
Mary Ellen Black

Production Manager:
Larry Main

Senior Project Editor:
Christopher Chien

Art/Design Coordinator:
Francis Hogan

Senior Editorial Assistant:
Dawn Daugherty

Library of Congress Card Number: 2004113844

A+ Guide to PC Operating Systems /
Michael W. Graves

ISBN: 1-4018-52491

NOTICE TO THE READER

Publisher does not warrant or guarantee any of the products described herein or perform any independent analysis in connection with any of the product information contained herein. Publisher does not assume, and expressly disclaims, any obligation to obtain and include information other than that provided to it by the manufacturer.

The reader is expressly warned to consider and adopt all safety precautions that might be indicated by the activities herein and to avoid all potential hazards. By following the instructions contained herein, the reader willingly assumes all risks in connection with such instructions.

The publisher makes no representation or warranties of any kind, including but not limited to, the warranties of fitness for particular purpose or merchantability, nor are any such representations implied with respect to the material set forth herein, and the publisher takes no responsibility with respect to such material. The publisher shall not be liable for any special, consequential, or exemplary damages resulting, in whole or part, from the readers' use of, or reliance upon, this material.

TABLE OF CONTENTS

PREFACE

The computer industry is far and away one of the fastest moving industries in the nation today. By the time one technology is just getting its feet off the ground, a new one is coming along to replace it. That's one of the reasons that CompTIA's A+ Certification Exam is updated frequently.

This certification requires that the candidate pass two different exams before becoming certified. These exams are the Core Hardware Exam and the Operating Systems Technologies Exam. The author's book *The A+ Guide to PC Hardware Maintenance and Repair* covers the material tested on the Core Hardware Exam. This book prepares the student for the Operating Systems Technologies Exam.

Using an upbeat, conversational tone to help engage readers' interest, the A+ Series by Michael Graves is written by an experienced teacher as well as a seasoned field technician. Not only does the author know the theory; he knows the practical applications and teaches what works and what does not work.

ORGANIZATION

Throughout its history, CompTIA has prided itself on being vendor neutral. The OS Exam is one exam in which the organization makes an exception. Only Microsoft products are covered. As such, Microsoft receives the majority of ink in this book.

The first chapter starts off with the underlying concepts of operating systems and how they work. This chapter is followed by two chapters of historical significance that receive minor coverage on the exam. These chapters cover DOS and Windows 3.x versions. Don't be too anxious to skip them by, however, because much of the material presented in these chapters comes into play in later chapters.

After the history lessons are reviewed, the text provides systematic coverage of the operating systems covered on the exam, in the order in which they were released. Each new OS is introduced by discussing what is new and different from the preceding operating system. After that comes a detailed discussion of the OS in general, including material concerning the user interface, OS architecture, and any relevant material surrounding configuration issues.

The last few chapters of the book cover networking, troubleshooting, and connecting computers to the Internet. In addition, the reader is given a brief introduction to Linux. Although that operating system will not be covered on the exam, Linux has gone from being the resident operating system on under 2 percent of the desktops worldwide to nearly 10 percent.

FEATURES

As you browse through the pages of *The A+ Guide to PC Operating Systems*, a few key qualities should pop out at you right away. The organization of the chapters is such that the reader is taken on a tour of operating systems from the early days of the PC all the way to the current day of Windows XP. While many A+ certification manuals concentrate only on the minimum information necessary to pass the exam, *The A+ Guide to PC Operating Systems* goes several steps further and provides insight into the underlying architecture of the operating systems, internetworking, and troubleshooting beyond the minimum.

The text includes the following features:

1. A+ Objectives mapped to the textbook are placed in the Introduction.

2. Each chapter begins with a list identifying the **Objectives** to be covered for the A+ Operating Systems Technologies Exam.

3. Computer technology is full of acronyms and technical terms that you need to understand, so each chapter integrates **Buzzwords, Tricky Terminology**, and **Acronym Alerts** to introduce and reinforce key terminology.

4. **Exam Notes** for the student are given throughout the text providing helpful hints in preparing for the A+ Exam.

5. A **Chapter Summary** offers a quick refresher and reviews key points from the text.

6. Each chapter concludes with two sets of questions, called **Brain Drain** and **64K$ Questions.** The first set is a series of challenging, essay-oriented questions, and the second set consists of a set of 20 multiple-choice, true/false, and short answer review questions.

7. A comprehensive **Glossary** and **Answers to Odd-Numbered Questions** are placed at the end of the book.

8. A **CD** placed in the back of the book includes **sample video clips** from the *Mastering the A+ Exam DVD Series* and **additional practice test questions.**

SUPPLEMENTS

Lab Manual. The OS Lab Manual consists of 14 Lab Exercises that involve the installation and/or configuration of WIN9x, WIN2K, and WINXP. In addition, students will explore the various tools provided by Microsoft for OS management and troubleshooting. Toward the end, readers will set up their own peer-to-peer network. (ISBN: 1401852531)

Instructor's CD. Textbook solutions and practice test questions are available on this CD-ROM. (ISBN: 1401852521)

A+ DVD Series: Mastering the A+ Exam. This comprehensive, five-part DVD series of 20 videos has been designed to assist viewers in preparing for the current A+ Exam. (ISBN: 1401858880)

ACKNOWLEDGMENTS

The Author and Thomson Delmar Learning would like to thank the following reviewers:

Shaikh Ali, City College, Fort Lauderdale, FL

Billy Graham, Northwest Technical Institute, Springdale, AR

Roger Peterson, Northland Community and Technical College, Thief River Falls, MN

Paul Wilson, DeVry University, Fremont, CA

A+ OPERATING SYSTEM TECHNOLOGIES

INTRODUCTION

CompTIA's A+ certification program is an extensive testing program designed to demonstrate the examinees' proficiency working with personal computers. In order to achieve full certification, the examinee must pass two exams. The first is the A+ Core Hardware examination. Material for this exam can be obtained in *The A+ Guide to PC Hardware Maintenance and Repair* by this same author.

The book you have in your hands prepares the candidate for the Operating System Technologies examination. This exam measures essential operating system competencies for an entry-level IT professional or PC service technician. This is not intended to be a "paper certification." It is assumed that candidates who attempt the exam go in with the equivalent knowledge of at least 500 hours of hands-on experience in the lab or field.

While the vast majority of CompTIA's certification programs are vendor neutral, this is one exam where it makes an exception. Operating systems covered on the exam include Microsoft products, including Windows versions 95, 98, 98SE, Me, 2000, and XP. Non-Microsoft operating systems are not covered.

The Operating System Technologies exam has been broken down into four different categories CompTIA calls domains. These domains are not given equal treatment or exposure on the exam. **Table I.1** itemizes the four domains and their relative predominance on the exam.

Each domain is subsequently broken down into a series of objectives. These objectives represent areas of knowledge for which CompTIA assumes the entry-level technician should be able to demonstrate adequate knowledge. The rest of this introduction, which lists more specifically the content that will be covered in each domain, has been extracted from the information available on CompTIA's Web site at www.comptia.org. I have added to the list chapters where you will find information addressing each objective.

Table I.1   OS Technologies Exam Domains

Domain	Percent of Examination
1.0 Operating System Fundamentals	28%
2.0 Installation, Configuration, and Upgrading	31%
3.0 Diagnosing and Troubleshooting	25%
4.0 Networks	16%
Total	**100%**

CompTIA A+ Operating System Objectives

DOMAIN 1: OPERATING SYSTEM FUNDAMENTALS

1.1 IDENTIFY THE MAJOR DESKTOP COMPONENTS AND INTERFACES AND THEIR FUNCTIONS. DIFFERENTIATE THE CHARACTERISTICS OF WINDOWS 9X/ME, WINDOWS NT 4.0 WORKSTATION, WINDOWS 2000 PROFESSIONAL, AND WINDOWS XP.

Content may include the following:

- Contrasts between Windows 9x/Me, Windows NT 4.0 Workstation, Windows 2000 Professional, and Windows XP (Chapters Four, Five, Six, Seven, Eight, Nine, Ten, and Eleven)
- Major operating system components (Chapters One, Two, Six, Eight, Ten, and Eleven)
  - Registry (Chapter Five)
  - Virtual memory (Chapters Three, Five, Eight, and Eleven)
  - File system (Chapters One, Five, Six, and Eleven)
- Major operating system interfaces (Chapters One, Two, Three, Four, Six, Eight, and Eleven)
  - Windows Explorer (Chapter Four)
  - My Computer (Chapters Four and Ten)
  - Control Panel (Chapters Four and Ten)
  - Computer Management Console (Chapter Twelve)
  - Accessories/System tools (Chapters Four, Five, Nine, and Eleven)
  - Command line (Chapter Three)
  - Network Neighborhood/My Network Places (Chapters Five and Ten)
  - Task Bar/Systray (Chapter Five)
  - Start Menu (Chapters Five, Nine, and Eleven)
  - Device Manager (Chapters Five, Nine, and Eleven)

1.2 IDENTIFY THE NAMES, LOCATIONS, PURPOSES, AND CONTENTS OF MAJOR SYSTEM FILES.

Content may include the following:

- Windows 9x specific files (Chapter Four)
  - IO.SYS
  - MSDOS.SYS
  - AUTOEXEC.BAT
  - COMMAND.COM
  - CONFIG.SYS
  - HIMEM.SYS
  - EMM386.exe
  - WIN.COM
  - SYSTEM.INI
  - WIN.INI
  - Registry data files (Chapter Four)
    SYSTEM.DAT
    USER.DAT
- Windows NT specific files (Chapters Six and Seven)
  - BOOT.INI
  - NTLDR
  - NTDETECT.COM
  - NTBOOTDD.SYS
  - NTUSER.DAT
  - Registry data files (Chapters Four and Six)

1.3 DEMONSTRATE THE ABILITY TO USE COMMAND-LINE FUNCTIONS AND UTILITIES TO MANAGE THE OPERATING SYSTEM, INCLUDING THE PROPER SYNTAX AND SWITCHES.

Command line functions and utilities include:

- Command/CMD (Chapters Four and Six)
- DIR (Chapter Two)
- ATTRIB (Chapter Two)
- VER (Chapter Two)
- MEM (Chapter Two)
- SCANDISK (Chapter Four)

- DEFRAG (Chapter Four)
- EDIT (Chapter Two)
- XCOPY (Chapter Two)
- COPY (Chapter Two)
- FORMAT (Chapter Two)
- FDISK (Chapter Two)
- SETVER (Chapter Two)
- SCANREG (Chapter Five)
- MD/CD/RD (Chapter Two)
- DELETE/RENAME (Chapter Two)
- DELTREE (Chapter Two)
- TYPE (Chapter Two)
- ECHO (Chapter Two)
- SET (Chapter Two)
- PING (Chapter Thirteen)

1.4 IDENTIFY BASIC CONCEPTS AND PROCEDURES FOR CREATING, VIEWING, AND MANAGING DISKS, DIRECTORIES, AND FILES. THIS INCLUDES PROCEDURES FOR CHANGING FILE ATTRIBUTES AND THE RAMIFICATIONS OF THOSE CHANGES (FOR EXAMPLE, SECURITY ISSUES).

Content may include the following:

- Disks
    - Partitions (Chapters One, Eight, and Eleven)
        - Active Partition (Chapter One)
        - Primary Partition (Chapter One)
        - Extended Partition (Chapter One)
        - Logical Partition (Chapters One and Eleven)
    - Files systems
        - FAT16 (Chapter One)
        - FAT32 (Chapter One)
        - NTFS4 (Chapters One and Six)
        - NTFS5.x (Chapters One and Eleven)
- Directory structures (root directory, subdirectories, etc.) (Chapter One)
    - Create folders (Chapter Five, Lab Manual)
    - Navigate the directory structure (Chapters One and Five, Lab Manual)
    - Maximum depth (Chapter One)

■ Files (Chapter One)

   ■ Creating files (Chapters One and Five, Lab Manual)

   ■ File naming conventions (Most common extensions, 8.3, maximum length) (Chapter One)

   ■ File attributes (Read Only, Hidden, System, and Archive attributes) (Chapter One)

   ■ File compression (Chapters One, Five, and Nine)

   ■ File encryption (Chapters Nine and Eleven)

   ■ File permissions (Chapter Six)

   ■ File types (text vs. binary file) (Chapter One)

1.5 IDENTIFY THE MAJOR OPERATING SYSTEM UTILITIES, THEIR PURPOSE, LOCATION, AND AVAILABLE SWITCHES.

Content may include the following:

   ■ Disk management tools

      DEFRAG.EXE (Chapters Five and Lab Manual)

      FDISK.EXE (Chapter One, Lab Manual)

      Backup/Restore Utilities (MSbackup, NTBackup, etc.) (Chapters Five, Six, Nine, and Eleven)

      ScanDisk (Chapter Five, Lab Manual)

      CHKDSK (Chapters Two and Five, Lab Manual)

      Disk Cleanup (Chapter Five, Lab Manual)

      Format (Chapter One, Lab Manual)

   ■ System management tools

      Device Manager (Chapters Five and Eleven, Lab Manual)

      System Monitor (Chapter Five)

      Computer Manager (Chapter Nine)

      MSCONFIG.EXE (Chapter Five, Lab Manual)

      REGEDIT.EXE (View information/Backup registry) (Chapter Four)

      REGEDT32.EXE (Chapter Four, Lab Manual)

      SYSEDIT.EXE (Chapter Four, Lab Manual)

      SCANREG (Chapter Two, Lab Manual)

      COMMAND/CMD (Chapters Two and Four, Lab Manual)

      Event Viewer (Chapter Eight, Lab Manual)

      Task Manager (Chapter Five, Lab Manual)

   ■ File management tools

ATTRIB.EXE (Chapter Two)

EXTRACT.EXE (Lab Manual)

EDIT.COM (Chapter Two)

Windows Explorer (Chapters Five, Six, Nine, and Eleven)

DOMAIN 2: INSTALLATION, CONFIGURATION AND UPGRADING

2.1 IDENTIFY THE PROCEDURES FOR INSTALLING WINDOWS 9X/ME, WINDOWS NT 4.0 WORKSTATION, WINDOWS 2000 PROFESSIONAL, AND WINDOWS XP AND BRINGING THE OPERATING SYSTEM TO A BASIC OPERATIONAL LEVEL.

Content may include the following:

- Verify hardware compatibility and minimum requirements (Chapters Four, Six, Eight, and Eleven)
- Determine OS installation options (Chapters Six, Nine, and Eleven)
  - Installation type (typical, custom, other) (Chapter Six, Lab Manual)
  - Network configuration (Chapters Six, Nine, and Eleven, Lab Manual)
  - File system type (Chapters One, Nine, and Eleven)
  - Dual boot support (Chapter Six, Lab Manual)
- Disk preparation order (conceptual disk preparation) (Chapters Six and Nine, Lab Manual)
  - Start the installation (Chapters Five, Six, and Nine, Lab Manual)
  - Partition (Chapters One, Two, Five, and Nine, Lab Manual)
  - Format drive (Chapters One, Two, Five, and Nine, Lab Manual)
- Run appropriate setup utility (Chapters Two, Five, Nine, and Eleven, Lab Manual)
  - Setup (Chapters One, Two, Five, and Nine, Lab Manual)
  - Winnt (Chapter Six)
- Installation methods (Chapters Five, Six, and Nine, Lab Manual)
  - Bootable CD (Chapters Five and Nine, Lab Manual)
  - Boot floppy (Chapters Five and Six, Lab Manual)
  - Network installation (Chapters Six and Eleven)
  - Drive imaging (Lab Manual)
- Device driver configuration (Chapters One, Two, Four, Five, Six, Nine, and Eleven, Lab Manual)
  - Load default drivers (Chapters Five and Nine)
  - Find updated drivers (Lab Manual)

- Restore user data files (if applicable) (Chapters Four, and Five, Lab Manual)
- Identify common symptoms and problems (Chapters Two, Three, Four, Five, Six, Seven, Eight, Nine, Ten, and Eleven, Lab Manual)

2.2 IDENTIFY STEPS TO PERFORM AN OPERATING SYSTEM UPGRADE FROM WINDOWS 9.x/ME, WINDOWS NT 4.0 WORKSTATION, WINDOWS 2000 PROFESSIONAL, AND WINDOWS XP. GIVEN AN UPGRADE SCENARIO, CHOOSE THE APPROPRIATE NEXT STEPS.

Content may include the following:

- Upgrade paths available (Chapters Four, Five, Seven, Nine, and Eleven)
- Determine correct upgrade startup utility (e.g. WINNT32 vs. WINNT) (Chapters Seven and Nine)
- Verify hardware compatibility and minimum requirements (Chapters Four, Six, Eight, and Eleven)
- Verify application compatibility (Chapter Six)
- Apply OS service packs, patches, and updates (Chapters Six, Seven, and Nine,
- Install additional Windows components (Chapter Eleven, Lab Manual)

2.3 IDENTIFY THE BASIC SYSTEM BOOT SEQUENCES AND BOOT METHODS, INCLUDING THE STEPS TO CREATE AN EMERGENCY BOOT DISK WITH UTILITIES INSTALLED FOR WINDOWS 9x/ME, WINDOWS NT 4.0 WORKSTATION, WINDOWS 2000 PROFESSIONAL, AND WINDOWS XP.

Content may include the following:

- Boot sequence (Chapters Two, Five, and Seven)
  - Files required to boot (Chapters Two, Five, and Seven)
  - Boot steps (9x, NT-based) (Chapters Two, Five, and Seven)
- Alternative boot methods (Chapter Four, Lab Manual)
  - Using a startup disk (Chapters Two, Four, and Seven, Lab Manual)
  - Safe/VGA-only mode (Chapters Five and Nine, Lab Manual)
  - Last Known Good configuration (Chapters Eight, Nine, and Eleven, Lab Manual)
  - Command Prompt mode (Chapters Two and Five)
  - Booting to a system restore point (Chapters Four and Eleven, Lab Manual)
  - Recovery console (Chapter Nine)
  - BOOT.INI switches (Lab Manual)
  - Dual boot (Chapter Six, Lab Manual)
- Creating emergency disks with OS utilities (Chapters Five and Eight, Lab Manual)
- Creating emergency repair disk (ERD) (Chapters Six and Nine, Lab Manual)

2.4 Identify procedures for installing/adding a device, including loading, adding, and configuring device drivers and required software.

Content may include the following:

- Device driver installation (Chapters Five and Nine, Lab Manual)
  - Plug 'n Play (PNP) and non-PNP devices (Chapter Four)
  - Install and configure device drivers (Chapters Five and Nine, Lab Manual)
  - Install different device drivers (Lab Manual)
  - Manually install a device driver (Lab Manual)
  - Search the Internet for updated device drivers (Chapter Ten)
  - Using unsigned drivers (driver signing) (Chapter Ten)
- Install additional Windows components (Chapters Four and Eleven)
- Determine whether permissions are adequate for performing the task (Chapter Seven, Lab Manual)

2.5 Identify procedures necessary to optimize the operating system and major operating system subsystems.

Content may include the following:

- Virtual memory management (Chapters One, Three, and Seven)
- Disk defragmentation (Chapters Two and Five, Lab Manual)
- Files and buffers (Chapter Two)
- Caches (Chapters Seven, Nine, and Thirteen)
- Temporary file management (Chapters Two, Three, Five, Six, and Eleven)

Domain 3: Diagnosing and Troubleshooting

3.1 Recognize and interpret the meaning of common error codes and startup messages from the boot sequence, and identify steps to correct the problems.

Content may include the following:

- Common error messages and codes
  - Boot failure and errors
    Invalid boot disk (Lab Manual)
    Inaccessible boot device (Chapter Nine, Lab Manual)
    Missing NTLDR (Chapter Nine, Lab Manual)
    Bad or missing Command interpreter (Lab Manual)

- Startup messages
    - Error in CONFIG.SYS line XX (Chapter Two, Lab Manual)
    - HIMEM.SYS not loaded (Lab Manual)
    - Missing or corrupt HIMEM.SYS (Lab Manual)
    - Device/Service has failed to start (Chapter Eight, Lab Manual)
- A device referenced in SYSTEM.INI, WIN.INI, Registry is not found (Lab Manual)
- Event Viewer – Event log is full (Chapter Eight, Lab Manual)
- Failure to start GUI (Chapter Four, Lab Manual)
- Windows Protection Error (Chapter Four, Lab Manual)
- User-modified settings cause improper operation at startup (Lab Manual)
- Registry corruption (Chapters Two, Three, Four, Eight, Nine, and Eleven)
- Using the correct utilities (Chapters Five, Six, Eight, Nine, Ten, and Eleven, Lab Manual)
    - Dr. Watson (Chapters Four and Eight, Lab Manual)
    - Boot disk (Chapters Two, Four, and Seven, Lab Manual)
    - Event Viewer (Chapter Eight, Lab Manual)

3.2 RECOGNIZE WHEN TO USE COMMON DIAGNOSTIC UTILITIES AND TOOLS. GIVEN A DIAGNOSTIC SCENARIO INVOLVING ONE OF THESE UTILITIES OR TOOLS, SELECT THE APPROPRIATE STEPS NEEDED TO RESOLVE THE PROBLEM.

Utilities and tools may include the following:

- Startup disks (Chapters Two, Four, and Seven, Lab Manual)
    - Required files for a boot disk (Chapters Two, Four, and Seven, Lab Manual)
    - Boot disk with CD-ROM support (Chapter Two, Lab Manual)
- Startup modes (Chapters Four, Five, and Nine, Lab Manual)
    - Safe mode (Chapters Four, Five, and Nine, Lab Manual)
    - Safe Mode with command prompt (Chapters Four, Five, and Nine, Lab Manual)
    - Safe mode with networking (Chapters Four, Five, and Nine, Lab Manual)
    - Step-by-step/Single step mode (Chapters Four, Five, and Nine, Lab Manual)
    - Automatic skip driver (ASD.exe) (Chapter Nine)
- Diagnostic tools, utilities, and resources (Chapters Five, Seven, Eight, Nine, and Eleven, Lab Manual)
    - User/installation manuals (Chapter Twelve, Lab Manual)
    - Internet/web resources (Chapter Fifteen, Lab Manual)
    - Training materials (Chapter Fifteen, Lab Manual)
    - Task Manager (Chapters Four and Fifteen, Lab Manual)

- Dr. Watson (Chapters Nine and Fifteen, Lab Manual)
- Boot disk (Chapters Two, Four, Nine, and Eleven, Lab Manual)
- Event Viewer (Chapter Nine, Lab Manual)
- Device Manager (Chapter Four, Lab Manual)
- WinMSD (Lab Manual)
- MSD (Chapter Two, Lab Manual)
- Recovery CD (Chapter Fifteen)
- CONFIGSAFE (Chapter Four)
- Eliciting problem symptoms from customers (Chapter Fifteen)
- Having customer reproduce error as part of the diagnostic process (Chapter Fifteen)
- Identifying recent changes to the computer environment from the user (Chapters Five and Fifteen, Lab Manual)

3.3 RECOGNIZE COMMON OPERATIONAL AND USABILITY PROBLEMS AND DETERMINE HOW TO RESOLVE THEM.

Content may include the following:

- Troubleshooting Windows-specific printing problems
  - Print spool is stalled (Lab Manual)
  - Incorrect/incompatible driver for print (Lab Manual)
  - Incorrect parameter (Lab Manual)
- Other common problems
  - General Protection Faults (Chapters Four and Fifteen, Lab Manual)
  - Bluescreen errors (BSOD) (Chapters Nine and Fifteen, Lab Manual)
  - Illegal operation (Chapter Fifteen)
  - Invalid working directory (Chapters One and Fifteen, Lab Manual)
  - System lock up (Chapters One, Five, Nine, and Fifteen, Lab Manual)
  - Option (Sound card, modem, input device) or will not function (Chapters Four and Fifteen, Lab Manual)
  - Application will not start or load (Chapter Fifteen, Lab Manual)
  - Cannot log on to network (option—NIC not functioning) (Chapters Thirteen and Fifteen)
  - Applications don't install (Chapter Fifteen)
  - Network connection (Chapters Thirteen and Fifteen, Lab Manual)
- Viruses and virus types
  - What they are (Chapter Fifteen)

- TSR (Terminate Stay Resident) programs and virus (Chapters Two and Fifteen, Lab Manual)
- Sources (floppy, emails, etc.) (Chapter Fifteen)
- How to determine presence (Chapter Fifteen, Lab Manual)

DOMAIN 4: NETWORKS

4.1 IDENTIFY THE NETWORKING CAPABILITIES OF WINDOWS. GIVEN CONFIGURATION PARAMETERS, CONFIGURE THE OPERATING SYSTEM TO CONNECT TO A NETWORK.

Content may include the following:

- Configure protocols
  - TCP/IP
    - Gateway (Chapter Thirteen, Lab Manual)
    - Subnet mask (Chapter Thirteen, Lab Manual)
    - DNS (and domain suffix) (Chapter Thirteen, Lab Manual)
    - WINS (Chapter Thirteen, Lab Manual)
    - Static address assignment (Chapter Thirteen, Lab Manual)
    - Automatic address assignment (APIPA, DHCP) (Chapter Thirteen, Lab Manual)
  - IPX/SPX (NWLink) (Chapter Thirteen)
  - Appletalk (Chapter Thirteen)
  - NetBEUI/NetBIOS (Chapter Thirteen, Lab Manual)
- Configure Client options (Chapter Thirteen, Lab Manual)
  - Microsoft (Chapter Thirteen)
  - Novell (Chapter Thirteen)
- Verify the configuration (Chapter Thirteen)
- Understand the use of the following tools (Chapter Thirteen)
  - IPCONFIG.EXE (Chapter Thirteen)
  - WINIPCFG.EXE (Chapter Thirteen)
  - PING (Chapter Thirteen)
  - TRACERT.EXE (Chapter Thirteen)
  - NSLOOKUP.EXE (Chapter Thirteen)
- Share resources (Understand the capabilities/limitations with each OS version) (Chapter Thirteen)
- Setting permissions to shared resources (Chapter Thirteen)
- Network type and network card (Chapter Thirteen)

4.2 IDENTIFY THE BASIC INTERNET PROTOCOLS AND TERMINOLOGIES. IDENTIFY PROCEDURES FOR ESTABLISHING INTERNET CONNECTIVITY. IN A GIVEN SCENARIO, CONFIGURE THE OPERATING SYSTEM TO CONNECT TO AND USE INTERNET RESOURCES.

Content may include the following:

- Protocols and terminologies
  - ISP (Chapter Fifteen)
  - TCP/IP (Chapter Thirteen, Lab Manual)
  - E-mail (POP, SMTP, IMAP)(Chapter Thirteen)
  - HTML (Chapter Fifteen)
  - HTTP (Chapter Fifteen)
  - HTTPS (Chapter Thirteen)
  - SSL (Lab Manual)
  - Telnet (Lab Manual)
  - FTP (Chapter Thirteen)
  - DNS (Chapter Thirteen, Lab Manual)
- Connectivity technologies
  - Dial-up networking (Chapter Fifteen)
  - DSL networking (Chapter Fifteen)
  - ISDN networking (Chapter Thirteen)
  - Cable (Chapter Fifteen)
  - Satellite (Chapter Fifteen)
  - Wireless (Chapter Thirteen)
  - LAN (Chapter Thirteen, Lab Manual)
- Installing and Configuring browsers (Lab Manual)
  - Enable/disable script support (Lab Manual)
  - Configure Proxy Settings (Chapter Thirteen, Lab Manual)
  - Configure security settings (Lab Manual)
- Firewall protection under Windows XP (Lab Manual)

CHAPTER 1

AN INTRODUCTION TO OPERATING SYSTEMS

In this first chapter, I'll be going over the fundamental basics of what an operating system (OS) is, what it does, and how it does what it does. In doing so, I'll also throw out a little history and perhaps dispel a few myths.

A+ OPERATING SYSTEM TECHNOLOGIES EXAM OBJECTIVES

I'm going to introduce a few topics covered on the CompTIA OS Exam. But trust me when I tell you, you'll be seeing these topics again in much greater detail in this chapter.

1.1 Identify the major desktop components and interfaces and their functions. Differentiate the characteristics of Windows 9x/Me, Windows NT 4.0 Workstation, Windows 2000 Professional, and Windows XP.

1.2 Identify the names, locations, purposes, and contents of major system files.

2.3 Identify the basic system boot sequences and boot methods, including the steps to create an emergency boot disk with utilities installed for Windows 9x/Me, Windows NT 4.0 Workstation, Windows 2000 Professional, and Windows XP.

JUST WHAT IS AN OS?

One of the first things I ask students coming into a class on operating systems is to define an operating system (OS). About ninety percent of the answers I get are variations on "It's what makes the computer work."

At first blush, this may seem like a fairly accurate answer. But consider this. If you install a newly formatted hard drive into a system, with no OS installed, and attempt to boot the machine, you will receive some variation on the message "Operating system not found." The very existence of this message proves that the computer is working. It knows enough to tell you that the OS doesn't exist.

Therefore, although the computer may not be doing what you want it to do, it is indeed working. So a more accurate reply to my question would be "The OS is what makes the computer do what you want it to do." Of course, CompTIA and the rest of the world want technicians to be a wee bit more technical than that when spewing out definitions, so the technical definition I'll offer is this: An *operating system* is the program running on the computer that manages all of the services required by applications that are to run on the system and interfaces with the hardware. These services include:

- The file system
- Processor control
- Memory management
- Device control
- Security

EXAM NOTE: Make sure you can spout off the major functions of the OS when it comes time to take the exam!

Different OSs handle these functions in different ways, and these factors become part of my later discussions. For now, I'd like to give brief descriptions of each one before I move on.

A FILE SYSTEM OVERVIEW

The file system is the method used by the OS to organize data on the hard disk. In order to efficiently sort this data, the file system consists of several nodes. A *node* is an addressable space on the hard drive. The different nodes are files, directories, and subdirectories. A *file* would be considered a collection of data that is intended to stay together, and generally speaking, if it becomes separated, it becomes either useless or almost useless.

A single document on your hard disk is a separate file from the other documents. Each image you store is a separate file. Files come in different types as well. User data files contain the information created or imported by users and can include text files, document files, images, databases, and so forth. Files with extensions of .txt and .doc are forms of text files. Files with a .dbf extension are just one example of database files. Appendix E has a listing of many of the most commonly seen extensions and what type files they are. Executable files are in a binary format and can't be read by typical text

BUZZ WORDS

Operating system: A program running on a computer system that manages all of the services required by applications that are to run on the system and interfaces with the hardware.

Node: Any one of several addressable types of allocated space on a hard disk that can contain the data that makes up a file.

editors. These would include files with extensions such as .exe and .com.

Each file is assigned certain defining characteristics called *attributes* (pronounced ăt´–tra–butes). These attributes tell the OS and applications running on the OS how to deal with the file. Among these attributes are Read Only, Hidden, Archive, and System. Read Only is fairly self-explanatory. It allows the file to be opened and viewed, but not overwritten or changed in any way. The Hidden attribute prevents the file from being reported by a standard directory listing, although in most graphical operating systems, an option is available to be able to view hidden files. (Kind of defeats the purpose, don't you think?) The Archive attribute tells the system that this particular file has been backed up, or archived, since the last time it was changed. A System file is very similar to a Read Only file, in that it cannot be overwritten, deleted, or edited. It goes one step further to identify that this particular file is integral to the OS and must not be changed or deleted.

> **BUZZ WORDS** —————
>
> **Attribute:** A property assigned to a file or directory on the system that defines certain characteristics of that file.
>
> **File:** A collection of data that is intended to stay together.
>
> **Directory:** A container node of a file system that can contain other directories or files.
>
> **Subdirectory:** Any directory that exists beneath another directory.

EXAM NOTE: Not only do you need to know precisely what an attribute is, but you need to know what the four primary file attributes are and what effect they have on a file relating to other system functions.

In general, it is bad practice to simply save all the files you ever create to the root directory of your hard drive. You need some method of storing those files in such a way that they will be easy to find later. For this, you make use of directories and subdirectories. A *directory* is a container node that can contain other directories or files, and a *subdirectory* is any directory that exists beneath another directory. With most graphical OSs, directories and subdirectories are frequently collectively referred to as folders.

On any given hard disk, the root directory is the managing node of any given file system. All else lies beneath. In the file systems used by most Microsoft OSs, the root directory is the drive letter followed by a colon and then a back-slash. C:\ is a typical representation of the root directory. In UNIX-based file systems, it is simply a forward slash (/). After the OS has been installed, a directory called root will be created. In Microsoft OSs, there is a maximum directory depth of twenty-one nested directories. In other words, you can have the Documents directory, and in that directory have a subdirectory of a subdirectory of a subdirectory, so on and so forth, up to twenty-one levels deep. Attempting to go beyond that limitation will result in an error message.

EXAM NOTE: Understanding how different OSs use paths to map to different files on a drive is very important. In later chapters, you'll see how a couple of OSs use a slightly different syntax for defining the path.

There are only certain files that should be stored directly in the root directory. These files vary with the OS and will be discussed in due time. But it is bad practice to simply dump files

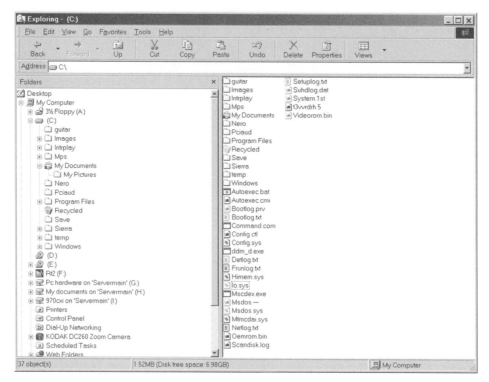

Figure 1.1   Windows Explorer is a graphical interface that allows the user to see at a glance how the hard disk has been organized.

to C:\ just because you don't know what else to do with them and you want to be able to find them easily later. The root directory can hold only a finite number of entries, and when this number is reached, the OS will report that the hard disk is full, even if a vast majority of the available space hasn't been filled with data.

Most of your files should be stored in an appropriate directory. For example, in Windows, your documents are stored in the My Documents directory by default. That makes them pretty easy to find, don't you think? Another directory created by Windows is the Program Files directory. Any time you install a new application written specifically for Windows, that application will create a subdirectory within the Program Files directory. That application will then copy any files and/or additional subdirectories it requires into that subdirectory. **Figure 1.1** shows how Windows Explorer allows the user to visually inspect the hierarchy of files on his or her hard drive.

PARTITIONING AND FORMATTING DRIVES

Before going into a lot of detail on the individual file systems, it is time to take a quick side trip into the world of hardware. The whole idea of having a file system is so that both the OS and the hard disk use the same rules for storing and locating files on the hard disk. Many of these rules relate to how the drive is partitioned. Once the file system has been selected the partitions must be formatted accordingly.

A partition is nothing more than a section of a disk. When you build a house, the main structure consists of four walls and a roof most of the time. However, it is pretty rare that those four walls contain only one room. Usually interior walls divide the house into several rooms.

Hard disks can be treated the same way. An 80GB hard disk can be divided into any number of different partitions of different sizes, and each partition will be recognized by the OS as a separate drive, even though it is not.

Partitions come in one of two forms: a primary partition or an extended partition. A *primary partition* is one that is defined in the master boot record of the hard drive and can be turned into a bootable partition. There can only be four primary partitions on any given physical disk.

Primary partitions can be further divided into *extended partitions.* How many extended partitions you can have is entirely dependent on the file system you select. With the vast majority of file sys-

tems, you will be limited by the number of letters in the alphabet. As I shall demonstrate later in this chapter, NTFS, version 5 does not carry that limitation.

I mentioned earlier that primary partitions can be made bootable. In order for a system to boot to any given partition, that partition must be made into an *active partition.* The active partition is typically the partition that boots the system.

Another term you might see thrown about is *logical partition.* This term might get confusing, because it is used in two completely different contexts, and in each context means something totally different.

In the PC world, logical partitions are only possible on NTFS formatted drives. A logical partition is a partition on one drive that is nothing more than a pointer that redirects the file system to a partition on a completely different physical drive. Logical partitions can carry a name other than a simple drive letter. For example \\DRIVEZERO might point to another physical disk on the system.

In the world of mainframe computers, a logical partition is not specific to the file system. Logical partitions take all system resources, including all available processors, system memory, and hard disk drives, and divides the system into several logical systems. Each of these logical systems is capable of running an independent OS, and each partition is capable of seeing the other partitions on the system.

FAT12 AND FAT16

FAT is an acronym for File Allocation Table. Therefore, it shouldn't come as much of a surprise that these two file systems center around the use of a small linear database of files and their locations on the hard disk called the file allocation table. The numbers at the end simply indicate how many bits are used for each entry in the table. FAT12 uses 12-bit entries and FAT16 uses 16-bit entries.

FAT16 was the file system used by the venerable MS-DOS, or simply DOS as it is usually called, operating system of yore. The first IBM PCs shipped with DOS on board. It was purely a command-line OS with no pretty pictures at all (ye-gads!!!).

EXAM NOTE: *Know your file systems!!!* CompTIA has several different ways in which to probe your knowledge of how the file systems differ and what limitations and/ or benefits each may bestow.

BUZZ WORDS

Disk slack: The amount of disk storage that is wasted by null files and/or small files stored on the hard disk.

Sector: The smallest data storage unit recognized by a disk on a hard drive. On magnetic media, the sector is consistently 512 bytes. It can vary for other types of optical media.

Cluster: Another term for the file allocation unit (FAU).

As you might imagine, FAT16 is fraught with limitations. The largest hard disk partition it can recognize is 2GB. The largest hard disk in general is 8GB, divided into four 2GB partitions. And it is seriously affected by something called disk slack. *Disk slack* is a fancy term for the amount of disk storage that is wasted by null files and/or small files stored on the hard disk.

A hard disk is divided into small units of data called *sectors*. A sector consists of 512 bytes of data. However, a hard disk formatted using the FAT16 file system can't read a single sector. Anywhere from four to as many as sixty-four sectors are collected together into file allocation units (FAU). Another term used interchangeably with FAU is *cluster*.

The number of sectors used by a single FAU is dependent on the size of the partition. **Table 1.1** lists the range of partition sizes used by FAT16 and the number of sectors used by FAUs in that partition. A single file can occupy as many FAUs as it needs, but a single FAU can never hold more than one file.

Now, examine Table 1.1 closely. A FAT16 hard disk formatted into 2GB partitions will have FAUs that are 32K in size. This means that, since a FAU can't hold more than one file,

Table 1.1 FAT16 File Allocation Unit Size by Partition Size

Partition Size	Sectors Used	FAU Size
16MB to 128MB	12-bit	4 sectors (Appx. 2KB)
128MB to 256MB	16-bit	8 sectors (Appx. 4KB)
256MB to 512MB	16-bit	16 sectors (Appx. 8KB)
512MB to 1GB	16-bit	32 sectors (Appx. 16KB)
1GB to 2GB	16-bit	64 sectors (Appx. 32KB)

FAU/Partition size relationships in FAT16

if that file is only a thousand bytes, then roughly 1K of that FAU will hold data and 31K will go unused.

Here is an extreme example of the impact this can have on the system. There used to be a CD running around that offered 10,000 different Windows icons. Icons are those little pictures you see on the Windows desktop that depict the programs installed. If you weren't happy with the icon Microsoft provided for MS Word, you could go to this disk and pick one you liked better.

A Windows icon ranges in size from under 800 bytes to as large as 2K. If you were to assume an average of 1K per icon, you would think that if you copied all 10,000 of those icons to the hard drive, it would occupy 10MB of space. However, since each icon represents an individual file, and since no more than one file can occupy a FAU, in reality those 10,000 tiny little files would eat up 320MB of space!

Another limitation of FAT12 and FAT16 often overlooked is the number of entries that can be stored in the root directory. Only 512 entries are allowed. An entry consists of either a directory or a file. Once this number is reached, the user receives a "disk full" message, regardless of how much data is stored on the drive. There is no limitation to the number of files and/or subdirectories that can stored in a directory.

> **EXAM NOTE:** It would be a good idea to be aware of the effect that file system selection has on disk slack. Also watch for questions on the exam that sneak the concept of the number of entries you can have in the root directory through the back door.

File names in FAT12 and FAT16 are limited to eight characters for the file name and three characters for an extension. This is often referred to as the *8.3 naming convention.* The extension is the portion of file name following the period. For example in the file novel.doc, the letters d-o-c constitute the extension. The extension is used to indicate the type of data held by a particular file. It is not necessary to use all eight characters for the name, nor is it a requirement to use all three characters for the extension. In fact, you can have a file name with no extension at all, although it is impossible to have a file with just an extension and no file name.

There are certain characters that are not allowed in FAT12/16 file names. These included [space] " * + , . / : ; < = > ? [\ and]. (Commas between characters have been intentionally omitted to avoid more confusion than you're already experiencing.)

FAT32

Like FAT12 and FAT16, FAT32 centers on the file allocation tables for the way it works. However, as the number at the end of the file system's name suggests, each entry in FAT32 is 32 bits wide. This greatly reduces many of the limitations of FAT16.

FAT32 still makes use of FAUs, the way the earlier systems did. However, it is much more efficient in its use of space. **Table 1.2** shows the relationship of partition size to FAU in FAT32.

Table 1.2 FAT32 File Allocation Unit Size by Partition Size

Partition Size	Sectors Used	FAU Size
<512MB–8GB	8 sectors	4KB
8GB–16GB	16 sectors	8KB
16GB–32GB	32 sectors	16KB
32GB–2048GB	64 sectors	32KB

FAU/Partition size relationships in FAT32

There is still a limitation to the number entries the root directory can store as well. However, this limitation is much larger; FAT32 can support up to 65,536 entries in the root. That doesn't, however, mean that you should just start arbitrarily dumping files into C:\. You'll still get the "disk full" error when you try to put in entry 65,537.

FAT32 also supports Long File Names (LFN). An LFN can be up to 255 characters long, including the extension. However, since the entry in FAT for any given file is only 32 bits, and much of that information is needed for other attributes, any given entry in FAT can only support thirteen characters. Therefore a filename with 128 characters would require eleven entries. Why eleven? 128 divided by thirteen is just a hair under ten! The eleventh entry is the 8.3-compatible entry that makes the file useable by older OSs and applications.

In order to maintain backward compatibility with FAT16 systems, an 8.3 filename is created for every LFN generated. This filename is created using a couple of techniques. First the OS eliminates all spaces and other characters allowed by FAT32, but illegal in FAT16. Next it truncates the filename by taking the first six legal characters, adding the tilde (~) and then adding an alphanumeric character as the eighth and final character of the naming portion of the filename. For example if you have on your hard drive a document named The Great American Mystery Novel.Doc, the 8.3 name for that file would be thegre~1.doc.

> **Exam Note:** You might want to expect one or more questions dealing with long file names and how 8.3-compatible file names are generated.

Therefore, great care should be taken in choosing file names if you know you're going to be sharing your files with users that either can't use LFNs or live on the other side of devices on the Internet that can't. Either way, the person who receives the file will receive a truncated file name. Now imagine if you have six different versions of The Great American Mystery Novel.Doc and you've decided to let your agent decide which one to submit. (Don't even try that in real life. There's not an agent alive that will let you get away with it!).

Your six different files are named The Great American Mystery Novel Version One.Doc, The Great American Mystery Novel Version Two.Doc, The Great American Mystery Novel Version Three.Doc, The Great American Mystery Novel Version Four.Doc, The Great American Mystery Novel Version Five.Doc, and The Great American Mystery Novel Version Six.Doc. The truncated file names for the first four files would look like this:

thegre~1.doc

thegre~2.doc

thegre~3.doc

thegre~4.doc

So what would you expect the other two versions to look like? Thegre~5.doc and thegre~6.doc, right? As you might imagine from the way I presented this, it couldn't be that easy, could it? After four regenerations of nearly identical file names, the OS keeps the first two characters of the filename, but for the remaining six characters generates a random collection of characters. Therefore, the last two files could be named just about anything that starts with TH and is eight characters long.

> **BUZZ WORDS** ───────────
>
> **Journaling:** A process used by certain OSs and applications by which any changes made to the basic infrastructure or code are recorded in a log prior to being enforced.
>
> **Lazy writing:** A disk-caching scheme that allows the OS to perform write operations to a disk at a time when the controller and disk aren't involved with read operations.

NTFS

The New Technology File System (NTFS) first became popular on an operating system with the release of Microsoft NT 4.0. That wasn't, however, the first release of NTFS. This particular file system evolved over the years as an offshoot of the High Performance File System (HPFS), an earlier file system developed by IBM for their now-defunct OS2 operating system.

NTFS is a vastly different file system than any of the FAT systems. It does, however, share some commonalities with FAT32. Among these are LFNs and large disk support.

It's the differences that interest us. NTFS was the first file system used in a Microsoft OS that incorporated a feature called *journaling*. Remember when you were a teenager and you kept a little notebook where you jotted down everything that happened to you? NTFS does the same thing. Every change made to the file system is recorded in a log file before it is allowed to be executed.

Second, an advanced feature called Discretionary Access Control (DAC) was introduced. DAC allows an administrator to enforce tight security standards on files and folders stored on the hard disk. That person can even place controls on what types of disk access and/or disk management a particular individual will be allowed.

Lazy writing is a disk-caching scheme that allows the OS to perform write operations to a disk at its leisure, when the controller and disk aren't occupied with more important read operations. (For a more detailed discussion of disk I/O operations, refer to *The A+ Guide to PC Maintenance and Repair*, also by this author.) The bright side to this technique is that it provides significant performance increases for the user. The down side is that if the system is shut down unexpectedly, such as from a power loss or an irate user, all data not yet written to the drive is permanently lost. Therefore, anytime you are running an OS that incorporates NTFS as part of its structure, you want to make sure you shut down gracefully. An uninterruptible power supply (UPS) is also a good investment.

NTFS gets away from the use of file allocation tables for data management and replaces it with a far more sophisticated Master File Table (MFT). NTFS stores a great deal of information concerning disk structure and many advanced attributes for each file. This information is stored in a collection of metafiles that become part of the MFT. A *metafile* is similar to a file except it consists of streaming data rather than packaged data. Metafiles exist in a format that isn't viewable by standard file management utilities. As such, the metafiles used by NTFS can't be mapped out or viewed the way conventional files are without using specialized utilities. **Table 1.3** lists the key metafiles of NTFS along with their functions.

Buzz Words

Metafile: A related string of streaming data that contains the information that is used to implement the file system structure. Also, a metafile is a structured graphical file, also containing streaming data.

Another interesting thing about NTFS is that, within certain parameters, FAU size can be configured. It has certain default sizes based on partition sizes that are listed in **Table 1.4**, but from within the OS, a person with administrative privileges can adjust these defaults.

One of the more useful features of NTFS for users with small disks is automatic file compression (AFS). AFS doesn't have to work on the entire disk to be useful. Users can pick and choose files and/or directories they want compressed and leave the rest of the disk alone. If files are selected for compression, when the user wants to access them they are automatically decompressed on the fly. After the user is finished with them and saves them back to disk, they are once again compressed. Although this does have a certain impact on performance, it isn't as bad as you might think.

NTFS 5.0 added some new twists. A complete discussion of all the new features added to NTFS would be quite extensive, useless (although perhaps interesting) to the average computer technician, and quite frankly beyond the scope of this book. But discussion of a few key features is in order.

Table 1.3   Important MFT Metadata Files

Metafile	Metafile Function
$.	Root directory
$Boot	Boot file
$Mft	Master file table (MFT) table of contents
$AttrDef	Attribute definition table
$Bitmap	Cluster bitmap file indicating the used/free status for each cluster in the file system
$MftMirr	Location of the copy of the metadata files elsewhere on disk
$LogFile	Transaction log (deployed as a circular buffer)
$Volume	Information about file system volume (including its name and NTFS version)
$BadClus	List of bad clusters
$Quota	Reserved for future use for disk quotas (used only in NTFS 5.0)
$Upcase	Unicode lowercase-to-uppercase conversion table (for translating file names)

The metafiles of NTFS

Table 1.4 FAT32 File Allocation Unit Size by Partition Size

Partition Size	Sectors Used	FAU Size
<512MB	1	512B
<512MB–1GB	2	1KB
1GB–2GB	4	2KB
2GB+	8	4KB

FAU/Partition size relationships in NTFS

One of these features is Native File Encryption (NFE). Individual users on a machine can select certain files and directories they don't want others seeing or accessing and scramble them. If another user is logged onto the machine, that user cannot see the files encrypted by other users that might share the machine. There will be a more detailed discussion of this feature in Chapter Eleven, Windows 2000 and Disk Management.

BUZZ WORDS ————————

Native File Encryption: A technology introduced into the NTFS file system that allows files and directories to be selectively scrambled for local storage.

A feature beloved by network administrators who are forced to deal with finite disk storage on their networks is disk quotas. The administrator can assign a maximum amount of disk space each individual is allowed to use. As users approach that quota, they are issued a warning that they are about to exceed their allotted disk space. When they actually reach their quota, they won't be able to write more data to the drive until they delete some old data they're no longer using or convince the administrator to increase their quota.

A COMPARISON OF FILE SYSTEMS

After such a lengthy discussion of the different file systems that have emerged over the years, I thought it might be useful if I collected some basic information into a table so that you might be able to compare them at a glance. **Table 1.5** offers those comparisons.

PROCESSOR CONTROL IN THE OS

A key concept to keep in mind throughout this book is that operating systems are written to specific microprocessors. While it is true that various OSs have been written to multiple platforms (Linux is a good example), the version written for Intel processors doesn't run on Power PC processors and vice versa. There are a number of powerful reasons this is the case, but two primary reasons are the command structure built into the processor itself and how many threads of code a processor is capable of handling. A thread is any particular series of instructions that must be run from beginning to end.

Table 1.5 A Comparison of File Systems

Feature	FAT16	FAT32	NTFS
File name convention	DOS 8.3	LFN system	LFN unicode
File size	232 bytes	232 bytes	264 bytes
Maximum volume size	2GB	2TB	16 exabytes
Directories	Unsorted	B-tree[1]	B-tree[1]
Compression	No	No	Yes
Security	None	None	Yes
Management	None	None	Disk quotas

[1]B-tree is a data searching algorithm that uses a storage architecture similar to a tree, with "branches" and "leaves" representing paths and objects.

Comparing the file systems

Exam Note: Know the difference between a thread and a process. Even if you don't see any related questions on the exam (which you might), these concepts will serve you in good stead later on down the road.

When an application is running on the system, the entire OS as well as that entire application is not running at once. That wouldn't be possible. Instead, a program runs in a series of smaller strings of code called processes. A process is simply a single grouping of code that must be run from beginning to end. What differentiates the process from the thread is that the process may consist of a series of different threads. A thread might be as small as a single line of code, whereas a process is more like an application within an application. Processes can include strings of code from the application, device driver routines, strings of data, or even commands issued by the firmware of devices installed on the system.

When multiple applications are running simultaneously on a system, the processor is going to be bombarded with many different requests to process this line of code or that. It is up to the OS to decide what processes are going to run at any given time. The OS is capable of initiating a process, canceling a process, or suspending one until a later time. In the event that two processes start to repeatedly call one another, it is up to the OS to break the infinite loop that will result if nothing is done.

Memory Management

A modern computer system is equipped with massive amounts of memory these days. And not all of it is conventional random access memory (RAM). RAM is that memory that you see reported as the machine boots. In addition to RAM, there is video memory, cache, and buffer memory installed on devices. The OS needs to know where every single piece of data that it might need is stored so that it can access it at the right time.

From the mechanical side of memory management, it is up to the OS to allocate memory for each application or process that starts and when it is finished to free that space for use. This is one area where some OSs have been notoriously inefficient and is the cause of many system crashes.

In order to accomplish the preceding task, the OS needs to keep track of what memory is being used for what process and what memory addresses are available for use. Another area of "memory" managed by the OS is something called a swap file (or paging file by some OSs). Because this isn't really memory, another term is virtual memory. This is an area of hard disk space that is treated by the OS as if it were memory. If physical RAM fills up and a new process needs to be opened, then processes not currently running on the system will be moved over to the swap file, freeing physical RAM for the new process.

A critical function of the OS is to protect the memory space allocated to specific processes. Each process running on the system needs to think that it's the only process running. If another process or application invades its space, both processes will crash and burn.

But memory mechanics isn't the only thing with which the OS has to be concerned. It also needs to set and enforce certain rules for memory usage. The OS will dictate when a process can be loaded into memory and how much memory that process will be allowed to use. And when the process is no longer needed by the application, the OS needs to unload it from memory.

DEVICE CONTROL

Now let's take a look at all those fancy new toys you installed on your system. How does the OS deal with those? The answer to that question is two-fold. It gets some of its instructions from the computer hardware and other instructions from the device driver installed on the system.

For a device to work, it must be supported by the system BIOS and the chipset on the motherboard. Once again, for more detail on these issues, a trip to a good hardware book is in order. If the computer won't support a device, it doesn't matter how many device drivers you install on the OS; the device won't work.

The device driver provides the advanced command set specific to that particular device. The OS will have a set of files that are general command sets for specific types of drivers. Windows makes use of an Application Programming Interface (API) for each device type. For example, most modern IDE hard disks, CD-ROMs, CD-RWs, DVDs, and the like are all under the control of the Advanced Technology API, or ATAPI. ATAPI provides the commands that all devices in this category have in common. For some devices, such as a simple CD-ROM, this is all that is needed. For more sophisticated devices, like an IDE tape drive, a device driver may need to be installed. The device driver, as stated earlier, provides the command set specific to that device.

EXAM NOTE: Know what APIs are and what their function in the OS is.

When an application running in the OS has need of the services of a particular device, the application will initiate a system call to the OS. A *system call* is simply a request for a service not directly provided by the application. The OS will then initiate an I/O operation to the specific device.

BUZZ WORDS —————

System call: A request for a service not directly provided by the application.

Table 1.6   Predefined IRQ Assignments

IRQ	Common Use
0	System timer
1	Keyboard
2	Cascade: switch over to 2nd IRQ controller
3	COM2, COM4 (2nd and 4th serial ports)
4	COM1, COM3 (1st and 3rd serial ports)
5	LPT2 (2nd parallel port)
6	Floppy disk controller
7	LPT1 (1st parallel port)
8	Real-time clock
9	Redirected IRQ2
12	PS/2 mouse port
13	Math coprocessor error signal
14	IDE hard disk controller

Knowing the IRQs your system is already using is key to preventing resource conflicts.

In order to keep track of where specific devices are located, the OS and the hardware make use of Interrupt Requests (IRQ), I/O addresses, and/or Direct Memory Access (DMA) channels. An IRQ is simply a signal that is used by devices, the CPU, and the OS to indicate that the services of a specific device are needed. This signal is nothing more than an electrical current that interconnects every device on the system to the CPU. It is like a doorbell that runs throughout the system. Each device is assigned an IRQ. When that device needs to communicate with the CPU or the OS, it will send a pulse down that wire. When the CPU is ready, it will process that request, calling on the OS if necessary. Some IRQs are assigned to default devices, and in order to avoid conflict, care should be taken when using these interrupts. **Table 1.6** lists the predefined IRQs and their assignments.

The *I/O address* is a logical location for the device. Every device on the system must have a unique I/O address. If two devices have I/O addresses that overlap, there will be a conflict and one or both of the devices will not be recognized by the system. An I/O address is really nothing more than a memory address. Data targeted for the device that holds the address is dumped into that memory space until the device comes to get it. Likewise, if the device is sending data to the OS, it deposits that data into the address in memory so that the CPU knows where to find it.

BUZZ WORDS

I/O address: A location in memory that identifies where data from a specific device will be stored as it moves from either the application or the CPU to the device and vice versa.

Sometimes, large amounts of data need to go directly to memory from either an application running on the system or from a device to memory. If the CPU has to process every byte of data that a sound card receives when it plays Canon in D in the background while I work, then the system is going to bog down, and playing music in the background won't be all that desirable. So instead, the system and the OS coordinate over DMA channels. The CPU arbitrates the transfer of the file to a specific memory location, or from a specific memory location to the device. After the data transfer has been initiated, data moves in a steady stream from source to target.

SECURITY

Security really amounts to who gets to do what and when they get to do it. Different OSs offer vastly different levels of security. Some security measures are OS specific and some are dependent on the file system in use.

The types of security that are available include the following:

- Password authentication
- File access restrictions
- Application access restrictions
- OS control and management
- System control and management

Since the levels and degree of security vary from OS to OS, I'll defer the discussions of security to the chapters on each specific OS.

OPERATING SYSTEM STRUCTURE

Controlling processors and drives, managing file systems, security, and memory—that's a lot of responsibility for just one program. Therefore, the programmers of an OS must make sure that it gets priority over all system resources. Over the years, a layered approach to designing OSs has emerged. And in fact, you can effectively say that your entire computer is a layered structure. Before breaking the OS down, I think it would be a good idea to examine how the system structure works.

The first thing that you need to understand is that the average users aren't the least bit interested in running the OS. For them, the OS is a minor convenience running in the background that occasionally comes in handy, but usually gets in the way. The average users are interested only in running programs.

But as I pointed out earlier, each program depends on the OS in order to run. The program needs the hardware on the system in order to do its thing, and it kind of needs the OS to help it out in that respect. In fact, in most modern OSs, programs aren't allowed to access the hardware at all. They must pass their requests on to the OS, which manages hardware functions.

Figure 1.2 shows the basic model of a computer system broken down from the applications to the basic hardware.

A modern OS such as Windows XP is broken down into several layers. Among these are:

- User interface
- Executive kernel
- Microkernel
- Hardware abstraction layer

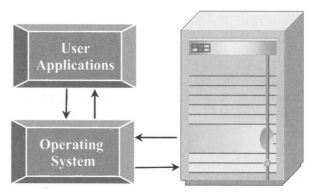

Figure 1.2 A computer system is a complex interaction between the applications, the OS, and the hardware.

The user interface these days is that pretty little screen that appears when your machine boots up. The term generally used for this is the graphical user interface (GUI). When the user interfaces with the GUI, either by clicking an icon or typing something into a command line, the OS will issue a series of instructions to the OS kernel. In the old days of MS-DOS, the kernel consisted of three very small files. Modern OSs are much more sophisticated. The kernel is broken down into two layers, the executive kernel and the microkernel. The executive kernel derives its name from the fact that it is the portion of the OS executing commands. When the executive kernel receives a command, it will issue a system call to one or more of several of its subcomponents. Although the names and variety of these subcomponents vary from OS to OS, there will inevitably be components that manage I/O, memory, process and processor control, and security. More sophisticated OSs add additional components.

The subcomponent processes the requests it receives and passes them on to the microkernel. If those requests are requests for more services to be provided on the OS level, they are passed on to the appropriate component. If they are hardware requests, then the appropriate device driver is called upon for its services.

In the days of DOS, this amounted to a direct access of the hardware by the application. Of course, DOS was not a multitasking OS (as you'll see in the next chapter). There were, however, programs written for DOS that emulated multitasking and provide more attractive and (sometimes) more efficient user interfaces. These were referred to as DOS shells. If two programs attempted to access the hardware at the same time there was a complete and total system crash.

Today's OSs are all multitasking, so that can't be allowed to happen. Therefore, the application isn't permitted to directly access the hardware. Hardware requests are passed onto the hardware abstraction layer (HAL). HAL is the only layer of the OS allowed to communicate with the hardware.

Defining HAL is more complex than a simple one-line description. HAL is a very complex layer of any modern OS. It consists of a collection of virtual device drivers, the APIs that I described earlier in the chapter. The virtual device driver is a file native to the OS that is designed to interface with a particular piece of hardware. In Microsoft OSs, the virtual device drivers are easily recognized by the fact that they end in a .vxd extension.

CHAPTER SUMMARY

Okay, I'll admit. So far, I haven't shown you how to install Windows XP and keep your sister out of your files. But as my uncle always told me, "You got to learn to run before you learn to crawl!" Like almost everything else he tried to teach me, he got it backward.

Essentially, in this chapter, you learned what the specific role of the OS is on the computer system. Probably as far as you are concerned, the most important thing you learned is that if an OS isn't installed, you can't play your favorite game. The most important thing you should have learned, as far as CompTIA is concerned, is that the OS controls all of the functions required by the applications you choose to run. These functions include file management, control of the microprocessor, memory management, control of devices installed on the system, and system security.

From a technician's standpoint, the most commonly encountered of these functions is the file system. That's why I devoted significantly more time and space to that issue than the others. Make sure you know your way around the file systems.

BRAIN DRAIN

1. List the five primary functions of the OS as they relate to the hardware and applications on the system.

2. Discuss the key limitations of the FAT16 file system.

3. How do LFNs work in FAT32? In your discussion, include FAT entry requirements and backward compatibility to DOS file names.

4. What are some of the ways NTFS differs from FAT in how it maps and defines files and directories on the system?

5. Discuss some of the additional features that distinguish NTFS 5.0 from NTFS 4.0.

THE 64K$ QUESTIONS

1. Which of the following is not a function of the OS?
   a. Memory management
   b. BIOS control
   c. Security
   d. Device management

2. The file name portion of a FAT16 filename could be up to _____ characters long.
   a. 8
   b. 12
   c. 32
   d. 255

3. What was the largest partition allowed by FAT16?
   a. 512MB
   b. 1GB
   c. 2GB
   d. 64TB

4. How long can a file name in FAT32 be, including the extension?
   a. 11 characters
   b. 64 characters
   c. 255 characters
   d. 1024 characters

5. What is the NTFS structure that houses the database that maintains file locations and attributes?

   a. FAT

   b. VFAT

   c. HPFS

   d. MFT

6. Which of the following is a correct example of a truncated file name derived from the file I_CANT_BELIEVE_THEYRE_MAKING_ME_WRITE_THIS.DOC?

   a. ICANTB~1.doc

   b. I_CANT~1.doc

   c. ICANTB1.doc

   d. I don't have any trouble believing it.doc

7. Native File Encryption is a function of _____.

   a. FAT32

   b. HPFS

   c. NTFS 4.0

   d. NTFS 5.0

8. An individual line of code from within an application that is running on the processor is called a _____.

   a. String

   b. Process

   c. Thread

   d. Stream

9. A part of the hard disk treated as if it were physical RAM is called _____.

   a. Virtual memory

   b. The swap file

   c. The paging file

   d. All of the above

10. Which of the following notifies the CPU that the OS wants to communicate with a specific device?

    a. System call

    b. IRQ

    c. DMA

    d. I/O address

11. Which of the following is not an example of an OS?

    a. MS Word

    b. MS-DOS

    c. Windows 3.1

    d. OS2

12. You open a file from a hard disk, make a few changes, and then try to save it. The OS won't let you save it under that name. Why is this?

    a. It is a system file.

    b. It is a hidden file.

    c. It is a read-only file.

    d. It is an archived file.

13. Your IT director asks you to copy the file IO.SYS from your hard disk to a floppy. You can't because _____.

    a. It is a system file.

    b. It is a hidden file.

    c. It is a read-only file.

    d. It is an archived file.

14. An FAU on a 2GB partition located on a FAT16 drive takes up _____ of space.

    a. 4KB

    b. 8KB

    c. 16KB

    d. 32KB

15. An FAU on a 2GB partition located on a FAT32 drive takes up _____ of space.
    a. 4KB
    b. 8KB
    c. 16KB
    d. 32KB

16. After copying a large number of files to your hard drive you get a message telling you your disk is full. But when you look, you have 2GB of free space. What happened?
    a. Your FAT somehow got corrupted while copying all of those files.
    b. Your system is incorrectly reporting free space.
    c. You have too many directories.
    d. There are too many entries in the root directory.

17. You have a 1.5GB partition on a FAT16 drive. You copy 10,000 files to the drive that are an average of 1000 bytes long. How much free space will you need on your drive to accomplish this?
    a. 10MB
    b. 15MB
    c. 160MB
    d. 320MB

18. Lazy writing is a technique used by the _____ file system.
    a. FAT16
    b. FAT32
    c. HPFS
    d. NTFS

19. Two features offered by NTFS –5.0 that didn't appear on NTFS –4.0 are _____ and _____. (choose two)
    a. NFE
    b. Selective file compression
    c. File-level security
    d. Disk quotas

20. Windows uses a(n) _____ to prevent the applications from directly accessing the hardware.
    a. InF
    b. RPG
    c. VXD
    d. DLL

TRICKY TERMINOLOGY

8.3 naming convention: A file naming scheme used by earlier file systems that permitted file names of up to eight characters, plus an extension of up to three characters.

Active partition: A primary partition on a hard disk drive that has been identified in the MBR as being the bootable partition.

Attribute: A property assigned to a file or directory on the system that defines certain characteristics of that file.

Cluster: Another term for the file allocation unit (FAU).

Directory: A container node of a file system that can contain other directories or files.

Disk slack: The amount of disk storage that is wasted by null files and/or small files stored on the hard disk.

Extended partition: Also called a logical disk drive, this is a partition contained within a primary partition.

File: A collection of data that is intended to stay together.

I/O address: A location in memory that identifies where data from a specific device will be stored as it moves from either the application or the CPU to the device, and vice versa.

Journaling: A process used by certain OSs and applications by which any changes made to the basic infrastructure or code are recorded in a log prior to being enforced.

Lazy writing: A disk-caching scheme that allows the OS to perform write operations to a disk at a time when the controller and disk aren't involved with read operations.

Logical partition: A pointer on a hard disk that identifies itself as a partition on the local drive, but in reality points to a partition on a remote disk.

Metafile: A related string of streaming data that contains the information that is used to implement the file system structure. Also, a metafile is a structured graphical file, also containing streaming data.

Native File Encryption: A technology introduced into the NTFS file system that allows files and directories to be selectively scrambled for local storage.

Node: Any one of several addressable types of allocated space on a hard disk that can contain the data that makes up a file.

Operating System: A program running on a computer system that manages all of the services required by applications

that are to run on the system and interfaces with the hardware.

Primary partition: Any one of four partitions on a hard disk drive that is defined in the MBR and can be converted into a bootable partition.

Sector: The smallest data storage unit recognized by a disk on a hard drive. On magnetic media, the sector is consistently 512 bytes. It can vary for other types of optical media.

Subdirectory: Any directory that exists beneath another directory.

System call: A request for a service not directly provided by the application.

Acronym Alert

AFS: Automatic File Compression. A technology built into NTFS that allows files and directories to be compressed and uncompressed on the fly.

API: Application Programming Interface. A collection of files used by Microsoft OSs that maintains and translates the basic command set required by all devices of a particular type.

DAC: Discretionary Access Control. A feature written into the NTFS file system that allows an administrator to apply security on a file or directory level.

DMA: Direct Memory Access. A technique by which a large amount of data is moved directly from an application or device to memory, without constant intervention from the CPU.

FAT: File Allocation Table

FAT16: File Allocation Table, 16-bit

FAT32: File Allocation Table, 32-bit

FAU: File Allocation Unit. The number of sectors that make up the smallest increment of data that can be read by a given file system.

HPFS: High Performance File System. A file system co-developed by Microsoft and IBM that was used in the now-defunct OS2.

LFN: Long File Name. A technology introduced into FAT32 and later OSs that allows file names up be up to 255 characters long, including the extension.

MFT: Master File Table. The database of information used by NTFS that stores file attributes and information defining file locations on the hard drive.

NTFS: New Technology File System. A file system introduced by Microsoft that incorporated a greater degree of security and more efficient file management procedures.

OS: Operating System

RAM: Random Access Memory. The physical memory installed on a computer system.

UPS: Uninterruptible Power Supply. A device that stores an electrical charge in a bank of batteries and is able to continue to provide current to a device for several minutes after a power failure.

CHAPTER 2

MS-DOS AND THE COMMAND PROMPT

First off, let me say that MS-DOS is no longer covered on CompTIA's A+ operating systems exam and hasn't been for a long time. A working knowledge of the command prompt is expected, however, and since the command prompt is a direct offshoot of the MS-DOS operating system, I feel very strongly that anyone who claims to be a working professional in the computer industry needs to have more than just a passing knowledge of the OS that started it all.

In this chapter, I will provide a brief history and overview of MS-DOS, followed by a discussion of some of the key commands still in use today by all of Microsoft's OSs anytime the command prompt is opened. And while the command prompt may not be a favorite place for the average computer user to spend much time, the working professional spends a good amount of time there. In addition to that, a vast amount of the technology used on the modern OS was derived directly from what you'll learn here. Get used to it, and get to know it well.

A+ OPERATING SYSTEM TECHNOLOGIES EXAM OBJECTIVES

There are two key CompTIA exam objectives covered in this section:

1.1   Identify the major desktop components and interfaces and their functions. Differentiate the characteristics of Windows 9x/Me, Windows NT 4.0 Workstation, Windows 2000 Professional, and Windows XP.

3.1   Recognize and interpret the meaning of common error codes and startup messages from the boot sequence, and identify steps to correct the problems.

A BRIEF HISTORY OF MS-DOS

MS-DOS got its start in May, 1979 at the hands of a hardware company called the Seattle Computer Company. SCC was one of those companies that got off to an incredible start, and but for a few bad decisions might have been the pre-eminent company in the personal computer industry. Its first product had been a memory card for a personal computer known as the S100. IBM had not yet entered the fray with its version of a personal computer, and dozens of companies were competing for a market dominated primarily by Commodore, Timex, Osborne, and Kaypro. (Aren't those all name brands we constantly throw about these days?)

The release of a processor board based on Intel's 8086 microprocessor led SCC to develop an OS that would support the new product. The fact that it managed to throw together a workable OS in under three weeks lead to the whimsical name of QDOS, which was short for Quick and Dirty Operating System.

On a similar note, Microsoft had started an 8086 software-development program. It had developed a version of the BASIC programming language intended to run on the 8086. SCC and Microsoft decided to join forces and see what might happen. SCC provided Microsoft with some samples of its product, and the BASIC project was completed. In the last two weeks of May 1979 Seattle Computer Company displayed the complete package, including its computer running the OS along with Microsoft's 86-BASIC, in June 1979 at the New York National Computer Conference.

In 1980, SCC released a new version of the DOS that it called 86-DOS version 0.3. By this time, Microsoft had purchased nonexclusive rights to market 86-DOS. In July 1981 Microsoft bought all rights to DOS from Seattle Computer, and the name Microsoft Disk Operating System (MS-DOS) was adopted.

When IBM released the IBM PC, it was in need of an OS that would run on the 8088 microprocessor it had chosen to power its computer. IBM approached Microsoft, who almost immediately realized that only a slight reworking of the code was necessary. In 1981, Microsoft signed a licensing agreement with IBM to ship MS-DOS with its newly released IBM PC. Thus began the reign of one of the most powerful business entities ever known.

Some of the key features of MS-DOS actually read today like a litany of its limitations. However, to put it in perspective, it's only fair to remind you that in its day, the average personal computer (prior to the release of the IBM PC) had a 4.7MHz microprocessor and supported a maximum of 64 kilobytes of RAM. For those of you with 256MB installed, that's less than one twentieth of the amount of data you can store on a floppy disk.

There was no such thing as a hard disk drive (not for PCs anyway), the CD-ROM hadn't been invented, and what the heck was a scanner or a digital camera? In the summer of 1981, those who were affluent enough to afford the roughly $6000.00 that a fully equipped IBM PC cost were absolutely delighted that they were able to bring the power of an actual computer into their homes or offices.

The IBM PC with DOS 1.0 installed supported a single-sided 5.25″ floppy disk drive, up to 1MB of RAM (640K of which could be used for programs), and, if you were really rich, you could buy a monitor that actually displayed four colors!

FAT12 was the file system used (FAT16 would replace it on the subsequent release of the IBM PC-XT). There was no support for hard disks, since none had yet been invented for the PC. It used the 8.3 file naming convention discussed in Chapter One, and the closest thing to a graphical interface was a dark green background with a very coarse and grainy C:\ taunting the new user to figure out what to do next. MS-DOS would remain the only available choice of OSs for computer users for the next nine years, until the release of Windows 3.0, although it would go through several generations of development. In fact, DOS is still alive and relatively well today, being resurrected every time someone opens the command prompt in virtually any version of Windows. **Table 2.1** lists the various versions of MS-DOS over the years, along with a brief description of each version.

THE STRUCTURE OF MS-DOS

As with all operating systems, MS-DOS centers around a relatively small kernel and provides subroutines (usually called utilities) for the upper layers of its work. In MS-DOS, the three files that make up the kernel are IO.SYS, MSDOS.SYS, and COMMAND.COM. By necessity, these files have to be located in the root directory. Each of these files plays a key role and is worthy of a brief discussion.

IO.SYS

IO.SYS is a hidden, read-only file that, as its name implies, was responsible for managing the input/output functions of the OS. For you to understand its key role a basic review of computer hardware is in order.

In order for a computer system to boot, it requires the services of a collection of files and programs that must be run prior to booting the OS. These files are located on a Programmable Read-Only Memory (PROM) chip. Collectively, the files are known as the Basic Input Output Services (BIOS). Some of the files stored on the BIOS chip provide command support to the CPU for all the devices installed on the computer system. These files are called *interrupts*. This can get a bit confusing because the same word is used to describe the process by which a piece of hardware requests the attention of the CPU. An example of a BIOS interrupt is the command set that supports hard disk drives. It is called Int13h (the letter h indicates that the number 13 is a hexadecimal value and not a decimal value).

To explain what I mean by a BIOS interrupt, the CPU, even today, only hosts a limited number of native commands. All of the other devices on the system, including RAM, serial ports, parallel ports, and floppy (and other) drives, function by way of their own separate command set. Devices can't issue commands to the CPU, but they need to think they can. So when a device on the system needs to request the services of the CPU or to send data to the CPU, it will issue its commands to the interrupt. The interrupt will process those instructions and translate them into instructions the CPU can understand.

The OS needs to be able to do the same thing. So IO.SYS consists of a number of different subroutines that interface with the BIOS interrupts to provide hardware support for the OS. These are referred to as the *BIOS extensions*. IO.SYS is not the only

BUZZ WORDS ———————

Interrupt: On a software level, it is a string of code that is called in order to perform a specific function. The BIOS uses software interrupts to manage hardware. On a hardware level, it is an electrical signal that notifies the CPU that a device needs to open communications (or vice versa).

Table 2.1   The Versions of DOS

Version	Date	Comments
1.0	1981	Renamed and slightly revised version of a program called QDOS, developed by Seattle Computer Company.
1.25	1982	Added support for double-sided floppy disks.
2.0	1983	First DOS version with support for hard disk drives and double-density 5.25" floppy disks with capacities of 360KB.
2.11	1983	Support for the Extended ASCII character set.
3.0	1984	Support for high-density (1.2MB) floppy disks; hard disk support increased to 32MB.
3.1	1984	Added network support.
3.3	1987	Added support for high-density 3.5" floppy disks, multiple partitions on hard disks, and for hard disks larger than 32MB.
4.0	1988	Provided support for partitions on hard disks up to 2GB, XMS support, and an optional graphical shell.
4.01	1989	A fix for the plethora of bugs that existed in version 4.0.
5.0	1991	Provided rudimentary support for expanded memory and allowed non-kernel portions of DOS to load in upper memory. It also allowed some device drivers and TSRs to run in the unused addresses of upper memory area between 640K and 1024K. Disk caching and support for 2.88MB floppy disks were also included. Included several utilities, including an a BASIC interpreter (a computer programming language popular at the time), a text editor, an undelete utility, and a hard-disk partition-table backup program.
5.0a	1992/3	A bug fix for 5.0.
6.0	1993	Mostly an increase in the number of utilities included. These included a disk-compression utility called DOUBLESPACE, a very rudimentary anti-virus program, and a disk defragmenter. It also finally included a MOVE command, MSBACKUP, and the ability to configure multiple boot configurations. Also included was a memory manager called MEMMAKER.
6.2	1993	SCANDISK, DISKCOPY, and SMARTDRIVE were added.
6.21	1993	DOUBLESPACE was removed in response to successful legal action from Stac Electronics. A voucher for an alternative disk compression program was included instead, and no compression application was present on the disks.
6.22	1994	Microsoft licensed a disk-compression package from VertiSoft Systems and called it DriveSpace.
7.0	1995	This version constitutes the command prompt of Windows 95. It provides support for long filenames when Windows is running.
7.1	1997	Released with Windows 95, Service Release 2; adds FAT32 support.

From its innocuous beginnings, MS-DOS eventually evolved into a relatively sophisticated operating system.

source of BIOS extensions. Many devices require device drivers to be loaded in CONFIG.SYS that provide extensions, and some devices even have code programmed into their firmware that provide them.

A critical subroutine of IO.SYS is one called SYSINIT. This is the last routine that IO.SYS loads during the boot process and is the file that goes out looking for. . .

MSDOS.SYS

MSDOS.SYS is often mistakenly referred to as the DOS kernel. This file provides file system services and memory management to the applications running on the system. In addition, it takes the upper-level instructions issued by applications and breaks them down into the simpler commands understood by IO.SYS.

In the last paragraph, I said that this file was mistakenly credited as being the kernel. There are many who would object to that phrase. However, MSDOS.SYS and IO.SYS rely on each other for many of their functions. When an application makes a request for an I/O operation with any given device, it comes in the form of a logical request. It is MSDOS.SYS that must intercept and interpret that logical request and convert it into a physical command. It subsequently passes that command onto IO.SYS, which executes it.

Processor control is also a key function of MSDOS.SYS. Which files get processed in what order is under its control. It also controls what registers within the CPU are responsible for processing a thread of code. In the old days of the 8088, this wasn't much of a challenge. There were only two sets of registers: one for data and one for instructions. As processors evolved and became more sophisticated, this responsibility became more critical.

COMMAND.COM

COMMAND.COM was the DOS command interpreter. It was a busy little file. On the OS side of the equation, it was responsible for managing both the resident commands and the transient commands. Don't let those terms throw you. They're not as complex as they sound.

The *resident commands* are commands built into COMMAND.COM's structure and can be executed without the aid of any external files. *Transient commands* are those that are run from an external executable. An example of a resident command is DIR. Search as you might, you won't find a DIR.COM, DIR.EXE, or DIR.BAT anywhere on your hard drive. Yet, when you type DIR at the C:\ prompt, your monitor spews out a listing of every file and/or subdirectory contained within. That's because DIR is a function of COMMAND.COM.

On the other hand, the FORMAT command is a transient command. There is a file called FORMAT.COM in the DOS directory. If you delete that file from the hard drive and type

FORMAT, you will get a message that says "Bad command or file name." It is not a direct function of COMMAND.COM.

The DOS Boot Process

Before I can effectively discuss how DOS boots, I must first take yet another excursion into the world of hardware. I'm going to describe the boot process in two steps. The first of these is to describe how your computer makes its way from a cold off position to the point where it can load the OS. After that, I'll describe the process DOS uses to load itself. If it will help you to understand the process better, consider these steps to be the hardware boot and the software boot (even though, in reality, it's all software).

The Hardware Boot

Earlier in the chapter, I mentioned that the system BIOS was critical in all system operations. Nowhere is that more evident than in system startup. Without the BIOS, the system couldn't start at all.

As I said before, the BIOS contains a number of different files that manage the devices on the system. In addition, there are three critical executable programs stored in BIOS. These are Power On Self Test (POST), Setup, and Bootstrap Loader.

Setup is a program that allows the user to adjust certain configuration settings related to the BIOS. That is more relevant to the hardware end of your training, and for a detailed discussion of Setup, I'll refer you to your favorite hardware book. POST and Bootstrap Loader are both part of the boot process and, therefore, need to be discussed before I move on.

POST is the first program your computer runs when it is first turned on. When you push the ON button, power is applied to the CPU, and the default command that is executed is for the CPU to go out to a specific address and run whatever program it finds there. That address is listed in hexadecimal as F000.FFF0h. This address is precisely 16 bytes below the uppermost address in conventional memory. Stored here is an instruction that jumps the system to the actual address of the BIOS chip. The program that the CPU finds and runs from there is POST.

POST actually accomplishes two functions. The first thing it does is to poll every device on the system to make sure it is up and running and functioning properly. If not, BIOS will generate an error message in one of two ways. If there is reason to suspect that the video subsystem has not successfully initialized, error messages are issued as beep codes. If video is available, error messages will appear on your display.

After the system devices have all initialized, BIOS will run the Plug 'n Play (PnP) scans. A *recognition scan* checks each expansion slot, USB connection, and serial and parallel port, as well as any other available connection, looking for any new PnP devices. The *allocation scan* assigns resources to

Buzz Words

Recognition scan: A BIOS routine that polls each device installed on a computer system to see whether that device is Plug 'n Play, and if so, what resources it currently claims.

any new device it discovers. Once again, a more detailed discussion of this process can be found in a hardware book.

When POST has finished the PnP scans, it hands the boot process over to the Bootstrap Loader. Bootstrap Loader checks all devices that have been identified in the BIOS as being bootable, looking for a master boot record (MBR). The MBR contains executable code that introduces the file system, defines how the disk has been partitioned, and includes a pointer to the first lines of executable code for the OS. Next comes the software portion of the boot process.

THE SOFTWARE BOOT

After the BIOS has completed its job and the code located in the MBR has been run, it hands control of the boot process over to the OS. The OS pointer in MBR locates the first file to be run. In the case of MS-DOS, this file is IO.SYS. In the days of DOS, this was a more primitive process. In order for MBR to find it, IO.SYS had to be the first file on the disk, following the file allocation tables.

IO.SYS loads itself into memory and will remain RAM-resident as long as the system is running. As I mentioned earlier, it contains the BIOS extensions for the system devices and provides the hardware support for the OS. It also runs a small program called SYSINIT, which locates and loads the next file in the boot sequence.

This file is MSDOS.SYS and must be the second file on the drive. MSDOS.SYS will go out looking for a file called CONFIG.SYS. CONFIG.SYS is actually an optional file and not required by the boot process. However, when present, CONFIG.SYS provides certain startup parameters, such as how many files can be opened at once, additional device drivers that may be required, and others. Later in this chapter will be a detailed discussion of CONFIG.SYS.

Finally, COMMAND.COM loads. COMMAND.COM will load another optional file called AUTOEXEC.BAT. AUTOEXEC.BAT loads any terminate and stay resident (TSR) programs required by the system. As its name implies, a TSR is a program that gets run, but when it's finished, stays loaded in memory just in case it's needed again. Once COMMAND.COM has been loaded, you get the screen shown in **Figure 2.1**.

Informative, isn't it? Now just dive right in and get to work.

Figure 2.1   The MS-DOS command prompt

MS-DOS AND MEMORY

We've grown so spoiled by modern OSs that even us old-timers sometimes forget exactly how limited DOS was in its use of memory. In its original incarnation, DOS could not read anything beyond 1MB of physical RAM. It wasn't until Version 5.0 that support for memory beyond 1MB became available. And even then there was an inherent limitation within the OS that would forever prevent it from being able to address memory beyond 64MB. Memory can be divided into three different types: conventional memory, expanded memory, and extended memory.

Conventional memory consists of the first megabyte of RAM. This is all that the original versions of DOS prior to 5.0 could address. Everything that DOS and the applications running on top of it required had to be loaded into this space. That included the system BIOS, device drivers, and, in those days before the invention of VGA, video memory, as well as the applications themselves. When the first prototypes of the IBM PC were originally being studied, the engineers decided to divide this 1MB of RAM into two areas: one area of 640K and one of 384K.

Applications had to share the lower 640K with key DOS files and some of the BIOS functions, including the interrupt pointers. The upper 384K, often called *upper memory*, was divided up into three 128K sections. The first 128K was used for video, the next 128K was where the BIOS copied itself, and the final block was where the supplemental BIOS of devices other than the motherboard could be copied. **Figure 2.2** shows a detailed map of conventional memory.

BUZZ WORDS

Conventional memory: The first megabyte of RAM, divided into 640K for running programs and 384K reserved for system use.

Upper memory: The 384K of conventional memory located above the 640K usable by applications.

High memory: The first 64K above the 1MB of conventional RAM, used as a paging window to Expanded memory.

Extended memory: All memory installed on a system above the 1MB of conventional memory.

Expanded memory: Memory beyond conventional memory that is under the direct management of a paging frame and a expanded memory manager.

Page frame: 64KB of high memory that is used for moving data down from addresses above 1MB into the 640K used by DOS programs.

Expanded memory was defined in the Expanded Memory Specification (EMS) and was DOS's first foray into using memory beyond 1MB. This was accomplished by creating a *page frame* of 64KB in the first 64K of RAM beyond 1MB, also known as *high memory*. This provided a window through which all of the information stored above 1MB could be accessed. For this to work an expanded memory manager (EMM) had to be installed and running on the system. The first and most popular of these was a product by Quarterdeck called QEMM386, which started the ball rolling. Microsoft would eventually come on board with the file EMM386.EXE.

Expanded memory needed be "protected" by the CPU. Data beyond 1MB needed to be sorted out according to what application was using it. And data from one application could never encounter data from another. This presupposed that you had a CPU that was capable of providing that protection, known as protected mode. The first Intel processor to provide protected mode was the 80286.

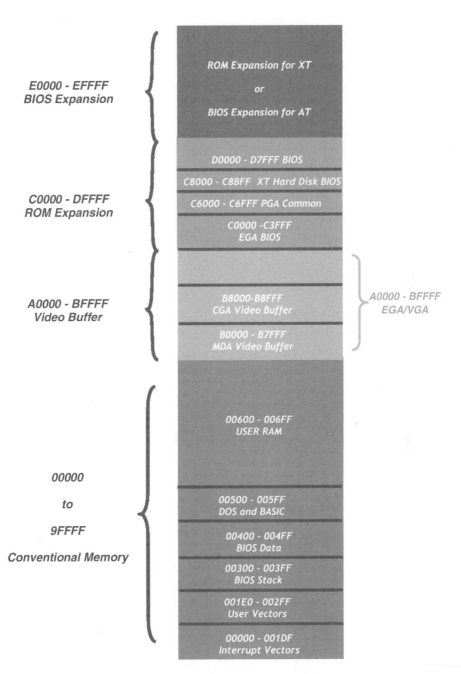

Figure 2.2   The DOS memory map

Data from expanded memory would be copied to the page frame and subsequently moved down into the lower 640K where the application could access it. The biggest limitation of this scheme was that an executable program could not run in expanded memory. It did, however, allow for significantly larger data files to be created and managed.

Extended memory was defined in the Extended Memory Specification (XMS). You would think XMS must take expanded memory to the next level. In reality, it's probably the other way around. Extended memory was simply any memory beyond 1MB. DOS needs help to get there and uses an EMM manager to provide that help. XMS provided a method by which DOS could read an additional 64K beyond the 640K originally provided for running apps. Under XMS, executable code can be loaded into the 64K of high memory. That ubiquitous Gate A20 that you frequently see as an optional setting in BIOS is the secret to using high memory.

Modern OSs were designed with extended memory in mind. XMS support was inherent in the code, and OSs actually load themselves above 1MB, so the issue of how to address beyond 1MB never arises. You'll see how these OSs use extended memory when I discuss it in their appropriate chapters.

NAVIGATING IN DOS

The file structure used in DOS is no more and no less complicated than what is used in the more modern OSs of today. It's identical. The key difference is that with DOS users don't have that pretty little Explorer window in which to view files, and they can't just grab onto files with the mouse cursor and drag them where they want. It's all command-line driven.

That means users have to understand the path. The path is nothing more than a verbal road map to the location of a file. Disk drives are divided into directories, subdirectories, and files. To find a file, DOS needs to know the correct order of the drive, directory, and each subdirectory, in order, leading down the file.

DOS drives are lettered from A to Z. However, by default, unless a line is added to CONFIG.SYS telling it otherwise, DOS will only recognize through Drive F. Drives can be either physical or logical drives. A physical drive is just what it sounds like. A floppy disk or a hard disk installed into the system is a physical drive. Drives A: and B: are reserved for floppy disk drives. The first hard drive in the system is Drive C:.

However, a hard disk can be divided into two or more partitions, and each partition is seen by the OS as a separate logical drive or *volume*. So if your hard disk is divided into three partitions, you would have drives C:, D:, and E:. Where it gets confusing is when you have two physical disks installed and each disk is divided into multiple partitions. In that case, the first physical disk is Drive C:, and the second physical disk is Drive D:. From that point all the partitions on the first physical drive will be lettered, followed by those on the second physical drive. Since this concept is probably confusing as all get-out, take a look at **Figure 2.3**. That should clarify it a bit.

Buzz Words ————

Volume: A single managed unit of storage on a computer system. This can be a single hard disk, if that disk has been formatted to only one partition, or it can be an individual partition on a disk.

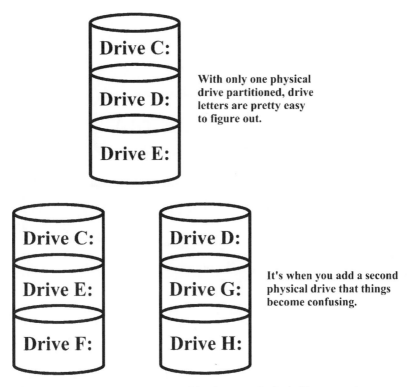

With only one physical drive partitioned, drive letters are pretty easy to figure out.

It's when you add a second physical drive that things become confusing.

Figure 2.3 New partitions on a drive become logical drives or volumes. When two or more physical disks are installed, figuring out which physical disk holds a particular logical drive gets confusing.

The most basic and fundamental directory is the *root directory*. This would be the entire partition on which all the files and directories are stored, and it is represented by a back-slash (\) in DOS. Generally, whenever the default prompt is used, the back-slash is preceded by the letter of the drive in which the partition resides. For example, the root directory of the first partition on the first physical drive would be seen as C:\. In MS-DOS, since the file system used was FAT16, there could only be 512 total entries to the root directory. As soon as you attempt to enter the 513th entry, you will get a message that says DISK FULL. If you had a 2GB partition and tried to copy 513 1KB files, that would only be 512KB of data, but if all those files were being dumped into the root directory, that would still be the message you get.

Therefore, it becomes essential to store files in directories. You can store as many files as you want in the directories, as long as there is sufficient space on the disk. Not only does this prevent the root directory from becoming overloaded, but it also makes your files easier to find. Any directory that is added directly to the root directory is called a primary directory. DOS installs

> **BUZZ WORDS**
>
> **Root directory:** The volume description into which all other directories and files will be stored.

Figure 2.4   Okay, so the last entry isn't a valid directory structure. What's wrong with a little humor here and there?

itself into a directory called DOS. Beneath the DOS directory, it is possible to create additional subdirectories. Subdirectories can be added to subdirectories as far deep as you wish (or need) to go up to the limitation of twenty-one nested directories. Files can be added anywhere along the line. Once again, the path is the road map from the root directory to the file, listing each directory and subdirectory along the line. **Figure 2.4** shows the path in action.

WORKING WITH THE COMMAND PROMPT

Okay, here comes the juicy part. You get to start working with the actual commands. And just in case you've been reading along in this chapter wondering whether I was ever going to get around to anything relevant, this is it. The command prompt is still alive and well and uses the same basic command structure today is it did in 1985. Certainly there has been some fine-tuning, but for the most part, the command prompt is a classic illustration of the old saying, "the more things change, the more they stay the same."

In WIN9x, the command prompt is reached in one of two ways. The first way is to click Start→Programs→MS-DOS Prompt. I find it easier to click Start→Run, and type **command** into the command line. In WIN2K and WINXP, the Start Menu shortcut is located in Start→Programs→Accessories→Command Prompt. With XP, unless you've been there recently, you'll have to click All Programs to get to Accessories. In either of the latter two OSs, the command prompt can also be reached with Start→Run and typing **cmd** into the command line.

Commands aren't as simple as they initially appear. For every command, there is a set of *switches* that allow that command to perform certain advanced functions. A switch, also called a *trigger*, consists of a letter preceded by a forward-slash. In Windows 2000 and later, the forward-slash has been replaced by the hyphen. The simplest switch, one that is common to all commands, is **/?**. While exploring the basic commands discussed in the following sections, you can always use this trigger to get a listing of every possible switch, along with a brief description of what that trigger accomplishes.

> **Buzz Words** ————————
>
> **Switch:** In reference to an OS, it is an additional parameter added to the end of a command that defines advanced functions for that command to perform. The switch turns a specific function on or off.
>
> **Trigger:** Another name for a switch.

One thing I'd like to point out is that I am not covering every command available. I have selected those that are most commonly used and described them as completely as I can. I used a computer running Windows 98 to create the screenshots used in the following sections. The descriptions are accurate, in spite of any difference in OS.

BROWSING COMMANDS

Some of the basic hard disk management functions a user faces are to make new directories on a disk as needed, and then be able navigate between directories. If a directory is no longer needed, there must be a way of getting rid of it as well. When a directory has been found, it's nice to be able to see what is in that directory without leaving the command prompt behind.

MD is short for Make Directory. Another command that works in the same way is MKDIR, but why type five letters when you can get away with two? The syntax is **MD {drive}{path}**. From the C:\ prompt, typing **MD TEST** will create the primary directory C:\TEST. If the TEST directory already exists and you type **MD TEST\TEXT**, a subdirectory of the C:\TEST directory called TEXT will be created.

After a while there are lots and lots of directories and subdirectories on a drive. The CD and CHDIR commands allow the user to navigate between the different directories on the drive. **CD** followed by a space and then a directory name assumes the directory name typed is a primary directory. If a primary directory of the name typed doesn't exist, you will get a message that says "Invalid Directory." It doesn't matter whether that was a valid name for a subdirectory or not. If you know the exact path to a subdirectory buried deep on your hard drive, you can type, for example, **CD\TEST\TEXT\CHAPTERS**. You will be moved directly to that directory.

Now, assuming you're using a default DOS configuration, your prompt should look like C:\TEST\TEXT\CHAPTERS> with a blinking line following it. If you type **CD..** at that prompt, you will be taken back one level to C:\TEST\TEXT. If you type **CD** at any level, you are taken back to the root directory.

RD or RMDIR allows you to eliminate the specified directory. However, for this command to work, the directory must be completely empty. There can be no files and/or subdirectories remaining, or you will get a message that says, "Invalid path, no directory, or directory not empty," and you will not be allowed to continue. If you wish to blow away a directory, all of its subdirectories, and the files within in one fell swoop, then you must use the DELTREE command described in the next section.

DEL, ERASE, AND DELTREE

If you need to delete commands from the command prompt, two commands useful for this purpose are DEL and DELTREE. DEL (or DELETE) and ERASE eliminate a single file and are pretty much the same command with different names. The correct syntax is **DEL {d:}{path}filename {/P}**. The /p trigger tells the system to prompt you before actually deleting the file. An example of this command in action would be **del c:\myfiles\novel.doc /p**. It will ask me if I'm sure, and if I type **Y** for yes, my great American novel will be erased, something my wife insists should have happened long ago.

DELTREE can be a bit more dangerous. It eliminates an entire directory, along with all the directories and files that reside beneath it. As with DEL or ERASE, the /p switch prompts the user to confirm that he or she actually wishes to perform this operation. Typing **deltree c:\myfiles** at the command prompt will eliminate the MYFILES directory, any subdirectories beneath it, such as the C:\MYFILES\NOVELS directory, the C:\MYFILES\COMPUTER directory, the C\MYFILES\PHOTOS directory, and all the other directories and every file that resides in those directories. Now what happens since I didn't use the /p switch? It still asks me if I'm sure I want to continue.

ATTRIB

In Chapter One, I discussed the various attributes a file may possess, including Hidden (H), Read-Only (R), System (S), and Archive (A). Many times these attributes are set by the OS or a program. However, there needs to be some way by which the user can edit the attributes if required. The ATTRIB command does that. The proper syntax for this command is: ATTRIB {+R +A +S +H} (DRIVE){PATH}{FILENAME} to assign the attributes to a file. It is not necessary to include each attribute in the command. To clear the attribute bits on any given file, replace the plus sign (+) with the minus sign (-). An example of this command at work:

```
ATTRIB +H +R  C:\MYFILES\NOVEL.DOC
```

This command will make the file named NOVEL.DOC, stored in the C:\MYFILES directory, a hidden, read-only file. Now my wife can't take it on herself to delete it for me.

MEM

This is a command that has lost much of its allure over the years. It's easier to obtain this information from other places in the OS. However, typing **MEM** at the command prompt will tell you how much memory is installed on the system. It also tells you how much conventional and extended memory you have and how much has been used.

SCANDISK AND CHKDSK

ScanDisk is a command line utility that checks for a number of different file system errors. It also can do a surface scan of the hard disk looking for surface errors or damaged sectors. In Windows, ScanDisk can also be run in graphical mode. From Windows Explorer, right-click the disk you wish to check and select <u>P</u>roperties from the pop-up menu. Click the Tools tab and in the Error-checking status section, click <u>C</u>heck Now.

ScanDisk is the more modern implementation of an earlier Microsoft utility called CHKDSK. CHKDSK was able to report disk size and usage, and it could report certain errors such as cross-linked files, but it could do nothing about them.

DEFRAG

DEFRAG is the Microsoft Disk Defragmenter. As files are opened and closed repeatedly over the life of the computer, they sometimes get scattered in small pieces over the hard disk. How this happens is covered in detail in *The A+ Guide to PC Hardware Maintenance and Repair*. For now, suffice it to say that scattering files like this can have severely negative impact on system performance. Typing **DEFRAG** at the command line will start a utility that puts as many files back into contiguous form as possible. Files that are open by the system can't be defragged, however.

DIR

The directory function was the fundamental method for locating files and directories in DOS. These days, Microsoft users rely on Windows Explorer, but I still find that if I haven't got a clue where a file I'm looking for is located, the command prompt is still the way to go. This simple command, used correctly with its associated switches, puts a lot of power at the fingertips of the user. The various options are as follows:

DIR {drive} {Path} (filename): allows the user to narrow the directory listings down to increasingly granular levels.

/p: Pause. When a full screen of listings appears, they will stop until the user presses the space bar.

/w: Wide. Displays five columns worth of listings but eliminates file and directory attributes. Can be used in conjunction with /p for directories with large numbers of entries. See **Figure 2.5**.

/a: Attributes. Displays the file or directory attributes after each listing.

/o: Order. Sorts the displayed listing into the order desired. In order to select the sort criteria, add after the letter O the letter N for name, S for size (smallest first), G for group, E for extension, D for creation date, or A for last access date.

/s: Search. Displays all files in the resident directory or those beneath it that fulfill the other search requirements used in the command.

/b: Bare. Displays no information other than file or directory name.

/l: Lowercase. Uses all lowercase. It must have been useful to somebody at some time or the other.

/v: Verbose. Displays all attributes of the file including size, time and date created, date last accessed, and file attributes.

```
Volume in drive C has no label
Volume Serial Number is 4323-11E5
Directory of C:\WINDOWS

[.]              [..]             [SYSTEM]         WINSOCK.DLL      SYSTEM.I~I
HWINFO.EXE       NETDET.INI       PIDGEN.DLL       SUBACK.BIN       W98SETUP.BIN
[HELP]           LICENSE.TXT      SUPPORT.TXT      [SYSTEM32]       MPLAYER.EXE
[CURSORS]        RUNHELP.CAB      [JAVA]           [COMMAND]        JAUTOEXP.DAT
NDDEAPI.DLL      NDDENB.DLL       SCRIPT.DOC       CLSPACK.EXE      DOSREP.EXE
DRWATSON.EXE     EXPLORER.EXE     EXTRAC32.EXE     FONTVIEW.EXE     GRPCONV.EXE
ODBC.INI         JVIEW.EXE        MSNMGSR1.EXE     NETDDE.EXE       PIDSET.EXE
SETDEBUG.EXE     SIGVERIF.EXE     TUNEUP.EXE       UPWIZUN.EXE      WINREP.EXE
WJVIEW.EXE       BACKGRND.GIF     CLOUD.GIF        CONTENT.GIF      HLPBELL.GIF
HLPCD.GIF        HLPGLOBE.GIF     HLPLOGO.GIF      HLPSTEP1.GIF     HLPSTEP2.GIF
HLPSTEP3.GIF     WINLOGO.GIF      [DRWATSON]       HTMLHELP.HTM     README.HTM
READM_01.HTZ     READM_02.HTZ     [CONFIG]         DELETEFI.INI     DOSREP.INI
HTMLHELP.INI     MSDFMAP.INI      DOSPRMPT.PIF     EXPLORER.SCF     ODBCINST.INI
CONFIG.TXT       DISPLAY.TXT      FAQ.TXT          GENERAL.TXT      HARDWARE.TXT
MOUSE.TXT        MSDOSDRV.TXT     NETWORK.TXT      PRINTERS.TXT     PROGRAMS.TXT
RECOVER.TXT      TIPS.TXT         [MEDIA]          REGTLIB.EXE      TELEPHON.INI
SMARTDRV.EXE     [CATROOT]        HIMEM.SYS        RAMDRIVE.SYS     LOGOS.SYS
LOGOW.SYS        1STBOOT.BMP      SYSTEM.INI       CIRCLES.BMP      FOREST.BMP
METALL~1.BMP     PINSTR~1.BMP     AC3API.INI       TILES.BMP        SETUP.BMP
POWERPNT.INI     CLOUDS.BMP       WIN.COM          CONFDENT.CPE     FYI.CPE
GENERIC.CPE      URGENT.CPE       MORICONS.DLL     MSOWS409.DLL     CTCCW.DLL
ASD.EXE          CALC.EXE         CLEANMGR.EXE     CONTROL.EXE      CVT1.EXE
CVTAPLOG.EXE     DEFRAG.EXE       DRVSPACE.EXE     EMM386.EXE       MM2ENT.EXE
NOTEPAD.EXE      PACKAGER.EXE     PBRUSH.EXE       PROGMAN.EXE      REGEDIT.EXE
RG2CATDB.EXE     RUNDLL.EXE       RUNDLL32.EXE     SCANDSKW.EXE     SCANREGW.EXE
MICHAELG.PWL     SNDREC32.EXE     SNDVOL32.EXE     TASKMAN.EXE      TASKMON.EXE
VCMUI.EXE        WELCOME.EXE      WINFILE.EXE      WINHELP.EXE      WINHLP32.EXE
WININIT.EXE      WINVER.EXE       WRITE.EXE        WUPDMGR.EXE      WINUPD.ICO
DRVSPACE.INF     IOS.INI          SCANREG.INI      [PIF]            STRAWM~1.BMP
ASPI2HLP.SYS     CMD640X.SYS      CMD640X2.SYS     DBLBUFF.SYS      IFSHLP.SYS
SFCSYNC.TXT      NDISLOG.TXT      TWAIN.LOG        [A3W_DATA]       CDPLAYER.EXE
CHARMAP.INI      CLIPBRD.EXE      DIALER.EXE       FREECELL.EXE     KODAKIMG.EXE
KODAKPRV.EXE     MSHEARTS.EXE     MSNCREAT.EXE     RSRCMTR.EXE      SOL.EXE
SYSMON.EXE       TOUR98.EXE       TWUNK_32.EXE     WINMINE.EXE      SERVICES.TXT
HIDCI.DLL        [SAMPLES]        COMMAND.COM      SCHEDLOG.TXT     SETVER.EXE
KHOOKER.INI      QTW.INI          ADMINIST.PWL     CONTROL.INI      WININIT.SAV
MSOFFICE.INI     SYSTEM.CB        [TEMP]           WIN386.SWP       PTDLL32.DLL
Press any key to continue . . .
```

Figure 2.5 Using the /w trigger in conjunction with the /p trigger enables you to display a lot of files on the screen at one time.

Switches can be used together to provide the greatest versatility. Also the asterisk character can be used as a wild card. What's a wild card? Simply put, the asterisk instructs the command to replace that character with any other character or collection of characters it finds in its place. For example the command DIR *.DOC will display a listing of every file in the resident directory that ends in a DOC extension. Not sure what directory a file is in, but you know it was a letter to Bill, so the filename starts with Bill and ends in DOC? Start at the C:\ prompt in the root directory and type `dir bill*.doc /s`. The DIR command will search every directory and subdirectory of your hard drive and display each result along with the directory in which it was found. Too many results? Add the /p switch and the screen will pause each time it fills up and wait for you to press the space bar to continue (**Figure 2.6**).

COPY, DISKCOPY, AND XCOPY

Once in a while it becomes necessary to create a copy of data you've created. There are two commands that perform this function and each one is slightly different. The COPY command takes a file and copies it from one location to another. Files can be copied between different drives and/or different directories. The syntax is **COPY {trigger} {source path}(source**

```
Directory of C:\My Documents

CHAPTE~1 DOC        75,776  08-29-03  9:30a Chapter19.doc
NEWRES~1 DOC        41,472  08-17-03 11:14a New Resume.doc
CHAPTE~2 DOC       163,840  08-31-03  6:31p Chapter19_1.doc
SEPTEM~1 DOC        21,504  09-25-03  8:19p September 25 letter to parents.doc
LABONE~1 DOC        72,704  09-26-03  3:03p Lab ONe.doc
         5 file(s)         375,296 bytes

Directory of C:\Program Files\Creative\EAX Demo

README   DOC       970,752  09-21-98  1:00a readme.doc
         1 file(s)         970,752 bytes

Directory of C:\Program Files\Infogrames Interactive\Civilization III

CIV30~~1 DOC        46,080  09-18-01  7:28p CIV 3 O-D I G.DOC
         1 file(s)          46,080 bytes

Directory of C:\Program Files\Microsoft Office\Templates\Business Planner Templa
tes

SAMPLE~1 DOC       633,344  03-10-99 10:37p Sample Business Plan.doc
SAMPLE~2 DOC        72,192  03-10-99 10:37p Sample Outline.doc
SAMPLE~3 DOC        35,328  03-10-99 10:37p Sample Marketing Strategy Document.d
oc
SAMPLE~4 DOC        37,376  03-10-99 10:37p Sample Marketing Materials Document.
doc
         4 file(s)         778,240 bytes

Directory of C:\Program Files\Microsoft Office\Templates\Business Planner for UK
 and AUS Templates

EXAMPL~1 DOC       475,136  03-10-99 10:35p Example Business Plan.doc
SAMPLE~1 DOC        65,024  03-10-99 10:37p Sample Plan Outline.doc
         2 file(s)         540,160 bytes

Directory of C:\WINDOWS

SCRIPT   DOC        38,400  04-23-99 10:22p SCRIPT.DOC
Press any key to continue . . .
```

Figure 2.6   Using wild cards and multiple switches is possible with virtually every command.

filename) {destination path} (destination filename). Paths and filenames need not be identical. For example the command copy a:\files\letter.doc c:\myfiles\letter2.doc takes the file named letter.doc located in the FILES directory on Drive A:, moves it over to the MYFILES directory of Drive C:, and renames it to LETTER2.DOC. Triggers include the following:

/a: Indicates an ASCII file

/b: Indicates a binary file

/v: Verifies that files are written correctly

/y: Prevents the system from prompting you before overwriting an existing file of the same name.

/-y: Forces the system to prompt you before overwriting an existing file of the same name.

Entire directories can be copied using wildcards. An example of this would the following: copy a:\win98*.* c:\temp will copy all files located in the WIN98 directory on the floppy disk in Drive A: to the TEMP directory on Drive C:.

DISKCOPY makes a duplicate of an entire disk. The correct format is **DISKCOPY {drive}** **{drive}**. The drives must be identical, so you cannot use DISKCOPY to move the contents of a floppy disk to a Zip drive. You can, however, copy from one floppy to another using the same drive. If you type **diskcopy a: a:** at the command prompt, all the contents of Drive A: will be copied to RAM, you will be prompted to insert the target diskette, and then the information will be copied from RAM back to Drive A:. There are three triggers for the DISKCOPY command:

/1: Copies only side one of the source disk.

/v: Verifies the integrity of the data on the target disk by comparing it to the source.

/m: Forces the process to make multiple passes between source and target diskettes using only RAM to store data.

The XCOPY command is good for copying entire directory trees. With this command, if you type **xcopy c:\myfiles a:** then the directory MYFILES, along with any subdirectory beneath it and all files contained within, gets copied. There are a lot of XCOPY triggers:

/a: Copies any file on which the archive attribute has been set but does not change the attribute.

/m: Copies any file on which the archive attribute has been set and changes the attribute.

/d:{date}: Copies only files that were created or changed after the specified date.

/p: Prompts the user before creating any new files.

/s: Copies only directories and subdirectories that actually contain entries.

/e: Copies directories and subdirectories even if they are empty.

/w: Prompts the user to press a key before copying a file.

/c: Continues copying even in the event of an error.

/i: If a destination does not exist, and more than one file exists in the target, the source is assumed to be a directory.

/q: Quiet. Does not echo file names while copying them.

/f: Full. Displays full source and destination file information while copying.

/h: Copies system and hidden files.

/r: Overwrites Read-Only files.

/t: Copies directory structure from source to destination but does not copy files.

/u: Update. Replaces files of the same name that exist in the destination.

/k: Copies attributes. If this switch is not used, Read-Only attributes will be removed.

/y: Overwrites existing files of the same name without prompting the user.

/-y: Does not overwrite existing files of the same name without prompting the user.

FORMAT

This command prepares a new hard disk or diskette to store files. It is the FORMAT command that creates the initial file allocation tables for any given disk. These tables are subsequently modified as data is added and/or removed. If the command is used with no triggers at all, the entire contents of the disk will be formatted using the default file system of the OS. As the disk is formatted, each FAU will be tested for integrity. Bad sectors will be marked as such and will not be made available for the OS to use when storing files. The syntax is **FORMAT {drive}**. The FORMAT command has a fairly large number of triggers.

- **/v:{label}**: Specifies a volume label (up to thirteen characters) that will be used to identify the disk (or partition) once the format is completed.

- **/q**: Quick format. Does not perform surface scan looking for bad sectors, but simply rewrites the FAT.

- **/F:{size}**: Specifies what size of disk is being formatted. For example if an old 720K 3.5″ floppy disk drive was all that you had in an older machine, a 1.44MB diskette could be formatted to that capacity by typing **format a: /F:720** at the command prompt.

- **/b**: Reserves enough space on the disk for future use by system files.

- **/s**: Copies the system files to the correct location on the disk after the format procedure is complete.

- **/t:{tracks}**: Specifies the number of tracks to be formatted on each side of the disk.

- **/c**: Tests clusters that are currently marked as bad.

SCANREG

A utility that exists in WIN98 that is very useful is SCANREG. This particular utility can be run from Windows or from the command prompt. However, there is one trick it can do from the command prompt that it can't do in graphical mode. Its basic function is to scan the registry for errors. Unfortunately, no matter how badly the registry might be corrupted, it never seems to find any errors.

The one trick it does well from the command prompt is to restore the system using an old copy of the registry. By selecting the option to View Backups, a user can select the last copy of the registry that started successfully and restart the system using those files.

MOVE

The move command is very similar to the copy command, except that once the selected file is copied to the target location, it is deleted from the original location. For example, the command **move c:\myfiles\novels\novel.doc c:\document\novels\novel.doc** will copy the file NOVEL.DOC from the c:\myfiles\novels directory to the c:\document\novels directory and then erase it from the c:\myfiles\novels directory.

SETVER

This is a command that isn't required as much any more, but does still come in handy once in a while. In the early days of DOS, many DOS programs would only run on certain versions (or later) of MS-DOS. So in order to ensure that the version of DOS currently running on the machine was suitable, the program would do a version check. Unfortunately, many programs were not programmed well enough to understand the concept of "or later." A program would require DOS 5.0 and the system would have 6.22. There would be no problem running that program on the system, but since the version reported was not identical to the version required, the program refused to run. SETVER looks at the version required by the program and, as long as the version running on the system is equal or later, reports that it is whatever the program wants it to be. So if that program that needed DOS 5.0 starts to install on a 6.22 box with the SETVER command in the AUTOEXEC.BAT file, the program checks the DOS version and SETVER reports back, "How convenient! I just happen to be DOS 5.0."

SYS

The SYS command transfers the key system (or kernel) files to the correct location on any formatted disk or diskette. The correct syntax is **SYS {drive}**. In DOS, if I may be so bold as to repeat myself yet again, these files are IO.SYS, MSDOS.SYS, and COMMAND.COM.

TYPE

This convenient little command allows the user to view the contents of any given file without the necessity of opening an editor of some sort. This is really only useful on text files, however, many of the different files used by DOS, including CONFIG.SYS, AUTOEXEC.BAT, any other batch file, and most .INI files are nothing more than text files. The syntax for the command is **TYPE {path}{filename}**.

VER

It's rather difficult to get too verbose describing this command. It reports what version of the OS is running, whether is be DOS or Windows.

EDIT

The EDIT command brings up the venerable old DOS editor. This is a pure ASCII text editor that completely lacks anything resembling basic formatting functions. However, for editing configuration files on the fly from the command prompt, there is nothing better.

CREATING CONFIG.SYS AND AUTOEXEC.BAT FILES

Brief mention of the CONFIG.SYS and AUTOEXEC.BAT files was made earlier in the chapter when discussing the boot process, and I threatened that I would cover them in more detail later on. It's time to carry out that threat. These files are optional startup files that are user-configurable and continue to be relevant even in today's modern OSs (although to an increasingly lesser degree).

As I said before, CONFIG.SYS is where certain user-configurable parameters relevant to the OS can be added. It can be compared to the BIOS Setup program, except the OS uses it during boot up. AUTOEXEC.BAT consists of a collection of executable commands that the user wants to run each time the system boots.

In both of these files, a key concept to remember is that each line in either of these files is run in the order in which it is placed within the file. This may seem like a no-brainer, but certain commands are dependent on another command. If loaded in the wrong order, the dependent command cannot run. I'll show you an example of this in just a bit.

Another thing to remember is that it is possible for a command in AUTOEXEC.BAT to be dependent on something loaded by CONFIG.SYS. If a file or parameter that was supposed to be loaded by CONFIG.SYS is either incorrect or not present, then that entry in AUTOEXEC.BAT will fail. I'll give you an example of that as well.

CONFIG.SYS

It is upon this venerable old file that the task of loading device drivers and custom system parameters falls. The device drivers loaded here would be basically any device not directly supported by the system BIOS. And there are a number of system parameters. There are also certain commands relative to configuration that must be run from CONFIG.SYS.

EMM386.EXE is one command that is run from CONFIG.SYS. If you think about it for a minute, it will make sense. For the system to be able to address expanded or extended memory, it must be configured to do so. And configuration is the purpose behind CONFIG.SYS (in case you were wondering where it got its name).

Device drivers are also loaded using one of two commands. DEVICE loads the driver into conventional memory. DEVICEHIGH loads the driver into upper memory as long as an expanded memory manager is loaded beforehand. This is an example of making sure that the lines in the file are arranged in the correct order. For example, the following CONFIG.SYS won't do what you want it to do because of the order.

```
DEVICEHIGH=C:\MOUSE\MOUSE.SYS
DEVICEHIGH=C:\CDROM\CDROM.SYS  /D:0001
C:\DOS\EMM386.EXE
```

The reason is that I've attempted to load the drivers into upper memory without the benefit of an expanded memory manager. The drivers will load; they'll just load into conventional memory.

Another thing that you may have noticed about the preceding example is that the entire path to the file must be listed. If not, CONFIG.SYS can't find the file to load it, and the device that requires that driver fails completely.

There are a few other commands that you can put into CONFIG.SYS that allow you to customize your configuration a bit. The following sections describe them.

FILES

DOS manages open files by way of something called a file handle. A separate file handle is required for each file that is opened. By default, DOS only loads eight file handles, which means that only eight files can be open at any given instant. Unfortunately, most programs needed to keep far more than eight files going at a time. By adding a line that reads **FILES=32** to CONFIG.SYS, you are creating thirty-two file handles. You can specify any number from eight to 255. The one thing to keep in mind is that for every file handle you open you are grabbing a certain amount of conventional memory. This amount varies with the number of file handles you create, as you can see in **Table 2.2**, so you don't want to be putting a value of 255 in every CONFIG.SYS you ever write. You'll be eating up 15K of valuable memory.

Table 2.2 Conventional Memory Used by the FILES= Statement

Files Value	Bytes Consumed
8 (Default)	192
10	496
15	608
20	896
25	1200
30	1488
35	1776
40	2080
45	2368
50	2672
55	2960
60	3260
65	3552
70	3856
75	4144

Increasing the number of files open in CONFIG.SYS consumes additional conventional memory.

BUFFERS

Whenever DOS is asked to perform an I/O operation, it needs a space to store the data it is moving. Some devices, such as disk drives, supported a form of buffering called read-ahead. Using read-ahead buffering, when the OS requests a sector of data, the device delivers that sector plus the next few sectors in the data stream. The more read-ahead buffers configured, the more additional sectors that are read. By default, DOS establishes the number of buffers on the basis of how much conventional memory is available. If there is 512KB of conventional memory, then fifteen buffers are created. No read-ahead buffers are created. The correct syntax is **BUFFERS={#CONVENTIONAL BUFFERS}, {#READ-AHEAD BUFFERS}**. To configure a system to use thirty conventional buffers plus an additional four read-ahead buffers, the following line should be added to CONFIG.SYS:

```
BUFFERS=30,4
```

As with the FILES command, a little caution is in order. Each buffer configured requires 532 bytes. More buffers means less available memory.

STACKS

Computer programs, including the OS, need a place where data can be temporarily stored until it is needed—or in many cases, needed again. DOS provides a collection of memory addresses just for this purpose. Data is stored in stacks and then retrieved on a first in, last out (FILO) basis. The proper syntax for configuring a STACKS command is **STACKS={#STACKS}, {SIZESTACKS}**. The acceptable range for the number of stacks is between eight and sixty-four, while the size of each stack can range from 32 bytes to 512 bytes. To configure a system to use nine stacks of 256 bytes, you would use the following line:

```
STACKS=9,256
```

Although this may appear to mean that you're configuring 9256 stacks, it does not. However, each of those stacks is more conventional memory you're eating up.

LASTDRIVE

When computers were first unleashed on the unsuspecting public, a fully loaded computer might have two floppy disk drives and, if the user was exceptionally affluent, a hard disk drive. CD-ROMs, DVDs, and Zip drives hadn't even crossed the minds of the most delusional of designers. Therefore, assigning drive letters beyond Drive F: was considered overkill. These were the same engineers that told us that one megabyte of RAM was more than anyone would ever need.

With multiple large hard disks divided into several partitions each, coupled with a CD-ROM and a DVD, we move into a different world. We need more drive letters. Add the following line to CONFIG.SYS:

```
LASTDRIVE=Z
```

Most of us will be all right now.

AUTOEXEC.BAT

There are certain programs that every computer needs to have running in the background in order to operate properly. For example, many mouse drivers run as executable programs in the background. For a CD-ROM to work, the program MSCDEX.EXE must be running at all times. These are the TSRs I described earlier in this chapter.

Imagine if every time you started your computer, you had to go through and start each and every one of these programs manually? Users would have to have sticky notes taped to their monitors reminding them of what they had to do to start their computers each morning!

Fortunately, that's not the way it works. AUTOEXEC.BAT is a batch file that runs each and every time the computer starts and launches all of these programs. Even today, if you still have older DOS programs that you're running, it may be necessary to create an AUTOEXEC.BAT, so the concept hasn't been totally beaten to death yet. There are a few commonly inserted DOS commands that routinely appear in this file, and those are the ones that I'll cover in this section. Keep in mind that virtually any program that you want to automatically launch every time a DOS-based computer starts can be added to AUTOEXEC.BAT. If the only thing you use the computer for is one program that only runs in DOS, add the command that runs that program as the last line and the computer will boot right to that program. Before I dive into the commands, I'd like to point out just a couple of things regarding the creation and execution of this file.

AUTOEXEC.BAT CONCEPTS

As with CONFIG.SYS, the lines that you add to AUTOEXEC.BAT will be executed in the order in which they appear in the file. Therefore, if one program needs to be running in order for another one to start, make sure you have them in the right order. Also, as I'll point out in a few moments, you can have lines of text appear as the computer boots, prompting the user for some action or the other or simply telling the user what's going on.

Sometimes while fine-tuning an AUTOEXEC.BAT file, you want to disable a particular line, but you don't want to eliminate it completely. If you add the command REM in front of that line, it treats the line as a remark rather than a command and does not run any executables contained in the line.

Batch files don't need to be a simple listing of existing commands. An experienced user can program very complex AUTOEXEC.BAT files using some of the batch file programming commands listed in the next section. Also, a batch file can call on another batch file, run that file, and then complete its own cycle. Let's take a look at some advanced batch file programming.

BATCH FILE PROGRAMMING

Creating a customized batch file will usually require knowledge and use of the batch file programming commands included in DOS. The following is a list of DOS commands and how they can be used.

@: Any text following the @ symbol will not be echoed on the screen. For example, the command @ECHO OFF prevents future commands in the batch file from being displayed on the screen as they are being processed, but in addition, the @ sign prevents the ECHO OFF command from being displayed.

:{SECTION}: By adding a colon in front of any word such as SECTION, the lines following the command up to the next similar entry form a category, also known as a label. This allows you to use the GOTO command to skip to certain sections of a batch file.

CALL: This brings up and runs another batch file within a batch file. When the batch file that is called is completed, the remainder of the original batch file is completed. If the batch file called cannot be found, an error message will be displayed.

CHOICE: Prompts the user to input a selection, based on predefined choices.

CLS: Clears the screen.

ECHO: Displays any text following the command on the screen. ECHO OFF stops commands from the batch file from being displayed as they're processed; ECHO ON causes them to be displayed. If you have not typed **@ECHO OFF** prior to using the ECHO command to display text on the screen, a command such as **ECHO You may now remove the floppy disk** will display "ECHO You may now remove the floppy disk" and "You may now remove the floppy disk." The command ECHO. (including the period) creates an empty line.

GOTO {LABEL}: Allows the batch file to redirect processing to a specific section. An example of GOTO would be to **GOTO END**.

IF: Checks for a certain condition. If that condition exists the batch file will perform the function included in the IF statement.

PAUSE: Stops processing of the batch file and prompts users to press any key when they're ready to continue.

REM: Allows you to place comments into the batch file without executing that line when the batch file is run.

%1: The percent followed by a numeric value, beginning with one, allows the insertion of a variable within the batch file. For example, if you write a batch file called greeting.bat and include the line **echo Good day, %1**, typing the command **greeting Master Graves** will output the text Good day, Master Graves.

The majority of DOS AUTOEXE.BAT files don't require anything as fancy as customized programming and generally include just a few DOS commands. Here are some of the more commonly used commands.

SET: Allows the user to specify an environment variable and then assign a value to that variable. Syntax is **SET {VARIABLE}={VALUE}**. An example: **SET TEMP=C:\FILES\TEMP** tells DOS that all temporary files will be stored in the C:\FILES\TEMP directory. That directory must exist in advance, however. MS-DOS will not automatically create it.

PATH: Loads a predefined listing of directories that COMMAND.COM should search any time a command is issued, looking for the executable code needed to execute the command. Syntax is **PATH {DRIVE:}{DIRECTORY;}{DIRECTORY;} {DIRECTORY;}** **{DIRECTORY;}**. An example: **PATH C:\;DOS; WINDOWS;CDROM; MYFILES**. In this example, if a command is issued, COMMAND.COM first looks in the root directory. If it doesn't find the code it needs there, it then looks in C:\DOS, C:\Windows, C:\CDROM, and finally C:\MYFILES. If it still hasn't found what it needs, the user gets the "Bad command or filename" message.

PROMPT: Defines how the command prompt will appear to the user. Includes a number of parameters for configuring the prompt. These parameters must be preceded by the $ symbol and include the following:

$Q	the equal sign (=)
$T	current time
$D	current date
$P	current drive and path
$V	OS version
$N	current drive
$G	greater-than sign (>)
$L	less-than sign (<)
$B	the pipe symbol (l)
$E	Backspace

The syntax is **PROMPT ${VARIABLE}${VARIABLE}**. An example: **PROMPT PGTD$B** will yield a prompt that looks like

```
C:\DOS> 10:30:45SAT 11-15-2004|
```

LOADHIGH: Instructs the program following the command to load into the upper memory area between 640K and 1MB. Syntax is **LOADHIGH {DRIVE}{PATH}{FILENAME}**. An example: the command **LOADHIGH C:\MOUSE\MOUSE.COM** will go the C:\MOUSE directory and run the MOUSE.COM program in upper memory.

SETVER: Allows COMMAND.COM to report to an application any DOS version request by the application, as long as it is equal to or later than the version actually running. Syntax is **SETVER {DRIVE}{PATH} filename x.xx**, where the drive and path specify the location of SETVER.EXE, filename indicates the program that requires the services of SETVER, and x.xx is replaced with the DOS version required by the application. An example: **SETVER C:\DOS WP51.COM 3.3** tells SETVER that SETVER.EXE is located in the DOS directory and if the user runs WP51.COM, this file needs to be told that DOS 3.3 is installed on the system.

MSCDEX: This is the DOS command that provides CD-ROM support and must be loaded on any machine with a CD-ROM drive installed. Syntax is **{DRIVE}{PATH}MSCDEX.EXE /D:XXXX**, where D specifies the device name and

XXXX is replaced with the name desired. The same variable /D:XXXX must be included as a switch in CONFIG.SYS in the line that loads the CD-ROM device driver.

CHAPTER SUMMARY

After you've read this chapter and tried some of the commands a few times, you should be starting to feel a little more comfortable dancing around in the command prompt. Never again will a black screen with that C:\ challenging you to figure out what to do next bother you in the least.

BRAIN DRAIN

1. Review the various versions of MS-DOS and come up with the following answers:
   a. What was the first version of DOS that supported 1.44MB floppy diskettes?
   b. What version supported the first hard drive?
   c. What year did MS-DOS provide the first support for memory beyond 1MB?
2. Describe the hardware boot process in detail.
3. Now describe the software boot process in detail, specifically using MS-DOS as the OS being booted.
4. Define the function and purpose of CONFIG.SYS and discuss some of the commands that might be used in that file.
5. Define the function and purpose of AUTOEXEC.BAT and discuss some of the commands that might be used in that file.

THE 64K$ QUESTIONS

1. What is the file loaded on the ROM BIOS chip that locates the MBR and turns the boot process over to the OS?
   a. POST
   b. IO.SYS
   c. Setup
   d. Bootstrap Loader
2. What is the first file called during the OS boot process in MS-DOS?
   a. COMMAND.COM
   b. SETUP.EXE
   c. IO.SYS
   d. MSDOS.SYS
3. Which DOS file is credited with being the kernel?
   a. COMMAND.COM
   b. SETUP.EXE
   c. IO.SYS
   d. MSDOS.SYS
4. Which DOS file hosts the internal instruction set supported by MS-DOS?
   a. COMMAND.COM
   b. SETUP.EXE
   c. IO.SYS
   d. MSDOS.SYS
5. How much conventional memory was available to a program running in MS-DOS?
   a. <640K
   b. 640K
   c. 728K
   d. 1MB

6. What was the area of memory above 640K and below extended memory called?

   a. Expanded memory

   b. DOS memory

   c. High memory

   d. Phantom memory

7. The function of DOS that provides a roadmap that leads to a specific file on a drive is known as the _____.

   a. Prompt

   b. Path

   c. VFAT

   d. File handle

8. If you wish to add a new device to a system running DOS, how do you introduce the device driver to the OS?

   a. You put it in CONFIG.SYS.

   b. You add it to the AUTOEXEC.BAT file.

   c. It runs as an application.

   d. The drivers load from a chip on the device.

9. A variable applied to a specific command that instructs that command to perform in a particular manner is known as a _____.

   a. Switch

   b. Pipe

   c. Hash

   d. Trigger

10. DOS was able to handle an unlimited number of nested directories.

    a. True

    b. False

11. If you wanted to erase an entire directory, along with all of its subdirectories and all the files contained within, which command would you use?

    a. DELETE /ALL

    b. DEL -A

    c. ERASE *.*

    d. DELTREE

12. DOS only provided for eight files to be open at once by default.

    a. TRUE

    b. FALSE

13. Which of the following is the correct syntax for a STACKS command?

    a. STACKS,9,256

    b. STACKS={9},{256}

    c. STACKS=9x256

    d. STACKS=9,256

14. How does adding /Q to the end of the format command made it perform its job quicker?

    a. It doubles the rotational speed of the disk.

    b. It bypasses the surface scan of the disk.

    c. It uses the existing FAT.

    d. It doesn't.

15. You've added a new device to your system. Which of the following must you do in order to make the device work properly under DOS?

    a. Run SETUP.

    b. Add a DEVICE= statement to AUTOEXEC.BAT to load the driver file.

    c. Add a DEVICE= statement to CONFIG.SYS to load the driver file.

    d. Nothing. It will load itself.

16. The TYPE command would display nothing at all if used on a binary file.

    a. True

    b. False

17. By default, DOS will keep _____ file handles active at once.

    a. 4

    b. 8

    c. 16

    d. Unlimited

18. Why wouldn't you use WordPerfect to edit a CONFIG.SYS file?

    a. Formatting codes could corrupt the file.

    b. WordPerfect can't recognized the file type used by CONFIG.SYS.

    c. WordPerfect would save the file using the wrong extension.

    d. You could if you wanted to.

19. Which of the following prompts is the result of PROMPT PG?

    a. C:

    b. C:\09:28PM

    c. C:\DOS

    d. C

20. What is the largest stack that can be managed by DOS?

    a. 32 bytes

    b. 128 bytes

    c. 256 bytes

    d. 512 bytes

TRICKY TERMINOLOGY

Allocation scan: A BIOS routine that reassigns resources to Plug 'n Play devices installed on a computer system.

BIOS extension: A string of code that interfaces the operating system to the BIOS interrupts.

Conventional memory: The first megabyte of RAM, divided into 640K for running programs and 384K reserved for system use.

Expanded memory: Memory beyond conventional memory that is under the direct management of a paging frame and a expanded memory manager.

Extended memory: All memory installed on a system above the 1MB of conventional memory.

High memory: The first 64K of memory beyond the 1MB of conventional memory, usually used as a paging file for access into extended memory.

Interrupt: On a software level, it is a string of code that is called in order to perform a specific function. The BIOS uses software interrupts to manage hardware. On a hardware level, it is an electrical signal that notifies the CPU that a device needs to open communications (or vice versa).

Page frame: 64KB of high memory that is used for moving data down from addresses above 1MB into the 640K used by DOS programs.

Recognition scan: A BIOS routine that polls each device installed on a computer system to see whether that device is Plug 'n Play, and if so, what resources it currently claims.

Resident command: In an OS, it is any command that is an integral part of the command interpreter and does not require an external executable program.

Root directory: The volume description, in which all other directories and files will be stored.

Switch: In reference to an OS, it is an additional parameter added to the end of a command that defines advanced functions for that command to perform. The switch turns a specific function on or off.

SYSINIT: A subroutine of IO.SYS that seeks out and runs MSDOS.SYS during the MS-DOS boot process.

Transient command: A command that is issued and run from an external source.

Trigger: Another name for a switch.

Volume: A single managed unit of storage on a computer system. This can be a single hard disk, if that disk has been formatted to only one partition, or it can be an individual partition on a disk.

Wild card: A character that instructs a command to replace that character with any other character or collection of characters it finds in its place.

ACRONYM ALERT

QDOS: Quick and Dirty Operating System

MS-DOS: Microsoft Disk Operating System

PROM: Programmable Read-Only Memory. A chip that contains permanently embedded code.

BIOS: Basic Input Output Services. The instruction set on a computer system that provides the startup code along with a number of routines that provide command support for the hardware installed on the system.

PnP: Plug 'n Play. An Intel/Microsoft technology that allows the computer system and OS to automatically detect and configure certain settings for PnP compatible hardware.

MBR: Master Boot Record. Information contained on the first one or two sectors of a hard disk that contain code that initializes the file system, defines disks and partitions, and provides a pointer to the OS.

TSR: Terminate and Stay Resident. Any program that is launched, performs a task, but then remains in memory in case its services are required again.

FILO: First In, Last Out.

CHAPTER 3

THE EVOLUTION OF WINDOWS AND WINDOWS BASICS

As the world moved on, so did the nature of operating systems. In the early 1980s there was a flurry of activity as a number of different companies competed furiously to create and dominate a market for a graphical operating system. Several different software companies, including Microsoft, developed applications with a graphical interface. But very few were rushing to the market with a true-blue OS.

Xerox Corporation had been producing a very high-end (for its day, anyway) computer called the Alto with a graphical interface since the early 1970s. However, since these machines boasted a starting price of $32,000 and up for a single machine, there is a justifiable argument that these machines didn't really qualify as personal computers. Apple Computer was the first to step up to the plate with a true personal computer that sported a GUI in 1983 with the LISA, short for *Logical Integrated Software Architecture*. (The story goes that the name really was in honor of Steve Jobs' secretary.) At $10K, it's hard to call this one a personal computer, too. Judging by the number that sold, I'd have to say that the public agreed with me in that respect. However, it paved the way for the tremendously successful Macintosh computer (named for Steve's favorite apple).

The majority of this chapter will concentrate on the various versions of Windows starting with 3.0, going through 3.11WFW. However, because I think you might find it interesting, I'm going to provide a little of the history leading up to the release of Windows 3.0.

A+ OPERATING SYSTEM TECHNOLOGIES EXAM OBJECTIVES

In spite of the fact that CompTIA announces that it does not cover Windows 3.x on the exam, much of the Windows technology that is covered was introduced in this version. Therefore, there is some very important exam material covered in this chapter:

1.1 Identify the major desktop components and interfaces and their functions. Differentiate the characteristics of Windows 9x/Me, Windows NT 4.0 Workstation, Windows 2000 Professional, and Windows XP.

2.4 Identify procedures for installing/adding a device, including loading, adding, and configuring device drivers and required software.

THE HISTORY OF WINDOWS

In 1982, a company called VisiCorp demonstrated a product they called VisiOn. It was a graphical user interface for MS-DOS that allowed point and click functionality. The product was full of bugs, ran only VisiCorp software, and was never a commercial success. Its real claim to fame was that present for the demonstration was a fellow by the name of Bill Gates. He was so impressed by the concept that he flew several top-level executives from Microsoft out to the Computer Dealer Expo (COMDEX) to see the demonstration. From that point on, it became a race to see who could reach the market first. Xerox, VisiCorp, Microsoft, IBM, and Tandy Corporation were just a few of the competitors trying to be the first to release a true graphical OS. And how many from that list are still writing OS applications?

The first commercial product to be released by Microsoft was Windows 1.0 (**Figure 3.1**). The idea behind this release was to provide bitmap displays supporting a menu-driven mouse-based environment. To call Windows 1.0 an operating system is a bit like comparing a bottle rocket to a spacecraft. In truth, it was nothing more than a DOS shell that provided mouse

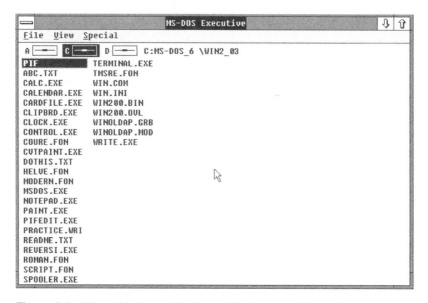

Figure 3.1 When Windows 1.0 shipped, it's biggest claim to fame was a graphical file manager.

support. It also shipped with a few rudimentary applications. These included a calendar, a notepad, a calculator, a clock, and a telecommunications program. A full install required just a hair under a megabyte of space, and the product shipped on five 360K 5.25″ floppy disks.

With the release of the 80286, Microsoft had the technology of higher-speed processors that supported protected mode to work with. While Windows 2.0 didn't take full advantage of protected mode, it did provide support for expanded memory and took advantage of computers with more than 1MB installed. This was the first OS to support a technology called *Dynamic Data Exchange* (DDE). Data could be moved between applications. Another addition was MS-DOS Executive, which provided a graphical method for browsing and launching files from a point and click environment.

Windows 2.03 was the first product to support the protected mode capabilities of the 80386. It also took advantage of extended memory. In essence, it was the predecessor to the version that would eventually make Microsoft a giant. The consumer had a choice of either 360K floppies or 720K 3.5″ floppies. A full install required 1.41MB.

WINDOWS 3.X VERSIONS

Windows first established itself as a mainstream desktop environment with the release of Windows 3.0 in 1990. Unlike version 2.03, which could take advantage of only some of the more advanced features of the 80386 microprocessor, Windows 3.0 took full advantage of this CPU.

It wasn't its computing power that appealed to the masses, however. It was the 16-color display that made the 4-color displays of the competition pale in comparison (**Figure 3.2**). It didn't hurt that Microsoft also showed their usual business savvy by releasing a Software Development Kit (SDK) that made programming applications for Windows 3.0 easier. The result was a plethora of new applications designed specifically for this new environment.

Some technological improvements that provided added horsepower to the 3.x products in general were hidden beneath the hood, but without them, Windows 3.x would not have enjoyed quite the success it did. One that was noticeable was the fact that MS-DOS Executive was replaced with a more powerful program called Program Manager (PM). PM was the predecessor of the Windows Explorer we all know and love today. Some of the hidden improvements included the following:

- Full support for virtual memory (swap files)
- A *Virtual Machine Manager* that supported virtual real mode operation for multiple programs in separate windows (more on that later)
- The ability to take control of the hardware from MS-DOS
- The ability to run programs in extended memory
- Cooperative multitasking

A key concept to keep in the back of your mind throughout the remainder of this chapter is that, in truth, none of the Windows 3.x products were true operating systems. They required

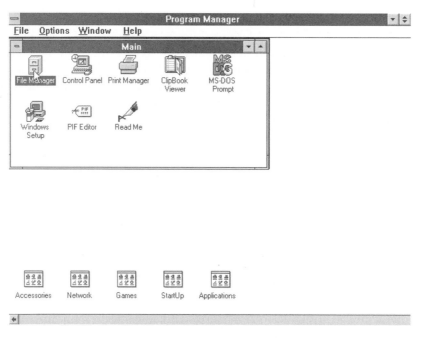

Figure 3.2 Windows 3.0 offered 16-color graphics and replaced the DOS Executive with Program Manager.

MS-DOS to be present in order to boot the system, and they still relied on the MS-DOS kernel. Therefore, the structure of Windows 3.x needs to be examined.

WINDOWS 3.X STRUCTURE

In Chapter One, An Introduction to Operating Systems, I pointed out that every OS has at its very core a collection of critical files around which the rest of the system is built. With MS-DOS, those files were IO.SYS, MSDOS.SYS, and COMMAND.COM. There are six critical files in the Windows 3.x foundation. **Table 3.1** lists those files and their functions.

Notice that WIN.COM isn't listed there? Although this file is essential for loading Windows, once loaded, this file steps aside and lets the core files take over. Which brings me to the boot process of Windows 3.x.

WINDOWS 3.X BOOT PROCESS

As I pointed out earlier, a computer system doesn't directly boot Windows 3.x. DOS must be running for any of these Windows products to function properly. Therefore, the first part of the boot process is identical to that of MS-DOS. Refer to Chapter Two, MS-DOS and the Command Prompt, for a detailed description.

Table 3.1 Windows 3.x Core Files

File Name	File Description
IO.SYS (loads with DOS)	A hidden read-only file located in the root directory of the active primary partition. Interfaces with system BIOS for hardware interaction.
MSDOS.SYS (loads with DOS)	A hidden read-only file located in the root directory of the active primary partition. Acts as the OS kernel.
COMMAND.COM (loads with DOS)	Read-only (but not hidden) file located in the root directory of the active primary partition. Manages the internal and external command structure for the OS.
KRNL386.EXE (loads with Windows)	Takes over control of I/O requests from IO.SYS. Handles memory management and CPU control.
USER.EXE (loads with Windows)	Creates and maintains windows on the screen for running programs. USER.EXE also handles requests regarding the icons and other components of the user interface. USER.EXE directs input to the appropriate application from the keyboard, mouse, and other input sources.
GDI.EXE (loads with Windows)	The graphics device interface, which executes graphics operations that create images on the system display and directs graphical output to other devices such as printers.

These six files are essential for Windows 3.x operation.

After DOS is loaded, the user enters **WIN.COM** at the command prompt. Since most dealers who configured Windows 3.x computers for their customers added WIN.COM as the final line to AUTOEXEC.BAT, this command was entered automatically, and to most users, it appeared that Windows loaded directly.

WIN.COM runs a quick check of processor functions to make sure that the processor supports protected mode and that all the basic processor subcomponents are available. It then starts the graphical interface of Windows, which is apparent to the user because of the pretty little Windows banner that appears on the screen (**Figure 3.3**).

At this point, WIN.COM passes control of the boot process over to a file called WIN386.EXE and steps aside. WIN386.EXE first switches the CPU over to protected mode, unless the user has inserted a switch in the WIN.COM command that instructs it not to do so. Next KRNL386.EXE is loaded.

When the kernel has successfully loaded, WIN386.EXE reads a file called SYSTEM.INI. This file controls and initializes all the resources for the computer. It contains system hardware settings and associated information. In addition, it maintains a list of drivers for each piece of hardware installed. It also contains information about each and every application installed on that system.

As soon as SYSTEM.INI has done its job, WIN386.EXE goes out looking for GDI.EXE and USER.EXE. Once these files are loaded, the full GUI is in place and operational. Next WIN386.EXE locates and loads PROGMAN.EXE, which loads the Windows Desktop. In doing so, it reads a file called WIN.INI. Another text file called PROGMAN.INI defines the desktop environment. Once PROGMAN.INI has loaded, Windows is ready for the user to start playing Minesweeper.

Multitasking in Windows 3.x

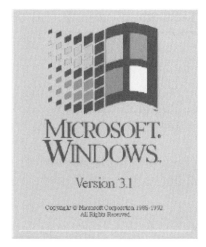

Figure 3.3   The Windows 3.x banner (3.11 for Workgroups in this illustration) indicates that WIN.COM has successfully started the GUI of Windows.

Windows 3.0 was the first Microsoft application to support true multitasking. Several previous third-party applications had provided task-switching capabilities, but there is a huge difference between task switching and multitasking. With *task switching* there are not two different programs running at once. While one program is running, it has full and complete control of the system. When the user switches over to another program, the first program must be closed.

So if the program was closed, how is it that users can get back to that program when they're ready to use it once again? Certain information, such as user data and what program threads were running at the time the program was exited, get stored to temporary files. When it is time to return to that application, those files are reopened, and users continue where they left off.

There are two problems associated with this approach. First off, the time involved in closing one program and opening another is noticeable enough to be annoying. Second, this does not permit data to be moved seamlessly from one application to another.

Multitasking keeps multiple programs open on the system at once. The CPU simply runs a series of instructions for one program and then switches over to another program and runs a few instructions for that one. Windows 3.0 and its siblings all use cooperative multitasking.

Cooperative multitasking places the responsibility for relinquishing control of the CPU and other resources onto the application running at the time. Programmers were required to place break points into their code that suspended the program so that another program could take over for a few clock cycles, until one of its break points was reached.

The problem with this approach is that if a routine needs to run from beginning to end (which most did) other applications running on the system appear to freeze up until the system is released by the application in control.

Still, multitasking did lead the way to Dynamic Data Exchange and Object Link Embedding (OLE), two features that turned Windows into a household name. DDE allows users to move data back and forth between applications. OLE allows an object such as an embedded table to be automatically updated if the source of that data changes, even if that source is another app.

WINDOWS MODES

The Windows 3.x versions were all designed to be able to run on anything from a 286-based PC and up. As such, there had to be some way in which the features specific to 386 and higher microprocessors could be switched off. To accomplish this, Microsoft designed Windows 3.x to run in three different modes. These modes were real mode, standard mode, and 386 enhanced mode. Which mode you selected dictated how much functionality your system had.

REAL MODE

As I've pointed out repeatedly, the early versions of Windows started out as nothing more than a point and click shell for MS-DOS. Versions prior to 3.0 had no memory management functions and couldn't even dream of multitasking. But then again, neither could any of the CPUs these versions were designed to run on. *Real mode* basically defines the behavior of an original MS-DOS program. It is capable of running only in the lower 640K of conventional RAM. No more than one application could be running on the computer at any given time. The presence of any data or command from another application would result in something called a non-maskable interrupt (NMI). An NMI occurs when something on the system has occurred which requires the CPU's immediate and instantaneous attention. If the CPU has a command loaded that knows what to do about the situation, the CPU fixes the problem and the system moves on along as if nothing ever happened. If the CPU *doesn't* know how to deal with the situation, it shuts off completely. An NMI generated by software always falls into the latter category.

So, to briefly summarize real mode: any program running in real mode must run in the lower 640K, it must be the only software running on the machine, it cannot share memory addresses with any other application, and it must have full control of the CPU. In the dark ages of computing, users with 8088 processors in their computers had no alternative to running in real mode. Machines with 80286 processors could run in protected mode, but in order to make use of virtual memory and run in enhanced mode, an 80386 processor or later was required.

BUZZ WORDS

Real mode: An operational mode for either a CPU or an OS in which only one application can be present on the system at a time and only 1MB of RAM can be addressed by that application.

Standard Mode

Standard mode took advantage of the protected mode functions of a 286 (or higher) processor. This allowed Windows to address up to 16MB of RAM, and it also allowed multiple applications that were designed for protected mode to run simultaneously (well, sort of, anyway). As you might imagine, this ability caused problems with programs that ran in MS-DOS's real mode. Also, DOS programs could only run full screen. They could not run in a window.

So if two programs are going to run at the same time on a Windows 3.0 machine, and one of those programs happens to be an MS-DOS program, then Windows has to make sure that the DOS program thinks that it is the only ticket holder in the theater. For that to happen, the user needs to be able to run in . . .

Buzz Words

Standard mode: An operational mode specific to Windows in which the OS could access expanded memory beyond 1MB and could task switch among multiple applications.

Enhanced mode: An operational mode specific to Windows that took advantage of advanced functions available in the 80386 microprocessor, including the ability to use virtual memory and to function in virtual real mode.

386 Enhanced Mode

As its name implies, 386 enhanced mode takes full advantage of the advanced functions of the 386 microprocessor. This mode supports extended memory addresses up to 4GB. It also adds support for virtual memory, and a Virtual Machine Manager (VMM) that runs in 386 enhanced mode allows multiple MS-DOS programs to run simultaneously. I'll be describing how this function works a little later in this chapter. In order to run in 386 enhanced mode, Windows has to have a minimum of 2MB of RAM available.

A key feature of enhanced mode operation is that programs can actually run in addresses beyond conventional memory. No longer is the programmer restricted to making a program run in a mere 640K of RAM. An expanded memory manager brought over from DOS and modified for use in Windows made this possible. The file is EMM386.EXE. Unless this file successfully loads, running in enhanced mode is not possible. Also, the user can enjoy the ability to run a word processor and a spreadsheet at the same time. OLE and DDE substantially reduce the amount of work a user has to do in order to complete a given task.

Windows Architecture

As I've said, technically speaking, Windows 3.x is not an operating system in the true sense. However, once loaded, it takes over the role of OS from DOS. As such, it becomes responsible for managing the core OS functions. Yet at the same time, it is also responsible for making sure that DOS is able to function when and where needed. The architecture of Windows was designed around those premises.

WINDOWS MEMORY MANAGEMENT

Windows may rely on DOS in order to start, but once loaded, it takes over the system completely, including the critical functions of memory management. Windows is capable of performing several tricks in order to more efficiently utilize the memory that is available and to assure that programs receive the amount and the type of memory they require. Among these techniques are the following:

- BIOS shadowing
- Expanded memory (discussed in Chapter Two)
- Upper memory blocks
- Memory mapping
- Virtual memory

BIOS SHADOWING

While shadowing is not exclusively the domain of Windows, it is a technique that Windows always used. Since the system relies heavily on the BIOS interrupts I discussed in Chapter One, calls are constantly being made to the BIOS chip. However, compared to RAM, the PROM chip used to store BIOS is unacceptably slow.

Windows takes the core hardware interrupts of BIOS and copies them to the middle 128K block of upper memory. This process of copying code to a secondary location is called shadowing. It differs from a direct copying function, because once the code is copied to the new location, the original addresses of the interrupts are disabled, and the new addresses in upper memory are used instead. On older machines the technique could improve the performance of hardware I/O operations a substantial margin.

UPPER MEMORY BLOCKS

The meticulously laid out map of upper memory that was used for DOS didn't make quite as much sense by the time Windows 3.0 was released. VGA was rapidly replacing EGA and CGA, so that region of memory wasn't used to the same extent. The top 128K had always been available for device drivers, but management of that space was notoriously inefficient in DOS. And since Windows managed memory more efficiently, it made more sense to use that space in other ways.

In Chapter Two, I discussed how EMM386.EXE provided access to memory addresses beyond 1MB. Another function of this program is to manage the upper and high memory areas. It divides upper memory into blocks called upper memory blocks (UMB). These blocks are created based on the amount of space required by the program intended to occupy them. The programs generally loaded into upper memory are things like device drivers and are generally quite small.

Typically UMBs are created in 8KB increments and cannot be larger than 64KB. A program running in UMB must be contiguous. If a 16KB program wants to run in upper memory and there are two noncontiguous 8KB blocks available, then that program cannot load.

The Windows version of EMM386.EXE does a much more efficient job of looking at the programs it wants to load in upper memory and then creating the UMBs needed. As a result more programs get loaded in upper memory.

MEMORY MAPPING

Windows 3.x had a couple of issues it had to deal with when managing the memory space above 1MB. For one thing, due to compatibility issues with DOS programs, it had to be able to support expanded memory. The page frame was a strictly defined 64KB address space through which everything moved from extended memory down into conventional memory and back. Programs running exclusively in extended memory obviously didn't need the page frame. They needed to be able to map everything to spaces above 2MB.

Windows got around potential memory conflicts by using a virtual address space of 4GB for every application opened. Since no system of the time had that much space available, there was a little bit of trickery involved here. The 4GB assigned is "pretend" space, but is mapped out with addresses the same as is physical memory. The physical memory is mapped out on a hardware level by the chipset's memory control circuit and on a software level by EMM386.EXE. EMM386.EXE can translate these virtual addresses into the real physical addresses occupied by the application or its data and use virtual memory to store any excess.

VIRTUAL MEMORY

Virtual memory is a method by which a chunk of hard drive space can be reserved for use by the OS and treated as if it is physical RAM. In the days when Windows 3.0 was first released a well-loaded computer consisted of a 127MB hard disk, 8MB of RAM, and a 386 microprocessor. While 8MB seemed like an immense amount of memory at the time, for a user running four or five apps at the same time, keeping DOS and Windows alive in the background, it wasn't enough.

So the *Virtual Memory Manager* (VMM) creates a hidden file on the hard disk called 386SPART.PAR. This is the file commonly known as the swap file (see **Figure 3.4**). When code or data is required by an actively running application, and there isn't enough physical RAM in which to store it, inactive code or data is moved from RAM to the swap file. When the application or data that had been banished to the swap file is once again needed, something else moves out of RAM to make room for it.

Of course, all of this data movement requires large numbers of hard disk I/O operations. These seriously impact system performance. Therefore, the more physical RAM the user has installed, the less the swap file is used. Increasing memory had (as it does today) much more impact on system performance than upgrading to a faster processor.

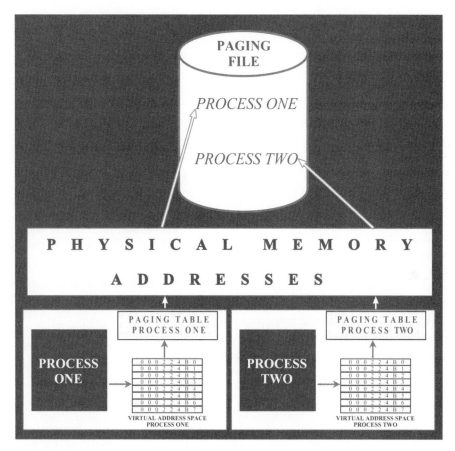

Figure 3.4   Virtual memory basically treats a portion of the hard disk as if it is physical RAM.

PROCESSOR CONTROL IN WINDOWS 3.X

When Windows is started in 386 enhanced mode, it is assumed that multitasking is going to be required. And sometimes that multitasking is going to involve older DOS applications that have to run in real mode. It will *always* require that the application share CPU time with core OS files.

One of the features of the 80386 microprocessor that made this all possible was the fact that Intel designers incorporated into the processor design four separate *privilege levels*. A privilege level basically determines the priority that any given line of code has over another line of code, assuming both want to run at the same time. These privilege levels are called *processor rings*. Processor rings are ordered on the basis of their current privilege level (CPL) and range from CPL-0 to CPL-3. A line of code running in Ring 0 (or CPL-0) has priority over Ring 1, which has priority over Ring 2, which has priority over Ring 3. Get the idea?

By having certain functions run in certain rings, the possibility that a renegade string of code from a poorly designed application might bring the entire system down is minimized. Windows specifications call for core system functions, such as the Virtual Machine Manager and the kernel, to run in Ring 0, where they enjoy maximum protection. In Windows 3.0, code running in real mode, such as DOS programs and BIOS code, run in Ring 3, and all other applications run in Ring 1. Starting with Windows 3.1 and in all subsequent 3.x releases, all the code running in Ring 1 is moved over to run in Ring 3. So essentially, Rings 1 and 2 are left under the control of the processor.

Microsoft products to this day continue to utilize this architecture. However, a slightly different vocabulary is used. Processes running in Ring 0 are said to be running in *supervisory mode*. These are the processes that require the most protection and the highest processor priority. All other processes, which would be running in Ring 3, are running in *user mode*.

BUZZ WORDS

Privilege level: A level of protection and priority that certain lines of code running within an OS have over other lines of code.

Processor ring: Another term for privilege level.

Supervisory mode: A process by which an OS runs code at the highest possible privilege level.

User mode: A process by which an OS runs code at a lower privilege level.

Virtual machine: An environment set up in system memory that emulates all functions of a working computer, providing the illusion that a program is the only code running on a computer system.

VIRTUAL MACHINES

To understand how an OS manages to juggle several different applications running at once along with their associated data, you must understand the concept of *virtual machines*. Like anything else virtual, a virtual machine doesn't really exist. But the things that require its services, such as applications, think that it does. Don't confuse a virtual machine with virtual memory. They're not the same. However, a virtual machine is capable of addressing virtual memory, so in that sense, they're virtually related.

A virtual machine is emulated in memory. The program running in that virtual machine is allotted its own share of CPU time and is under the impression that it owns the CPU. It just can't figure out why there are times in which the CPU seems to have gone to sleep. It doesn't know about the other programs that think *they're* the only ones the CPU will deign to address.

The OS intervenes on behalf of each virtual program for every service it requires. It has to. The virtual machine has absolutely no access to any code running in Ring 0. So if the program issues a hardware interrupt, it issues it to the VMM.

What happens if two different applications attempt to run at the same instant? That depends entirely on the CPU. Some of the more modern CPUs have multiple pipelines and can process more than one thread of code at the same time. On one of these processors, both apps will run concurrently. On earlier CPUs without this capability, the VMM intercepts both calls and based on priority, determines which one runs first.

VIRTUAL DEVICE DRIVERS

It only makes sense that if you're going to have a virtual machine, then you're going to have to use virtual device drivers (VDD). In the old days of DOS, the device driver basically acted as an extension to the BIOS and, in essence, any application running in DOS could directly access the hardware. However, in the days of DOS, two programs could never run at the same time, and therefore, there was no possibility that a device would receive two hardware calls at the same time. Such an event would result in one of those NMIs I discussed earlier.

In order to maintain backward compatibility with DOS programs, Windows 3.x requires that AUTOEXEC.BAT and CONFIG.SYS files contain any relevant information for a device and load DOS drivers. However, in order to make sure the system remains stable while multitasking, when any program (including a DOS program) is loaded into a virtual machine, it is assigned a VDD. The VDD intercepts any hardware calls, and the VMM issues calls directly to the hardware. In Windows 3.x these driver files end in a .386 extension.

DYNAMICALLY LINKED LIBRARIES

A concept Windows 3.0 borrowed from the world of UNIX was that of the Dynamically Linked Library (DLL). These are also called dynamic link libraries. Since many programs might require exactly the same subroutines or code as another at any given time, rather than write this code into each and every application that runs under Windows, that code is stored in a *library*. The library serves as a repository for this information. When an application requires the services of a particular DLL, it issues a call for a subroutine, and the OS intercepts that call and loads the appropriate DLL in its place. The app neither knows nor cares that what it originally requested wasn't exactly what it got. Its needs were fulfilled either way.

There are a couple of advantages to using DLLs. For one thing, DLLs can be changed to accommodate new programs and/or services that may be developed. For example, a company might write a DLL to provide a direct link to the virtual driver for a its brand of digital cameras. When that DLL was first conceived, there were only a handful of models of that camera available. As the manufacturer comes out with more advanced models, it takes the DLL, adds the new subroutines, and replaces the older file with the newer one when users install the device drivers for their new toys.

A second advantage of a DLL is that it only gets loaded into RAM when and if it is needed. When the driver call for that camera is made, the DLL is dynamically loaded into RAM (bet you wondered where that part of the name came from), runs, and is unloaded when its task is completed. This prevents resource requirements for an OS from being any greater than they already are.

BUZZ WORDS ———————

Library: In programming, a collection of subroutines that are required by several or all applications running on a computer. By storing this code in a single file, it does not need to be duplicated many times over.

CHAPTER SUMMARY

In the past several pages you have been introduced to a number of the concepts that would go on to make Windows what it is today. Although it is totally unnecessary for a technician these days to understand how Windows 3.1 is installed and how to run the OS, an understanding of its basic architecture goes a long way in understanding some of the concepts that will be introduced later in this book.

BRAIN DRAIN

1. Several times in this chapter, it was pointed out that Windows 3.x products were not true OSs. Explain why this is so.

2. It was also pointed out that Windows 3.x takes over the role of OS once it is loaded. Discuss several ways how it does that.

3. Discuss the concept of the virtual machine. Why is it that several virtual machines can be running on a single computer at any given time?

4. What is a DLL, and why is it so important to the Windows environment?

5. How do virtual device drivers differ from a "real" device driver?

THE 64K$ QUESTIONS

1. Steve Jobs named the LISA after _____.

   a. His wife
   b. His daughter
   c. His mother
   d. His secretary

2. What is one key reason why most people today won't load Windows 1.0 onto their computer just to see what it could do?

   a. It only runs under DOS, and DOS won't run on today's machines.
   b. The presence of memory over 1MB causes WIN.COM to fail.
   c. It had no VGA drivers, and most of us today don't have an old EGA video card and monitor lying around.
   d. It would corrupt their current OSs.

3. Which of the following features of the 80386 microprocessor did Windows 3.x exclusively take advantage of when running in 386 enhanced mode?

   a. Protected mode
   b. The 32-bit address bus
   c. Virtual real mode
   d. Virtual memory

4. DOS has already been loaded on the system and the user types in the command **WIN**. What is the first file to be loaded by WIN.COM?

   a. WIN386.EXE
   b. KRNL386.EXE
   c. USER.EXE
   d. GDI.EXE

5. Windows 3.x versions all use _____ in order to give the user the sense that multiple programs are running at the same time.

a. Pre-emptive multitasking

b. Cooperative multitasking

c. Task switching

d. Preoperative multitasking

6. The core OS files in Windows 3.x all run in _____.

a. Ring 0

b. Ring 1

c. Ring 2

d. Ring 3

7. Applications in Windows 3.x all run in _____.

a. Ring 0

b. Ring 1

c. Ring 2

d. Ring 3

8. Which operational mode of Windows requires an 80386 (or higher) processor in order to function?

a. Real mode

b. Standard mode

c. Enhanced mode

d. Virtual mode

9. Which operational mode of Windows takes advantage of memory beyond 1MB but cannot address virtual memory?

a. Real mode

b. Standard mode

c. Enhanced mode

d. Virtual mode

10. Which Windows feature allows the user to put an Excel table into a Word document that will automatically update in Word every time the user changes the source data in Excel?

a. OLE

b. DDX

c. OSI

d. DDE

11. Which operational mode of Windows did legacy DOS applications run in?

a. Real mode

b. Standard mode

c. Enhanced mode

d. Virtual mode

12. Which of the following functions in Windows ensured that DOS programs never knew that other applications were running on the system?

a. The legacy DLL

b. The VMM

c. WIN.COM

d. EMM386.EXE

13. Which of the following Windows functions allowed memory beyond 1MB to be utilized?

a. The legacy DLL

b. The VMM

c. WIN.COM

d. EMM386.EXE

14. A file that provides a unified set of instructions to a number of different applications is known as an _____.

a. DLL

b. VXD

c. API

d. INI

15. Which Windows feature allows the user to move data seamlessly from one application to another on the fly?

a. OLE

b. DDX

c. OSI

d. DDE

16. The reason several DOS applications can be run at the same time in Windows 3.x is that _____.
    a. Windows drops back to task switching when DOS programs are involved
    b. Cooperative multitasking prevents each DOS app from seeing one another
    c. Each app runs in a separate virtual machine
    d. They can't.

17. What is the default size of a typical UMB?
    a. 8K
    b. 12K
    c. 16K
    d. 32K

18. Where was information stored in virtual memory located in Windows 3.x?
    a. A hidden partition created when Windows was first installed
    b. A file called VMM.DLL
    c. A file called 386SPART.PAR
    d. A file called SYSMEM.VMM

19. What was the typical extension for a virtual device driver in Windows 3.x?
    a. .VXD
    b. .DLL
    c. .VDD
    d. .386

20. A process running in Ring 0 is said to be running in _____.
    a. User mode
    b. Supervisory mode
    c. Restricted mode
    d. Access mode

TRICKY TERMINOLOGY

Cooperative multitasking: The ability of an OS to simultaneously run more than one program, placing responsibility on the application for relinquishing control of the system.

Enhanced mode: An operational mode specific to Windows that took advantage of advanced functions available in the 80386 microprocessor, including the ability to use virtual memory and to function in virtual real mode.

Library: In programming, a collection of subroutines that are required by several or all applications running on a computer. By storing this code in a single file, it does not need to be duplicated many times over.

Multitasking: The ability of an OS to simultaneously run more than one program at once.

Privilege level: A level of protection and priority that certain lines of code running within an OS have over other lines of code.

Processor ring: Another term for privilege level.

Real mode: An operational mode for either a CPU or an OS in which only one application can be present on the system at once and only 1MB of RAM can be addressed by that application.

Standard mode: An operational mode specific to Windows in which the OS could access expanded memory beyond 1MB and could task switch multiple applications.

Supervisory mode: A process by which an OS runs code at the highest possible privilege level.

Task switching: The ability of an OS to close a program, run another, and then return to the same point in the program previously closed.

User mode: A process by which an OS runs code at a lower privilege level.

Virtual machine: An environment set up in system memory that emulates all functions of a working computer, providing the illusion that a program is the only code running on a computer system.

ACRONYM ALERT

COMDEX: Computer Dealer Exposition. An annual trade show for businesses in the computer industry.

CPL: Current Privilege Level. The level of priority at which code is running on machines. It is the method by which processor rings are defined.

DDE: Dynamic Data Exchange. A technology for exchanging data between two autonomous programs running on a single computer.

DLL: Dynamically Linked Library. A file that contains a collection of subroutines that can be called on the fly by any application running on the system that requires the services it provides and then can be flushed from memory when its task is finished.

NMI: Non-Maskable Interrupt. Any software or hardware induced interrupt that requires instantaneous attention from the CPU.

OLE: Object Linking and Embedding. A technology that allows an object to be created in one application, imported into a second application; should the properties of the object ever change in the first, it is automatically updated in the second.

PM: Program Manager. A file and application management utility provided in Windows 3.x products.

SDK: Software Development Kit. A collection of utilities and programs provided by an OS manufacturer that makes the development of applications to run on its OS much easier.

UMB: Upper Memory Block. A segment of memory created by an extended memory manager in the address range between 640K and 1MB of conventional memory.

VDD: Virtual Device Driver. A piece of software running within an OS that emulates a hardware device driver.

VMM: Virtual Machine Manager and Virtual Memory Manager. The first is a piece of software running within an OS that creates, maintains, and breaks down in memory an environment that emulates an actual computer. The second is a piece of software running within an OS that creates and manages the swap file on a hard drive.

CHAPTER 4

INTRODUCING WIN9x

The Windows versions from 3.0 to 3.11WFW provided a useful and formidable entry into the GUI for Microsoft. Unfortunately, they lacked the punch and the stability offered by some of its competitors: most notably the Apple Macintosh. As the 80386 gave way to the 80486 there was no driving need to change OS technology. The 486 was little more than a 386 on steroids.

However, when the Pentium was released in 1993, it offered several features not supported by Windows 3.x. The most notable of these features was the presences of multiple processing pipelines. The CPU could process several lines of code at the same time, but Windows could not. At about the same time, Intel threw another wrench into the works. That wrench was called Plug 'n Play.

Microsoft's original intent had been to release a 32-bit multi-threading OS in 1992. Delays in development and production haunted the product practically from its inception, but once Windows 95 (WIN95) was released in the summer of 1995, it was an unmitigated commercial success. It sold more than a million copies in the first day and essentially put an end to competition in the OS world for nearly a decade.

This chapter will cover the various versions of WIN9x. The more advanced users among you will know these versions as the 4.xx.xxxx versions. The number four indicated that they were in reality Windows Version 4. The two digits following the 4 indicated sub-versions, and the final three or four digits were revision numbers.

For the most part, the core remains essentially the same. There are, however, some differences between versions that should be pointed out.

A+ OPERATING SYSTEM TECHNOLOGIES EXAM OBJECTIVES

In this chapter, I will cover the following CompTIA exam objectives:

1.1 Identify the major desktop components and interfaces and their functions. Differentiate the characteristics of Windows 9x/Me, Windows NT 4.0 Workstation, Windows 2000 Professional, and Windows XP.

2.1 Identify the procedures for installing Windows 9x/Me, Windows NT 4.0 Workstation, Windows 2000 Professional, and Windows XP, and bringing the software to a basic operational level.

2.2 Identify steps to perform an operating system upgrade from Windows 9x/Me, Windows NT 4.0 Workstation, Windows 2000 Professional, and Windows XP. Given an upgrade scenario, choose the appropriate next steps.

Hardware Requirements and New Features of WIN95

Contrary to popular belief, WIN95 was not the first Microsoft OS to feature a GUI. Windows NT 3.1 earned that honor in 1993. However, that OS was designed for high-end workstations and network environments and didn't get a lot of public exposure. Its lifespan was relatively short, it is rarely, if ever, seen today, and it isn't covered on any certification exams. Therefore, I won't be covering NT 3.1 in this book.

WIN95 was the first graphical OS to capture the public's fancy. Previous versions of Windows had required MS-DOS to be properly configured and running on the computer before they could load. WIN95 stands on its own. It is a 32-bit OS as well and, therefore, could take full advantage of emerging processors.

Minimum Hardware Requirements for Installation

Microsoft's intent had originally been for WIN95 to run on any machine that had been capable of running WIN3.x in 386 enhanced mode. In this respect, it fell a little short. The requirements were a bit more stringent. Still, by today's standards the requirements were quite modest. In order to run WIN95 a computer needs the following at the minimum:

- 20MHz 386DX microprocessor
- 4MB of RAM
- 1.44MB floppy diskette drive
- 85MB free hard disk space (for local installation)
- VGA graphics

Exam Note: For virtually all of the Microsoft OSs, CompTIA expects you to know the minimum hardware requirements for installation. Know them all. You never know which OS it will hit you with.

Just having hardware that meets the minimum specifications is no guarantee that a computer will successfully run WIN95. The hardware also has to support virtual device drivers exclusively. As a result, Microsoft would only support the product if a customer's computer consisted entirely of hardware that was included in its Hardware Compatibility List (HCL).

NEW FEATURES

For the user whose computer satisfied all the requirements, a plethora of new features were available. Some of these new features focused on OS stability, while others focused on the user experience. All of them collectively were really little more than a brief glimpse of what was to come.

PLUG 'N PLAY

Plug 'n Play (PnP) was a new standard incorporated into WIN95 that (in theory, at least) allows a user to install a new piece of hardware and have the OS automatically configure the device. The first versions of PnP worked pretty well as long as the user was using:

- A device that was fully PnP compliant
- A computer with a PnP-compliant BIOS
- A PnP-compliant OS

Anyone who ever fought with a device installation when even one of these three critical elements was missing understands fully why, in its early stages, PnP developed the nickname Plug 'n Pray. When it did work, it was a blessing. A device was automatically recognized by the BIOS during POST and assigned an IRQ. Windows automatically detected the new device once it was loaded and launched a device installation wizard that led the user through the process of driver installation.

> **EXAM NOTE:** It is very likely that you might get a question relating to the three essential elements required for PnP to be 100% functional. Even though many consider this to be a hardware issue, you can expect to see it on the OS exam as well.

In the early stages of PnP there were three types of devices that could be auto-configured by PnP:

- PnP-compliant ISA devices
- PCI devices
- PCMCIA devices

All PCI and PCMCIA devices were designed to be PnP compliant by default. ISA devices were not PnP compliant by nature, and the capabilities had to be incorporated into the device.

FAT32

Previous Microsoft desktop offerings had supported only the FAT16 file system. Windows NT 3.1 had introduced the NTFS file system, but as I mentioned earlier, that OS didn't see much use on the desktop environment. FAT32 appeared in Service Release 2 (SR2) of WIN95 and offers all of the advantages of that file system. For a more detailed discussion, refer back to Chapter One, An Introduction to Operating Systems.

PRE-EMPTIVE MULTITASKING

Instead of using the cooperative multitasking used by WIN3.x, WIN95 uses *pre-emptive multitasking*. No longer are the applications in charge of when, where, and how they give up control of the system. A *task scheduler* runs as an integral part of the OS and makes sure each and every application running on the system has an equal chance at system resources.

EXAM NOTE: Be able to distinguish between cooperative multitasking and pre-emptive multitasking. It's a popular exam topic.

INTEGRATED 32-BIT TCP/IP

WIN95 is the first OS in which TCP/IP was included as a default networking protocol. Windows 3.11WFW provided support only for Microsoft's native NetBEUI protocol and its own version of IPX/SPX in order to allow it to work on Novell networks. For 3.11 to run on a TCP/IP network, the protocol had to be installed separately.

INTEGRATED MULTIMEDIA CAPABILITIES

Microsoft incorporated into WIN95 several new features specific to the enjoyment of multimedia applications. For one thing, CD-ROM support and the CDFS file system were part of the default installation. A new video playback engine called Video for Windows was also part of the OS.

WIN9X STRUCTURE

In nearly every respect, WIN95 was a dramatic departure from the 3.x products. One of the more glaring differences is that it is a true OS and not simply an application running on top of DOS. Second, it was the first consumer-level 32-bit OS from Microsoft to hit the market. In order to maintain backward compatibility with WIN3.x and MS-DOS, certain key elements from each were carried over.

KERNEL FILES

If you recall from Chapter Three, The Evolution of Windows and Windows Basics, Windows 3.x relied on the three core files of MS-DOS, IO.SYS, MSDOS.SYS, and COMMAND.COM, to

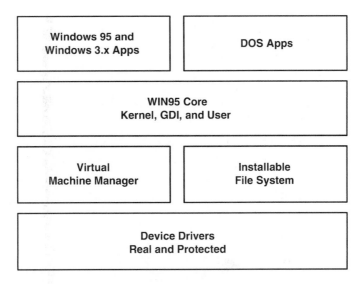

Figure 4.1   WIN95 Architecture

be fully loaded and operational before Windows could be run. And then Windows ran as a separate application. The three core files of WIN3.x were KRNL385.EXE, GDI.EDE, and USER.EXE.

For the purposes of backward compatibility, Windows retains all of these files. These files continue to make up the core of WIN9x (**Figure 4.1**). However, their significance and, in one case, even the structure differs greatly. First consider the core files retained from MS-DOS.

> **EXAM NOTE:** If there were Ten Commandments for passing the OS exam one of them would very likely be, "Thou shalt know the six core files of WIN9x backward and forward."

IO.SYS

In WIN95, IO.SYS has been retooled and actually performs the functions for which IO.SYS and MSDOS.SYS had been responsible in the days of DOS. All of the information required to start the computer following a successful POST is contained in this one file. Now, if you recall from Chapter Two, MS-DOS and the Command Prompt, IO.SYS had been responsible for calling up CONFIG.SYS, and MSDOS.SYS loaded AUTOEXEC.BAT.

WIN95 requires neither CONFIG.SYS nor AUTOEXEC.BAT in order to boot. They're both present for that elusive goal of backward compatibility. WIN95 extracts its system information from a structure called the registry, which I'll be covering in detail later in this chapter.

MSDOS.SYS

If MSDOS.SYS has been combined with IO.SYS, then why is there still a file by that name? Once again, it's for backward compatibility. Microsoft had no illusions that people who had spent the last several years accumulating expensive software for their Windows 3.1 computers were going to upgrade to WIN95 if they knew they would have to shell out several hundred (or even several thousand) dollars for all new software.

In WIN95, MSDOS.SYS exists as an ASCII text file with a structure very similar to one of the INI files used by WIN3.x. **Figure 4.2** shows the default MSDOS.SYS open in a DOS editor. As you can see from the text in the illustration, this file must be a minimum of 1024 bytes long. According to Microsoft, a file smaller than this size is likely to be seen by many antivirus applications as being infected and will be quarantined. The array of Xs following that final statement is there for a reason as well. As long as the file size of 1024 bytes remains consistent, there are a number of statements that can be added to MSDOS.SYS that will fine-tune or modify the performance of windows. **Table 4.1** lists some of those statements and the effect each has on the system.

Making any changes to MSDOS.SYS does require that the attributes of Hidden, Read-only, and System be reset to 0. You cannot do this from Windows Explorer or even from a command prompt once Windows has booted to the GUI. In order to change the attributes on this file, you must boot into DOS mode and make the changes from there.

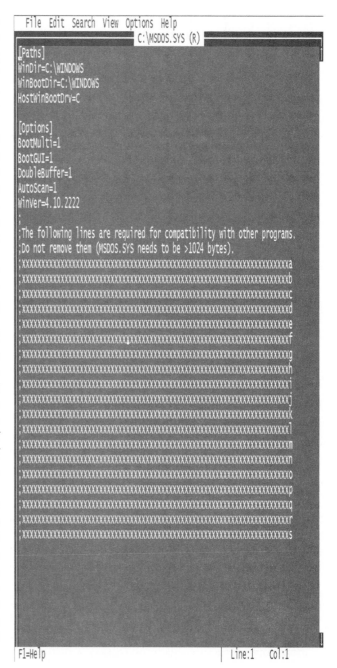

Figure 4.2 MSDOS.SYS is an ASCII text file in WIN9x.

COMMAND.COM

COMMAND.COM retains the same role in WIN9x as it did in MS-DOS. It is the command interpreter for DOS. WIN9x carries with it a version of DOS called DOS 7.0. This version is

Table 4.1   Custom Entries for WIN9x MSDOS.SYS

Entry	Description
Autoscan=	Disable | "BYPASS" ScanDisk check after system lockup (OSR 2.x + Win98/Me ONLY)
BootDelay=0/1	Skip 2 seconds boot delay (In Win98/Me defaults to 0)
BootGUI=0/1	Boot to MS-DOS mode
BootKeys=0/1	Enable/Disable Startup Menu keys
BootMenu=0/1	Display WIN9x Startup Menu
BootMenuDefault=0/1	Select Normal boot option (loads WIN9x)
BootMenuDelay=0/60	Boot delay (in seconds)
BootMulti=0/1	Enable/Disable Dual-Boot
BootWin=0/1	Enable/Disable WIN9x as OS
DblSpace=0/1	Enable/Disable DoubleSpace
DisableLog=0/1	Enable/Disable BOOTLOG.TXT creation
DoubleBuffer=0/1	Enable/Disable Double Buffer
DrvSpace=0/1	Enable/Disable DriveSpace
HostWinBootDrv=	Set Host WIN9x OS Boot Drive
LoadTop=0/1	Enable/Disable loading of COMMAND.COM in upper memory
Logo=0/1	Display/Not Display Windows Logo during boot
Network=0/1	Enable/Disable boot with Network/TCP/IP support
SystemReg=0/1	Enable/Disable System Registry scan
WinBootDir=	Set WIN9x OS Boot Directory
WinDir=	Set WIN9x OS Directory
WinVer=4.xx.xxxx	Windows 98/Me version check (Win98/Me ONLY)

Entries containing 0/1: 0 disables the function and 1 enables it.

actually a bit scaled down from Version 6.2 and does not support all of the same commands. Still, it provides all of the requisite services of the command prompt.

COMMAND.COM is used only when a command prompt is opened. In GUI mode, WIN.COM acts as the command interpreter. Since WIN9x supports multiple MS-DOS windows being open at once, it is possible for several different instances for COMMAND.COM to be open at the same time.

INI FILES

Also described in Chapter Three were several different .INI files. Two key files were SYSTEM.INI and WIN.INI. WIN9x retains these files for backward compatibility with programs designed for WIN3.x. They have exactly the same structure and perform the same functions.

The WIN9x Kernel

After you get into the WIN9x kernel, things start to change a bit. Microsoft touted WIN95 as being a 32-bit OS. Windows broke a long-standing tradition in one respect in order to provide this 32-bit support. It stopped supporting older CPUs. If you didn't have a 386DX (or faster) microprocessor, WIN9x didn't run. Calling WIN95 a 32-bit OS was sort of true. However, if I want to be a little more accurate, it really should be called a 16-bit OS with a 32-bit overlay.

> **Exam Note:** Be able to define the process of thunking. Whether you like it or not, it's a real word.

By this, I mean that the OS was built on the basis of older 16-bit technology. Other files were sewn into the OS to provide 32-bit functionality without losing the OS's ability to run 16-bit software. In order to accomplish this, Microsoft developed a technique it called thunking. *Thunking* is merely the translation of 32-bit commands into 16-bit format and vice versa. For every 16-bit kernel file, there is a 32-bit file (see **Figure 4.3**). The files involved are KERNEL32.DLL, KRNL386.EXE, USER.DLL, USER.EXE, GDI.DLL, and GDI.EXE. The DLLs are all 32-bit components, while the EXE files are 16-bit.

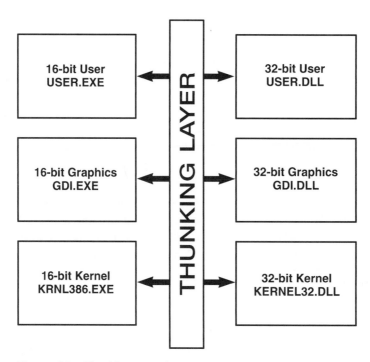

Figure 4.3 Thunking at work.

If a 16-bit application or device is communicating with a 32-bit process, it first communicates with the 16-bit entity, which translates the request and passes it on to the 32-bit version.

Two other features incorporated into the WIN9x architecture were a beefed-up Virtual Machine Manager (VMM) and an Installable File System (IFS). While the VMM provides a similar functionality to the one used in WIN3.x, since it now has the responsibility of sorting out 32-bit applications from 16-bit Windows applications and older DOS apps, Microsoft made it a bit more sophisticated. IFS allows file systems not native to the OS be added. This would include the file system used by various CD formats and the Network File System (NFS) used by networking clients.

> **BUZZ WORDS** ——————
>
> **System virtual machine:** An environment in Windows that emulates a complete computer system and houses all of the critical processes and functions of the OS.

THE WIN95 VIRTUAL MACHINE MANAGER

In Chapter Three, when I was discussing the various modes in which Windows could run, I pointed out that the three basic modes were real, standard, and 386 enhanced modes. WIN95 also included the pre-emptive multitasking I discussed earlier in the chapter. So now, when multiple applications are running on the system, VMM has to keep track of which are 16-bit and which are 32-bit; it has to manage real and protected mode operations running at the same time, and now it has to assure that applications that employ cooperative multitasking don't interfere with those that use pre-emptive multitasking.

As with WIN3.x, the WIN95 VMM accomplishes this by running apps in separate virtual machines. A couple of key things to remember are these: VMM runs in Ring 0, while the machines it creates and manages all run in Ring 3. When WIN95 first boots, it creates its first virtual machine for itself. System services and kernel files all run in this *system virtual machine*. Any WIN95 apps that are started will open a separate VM that runs inside of the system VM.

WIN3.x apps will all run within the same VM. If a WIN3.x application is started, a single VM will be created in which all 3.x apps will subsequently load. This allows the WIN3.x apps to make use of the cooperative multitasking they require. However, it also has the negative effect that, if any WIN3.x app crashes, they all do. And in doing so, they will most likely take all 16-bit support down along with them. **Figure 4.4** illustrates the concept behind the WIN95 Virtual Machine structure.

Each DOS application runs in a separate virtual machine that resides outside of the system machine. DOS VMs occupy no more than 1MB of RAM, divided into 640K of conventional memory and 384K of upper memory, and run in real mode. They can also be configured to use expanded memory, if so desired. For every DOS app on the system, a program information file (PIF) will be created. When users edit the properties of a DOS application, they are editing the PIF. Use of expanded memory is one of the options available (see **Figure 4.5**). Obviously, for this to work, protected mode must be enabled. But the executable cannot run outside of its 1MB shell.

WIN95 can open as many of these real mode virtual machines as the user sees fit, but only one can ever be active at a time. Within each machine a separate instance of IO.SYS, MSDOS.SYS,

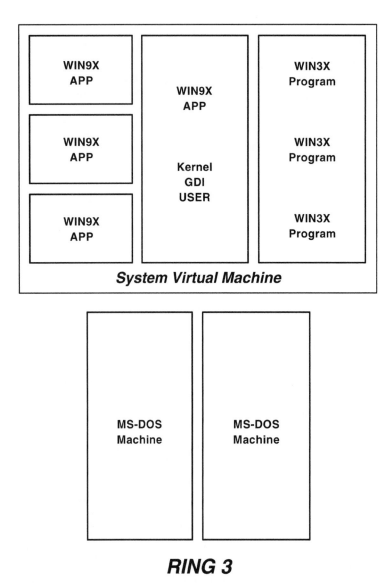

Figure 4.4   The WIN95 Virtual Machine Manager at work.

and COMMAND.COM will run. A separate copy of each DOS device driver required by the system will also be running within each DOS virtual machine. And when one of these apps is active, no other application will attempt to access the CPU.

INSTALLABLE FILE SYSTEM

A critical component of WIN95 is the installable file system (IFS). Under MS-DOS and Windows 3.1, applications and system components that needed to handle file I/O requests had

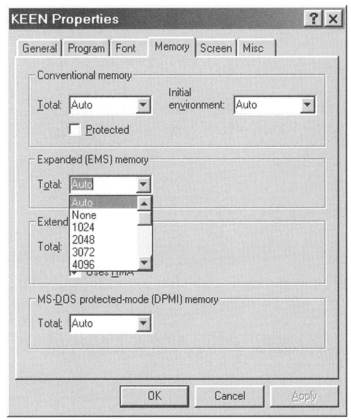

Figure 4.5 For every DOS program, there is a PIF file that describes how that program runs.

to make a direct call to the BIOS in order to fulfill those requests. The file system drivers of WIN95 exist as virtual device drivers running in Ring 0, instead of as real-mode MS-DOS drivers. Not only does this allow file system drivers to run in 32-bit protected-mode, it beefs up WIN9x networking capabilities.

> **EXAM NOTE:** Make sure that you're aware that a key function of IFS is to load the network redirectors.

For any OS to join a network a piece of software called a *client* must be installed and running. An integral part of the client is the *redirector*. So what is a redirector? On a non-networked system, any time your computer goes out looking for any system resource, it knows it will find it locally. On

BUZZ WORDS

Client: A piece of software running from within an OS that allows the device to connect to a network.

Redirector: An OS function (usually running within a client) that intercepts hardware and software calls that are intended for remote devices and points them in the right direction.

a network, the user might be requesting the services of a piece of hardware on the other side of the building, or even the other side of the world, for that matter. The redirector examines a request and determines whether that request can be fulfilled locally. If not, it redirects that request to the appropriate destination. Hence the name.

IFS also supports a 32-bit virtual file allocation table (VFAT) driver, the 32-bit CD-ROM file system (CDFS) driver, and integrated 32-bit network redirectors for Windows NT and NetWare servers. With an IFS, third-party vendors can add specialized file systems under the IFS Manager. Applications and system components are now accessing the hard disk file system through VFAT, instead of making a direct hardware call (which is prohibited in WIN9x and later Microsoft OSs).

THE WINDOWS REGISTRY

In all previous versions of Windows, certain system settings and parameters were all incorporated into the .INI files. During the boot process these files were read and as a result, device drivers and parameters were loaded. .INI files were also responsible for mapping the locations of critical system files and where applications loaded on the system could be located.

> **Buzz Words**
>
> **Registry:** In Windows, it is a relational database that contains all system and application settings and/or parameters.

This was a functional method, but it was resource intensive and provided additional overhead on the system that WIN9x could not afford. As a result, all of this responsibility was migrated over to the registry. The *registry* acts as a relational database of every setting, parameter, device driver, or file location the system requires for full functionality.

The registry consists of a series of six primary registry keys. A key consists of a specific category of setting relevant to a specific area of Windows functionality. Any number of subkeys can exist beneath the primary keys. All of this information is initialized when Windows is first installed and is constantly being updated every time a new piece of hardware or software is installed and every time a user makes a change to the system configuration. It is all stored in two primary files: USER.DAT and SYSTEM.DAT. In WIN95, a backup of each of these files existed, but carried .DAO extensions. Windows 98 increased the number of backup files from one to three.

REGISTRY ORGANIZATION

There are six primary keys in the registry. These are HKEY_CLASSES_ROOT, HKEY_CURRENT_USER, HKEY_LOCAL_MACHINE, HKEY_USERS, HKEY_CURRENT_CONFIG, and HKEY_DYN_DATA. Each of these primary keys holds specific information critical to the system. Oddly enough, one of these keys does not get stored in the .DAT files I just mentioned. I'll get to that in a minute.

Beneath the primary key are subkeys. These are frequently referred to as hives. Each hive contains sections specific to the properties of a particular function within the OS. For example, later on, when I discuss the primary key called HKEY_LOCAL_MACHINE, I mention that this key holds information specific to hardware and software. One of the subkeys is called Software. Beneath this folder are additional folders for each and every brand of software installed on the system, as well as folders for software Microsoft thinks you are likely to install later. The folder specific to Microsoft (or any other brand) would be called a hive file.

EXAM NOTE: You need to know all six primary keys of the Windows Registry.

HKEY_CLASSES_ROOT

HKEY_CLASSES_ROOT provides the information that OLE requires in order to work. It also stores the mappings used by different programs when the user takes advantage of the drag-and-drop functionality offered by Windows. Other information, including how different applications deal with different file types based on their extensions, is stored in this key.

HKEY_CURRENT_USER

HKEY_CURRENT_USER contains information specific to the preferences of the user logged onto the machine. WIN95 is capable of storing the settings for each person who creates an account on a machine. The various settings, preferences, desktop configuration, and applications groups for a specific individual make up that user's *profile.*

HKEY_LOCAL_MACHINE

HKEY_LOCAL_MACHINE stores information specific to the hardware and software running on the machine. For most technicians, this key is where the majority of registry changes you'll ever make will take place.

HKEY_USERS

HKEY_USERS is where the information for all users that have a profile on a specific machine will be stored. If two or more users have created profiles on a machine, this key will be different from that of HKEY_CURRENT_USER. Each profile will point to a specific set of subkeys. When a user logs on, this subkey will form HKEY_CURRENT_USER. If there is only one profile, there will be little or no difference between the two keys.

HKEY_CURRENT_CONFIG

HKEY_CURRENT_CONFIG loads a specific hardware profile. As Windows supports multiple user profiles, it also supports more than one hardware configuration on a single machine.

For example, you might have a computer with two video cards. When you are running your photo editor, you keep your image on one monitor and the software menus on another. But when you're only using your word processor, you have no use for the second monitor. By creating a separate profile in which the second video card is disabled, when Windows is booting you have the option of selecting the hardware configuration of your choice.

HKEY_DYN_DATA

HKEY_DYN_DATA is the one key that is not permanently stored on a hard drive. It is configured on the fly as the system boots, based on what user has logged onto the system and what specific hardware profile has been selected. It stays RAM-resident until Windows is shut down.

THE REGISTRY EDITOR

For the most part, the registry is best left alone. Most configuration changes can be made in the OS within different applets or fields that I'll discuss in Chapter Five. However, once in a while, it is necessary for a technician to manually edit entries in the registry. This is done through a command-line utility called REGEDIT. Later versions of Windows also included REGEDT32. REGEDIT was included in the first version of WIN95 as a 16-bit registry editor and has been included in every version of Windows released since that date. As its name implies, REGEDT32 is a 32-bit editor. REGEDIT is somewhat limited:

- You can't set security on registry values.
- Not all entries can be edited. Entries whose value types are marked REG_EXPAND_SZ or REG_MULTI_SZ contain binary data. Attempting to edit them will render them useless.
- Individual keys cannot be saved or restored as hive files.

REGEDT32 allows for securing registry keys and editing binary entries (although I recommend that you avoid this practice unless directed by help desk professionals!). It does not, however, allow the user to import or export .REG files. These are files that contain precoded registry entries, and are often provided by help desk personnel to fix specific problems.

In some instances, this can be a tricky and potentially hazardous adventure. There are some settings in the registry that consist of hexadecimal notation that points to specific OS functions or identifies specific hardware and/or application calls. Changing a single character can make an application or piece of hardware act up or possibly not work at all. It is conceivable that some changes could even cause your system to refuse to boot.

That's why it's a good idea to back up the registry before you play around in it. The Registry Editor allows you to back up and restore certain parts of the registry or even the entire registry. And it is where you make all the changes that might cause you to have to restore it.

Some entries are benign enough. For example, if you installed a particular piece of software and then decided you didn't like it all that much after all, chances are pretty good you're going to uninstall it. Unfortunately, uninstalling software does not back out all the changes to the

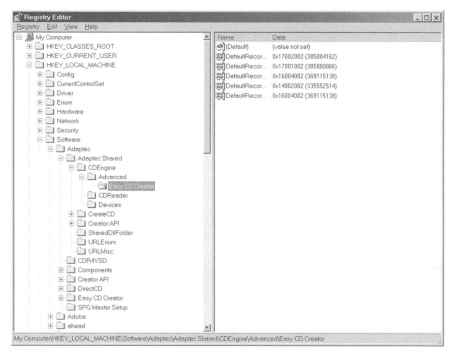

Figure 4.6   The registry maintains information on every piece of software you've ever installed, including software that no longer exists on your system.

registry that installing the program initiated to begin with. As you can see in **Figure 4.6**, under HKEY_LOCAL_MACHINE>Software, every application you've ever installed creates a folder with its settings. If the application is no longer installed, it's pretty safe to delete that folder.

ConfigSafe

Registry corruption is such a common issue in Windows that third-party manufacturers have made a killing by providing failsafe software to protect the end user. One of the most popular of these that is worth mentioning is a product called ConfigSafe by a company called Imagine-Lan.

ConfigSafe tracks changes to a system's configuration over time. In the event of a system failure, or should the system suddenly start experiencing repeated system crashes, the software allows users or technicians to quickly restore a problem system to a working configuration.

ConfigSafe currently offers versions that support Windows 95/98/Me and Windows NT/2000/XP operating systems. ConfigSafe works by taking a *snapshot* of a system's configuration. This can be done at any specific point by the user, and the

> **Buzz Words**
>
> **Snapshot:** In reference to an OS, it is a small binary file that contains information useful in replicating the organization and structure of an application or configuration.

program will automatically do so whenever there is a configuration change. The snapshot stores information about the system's configuration at that exact point in time. Some examples of information tracked are as follows:

- Configuration files (WIN.INI, SYSTEM.INI, AUTOEXEC.BAT, CONFIG.SYS)
- System changes (memory, processor, Windows version)
- Drives (hard drives, CD-ROMs, network connections)
- Directories
- Windows registry
- System assets (for example, the Windows desktop)

Should the end user or a technician discover that some change to the system has rendered it unstable, he or she can "go back in time" to one of the snapshots taken when the system was working properly and restore those versions of the system files. The system will now work properly. As I will discuss in Chapter Eleven, Introducing XP, XP has incorporated a similar feature called System Restore into the OS, so that a third-party utility is no longer needed.

WIN9X VERSIONS

Starting with its initial release on August 4, 1995, and all the way through to the release of Windows 2000 (oddly enough, in the year 2000), Windows enjoyed a five-year reign as the most popular OS in the world. Several different versions appeared over those five years, and many of them continue to exist on machines to this day. Therefore it is important for the technician to be able to navigate all of them.

WIN95 SR2

Most of the features of the initial release of WIN95 were discussed in detail in earlier sections of this chapter. Therefore, it isn't necessary to go over it all again. So I'll begin my discussion of the various versions with WIN95-SR2.

FAT32 had originally been intended to be a part of WIN95 in its initial release. However, problems integrating the file system into the OS were threatening to delay a release that had already been put off several times over the previous eighteen months. Therefore, the decision was made to release WIN95 without this important feature. Therefore, FAT32 support first appeared in SR-2.

SR-2 also featured the first release of a new graphics API by Microsoft called DirectX. DirectX consists of a collection of various routines that allow different multimedia components, such as the video card, CD-ROM, and sound card, to share common command sets and to seamlessly communicate with one another.

Another feature that was provided for SR-2, but that was only available as a download from Microsoft at first, was USB support. In 1996, Microsoft released WIN95 OSR2.5, which included USB on the CD. What a lot of users didn't realize was that this feature was required in order to get AGP video cards to function as well.

WINDOWS 98

As with the remainder of the WIN9x products, WIN98 was not really a technical improvement over WIN95, but rather an improvement that sported added features. The basic core of the product didn't change much. Most of the new features benefited the users whose computers were high-priced home video arcades rather than business tools. As such, the thrust of Microsoft's marketing campaign was targeted at the home user rather than the corporate environment.

WIN98 upped the ante in terms of installation requirements as well. Its added features put a little more strain on hardware and as a result, Microsoft was a little less liberal in stating minimum requirements. WIN98's published requirements included the following:

- 66MHz 80486DX microprocessor
- 16MB of RAM
- 140MB free hard disk space (minimum install)
- 1.44MB 3.5″ floppy diskette drive
- VGA monitor

WIN98 was the first OS to recognize the impact of the Internet on the average home user, and it sewed a new version of Internet Explorer so tightly into the OS that uninstalling it could render the system unstable (although independent programmers would release a bevy of shareware products on the market that claimed to perform this feat). Microsoft also added support to some newly emerging technologies and dramatically increased PnP capabilities by expanding the database of built-in device drivers. For the most part, however, WIN98 was little more than a collection of utilities bundled with WIN95 and given a pretty new face.

One of these utilities was an improved backup/recovery program that Microsoft licenses from Seagate (**Figure 4.7**). While it did not support scheduled unattended backups, it did provide support for a variety of different backup devices. There was also a file system converter that was capable of a one-time FAT16 to FAT32 conversion. Just don't change your mind once the conversion is completed. The process isn't reversible.

For those times when PnP didn't work, and the user couldn't get a piece of hardware to work, there was the System Troubleshooter. While this utility did very little to actually solve a problem for the user, it did lead users through a systematic approach to figuring out what went wrong and gave tips on how they might fix problems.

A System File Checker could monitor critical system files and if any change in version number or file size was detected, automatically restore the file to its original version. Unfortunately, if the utility detected a change that was the result of a piece of software that was intentionally installed, the results were occasionally (although rarely) undesirable.

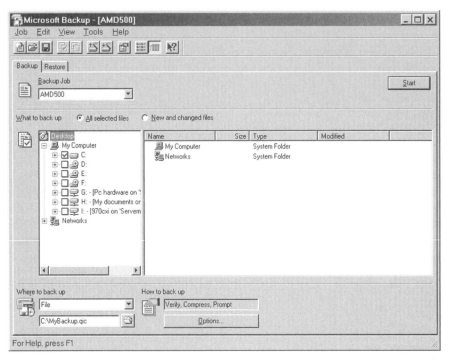

Figure 4.7 The Windows 98 backup utility provided an easier way for users to recover from a hard drive failure.

Dr. Watson was a utility that monitored system errors and generated a text log. The first thing the utility did on its first execution was to create a snapshot of the system. This snapshot consisted of a complete list of drivers running on the system. In the advanced view (**Figure 4.8**), the user could view a complete listing of virtually everything going on within the system at the time the snapshot was made. It worked by intercepting software interrupts. If the system failed abruptly, the last entry in the log would be the guilty culprit.

WINDOWS 98SE

Was Windows 98SE really a new version? Or was it more of a bug fix for Windows 98? Fortunately, as a writer, that's not up to me to decide. Its greatest claim to fame was really that it was more stable than its predecessor. There were a few new features added.

For one thing, a product that Microsoft had previously sold separately, Windows 98 Plus, was incorporated into the package. This allowed the user to select from a large variety of themes and to pick from a number of different pretty pictures for their desktop wallpaper.

The version of Internet Explorer was upgraded to 5.0, and DirectX 6.1 was added during the installation. In an attempt to fend off the image Microsoft had created for itself that Windows 98 could not be taken seriously as an OS for the working environment, it included a piece of software

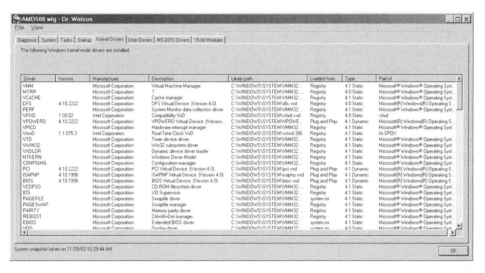

Figure 4.8   Dr. Watson was Windows 98's resident troubleshooter.

called NetMeeting. This allowed teleconferencing over the Internet using both audio and video data streams. While this first version was admittedly primitive by today's standards, it did lead the way to the more sophisticated conferencing features taken for granted today.

The new version of DirectX may have been the most under-rated improvement of all the WIN98SE features. In addition to allowing the OS to take advantage of the latest and greatest toys on the market (mostly targeted at gamers), it also provided the first user-level offering for Internet Connection Sharing (ICS). Microsoft took a look at the increasing numbers of households in the US and abroad that boasted multiple computers and offered this audience a way to get two or more computers on the Internet at the same time.

WINDOWS ME

Windows Millenium, or WINMe as it was more commonly known, turned out to be quite a controversial product. In many respects, it was Microsoft's way of moving the consumer out of the world of backward compatibility. It incorporated some of the technology that was present in the already-released Windows 2000, abandoned some of the features that supported legacy programs, but still maintained a comfortably familiar look and feel. In some respects, this caused more problems than it provided solutions.

One of the key architectural changes was that this version of the OS no longer supported real mode. If you wanted to run an older DOS program on Me, you were on your own. And while it gave the impression of being a faster OS because of how much faster it booted, when running 32-bit apps it was measurably slower than WIN98.

It was the first Microsoft product to implement Universal Plug 'n Play. By the time Me was released, Microsoft had released development of PnP to the UPNP Forum. One of the first things this body did was to make some minor modifications to PnP in order to allow the technology to be incorporated into other brands of OS such as Linux. Some of the older versions of PnP devices and BIOS versions performed unpredictably in the UPNP environment. If anything, these devices could be more troublesome to install than an older legacy device with no PnP capabilities whatsoever.

But WINMe is not without its plus side. System File Protection (SFP) prevents a poorly written application from deleting or overwriting critical system files. The *cabinet (CAB) files* used by the OS during installation were stored locally on the hard drive by default. CAB files are single compressed files that store a large number of smaller files. Should a critical file be altered in any way, SFP would regenerate that file on the fly.

System Restore is another new feature in Me that has saved many an adventurous experimenter. Suppose a user purchases a new toy and the install goes awry. This utility allows the user to step back in time, so to speak, to a system configuration prior to the installation that worked properly and then try the installation again. And fail again.

SUMMARY OF WIN9X VERSIONS

If the WIN9x versions proved nothing else, they proved the old adage that "the more things change, the more they stay the same." Until WINMe came around, there were no real structural changes at all. So to summarize the changes made in Windows between the years 1995 and 2000, I have put together **Table 4.2**. I hope you find it useful.

Table 4.2   History of WIN9x Releases

Version	Release Date	Improvements	Version Number
WIN95	August 1995		4.00.950
WIN95 SP1	February 1996	Bug fix for WIN95	4.00.950A
WIN95 OSR2	August 1996	FAT32	4.00.950B
WIN95 OSR2.1	April 1997	USB as download	4.00.950B + USB
WIN95 OSR2.5	November 1997	IE4 and incorporated USB	4.00.950C
Windows 98	June 1998	DVD, DirectX	4.10.1998
Windows 98 SE	May 1999	IE5, ICS, DirectX 6.1, NetMeeting	4.10.2222A
Windows Me	September 2000	UPNP, SFP, System Restore	4.90.3000

The WIN9x series went through a number of changes from its inception to the final death knell.

CHAPTER SUMMARY

So, if you were looking for a tour of WIN95 and all of its features, you were probably pretty disappointed in this chapter. What I covered here is the core technology behind the WIN9x series and a brief review of the evolution of Windows 4.xx.

The 4.xx versions of Windows provided some very important technological breakthroughs over the 3.xx versions of yesteryear. A couple of key points to this chapter are how Windows now handles multitasking and its usage of memory.

BRAIN DRAIN

1. Discuss the differences between cooperative multitasking and pre-emptive multitasking.

2. What is a key reason for placing all WIN3.x apps into a common virtual machine?

3. Draw a rough diagram of how the WIN9x Virtual Machine Manager handles different applications, including legacy DOS apps, WIN3.x, and WIN9x apps.

4. Why was Plug 'n Play so problematic with certain devices in its early years?

5. Discuss how WINMe was responsible for a number of gray hairs in the heads of technicians worldwide.

THE 64K$ QUESTIONS

1. WIN95 was originally intended for release in the year _____.
   a. 1995
   b. 1994
   c. 1993
   d. 1992

2. Even if a consumer's hardware met the minimum requirements for WIN95, Microsoft still wouldn't provide support if _____.
   a. The computer was made prior to 1995
   b. Any of the hardware was not listed on the HCL
   c. The computer didn't have a 32-bit bus
   d. Any of the hardware was listed on their UCL

3. WIN95 required, at the minimum, _____.
   a. A 16MHz 386SX processor
   b. A 20MHz 386SX processor
   c. A 16MHz 386DX processor
   d. A 20MHz 386DX processor

4. WIN95 required, at the minimum, _____.
   a. 2MB of RAM
   b. 4MB of RAM
   c. 8MB of RAM
   d. 16MB of RAM

5. WIN95 required, at the minimum, _____.
   a. 16-color CGA
   b. EGA
   c. VGA
   d. SVGA

6. WIN95 required, at the minimum, _____ (for a full installation).

   a. 85MB free hard disk space

   b. 120MB free hard disk space

   c. 240MB free hard disk space

   d. 540MB free hard disk space

7. Which of the following was not a requirement for full PnP functionality?

   a. A PnP BIOS

   b. A PnP device driver

   c. A PnP device

   d. A PnP OS

8. Pre-emptive multitasking adds the services of _____.

   a. A virtual machine manager

   b. A task scheduler

   c. An event scheduler

   d. A process timer

9. Which protocol was incorporated into WIN95 for the first time in Microsoft's history?

   a. NetBEUI

   b. IPX/SPX

   c. Banyan Vines

   d. TCP/IP

10. Which of the following files became a text file in WIN95?

    a. MSDOS.SYS

    b. COMMAND.COM

    c. IO.SYS

    d. WIN.INI

11. WIN95 did not incorporate any version of MS-DOS into its structure.

    a. True

    b. False

12. The 32-bit graphics drivers were managed by _____.

    a. USER.DLL

    b. GDI.EXE

    c. GDI.DLL

    d. KERNEL32.DLL

13. A 16-bit mouse driver would interface with _____.

    a. USER.DLL

    b. GDI.EXE

    c. GDI.DLL

    d. KERNEL32.DLL

14. Opening a new DOS window was the responsibility of _____.

    a. KRNL386.EXE

    b. KERNEL32.DLL

    c. The Virtual Memory Manager

    d. The Virtual Machine Manager

15. Multiple networking clients on a single computer were made possible by the addition of _____.

    a. The Virtual Memory Manager

    b. The Virtual Machine Manager

    c. The Installable File System

    d. The Network Device Interface

16. What version of WIN9x was the first to provide support for FAT32?

    a. Windows 95

    b. Windows 95 SR2

    c. Windows 98

    d. Windows 98SE

    e. None of the above

17. What version of WIN9x was the first to provide support for USB?

    a. Windows 95

    b. Windows 95 SR2

c. Windows 98

d. Windows 98SE

e. None of the above

18. What version of WIN9x was the first to provide support for DVD?

a. Windows 95

b. Windows 95 SR2

c. Windows 98

d. Windows 98SE

e. None of the above

19. What version of WIN9x was the first to provide support for DirectX?

a. Windows 95

b. Windows 95 SR2

c. Windows 98

d. Windows 98SE

e. None of the above

20. What version of WIN9x dropped support for real mode operation?

a. Windows 95

b. Windows 95 SR2

c. Windows 98

d. Windows 98SE

e. None of the above

TRICKY TERMINOLOGY

Cabinet file: A compressed file that holds a large number of smaller files that can be uncompressed and installed as needed.

Client: A piece of software running from within an OS that allows the device to connect to a network.

Pre-emptive multitasking: A way to manage multiple applications on a computer system that puts the responsibility for releasing system resources onto the OS.

Profile: Various settings and preferences specific to a particular user or piece of hardware on a system.

Redirector: An OS function (usually running within a client) that intercepts hardware and software calls that are intended for remote devices and points them in the right direction.

Registry: In Windows, it is a relational database that contains all system and application settings and/or parameters.

Snapshot: In reference to an OS, it is a small binary file that contains information useful in replicating the organization and structure of an application or configuration.

System Virtual Machine: An environment in Windows that emulates a complete computer system and houses all of the critical processes and functions of the OS.

Task scheduler: A system file that determines how long a particular application can retain control of system resources.

Thunking: A Microsoft process of translating 16-bit commands and data into a 32-bit format, and vice versa.

ACRONYM ALERT

CAB: Cabinet. A compressed file that houses a number of smaller files that can be independently extracted as needed.

CDFS: CD-ROM File System

HCL: Hardware Compatibility List. A list of devices that have been approved by an OS manufacturer for use with a specific product.

ICS: Internet Connection Sharing. A service that allows multiple computers to simultaneously use a single hookup to the Internet.

IFS: Installable File System. A feature in WIN9x and later OSs that allows network redirectors and third-party file systems to be installed as needed.

PIF: Program Information File. A small descriptor file that tells Windows how a specific DOS application is going to behave.

SFP: System File Protection. A Windows utility that prevents critical OS files from being deleted or overwritten, and if they are, can replace them on the fly.

UPNP: Universal Plug 'n Play. Revised PnP standards that are constantly monitored and updated by the UPNP Forum.

VFAT: Virtual File Allocation Table. A software driver that emulates the file allocation tables stored on a hard disk and prevents applications from making direct calls to the hardware.

CHAPTER 5

MANAGING WINDOWS 9X

In the previous chapter, I discussed the structure and architecture of the WIN9x products. Here I will go through the installation and configuration of WIN95, and, where relevant, discuss how these procedures may differ for other WIN9x products. After that, there will be a brief discussion of the WIN9x user interface and a more detailed discussion of WIN9x use and management.

In previous chapters, most of the discussion has revolved around OSs that are no longer in use. That is no longer the case. While the WIN9x products are long discontinued, they proved to be a viable enough product that, as of this writing, there are an estimated 20,000,000 computers still running one or the other of these venerable old systems.

A+ OPERATING SYSTEM TECHNOLOGIES EXAM OBJECTIVES

There is also a lot of coverage on the CompTIA exam concerning these products. Among the topics you might see from this chapter are the following:

1.1 Identify the major desktop components and interfaces and their functions. Differentiate the characteristics of Windows 9x/Me, Windows NT 4.0 Workstation, Windows 2000 Professional, and Windows XP.

1.2 Identify the names, locations, purposes, and contents of major system files.

2.1 Identify the procedures for installing Windows 9x/Me, Windows NT 4.0 Workstation, Windows 2000 Professional, and Windows XP and bringing the operating system to a basic operational level.

2.2 Identify steps to perform an operating system upgrade from Windows 9x/Me, Windows NT 4.0 Workstation, Windows 2000 Professional, and Windows XP. Given an upgrade scenario, choose the appropriate next steps.

2.3 Identify the basic system boot sequences and boot methods, including the steps to create an emergency boot disk with utilities installed for Windows 9x/Me, Windows NT 4.0 Workstation, Windows 2000 Professional, and Windows XP.

2.4 Identify procedures for installing/adding a device, including loading, adding, and configuring device drivers and required software.

3.1 Recognize and interpret the meaning of common error codes and startup messages from the boot sequence, and identify steps to correct the problems.

3.2 Recognize when to use common diagnostic utilities and tools. Given a diagnostic scenario involving one of these utilities or tools, select the appropriate steps needed to resolve the problem.

> **BUZZ WORDS** ————————
>
> **Clean install:** The fresh installation of an OS over a newly partitioned and formatted hard disk.
>
> **Upgrade:** The replacement of an older OS with a newer, migrating as many settings and applications as possible.

INSTALLING WINDOWS 95

When WIN95 was first released, there were two different approaches commonly used in installing the product. Since there were a plethora of people who owned computers with WIN3.x already installed, the *upgrade* path was popular with them. However, for users to expect the most reliability and stability out of their systems, Microsoft suggested a *clean install*. Even though it is unlikely that you'll ever encounter a situation in which you'll be upgrading a WIN3.x system to WIN9x, I'm going to provide a brief discussion of the procedures. I'll start with the clean install.

PERFORMING A CLEAN INSTALL

The first thing you ever want to do when performing any clean install is make sure you have a clean hard drive or partition onto which the OS can be installed. If a previous installation of Windows existed, then you want to repartition that disk prior to performing a clean install. Don't just format the disk. For most Microsoft OSs, the partitioning utility of choice will be FDISK.

After you have FDISKed the hard disk and formatted it, you are ready to perform your installation. WIN95 distributions did not ship on bootable CDs; therefore, it is essential to boot to the WIN95 Startup Diskette enclosed in the product. Place the CD-ROM into the drive and from the command prompt, type **D:\Setup** (where D: represents the correct drive letter for your CD drive). The rest is a matter of following the yellow brick road. If you are using the lab manual designed to accompany this book, you'll be doing an installation of Windows 98.

PERFORMING AN UPGRADE

Performing an upgrade of Windows 3.x or MS-DOS to WIN95 is a bit different than a clean install in a couple of respects. The upgrade migrates all configurations, personal preferences, and

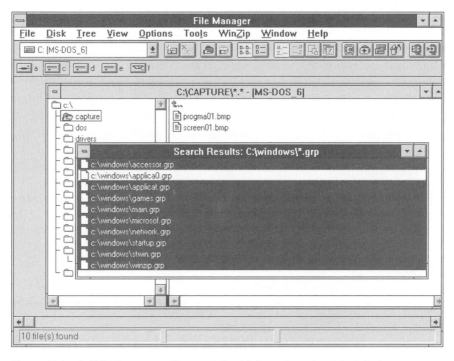

Figure 5.1   In WIN3.x, group files contained information about installed applications that was useful in migrating those apps into a WIN95 install.

applications that were installed under the old OS, making the new installation as close to what the user is accustomed to as possible.

From a DOS installation, the Setup program derives the majority of the information it requires for this migration from CONFIG.SYS and AUTOEXEC.BAT. In an upgrade from WIN3.x, it also scours files such as SYSTEM.INI and WIN.INI and migrates desktop settings and applications. It also uses a WIN3.x utility called Program Manager (PM) for locating applications. PM maintained a series of descriptor files called group files. There were files with a .GRP extension (**Figure 5.1**) that defined the groups in which the applications were installed. Setup uses these to migrate path information and program configuration.

Certain device settings could be migrated as well. Printers could be migrated, and some devices designed for Windows such as modems and sound cards were occasionally migrated successfully. For the most part, however, nonprinter devices were best installed separately after the Windows 95 installation was completed.

The biggest problem with the WIN95 upgrade was that it also migrated any problems that existed. Also, if a program or device was incompatible with the 32-bit drivers of Windows, there were occasionally problems uninstalling the offending resource and reinstalling it under WIN95. Some hardware devices simply weren't compatible with WIN9x and couldn't be used at all. The remainder of this section will deal with a clean install and will only point out issues specific to an upgrade where relevant.

Completing an Installation

Aside from those rather important differences, the process of installing WIN95 was the same regardless of which option was chosen by the user. A big difference for WIN3.x users upgrading from the WIN95 Upgrade CD was that they did not start from the command prompt. There were a few additional steps involved in the upgrade while Setup located and migrated pre-existing settings, but the primary stages of installation remained the same. DOS users and those performing a clean install would generally have to start from the command prompt.

Command Line Switches

Command line switches allowed the user to select certain installation options before Setup began to do its thing. These switches are applied just like the switches used in MS-DOS. **Table 5.1** lists the various switches and the effects they had on installation.

Table 5.1   Windows 95 Setup Switches

Switch	Function
/?	Provides descriptions for these switches in case you don't have this book at your fingertips.
/c	Instructs Setup not to load the SmartDrive disk caching utility.
/d	Prevents Setup from using earlier versions of Windows in the initial phases of installation.
/id	Prevents Setup from performing a test to see whether the minimal amount of free hard disk space is present.
/in	Prevents Setup from running the Network Setup Module.
/iq	Prevents Setup from performing a ScanDisk quick-check when running Setup from DOS.
/is	Prevents Setup from performing a ScanDisk quick-check when running Setup from Windows.
/iw	Prevents Setup from running the End User License Agreement.
/t:[dir]	Where DIR specifies a designated directory, this switch instructs Setup where to store temporary files during installation.
[batchfile.bat]	Where the actual name of the batch file is used, it runs the specified batch file containing specific setup instructions.
/NOSTART	Instructs setup to load a minimal set of files and then exit without installing Windows.

The Windows Setup switches allow the user to modify the way Setup runs in a specific fashion.

WINDOWS 95 SETUP PHASES

There are four separate phases to the installation of WIN95. The first three involve preparing your computer for the WIN9x GUI. The final phase occurs after a reboot, when the user is in graphical mode. These phases are:

- Startup
- Information gathering
- File copy
- Final system configuration

Startup and Information Gathering If Setup is run from a command prompt, the first thing it will do is search your computer for previous installations of any version of Windows. If one is found, you will be given a suggestion to start Windows and run Setup from there. If no Windows installation is found, Setup installs a base configuration of WIN3.1 files and moves on to perform a series of basic system checks (**Figure 5.2**).

These checks are designed to confirm that the system onto which you're attempting to install WIN95 has the minimum requirements. Should it find a problem, such as insufficient

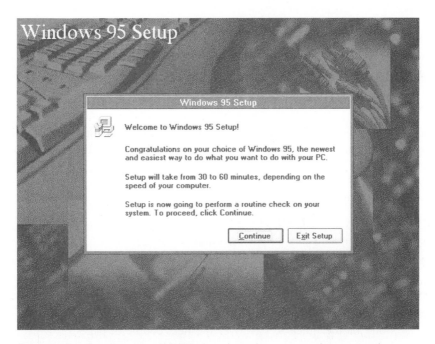

Figure 5.2 The first thing WIN95 does is make sure you have enough computer to run it. The sign of things to come!

drive space or insufficient memory, Setup will issue an error message indicating what type of problem it found.

Next Setup checks for an XMS manager such as EMM386.EXE. If one is not present, Setup installs it. Setup also looks for a disk caching utility such as SmartDrive. Once again, if not present, one will be installed.

Now, Setup scans CONFIG.SYS and AUTOEXEC.BAT, looking to see what TSRs are running on the system. In the event that it detects any programs that could potentially cause a conflict (and this would include incompatible drivers), Setup will issue a warning message. During this phase, it is also checking both files for device information on installed hardware so that it can load any necessary drivers.

File Copy This is the part of the process where most users go out for a cup of coffee and a donut. On older computers, this process can take quite some time. At the very end of the file copy stage, the user will see a series of Setup prompts. The information provided in these fields will be used in the creation of the registry later on.

Final System Configuration It's too late to turn back now. If you were running WIN3.x or DOS before, your OS has been permanently changed. The MBR on the hard drive is rewritten to point to WIN95. Also the registry is fully configured and written to the hard drive. On the next boot, your system will initialize from the registry for the first time and perform a PnP scan for hardware.

Once the hardware setup phase has been completed, which may or may not require yet another reboot, you will be offered the opportunity to take a tour of Windows. In the lower left-hand corner of that window is a check box; leave that box checked if you want to see this window each time Windows starts.

WINDOWS 98 SETUP PHASES

WIN98 and WINMe users will see some extra stages during their installation. First off, these versions separate the startup preparation from the information-gathering phase. Also, since WIN98 is Plug 'n Play, it adds a hardware detection phase. Here is the order of WIN98 Setup:

- Preparing to run Windows 98 Setup
- Collecting information about your computer
- Copying Windows 98 files to your computer
- Restarting your computer
- Setting up hardware

Even the phases that look like they should be identical to WIN95 Setup phases have some differences. So don't be too quick to pass over the next couple of pages.

Preparing to Run Windows 98 Setup What happens here depends on whether you're upgrading from WIN95 or running Setup from a command prompt. If Setup is run from

WIN95, a directory called WININST0.400 is created. Two files, called PRECOPY1.CAB and PRECOPY2.CAB, are copied into this directory. These files contain setup and information files that Setup will extract and use later in the installation process.

If you're installing Windows from a command prompt (and this would include installation from a Startup diskette), then there is no previous installation of Windows. Since Setup is going to be looking for certain files, it copies a file called MINI.CAB. This file is a compressed bare-minimum installation of Windows that Setup can use.

Collecting Information About Your Computer   This phase also has a bit of variation, depending on whether Setup is being run from DOS or Windows. From DOS, users will be prompted to read and agree to Microsoft's licensing agreement. Next they will be asked what directory they would like WIN98 installed into. The default C:\WINDOWS will already be filled out, but it is possible for users to install Windows into any directory they chose. They must then supply a directory for temporary files. Once again, the one Setup suggests should be used unless there are qualifying reasons (such as a previous OS that you wish to preserve) for not doing so. The last part of this phase is to prepare an Emergency Startup Diskette.

Those running Setup from Windows 95 will first see the license agreement. Then ScanDisk will run a check on the system to ensure that all is well. ScanReg scans the WIN95 registry and prepares the WIN98 registry. Then the user is prompted to prepare an Emergency Startup Diskette.

Copying Windows 98 Files to Your Computer   This phase isn't really that much different that the WIN95 file copy phase. It uses the information it found in the prior phases to determine what files need to be copied, and, until it's finished, the user can return his or her attention to the playoffs.

Restarting Your Computer   This *sounds* like a simple enough phase, right? A bar starts ticking off fifteen seconds, after which your computer will restart automatically. If you're in too much of a hurry to wait fifteen seconds, you can press the spacebar and the system will reboot immediately.

It's what is happening *during* reboot that matters, though. Setup takes any information it was able to extract from CONFIG.SYS, AUTOEXEC.BAT, and any .INI files from previous OS installations and integrates them into the WIN98 registry. If any device drivers are found that Setup knows to be incompatible with WIN98, Setup edits these entries to be preceded by a REM (remark). This prevents them from being loaded during this and any subsequent reboots of the system.

Setting Up Hardware and Finalizing Settings   During this phase, Setup utilizes the PnP abilities of WIN98 to automatically detect any PnP hardware installed on the system, copy the appropriate files, and make any necessary entries to the Windows registry. During an upgrade, information from .INI files and/or the WIN95 registry is used to collect information about non-PnP devices. Any settings it finds in these locations are retained. On a clean install, non-PnP devices will have to be installed separately after installation is completed.

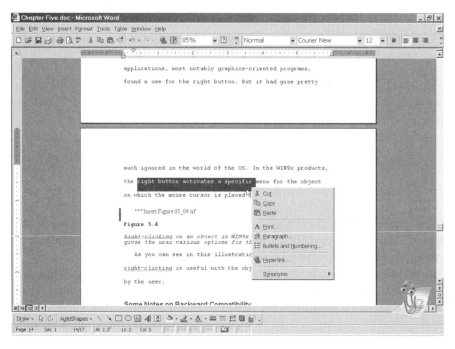

Figure 5.3   Right-clicking an object in WIN9x brings up a menu that gives the user various options for the selected object.

WIN9X AND THE MOUSE

All of Microsoft's previous versions of Windows provided mouse support. WIN95 was the first Microsoft OS to take this ingenious little device and move it from a role of a convenient toy to a powerful tool. Having finally realized that the mouse was equipped with two buttons (sometimes three), Microsoft finally provided a role for the right mouse button.

The left button (the one generally manipulated by the index finger on right-handed people) has always been used for selecting objects and launching applications. Some applications, most notably graphics-oriented programs, found a use for the right button. But it had gone pretty much ignored in the world of the OS. In the WIN9x products, the right button activates a specific menu for the object on which the mouse cursor is placed (see **Figure 5.3**).

As you can see in this illustration, the process of right-clicking is useful with the objects and data created by the user. Another term to be familiar with is double-clicking. Many actions require that the left mouse button be clicked twice in succession. This is the infamous double-click.

MAKING YOUR WAY AROUND WINDOWS

For the rest of this chapter, I'm going to be going over the various elements of WIN9x as they affect the user. From here on, unless otherwise specified, I'll be using WIN98 as the subject of

SOME NOTES ON BACKWARD COMPATIBILITY

Several times in the course of this book, I've mentioned things that were done or features that were retained from previous OSs in order to maintain backward compatibility with older systems. In the first couple of decades of the personal computer, Microsoft and Intel had a tacit agreement that new advances in computing would not render existing systems and/or software totally obsolete. They realized the backlash that would occur if users had to replace an entire computer system just to use an OS or program or had to replace thousands of dollars worth of software just because they had upgraded to a new computer and OS.

With that objective in mind, each advance in CPUs and each advance in OS was designed with some method integrated into it that allowed older technology to coexist with the new. For Microsoft, achieving this goal with WIN9x was a daunting task. In Chapter Four, I discussed how the VMM was redesigned with this goal in mind. I also discussed the changes made to MSDOS.SYS.

A key point to be made here is that WIN9x does not use AUTOEXEC.BAT and CONFIG.SYS, nor any of the .INI files previously found in WIN3.x products for its own purposes. These files are all retained to make DOS and WIN3.x programs run on the WIN9x platform. Therefore, when running programs designed for WIN9x on WIN9x, nothing you do to any of the previously mentioned files will have any impact whatsoever.

On the other hand, if you choose to run an older DOS program on WIN9x after having completed a clean install, you might find it more of a challenge than you might have expected. A clean install of WIN9x does not load any devices drivers into either CONFIG.SYS or AUTOEXEC.BAT. When your DOS program tries to run, it's going to be looking to those files for its driver information the majority of the time. Devices such as a CD-ROM drive or a sound card will need to have DOS drivers installed and the appropriate lines added to these files.

my discussion. It is far more likely that you, as a technician, will be running into that particular version than any other. The various aspects of Windows I'll be discussing include the following:

- The desktop
- Menus
- Control Panel
- Windows Explorer
- Hot keys
- Help

The information I give you in this chapter is rather important even if you feel you'll never spend any time with WIN98. The basic design of this OS formed the template that Microsoft has continued to follow in subsequent versions. In later chapters, as I discuss more recent OS releases by Microsoft, I'll be pointing out new features and differences. I'm going to be assuming you already know the information provided in this chapter.

BUZZ WORDS

Icon: A small picture linked to an application shortcut.

THE DESKTOP

The Windows desktop (**Figure 5.4**) provides the launch pad where everything else you ever do in Windows begins. The various aspects of the desktop have come to be things now taken for granted, and, therefore, people probably don't really know as much about them as they should. As a technician, you need to know your way around the system extremely well. After all, it's really quite embarrassing to be on a customer's site, poking around in their computer, mumbling, "Now where did they put Device Mangler in *this* version?"

The Desktop consists of several different components, each with a specific task. The main desktop screen is only one of these components. There are also the Start menu, the taskbar, and the toolbar.

THE DESKTOP REGION

The largest area of the desktop is devoted to the main desktop region. This area is where the pretty little pictures that represent your programs are stored. These pictures are called *icons*. In

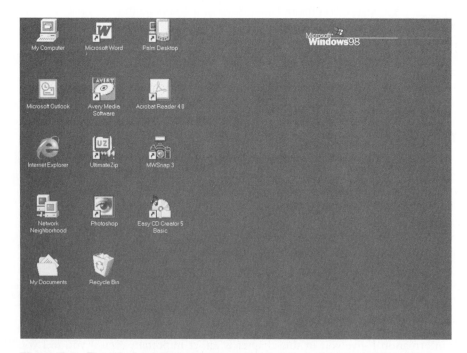

Figure 5.4   The Windows Desktop acts as the launch pad for everything else you do in Windows. Know it well!

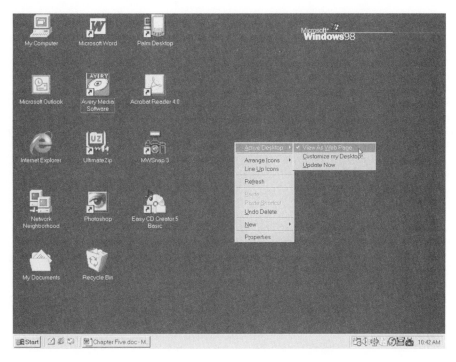

Figure 5.5   Right-clicking the Windows Desktop brings up a menu for configuring the desktop options.

WIN95, double-clicking an icon launches the program. In WIN98 and later, the user can configure an *Active Desktop.* If an Active Desktop is configured, users can configure their desktops to act as if they are Web pages. In this case, a single click on an icon launches the program (**Figure 5.5**).

Right-clicking the desktop and selecting Properties opens the Display Properties dialog box. From here, you can configure a wide variety of options affecting the look of your desktop and applications. You can also get to this dialog box from the Control Panel, and I will cover all the options it offers fully when I address all the applets you can access through Control Panel.

> **BUZZ WORDS**
>
> **Active Desktop:** A method of configuring the Windows desktop to behave as if it is a Web page, allowing single-click activation of icons and other Web-like features.

THE START MENU

The Start Menu (**Figure 5.6**) is more than just a place for launching programs that don't have an icon. Here is also where you go to shut down your computer. If you're on a network, or have set up multiple user profiles, an option for logging off as one user and logging on as another is also available.

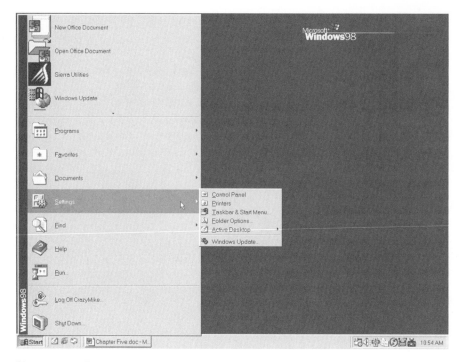

Figure 5.6   The Windows Start Menu

Clicking <u>R</u>un in the Start Menu opens a command line interface that allows users to type in a command the same way they would if they were at the command prompt. Unlike the command prompt, the <u>R</u>un option also allows users to use Windows Explorer to browse their computers looking for the application or command they wish to launch.

<u>H</u>elp opens the Windows Help. Since I'll be covering that in more detail in a later section, I'll pass on discussing it for now.

The <u>F</u>ind option is where users can go to browse for files or folders. They can also browse the network looking for another computer, or they can search for resources on the Internet with this tool. The Find → People option opens users' address books and allows them to search for information about the individuals stored there. An option that appears if you have Microsoft Outlook installed is Find → Using Microsoft Outlook. Using this option, you can look for files, folders, computers, people, or your car keys.

The <u>S</u>ettings option on the Start Menu is an important one for technicians. Here is where you can find shortcuts to Control Panel, the Printers menu, and a place to configure your Taskbar to your liking, as well as another way of getting to the Folder Options that I discussed earlier. On WIN98 and later, you can also configure your Active Desktop from here or link directly to Microsoft's Updates Web site (assuming you have an active Internet connection.)

<u>D</u>ocuments basically has only one default shortcut, and that is to the My Documents folder on your hard drive. However, it also maintains a list of recently opened documents. So if you've been working on Chapter Five of your OS book for several days, instead of opening your word

processor and going through the rigmarole of browsing to the document through the menus and Windows Explorer, you can just click the document. The correct program will automatically open, and that document will load.

The Favorites option is a direct link to Internet Explorer's Favorites menu. If you click any of the items listed under this option, WIN98 will automatically launch whatever version of IE you have running on your machine and browse to that Web site.

Programs is where shortcuts to all of the programs installed on your system can be found. Even if an icon has not been created on the desktop for a particular application, the installation program will generally place a shortcut here. You can also create shortcuts for your desktop from this component. Right-click the application and select Create Shortcut. A second entry for that application, with its name followed by the number two in parentheses (2), will appear. Drag and drop that entry over to the desktop. An icon will magically appear.

Above the Programs entry there is a separator bar, and above that bar are shortcuts to common tasks. These tasks include creating a new document, yet another shortcut to Windows Update, and just about any other thing that some program you installed chose to add. For example, in my Start menu, I have a shortcut to Sierra Utilities. This is because I installed a game from Sierra Entertainment, Inc. I didn't particularly care for it, so I uninstalled it. (Okay, I'll admit it. It was too hard, and I couldn't figure out how to win!!!) Uninstalling the game, however, did not uninstall the Sierra Utilities entry, and I've been too lazy to do it since then.

THE TASKBAR

Starting with WIN95, and in every version since, Microsoft OSs have sported a taskbar that, by default, appears at the bottom of the screen. For every application you open, a button for that app appears in the taskbar. In **Figure 5.7**, I've opened several different applications.

When you right-click the taskbar, the menu that appears gives you several options. You can manage the toolbars (discussed in the next section); you can choose to either cascade your windows (as shown in **Figure 5.8**) or tile them (as shown in **Figure 5.9**). Note that the menu items from Photoshop didn't cascade or tile along with the program.

Another useful function found here is the ability to minimize all windows. This takes you straight back to an uncluttered desktop without the hassle of having to minimize each window one at a time.

On the left side of the task bar are usually several shortcuts to frequently used applications, such as Internet Explorer and Outlook. Other applications you install may choose to insert an icon here. If you don't want it there, right-click it and select Cut. The middle section of the

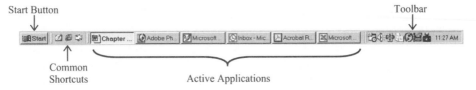

Figure 5.7 Clicking one of the buttons on the taskbar takes you straight to that application.

Figure 5.8
Cascading your applications makes the various windows appear like a hand of cards spread out.

Figure 5.9
Tiling your applications places them all in nice even little squares distributed across your desktop.

taskbar is where the shortcut buttons for applications active on your system will appear. And to the left is the Toolbar.

THE TOOLBAR

On the lower right-hand corner of your screen is a small section of the Taskbar known as the Toolbar. Here is where the user can open and manage some of the TSRs of Windows. One of the useful functions here is Time/Date. These are the programs that automatically launch every time you start Windows. It's also a source of some of your biggest headaches.

It seems that every application you ever install assumes that the only reason you purchased a computer was to run that particular program. Therefore, it adds itself to your Startup folder. This is a folder where Windows places shortcuts to these apps that automatically launch.

Each one of these TSRs takes up memory and swap file space. And each one adds several more seconds to the amount of time it takes Windows to load. A good housekeeping task is to occasionally weed out the Startup items you don't need, keeping only those that are useful to you. WIN98 and WINMe have a useful utility called MSCONFIG (which I'll be discussing in a few pages) that allows you to manage this and several other Windows functions.

MENUS

One of the key features of Windows that made it a successful OS was the fact that Microsoft insisted that all applications written for the WIN9x (and later) platform maintain a degree of consistency in organization and appearance. This common functionality is known as the Common User Interface (CUI). Under the CUI, this includes how the menus used in applications look and feel.

Each Windows application features a base menu bar at the top of the screen. Although there are certain differences allowed among applications based on the specific functions of those applications, for the most part, the base menu bar of any given application will share most of the same options, and those options will all appear in the same order on the menu. **Figure 5.10** illustrates the base menu bar for Microsoft Word compared to that of Adobe Photoshop.

Another toolbar that can be specific to the application is the base icon toolbar. This consists of a secondary toolbar (usually located directly beneath the base menu bar) that consists primarily of icons. To get a description of the function of any given icon, the user rests the cursor over that icon, and a description will appear (**Figure 5.11**). Various other toolbars and menu bars are permitted and frequently seen, but they must follow the same conventions described previously.

File Edit View Insert Format Tools Table Window Help

The base menu of Microsoft Word

File Edit Image Layer Select Filter View Window Help

The base menu of Photoshop

Figure 5.10   The base menu bar for Microsoft Word compared to that of Photoshop

Print (HP LaserJet 4)

Figure 5.11   The base icon toolbar

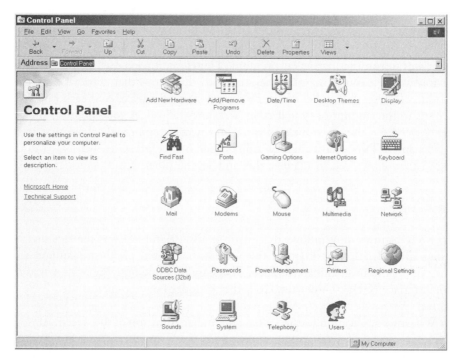

Figure 5.12   Control Panel

CONTROL PANEL

For the technician, Control Panel (**Figure 5.12**) is one of the key places to get to know well. This is where the various settings in Windows can be found in one tidy location. Here you find a collection of applets for managing and configuring virtually every part of your machine.

The next several pages are going to deal with the primary applets of Control Panel. I'm not going to attempt to go through all of them for three reasons. First of all, not all of them are critical to a technician. Second, there are applets that are added by applications and devices that the user installs onto the system. And finally, since I plan on discussing Control Panel only once in this book, and this feature varies slightly among versions of the OS, I figure it's easier to point out differences as I go.

Figure 5.13   The Add New Hardware Wizard

ADD NEW HARDWARE

In Windows 2000 and XP this applet is known as Add/Remove Hardware. Normally, when PnP is working properly, when a new device is added to the system, Windows picks it up on the next boot and starts the Add New Hardware Wizard (**Figure 5.13**). At this point, Windows either locates the drivers it needs in the INF directory, or it prompts the user to insert the disk containing the drivers. If for any reason Windows fails to detect a new device, or should the user not install the drivers at that time, the Add New Hardware Wizard can always be started from this applet. It leads you through the procedures of detecting and installing new hardware.

ADD/REMOVE PROGRAMS

One of the advantages of Windows is that it recognizes and makes use of Autorun applications on a CD. Autorun applications are the little snippets of code that cause a program to automatically launch simply by inserting the CD. This makes it very easy to install applications these days. It will probably grieve you to no end to learn that this is the least desirable way to install an application. Add/Remove Programs (**Figure 5.14** and **Figure 5.15**) should be used for installing programs as well as removing them.

When you use this applet to install programs, it generates an uninstall script. The uninstall script is a small file that maintains a log of every new directory that was created on the hard drive and what files were installed into those directories. It also logs what common files were overwritten with newer versions, and it records any changes that were made to the registry during the installation of that program.

Later on, when you realize just how bad that program really is, Windows does a better job of removing all traces of that application when you uninstall it. Although it is true that some

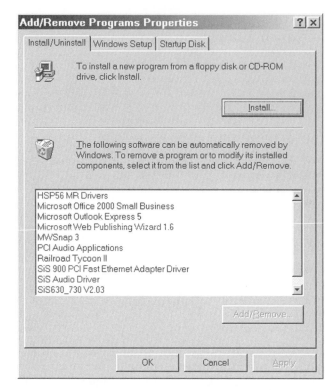

Figure 5.14 The Windows 98 Add/Remove Programs applet

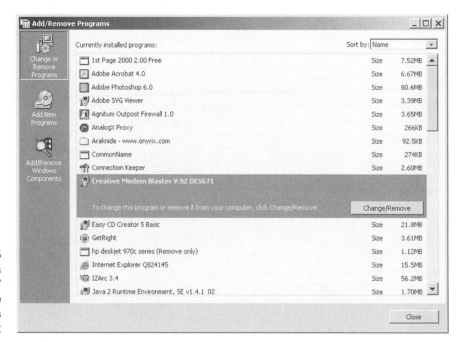

Figure 5.15
The Windows
2000 Add/
Remove
Programs
applet

of the new installer utilities used by software companies now provide this function, not all do. Windows 2000 and XP use a beefier version of the Windows Installer that generates these scripts whether you use Add/Remove Programs at the install or not.

Removing a program is a simple matter of opening the applet, highlighting the program you wish to blow away, and clicking the Add/Remove button (the Change/Remove button in Windows 2000 and XP). The applet asks you whether you're really sure you want to do this, and when you click OK, it's bye-bye program. That's happened to just about every game I've bought lately. Isn't *anyone* out there writing a decent computer game any more?

THE DATE/TIME APPLET

Hopefully, the Date/Time function (**Figure 5.16**) won't require a lengthy technical discussion. This is where you adjust your Windows clock and calendar settings. One other setting you can adjust here is whether or not you want your computer to automatically adjust for Daylight Savings time. If you live in one of the states that do not recognize Daylight Savings time, then you'll find it very annoying to have your clock changed twice a year. Right-clicking the time display in your toolbar and selecting Properties can also access this function.

THE DISPLAY APPLET

Should you wish to adjust the resolution or color depth on your monitor, the Display applet (**Figure 5.17**) is where you'll want to go. The Display applet is one of those applications that

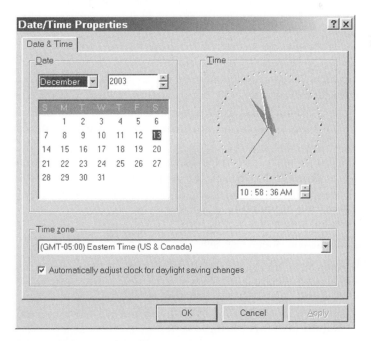

Figure 5.16   The Date/Time applet

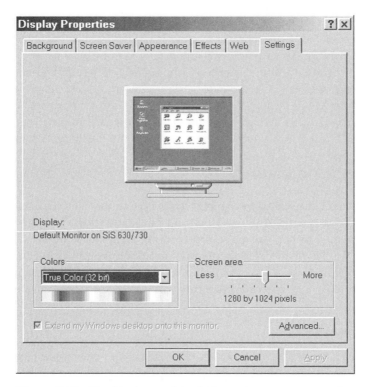

Figure 5.17 The Display applet might vary in appearance and available options from one machine to another, depending on the graphics adapter that is installed.

can vary in appearance and options, depending on what graphics adapter you have installed on your system. Some graphics adapters can be adjusted for advanced properties such as gamma (image density), moiré (a circular distortion that can occur), and other properties. Therefore, it is possible that when you open Display on your system, you may get a somewhat different screen than you see in the illustration.

The system I used to make these illustrations has a pretty fundamental display adapter installed and offers only the basic options. These are Background, Screen Saver, Appearance, Effects, Web, and Settings. Background is where you pick which pretty picture you wish to be part of your desktop. You can make your own background if you wish. Just browse to an image on your hard drive that you prefer and select it.

Screen savers are programs that blank the screen and then run animated little images across the screen in random patterns. This is necessary on cathode-ray tube (CRT) monitors to prevent a phenomenon called *burn-in*. Burn-in occurs when the same screen is left open on the monitor for an extended

Buzz Words

Burn-in: The tendency for a CRT monitor to permanently etch an image onto the inner surface of the tube if the image stays on the screen for too long a period.

period, and the phosphorous layer on the inside surface of the CRT is permanently etched with that image. This is not so much of a factor with LCD monitors.

The Appearance tab allows you to adjust virtually every aspect of the Windows desktop. This includes the size and font used for menus, icons, and buttons as well as the different sizes and colors of borders and bars. It's a great place for users to play around without hurting anything.

You can create an active desktop by clicking the Web tab. With an active desktop, icons are activated with a single click, and the overall effect is that of the desktop being like a Web page. In fact, by selecting a URL from the Internet, the desktop becomes that Web page. This is useful for companies that make computers accessible to the public. Having their Web page as the desktop background is great promotion.

In the Settings tab, you can adjust things like color depth and monitor resolution. If the computer is equipped either with two graphics cards, or with a dual-output graphics card, dual-monitor displays can also be set up here. The Advanced tab will bring up settings specific to the graphics adapter as well as some system settings common to all adapters. These include adjustments such as the smoothing of screen fonts, what size screen fonts the user wishes to use, and whether or not a restart of the machine is necessary to apply display changes.

FONTS

The term "font" is one of those words that get misused a lot. Many people mistake the typeface for the font. The *typeface* is the basic shape of the letters and numbers that appear on the page. For example, Times New Roman is a typeface. The *font*, technically speaking, is a particular size and style of that typeface. 12-point italic Times New Roman is a font.

> ### BUZZ WORDS
>
> **Typeface:** The basic shape that letters and numbers of a particular character set will assume.
>
> **Font:** The size and characteristic (such as bold or italic) of a particular typeface.

One of the best features of any GUI OS is the ability to use different typefaces in documents and to be able to see what that document is going to look like on the screen before it is printed. If a user is involved in desktop publishing, it is likely that he or she makes use of a number of different typefaces. The Fonts applet (**Figure 5.18**) is where different typefaces can be installed or removed. As you can see in this illustration, it is also where you can view that typeface to see what it looks like. This preview page can be printed up as a sample page if desired.

INTERNET OPTIONS

I guess there's no doubt that a large reason for the popularity of PCs can be attributed to the popularity of the Internet. Internet Options (**Figure 5.19**) is where you go to configure an Internet connection and then make it behave the way you want it to.

This applet consists of six different tabs. The General tab is the one to appear on top by default. Here you can select the URLs that your browser will load when it first starts. It's also where you manage the temporary files that build up on a computer over time. In order to allow frequently used pages to load faster, the files for that page are downloaded and stored locally on

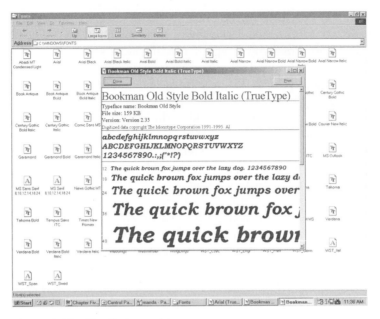

Figure 5.18   The Fonts applet

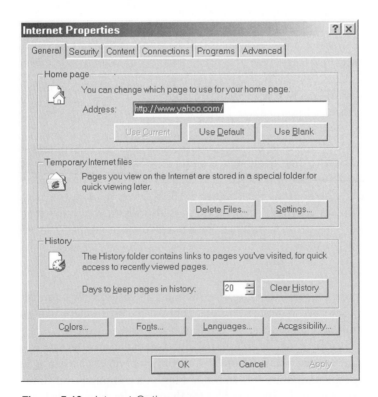

Figure 5.19   Internet Options

the user's hard disk. The Delete Files button does just what it says it's going to. When you click it, the folder that holds all those files is emptied. The Settings button allows you to dictate the maximum amount of hard drive space that these files will be allowed to occupy and, if you choose, select a different folder where those files will be stored.

The History section allows you to figure out how many days worth of temporary files will be stored before the older ones are overwritten. This is also how your Web browser keeps that pull-down list in the address bar up to date. Clearing the history doesn't delete the files, but it will empty out the pull-down menus.

The other buttons along the bottom of this tab allow you to configure what colors and fonts you like on your browser and what language you want to display. The Accessibility button allows you to configure the display for people with poor eyesight.

The Security tab is where you can configure what types of material you want to allow users on this system to access. Microsoft is fully aware that downloading applications, screensavers, macros, and so on is a likely way to pick up viruses and other malignant software. Here is where you can control what actions a user can take when browsing the Internet.

The Privacy tab lets you configure how your system handles cookies. Cookies are small files that some Web administrators place on your system that allow them to track your activity while on their site. Unfortunately not all cookies limit their activity to the host site that dumped them on your system. Some cookies track you wherever you go. Here you can block all cookies, have the system prompt you yea or nay when a cookie is on its way, or let them all come aboard.

The Content tab lets you configure the type of material that can be viewed. If the Content Advisor is enabled, you can filter sites based on language, nudity, sexual content, or violence. This can be a particularly good feature for families with children. On the other hand, one of my children was assigned to write a paper on the Ku Klux Klan but was unable to use school computers because all sites that even mentioned the group were blocked. A little care is in order here.

The Connections tab is where the methods by which the system accesses the Internet are configured. This includes dialup connections and proxy settings.

The Programs tab lets you configure which program is the default program to run and/or edit certain types of files. You can tell Windows what program edits HTML files, what your email client happens to be, what program handles your calendar and contacts, where your newsgroup reader is located, and how virtual meetings are handled.

Last is the Advanced tab. Here is where you find all the other settings that didn't fit nicely into a particular category. There are more than fifty different configuration settings in this tab. To cover them all in detail is somewhat beyond the scope of this book.

KEYBOARD

The Keyboard applet (**Figure 5.20**) is one of the simpler applets in Control Panel. Here you can configure how fast keys should repeat characters when held down and how fast the cursor within a document page blinks. On the Language tab, you can pick what language you prefer.

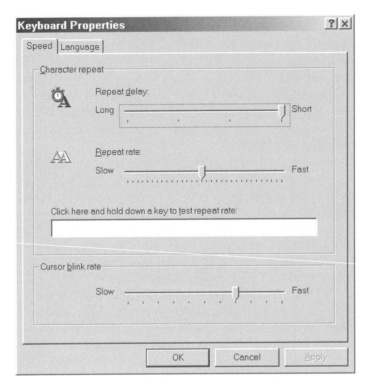

Figure 5.20 The Keyboard applet

MAIL

Configuring an email account in Windows needn't be all that hard. Oddly enough, it's done in the Mail applet shown in **Figure 5.21**. The one thing that might make it little more challenging is that you need some information from your Internet service provider concerning its systems. Most ISPs are willing to provide that information, but you bump into a few that won't go that extra step. In the latter case, you need to rely on them for assistance. That assistance usually arrives in the form of a disk.

The window in Figure 5.21 doesn't look like much. There's no place for configuring an address or anything. Clicking the Add button runs you through a wizard for setting up your new account. For an existing account, you highlight the account you wish to reconfigure and click Properties. That will bring up the screen shown in **Figure 5.22**, where the various settings are configured. Some information that you will need from your ISP is the server names for their incoming and outgoing mail servers. For many ISPs one server performs the same function. A server name commonly looks something like *mail.ISPname.net.*

MODEMS

As DSL and cable modems become increasingly popular, the Modem applet (**Figure 5.23**) is seeing less of a workout. Still, for people who live out in the boonies, modems are all too often

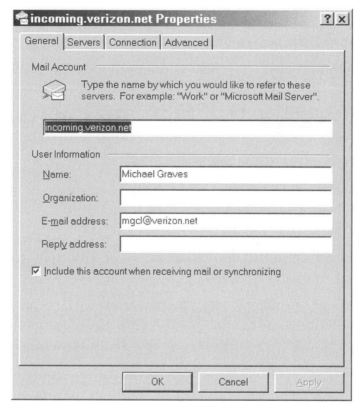

Figure 5.21 The Mail applet

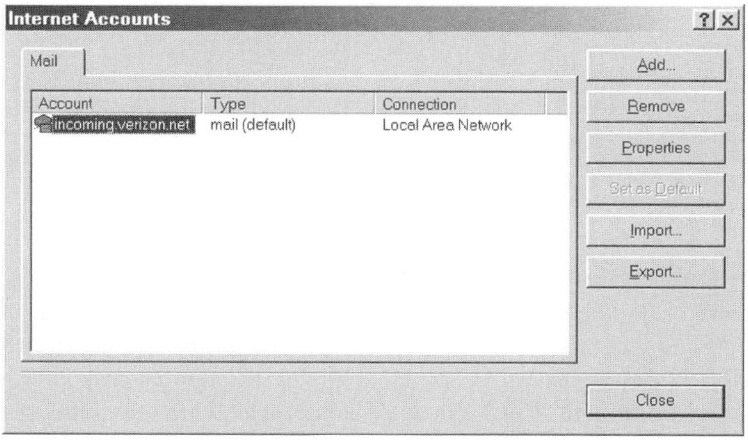

Figure 5.22 Configuring a mail account

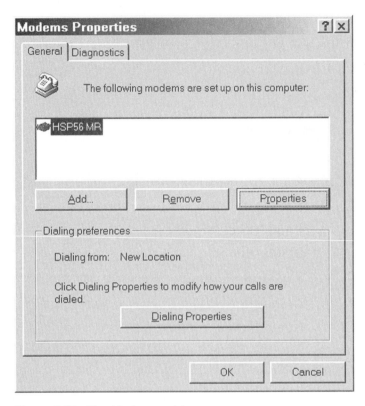

Figure 5.23 The Modem applet

the only choice for connecting to the outside world. So a good technician needs to be able to configure them.

Clicking the Add button starts the Add/Remove Hardware wizard, which detects the modem and prompts you for the CD if it can't find the drivers. As surprising as this may sound, the Remove button is the one you click should you wish to uninstall a modem. The Properties button allows you to configure settings such as maximum speed, how loud the modem speaker squawks, the size of the transmit and receive buffers used during a session, whether or not to use parity, and how many data bits to use. In general, the default settings are best left alone unless a particular server requires different settings. In that case, the provider will let you know.

MOUSE

One rarely thinks of the lowly little mouse as requiring any special attention. However, you'd be amazed at the number of settings that can be changed on this device. In the Mouse applet (**Figure 5.24**), you can adjust the speed required for the double-click of your mouse and whether it is a device for a right-handed or a left-handed user. Different options for pointers and the infamous hourglass can be selected, and mouse speed can be adjusted.

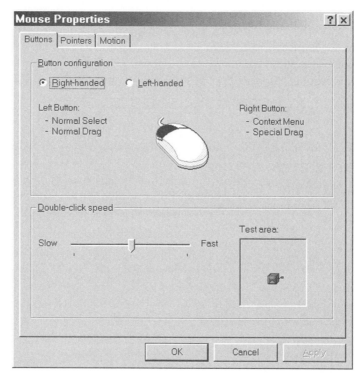

Figure 5.24   The Mouse applet

MULTIMEDIA

Multimedia (**Figure 5.25**) is another of those applets with a fairly sizeable number of options available. Here is where you can select which device performs which functions. The advanced properties vary with the device, but as an example, for a particular sound card you might be able to select whether a single pair of speakers is installed or whether the system is equipped with a full-blown 5.1 surround-sound system. The Video tab simply allows you to select whether video clips are shown full screen or in a window. The MIDI (an acronym for *musical instrument device interface*) tab provides the different options for voice selection. Unless there is a driving reason for changing it, the default is usually best left in place here. The CD Music tab is where you tell Windows which CD drive to use for playing music, should more than one drive be installed. The Devices tab lists each multimedia device installed on the system and allows you to configure the appropriate properties.

THE NETWORK APPLET

The Network applet (**Figure 5.26**) is another busy place for the professional technician. This is where you will configure and troubleshoot network hardware, clients, and protocols. And because network issues constitute a large percentage of problems in the corporate or institutional

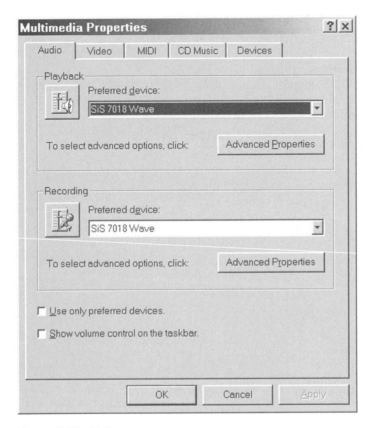

Figure 5.25 Multimedia

environment, it's a good idea to be comfortable with this applet. This applet is accessed by right clicking Network Neighborhood on the desktop (My Network Places in Windows 2000 and XP) and selecting Properties. A detailed discussion of everything that goes on in here is far beyond the scope of this book. For that, refer to *The Complete Guide to Networking and Network+*, by this same author. A brief tour is in order here, and there will be a more detailed description later in this book.

The Configuration tab is where you would add a NIC, a networking client, or a new protocol. Obviously, you do this by clicking the Add button. If you highlight an existing resource, the Remove and Properties buttons will become active. The function of the Remove button is self-evident. The Properties button is where the specific resource can be configured.

The Identification tab is where you configure the network name for the computer and identify what particular workgroup the computer will join. Windows 2000 and XP machines do not have the Identification tab in the Network Properties. With those two OSs, identification is a System property.

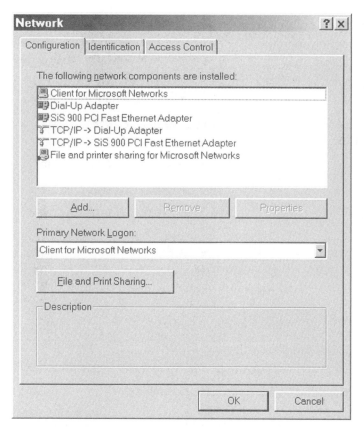

Figure 5.26 The Network applet

Access Control is where you define whether or not security on files will be Share Level or User Level security. With Share Level security, the user places permissions on the file or folder, and those permissions and any passwords the user assigns determine who may or may not access that resource. User Level security checks a User ID and password against a security database stored on a server and allocates permissions based on the individual users' privileges.

POWER MANAGEMENT

In this day and age of ecological awareness, users need to be conscious of the amount of energy they consume. By properly configuring the Power Management applet (**Figure 5.27**), at least their computer will do its part.

In this applet you can select specific time intervals for how long a specific device remains idle before reverting to sleep mode. In sleep mode, only the minimal amount of power is applied to the system to protect the data. Unnecessary devices are powered down. Intervals range from Always On (in which the system never powers down) to as short as one minute.

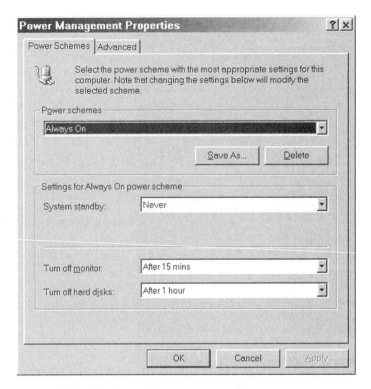

Figure 5.27 The Power Management applet

PRINTERS

As you can see in **Figure 5.28**, clicking Printers doesn't open an applet, but rather a folder. The Add Printer icon launches a wizard that allows you to install a new local printer or to browse to an existing printer on the network and install that printer locally.

When a printer is installed, you can click the printer's icon with the left mouse button to manage the print queue for that particular printer. This is where you can delete pending print jobs or assign priorities to print jobs. You can also right-click the icon and select Properties to configure the printer. Different printers offer different configuration options, depending on their capabilities.

SOUNDS

The Sounds applet (**Figure 5.29**) is where you go to change what sound is played for any given event in Windows. (Or if you're like me, it's where you go to turn the pesky things *off*!) If you selected the various Windows themes as you were installing Windows, then you have the option of selecting those from the different sound themes here as well.

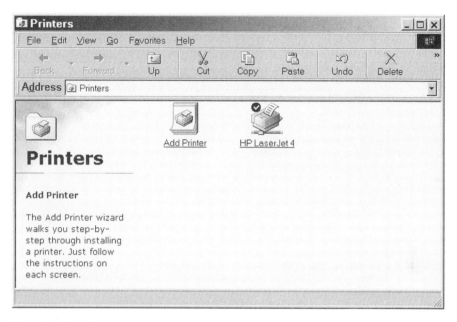

Figure 5.28   The Printers folder

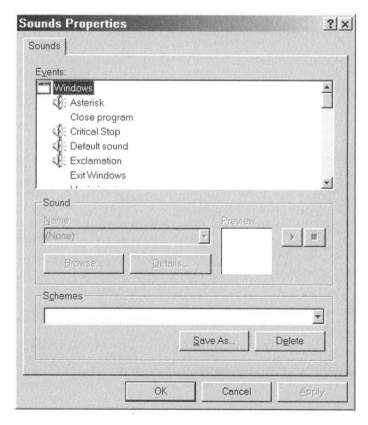

Figure 5.29
The Sounds applet

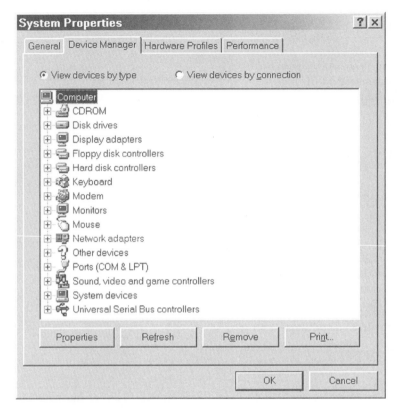

Figure 5.30 The System applet

SYSTEM

The System applet (**Figure 5.30**) is by far the most frequently visited Control Panel app for any technician. The General tab provides basic information about the computer system, including the version of OS running, how much RAM is installed, and what kind of CPU powers the system. It also provides the serial number for the specific OS installation.

Device Manager provides configuration settings for the different pieces of hardware installed on the system. If you elected to purchase the lab manual that accompanies this text, you will have the pleasure of spending quite a bit of time poking around in this section.

Because Windows allows more than one hardware configuration to exist on a single computer, there needs to be a way of deciding which hardware configuration you want to use at any given time. The Hardware Profiles tab allows this.

The Performance tab allows you to adjust certain settings critical to system performance. These include making adjustments to file systems used by the various storage devices installed on the system, setting hardware acceleration for your graphics adapter, and managing the swap file.

WINDOWS EXPLORER

One of the key features of Windows that all too often gets taken for granted is Windows Explorer. Explorer is a GUI shell that places all file and directory management functions into a single application that is intuitive and easy to manage.

To fully take advantage of the power Explorer offers, it is necessary to understand the seven important elements of the Explorer application. **Figure 5.31** points out the location of each of these elements:

- The folders (or navigation) pane
- The details (or contents) pane
- The title bar
- The menu bar
- The toolbar
- The address bar
- The status bar

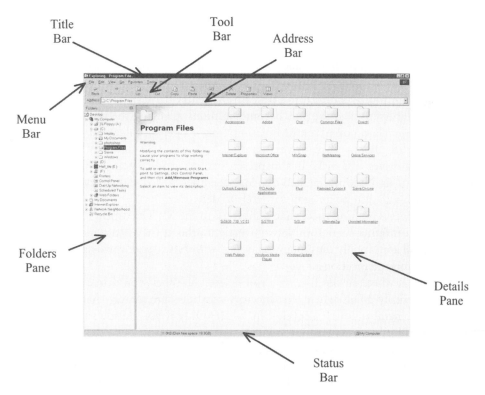

Figure 5.31   The essential elements of Windows Explorer

The title bar basically just displays what folder is currently opened or highlighted. It doesn't, however, show the full path. The menu bar is identical to the menu bars I discussed earlier in the chapter, as is the toolbar.

The address bar is something different for Explorer. Not only can this be used to type a path and/or file name, it can also be used to locate Internet sites or other machines on the network. In the absence of a full-fledged browser, it makes an acceptable substitute. The status bar provides such information as the size of the file currently highlighted and how much free space remains on the selected disk.

The two features of Explorer I want to spend the most time discussing are the folders, or navigation, pane and the details pane. These are the most heavily used features of Explorer. After that, I will cover a few of the more commonly used menu items.

THE FOLDERS PANE

The folders pane is the tool that allows the user to locate specific resources, both on the local computer as well as across the network. These resources are displayed starting with the desktop and then expanding into wider and more diverse resources. They are organized into a tree structure similar to that of the file systems I discussed earlier in the book. This shouldn't come as too much of a surprise, since what you're basically viewing is the file system for every device available to the system.

The basic resources offered for browsing are My Computer, My Documents, Internet Explorer, Network Neighborhood, and the Recycle Bin. In front of each of these resources (except for Recycle Bin) is a checkbox, usually containing a plus sign (+). The plus sign indicates that there are one or more subdirectories beneath that entry that can also be viewed. If you click the plus, the folder opens, and the plus becomes a minus. Clicking the minus closes the folder.

If you click the checkbox next to My Computer, it opens a folder for each drive on your computer, including floppy disk drives, hard disk drives, CD and DVD drives, and any removable media drives you own. It also presents folders for Printers, a shortcut to Control Panel, one for Dial-up Networking, and one for Scheduled Tasks. If you have an active Internet connection, there will also be an icon for Web folders.

My Documents is nothing more than a shortcut to the My Documents folder on your hard drive. Ditto with Internet Explorer. Network Neighborhood (My Network Places in WIN2K and WINXP) will appear only on systems equipped with NICs, and it will appear whether there is an active network connection or not.

Recycle Bin is where all the files that you delete go. When you delete a file in Windows, the data doesn't really go anywhere. Its directory attributes are merely changed to reflect that the file is now a member of the Recycle Bin folder. Only if you decide to erase the file from Recycle Bin is that file permanently erased.

Another task that be accomplished from the folders pane include moving entire directories from one location to another. As you can see in **Figure 5.32**, right-clicking a folder brings up a pop-up menu. From this menu you can open the folder, which brings the contents of that folder, including all subdirectories and files, into a separate window. You can also explore that folder, which opens the folder in the details pane on the right-hand side of the screen. The Find option

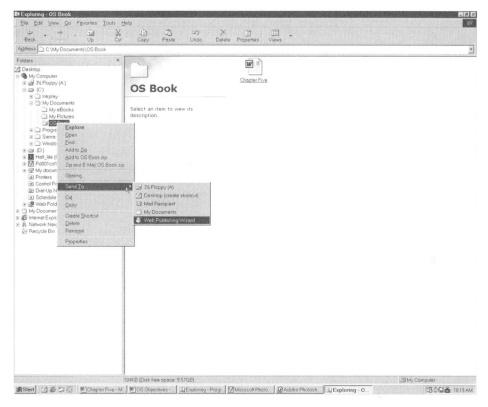

Figure 5.32 Working with the folders pane

opens Explorer's search engine and allows you to look for specific files or directories within the folder. From there, that search can be expanded to include the entire system, if desired.

On a networked computer on which File and Print Sharing has been enabled (more on that in Chapter Thirteen, Networking Computers), a user with appropriate rights can also share that directory for others on the network to use. The Cut and Copy commands need to be used with discretion, because they affect the entire directory that has been selected, including all files and subdirectories contained within. Cut deletes the directory from its current location. After you have selected a new location, a new command, Paste, will appear the next time you right-click a new location. This moves the directory from the previous folder to the new location, and it no longer exists in the first location. Copy allows you to make an identical copy of a folder while retaining the original copy in its previous location.

If you have browsed to a network location, another item that will appear on this menu is the Map Network Drive command. This is useful on networks where data is stored on servers. You can browse to a folder that contains data frequently used, and by mapping that folder as a network drive, it looks, feels, smells, and tastes just like a local hard disk to both the user and the computer. That folder is now directly accessible from the File menu of all Windows applications as a drive letter.

The Delete command moves the folder and all its contents to the Recycle Bin. First you'll be asked whether you're really sure you want to make such a drastic move. Then you will be prompted again for any executable or system files before the folder is deleted. Selecting the Yes to All button stops those prompts.

The Rename command is pretty self-explanatory. However, there can be unexpected side effects of renaming a folder. If it is a system folder, such as the Windows directory, you'll first be prompted that renaming it can stop the system from functioning properly, and Windows won't let you do it. If you rename a shared folder, not only will it no longer be shared, but should you elect to share it out once again under the new name, all permissions will have to be reconfigured. Those out there who have mapped this folder as a network drive will not be happy.

The Properties command can be an interesting tool when used properly. It has two tabs: the General tab and the Sharing Tab. The General tab tells you how many files and subdirectories exist within that folder. It tells you how many bytes of data reside within that folder as well as how much disk space is being occupied by that data. If there is a huge discrepancy between these two numbers, it can mean one of two things. It's time to convert from FAT16 to FAT32, if you haven't already, or you may have a problem with your file system, and it's time to run ScanDisk.

Also on this tab you can see the folder's attributes. On WIN98 and later there is also an option for Enable thumbnail view. If this option is selected, when a file is selected from the Contents Pane, a small image of that file will appear. (Note that the latter feature is not installed by default in a Typical installation and must be either selected optionally during installation, or installed later before it is available.)

THE CONTENTS PANE

The contents pane is where you go to see details and manage more specific resources on a computer. Here individual files can be copied, moved, renamed, created, or erased. Right-clicking a specific file or subdirectory will bring up a menu identical to the one I just discussed in the previous section. Rather than repeat the last few pages, I'll just move on to the differences.

Right-clicking a part of the contents pane other than over an icon will bring up a menu specific to the functions of this pane. As with all other Windows menus, an arrow pointing to the right indicates submenus that can be opened. **Figure 5.33** shows the New option selected.

The View option allows you to select how you want files and folders to be displayed on the screen. As Web Page enables a single click of the mouse to open a file or folder. The graphic in the upper left corner and the description of the folder also disappears. The Thumbnails option puts the icon for each file or folder into a separate bitmap. If it is a registered graphics file, a small reproduction of the image appears within the box. Other file types will simply show the icon of the program that has been configured to open that type of file in the folder options (which I'll discuss in a few paragraphs.)

The Large Icons and Small Icons options are fairly self-explanatory. They determine how big the pretty picture that represents the file will appear in the contents pane. The two options that are interesting are List and Details. List simply places the files in rows, with a small icon

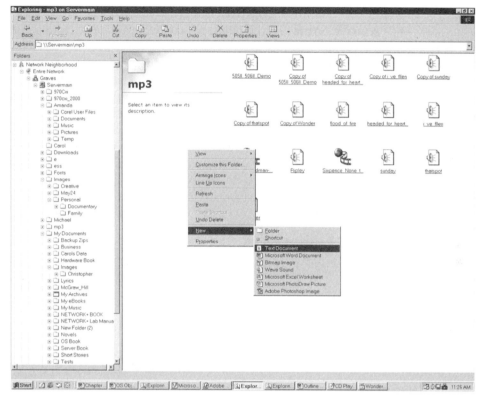

Figure 5.33   Right-clicking the details pane enables a whole new set of options for the user

to indicate file type. Details arranges files and folders in the directory by name, size, type, and the date on which it was last modified.

If you are using the Detail view, at the top of each column is a button labeling the column. If you click the button for Size, then all the files are sorted in size, from smallest to largest. Click the Size button a second time, and now they're sorted from largest to smallest. Click the Type button, and files are sorted by their extension. The Modified button sorts by date last modified. Clicking once on this button sorts by most recent; clicking a second time sorts by least recent.

The Customize this Folder option allows you to configure a specific folder to been seen as a Web page. Or you can choose a background image to appear behind the files and folders list.

The third command in the pop-up menu allows you to arrange the icons in the pane by a specific order. Files can be arranged by Name, Type, Size, or Date regardless of the view mode selected. This is identical to the function I discussed when viewing the folder in the Details mode. The Line Up Icons command simply tidies up the screen, without resorting icons.

Next, you have a Refresh command. Now what good would that be when viewing files on a hard drive? Are they likely to change while you watch? If you're looking at a remote location, such as a file server, they very well might. And if you're waiting for someone to post a file for you, simply having Explorer open won't help. You'll need to refresh the screen periodically to see when that file finally appears. You can accomplish the same thing by pressing the F5 button on your keyboard.

The Cut and Paste commands are identical to the ones I discussed in the section on the folders pane. An interesting item that comes next is the New command. What you see listed on this option can depend entirely on what applications you have installed on your system. By default, you can create new folders within a folder, new shortcuts, and new text documents. If you've installed a word processor such as Microsoft Word, then the option to create a new Word document becomes available. Many other applications add options to this menu as well. When you select New and then Word Document, Explorer launches Microsoft Word and allows you to start working from there.

Properties opens the same screen that you saw in the folders pane when you right-clicked a particular folder and selected Properties.

THE EXPLORER MENU

For the most part, the items found in the main menu of Windows Explorer are identical to items discussed in previous sections of the chapter. To show you where the items can be found, I've created a montage in **Figure 5.34** showing each of the menu items opened simultaneously. (Remember! I'm a trained professional. Don't try this stunt at home!)

A couple of items I want to discuss in greater detail are Folder Options (found under both the Tools menu item and the View menu item in WIN98) and the Go menu. Both of these applets offer you some added power that often goes unused.

FOLDER OPTIONS

Although I've already discussed the contents of the three tabs in the Folders Options dialog box in a previous section, I want to take a more detailed look at the View tab and the File Types tab. There are a couple of things you can do in here that can be done nowhere else.

Figure 5.34 Windows Explorer with all the menus open at once

In the View tab there are two sets of advanced settings. One is for Files and Folders, and the other, Visual Settings, allows you to adjust certain settings relevant to Explorer's appearance. At this point, I'm only interested in the Files and Folders section.

Earlier in this section, I mentioned how the title bar only shows the name of the folder you are in. One of the options you can select is to show the entire path. This is an option I prefer to have selected on a Windows machine I'm using, except when I'm making illustrations that show Windows default settings.

Notice that there are three different options for viewing hidden and/or system files. One of the options hides only files whose attributes are set for Hidden, and the other hides those with the attributes of Hidden and System. The last option displays all files. If you need to copy all the files in a directory from one location to another, and elect to use Windows Explorer for this task rather than doing it from a command prompt, then you need to adjust this setting to show all files. When you select all the files in the details pane, files that are not displayed are not selected and, therefore, not copied.

By default, Windows is configured to not show extensions for commonly used file types. This means that in Explorer, Novel.doc only appears as Novel, with the icon of your word processor above or next to it. Checking this box forces Windows to show all file extensions. The other settings in this section are fairly self-explanatory and are of little use to the technician.

In the File Types tab, the user can change how the extension of a file affects that file's behavior. In the details box of this window, you see the extension for the file type that has been selected in the Registered files types list along with its content type. Content type basically indicates whether the file is a document, an application, image file, or whatever. This is generally not something you want to change. Where it says Opens with, you see what program (if any) will automatically launch if you double-click that file in Explorer (or single-click if you are in Web mode).

You can change these settings (except for the extension itself, of course) by clicking the Edit button. You can also change the icon that is displayed in Explorer if you so desire. In the Edit File Type window, there is another Edit button. Clicking this allows you to change what program runs a particular file type. You can change what actions Windows performs when you double-click an icon by clicking the Add button.

HOT KEYS

Windows has been designed to be a point-and-click environment in order to make it easier to use. In a way, this is Microsoft's way of acknowledging that the majority of people who use computers have no intention or desire to learn *how* to use them beyond the minimal level they require.

However, excessive use of a mouse has two negative effects. One of these is repetitive stress injury. This is a physical ailment that many people develop from repeating the same motions over and over again. The second negative effect isn't quite as serious, but is still something to consider. And that is the fact that reaching for the mouse, navigating the cursor to the place where it needs to be, and then performing whatever function is needed can often be much slower than simply pressing a couple of keys.

Windows is programmed with a large number of predefined key sequences that, when pressed, accomplish some function that might require searching through several levels of menu items to find if using the mouse. These are called hot keys. Some of the Windows hot keys involve only a single keystroke. However, most involve some combination of the <Ctrl> or the <Alt> keys along with one or more other keys on the keyboard. For example, when I want to type in *italics*, I don't use my mouse to click the italics button in the tools menu. That would seriously impact on my blazing typing speed (126 mistakes per minute, thank you very much!). I press <Ctrl>+I to get the same effect. Appendix A contains a table listing the most commonly used hot keys.

MSCONFIG

Earlier in the chapter, I mentioned a utility present in WIN9x that would allow the user to manage the TSRs that started automatically. That utility is MSCONFIG (**Figure 5.35**), and it does a lot more than just that. There are several tabs in this section, but for most technicians, only two are truly relevant in most situations.

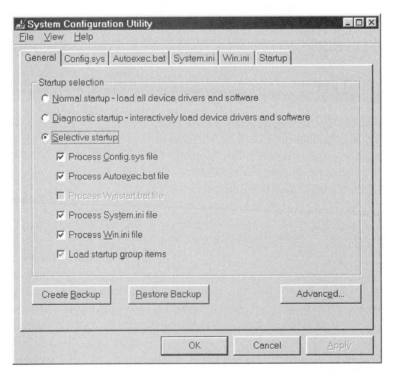

Figure 5.35 The MSCONFIG utility is an easy way to edit the startup parameters and other aspects of your system.

The General tab is the first to appear when you launch the application by clicking Start →
Run and typing **MSCONFIG**. Here you can select between a normal startup, a diagnostic startup,
or a selective startup. Obviously, a normal startup is the default, and, unless there is a good
reason, it is the one that you should retain. A diagnostic startup does come in handy when you
have a system that starts fine in Safe Mode but won't start normally. While the procedure can
be time-consuming, using the diagnostic startup enables you to selectively load drivers. By
leaving drivers out, one at a time, on successive reboots, it is possible to locate the offending
device and decide what to do about it. Selective startup allows you to tell Windows which file
to load and which ones not to load during startup. This can be useful if you have an old DOS
program that you run regularly.

Create Backup and Restore Backup are for creating or restoring backups of the configuration file that's created by MSCONFIG. There is an Advanced button that takes you to a
number of settings that in most cases should be left alone. These are mostly settings relating to
hardware and are best covered in a hardware book.

The four tabs for CONFIG.SYS, AUTOEXEC.BAT, SYSTEM.INI, and WIN.INI allow
you to view and edit these specific files. This is usually unnecessary, since WIN9x applications
do not make use of these files. They exist for backward compatibility with older DOS and
WIN3.x programs.

Finally, the Startup tab is where you go to enable or disable the applets that start automatically
every time Windows loads. Although not 100 percent complete, there is a table in Appendix A
that shows some of the items commonly located in the Startup menu along with descriptions.

WINDOWS HELP

Microsoft has incorporated a help function of some form since the earlier incarnations of
MS-DOS. In DOS, it consisted of typing the command you wanted help with followed by
/?. Doing that listed the possible triggers for that command. With WIN3.x, the help function
became more of a formatted text document. These days, Windows help (**Figure 5.36**) is a full-
blown application. It is a relational database of topics that cover a vast majority of the common
problems people face.

Topics are hyperlinked between one another where relevant so navigation between topics
is much easier. By hyperlinked, I mean that clicking a hyperlinked topic automatically redirects
you to another page with more or related information on the topic. In addition, Windows help
can hyperlink you to a number of different troubleshooters. Hardware troubleshooters help
diagnose problems with misbehaving devices, and the Network Troubleshooter can help you
figure out why you can't log on to the domain.

Windows help is also context-sensitive. That means if you are in a particular function or
application and press the F1 key, a window will appear with tips relevant to what you were doing
when you pressed the key. If you wish more general help, you can get there by clicking
Start → Help. If it is the first time you've used help, you might have to wait a couple of seconds
while the application indexes the topics for the first time. After that, you're off and running.

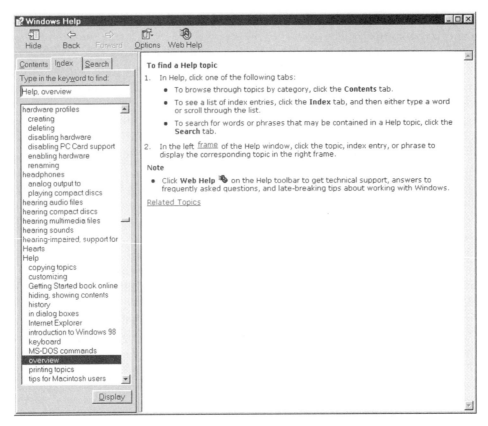

Figure 5.36   The Windows Help function provides literally volumes of information that is context sensitive.

Chapter Summary

Okay, I'll admit. This was a long chapter. However, since it prepares you for much of what is to come, that simply means that you've gotten the basics out of the way. For the rest of the book I can concentrate on specifics.

By the time you've finished this chapter, you'll have a pretty good idea of how to get around Windows. The nice thing about later versions is that, for the most part, they stick to a very similar format and structure. Making a move from an older OS to a newer version isn't quite as painful as it might be. However, Microsoft does like to slip in a few changes here and there, so there will still be much to discuss in the chapters to come.

Installing the OS was the first thing I covered. This is one area that does change somewhat with future versions, so I'll be looking at those differences. An understanding of the Windows Desktop is critical, but fortunately, it also comes easily. There are also a good number of questions on the CompTIA exam relevant to the desktop, so don't slack off on the subject just because you think you know it. And *really* make sure you understand Control Panel.

One of the topics I covered in this book that I rarely see covered in other books is that of hot keys. This is a sad omission because someone who truly understands hot keys and knows them well is far more productive than the user who is chained to a mouse.

BRAIN DRAIN

1. Discuss the differences between a clean install and an upgrade. While you're at it, discuss the pros and cons of each type of installation.

2. What are the different setup phases for Windows 95 and what is happening to your computer at each phase?

3. Now discuss the different setup phases for Windows 98 and how they differ from Windows 95.

4. Discuss how an understanding of the Taskbar can help you determine why a computer takes its own sweet time every time it boots up.

5. How did Microsoft take the mouse from a cute little toy to a powerful tool with the release of Windows 95?

THE 64K$ QUESTIONS

1. During an upgrade, Windows 95 could extract information about programs installed to WIN3.x by opening and reading the _____.
   a. Registry
   b. SETUP.INI file
   c. Group files
   d. CONFIG.SYS and AUTOEXEC.BAT

2. You want to run the Windows Setup program from a command prompt and want it to skip the network configuration portion of Setup. What command would you type?
   a. `SETUP /NONET`
   b. `SETUP /IN`
   c. `SETUP /N`
   d. `SETUP /IS`

3. Which of the following is not a setup phase for WIN95?
   a. Startup and information gathering
   b. File copy
   c. Final system configuration
   d. Hardware setup

4. What is the first thing the WIN95 Setup program does after it is launched?
   a. Perform a system check
   b. Install the Setup Wizard
   c. Prompt the user for the License Key
   d. FDISK the hard drive

5. How does Windows setup remove AUTOEXEC.BAT or CONFIG.SYS lines that may cause problems during an upgrade?
   a. It deletes them completely.
   b. It places a REM statement in front of the offending command.
   c. It places a NO statement in front of the offending command.
   d. It doesn't.

6. The right button on the mouse can do what in WIN9x?
   a. Highlight an entire line with a single click.
   b. Move to the next active window.

c. Bring up context-sensitive help.

d. Bring up a menu specific to the object clicked upon.

7. In order to bring up Display Properties, the user can _____.

a. Right-click the Desktop and click Properties

b. Open My Computer and click Display Properties

c. Click Start → Control Panel → System → Display Properties

d. Click Start → Settings → Control Panel → Display Properties

8. A user's desktop that is setup for single-click activation of a menu item has been configured to be _____.

a. A Web page

b. An interactive desktop

c. An active desktop

d. You can't do that.

9. Control Panel can be accessed from which two of the following places?

a. My Computer

b. An active desktop

c. The taskbar

d. The Start menu

10. How would you create an icon on the desktop for a program that appears in your Start menu, but not on the desktop?

a. Dragging and dropping the Menu item over to the desktop.

b. From the Application's menu, clicking Tools → Create Shortcut.

c. Right-clicking the Desktop, selecting Create New Shortcut, and typing in the application's name.

d. Clicking Start → Programs, right-clicking the Application's name, and selecting Create Shortcut. When a new item appears on the menu with the application's name followed by (2), drag and drop it over to the desktop.

11. You've just installed a new sound card and it places a handy little applet somewhere on your computer that allows you to adjust volume without constantly reaching up to the speakers. Where is the icon for that program most likely to be placed?

a. On the Start menu

b. On the Desktop

c. On the Taskbar

d. On the Toolbar

12. You've installed about a hundred different things that all assume that you want them to automatically start every time you run Windows. What handy little applet did Microsoft include with WIN98 that allows you to easily reconfigure startup options?

a. SCANREG

b. MSCONFIG

c. START.BAT

d. SYSCONFIG

13. Windows applications are consistent among themselves because of a feature built into Windows called the _____.

a. GUI

b. CUI

c. UID

d. IRD

14. How does using Add/Remove Programs (in WIN95) to install software differ from simply allowing

a CD's autorun feature to install it automatically?

   a. It forces all programs to be installed into the Program Files directory.

   b. It creates an Uninstall script.

   c. It allows greater user control of what files are installed.

   d. It doesn't.

15. Which Control Panel applet allows the user to turn off Daylight Savings Time?

   a. System

   b. Regional Settings

   c. Users

   d. Time/Date

16. Which of the following can't you browse to from Windows Explorer?

   a. A networked printer

   b. A Novell server

   c. An Internet location

   d. You can browse to any of those.

17. What are two methods of mapping a folder on the network server to your local machine so that it appears as though it were a local drive?

   a. In the folders pane of Windows Explorer, right-click the remote resource and select Map Network Drive.

   b. In the contents pane of Windows Explorer, right-click the remote resource and select Map Network Drive.

   c. Add the location to the Favorites menu.

   d. Click Tools → Map Network Drive.

18. Which of the following keys is not used in a key combination for a keyboard shortcut?

   a. <Alt>

   b. <Enter>

   c. <Shift>

   d. <Ctrl>

19. Which of the following shortcuts selects all text in an open document?

   a. <Alt>+A

   b. <Alt>+S

   c. <Ctrl>+A

   d. <Ctrl>+S

20. <Ctrl>+<Alt>+<Delete> _____ on a WIN9x computer.

   a. Opens the Task Manager

   b. Opens a Close Program window

   c. Resets the computer

   d. Is used when you first log onto the computer

TRICKY TERMINOLOGY

Active Desktop: A method of configuring the Windows desktop to behave as if it is a Web page, allowing single-click activation of icons and other Web-like features.

Burn-in: The tendency for a CRT monitor to permanently etch an image onto the inner surface of the tube if the image stays on the screen for too long a period.

Clean install: The fresh installation of an OS over a newly partitioned and formatted hard disk.

Font: The size and characteristics (such as bold or italic) of a particular typeface.

Icon: A small picture linked to an application shortcut.

Typeface: The basic shape that letters and numbers of a particular character set will assume.

Upgrade: The replacement of an older OS with a newer, migrating as many settings and applications as possible.

ACRONYM ALERT

PM: Program Manager. An applet in WIN3.x that acted as a DOS shell for file and program management functions.

CUI: Common User Interface. A feature of many OSs that dictates how certain functions related to user interaction with the programs are handled, ensuring that all applications have a similar look, feel, and function.

MIDI: Musical Instrument Device Interface. A connector for hooking up computerized musical instruments to a computer system.

CHAPTER 6

THE WORLD OF NT

As I pointed out in the previous two chapters concerning the WIN9x products, one of Microsoft's main concerns had been that of maintaining backward compatibility with previous products. As such, the WIN9x products (except for WINMe) were hybrid OSs, consisting of a 16-bit component plus a 32-bit component. To further enhance their ability to run DOS applications, these products shipped with DOS 7.0.

With the release of Windows NT 3.51, this all changed. Although NT did have a command prompt, it did not support any version of DOS. It was a purely a 32-bit OS with only rudimentary support for 16-bit code. Microsoft's goal here was to provide a faster OS that exhibited greater stability. Windows NT (WINNT) was the first in a growing line of products that have pursued that goal.

A+ OPERATING SYSTEM TECHNOLOGIES EXAM OBJECTIVES

CompTIA exam objectives covered in this chapter include the following:

1.1 Identify the major desktop components and interfaces and their functions. Differentiate the characteristics of Windows 9x/Me, Windows NT 4.0 Workstation, Windows 2000 Professional, and Windows XP.

1.2 Identify the names, locations, purposes, and contents of major system files.

1.4 Identify basic concepts and procedures for creating, viewing, and managing disks, directories, and files. This includes procedures for changing file attributes and the ramifications of those changes (for example, security issues).

2.1 Identify the procedures for installing Windows 9x/Me, Windows NT 4.0 Workstation, Windows 2000 Professional, and Windows XP and bring the operating system to a basic operational level.

2.2 Identify steps to perform an operating system upgrade from Windows 9x/Me, Windows NT 4.0 Workstation, Windows 2000 Professional, and Windows XP. Given an upgrade scenario, choose the appropriate next steps.

2.3 Identify the basic system boot sequences and boot methods, including the steps to create an emergency boot disk with utilities installed for Windows 9x/Me, Windows NT 4.0 Workstation, Windows 2000 Professional, and Windows XP.

2.4 Identify procedures for installing/adding a device, including loading, adding, and configuring device drivers and required software.

3.1 Recognize and interpret the meaning of common error codes and startup messages from the boot sequence, and identify steps to correct the problems.

3.2 Recognize when to use common diagnostic utilities and tools. Given a diagnostic scenario involving one of these utilities or tools, select the appropriate steps needed to resolve the problem.

3.3 Recognize common operational and usability problems and determine how to resolve them.

THE HISTORY OF NT

While there would not be an official release of a product with NT in the name until 1993, Microsoft began work on the concept of a 32-bit OS in 1988. A gentleman by the name of David Cutler, Sr., moved over to Microsoft from Digital Equipment Corporation (DEC), bringing to Microsoft a profound knowledge of OS architecture. Most notably, Cutler had been involved with the development of DEC's Virtual Memory System (VMS).

By 1991, Microsoft had developed a version of NT that it considered stable enough to demonstrate at the Microsoft Windows Developers Conference. Designated NT 3.0, it was never deemed stable enough for a public release, but it still possessed most of the features that were to become the NT core.

What happened to versions 1.0 and 2.0? They never existed. Microsoft doesn't explain the reasoning behind their version numbering system, but here are the two most popular explanations:

1. They wanted the version numbers to coincide with Windows 3.0 and 3.1 desktop OSs.

2. Because the similarities between NT and VMS were so strong, the version number was selected to coincide with the current version of VMS.

Fortunately for me, it isn't up to me to decide. Fortunately for you, it isn't something that's covered on the exam. I simply thought it interesting enough to mention.

In July of 1993, Microsoft released the first version of NT designed for public consumption, Windows NT 3.1. There were two separate releases of this OS. NT 3.1 was an OS designed for high-end desktops, and NT 3.1 Advanced Server was Microsoft's first foray into a true network operating system (NOS).

NT 3.1 could never be mistaken for a bastion of stability in any respect. It had a number of issues that prevented it from really taking off as an enterprise-level product. Still, for Microsoft, this OS broke new ground in several respects.

- It was a true 32-bit OS.

- It was the first OS to implement pre-emptive multitasking.

- The NTFS file system provided much greater local security.

- Domain Server security provided network level security that had previously not existed on any Microsoft product.

- File and Print services provided network-wide access to files and printers distributed across the network.

- It supported multiprocessor systems.

- Virtual memory support was an embedded function of the OS.

- It was the first Microsoft OS to have versions designed to run on non-Intel microprocessors.

On a more familiar note, one of the biggest claims to fame for NT was that it became the foundation over which future Microsoft products would be developed. It was the first to abandon 16-bit code as part of the architecture, although it did continue to provide support for running 16-bit applications. More notably, it was the first OS to separate the hardware interface from the applications interface. Applications could no longer make direct calls to the hardware.

EXAM NOTE: It is a key point that NT was Microsoft's first true 32-bit OS. WIN9x was touted as being a 32-bit architecture, but in reality it was a hybrid OS, running both 16-bit and 32-bit code.

Microsoft continued to work out the kinks in the NT code, and a year later, in September of 1994, NT 3.5 was released. This version proved to be much more stable. More notably 3.5 also introduced internetworking capabilities that allow Microsoft networks to mingle with Novell and UNIX networks. NT 3.5 was followed up in July of 1995 with NT 3.51.

More than just a bug fix, NT 3.51 introduced some new capabilities to NT. Features were added to make the OS more accessible to people with hearing or sight impairments. Support for the BackOffice product line made it easier to manage network applications and licensing. A desktop version of the OS, NT 3.51 Workstation, was designed to accommodate applications written for the newly released WIN95. It also provided hardware support for the new Personal Computer Memory Card International Association (PCMCIA) devices.

Still, even with all these improvements, the IT industry wasn't exactly moving toward NT in droves. If anything, there was exactly the opposite direction of movement. In 1996, Microsoft successfully reversed that trend with the release of NT 4.0. With many of the features that made WIN95 so popular, along with a massive improvement in stability, NT 4.0 became the mainstay for servers and high-end workstations for the next four years and contributed greatly to Microsoft's ascending dominance in the OS industry. The remainder of this chapter will deal exclusively with NT 4.0, as all other versions are considered obsolete.

NT'S TENUOUS RELATIONSHIP WITH VMS

VMS is an OS that isn't covered in the A+ exam, but nonetheless, it deserves an acknowledgment here. It is frequently credited as being the most stable OS ever written. (At one point in time, there was a computer system running VMS that had run non-stop for twelve years without a reboot.) Because of its stability, the OS still sees a lot of use in computing environments where the system can never go down.

Since Cutler was so heavily involved in the VMS project at DEC (and since he brought a big chunk of his programming team with him from DEC to Microsoft), it should come as no surprise that similarities between the two OSs abound. There are many characteristics of the two OSs that are virtually identical in both form and function:

- A process scheduler that imposes thirty-two priority levels
- A process called boosting that prevents a process from hogging the CPU
- Symmetric multiprocessing support
- Memory mapping imposed on files
- Demand-paged virtual memory for physical memory management
- Device drivers built in a layered model
- I/O commands issued asynchronously in a packet-based structure
- All resources, including files, devices, and users represented as objects managed by an Object Manager
- A tighter security subsystem that links to the Object Manager to control user access based on access control lists (ACL)
- Hardware diagnostics—in VMS the utility is called Monitor, in NT it's called Performance Monitor.
- A hard disk backup utility

VMS, on the other hand, isn't exactly what one would call user-friendly. Cutler and his team approached this issue, as well as the native file system of VMS, which would have been completely unfamiliar to users already immersed in the Microsoft world. To ensure that NT would be a friendlier environment to existing Windows users, Microsoft embedded the WIN32 API and the NTFS file system. The result was a more stable OS with a familiar look and feel.

SYMMETRIC MULTIPROCESSING

NT 4.0 incorporated most of the features of previous versions of NT, but in many cases it took these features to a higher lever. Earlier in the chapter I provided a bulleted list of the ways that NT is similar to VMS. One feature that deserves a closer look is that of *symmetric multiprocessing* (SMP).

This .44 caliber term basically means that the OS is capable of utilizing the services of more than one microprocessor. When a system can do this, it runs faster and responds to user requests

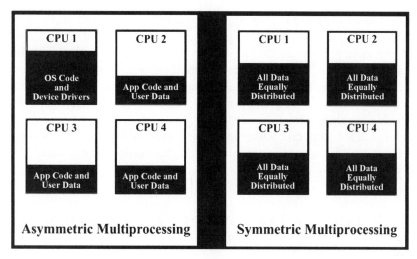

Figure 6.1   With ASMP, the OS code and device drives all run on one CPU while application code and user data is evenly distributed among the remaining processors. With SMP, all data is distributed equally.

more quickly. However, different OSs over the years have made use of two different forms of multiprocessing. Those two forms are asymmetric and symmetric multiprocessing (**Figure 6.1**).

Asymmetric multiprocessing (ASMP) operating systems typically utilize the primary microprocessor (Processor 1) for the execution of operating system code. The other processors in the system run application code or process user data. Typically, an ASMP-configured machine has more than one processor, but the processors do not necessarily have access to the same memory addresses, or even the same amount of memory for that matter.

EXAM NOTE: Be prepared to be able to identify the differences between symmetric and asymmetric multiprocessing.

BUZZ WORDS —————————

Asymmetric multiprocessing: A method by which an operating system makes use of more than one processor, loading OS code onto one processor and application code and user data onto all others.

Symmetric multiprocessing: A method by which an operating system makes use of more than one processor, distributing all code equally across all available processors.

The vast majority of operating systems that support multiprocessing make use of SMP. This includes all versions of Windows NT. SMP allows the operating system code, application code, or user data to run on any free processor. Most hardware configurations share all available memory between all available processors.

In Chapter One, I discussed the difference between threads of code and processes. NT 4.0 makes use of multiple threads within a single process wherever possible. As a result, different threads from the same process can be running on different CPUs at the same time.

SMP is a much more efficient utilization of multiple processors because operating system code has a tendency to hog the processor. Allowing the operating system to run on only one processor frequently results in that one processor becoming overloaded, while the others are sitting back twiddling their virtual thumbs.

All versions of NT 4.0 can take advantage of multiprocessor systems. However, the different versions have different limitations in the number of processors they can address. This will be discussed in the next section.

NT 4.0 Versions: Hardware Requirements and OS Features

Microsoft shipped several different versions of NT 4.0 over the life of the product line. Each version offered different capabilities, and each one exhibited its own unique system requirements for successful installation and operation. These are the different versions I'll discuss in this chapter:

- NT 4.0 Workstation
- NT 4.0 Server
- NT 4.0 Server, Enterprise Edition
- NT 4.0 Terminal Server

It should be noted that there were also a number of different service packs that were issued over the life of the product. Installation of a service pack impacted the minimum hardware requirements in some cases. Later in the chapter, as I discuss service packs, I'll point out some exceptions.

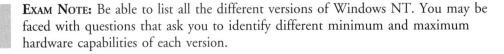

EXAM NOTE: Be able to list all the different versions of Windows NT. You may be faced with questions that ask you to identify different minimum and maximum hardware capabilities of each version.

NT 4.0 Workstation

NT 4.0 Workstation (NTWS) was the OS of choice for many high-end workstations during its era. Although it could only address two processors, it was still one of the few over-the-counter OSs that supported SMP.

Another interesting addition to NTWS was Remote Access Service (RAS). The user could configure a NTWS machine to accept an incoming connection from a remote computer. While NTWS was limited to only one RAS connection at a time, this was still an improvement over previous OSs. And as with all other versions of NT 4.0, NTWS could be installed on computers

Table 6.1 Minimum and Maximum Hardware Requirements, NTWS

Device	Minimum	Maximum
Processor	Single 486-DX33	Two >486-DX33
Hard Disk (CISC/RISC)	110MB/148MB	16EB
Memory (CISC/RISC)	12MB/16MB	4GB
Graphics	VGA	VGA
Pointer	Mouse or trackball	Mouse or trackball

Minimum and maximum hardware requirements for NTWS 4.0. Note that the minimum requirements differ between a CISC installation and a RISC installation.

powered by Intel (and compatible), DEC Alpha, Motorola Power PC, or Silicon Graphics (and compatible) MIPS processors. **Table 6.1** lists the system requirements for NTWS.

NT SERVER 4.0

NT Server was designed to be a full-blown NOS, providing a scalable architecture that would allow networks to enjoy virtually unlimited growth. With NT 4.0 Server, Microsoft bet the bank on a domain model of networking. Under this model, all users, servers, workstations, and other devices that were under the administrative control of a single collection of security data became the domain. This information was stored on one computer called the primary domain controller (PDC). The PDC provided security control and logon authentication services for every user and device on the domain. Other computers, called backup domain controllers (BDC), can maintain copies of this database, but only the PDC maintains an original. This information is stored in the Security Account Manager (SAM). However, SAM is part of the registry, and there is a built-in limitation to the maximum size to which the registry can grow.

SAM AND THE REGISTRY

By default, NT sets the maximum registry size to 25 percent of the paged pool. The paged pool consists of all data currently stored in RAM that can be written to the hard disk in order to free up physical RAM. The maximum size of the paged pool in NT 4.0 is 128MB; therefore, the default maximum size of the registry is 32MB.

If the administrator requires a larger registry, it is simply a matter of changing one of the entries in the registry. This can be done by editing the registry, but it's safer and easier to use Control Panel. In the System Applet, under Performance, registry size can be configured either in megabytes or as a maximum percentage (up to 80 percent of the paged pool). The minimum size that be configured is 4MB. Since the paged pool is limited to 128MB, then the maximum size is 102.4MB.

Table 6.2 Minimum and Maximum Hardware Requirements, NT Server

Device	Minimum	Maximum/ NT Server	Maximum/ Enterprise	Maximum Terminal Server
Processor	Single 486-DX33	Two >No max. speed	Eight >No max. speed	Four >No max. speed
Hard Disk (CISC/RISC)	125MB/160MB	16EB	16EB	16EB
Memory (CISC/RISC)	16MB/16MB	4GB	8GB	4GB
Graphics	VGA	VGA	VGA	VGA
Pointer	Mouse or trackball	Mouse or trackball	Mouse or trackball	Mouse or trackball

Minimum and maximum hardware requirements for NT 4.0 Server versions.

Hardware requirements for the server versions vary in maximum capabilities. However, minimum requirements are consistent. **Table 6.2** lists minimum and maximum requirements for the different server versions.

NT SECURITY

Increased security was a key issue for Microsoft during the developmental phase of NT 4.0. This security tightening began at the logon screen and worked its way down into the basic architecture of the OS.

LOGON SECURITY

Previous versions of the software had users logging on from a prompt that was little more than an elegantly designed DOS screen. As a result users and network administrators could easily find themselves victims of a malicious piece of software called a Trojan Horse. A *Trojan horse* is a piece of software that mimics the look and function of another piece of software familiar to users, but in reality it is performing a completely different function all together.

One of these Trojan horses particularly embarrassing to Microsoft was a program that was designed to look, feel, taste, and smell just like the logon screen for Windows NT. When users typed in their user IDs and passwords, nothing appeared to happen. All too frequently, this resulted in a

BUZZ WORDS ─────────

Trojan horse: A malicious program designed to mimic another commonly recognized program, but that is, in fact, performing some other action in the background without the knowledge or consent of the user.

frustrated user calling the network administrator down to fix the problem. And what was the first thing this person would do? Type in his or her user ID and password, of course! But the program wasn't doing nothing. It was doing something. It collected all those user IDs and passwords into a file that the attacker could come and collect at leisure.

> **EXAM NOTE:** My discussion of OS security and the logon process is probably a bit more detailed than really required for the CompTIA exam. However, it's basic OS information with which any IT professional should be comfortable. One key point that is brought up on the exam a lot is the logon security added to protect against Trojan horses. File system security is also covered.

With the release of NT 4.0, logging onto the system is mandatory. To do so, the user must press <Ctrl>+<Alt>+<Delete> to begin. On older DOS-based computers and those with DOS programs, this key sequence resets the computer. With NT it brings up the logon screen. This is the door that locks out the Trojan horses, because as DOS-based programs, the key sequence will give them away.

PERMISSIONS AND PRIVILEGES

The basis for internal security on an NT network is grounded in the concept of permissions and privileges. This is one of those situations where two words mean the same thing, only different. *Permissions* apply to various resources on the network and whether or not a specific user has access to a specific resource, and if so, just how much control that user can have over the resource. *Privileges* dictate what actions or functions a user can perform on his or her own system or on the network in general.

PERMISSIONS

Permissions have been around the OS world for a long time and tend to vary slightly from one OS to the next. The Microsoft world is divided into two different forms of permissions. There are share level and user level security.

Share Level Security *Share level permissions* are attributes that are assigned directly to a specific resource on the network. For any given resource, there will be a specific password that will allow access. Access comes in one of four different forms.

Read permission allows you to access and view the object, but not to modify it in any way. You cannot edit, delete, or rename the object. If changes are made to a file with Read permission, that file cannot be saved under the same name.

BUZZ WORDS

Permissions: The degrees of access a particular user has been granted to a specific resource on the network.

Privileges: The rights a particular user has been granted to perform specific functions or tasks on a system or the network in general.

Share level security: A method of protecting resources on the network that involves applying the security attributes, such as password protection, to the object itself. As such, each secured object on the system may have a unique password.

Full Control permission allows you to do what you will with the file. You can edit, delete, or rename the file. You can even change the permissions on it, should you so desire.

No Access permission should be fairly self-explanatory. A file with No Access assigned to it cannot be opened at all.

Depends on Password gives you specific permissions based on what password you supply. There will be one password for Full Control and another for Read.

A problem inherent with share level security is that for every resource, there is a password. If 200 users have all created 10 files, each with a different password, then if you want to be able to access all 2,000 files, you need to know 2,000 passwords. That's handy, isn't it?

BUZZ WORDS

User level security: A method of securing resources on a system or network that involves assigning the security attributes to an account provided to the user. After the user has logged on, access to resources is provided based on the permissions assigned to the account.

Credentials: Information provided by the user, including but not restricted to the user ID and password, that grants that user access to a system or network.

User Level Security That's why network OSs all employ *user level security*. With user level security, the user is assigned a user ID and password. These are the user's *credentials*. When the user logs on, he or she types in the credentials, and from that point forward, the permissions granted to that user control access to any given resource on the network. As a result, user level security makes heavy use of file system security.

With file system security, file and folder level permissions are used. But unlike share level security, access is controlled by a centralized security database. This is the SAM I discussed earlier. File system security is much more granular than share level. Any given permission on a resource can be specifically denied to a given user or group. There are also a number of other different permissions that can be assigned:

- *Read*: Similar to the Read permission in share level security.
- *Write*: The user can edit the file but cannot delete it or rename it.
- *List Contents*: A user with this permission can view a directory listing of a given folder but cannot access the individual files.
- *Read and Execute*: Applications can be secured as well as data files. If the administrator denies this permission to a user or group, then that application cannot be run.
- *Modify*: A Modify permission allows the user to open, edit, rename, or even delete the file. This is not, however, the same as full permission.
- *Full Control*: Full Control grants the user all the abilities granted by Modify permission. In addition, the user with Full Control can change permissions on a resource and take ownership of a resource. In essence, Full Control is putting the security of that file into the users' hands. By default, the original creator of a file has Full Control, as does anyone with administrative privileges on the network. More on privileges later.

The more astute reader may notice that there is no mention of a No Access permission in the preceding list. No Access would be the permissions level one might expect to see that blocks a user from even knowing a file or directory even exists. The administrator can accomplish No Access simply by denying Full Control.

PRIVILEGES

There is, however, more to network security than simply accessing data. There is a lot of administration that needs to be done and a lot of administrative functions that the administrator doesn't want just anybody doing. For example you don't want just anyone to have the right to go in and change other peoples' passwords. You don't want just anyone to have the right to shut down the server.

Privileges are administrative rights allowed by the system. These can either be assigned directly to a user on an individual basis, or they can be assigned by adding a user to one of NT's built-in groups. Most administrators prefer the latter approach. Built-in groups in NT vary slightly between NT Workstation and the versions of NT Server. **Table 6.3** lists the built-in groups for all versions along with the privileges that go with those groups.

SAM AND THE LOCAL SECURITY AUTHORITY

Earlier in the chapter, I discussed how account information was stored in the SAM. Here, I will talk about how SAM is used to keep the network secure, with a little help from another piece of NT architecture called the Local Security Authority (LSA).

I'll start with how a user's account is actually managed by SAM. When the network administrator first creates an account for a new user, that user is assigned a user ID and (usually) a password. Most users think that it is this user ID and password that is their key to the network. As far as they're concerned, it is. But SAM could care less about that. It's looking at a number called the Security Identifier (SID) that is generated by the system when the account is created. As long as that account remains on the system, that SID follows the user wherever he/she goes.

When the user first logs onto the system (after having pressed <Ctrl>+<Alt>+<Delete>, of course), a process called WinLogon passes the user ID and password that are entered to LSA. LSA compares the information provided by the user to that which is stored in SAM. If the data is correct, the user is allowed onto the system. If not, that user is rejected. Across a network, LSA will transmit this information to either a PDC or a BDC.

When a user is successfully logged on, LSA will generate a security access token that validates the user's session on the network. That token is the key to network resources. If the user logs off and then back on, a new token will be generated. The token includes the following:

- The user's SID
- The SID for any user groups to which the user has been assigned
- The list of permissions and privileges assigned to that user

Table 6.3 NT Built-in Groups

Local Group Name	Default Members	Who Can Modify?	Inherent Privileges	Available on Domain Controller (DC) or Workstation (WS)
Account Operators	None	Administrators, Account Operators, Server Operators	Create, delete, modify user accounts and groups. Cannot modify the Administrators or Server Operator groups	DC
Administrators	Domain Administrators, Administrators	Administrators	Create, delete, or manage user accounts and groups. Manage resource shares. Grant resource permissions. Install programs, OS patches, and device drivers.	WS, DC
Backup Operators	None	Administrators	Backup and restore servers and workstations. Logon locally. Shut down the server.	WS, DC
Guests	Guest	Administrators, Account Operators	None defined.	WS, DC
Power Users	None	Administrators, Account Operators	Install programs, OS patches, and device drivers. Manage local printers.	WS
Print Operators	None	Administrators	Share and remove sharing printers. Manage printers. Logon locally. Shut down servers.	DC
Replicator	None	Administrators, Account Operators, Server Operators	Used with the Directory Replication Service.	WS, DC
Server Operators	None	Administrators	Share and remove sharing resources. Format the server disks. Logon locally. Backup and restore servers. Shut down servers. Lock and unlock servers. Install programs, OS patches, and device drivers.	DC
Users	Domain Users	Administrators, Account Operators	None defined.	WS, DC

The built-in groups in NT are a convenient way of managing user privileges.

Now that the token has been generated, WinLogon opens a new session of EXPLORER.EXE. The access token assigned to the user is attached to this process, and from that point forward, everything the user attempts to do must be validated by the token.

THE SECURITY DESCRIPTOR

Users aren't the only targets of system security. NT security treats every single resource on the system,

> **BUZZ WORDS** ————
>
> **Security descriptor:** A token attached to a resource that defines security attributes assigned to that resource.
>
> **Object:** In reference to an OS, an object is any resource, user account, or group account present on the system or network.

including the users, as *objects*. All of these objects are defined by a specific security descriptor. The *security descriptor* is a token that defines the security attributes of a specific object. In many cases, by default, this security is minimal unless the administrator chooses to increase it. The security descriptor comprises four components.

The first two are the individual SID and the group SID discussed in the previous section. Another component called the discretionary Access Control List (ACL) identifies what users and groups are allowed to access a particular object. The system maintains its own ACL, conveniently named the System ACL, that oversees all security descriptors. The System ACL is used by the system for internal security audits when defined by the administrator and is what allows an administrator to set and enforce security policies over the entire network.

Now let's go back to those discretionary ACLs for a moment. As I mentioned, it is the discretionary ACL that defines what users and groups are allowed to access a specific object. I called it a list, but what is it a list of? The ACL consists of a series of Access Control Entities (ACE). Each of these entities either grants or denies access to the object for a specific user or group. It does this on the basis of the permissions granted to that user.

ACCESS VALIDATION

The process of access validation is what makes all of the preceding work the way it does. When the user attempts to access an object for the first time, an NT function called the Security Reference Monitor (SRM) examines the user's access token and compares it to the object's ACL. Each ACE in the ACL is read in the order it is listed. No Access entries are all listed first. This reduces system overhead for processing requests that won't be honored anyway. Once any ACEs in the ACL specific to the user's token indicate that the buzz should be allowed access, SRM opens the object to the user. Is it just me, or are there too many acronyms in this industry?

NT DOMAIN MODELS

As a result of these registry limitations, there is an inherent limitation to the number of user accounts that can be stored on a single machine. If the network begins to get too large for a single PDC to manage, the administrator has several options available. These options appear as the different domain models available to NT. Microsoft defines four different domain models:

- The Single Domain
- The Single Master Domain
- The Multiple Master Domain
- The Complete Trust

But before I get into a heavy discussion of NT's domain models, perhaps it would be a good idea to define the concept of a domain. Earlier Microsoft OSs, starting with Windows for Workgroups 3.11, included rudimentary built-in networking support. These OSs depended upon the concept of the workgroup for network management and communication. Simply put, a *workgroup* is a collection of devices on the network that share common resources and (usually) common responsibilities. This concept was fine for small networks but was virtually unusable for enterprise level networking.

The *domain* allows for much greater expansion and tighter control of the network. The domain consists of all users and resources that are under the oversight of a single administrative unit. Since large numbers of smaller networks can be combined into a single large network and still be under the control of a single PDC, domains can become quite large.

THE SINGLE DOMAIN

Under the Single domain (**Figure 6.2**), there is only one PDC that controls the entire network. All changes to the network infrastructure must be recorded on the PDC. This is where the master copy of SAM is stored. Additional BDCs may be used for balancing the load of logon requests for networks with large numbers of users. However, BDCs only maintain copies of SAM. These copies are updated from the PDC periodically in a process called synchronization, where the PDC checks with all BDCs on the network. If SAM has changed since the last synchronization, a new copy will be sent.

THE SINGLE MASTER DOMAIN

With the Single Master domain, there is still only a single PDC that houses the SAM that manages user accounts. However, there are one or more additional domains called Resource domains that maintain the security for some aspect of the network other than users. An example of a Resource domain would be as follows (and as illustrated in **Figure 6.3**). An organization might have a very large managed database with extremely critical security requirements. Access requirements for this database vary greatly from user to user. The network administrator has a

PDC
MYCOMP Domain

BDC
MYCOMP Domain

PDC Copies SAM

to BDC with changes

Brenda's logon can be
processed by BDC or PDC

Figure 6.2 While additional BDCs can help distribute the load of logon
authentication across a large network, there is only one PDC that
manages the master SAM.

reputation for being the best there is at overall network design, management, and maintenance. Unfortunately, what he knows about database management can be engraved on the sharp edge of a razor blade—with room left over for the Gettysburg Address.

Fortunately, the company also has an expert database administrator. She's the best there is at what she does, but neither knows, nor cares, what goes on in the overall workings of the network. The Single Master domain model provides the perfect solution. Two domains are

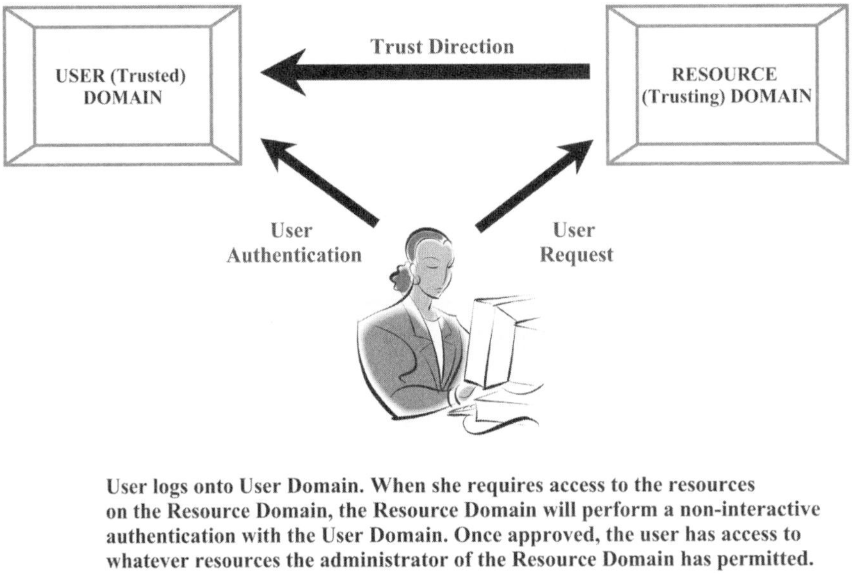

User logs onto User Domain. When she requires access to the resources on the Resource Domain, the Resource Domain will perform a non-interactive authentication with the User Domain. Once approved, the user has access to whatever resources the administrator of the Resource Domain has permitted.

Figure 6.3 With a single master domain, there is still only one PDC handling logon authentication, but this PDC represents an independent domain. Network resources are secured on separate domains.

created. The network manager assumes control of the user domain while the database administrator takes over the resource domain. Then the two administrators establish a trust between their separate domains.

A trust is a link between two domains over which user authentication is performed on one domain, but the permissions and privileges associated with that user's accounts are honored on another domain. In a trust relationship, there is a trusting domain and a trusted domain. The trusting domain is the domain that allows user authentication to occur over there on somebody else's domain. It trusts the authentication to be accurate. The trusted domain is the domain that maintains the SAM for the user account that is being verified.

Trusts are only one-way. There is no such thing as a two-way trust in the Windows domain structure. For a two-way trust to exist, a separate trust must be established in each direction on an NT network. For that to occur, the administrators of each domain must be actively involved, or one or the other of the administrators must know the user name and ID of the other.

Another thing about trusts in an NT 4.0 network is that trusts are nontransitive. This means that if I set up a trust between Domain A and Domain B, and then another trust between Domain B and Domain C, a trust between Domain A and Domain C will not be created by default. If I want that trust to exist, I will have to create it separately.

Under the Single Master domain model, there can be as many Resource domains as the organization requires, but as I've already pointed out, there will be only one Master domain that is managing authentication. Setting up multiple Resource domains allows for a tighter reign on security.

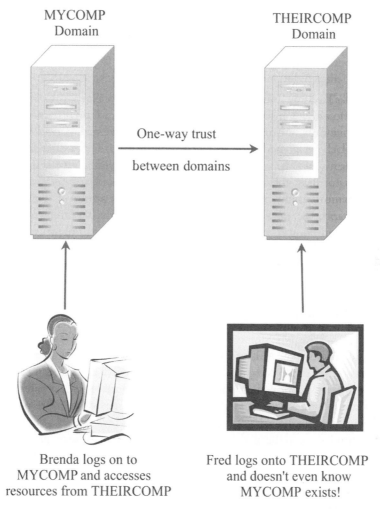

MYCOMP
Domain

THEIRCOMP
Domain

One-way trust

between domains

Brenda logs on to
MYCOMP and accesses
resources from THEIRCOMP

Fred logs onto THEIRCOMP
and doesn't even know
MYCOMP exists!

Figure 6.4 Larger organizations may benefit from the load balancing
and added security of a Multiple Master domain.

THE MULTIPLE MASTER DOMAIN

Some organizations reach the point where a Single Master domain isn't sufficient. This can occur when the number of user accounts and groups exceeds that which a single PDC can manage. And it can also happen when security issues dictate that different groups of users be separated from other users on the network. This is where the Multiple Master domain (**Figure 6.4**) comes into play.

With the Multiple Master domain, two or more PDCs are configured, each managing a different domain. Each of these domains is handling user authentication. However, unless trusts are established between the different domains, they can't see one another on the network.

For example, a company might have an office set up in Baton Rouge and another set up in Atlanta. The network in each office is managed by its own domain. The Baton Rouge office is BRCOMP and the Atlanta office is ATLCOMP. When a user logs on in Atlanta, if there is no trust established between Atlanta and Baton Rouge, then that user isn't even aware that the BRCOMP domain even exists.

This structure gives the administrators a bit of leeway in how they want to handle user access. For instance, if there is a pressing demand for the BRCOMP users to be able to access resources in the ATLCOMP domain, but not the reverse, then the administrators of the two domains might want to establish a single trust in which ATLCOMP domain trusts the BRCOMP domain, but not vice versa. ATLCOMP shares out the resources required by BRCOMP and then assigns permissions as it sees fit.

As with the Single Master domain, Resource domains can also be established to manage specific resources on the network. These are handled in exactly the same manner as I discussed in the section on the Single Master domain. As a result, a very complex network might have five Master domains and a dozen different resource domains, or even substantially more. Networks are practically limitless in terms of scalability.

The Complete Trust

The most complex of the NT domain models is the Complete Trust (**Figure 6.5**). In this scenario, a number of different Master and Resource domains are created, and every domain on the network trusts every other domain on the network in both directions. This model requires a literal maze of trust relationships and a massive amount of administration in terms of individual user and/or group access requirements between the domains.

Generally, this approach is not the most favorable, and where it exists, it usually exists by accident. An example would be a network that just seemed to keep growing. As each new domain was added, the administrators simply decided it was easier to simply establish trusts in each direction between their own domain and the new one. This prevents the administrators from having to make too many complex decisions, but it does lead to an overly complex and cumbersome network that is full of security holes.

Installing NT 4.0

As with previous Microsoft OS versions, there are two ways to install NT as the only OS on the system. The best and safest method is the clean install. However, as with other Windows versions, there is also the option for an upgrade. All of the possible problems that exist with upgrades are also apparent in an NT upgrade.

A third option with NT is to create a dual-boot system. This option allows the user to boot the system either to NT or to another OS installed onto another partition on the hard disk. I will discuss dual-boot systems toward the end of this chapter.

Regardless of the installation method you chose, there will be four separate phases to the NT installation process:

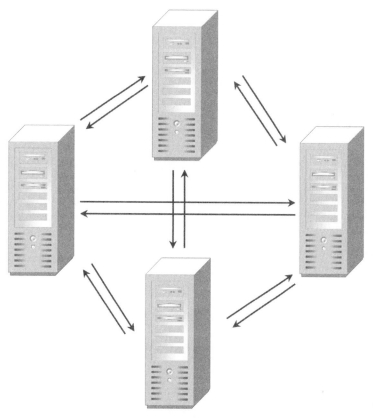

Figure 6.5   The complete trust is not considered to be an ideal structure for a network.

CREATING THE BOOT DISKETTES FOR NT 4.0

Many older machines won't boot to the CD, so it is essential for those users to have access to the installation disks. Even if you can successfully boot to a CD, it is a very good idea to keep a set of these diskettes on hand at all times. In recovery mode, the CD drive is quite often not readable.

To create the three boot diskettes for NT, have three blank formatted 1.44MB floppy diskettes available and label them "NT Installation Disk One," "NT Installation Disk Two," and "NT Installation Disk Three." Insert the CD into the drive of any working DOS or Windows machine. Open a command prompt and browse to the i386 directory on the CD-ROM. From the command prompt, type **WINNT /OX**. (The command is not case-sensitive). Read the prompts carefully. You'll note that the process creates disk three first, then disk two, and finally the boot diskette.

- The initial phase
- The text phase
- The GUI phase
- Finalizing the installation

THE INITIAL PHASE

The initial phase begins in one of two ways. If this is a clean installation onto a new hard drive then the installation file that will be used is WINNT.EXE. For the installation to succeed, the hard disk must already be prepared with a DOS partition to hold temporary files. This is a 16-bit file, and it only recognizes FAT16 for this installation partition. Therefore, if the FDISK utility from a WIN9x boot diskette was used to prepare the hard disk, and Large Disk Support was selected, then WINNT.EXE will not be able to recognize the disk.

If the computer can boot to a CD-ROM drive, then the installation procedure is as simple as inserting the NT 4.0 CD into the drive and booting the computer. If for any reason the system cannot boot to a CD, then the user will have to use the installation diskettes. This is a set of three diskettes that shipped with the product. If the diskettes have been lost or damaged, do not despair. They can be recreated on any DOS or Windows-based machine. See the sidebar for instructions.

After the system has booted, WINNT.EXE will create a temporary directory called win_nt.~ls. This is where all the files required for installation will stored for the remainder of the process. Once installation has been completed, WINNT.EXE deletes that directory and all the files it holds. Once in a while, if for any reason an installation is aborted and subsequently resumed at a later time, this temporary directory remains on the hard drive. When installation is complete, if that directory is still there, it is safe to remove it.

THE TEXT PHASE

After all the files are copied, you are prompted to remove any floppy diskettes from the drive and the system reboots. Now the installation enters the text phase. A program called NTDETECT.EXE scans the system for any installed hardware and generates a list of drivers that will be installed. (Note that NT 4.0 is not a PnP OS.) You will be prompted to press F5 if there are any hardware devices that are not internally supported by NT, such as SCSI adapters, which require installation of third-party drivers. This notifies WINNT.EXE that during the driver installation, it should prompt you to insert the floppy diskette with those drivers. Note that WINNT.EXE will not read drivers from a CD-ROM during installation.

If the system onto which you are installing NT is a multiprocessor machine, it is likely that you will be prompted to enter a disk supplied by the motherboard or system manufacturer. SMP machines require an updated version of a file called HAL.DLL. If this is not installed during the initial installation, it can be added later. But until that time, the system will be making use of only one CPU.

In a server installation, this is also the phase in which you are asked to enter the type of licensing you wish to use. The two options are Per Server and Per Seat. With Per Server licensing, the administrator fills in the number of Client Access Licenses (CAL) that have been purchased. Only that number of users can access the server at one time. This is useful for organizations that use shift workers. For example if there are three shifts of 100 users, but each user has a dedicated computer assigned, there might be 300 computers, but only 100 users will ever be logged on at any one time. Per seat requires a CAL for each workstation on the system.

Finally, during this phase you are asked to select the partition on which you want NT installed. WINNT.EXE also asks whether you prefer to use FAT or NTFS. Note that this is FAT16, and if this file system is selected, the subsequent limitations of that system are selected as well. NT does not support FAT32. After the partition and file system have been selected, a quick scan of the disk is performed and the system reboots once again. If the NTFS file system was selected, during this reboot a utility called CONVERT.EXE converts the hard disk partition's file system from FAT to NTFS. This might take a few minutes.

THE GUI PHASE

When the reboot is completed, the NT installation enters the GUI phase. Now you have access to all those pretty little boxes with the Next and Back buttons. The mouse has suddenly come alive, and everything is now point and click. During this phase you will be prompted to enter a computer name and password for the administrator account. Other wizards automatically open that run through the installation of any modems and set up networking.

At one point you are asked whether the computer should obtain its address automatically from a DHCP server. DHCP stands for the Dynamic Host Configuration Protocol, which is a protocol that automatically hands out IP addresses (and other information) for networks using the TCP/IP protocol. If this is an NT 4.0 Workstation installation and you know for sure that there is a DHCP server on the network, you might want to select this option. If this is a server installation, a static IP address should always be assigned. For more information on configuring TCP/IP, refer to *The Compete Guide to Networking and Network+*, by this same author.

Toward the end of the GUI phase, you will be asked whether you wish to create an Emergency Repair Diskette (ERD). The ERD is useful for repairing an NT installation gone bad and will be required if you wish to perform one of those dual-boot installations to which I alluded earlier in the chapter. The cautious type selects Yes for this option and inserts a blank, formatted 1.44MB floppy diskette into the drive.

I don't. I wait until the installation is completed and all third-party device drivers are successfully installed, and then I create the ERD manually. I'll have instructions on how to do this later in the chapter. But take note that the ERD should be updated any time system configuration changes or after the addition of new accounts. The ERD is definitely not a one-size-fits-all type of disk.

After the GUI phase is completed, the system reboots yet again. This time it boots to a working NT machine. However, for the vast majority of users, this isn't the end of the installation process.

Finalizing the Installation

This is a phase that doesn't seem to appear an a lot of the books I've seen. However, before the system can be used, there is generally a bit more work to do. Any third-party device drivers that weren't detected by NTDETECT.EXE must be installed before the device will work properly.

Typically the graphics card will have to be installed separately. Until this happens the system will only be capable of 640×480 resolution at sixteen colors. This is because NT does not maintain a substantial collection of drivers for video adapters and simply installs standard VGA.

Many network cards need to be installed separately. You'll know if yours is one of those, because during the GUI phase you weren't asked to set up networking. Therefore, if your NIC didn't install, you'll have to do it manually. There will be a discussion of installing device drivers in NT in Chapter Seven, Windows NT Architecture. When this process has been completed and you have a fully configured NT system, it is now time to create (or update) the ERD.

Creating or Updating the ERD

I cannot emphasize the importance of having an updated ERD for Windows NT. Just installing an NT system is work enough. All of the configuration and creation of user accounts adds to that burden. The less work you have to redo should you have to rebuild the system, the happier you'll be.

The ERD contains all the configuration data for the system, along with a list of user and group accounts that have been added. Proper use of this disk allows the administrator, in many cases, to repair a corrupted system without losing everything.

ERDs are managed through a utility called RDISK. There is no icon for this utility, and it doesn't have an entry in the Start menu (although if you desire, you can create either one). To run RDISK for the first time, you must open a command prompt (or click Start → Run) and type **RDISK** in the command prompt.

A little window will open with two buttons. One says Update Repair Info and the other says Create Repair Disk. If you select the first option, you will need to have your existing ERD in hand. It won't create a new one from scratch. That is the purpose of the second option.

The Dual-boot System

Once in a while, it becomes necessary to have access to more than one OS at any given time, but there is only one computer on which an OS can be installed. For example, you may be perfectly comfortable with your existing OS, but it becomes necessary for some reason to introduce a new one. A dual-boot system gives you access to the OS you're comfortable with until such time as you have mastered the new one.

If you wish to create a dual-boot system running NT 4.0 as one of the OSs, then there is a specific order in which you must do things. And there are a couple of things to be considered. You have to prep your hard drive, and the order in which you install the OSs is important.

If you are planning to dual-boot your system, you might want to consider this when preparing your hard drive. Although it isn't absolutely necessary to have NT on a different partition if both it and your other OS are using FAT16, I would still strongly advise it. Putting each OS on a separate partition is absolutely necessary if NT is going to be on an NTFS partition. In fact, I would strongly recommend a dedicated disk drive.

With NT you need to complete the NT installation first and make sure that it's properly configured. All device drivers should be installed, and configurations adjustments such as display settings should be to your satisfaction. Now either update the ERD or create a new one.

Reboot the machine to the installation disk of the second OS and perform that installation. When that is completed, you'll be aghast to realize that all your hard work installing NT was to no avail. The new OS wiped it out!

Don't panic. Simply start the NT installation either from the CD or by booting to the boot floppies. However, this time, instead of selecting a fresh installation, tell WINNT.EXE (or WINNT32.EXE if you're running from another Windows application) that you want to repair an existing installation. That will be the second option on the checklist. Have your ERD ready and follow the prompts as they appear. When your machine reboots after completion, during the boot process you will be presented with a menu giving you thirty seconds to pick which OS to load. If you don't make a selection, NT 4.0 will load by default.

When making a dual-boot system, decide in advance whether or not you're going to need to be able to access files created by one OS when running the other. Not all file systems work well together, as I've already pointed out. If you're setting up a dual boot between NT 4.0 and WIN9x, it can be particularly problematic. Choosing NTFS as the file system for NT will prevent the WIN9x installation from even seeing that the NT partition is present on the system. Likewise, selecting FAT32 for WIN9x will prevent NT from seeing the WIN9x partition. The only mutually accessible file system between the two OSs is FAT16.

PROFILES IN NT

NT is designed to be an OS that supports a multitude of users. This is true whether it's NT Workstation or one of the server versions. In order to ensure that each user has his or her own unique operating environment, NT makes use of separate profiles for each user. A profile is simply an overview of individual user settings and preferences.

As I discussed in an earlier chapter, the registry contains two different root keys to define users. HKEY_CURRENT_USER defines the user that is currently logged on, while HKEY_USERS contains the information for every user that has an account on the system. To create individual user profiles, NT also stores this information in the %SystemRoot%\PROFILES folder in a file called NTUSER.DAT.

Profiles can be treated in one of two different ways. A more permissive administrator will allow each user to create a unique profile that reflects individual work habits and personality. This might include the ability to install personalized screen savers, desktop backgrounds, and programs. Conversely, an administrator might think this practice is too risky and may prefer to enforce a standard profile. This is something that NT allows as well.

Chapter Summary

Microsoft's first implementation of a true 32-bit OS launched the company's ascendancy to the position it now holds as the largest manufacturer of operating systems in the world. The server versions of Windows represented its first line of NOS that genuinely addressed the needs of an enterprise.

In this chapter I introduced some of the key features of the different versions of the OS. I spent a great deal of time on the security implementations Microsoft added and defined its different domain models. This is all information that will serve you in good stead in later chapters, as these are features that will be compared and contrasted in discussions of later Microsoft operating systems.

Brain Drain

1. Discuss the differences between symmetric and asymmetric multiprocessing. Why is one more efficient than the other?

2. How is a BDC different than a PDC? And why might a larger network need several BDCs?

3. Discuss some of the security enhancements Microsoft incorporated into NT.

4. How are privileges and permissions different from one another? Discuss some examples of each.

5. List the different domain models supported by NT and describe the differences.

The 64K$ Questions

1. The first version of an NT product was demonstrated in _____.
   a. 1984
   b. 1991
   c. 1993
   d. 1994

2. The first version of NT to be released was NT 3.5. There never was a version 3.0.
   a. True
   b. False

3. The NT feature that provided security on a file or folder level was called _____.
   a. File and Print Services
   b. Domain Server Security
   c. SMP support
   d. NTFS

4. A system that runs OS code on one processor and application code and user data on a second processor is an example of _____ multiprocessing.
   a. Asymmetric
   b. Symmetric
   c. Hierarchical
   d. Demand Priority

5. NT 4.0 Server, Enterprise Edition can support up to _____ processors.
   a. 2
   b. 4

c. 8

d. 16

6. NT 4.0 Workstation requires a minimum of _____ RAM in order to run on a RISC machine.

a. 8MB

b. 12MB

c. 16MB

d. 32MB

7. NT 4.0 Server requires a minimum of _____ RAM in order to run on a RISC machine.

a. 8MB

b. 12MB

c. 16MB

d. 32MB

8. In order to install NT 4.0 Workstation, you need a minimum of _____ free hard disk space.

a. 85MB

b. 110MB

c. 125MB

d. 150MB

9. In an NT domain, the machine that maintains a copy of the security database that is updated periodically is called a _____.

a. Primary Domain Controller

b. Backup Domain Controller

c. Security Accounts Manager

d. Domain Controller

10. A piece of software that looks like a friendly game of Pac Woman but that is actually harvesting emails from your system while you play would be called a _____.

a. Virus

b. Worm

c. Back door

d. Trojan horse

11. In order to get to the logon screen in Windows NT 4.0 (any version) you must first _____.

a. Type in a unique security authenticator

b. Provide your user credentials

c. Press <Ctrl>+<Alt>+<Delete>

d. Press <Shift>+<F5>

12. As a user, you have been granted the ability to add new users to the network. From an OS standpoint you have been given _____.

a. A new permission

b. A promotion

c. A new privilege

d. More work to do for the same pay

13. You have created a new file on the system and assigned one password on the file that allows the users who access it full control and another password that only lets them read the file. This is an example of _____.

a. Workgroup security

b. File and folder security

c. Share level security

d. User level security

14. When the administrator first creates a new account on an NT system, NT assigns a unique _____ to that account.

a. SID

b. SAM

c. SLC

d. SAC

15. In order to tighten up security on your network, your administrator has divided the network into two separate domains. One of these domains is where all the users log on, and the other hosts the company's database servers. This is an example of _____ .

    a. The Single domain

    b. The Single Master domain

    c. The Multiple Master domain

    d. The Complete Trust

16. NT 4.0 trusts are said to be _____ .

    a. Transitional

    b. Transitory

    c. Nontransitional

    d. Nontransitory

17. In order to install NT onto a machine, it is best to start with a freshly prepared hard disk on which no partitions have been defined. This allows NT to prepare the drives using its own utility.

    a. True

    b. False

18. NTDETECT runs during the _____ phase of the installation.

    a. Initial

    b. Text

    c. GUI

    d. Finalizing installation

19. The licensing mode is selected during the _____ phase of the installation.

    a. Initial

    b. Text

    c. GUI

    d. Finalizing installation

20. Before attempting to create a dual-boot system between NT 4.0 and another OS, you must first make sure you have a fresh _____ .

    a. ERD

    b. Partition

    c. Formatted diskette

    d. Cup of coffee

TRICKY TERMINOLOGY

Asymmetric multiprocessing: A method by which an operating system makes use of more than one processor, loading OS code onto one processor and application code and user data onto all others.

Credentials: Information provided by the user, including but not restricted to the User ID and password, that grants that user access to a system or network.

Domain: A collection of all resources and users that fall under the control of a single administrative unit. In the case of Windows NT, the administrative unit would be the PDC.

Object: In reference to an OS, an object is any resource, user account, or group account present on the system or network.

Permissions: The degrees of access a particular user has been granted to a specific resource on the network.

Privileges: The rights a particular user has been granted to perform specific functions or tasks on a system or the network in general.

Security descriptor: A token attached to a resource that defines security attributes assigned to that resource.

Share level security: A method of protecting resources on the network that involves applying the security attributes, such as password protection, to the object itself. As such, each secured object on the system may have a unique password.

Symmetric multiprocessing: A method by which an operating system makes use of more than one processor, distributing all code equally across all available processors.

Trojan horse: A malicious program designed to mimic another commonly recognized program that is, in fact, performing some other action in the background without the knowledge or consent of the user.

User level security: A method of securing resources on a system or network that involves assigning the security attributes to an account provided to the user. Once the user has logged on, access to resources is provided based on the permissions assigned to the account.

Workgroup: A collection of devices on the network that share common resources and responsibilities.

ACRONYM ALERT

ACE: Access Control Entity. An individual entry of the ACL defining a specific object and its security attributes.

ACL: Access Control List. A data token attached to the descriptor of a specific object on the network that defines what users and/or groups are allowed to access that object and what degree of access they are allowed.

ASMP: Asymmetric Multiprocessing. The ability of an OS to use more than one processor, where the OS code runs on one processor and all other application code and user data is distributed across the remaining processors.

BDC: Backup Domain Controller. Any server on an NT domain that houses a copy of the security database that is periodically updated by the PDC.

CAL: Client Access License. A license granting one user permission to access a system or network.

DEC: Digital Equipment Corporation

ERD: Emergency Repair Diskette. A floppy diskette that holds system configuration and account information for a machine running NT (or later) operating systems.

LSA: Local Security Authority. An NT service that manages the logon process and all subsequent access to system or network resources.

NTWS: NT Workstation

PCMCIA: Personal Computer Memory Card International Association

PDC: Primary Domain Controller. The server in an NT domain that houses the master security database.

RAS: Remote Access Services. An NT service that allows a direct dial-up connection from a remote computer to access the host system.

SAM: Security Account Manager. An encrypted file stored within the registry of NT that hold the security attributes for all user and group accounts.

SID: Security Identifier. A unique number generated and assigned to an object on the system or network that allows LSA to manage the security for that object.

SMP: Symmetric Multiprocessing. The ability of an OS to run OS or application code equally distributed across all available CPUs.

SRM: Security Reference Monitor. An NT service that compares a user's access token to the ACL and either allows or denies access to a specific resource accordingly.

VMS: Virtual Memory System. An OS written by DEC.

CHAPTER 7

WINDOWS NT ARCHITECTURE

As you might imagine, since the NT operating systems were composed entirely of 32-bit code, some changes to the OS architecture had to be made. It wasn't entirely the 32-bit code that forced certain architectural changes either. Changes to security functions that I discussed in Chapter Six, An Introduction to Windows NT, as well as to the way the OS interfaced with the hardware, required changes as well. Even the overall boot process is different between NT and the WIN9x versions. This chapter will discuss some of the internal technology that makes NT what it is. A lot of what is covered in this chapter relates to later chapters in this book pertaining to the Windows 2000 versions and Windows XP as well, so don't be too quick to pass this information over.

A+ OPERATING SYSTEM TECHNOLOGIES EXAM OBJECTIVES

The CompTIA exam objectives covered in this chapter include the following:

1.1 Identify the major desktop components and interfaces and their functions. Differentiate the characteristics of Windows 9x/Me, Windows NT 4.0 Workstation, Windows 2000 Professional, and Windows XP.

1.4 Identify basic concepts and procedures for creating, viewing, and managing disks, directories, and files. This includes procedures for changing file attributes and the ramifications of those changes (for example, security issues).

2.1 Identify the procedures for installing Windows 9x/Me, Windows NT 4.0 Workstation, Windows 2000 Professional, and Windows XP and for bringing the operating system to a basic operational level.

2.2 Identify steps to perform an operating system upgrade from Windows 9x/Me, Windows NT 4.0 Workstation, Windows 2000 Professional, and Windows XP. Given an upgrade scenario, choose the appropriate next steps.

2.3 Identify the basic system boot sequences and boot methods, including the steps to create an emergency boot disk with utilities installed for Windows 9x/Me, Windows NT 4.0 Workstation, Windows 2000 Professional, and Windows XP.

2.4 Identify procedures for installing/adding a device, including loading, adding, and configuring device drivers and required software.

3.1 Recognize and interpret the meaning of common error codes and startup messages from the boot sequence, and identify steps to correct the problems.

3.2 Recognize when to use common diagnostic utilities and tools.

THE NT BOOT PROCESS

In NT, getting a computer up and running from the off position to being ready for user input is a far more complicated process than it is for WIN9x systems. There are actually two separate steps involved. The first step is the boot process, in which the computer is raised from the dead and a basic OS is loaded. The second step is called the load process. This is where the system initializes, allows the user to log on, and loads any programs that are configured to automatically run.

THE BOOT PROCESS

For the NT boot process to be successful, a number of files need to be present on the root directory of the hard drive. These files are placed there during the installation process, and therefore, it's a good idea to leave them there. The following is a list of these files, followed by a brief description.

- *BOOT.INI:* This file provides the full path to the NT core files. It also generates the menu at startup that allows the user to select which OS to launch. In a system that is purely NT, the choices are NT 4.0 and NT 4.0 VGA Mode. In the event that the system is set up for multi-boot, these options will be included in the menu, and the paths to the core files for the alternate OS will also be provided. BOOT.INI attributes are read-only and system.

- *NTLDR:* This is the OS loader. After an OS has been selected, NTLDR launches the requisite file. In a multi-boot environment, many other OSs cannot launch without the services of this file. Its attributes are hidden, system, and read-only.

- *BOOTSECT.DOS:* Present on multi-boot systems. The boot sector of the hard drive as it existed prior to the installation of NT is copied to this file. When the earlier OS is selected for boot, BOOTSECT.DOS plays the role of the master boot record for that OS. Its attributes are hidden and system.

- *NTDETECT.COM:* This utility examines the system's hardware and builds the list of device drivers that NT will need to load. This information is passed on to NTLDR. Its attributes are hidden, read-only, and system.

- *NTBOOTDD.SYS*: This file is only present on systems that boot from a SCSI device on which the SCSI BIOS has been disabled. It acts as a device driver for the boot device. There are no specific attributes required for this file.

In addition to the files located in the root directory, two other files are called on by NTLDR:

- *NTOSKERNEL.EXE*: This is NT's base kernel file. It manages I/O and file system functions and is located in the WINNT\SYSTEM32 directory.
- *SYSTEM*: This file directs the loading of device drivers and OS services during the boot process and manages those drivers and services while the system is running. It is located in the WINNT\SYSTEM32\CONFIG directory.

The actual boot process in NT as a bit more complex than the process I described in Chapter Four for WIN9x. The first step is the system POST. After that has been completed, the file that the MBR goes out looking for is NTLDR. One of the key services this file offers is to act as a rudimentary file system manager. It is capable of reading FAT12, FAT16, CDFS, and NTFS. NTLDR initializes the proper file systems and then goes out looking for BOOT.INI. After it finds it, it loads that file and displays the boot menu for the user. After the user has made his or her selection, one of two things will happen.

EXAM NOTE: As in previous discussions of operating systems, it is very likely you will be tested on the boot process of NT. Know the files that are required and the order in which they're run.

Should the user select an alternative OS, NTLDR runs BOOTSECT.DOS. NTLDR will then pass control of the boot process over to BOOTSECT.DOS and exit. From that point the boot process of the selected OS will continue. For the users that select NT, NTLDR will load and run NTDETECT.COM. This file checks all the hardware, and this is where the user sees a bit of system activity. Keyboard lights flash, and if there is a printer or tape drive installed, these devices will most likely blink or perhaps even make noise. The floppy disk light will flash as well. When NTDETECT is done, it passes the information it gathered on to NTLDR, which generates the hardware hive in the registry.

The last part of this process is for NTLDR to initialize NTOSKERNEL.EXE and hand off the hardware information it collected to that file. NTOSKERNEL.EXE is now in control of the machine, and NTLDR exits. Technically speaking, that is the end of the boot process. The system still isn't in a position for the user to take over and start working, though. Next comes the load process.

A TOUR OF **BOOT.INI**

As I mentioned earlier, the BOOT.INI file is critical for the correct loading of NT. So just what is that file? If you were to open the file for viewing, it would look something like **Figure 7.1.**

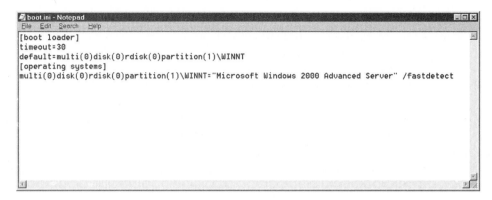

Figure 7.1 BOOT.INI determines both the parameters of the boot process and provides NTLDR with the correct ARC paths to all OSs loaded on the system.

This file isn't quite as intimidating as it first appears. Something you need to understand is that BOOT.INI uses the ARC file naming convention and ordinal counting. And that clarified everything didn't it?

ARC is an acronym for Advanced RISC Computing and is the file system used by operating systems such as UNIX and Linux. I'll describe that over the next few paragraphs. Ordinal counting simply means you start counting at zero instead of one. So the first drive in the system is Drive 0 and the second one is Drive 1. Makes sense.

Now let's translate the lines of BOOT.INI. The lines enclosed in brackets— **[boot loader]** and **[operating systems]**—are simply headers for separate sections of the file. All lines following **[boot loader]** define boot process parameters, and all lines following **[operating systems]** lay out the ARC path to each OS installed on the system. In the example shown in the figure, there is only one OS installed. In a moment, I'll show how another line can be added that defines a second OS on the system.

timeout=30 defines how long the user will have to select an OS during the boot process. Thirty seconds is the default. This means that the boot menu that appears will count down 30 seconds before the default OS loads. You can use the up and down arrows on the keyboard to select an OS and press <Enter> at any time to start the OS of your choice. That can be a bit annoying to someone with only a single OS loaded. Hmmm, which one do I want to load? I can't decide! **timeout=0** eliminates the 30-second countdown.

EXAM NOTE: You are very likely to be asked to break apart an ARC path on the OS exam. Understand what each section of the path points to and that the OS can never reside on partition(0).

default=multi(0)rdisk(0)disk(0)partition(1)\WINNT is the line that defines the ARC path to the default OS. An ARC path is divided into five parts. **multi(0)** indicates that the first, or primary, hard disk controller is the host for the boot drive. If the OS is installed on a drive located on a secondary controller, this portion would read **multi(1)**. Computers equipped with SCSI controllers will read **SCSI(0)** or **SCSI(1)** instead of multi.

Rdisk(0) indicates the node number that the disk occupies on the defined controller. For example, the illustrated BOOT.INI file indicates that it is the primary drive on the first controller. IDE controllers are true multi-disk controllers, and that number will always read 0. If it was the second drive on a SCSI chain, that section would read **rdisk(1)**. The third drive on a SCSI chain would be **rdisk(2)** and so on and so forth.

Disk(0) tells you which disk at a particular node address houses the system files. Since IDE controllers might host two different drives at the same node address, **disk(0)** indicates it is the master drive on that port. **Disk(1)** would indicate a slave drive. SCSI drives only support one drive per node and, therefore, will always read **disk(0)**.

Partition(1) states that the system files are located on the first partition of the drive that was defined in previous sections. ("Now, wait a minute," the astute reader thinks. "I thought in ordinal counting the first partition would be **partition(0)**!") Microsoft operating systems define **partition(0)** as being the hard disk in its entirety, including all partitions and unpartitioned space such as the MBR and the file system tables. Therefore, the first usable partition is **partition(1)**. WINNT defines the directory on that partition that houses the system files.

Now under the **[operating systems]** portion of BOOT.INI, you see two things. First of all, each OS installed will have its ARC path defined. A user with WIN98 installed on the first partition of the slave of the primary IDE port would have a line that reads **multi(0)rdisk(0)disk(1)partition(1)\WINDOWS="Windows 98"** listed in that section as well. The second thing defined in this section is what name will be given the OS in the boot menu. That is the text enclosed in the quotes. If I type **Old Operating System** between the quotes, then during the boot process, I will have the choice of **Windows NT 4.0** or **Old Operating System** to choose from.

THE NT LOAD PROCESS

There are four phases to the load process:

- Kernel Load
- Kernel Initialization
- Services Load
- Subsystem Start

The Kernel Load phase initializes the HAL and effectively tucks all the system hardware away and out of sight of any applications running on the system. The file SYSTEM.DAT (which is the part of the registry that controls system functions) is loaded and scanned for a list of drivers and services that must be started.

Kernel Initialization is that part of the boot process that displays little more than a blue screen. The list of drivers and services generated during the Kernel Load phase is initialized, and the files for the drivers are located and loaded. The CurrentControlSet section of the registry is generated and loaded as well.

The Services Load Phase takes over and, as the name implies, takes the list of system services and locates and runs the files associated with those services. Note, however, that these services are not actually launched at this time. Not all services are necessarily required in order for the system to run. A file called SMSS.EXE is loaded and executed. This is the Windows Session Manager. It prepares a list of all programs listed in the Startup menu and prepares the system to launch those applications. They won't actually be launched, however, until the user has successfully logged on.

Finally, the Subsystem Start phase loads LSASS.EXE. This is the Local Security Authority (LSA) that I discussed in the previous chapter. This brings up the dialogue box that instructs the user to press <Ctrl>+<Alt>+<Delete> in order to log on. Another file loaded during the Subsystem Start phase is SCREG.EXE. This is the Windows Service Controller. It scans the registry looking for all the services that are set to load automatically and launches those services.

The final part of the boot process is the user logon. This is where the user presses <Ctrl>+<Alt>+<Delete> and enters his or her credentials. LSA compares these credentials to the entry for that user in SAM. If the information matches, the user logon is accepted. If not, a message is generated notifying the user that the user ID and/or password entered was not recognized by the system. After a user has been authenticated, the desktop loads, and the programs that are part of the Startup menu are finally launched. The system is ready to go.

NT ARCHITECTURE

One of the key factors that made NT such a success was the fact that it was so much more stable than previous Microsoft OSs. People liked the point-and-click ease of the WIN9x versions. But they weren't exactly ecstatic about having to restart their computers three and four times a day because of system crashes and application errors. For many organizations, the occasionally erratic behavior of the WIN9x versions was totally unacceptable. NT was the better choice.

Key changes made to the NT architecture were responsible for this increased stability. To begin with, NT is basically divided into two separate parts—Kernel Mode and User Mode. *Kernel Mode* is responsible for managing system functions, while *User Mode* manages the logon process, security, and application functions. An overview of NT's architecture is provided in **Figure 7.2.**

KERNEL MODE

One of the primary reasons NT is more stable than previous products released by Microsoft is that the hardware is completely isolated from the applications. The WIN9x versions had taken steps in this direction, but NT made the process complete. Applications cannot directly communicate with hardware. Plain and simple.

BUZZ WORDS

Kernel Mode: An operational mode for an OS that manages system functions.

User Mode: An operational mode for an OS that manages applications and security functions.

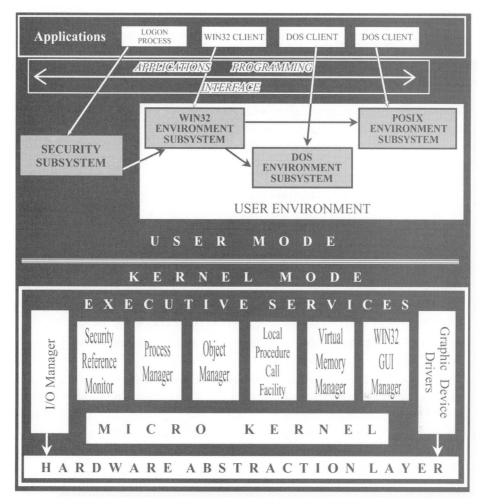

Figure 7.2 An overview of NT architecture

Kernel Mode can be broken down into three basic components. Each of these components brings user data and commands progressively closer to the point of being able to interface with the hardware. These three components are listed here:

- Executive Services
- Micro Kernel
- Hardware Abstraction Layer

If you recall from Chapter Three, The Evolution of Windows and Windows Basics, I included a lengthy dissertation on the different processor rings. NT has clearly defined how processor rings are used. All Kernel Mode processes run in Ring 0.

Executive Services

Executive Services does not derive its name from the fact that it wears a suit and tie and commutes from the suburbs to work every day. This is the layer of the OS that is responsible for executing commands. Every device driver, service, or application is under the control of Executive Services. But other critical services are at its command as well. The various services managed by Executive Services include the following:

- *Hardware device drivers:* Generate the commands that will eventually be sent to the hardware.
- *The Security Reference Monitor:* Tracks user activity and allows access to only those resources for which the user has the appropriate permissions.
- *The Virtual Memory Manager:* Controls the paging file created by NT for temporary storage of data not required in physical RAM at the moment.
- *The Object Manager:* Provides resource management support needed by virtually every other subsystem for both logical and physical resources on the system.
- *The I/O Manager:* Controls input/output requests from applications running on the system and, conversely, manages data being returned by the devices on the system.
- *Process Manager:* Controls which processes (refer back to Chapter One for a discussion of the differences between a process and a thread) are active on the system at any given time.
- *Local Procedure Call Facility:* Provides a communications platform for applications to local resources. This would include interaction with other applications and interaction between the applications and the OS.
- *Configuration Manager:* Manages the system registry and directs calls and functions to the I/O Manager in order to prevent resource conflicts.
- *Cache Manager:* Manages NT's file system cache. By mapping specific memory to specific functions, NT is able to manage existing cache memory more efficiently and utilize system memory as cache memory where needed.

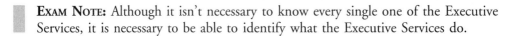

Exam Note: Although it isn't necessary to know every single one of the Executive Services, it is necessary to be able to identify what the Executive Services do.

The Micro Kernel

The Micro Kernel acts as the central core for the entire operating system. It controls the functions of the Executive Services layer, dictating what service will be called when. It also directly manages all I/O functions between the applications and HAL.

THE HARDWARE ABSTRACTION LAYER

This is the layer that actually isolates applications from the physical devices on the system. When a device driver makes a system call to a particular piece of hardware, it actually sends that command to a program called an Application Programming Interface (API). The API is a piece of software that collects commands generated by applications and translates them from the upper-level programming languages used by applications to the machine-level languages used by hardware.

APIs take it a step further. Since a number of different devices might use a similar command set, HAL uses the APIs to treat all devices of a particular type as if they were the same device. For example, the Advanced Technology API (ATAPI) provides hardware support for a vast majority of devices that make use of the IDE interface. This includes devices such as hard disks, CD-ROMS, CD-RWs, and the list goes on and on. (For more detailed information on APIs and IDE, see *The A+ Guide to PC Hardware Maintenance and Repair*, by this same author.)

After HAL has translated the commands from the application, it can then issue the simpler commands directly to the device. On the flip side, data and/or commands coming from the hardware must be processed by HAL and translated to the upper-level languages understood by the applications.

A key function of HAL that is often overlooked is this: While modern OS have absolutely no problem whatsoever running multiple applications on the system, the devices themselves can only communicate with a single application at a time. Therefore, in a multitasking system, it is the responsibility of HAL to monitor the traffic of multiple applications back and forth between the individual pieces of hardware.

USER MODE

NT architecture is based on a layered model. The Kernel Mode processes that I just discussed can be considered the bottom layer of the cake. The next layer up would be the User Mode processes. These are the NT services that intercept requests from the applications or from user input and transfer them over to the Kernel Mode processes that I just discussed.

User Mode processes are considered to be non-privileged, and as such, run in processor Ring 3. To better understand User Mode, just remember that it is broken down into two basic types of services. These are user environment services and security services.

The user environment services define what types of applications can run on the computer. Technically speaking, it isn't actually the user environment that is being defined, but rather an environment in which the user's applications can run. NT has been written to support the following OS environments:

- MS-DOS
- 16-bit Windows
- 32-bit Windows
- POSIX
- OS/2

If you're wondering about POSIX and OS/2, don't be too paranoid about running into these types of applications any time soon. POSIX is an acronym for *Portable Operating System Interface* (and no, I don't know where the X came from). It is a platform designed to make applications written for different forms of UNIX OS versions, as well as certain other OSs, compatible with one another. As a result, with POSIX support enabled, an NT user could run UNIX applications. OS/2 was an OS designed by IBM to run on personal computers.

EXAM NOTE: A common subject for NT-related exam questions relates to the OS environment. Know which OS environments are supported by NT. Also make sure you remember what POSIX stands for.

The security component of User Mode starts with the <Ctrl>+<Alt>+<Delete> logon function. From that point on, the security component maintains a constant link with SRM. Once the user's credentials have been verified and accepted, the authentication token that I discussed in the previous chapter is generated. This token identifies the correct user profile to load from the registry, ensuring that the user sees the same desktop every day. From that point forward, SRM uses that token to verify user permissions and/or privileges for every action the user attempts on the system or network.

MANAGING PHYSICAL RESOURCES IN NT

In this section, I am going to discuss how NT manages the physical resources of the computer system. This will include the processor(s), memory, and hard disks. Much of the technology that NT uses was derivative of WIN9x, but in most cases it has been modified or refined for NT's advanced architecture. Therefore, if some of this seems familiar, start digging for the differences.

PROCESSOR CONTROL

In previous chapters, I've discussed how various Microsoft versions take advantage of processor rings to enhance stability. There is more to processor management than processor rings. NT exacerbated the complexity of managing processors by introducing SMP. Now it's quite possible that the machine is going to have more than one CPU to keep track of. To further emphasize the complexity of this responsibility, consider that the processor(s) are not only managing application and user data; they are also playing conductor to the orchestra of hardware devices that make up the system.

On a hardware level, distribution of interrupt requests across multiple CPUs was made possible by rebuilding the I/O subsystem of the OS from the ground up. A central engineering feature of this subsystem is SMP support. NT manages this by maintaining two separate versions of HAL.

When NT 4.0 is installed on a single-processor system, the basic version of HAL is installed. This version consists of an interrupt handler that targets a single CPU and the main file that supports the HAL, which is a file appropriately named HAL.DLL. If NT is installed on a multiprocessor system, a different version is installed. The file for this version of HAL is

HALMPS.DLL. Along with these two primary files are a number of different driver files that are substituted as well.

The end result is that upgrading a machine from single-processor support to SMP support isn't quite as simple as copying a couple of new files onto the system. Therefore, for most people, an upgrade requires reinstalling the OS. Microsoft did provide a utility with NT to assist the user in performing this upgrade. This utility is UPTOMP.EXE. Unfortunately, this file was provided only in the resource kit and not on the original CD.

A feature added to NT that ensured that application and user data got their fair share of CPU time was the NT Scheduler. As with the I/O Manager, NT Scheduler was designed from the ground up with SMP support as part of its basic structure. Whether you have one processor or sixteen, the process of running applications or processing data is going to be the same.

NT was designed to function with pre-emptive multitasking. As such, it is up to the OS to determine how much time a particular string of code will be allowed to tie up the CPU. NT is designed to be a multi-user as well as a multiprocessor environment. However, it's also designed to be a *real time OS*. This means that it needs to be able to perform specific threads of code at a specific time. An example of real time processing would be the systems at an automated factory.

Here is an example of real time processing at work. Here in Vermont there is a company that produces engraved metal furniture. Their product line includes tables that feature incredibly detailed illustrations and designs etched onto the surfaces. These designs are all computer rendered. The application that controls the etching process must be able to manipulate the equipment in extremely precise movements; otherwise the etching will be flawed. This, too, is a function of the NT Scheduler.

This is where being able to set priorities on specific threads of code becomes essential. The NT Scheduler assigns each thread that is called a priority between 1 and 31. Higher numbers represent higher priorities. Therefore, a thread with a priority of 16 will be run before a thread with a priority of 12. Priority 0 is reserved for the System Idle function, which will cause this thread to run only when no other thread is present on the system. Priorities 16 through 31 are reserved for real time functions. Priorities can be assigned either by the OS (for system generated threads) or by the application (as in the example related previously).

When the thread receives its allotted CPU time, it will be given specific time slots to run. These time slots are very short, and vary between Workstation and Server versions. Threads on NT Server versions are typically 120ms in duration, while the threads on NT Workstation can run in 20ms, 40ms, or 60ms increments. Multiple threads running on a system will still appear to run seamlessly because the time slots occur so frequently that they appear to the user to be continuous.

The problem Microsoft engineers foresaw with this technique was this: If a particular thread has a very low priority, and there are a number of high-priority threads running on the system,

BUZZ WORDS

Real time OS: An OS designed to be able to perform specific functions at the precise time at which those functions are needed.

Priority boosting: A process by which the privilege level of a thread of code is promoted to a higher level in order to enhance its chances at the CPU.

the low-priority thread may never have the opportunity to run. A process called *priority boosting* prevents this from happening. Periodically a service running in NT called the Balance Set Manager scans the system looking for CPU-starved threads. When it finds one, it doubles the priority number of the starved thread. If the next time the Balance Set Manager runs, that thread still hasn't had a shot at the CPU, it will be boosted again. This process repeats until the thread is finally run.

Another method by which a thread can receive a boost is from an event-induced boost. An example of this would be a process that was waiting for user input from the keyboard or mouse. Rather than shut the entire system down for the whole time the user is out getting coffee and donuts, these threads start out with a very low priority. When the user performs the action the thread has been waiting for, the thread's priority is bumped. For keyboard and mouse events, it amounts to a six-point boost in priority.

Memory Management

One of the biggest advances in NT was the way it managed memory. Unlike previous Microsoft OS versions that depended on an age-old separation of memory between conventional and extended memory, NT uses a flat memory model. By this, I mean that once NT is up and running, each application that is launched is assigned a specific address space and that application runs within that space. That address space will appear to the applications to be 4GB per application, with 2GB being allocated to the application processes, and 2GB allotted to system processes needed to support the application. This is true whether you have 64MB installed or GB installed. How does it do this? It's simple. NT lies to the applications.

> **Note:** Starting with Service Pack Three, it became possible for the user to configure the virtual address space of NT a little differently. 2GB was far more space than was needed for an OS that only took up 300MB in its entirety. After SP3 was released, it became possible to allocate 1GB to OS functions and 3GB to applications. For the most part, that amounted to fixing a problem that didn't exist. Every paper I've ever read on the subject came to the conclusion that making this change had little or no effect on the stability or the performance of the OS.

This vast space assigned by NT is known as the *memory pool* and consists of physical memory and virtual memory. As with WIN9x, virtual memory is hard drive space that has been reserved as a place to move items in physical memory when they're not being used in order to make space in physical memory for items that are needed immediately. In WIN9x, the term for this hard drive space is the swap file. In NT, Microsoft engineers got fancier. It's now called the ging file.

> **Exam Note:** Make sure you can identify the key points for virtual memory management in NT. Make special note of the memory pool and the 4GB virtual address space.

Buzz Words

Memory pool: The total address space available to an OS and the applications running on top of it.

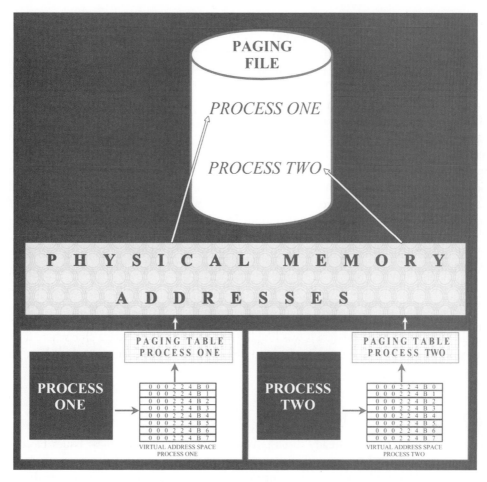

Figure 7.3 Windows has some pretty nifty tricks for convincing an application that it has 2GB of free memory on a computer that doesn't.

All memory functions in NT are under control of the Virtual Memory Manager (VMM). The functions of NT's VMM are identical to those of the WIN9x VMM that I discussed in Chapter Four, but the structure of the file is different. In NT there is only a single 32-bit memory manager. In the following discussion of how Windows manages memory, it might help if you occasionally refer to **Figure 7.3**.

VMM maps all available physical addresses, both physical RAM and paging file space. The applications are given a range of *virtual addresses* that they will use. Now, if you're following this correctly, you've already seen the minor glitch in this scheme. There are obviously more virtual addresses assigned than there can possibly be physical addresses on the system.

So, when a process is given an address range that starts at byte number 2,000,000,000, this is provided to the system as a binary address of 1110111001101011001010000000000. VMM locates a contiguous physical address large enough to store the code for that process and records the physical address. Let's say for example, that this actual physical address starts at byte number 120,540,000. VMM records the binary equivalent of this address, which would be 111001011110100101101100000. For every call to the virtual address, VMM translates this call to the actual address in which the data is stored.

If there is no contiguous space in RAM large enough for this process, then some process that is not currently being used will be moved from RAM to the

paging file, and the RAM it previously occupied will be cleared for the new process. If there are more applications, with their associated processes, running on the system than there is physical RAM and paging file combined, then data from the paging file is simply dumped to make room for the new applications. The data to be dumped is determined by how recently it has been accessed. The data least recently used is what goes.

Now what happens to the application that might have needed the data that was dumped? VMM is still telling that application that the data is there. And if that application becomes active once again and requires that data, it will issue a call to the virtual address. VMM translates the virtual address to the physical address and sees that that address no longer holds data associated with the application making the request. VMM will then issue a *page fault*. All this means is that the paging file didn't have the data it was looking for, and it doesn't have a clue where it is. The system will issue a new I/O request to the hard drive to look for the data, and the whole process will start all over.

Hard Disk Management Under NT

In previous chapters I have already discussed some of the major technical issues faced when managing hard disks in NT. One of these issues is the file systems NT supports, and another is the fact that NT need not be loaded onto the root drive in order to run. From the outset, this makes it appear that managing disks in NT becomes more difficult. It needn't be all that challenging as long as you keep some basic concepts in the back of your mind when administering disks.

First off, when installing NT, it is not possible to create an NTFS partition on the fly. Therefore, for the initial installation of NT to succeed, there needs to be a FAT16 partition present. If the NTFS file system has been chosen, that FAT16 partition will be converted to NTFS during the installation process. If FAT was chosen and the user later chooses to convert the drive to NTFS, it is possible to do a one-time conversion of the drive from FAT to NTFS using the Convert utility. It is not possible to convert an NTFS drive to FAT16. FAT32 is not supported.

FAT16 partitions created by NT are somewhat different than those created by earlier OSs. If you recall the discussion of file systems from Chapter One, An Introduction to Operating Systems, you'll remember that the largest partition supported by FAT16 is 2GB. This is due to the fact that the largest cluster readable by DOS and earlier Windows versions was 64 hard disk sectors, or 32KB. NT supports 64KB clusters, and, therefore, a FAT16 partition can be as large as 4GB.

After the OS is installed, a large hard disk can then have the remainder of its available space formatted as a single NTFS partition. For example, if you are installing NT onto an 80GB hard disk, you would have to create one smaller FAT16 partition for the installation of NT and leave the remainder of the drive unallocated. A utility called Disk Administrator can then be used to configured the remaining drive space.

Now what about this Disk Administrator? Just what is it, and how does it work? In a nutshell, it's a utility that allows the user to add and remove and/or format partitions on the fly without having to reboot the system.

The first time you run Disk Administrator (**Figure 7.4**), it asks for your permission to configure your system. At this point it adds a signature to the disk. This signature consists of four bytes of data that are added to the first physical sector on the hard disk. The signature identifies a specific volume on the drive and follows the physical disk wherever it goes, even if it is moved to a different hard disk controller on the same system. For Disk Administrator to perform any of its advanced magic, you need to allow this signature. Conversely, if your alternate OS on a dual-boot system includes UNIX, VMS, or Linux, you need to refuse this permission. The signature will corrupt the partition tables for these OSs.

There are two partitions that cannot be deleted or formatted in Disk Administrator. These are the *root partition* and the *system partition.* The root partition is the partition with all of the key files necessary for NT to boot. These files were listed earlier in the chapter. The system partition is the directory into which NT was installed.

In the majority of installations these partitions are one and the same, but not always. For example, in a dual-boot system, you might have WIN98 installed on the first partition and NT installed onto the second. Under these circumstances, neither of these partitions can be deleted

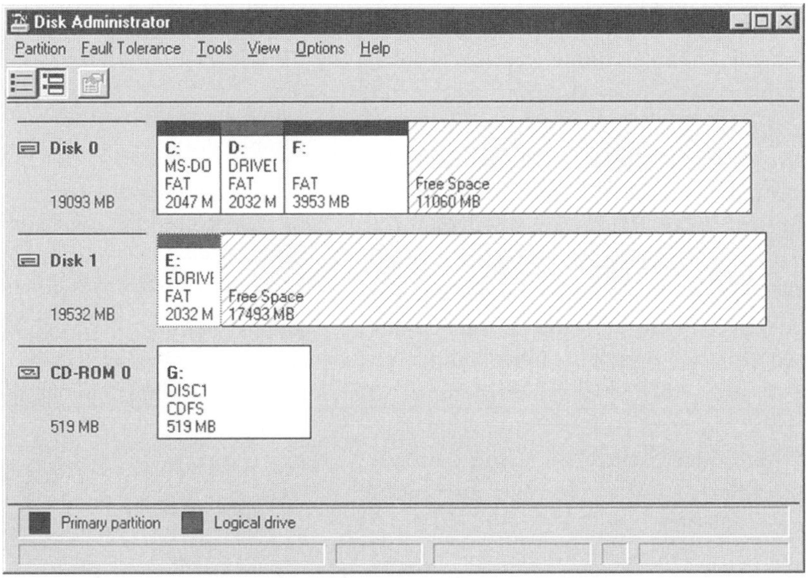

Figure 7.4 The Windows NT Disk Administrator

or formatted by Disk Administrator because the root files exist on the WIN98 partition and the system files on the NT partition.

Nonallocated space on hard drives can be managed any way the user sees fit. New partitions can be added and formatted in either FAT16 or NTFS, and logical DOS drives can be corporated into these partitions.

> **CAUTION:** If you are one of those people (like me) who likes to experiment with different operating systems and are always changing OSs, there is one thing you should know about Disk Administrator. When you add logical DOS drives to an NTFS partition, you will render the partition unreadable by Microsoft's FDISK utility. FDISK will see that a non-DOS partition exists, but when you attempt to delete it, FDISK reports that the logical DOS drives must be deleted first. However, since FDISK can't read NTFS, it can't delete the logical drives. In order to recover the hard disk, you need to start the installation of NT (or any later version of Microsoft OS) and delete all partitions through Disk Manager. Another option is to use a third-party utility, such as PowerQuest's Partition Magic.

As additional disks are added to the system, Disk Administrator will prompt the user to sign these disks as well. Once the disks have been signed, there are a number of different tricks that become possible for the user. Its best trick is the ability to manage *volume sets*. Although there are different types of volume sets, they all amount to the same. Multiple partitions or physical disks are combined to create what appears to the system as a single disk drive. The most commonly seen volume sets are spanned volumes, striped volumes, and mirrored volumes.

A *spanned volume* occurs when a user creates a logical single drive that incorporates unallocated space for more than one physical disk. For example, if you have three different hard disks installed in a computer and each disk has some free space on it, Disk Administrator will allow you to merge the free space into a single logical drive (see **Figure 7.5**).

A *striped volume* is similar to a spanned volume in that one logical drive is distributed across multiple physical disks. The striped volume differs in the fact that data is broken up into small chunks (called stripes) and distributed equally across all the drives in the set. Striped sets can be used either to enhance hard disk performance on a system or to add a degree of fault tolerance to the system. The *mirrored volume* exists when two different drives house exactly the same data. As new data is added to one drive, it is automatically copied to all other drives in the mirrored volume.

BUZZ WORDS ─────────────

Volume set: A single logical disk drive that is created when multiple partitions or physical disks are combined.

Spanned volume: A larger logical drive that is created by combining space located on two different partitions or disks.

Striped volume: A logical drive that is created by storing data in chunks that are distributed among multiple physical drives.

Mirrored volume: A single logical drive that is made of two disks, both of which contain identical data.

Figure 7.7 Disk mirroring simply duplicates the data on two separate disk drives.

RAID 0

Of all the levels listed in Table 7.1, only three are actually in common use. RAID 0 provides no fault tolerance. It simply stripes the data across multiple drives, as shown in **Figure 7.6**. It's key reason for existing is that it provides for extremely good drive performance. For machines designed exclusively for doling out data to large numbers of users, or one on which large files need to be opened quickly, this might be a viable choice. Just make sure you have a suitable backup strategy in place.

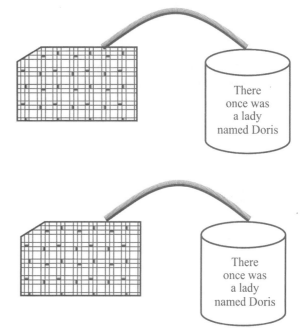

RAID 1

RAID 1 does provide a degree of fault tolerance in that the data is duplicated on two different drives. This duplication covers everything from the MBR to the last byte of data on the drive. With RAID 1 implemented, every bit of data written to Disk One is also written to Disk Two. If either disk fails, the other disk is available, and the system does not go down.

RAID 1 can be implemented two ways. *Disk mirroring* involves putting two separate drives on the same controller. The other implementation of RAID 1 is *disk duplexing*. This is identical to disk mirroring in every respect, except that each disk is

Figure 7.8 Disk duplexing is the same as mirroring, only each disk is on a separate controller.

BUZZ WORDS

Disk mirroring: Exactly duplicating the data on a system on two different drives hanging off of a single controller.

Disk duplexing: Exactly duplicating the data on a system on two different drives, each hanging off of a separate controller.

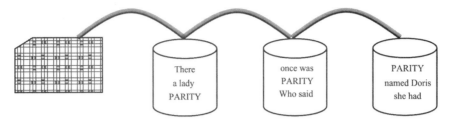

Figure 7.9 A RAID 5 implementation. As with RAID 0, in actual practice all data blocks would be the same size.

on its own separate controller. The thought here is that should the controller be the cause of failure, both drives would go down. By putting each drive on its own controller, failure of a single controller will not bring the system down. **Figure 7.7** and **Figure 7.8** illustrate the difference between mirroring and duplexing.

BUZZ WORDS ─────────

Parity block: A mathematical image of data that can be used to reconstruct that data in the event it is lost.

RAID 5

The RAID level most commonly used by network administrators is RAID 5, which requires a minimum of three hard disks. The maximum number of drives you can use depends on whether you are using a hardware controller or the software RAID included in NT or Novell. Software raid can make use of up to thirty-two drives. Your hardware will dictate its own limitations.

RAID 5 resembles RAID 0 in that it spreads the data across the drives equally. It adds fault tolerance because for each block of data copied to the array, it generates a mathematical image of that data called a *parity block*. The parity information is also distributed evenly across the drives. If a single drive fails, the system continues as if nothing had happened. The parity information is used to rebuild all data in its entirety. As soon as the dead drive has been replaced, the array can be rebuilt. It should be noted, however, that while the faulty drive is still in place you have no fault tolerance. **Figure 7.9** shows you how RAID 5 works.

RAID 0/1

The RAID levels I've been discussing so far have all been what are called single RAID levels. In order to provide maximum security for your data, it is also possible to configure nested RAID levels. These are when you combine two different RAID levels onto a single machine. The most commonly used nested raid level is RAID 0/1.

In this implementation, you create a RAID 0 array of however many disks you require in order to provide for disk performance. Then, in order to implement some level of fault tolerance, you duplex the RAID 0 array on a separate controller. In the event that one disk fails, that entire side of the mirror is broken, and the system is dependent on the other side until the defective disk is replaced. See **Figure 7.10**.

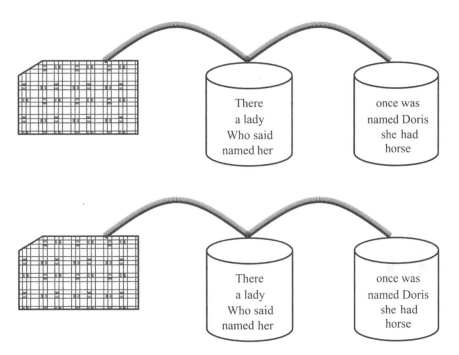

Figure 7.10   A RAID 0/1 implementation gives you the best of RAID 0 and RAID 1.

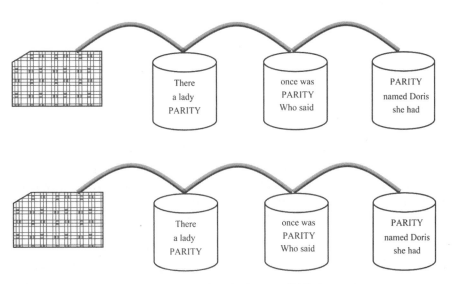

Figure 7.11   A RAID 50 implementation duplexes a RAID 5 array.

RAID 50

RAID 50 is another combination of multiple RAID levels. Two separate RAID 5 arrays are implemented, using anywhere from three to thirty-two disks. Then, a separate, identical collection of disks duplexes that array. **Figure 7.11** illustrates how this works. As you might imagine, implementing this configuration can be a more costly approach. However, your data is about as secure as it can get. In order for the data to be completely unavailable, a total of four different drives would have to fail at the same time. Failure of one drive in either array wouldn't generate so much as a flutter in the system. Should two drives in the same array fail simultaneously, the second array will automatically take over. To have a disaster resulting in total system failure, two drives in each array would have to go down at the same time. If this happens, you can only hope you have a good tape backup as well as a new server. You're going to need both.

MANAGING DEVICES IN NT

The key to understanding device management in NT (or any other OS, for that matter) is that no matter how complicated the OS seems be to, the devices all have the same requirements. To refresh your memory, on a hardware level, the devices will all require an assigned IRQ and I/O address. Some devices will require, in addition, a DMA channel and a range of system memory addresses. If you need review on these principles, refer back to Chapter One.

It's how these resources are managed that vary from OS to OS. NT, from outward appearances, seems to be identical to the WIN9x OS versions that were discussed in previous chapters. However, there are some key differences.

First of all, NT is not PnP-compliant. NTDETECT provides functionality that is similar PnP, but it is severely limited in the types of devices it can detect. There are a great many devices that are not properly detected by NTDETECT. For these devices, it is essential to be able to manually install device drivers.

> **EXAM NOTE:** Pay special attention to the fact that NT is *not* a PnP OS. Not knowing that might trip you up on a couple of questions.

Two NT utilities that make this job a bit easier are Add New Hardware and Windows NT Diagnostics. Add New Hardware differs very little from the utility of the same name that I discussed in Chapter Five, Managing Windows 9x. NT Diagnostics can come in handy when attempting to resolve a resource conflict for a new device that won't come in handy.

NT Diagnostics can be accessed in one of two ways. Click Start→Programs→Administrative Tools Common→NT Diagnostics, or click Start→Run and type **winmsd** into the command line. Either approach will get you the screen illustrated in **Figure 7.12**. The various tabs seen at the top of this applet are briefly described in **Table 7.2**.

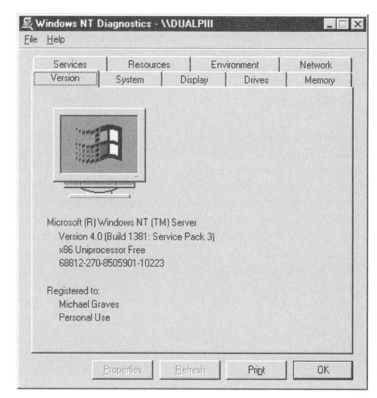

Figure 7.12
NT 4.0 ships with its own diagnostics utility.

Table 7.2   Contents of NT Diagnostics Utility

Tab	Information Contained
Version	OS version, latest service pack, serial number, and to whom registered
System	Number and type of processors and BIOS version
Display	Display adapter settings, type of adapter, installed memory on adapter, the chipset, and driver files
Drives	Information about all physical and mapped network drives on system
Memory	The amount of physical memory installed, size and location of paging file, how much data is stored in memory (File Cache), how much data is stored in the paging file (Commit Charge), and how much RAM is used by system processes
Services	A list of all services installed on the system and whether they are running or stopped
Resources	Information about IRQ, I/O address, and DMA settings
Environment	Identifies file for a command prompt, various processor information, path to system files, path to library files, and path to root directory
Network	User access level, whether computer is on a workgroup or a domain, version, number of logged on users (locally), and User IDs for those users

NT 4.0 ships with a basic diagnostics utility that contains valuable information about the system.

As far as device management is concerned, the information you'll be most concerned with is contained in the Resources tab. This is where you see what is already used in the system. That way you can identify possible resource conflicts.

CHAPTER SUMMARY

The information found in this chapter is going to provide the foundation for much of what you will see in later chapters. Subsequent versions of Microsoft OSs, including Windows 2000 and XP, rely very heavily on the underlying technology of NT.

There are several key points to remember from this chapter. First and foremost is understanding the boot process. This information is critical to troubleshooting NT, and it also makes a frequent appearance on the exam. Another critical area covered is that of virtual memory.

RAID levels are also heavily covered on the exam, but more importantly, any technician who doesn't know about RAID isn't really a technician at all. At the minimum, you need a solid understanding of RAID levels 0, 1, and 5.

Device management in NT makes up a large part of many technicians' jobs. And I know what you're thinking. When will I ever see NT actually deployed? The answer is, you never know. As of this writing, Microsoft estimated that there were still approximately 10 million desktops with NT 4.0 Workstation installed. And hundreds of thousands of organizations have resisted the commercial clamor for them to upgrade their existing NT 4.0 servers.

BRAIN DRAIN

1. Discuss several ways that the NT boot process differs from that of WIN9x.

2. What is the NT load process? Discuss it in detail.

3. What are the two operating modes of NT? Discuss them in as much detail as you can muster.

4. What does Microsoft mean when it discusses the OS environment? How does NT maximize the options for the OS environment?

5. Discuss memory management in NT and how the concept of virtual memory is critical to the OS.

THE 64K$ QUESTIONS

1. Which of the following files is not a part of the NT boot process?
   a. WIN.COM
   b. BOOT.INI
   c. NTLDR
   d. NTDETECT

2. If you have created a multi-boot system, which of the following files will contain the information needed in order to boot the other OS?
   a. NTBOOTDD.SYS
   b. NTDETECT
   c. BOOTSECT.DOS
   d. BOOT.INI

3. What file system is not supported by NT?
   a. FAT12
   b. FAT16
   c. NTFS

d. FAT32

4. The file path system used by NT in the BOOT.INI file is _____.

a. ARC

b. ANC

c. FAT

d. HPFS

5. Which of the following is not a phase of the NT load process?

a. Kernel Load

b. Subsystems Start

c. Services Load

d. File System Initialization

6. User Logon is initiated _____.

a. By logon screen that prompts for User ID and password.

b. By screen that prompts the user to press <Ctrl>+<Alt>+<Delete>

c. Prior to NT booting

d. User Logon is only initiated if configured to do so by the Administrator.

7. Kernel Mode services run at processor _____.

a. Ring 0

b. Ring 1

c. Ring 2

d. Ring 3

8. User Mode services run at processor _____.

a. Ring 0

b. Ring 1

c. Ring 2

d. Ring 3

9. The Executive Services run at _____.

a. Ring 0

b. Ring 1

c. Ring 2

d. Ring 3

10. An API runs as a service of the _____.

a. I/O Manager

b. Executive Services

c. HAL

d. Configuration Manager

11. UNIX applications running in the NT environment are known as _____ apps.

a. POSIX

b. UNIXServe

c. UNINT

d. POSIT

12. The service running in NT that prevents a renegade application from hogging processor time is called the _____.

a. Task Scheduler

b. Task Manager

c. NT Scheduler

d. Thread Scheduler

13. Threads of code that are time sensitive can be assured of getting first crack at the processor because they will be given a priority _____.

a. Of 1

b. Of 31

c. Between 0 and 15

d. Between 16 and 31

14. A process that has not been allowed access to the CPU for an extended

period of time is given an increased priority through a process of _____.

a. Thread promotion

b. Priority boosting

c. Priority override

d. It isn't given any increased chance.

15. On a system with 128MB of installed RAM, an application in NT will be assigned an address space equal to _____.

a. The amount of free RAM divided by the number of concurrently running applications

b. The amount of free RAM divided by the number of concurrently running applications plus an equal division of free paging file space

c. 16MB

d. 2GB

16. Two hard disks configured to maintain identical copies of one another are a form of _____.

a. RAID 0

b. RAID 1

c. RAID 5

d. RAID 0/1

17. If a computer has been configured to divide all data equally between two or more hard drives, with no allowance for data recovery, this computer has been configured for _____.

a. RAID 0

b. RAID 1

c. RAID 5

d. RAID 0/1

18. A computer with five hard disks on which data is equally divided between all drives, with parity information that can be used for data recovery also divided across all drives, has been configured for _____.

a. RAID 0

b. RAID 1

c. RAID 5

d. RAID 0/1

19. If you want to see what IRQs are being used by your system under NT, you would use _____.

a. Device Manager

b. Configuration Manager

c. Resource Manager

d. NT Diagnostics

20. NT 4.0 is an example of a true PnP OS.

a. True

b. False

TRICKY TERMINOLOGY

Disk duplexing: Exactly duplicating the data on a system on two different drives, each hanging off of a separate controller.

Disk mirroring: Exactly duplicating the data on a system on two different drives hanging off of a single controller.

Executive Services: The layer of the operating system responsible for running commands.

Kernel Mode: An operational mode for an OS that manages system functions.

Memory pool: The total address space available to an OS and the applications running on top of it.

Mirrored volume: A single logical drive that is made of two disks, both of which contain identical data.

Page fault: A noncritical error state that occurs when the OS looks for data in the paging file and fails to locate it.

Parity block: A mathematical image of data that can be used to reconstruct that data in the event it is lost.

Priority boosting: A process by which the privilege level of a thread of code is promoted to a higher level in order to enhance its chances at the CPU.

Real time OS: An OS designed to be able to perform specific functions at the precise time at which those functions are needed.

Spanned volume: A larger logical drive that is created by combining space located on two different partitions or disks.

Striped volume: A logical drive that is created by storing data in chunks that are distributed among multiple physical drives.

User mode: An operational mode for an OS that manages applications and security functions.

Volume set: A single logical disk drive that is created when multiple partitions or physical disks are combined.

ACRONYM ALERT

API: Application Programming Interface. A set of uniform commands common to a group of devices of the same type.

ARC: Advanced RISC Computing

ATAPI: Advanced Technology Application Programming Interface. The API that controls IDE devices.

LSA: Local Security Authority. A Microsoft service that authenticates users' rights.

POSIX: Portable Operating System Interface

RAID: Redundant Array of Independent Disks

VMM: Virtual Memory Manager. A service of an OS that maps hard drive space out and presents it as being available physical memory.

CHAPTER 8

ADMINISTRATIVE TOOLS IN NT

With the release of NT, users found themselves with several new tools to help keep their systems running at their best and to help figure out problems that might exist. Among these are Dr. Watson, the Event Viewer, Performance Monitor, and Network Monitor. These four items are the most commonly used of the Administrative Tools in NT. Even when these fail, NT has a built-in tool for helping the troubleshooting process. To most users, this last tool is affectionately known simply as the "blue screen of death." Most people, when faced with the blue screen, moan loudly and shut the machine off. But it can actually provide some useful information, if you know how to read it. The final thing I'll tackle in this chapter will be a brief overview of the rest of the set of administrative tools NT provides.

A+ OPERATING SYSTEM TECHNOLOGIES EXAM OBJECTIVES

CompTIA exam objectives covered in this chapter include the following:

2.3   Identify the basic system boot sequences and boot methods, including the steps to create an emergency boot disk with utilities installed for Windows 9x/Me, Windows NT 4.0 Workstation, Windows 2000 Professional, and Windows XP.

3.1   Recognize and interpret the meaning of common error codes and startup messages from the boot sequence, and identify steps to correct the problems.

DR. WATSON

Everyone has experienced system crashes before, and had applications crash. In previous versions of Windows, you basically just had to live with it and move on. NT provided a tool for diagnosing the cause of application crashes. This tool is called Dr. Watson. Dr. Watson automatically launches itself whenever an application stops responding to the system. It then generates a log file called drwtsn32.log that holds information specific to the condition of the system at the time of the crash. I should point out that Dr. Watson exists in Windows 98 as well. However, it's deeply integrated into the system in NT.

Dr. Watson can also create something called a *crash dump file*. The crash dump file is a byte for

> **BUZZ WORDS** ——————
>
> **Crash dump file:** A direct copy of the entire contents of system RAM copied to a file on the hard disk.

byte copy of the entire contents of system memory that is written to the hard disk. To the average user, this file is all but meaningless. But in the event of a disastrous system crash on a mission critical system, this file can be retrieved and sent to Microsoft for analysis. (There is a significant fee for this service.)

> **EXAM NOTE:** Understand what a crash dump is and what it can be used for. But don't bother trying to understand how to read one unless you're an accomplished programmer.

There are a number of ways you can tweak Dr. Watson to work for you instead of for itself. The following few pages will take you on a tour of this often-ignored utility.

CONFIGURING DR. WATSON

Configuring Dr. Watson first requires starting the utility. In order to start Dr. Watson, click Start→Run and into the command line, type **drwtsn32**. You can do the same thing from a command prompt if you prefer. Either way will result in a window similar to **Figure 8.1**.

As you can see, there are several options. The first is the Log File Path. This is the directory in which the log file will be stored. In the illustration the path selected is called *%windir%*. This refers to the system directory. If you perform a typical installation, allowing Setup to use all of the default paths, then this directory will be C:\WINNT. If you chose to install to a different drive or direction, you'll need to know what that path was. Many administrators change this directory to C:\. That way, in the event of a system crash, it's easier to find the file.

The next entry is Crash Dump. This indicates the directory and filename where the crash dump will be stored in the event of a total system crash. The default directory is *%windir%\user.dmp*.

Below this, you see two number boxes. One is for Number of Instructions and the other for Number of Errors to Save. The default for both is 10. The Number of Instructions entry allows the user to configure how many program threads that were executed prior to the error state will be recorded. Number of Errors to Save actually doesn't refer to Dr. Watson's log file, but rather to Event Viewer. In addition to creating the log, Dr. Watson will write errors to another utility called Event Viewer (discussed later in this chapter.)

Beneath the instructions and errors options are six other options that are selected simply by checking the boxes. These options include the following:

- *Dump Symbol Table*. Records each application module running at the time of the crash, along with every program thread and the memory address at which that thread was running.

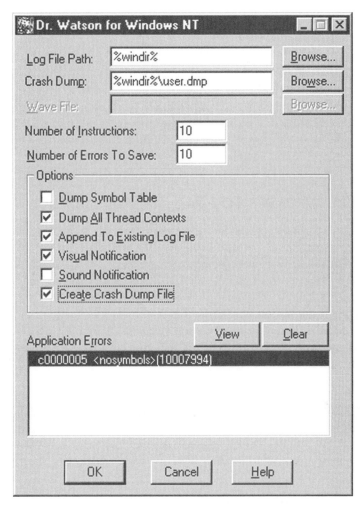

Figure 8.1   The Dr. Watson utility is a good tool for troubleshooting the probable cause of application errors.

■ *Dump All Thread Contexts*: By default only the offending thread is recorded. By clicking this box, all threads running at the time of the failure will be recorded.

■ *Append To Existing Log File*: When this box is checked, information is added at the bottom of a constantly growing file. If unchecked, the new log file will overwrite the old one.

■ *Visual Notification*: If checked, when a failure occurs, a popup box will appear for five seconds, notifying the user of the event. If the OK is not clicked, the box will automatically disappear.

- *Sound Notification*: When an event occurs, Windows will play a sound file through the speakers.
- *Create Crash Dump File*: If unchecked, the crash dump file discussed earlier in this section will not be created.

At the bottom of the window is a text box labeled Application Errors. Any errors recorded in Dr. Watson's log will be listed here. Above the text box are two buttons. Clicking View allows the user to open Dr. Watson's log in a separate window and browse the entire file. Clicking Clear will erase the log file and start a new one.

A Tour of Dr. Watson's Log File

The log file that Dr. Watson generates can contain a plethora of useful information, if you know how to read it. To the beginner's eyes, it simply causes headaches. In this section, I'll provide the information that might prevent those headaches.

The log file is broken down into several sections, and each section contains specific information. **Figure 8.2** shows the opening two sections of the file. It always starts out with Microsoft's copyright information. You would never want to forget about that. Next will be the line that reads `Application exception occurred`. As if you didn't already know. The file then identifies the application that generated the error (although not always in a fashion that the user can understand), the time and date at which the error occurred, and the type of error

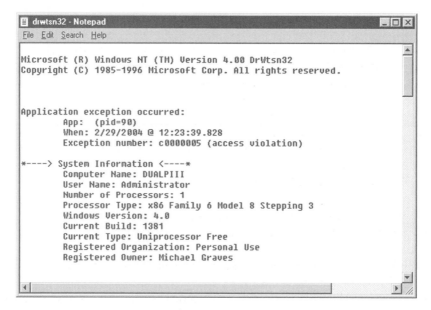

Figure 8.2 The first couple of sections of Dr. Watson's log file are the most informative to the average technician.

Figure 8.3 The Dr. Watson log lists all threads that were running at the time of the program fault.

that occurred. Following the opening sequence is some basic information about the system configuration.

After the system information section, the log file provides a list of all open threads at the time of the event (**Figure 8.3**). The number on the left side of the column is the Task Identifier and on the right is the name of the process running. This list is for information purposes only and does not indicate that these threads were at fault.

Now comes a list of all the program modules that were running on the system at the time of the error and the range of memory addresses that these modules occupied. (Note that in **Figure 8.4**, the list of modules contains only debug files, because the system from which this log file was obtained had no program errors.)

The State Dump section (**Figure 8.5**) is where Dr. Watson finally starts to dig into the problem. This section is divided into four columns. The first is the address of the instruction; the second is the machine code (in hexadecimal), while the last two are programming code. The only thing that matters to you as a technician is the line that says FAULT in front of it. That is the instruction that crashed the system. Microsoft's TechNet Web site contains a database of different fault codes and what they mean. Therefore, you can use this information on its Web site to troubleshoot the problems.

Following the State Dump are three other sections. These are the Stack Back Trace, the Raw Stack Dump, and the Symbol Table. These are useful only to programmers and will not be discussed here.

```
(77f60000 - 77fbc000) dll\ntdll.dbg
(77f00000 - 77f5e000) dll\kernel32.dbg
(77e70000 - 77ec4000) dll\user32.dbg
(77ed0000 - 77efc000) dll\gdi32.dbg
(77dc0000 - 77dfe000) dll\advapi32.dbg
(77e10000 - 77e62000) dll\rpcrt4.dbg
(10000000 - 10000000)
(77d80000 - 77db2000) dll\comdlg32.dbg
(77c40000 - 77d7c000) dll\shell32.dbg
(77bf0000 - 77c3f000) dll\comctl32.dbg
(77b20000 - 77bd2000) dll\ole32.dbg
(65340000 - 653bc000) oleaut32.dbg
(77a90000 - 77a9b000) dll\version.dbg
(779c0000 - 779c8000) dll\lz32.dbg

State Dump for Thread Id 0x5b

eax=00000000 ebx=00000000 ecx=00000000 edx=ffffff01 esi=01010044 edi=0
eip=10007994 esp=0012fae4 ebp=00e00048 iopl=0         nv up ei pl nz a
cs=001b  ss=0023  ds=0023  es=0023  fs=0038  gs=0000              efl=0
```

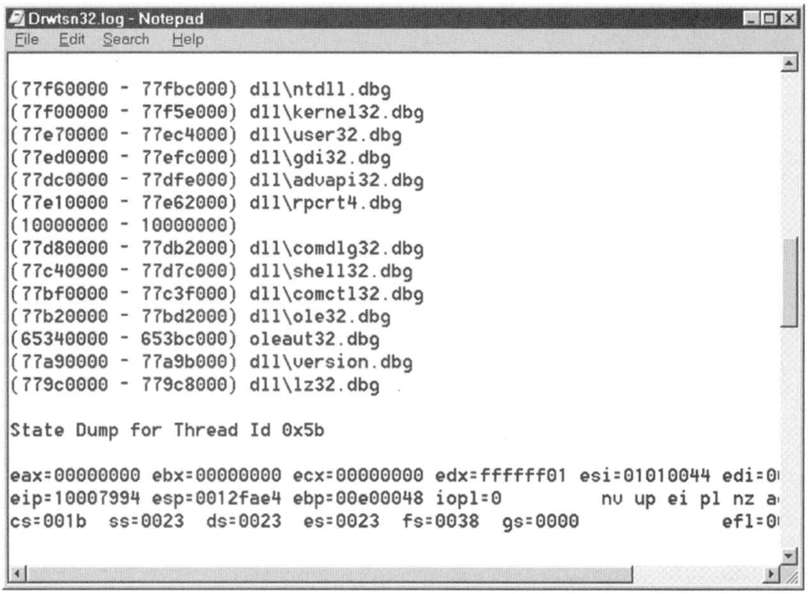

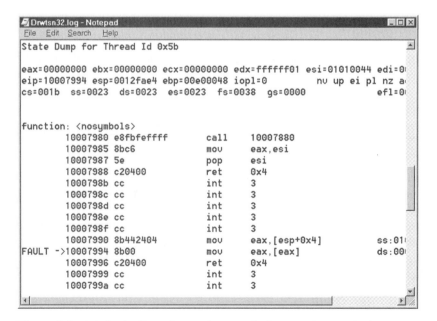

Figure 8.4 The Dr. Watson log now lists all program modules running on the system.

```
State Dump for Thread Id 0x5b

eax=00000000 ebx=00000000 ecx=00000000 edx=ffffff01 esi=01010044 edi=0
eip=10007994 esp=0012fae4 ebp=00e00048 iopl=0         nv up ei pl nz a
cs=001b  ss=0023  ds=0023  es=0023  fs=0038  gs=0000              efl=0


function: <nosymbols>
        10007980 e8fbfeffff       call    10007880
        10007985 8bc6             mov     eax,esi
        10007987 5e               pop     esi
        10007988 c20400           ret     0x4
        1000798b cc               int     3
        1000798c cc               int     3
        1000798d cc               int     3
        1000798e cc               int     3
        1000798f cc               int     3
        10007990 8b442404         mov     eax,[esp+0x4]              ss:01
FAULT ->10007994 8b00             mov     eax,[eax]                  ds:00
        10007996 c20400           ret     0x4
        10007999 cc               int     3
        1000799a cc               int     3
```

Figure 8.5 It is in the State Dump that you finally see what crashed the program.

THE EVENT VIEWER

One of the better troubleshooting tools provided by WINNT is one called Event Viewer. Event Viewer collects information on different activities that are generated by either hardware or software action. These events range from benign to critical, and Event Viewer frequently can provide information that helps the administrator diagnose what led up to the event.

Event Viewer reports three degrees of severity in its logs, as illustrated in **Table 8.1**.

Table 8.1 Event Viewer Severity Classifications

Symbol	Severity	Description
	Information	Information describes the successful operation of an application, driver, or service.
	Error	A significant problem, such as loss of data or loss of functionality.
	Warning	An event that is not necessarily significant, but may indicate a possible future problem.

There are three ways to get to Event Viewer. The first is to click Start→Programs→ Administrative Tools→Event Viewer, and another is to click Start→Run and type **eventvwr** into the command line. The third way is to type that same command at the command prompt. However you get there, the result will be similar to the screen shown in **Figure 8.6**.

The NT Event Viewer maintains three separate event logs. These are the Application Log, the System Log, and the Security Log. I've already mentioned that the Application Log is where Dr. Watson stores the event notifications that it generates when an application error occurs. The security log is only used if the system administrator has enabled a function called auditing. Auditing is a method by which a user's activities on the system can be tracked. A large number of events, including logon attempts, attempts to access system resources, and literally hundreds of others, can be tracked in NT. It is the Security Log that hosts the event notifications that are generated by auditing.

> **EXAM NOTE:** Make *sure* you know all three of the logs maintained by the NT 4.0 Event Viewer, as well as the type of information that is stored in each log.

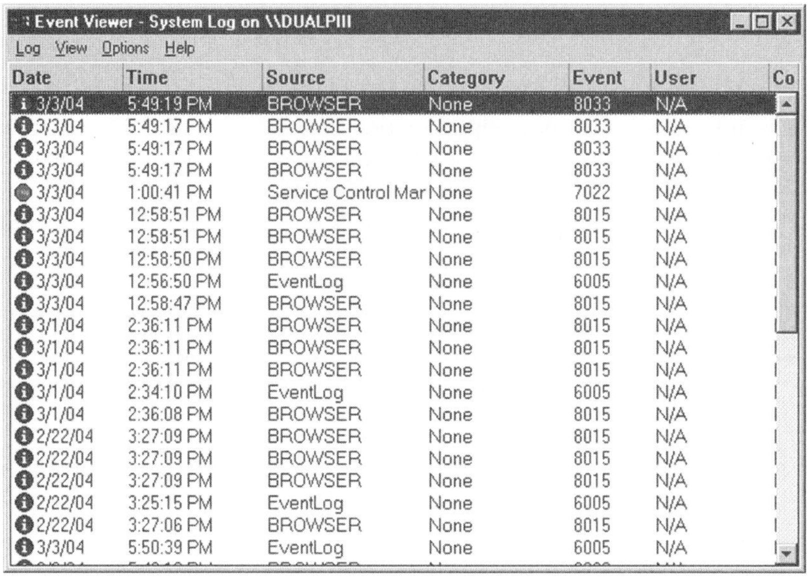

Figure 8.6   The Windows NT Event Viewer

The log that is used most frequently is the System Log. Here is where situations relating to system and network performance can be analyzed. When an error is generated, an event message similar to the one shown in **Figure 8.7** will be generated. Within this message is frequently good information relating to what caused the error.

TROUBLESHOOTING THE NOS THROUGH EVENTS

When you're first getting started with this network administration thing, it can appear to be overwhelming at first. You'll soon get over that. You'll find that all providers of network operating systems provide a substantial amount of support for their products. In Windows NT, 2000, and XP, the Event Viewer provides information on what caused a failure. If this doesn't help, you can take it a step further and make use of Microsoft's TechNet services on the Web page (currently at www.microsoft.com/technet/). A search of key words from the message is very likely to bring up several articles related to your problem. Novell offers very similar services, and Linux help can be obtained from Red Hat, Mandrake, and numerous other Linux vendors.

Another good resource for Microsoft users is the Windows 2000 or Windows XP Resource Guide. Again, Novell provides similar references for its NOS. In this kit you will find reams of information. Nearly every error message generated by the NOS is explained, and most causes of service or driver failure can be found in this guide. These are not inexpensive books, but compared to the cost of your NOS and/or the cost of the administrator's time, the resource guide is an essential tool for any administrator.

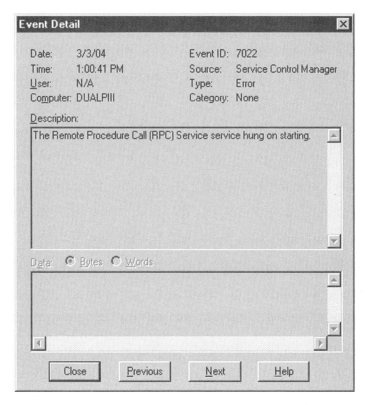

Figure 8.7   An error notification in the NT Event Viewer System Log

PERFORMANCE MONITOR

Performance Monitor is an application that ships with Microsoft server products that can monitor a huge number of system variables. Variables are broken down into groups called *system objects*. Within these objects are the *counters* themselves. The actual number of items that can be monitored is vast and to attempt to cover them all would require a complete volume in and of itself. However, a few items are of sufficient value to the network engineer to justify a brief discussion.

While Performance Monitor is not necessarily limited to monitoring hardware statistics, it is very useful in that respect. It can measure certain statistics concerning your processor, your memory, and the network interface. **Figure 8.8** is a graphic of Performance Monitor keeping track of system resources while I processed an image.

BUZZ WORDS

System object: On a system in general, it is any hardware or software entity to which specific properties can be assigned. In Performance Monitor, it is a category of events that can be monitored.

Object counter: In Performance Monitor, it is the specific property or variable for which data is being collected.

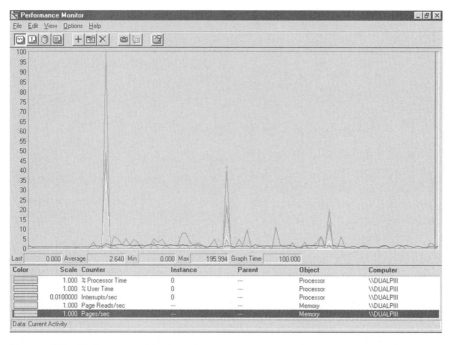

Figure 8.8 Performance Monitor allows you to collect data on the amount of strain specific aspects of your system's software or OS are experiencing.

Performance Monitor can be used in this way to generate a report that can let you know whether it is time to increase the amount of memory installed in a server, whether a second processor is in order, or whether your bandwidth is insufficient for your needs. To do this there are several key functions to watch.

EXAM NOTE: It isn't really necessary to know all of the different objects that can be studied by Performance Monitor. All you really need to know for the exam is the function of the tool and how it can be used to isolate problems. The rest of the information contained in this section is for the real-world user.

There are two system objects with very similar names that are not very similar in what they do. One is process, and the other is processor. Process keeps tab of the different processes from different applications running on the server, while Processor watches certain performance variables of the CPU. Both are useful to monitor if you think that your CPU might be a bottleneck.

Under Process, one of the key counters to watch is % Processor Time. This is the percentage of elapsed time that all of the threads of a specific process used the processor to execute instructions (the basic unit of execution in a computer). A thread is the object that executes instructions, and a process is a virtual object that is created when a program is run. If this value continually runs much higher than 60 percent, you should get a noticeable increase in performance if you add a second processor. On that note, if you already have multiple processors, it is possible to get values beyond 100 percent. Maximum percentage totals would be 100 percent times the number of processors installed in the system.

Another counter that can indicate the need for an additional processor is found in the Processor object. Unfortunately for beginners, the counter has the same name as the one I just discussed: % Processor Time. The difference here is that under the Process object, the variable describes the amount of processor time used by specific processes. Under the Processor object, it describes the amount of processor time used by *all* non-idle processes on the machine. (Each processor has an Idle thread that consumes cycles when it has no other threads to run.)

Under the Memory object, there are two key counters to watch. One is Pages/sec. Pages/sec is the number of pages read from (a *page read*) or written to (a *page write*) disk to resolve hard page faults. A hard page fault occurs when the CPU requires code or data that is not resident in physical

BUZZ WORDS

Page read/write: When physical RAM in a system becomes full, data will be temporarily stored in a file called the paging file. A Page Read is a read operation from this file, while a Page Write is when data is moved from RAM to the paging file.

Page fault: A non-critical error state that occurs when the OS looks for data in the paging file and fails to locate it.

Hard fault: A situation in which data sought by the CPU was neither in memory nor in the paging file. As a result a new hard disk search must be initiated.

Soft fault: The data requested by the CPU is in memory, but not part of the current working set of data. As a result, a new memory search must be initiated.

memory and was not found in the page file. This indicates that, somewhere along the line, the processor expected to need that data, but there was insufficient memory to store it in RAM or the paging file. Any time this happens, the CPU experiences extensive and unnecessary delays.

The second counter to watch is Page Faults/sec. This is somewhat like pages per second, but lets you know how many times the system hit the paging file looking for data that wasn't there. There are two types of page faults. A *soft fault* is where the data was actually present in memory, but not part of the working set. They generally don't affect the system too badly. A *hard fault* requires a search and retrieval by the hard drive and is an even more significant delay than a simple page read. Excessive Pages/sec and Page Faults/sec are indications that you need to install more RAM in your system.

The Network Interface Object can let you know how heavily the interface to the server is being hit. Two counters to monitor are Bandwidth and Output Queue Length. Bandwidth suggests how much of your available bandwidth is being used. Output Queue Length shows how many packets are resident in the buffer. You want this to be zero. One is acceptable, but two or more means you have a problem and need to locate the source of the bottleneck.

As I said earlier, there are literally hundreds of different counters in Performance Monitor. A good network engineer will make a more detailed study of this handy little application and put it to use.

Network Monitor

Most of Microsoft's OSs, since the days of Windows 9x, have shipped with a utility called Network Monitor (**Figure 8.9**). Network Monitor is a diagnostics tool that monitors traffic on the LAN and collects information by capturing packets and analyzing the headers and, in some cases, the contents of the packets.

Basic information displayed includes the following:

- The source address of the frame
- The destination address of the frame
- The protocols used in sending the frame
- The payload

The interesting thing is that Network Monitor is not installed by default. In order to use this service, it must first be installed. To do this, open Control Panel, click the Network applet, and then click the Services tab. Now click <u>A</u>dd and select Network Monitor Tools and Agent. Make sure the NT CD is in the drive. After the files have been copied, you'll be prompted to restart your computer. Upon completion of the reboot cycle, Network Monitor will appear in the Administrative Tools (Common) menu.

Exam Note: A question that frequently appears on the exam in various forms is one that checks to make sure you are aware that Network Monitor does not appear in a default installation. Keep that in the back of your mind.

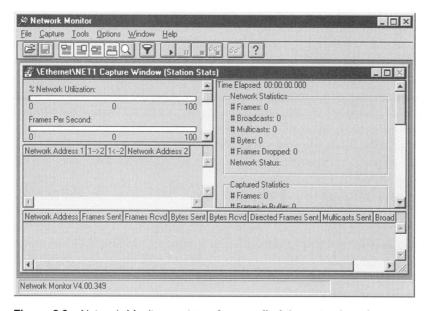

Figure 8.9 Network Monitor captures frames off of the network and provides the tools by which an engineer can analyze the frame.

In order for Network Monitor to work, the NICs installed in the computers need to work in *promiscuous mode.* This term is a colorful way of describing a mode of operation in which a network interface card (NIC) will accept all packets that arrive, regardless of intended destination.

Although Network Monitor will capture all packets passing through the NIC in a default configuration, it can be configured to filter packets on a large number of criteria. These criteria include addresses, protocols, NetBIOS names, and the list goes on.

Unfortunately, the version of Network Monitor that comes with Windows OSs is much like some of the evaluation software that can be downloaded off the Internet. Many of the functions displayed are disabled, working only on the version that ships with Microsoft's Systems Management Server (SMS).

> **BUZZ WORDS** ─────────
>
> **Promiscuous mode:** An operating mode for any network interface in which all incoming packets will be accepted, even if they are not intended for that specific interface.
>
> **Stop code:** A number assigned to a particular catastrophic event, along with certain parameters that further define the event.

INSIDE THE BLUE SCREEN OF DEATH

When NT does crash and burn, it at least has the decency to leave behind one final message lingering on your screen. This is the infamous blue screen of death (BSOD) shown in **Figure 8.10**. Most people, upon being faced with a BSOD, either start panicking or begin lamenting their now lost data. Before you shut the machine down, you might want to take a look at the information presented on that screen.

There are five sections of the BSOD. The first section indicates precisely what failed. It simply doesn't tell you in English. The first line on the screen begins with ✱✱✱ **STOP**, followed by a rather long number. After this number are some additional numbers in parentheses, and finally a description strung together by underscores. In truth, this is the only section that contains information useful to the hardware technician or network engineer.

The second section identifies the CPU, and in the third section you get a list of all drivers that were running on the system at the time of the crash. The fourth section is a copy of each byte of data that was housed in the system stacks at the time of the crash. The stacks are areas of system memory reserved for the CPU to temporarily hold data until it needs it again. The last section simply tells you to try again, and, if necessary, to start in debug mode. Unless you are a seasoned programmer with experience writing code for operating systems, these last three sections will be about as useful to you as an ejection seat in a helicopter. So let's go back to that first section.

The number following ✱✱✱ **STOP** (in the illustration, the number shown is `0x00000019`) is a *stop code*. The only part of that number you really need is the 0x and any characters that follow the string of 0s. These characters are hexadecimal and, therefore, may contain the numbers 0–9 or the letters A–F. The stop code in the illustration would be referred to as Stop 0x19. A number of 0x0000000A would be Stop 0xA. You can look up stop codes on Microsoft's Web site.

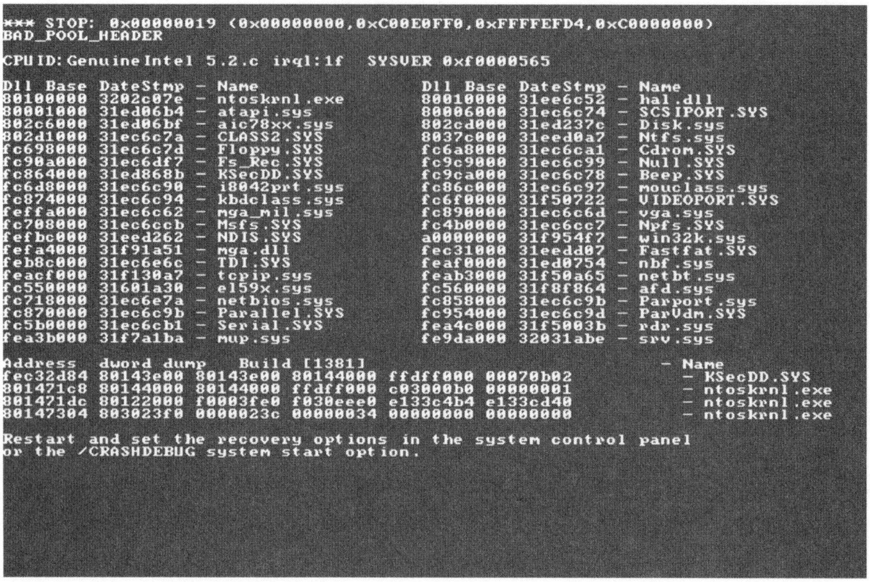

Figure 8.10   The blue screen of death contains information relating to the event that caused your system to crash.

The numbers in the parentheses are the stop code parameters. These parameters are also listed in hexadecimal and indicate, in order:

- The memory address of the error
- The IRQ level that was active
- The type of access that was being attempted (i.e., read or write)
- The address of the function that requested the function listed in the first parameter

There are several hundred stop codes listed on Microsoft's TechNet Web site. Fortunately, about 99 percent of all BSODs are the result of a few errors. **Table 8.2** lists the most commonly seen stop codes, their explanations, and possible fixes when they appear.

The parameters are rarely useful to the average technician in terms of troubleshooting. They are useful when searching TechNet for information. Some stop codes exhibit different parameters, depending on the failure, and by searching the knowledge base using the specific parameters, you get more specific help.

THE OTHER ADMINISTRATIVE TOOLS

One thing that differentiates NT from "lesser" operating systems is the array of tools that are provided to assist the user or administrator in the process of system and/or network administration. As you might expect, the collection of tools that ships with NT Workstation is not quite

Table 8.2 Blue Screen Stop Codes and their Meanings

Stop Code	Description	Explanation
0x19	BAD_POOL_HEADER	Frequently appears as a one-time failure, and the machine boots fine afterward. Can be the result of a failed remote procedure call, a corrupted driver, or an invalid application instruction. If it occurs repeatedly, try Last Known Good. If this fails, it's time for the backup/restore procedure.
0x1E	KMODE_EXCEPTION_NOT_HANDLED	A device driver has attempted an illegal CPU function. Either that or an application issued an instruction that could not be decompiled by NT. Unfortunately, you'll probably never know which. The error may or may not repeat itself.
0x35	NO_MORE_IRP_STACK_LOCATIONS	Either someone has attempted to access a shared resource on this computer for the first time and the remote procedure call failed, or you've just installed a new virus scanner. If it is the first situation, rebooting the machine will resolve the issue, and you'll probably never see it again. If it's the latter, you may need to check with the software vendor for a patch.
0x51	REGISTRY_ERROR	Oh, oh!! The registry is corrupted. If you're lucky, during the boot process, you can press F8 and select "Last Known Good." As long as there hasn't been a reboot that got as far as the logon screen since the last known good, this will restore that copy of the registry. If there has been, then I hope you have a backup.
0x77	KERNEL_STACK_INPAGE_ERROR	Information requested from the paging file could not be read. This can be the result of the data simply being corrupted, or it can be the result of a bad sector on the drive. Worst-case scenario is your controller is failing. Reboot the machine. If it is a bad sector, NT will mark it bad, and life will move on. If it's a bad controller, you may or may not get it again.
0x7B	INACCESSIBLE_BOOT_DEVICE	BOOT.INI is pointing to a partition that does not exist. If a new drive has just been installed, this simply means that drive letters changed. Edit BOOT.INI to point to the correct drive letter. Unfortunately, it can also mean a failed drive.
0x7F	UNEXPECTED_KERNEL_MODE	See 0x1E
0x80	NMI_HARDWARE_FAILURE	The CPU was just issued a nonmaskable interrupt that it couldn't handle. It's virtually always related to bad memory. A failed parity or ECC memory module will cause this; mixing parity with non-parity or ECC and non-ECC in the same system will also cause it. Replace the offending memory with good memory and reboot.
0xA	IRQL_NOT_LESS_OR_EQUAL	A device driver has attempted an illegal memory access function. Reinstall the device driver.

Most blue screens result from one of these stop codes.

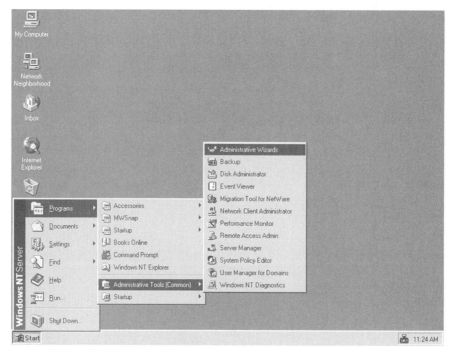

Figure 8.11 The NT Administrative Tools menu

as robust as that which NT Server sports. So in the following few pages, I'm going to list the tools that ship with Server. As I go, I'll point out the ones that do not ship with Workstation. I would also like to point out that because this is not intended to be a instructional manual on NT, I'm only going to give an overview of each tool and not spend a great deal of time on how to use each one.

To get to the Administrative Tools in NT, click Start→Programs→Administrative Tools (Common). The list of available tools appears in a menu, as shown in **Figure 8.11**. The list of tools in NT 4.0 includes the following:

- Administrative Wizards (Server only)
- Backup (Workstation and Server)
- Disk Administrator (Workstation and Server)
- Event Viewer (Workstation and Server)
- Migration Tool for Netware (Server only)
- Network Client Administrator (Server only)
- Network Monitor (Workstation and Server, but must be installed separately before it is available)
- Performance Monitor (Workstation and Server)

- Remote Access Admin (Workstation and Server)
- Server Manager (Server only by default; can be added to Workstation for remote server administration)
- System Policy Editor (Server only)
- User Manager for Domains (simply User Manager on Workstation)
- Windows NT Diagnostics (Workstation and Server)

As the list indicates, the available tools vary between the Server versions of NT and NT Workstation. In a couple of cases, a tool can be added to Workstation.

Some of the Administrative Tools were discussed previously and will not be rehashed here. This includes Backup. The backup tool in NT 4.0 is virtually identical to the one in WIN98. That was discussed in Chapter Four, Introducing WIN9x. Disk Administrator and NT Diagnostics were discussed in Chapter Seven, Windows NT Architecture. Performance Monitor, Network Monitor, and Event Viewer were all discussed earlier in this chapter.

ADMINISTRATIVE WIZARDS

The Administrative Wizards applet (**Figure 8.12**) is a method by which eight of the most common administrative tasks can be accomplished by a user with little or no training. You select a task, and the Wizard provides step-by-step instructions for accomplishing that task. Naturally, you must have the appropriate privileges assigned, or the Wizard will bump you out.

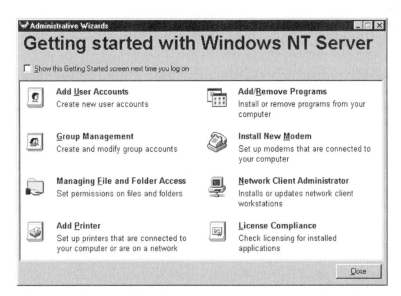

Figure 8.12   The NT Administrative Wizards applet allows even an untrained user to perform certain otherwise complex tasks.

Note that for each of these tasks there is an appropriate Administrative tool for accomplishing that same task. In most cases the Administrative Tool is going to offer some more advanced options not available in the Wizards.

CAUTION: If you are administering an NT 4.0 Small Business Server network and plan on using the Wizards on a regular basis, you should be cautious of using the Administrative Tool with Wizards you want to use. A small glitch in the software exists. If you ever use the Administrative Tool for a specific task, for some reason the Wizard will frequently (although not always) become disabled.

Migration Tool for NetWare

At the time NT 4.0 was released, a company called Novell had an iron grip on the network server market. One of the goals Microsoft set for NT was to take some of this market share away from Novell. They were aware that very few network administrators were willing to rebuild a network from scratch simply so they could have the pleasure of using a Microsoft product. Microsoft needed a way of importing key network settings and resources from a NetWare server over to a Microsoft NT server.

The Migration Tool for NetWare was Microsoft's answer. This tool imports user accounts along with their associated permissions and privileges, security settings on various files and other resources, and all path information. The tool even had a facility for doing a test migration prior to attempting the real thing. During the test, any errors were detected and recorded in a log. This allowed the administrator to find these errors and fix them before performing the final migration.

Network Client Administrator

For a computer to become a member of any given network, the appropriate client software must be installed. The client software acts as the user interface between the workstation and the network server, and it also acts as a redirector. The redirector is a piece of software that looks at user requests and determines whether those requests can be fulfilled on the local machine or whether they require the services of some remote resource. If it is the latter, the client will issue a remote procedure call to the remote device.

Client software is specific to the OS running on the host computer and to the NOS running on the server. For example, if you have a Novell server and a WIN98 machine, the WIN98 machine would have to have the Microsoft Client for Novell NetWare installed. For an NT network, the Client for Microsoft Networks would be required.

The Network Client Administrator allows the administrator to create a bootable floppy diskette. This diskette then can be used to accomplish several tasks. It can install client software, ensuring that all hosts on the network have identical configurations. It can also be used to remotely install WIN9x OSs onto a host computer from a network location. And it can be used to install the Administrative Tools I've been discussing onto a WIN9x machine. Doing this would allow the administrator to remotely administer the network from a WIN9x workstation.

REMOTE ACCESS ADMIN

A feature of NT 4.0 that was popular with administrators was its ability to allow a user to log onto the network from a remote location. For example, if you were unable to make it in to work one day, you could log onto the network over a modem and work from home. For this to happen, two things need to be configured. The server has to have Remote Access Services (RAS) installed and configured, and the user's account has to be configured to allow access from outside the network. Remote Access Admin is the utility that allows easy configuration of RAS and user accounts.

SERVER MANAGER

Server Manager is where the administrator goes to administer NT domains and computers. One of the tasks that can be accomplished here is promoting a BDC to a PDC. In the event that the PDC goes down, or needs to be taken down for service, one of the BDCs can take its place. The administrator can also synchronize the PDC to all BDCS. By this, I mean that the SAM can be force-fed to the BDCs without waiting for the usual cycle. Server Manager is also where computers are added or removed from the domain (although a computer can also be added to the domain remotely). And certain other tasks, such as viewing connected users and in-use shares and resources, configuring administrative alerts, managing services and shares, and sending pop-up messages to connected users, can be accomplished here.

SYSTEM POLICY EDITOR

System Policy Editor is a utility that allows the administrator to create, edit, and manage policies that control the actions of individual users or computers, or that affect the entire network. A policy is a defined set of rules that control, restrict, and configure user desktop settings, profiles, and system configurations. System Policy Editor creates a file that overrules the local registry with new settings, so be cautious when you use it. For example, instead of editing default user and computer policies, create policies for specific users, computers, or groups on which you want to impose policies. If you get carried away with your policy, you can wind up prohibiting everyone, including administrators, from doing anything on a particular computer. This would include being able to override the policy you just created.

USER MANAGER FOR DOMAINS

User Manager for Domains is where the administrator goes to create and manage individual user accounts as well as group accounts. Throughout this book, I have pointed out that certain OSs allow the administrator to define permissions and privileges for any given user. This is where these tasks are performed in NT. The administrator can configure certain options as well. These options would include group membership of individual accounts, profile settings, and a pre-defined home directory for each user. It can also include logon script pointers, access scheduling, workstation privileges, and RAS restrictions.

Exam Note: Of all the Administrative Tools available in NT, the one that seems to get the most exposure on the Exam is User Manager. Understand its functions.

You can also control system policies regarding accounts, user rights, and audits. The account system policy sets parameters for user passwords and account lockouts for failed logon attempts. The user rights system policy sets rights for each group or user, such as accessing computers over the network, changing the system time and device driver controls, adding new software, and even shutting down the system. Another feature available from this tool is auditing. The administrator can select from a rather extensive list of events that he or she wants to watch. The events can be monitored for successful attempts, unsuccessful attempts, or both. Any time an audited event is detected by the server, an entry is added to the Security Log in Event Viewer.

Chapter Summary

Although this may be one of the shorter chapters in this book, it is nonetheless a very important one. Most of the tools discussed in this chapter carry over into subsequent versions of Microsoft OSs with little or no change. Therefore, as the book progresses, I will only be pointing out new additions or changes that occur.

This is also a chapter that holds a lot of information that shows up on the CompTIA exams. Even though NT is no longer "officially" considered an exam objective, there is still a great deal of coverage on the Administrative Tools. From the standpoint of practical applications, since there is still a large number of computers out there in the world that use NT 4.0, you need to be prepared when you run into one.

Brain Drain

1. What are some of the different actions that are taken by Dr. Watson when there is an application error on the system? How are they useful to the user?

2. Discuss how Event Viewer can be used as a troubleshooting tool.

3. You suspect that CPU performance has become a serious bottleneck in the system. How can you use Performance Monitor to back up your suspicions?

4. There is a computer on the network that is broadcasting thousands of random packets onto the network each second. How can you use Network Monitor to determine which computer on the network is responsible?

5. Discuss as many of the Administrative tools as you can think of. Point out how they are useful to the system administrator.

The 64K$ Questions

1. A crash dump is _____.

    a. A critical system error that results in a blue screen

    b. A sudden loss of all information from RAM, resulting in a system crash

c. A byte-by-byte copy of all information stored in RAM to the hard drive that occurs after a fatal system error

d. A place where they haul all the cars after a Demolition Derby

2. The entry *%windir%* _____.

a. Refers to the location of the NT Boot files

b. Refers to the location of the NT System Files

c. Always points to the WINNT directory

d. Always points to the root directory

3. When a fatal system error does occur, NT will copy all the information in RAM to a file. By default that file is stored in the _____ directory.

a. Root

b. WINNT

c. %windir%

d. WINNT/SYSTEM32

4. Which of the following is not a log maintained by the NT 4.0 Event Viewer?

a. Application

b. System

c. Security

d. Services

5. The individual variables that can be watched by Performance Monitor are called _____.

a. Threads

b. Object counters

c. System objects

d. Objects

6. A variable that Performance Monitor can study to keep track of memory

performance is Pages/sec. This variable measures _____.

a. How many times the CPU requests data that does not exist in RAM

b. How many times the CPU requests data that does not exist in the paging file

c. How often the Virtual Memory Manager writes data to the paging file

d. How often the Virtual Memory Manager reads or writes data to the paging file

7. Page faults/sec is a variable that measures _____.

a. How many times the CPU requests data that does not exist in RAM

b. How many times the CPU requests data that does not exist in the paging file

c. How often the Virtual Memory Manager writes data to the paging file

d. How often the Virtual Memory Manager reads or writes data to the paging file

8. In order to function properly, Network Monitor requires that the system be equipped with a NIC that _____.

a. Features a boot PROM

b. Works in promiscuous mode

c. Supports full-duplex operation

d. Sits in a PCI slot

9. Network Monitor automatically loads when you install NT for the first time.

a. True

b. False

10. The blue screen of death is divided into _____ different sections.

    a. Three

    b. Four

    c. Five

    d. Six

11. Of these sections, _____ of them might be useful to the average technician.

    a. One

    b. Two

    c. Three

    d. Four

    e. Five

    f. Six

12. The code presented on the blue screen that specifically identifies the event that crashed the system is known as the _____.

    a. Stop code

    b. Crash dump

    c. Event identifier

    d. Event parameter

13. Which of the following Administrative tools will be found in NT Server, but not on NT Workstation?

    a. User Manager

    b. Network Client Administrator

    c. Disk Administrator

    d. Remote Access Admin

14. A redirector is a piece of software that is a function of the _____.

    a. Network client

    b. NOS

    c. Network-aware application

    d. Network protocol

15. RAS is a service that exists on Server versions of NT only.

    a. True

    b. False

16. In order to promote a BDC to PDC, the administrator would go to _____.

    a. Administrative Wizards

    b. System Policy Administrator

    c. Remote Access Admin

    d. Server Manager

17. Which two of the following tasks can be accomplished from the boot diskette created by Network Client Administrator?

    a. Restore the registry.

    b. Install an OS onto a workstation remotely.

    c. Install a client onto a workstation remotely.

    d. Rebuild the SAM.

18. Which of the following tools allows the Administrator to send a message across the network to a specific user?

    a. Administrative Wizards

    b. System Policy Administrator

    c. Remote Access Admin

    d. Server Manager

19. The Policy Editor is where the administrator would go in order to enable auditing.

    a. True

    b. False

20. Two ways to add a new user to the network in NT 4.0 Server are _____ and _____.

    a. Type **useradmin** from the command prompt

b. Run the Administrative Wizards

c. Go to Server Manager

d. Go to User Manager for Domains

TRICKY TERMINOLOGY

Crash dump: A direct copy of the entire contents of system RAM copied to a file on the hard disk.

Hard fault: A situation in which data sought by the CPU was neither in memory nor in the paging file. As a result, a new hard disk search must be initiated.

Object counter: In Performance Monitor, it is the specific property or variable for which data is being collected.

Page fault: A non-critical error state that occurs when the OS looks for data in the paging file and fails to locate it.

Page read/write: When physical RAM in a system becomes full, data will be temporarily stored in a file called the paging file. A Page Read is a read operation from this file, while a Page Write is when data is moved from RAM to the paging file.

Promiscuous mode: An operating mode for any network interface in which all incoming packets will be accepted, even if they are not intended for that specific interface.

Soft fault: The data requested by the CPU is in memory, but not part of the current working set of data. As a result, a new memory search must be initiated.

Stop code: A number assigned to a particular catastrophic event, along with certain parameters that further define the event.

System object: On a system in general, it is any hardware or software entity to which specific properties can be assigned. In Performance Monitor, it is a category of events that can be monitored.

ACRONYM ALERT

BSOD: Blue Screen of Death. The last message NT (and later Microsoft OSs) manages to choke out in its dying breath.

NIC: Network Interface Card

RAS: Remote Access Services. A service that allows clients to log onto the network from locations physically isolated from the network.

CHAPTER 9

AN INTRODUCTION
TO WINDOWS 2000

Up until now, this book has served primarily as a history of operating systems. Starting with Windows 2000 (WIN2K) I am going to start treating these discussions as current events rather than history. There are vast numbers of machines in the world on which WIN2K serves as the OS. In fact, I have seen several instances where large organizations migrated to Windows XP, which is a more recent OS, and then reverted back to WIN2K because they felt it was more suitable for their operation.

WIN2K and NT share a lot of common ground. That is to be expected since WIN2K is based entirely on the NT kernel. However, there are a number of significant differences, both in internal architecture and in the user interface that need to be discussed. In this chapter, I'll go over the differences and similarities. In addition, I'll cover some different installation methods for WIN2K and compare the boot process to that of NT. Finally, I will go over some methods of troubleshooting the boot process.

A+ OPERATING SYSTEM TECHNOLOGIES EXAM OBJECTIVES

CompTIA objectives covered in this chapter include the following:

1.1 Identify the major desktop components and interfaces and their functions. Differentiate the characteristics of Windows 9x/Me, Windows NT 4.0 Workstation, Windows 2000 Professional, and Windows XP.

1.2 Identify the names, locations, purposes, and contents of major system files.

1.3 Demonstrate the ability to use command-line functions and utilities to manage the operating system, including the proper syntax and switches.

2.3 Identify the basic system boot sequences and boot methods, including the steps to create an emergency boot disk with utilities installed for Windows 9x/Me, Windows NT 4.0 Workstation, Windows 2000 Professional, and Windows XP.

2.4 Identify procedures for installing/adding a device, including loading, adding, and configuring device drivers and required software.

3.1 Recognize and interpret the meaning of common error codes and startup messages from the boot sequence, and identify steps to correct the problems.

THE WIN2K VERSIONS

In many respects, WIN2K is really nothing more than a hybrid of NT and WIN98. It takes the 32-bit infrastructure of NT along with its core architecture and then adds the PnP and multimedia capabilities of WIN98. For the most part, the interface is that of WIN98, although the seasoned WIN98 user is going to discover that some familiar utilities have changed, at least one notable one has disappeared, and several have been moved to different places.

WIN2K, like WINNT, ships in several different versions. **Table 9.1** lists those different versions and identifies their different memory and CPU requirements, their maximum capabilities, and their hard disk requirements. Over the next few pages, I'll give an overview of each of the versions.

WIN2K PROFESSIONAL

This is the OS that was intended for stand-alone computers or hosts on a network. This is the version of WIN2K you would want to install for running basic applications. For users migrating from WIN98, there are pros and cons. Anyone who has affection for older DOS or 16-bit Windows applications won't like it. At best, it's difficult to get these apps to run. In many cases, it's all but impossible for anyone but the most advanced user.

Table 9.1 A Comparison of the WIN2K Versions

Version	RAM (min/rec/max)	CPU (min/# supported)	HDD Requirements
Professional	64MB/4GB	P166/2	650MB for installation/ 2GB min recommended
Server	128MB/256MB/4GB	P166/4	1GB
Advanced Server	128MB/256MB/8GB	P166/8	1GB
Datacenter[1]	256MB/512MB/64GB	PIII Xeon/16 (32 via OEM)	2GB

[1] Datacenter information is included for comparison only. This OS is **not** available unbundled from a configured server.

The four different versions of WIN2K

On the other hand, many of the features added to WIN2K enhance productivity and increase security. Therefore, in the working environment, as long as updated productivity software is used, it is often the better choice. There were a large number of new features added to WIN2K to make this true. I've listed the most significant new features here, along with a brief description of what they are.

- *Automated Proxy.* Automatically locates a proxy server and configures Internet Explorer 5.01 (or later) to connect to the Internet through that server.
- *Driver Certification.* Informs the user as to whether or not a device driver has been tested and certified by Microsoft and gives the user the option of continuing or not.
- *Encrypting File System (EFS).* Allows individual files and/or folders to be encrypted so that only the owner of the files can view them.
- *Group Policy.* Allows administrators to define the computing environment, including such aspects as security, user rights, desktop settings, applications, and resources, either locally or across the network. Group Policy works in conjunction with the Active Directory service and requires a Windows 2000 Server to be on the network.
- *Hibernate.* Copies the entire contents of RAM to a file on the hard drive, retains the paging file intact, and then shuts the system completely down. When the system is reactivated, hibernate mode is able to restore all programs and settings exactly the way they were before the system shut down.
- *Hot Docking.* Allows a user to dock or undock a notebook computer without changing hardware configuration or rebooting.
- *IEEE 1394.* Provides FireWire support.
- *IP Security Support (IPSec).* Provides encryption of data over TCP/IP.
- *IrDA Support.* Provides secure, wireless communications between devices using the infrared communication.
- *Kerberos Support.* Provides industry-standard and high-strength authentication with fast, single logon multi-platform networks consisting of different operating systems such as UNIX, the most recent versions of NetWare, and Windows.
- *Microsoft Installer.* Works alongside the Windows Installer Service. Installation and removal of software is managed by the OS, minimizing the risk of user error and possible corruption of the registry.
- *Microsoft Management Console (MMC).* Provides a centralized and consistent environment for management tools.
- *Multilingual User Interface (MUI).* Allows the user interface to be presented in any one of several languages.
- *Offline Files and Folders.* Mirrors documents stored on a remote machine to the local machine and allows the user to disconnect from the network.
- *Offline Viewing.* Makes entire Web pages with graphics available for viewing offline. The user can view Web pages on the system when there is no network or Internet connection.

- *Personalized Menus:* Adapts the Start menu to show only the applications most recently used.

- *Plug 'n Play:* PnP was described in detail in Chapter Four, Introducing WIN9x.

- *Preview Windows for Multimedia:* Allows the user to preview a snapshot of a multimedia file in Windows Explorer before opening the file.

- *Recovery Console:* A command-line console that allows the user to start and stop services, format drives, and read and write data on a local drive. Other administrative services are provided as well.

- *Reduced Reboot Requirements:* Eliminates many situations that required a system reboot in previous OSs. Many software installations also will not require reboots.

- *Remote Installation Services (RIS):* Permits an operating system to be installed over the network. RIS also allows administrators to dictate standard settings in accordance with organizational requirements. RIS requires a Windows 2000 Server to be present on the network, but it does not need to be installed on each client computer.

- *Scalable Memory and Processor Support:* Supports up to 4GB of RAM and up to two symmetric multiprocessors.

- *Setup Manager:* Provides a graphical wizard that guides administrators through the process of creating installation scripts.

- *Smart Card Support:* Integrates smart card capabilities into the operating system.

- *Synchronization Manager:* Allows the user to compare and update offline files and folders with those on the network.

- *System Preparation Tool:* Helps administrators clone computer configurations, systems, and applications, resulting in simpler, faster, and more cost-effective deployment.

- *Troubleshooting Wizards:* Leads the user through some basic troubleshooting processes in order to isolate a problem.

- *Universal Serial Bus (USB) Support:* Lets the system interface with USB devices.

- *Windows File Protection:* Protects core system files from being overwritten by application installs. Should a file be overwritten, Windows File Protection can automatically replace that file with the correct version.

- *Windows NT Security Model:* See Chapter Six, The World of NT, for a description of the NT security model.

- *Disk Defragmentation:* This old friend from WIN9x had disappeared from NT. However, fragmentation can have more impact on servers than it does workstations. Defrag can be done on the fly while users continue to access the network.

- *Safe Mode Boot:* Another old friend from WIN9x that returns in W2K. Booting in Safe Mode allows users to troubleshoot the system during startup by changing the default settings or removing a newly installed driver that is causing a problem.

- *Backup and Recovery:* A more advanced backup utility than was present in WIN9x, this utility allows unattended backups.

WIN2K SERVER AND ADVANCED SERVER

These two products were Microsoft's mainstays in the NOS market for three years. Even the release of XP Server did nothing to slow their sales. It wasn't until the release of Windows 2003 server products that IT professionals' attention began to turn elsewhere.

The enhanced security offered by the WIN2K products was adequate reason for many organizations to make the move from NT. For many others, just the idea of having a Plug 'n Play server was attractive.

W2K Server is the basic server product offered in this line and is more than adequate for even large networks. It offers all of the advantages of NT 4.0 and then adds features such as the Encrypted File System (EFS), Kerberos and IPSec security, and much more. W2K Advanced Server goes even further. With Advanced Server multiple servers can be combined into a single "super server" using clustering services. Servers with as many as eight CPUs and up to 8GB of RAM are possible. The features are so many and varied that it's best if I simply provide a list of features, followed by short descriptions of each one. The server products include all of the features listed in W2K Workstation, as well as the following advanced features:

- *4GB Memory Support (8GB for Advanced Server)*: Larger amounts of memory serve to improve performance of applications and NOS functions.

- *4-way Symmetric Multiprocessor Support*: Scale up by utilizing the latest 4-way SMP servers for more processing power. Windows 2000 Advanced Server delivers support for up to 8-way SMP servers.

- *Active Directory Integration*: Active Directory incorporates the underlying security infrastructure into an encrypted relational database that serves as the focal point for network security.

- *Active Server Pages (ASP) Programming Environment*: A scripting language that allows a server to run interactive Web-based applications.

- *Application Certification & DLL Protection*: Applications certified to run on Windows 2000 Server are tested by Microsoft to ensure high quality and reliability. Protects DLLs installed by applications from conflicts that can cause application failure.

- *Automatic Restart*: Administrators can configure services throughout the operating system to restart automatically if they fail.

- *Centralized Desktop Management*: Manage users' desktop resources by applying policies based on the business needs and location of users. IntelliMirror management technologies install and maintain software, apply correct computer and user settings, and ensure that users' data is always available.

- *Cluster Administrator (Advanced Server)*: Run Cluster Administrator from any Windows NT or Windows 2000 system to remotely control multiple clusters from a single location.

- *Cluster Service (Advanced Server)*: 2-node Cluster Service can be configured to maintain a backup server to keep the network running in the event of hardware or software failure, or failure of critical applications, including databases, knowledge management, and file and print services.

■ *Component Object Model + (COM+)*: A collection of integrated services and features that makes it easier for developers to create and use software components in any language, using any tool. COM+ includes Transaction Services and Message Queuing Services for reliable distributed applications.

■ *Delegated Administration*: Active Directory allows administrators to assign selected administrative privileges to appropriate individuals in order to distribute the management and improve administration efficiency.

■ *Directory Synchronization Tools*: These tools make it easier for the administrator to maintain and synchronize data between Active Directory and Microsoft Exchange or Novell servers running Network Directory Services (NDS).

■ *Directory-Enabled Applications*: Developers can use a number of standard interfaces to write applications that utilize information stored in the Active Directory service about users, other applications, and devices. All Active Directory functions are available through the Lightweight Directory Access Protocol (LDAP), the Active Directory Service Interface (ADSI), and the Messaging Applications Programming Interface (MAPI) for extending and integrating with other applications, directories, and devices.

■ *Disk Quotas*: Administrators can set limits on the amount of disk space usage each user and/or volume can consume and then strictly enforce those limits.

■ *Distributed File System (DFS)*: Build a single, hierarchical view of multiple file servers and file server shares on a network. DFS makes the entire network look like a really big hard disk to the average user.

■ *Dynamic System Configuration*: Add new volumes, extend existing volumes, break or add a mirror, or repair a RAID 5 array while the server is online, without impacting the end-user.

■ *Hierarchical Storage Management*: This service automatically migrates data that hasn't been accessed for a while to alternative storage locations, maximizing disk space for the most heavily accessed data on the disk.

■ *High Throughput and Bandwidth Utilization*: Increased bandwidth support combined with decreased overhead increases overall network performance.

■ *IIS Application Protection*: Application protection keeps Web applications running separately from the Web server itself, preventing an application from crashing the Web server.

■ *IIS CPU Throttling*: Prevents a single application and/or Web site from dominating available CPU process time.

■ *Integrated Directory Services*: Microsoft's implementation of LDAT, Active Directory is a scalable, standard-compliant directory service that makes Windows 2000 easier to manage, more secure, and more interoperable with existing investments.

■ *Internet Information Services 5.0 (IIS)*: Integrated Web services enable users to easily host and manage multiple Web sites on a single server. Web-based business applications and file and print services can be extended over the Internet.

- *Internet Printing*: Print jobs can be transmitted over the Internet to a URL.
- *Kernel-Mode Write Protection*: Helps prevent errant code from interfering with system operations.
- *Kill Process Tree*: Stop all processes related to an errant process or application without rebooting the system.
- *Multi-Master Replication*: Unlike NT 4.0 where there was only a single master copy of SAM, Active Directory uses multi-master replication to ensure high scalability and availability in distributed network configurations. There are no longer specific PDCs and BDCs. All authentication servers maintain master copies and then synchronize with other authentication servers on the network.
- *Multimedia Delivery Platform*: With integrated Windows Media Services, administrators can distribute high-quality digital media content across the Internet and intranets. This includes the simultaneous delivery of live and on-demand content to a large number of users.
- *Network Load Balancing (NLB) (Advanced Server)*: Multiple servers can be configured to share the burden in high-traffic areas of the network.
- *PKI Group Policy Management*: Centrally manage domain-wide PKI policies. Specify which Certificate Authorities a client will trust, distribute new root certificates, adjust IPSec policy, or determine whether a user will be required to use smart cards to log on to a particular system.
- *Public Key Infrastructure (PKI)*: The Certificate Server is a critical part of a public key infrastructure that allows customers to issue their own x.509 certificates to their users for PKI functionality such as certificate-based authentication, IPSec, secure email, and so on. Integration with Active Directory simplifies user enrollment.
- *Remote Management with Terminal Services*: Allows Terminal Services to be safely used for remote administration purposes. Up to two concurrent sessions are supported.
- *Routing and Remote Access Service*: Connects remote workers, telecommuters, and branch offices to the corporate network through dial-up, leased line, and Internet links.
- *Security Configuration Toolset (SCTS)*: A management console that allows the administrator to use Group Policy to set and periodically update security configurations of computers on the network.
- *Terminal Services*: Windows-based applications run on the server rather than from the workstation. This maximizes performance in low-bandwidth networks
- *Virtual Private Networking (VPN)*: A full-featured gateway that encrypts communications to securely connect remote users and satellite offices over the Internet. Now with an updated PPTP support and advanced security with Layer 2 Tunneling Protocol.
- *Web Folders*: Web Folders provide the utilitarian comfort of an Explorer-like interface to the Web using Web Document Authoring and Versioning (WebDAV). This service enables the user to extend drag and drop capabilities to Web publishing.
- *Windows DNA 2000*: Windows Distributed InterNet Applications Architecture (Windows DNA 2000) is an application development model for the Windows platform.

With this architecture, programmers can build secure, highly scalable cross-platform applications.

- *Windows Management Instrumentation:* A uniform model through which management data from any source can be managed in a standard way. Windows Management Instrumentation (WMI) provides this for software such as applications, while WMI extensions for the Windows Driver Model (WDM) provide this for hardware or hardware device drivers. WMI in Windows 2000 enables management of even more functions.

- *Windows NT 4.0 Domain Migration Tools:* Allows the administrator to migrate an NT 4.0 domain to W2K with a minimum of effort.

- *Windows Script Host (WSH):* A command line utility that allows the administrator to manage scripts.

- *XML Parser:* Support for the Extended Markup Language. This is the latest in interactive Web page scripting languages.

W2K DATACENTER

Microsoft Windows 2000 Datacenter Server is designed for enterprises that demand the highest levels of availability and scalability. An organization that is running extremely large mission-critical databases or is involved in the processing of a large volume of real-time transactions might consider this product.

Windows 2000 Datacenter Server is the most powerful and functional server operating system ever offered by Microsoft. In fact, it's so powerful, you're not even allowed to buy it! Not by itself, anyway. This NOS comes bundled with preconfigured servers provided by a select number of vendors that have been approved by Microsoft. It supports SMP servers of up to thirty-two CPUs and up to 32GB of physical memory. The latter is accomplished through a technology Microsoft calls Physical Address Extension (PAE). It provides both 4-node clustering and load balancing services as standard features.

Because W2K Datacenter is such a specialized NOS, the only thing you really need to know about it for the CompTIA exam is that it exists, how many processors it supports, and how much RAM it supports. The advanced features of this NOS are beyond the scope of this book.

INSTALLATION METHODS FOR W2K

As with previous versions of Windows, WIN2K can be installed as either an upgrade to an existing Windows operating system or as a clean install. And once again, unless there are overwhelming reasons for performing an upgrade, I'm going to once again strongly recommend the clean install.

Regardless of which installation you select, there are three options available for installing WIN2K:

- Setup boot disks
- CD-ROM
- Network installation

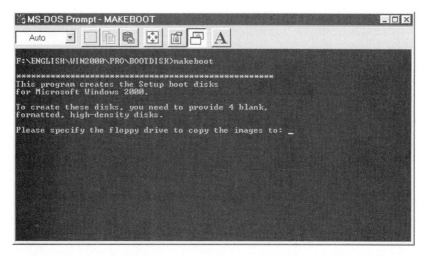

Figure 9.1   The MAKEBOOT utility is located in the BOOTDISK directory of the WIN2K Installation CD.

SETUP FLOPPIES AND CD-ROM INSTALLATION

The setup boot disk installation method requires the use of four setup floppy disks. As with NT, these disks can be made from the WIN2K installation CD on any machine running a Microsoft operating system. The command for creating those disks is different for WIN2K, however. You can create the WIN2K installation floppies in one of two ways. The files required for creating these disks are located in the bootdisk directory of the WIN2K installation CD. The command is MAKEBOOT.BAT. You can either browse to this file in Windows Explorer and double-click, or you can click Start→Run and type **D:\bootdisk\makeboot** (where D represents the actual drive letter of your CD-ROM drive). You'll get a screen like the one in **Figure 9.1**. You will need four blank formatted floppy diskettes available to complete the process. If there is data on a disk, MAKEBOOT will reject it.

The setup boot disk method of installation will be required if the computer on which the operating system is to be installed does not support the bootable CD-ROM format. If your system supports booting from a CD (which they all have done for several years now), the easier method is to boot from the CD-ROM and let Setup take it from there. Many machines that are capable of doing this simply haven't been configured to do so. Therefore, if your machine is not booting to the WIN2K installation CD, before going to the trouble to make the floppies check your CMOS settings to ensure that your computer is configured to boot from CD.

NETWORK INSTALLATION

One of the newest features of WIN2K, in both the Server and Workstation versions, is that the installation files can be located on a remote server, and a large number of computers can be configured at the same time over the network. The remote location on which the installation files will be stored is called a *distribution server*. The client computers wishing to install the WIN2K OS will need to be able to boot to an appropriate network client. This can be done in one of two ways.

The easiest way is if you're performing an upgrade on machines with an existing Microsoft OS installed. Simply boot the machine, log on to the

network, and browse to the distribution server. Double-click WINNT32.EXE and let the fun begin. For machines requiring a clean install, the process is a bit more complicated.

For a clean install to a fresh system over the network, you must have a network card that is PXE-compliant. This means that the NIC supports the BootP protocol. BootP is a protocol that allows a computer to boot from files stored on a remote device. If it was made in the last several years, it most likely does. Next, you must create a boot disk that loads a NIC driver and a basic network client that can then connect to the distribution server. How this is done varies slightly among manufacturers, but many make it easy. For example, on its support site, 3Com provides a utility called MBADISK.EXE that creates the floppy for you. When you run this utility, as it creates the disk it asks you to configure what protocol to use. (I'll be discussing network protocols in more detail in Chapter Thirteen, Networking Computers.) The default protocol is the Preboot Execution Environment (PXE) protocol. This is a newer implementation of the BootP I mentioned earlier. Either of these protocols works by sending a broadcast out over the network, looking for a distribution server. This server then provides the essential information for booting the network client.

At this point, most professional administrators rely on scripts that they create in order to make the process work smoothly. However, scripting an unattended installation is beyond the scope of a book on basic operating systems. For more information on how to do this, refer to a good reference on your specific NOS.

After the network client machine has been booted to the distribution server, the installation can be performed in a manner similar to that of the floppy diskette or CD-ROM installation. You do need to remember to remove the network boot diskette from the drive before the first system reboot, unless you want to start all over again.

The Windows 2000 Upgrade

There are situations where an upgrade is the best way to go, assuming that it's possible. The different versions of WIN2K have different requirements in terms of what previous OSs can be upgraded. If you are installing a WIN2K Professional OS, you can upgrade from the following:

- Windows 95 (any release)
- Windows 98 (any release)
- NT 3.51 Workstation
- NT 4.0 Workstation

You may *not* upgrade to WIN2K Professional from these OSs:

- MS-DOS (any version)
- WIN3.x (any version)
- WINMe

If you are upgrading a network operating system the requirements are slightly different. You *may* upgrade to WIN2K Server or Advanced Server from the following NOS versions:

- NT Server 3.51
- NT Server 4.0
- NT Server 4.0 Enterprise Edition
- NT Server 4.0 Terminal Server Edition

You may *not* upgrade from these:

- MS-DOS (any version)
- WIN3.x (any version)
- WIN9x (any version)
- NT Workstation (any version)
- NT Server 3.51 for Citrix
- Microsoft BackOffice Small Business Server (any version)

> **BUZZ WORDS** ──────────
>
> **Report phase:** A part of the WIN2K installation procedure that seeks out and logs programs and device drivers that are likely to cause problems.

There is no upgrade path for Datacenter. But since that is available only on preconfigured servers, that should come as no surprise.

When performing an upgrade, an additional phase is added to the installation procedure. This is called the *report phase.* During this phase, WINNT.EXE (or WINNT32.EXE) will scan the system registry and all .INI files looking for installed components, software, and device drivers. Any inconsistencies that it finds at this time, such as programs that are known to not run on WIN2K or incompatible device drivers, are reported to the user. It also generates an installation script based on the information it finds.

After the user has prompted the setup program to continue, it will keep track of all registry settings, user profiles, user accounts and associated security settings, and path locations. All of this will be migrated into the new installation.

THE WIN2K BOOT PROCESS

If you were to watch two machines, one running WINNT and the other WIN2K, booting side by side, it would be very easy to think that the boot process between the two OSs was identical. In terms of the files that are required during the boot process, there are no differences. But the boot process is somewhat different in the steps that it takes to load different files. The boot process can essentially be broken down into two steps. The first step is the hardware boot, and the following things happen:

■ During the hardware boot, POST checks all hardware devices on the system, including memory, video, and all communications ports.

■ PnP scans for any new hardware that has been installed since the last POST.

■ Bootstrap Loader searches for a viable master boot record.

Once the MBR has been located, the hardware boot phase has come to an end. The rest of the process involves loading all the necessary software to make the system work well enough to initiate the Kernel Load. In step two these things happen:

■ The MBR locates and reads BOOT.INI.

■ If WIN2K is selected, NTLDR is located and loaded.

■ If an earlier OS is selected, BOOTSECT.DOS is located and loaded.

Since I'm not interested in earlier OSs at this point in time, I'll assume WIN2K has been selected and take the process from there. As with NT, WIN2K locates and loads NTLDR, and the Kernel and Executive Systems begin to initialize. This can be broken down into three phases, the Kernel Load, the Kernel Initialization, and the Services Load.

KERNEL LOAD

This brings you to Step Three, Kernel Load. The first thing that NTLDR does is to locate and load NTOSKRNL.EXE, followed by HAL.DLL. If the user has more than one hardware profile configured, a menu will appear prompting the user to select which profile to load. NTLDR reads the system registry key into memory and selects the hardware configuration and control set that will be used based on the profile selected by the user. NTLDR scans the registry looking for any device drivers that have a start value of 0x0 and loads them.

> **NOTE:** By adding the switch /SOS to BOOT.INI, the user can see the drivers listed on the screen as they are loaded. This can be useful in troubleshooting if, for any reason, Windows doesn't want to load. It's easy to see what driver is trying to load when the system hangs.

KERNEL INITIALIZATION

After NTOSKRNL.EXE has been initialized, a copy of the current control set is made and transferred into memory as the Clone control set. The information collected by NTDETECT.COM during step two is used to create the HARDWARE key in the registry. The device drivers loaded in step two are initialized, and NTOSKRNL.EXE will now scan the registry looking for device drivers that have a start value of 0x1.

SERVICES LOAD

This step begins when NTOSKRNL.EXE loads the Session Manager (SMSS.EXE). SMSS.EXE reads a section of the registry with the heading of BootExecute and runs the programs listed in that section. Next, a file called WINLOGON.EXE is located and loaded. This launches LSASS.EXE. The familiar window that prompts the user to press <Ctrl>+<Alt>+<Delete> to log on appears. You'd think that the Services Load procedure is finished at this point. But you'd be wrong. The Service Controller (SCREG.EXE) now scans the registry for services with a start value of 0x2, and loads them. When these files are loaded and running, this phase has ended.

BUZZ WORDS

Control set: A collection of registry settings that defines the system configuration for Windows during the boot process.

LOGON

Finally, the user gets to make use of that logon prompt. Here is where the user types in his or her credentials and is either allowed onto the system or not. LSASS.EXE compares the information typed into these fields with information stored in SAM.

In WIN2K, the boot is not logged as successful until there has been an attempt at a logon. Note that it does not have to be a successful logon, merely an attempt. As far as the boot process is concerned, whether or not LSASS.EXE authenticates the user or not, once the credentials have been typed in and either accepted or rejected, it's considered a successful logon. After a successful logon is registered, the Clone control set that was created in the Kernal Initialization phase is copied to a new control set. A *control set* is a collection of registry settings that define system configuration information such as what device drivers to load and any parameters that have been set for those drivers. The next time the system boots, it becomes available as an advanced boot option in the later half of Step 2. **Figure 9.2** shows the control sets in the Windows registry.

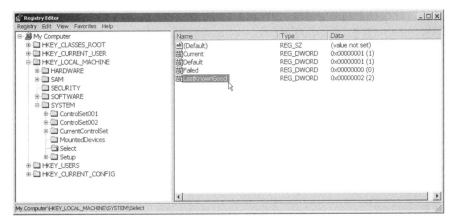

Figure 9.2   Windows 2000 (and up) maintains multiple control sets. A line in the registry (highlighted) identifies which control set contains Last Known Good information.

ABOUT CONTROL SETS

The Windows registry maintains all the information relating to the service configuration of the OS, such as drivers, customized driver settings, and so forth in a hive in the registry called a control set. Control sets are stored in HKEY_LOCAL_MACHINE>SYSTEM. There are usually three control sets (although there can be more) stored. These control sets are identified with the names ControlSet001, ControlSet002, and CurrentControlSet. The CurrentControlSet contains the parameters that are necessary for the system to boot up correctly.

ControlSet001 is created when the system is first configured. Later on down the road, if any changes are made to the system configuration, a copy of the original control set is made into the registry and called ControlSet002. A new set with the changes is called ControlSet001. Under HKEY_LOCAL_MACHINE>SYSTEM>SELECT is a registry key labeled LastKnownGood. This entry identifies which control set to load in the event that the user selects Last Known Good as an advanced boot option.

ADVANCED BOOT OPTIONS

During Step 2 of the boot process, a message appears at the bottom of the screen telling the user that in order to view the Advanced Boot Options, he or she should press F8. F8 brings up a menu that allows the user to boot WIN2K in a number of different modes. These options are listed, along with brief descriptions, in **Table 9.2**.

CHANGES TO THE USER INTERFACE

Primarily, WIN2K was designed to add a WIN98 desktop to a WINNT environment. All of the user functionality, including right-button mouse functions, menu structures, and icons migrated from the older OS to the newer. There were a few changes that must be noted. Some of the things I'll be looking at in this section include the Start menu, Administrative Tools, and Control Panel. I'll also take a look at some utilities that have been either added or modified greatly in WIN2K and some changes that have been made to common file locations, such as My Documents and the Desktop.

START MENU

The Start menu saw a lot of changes in the transition from WIN9x/NT to WIN2K. WIN2K borrowed the concept of personalized menus from WINMe. Certain items that were originally not part of the Start menu were added. In addition, there are more ways in which the Start menu can be customized (see **Figure 9.3**). By clicking Start→Settings→Task Bar & Start Menu, and then selecting the Advanced tab, a number of different options can be configured:

- *Display Administrative Tools:* Includes the Administrative Tools as menu items.
- *Display Favorites:* Web sites bookmarked in IE Explorer's Favorites menu are displayed.
- *Display Logoff:* An option to log off as user is included.
- *Expand Control Panel:* Generates a sub-menu in the Control Panel option that includes a shortcut to each applet within the control panel.
- *Expand My Documents:* Shows most recently opened documents.
- *Expand Network and Dialup Connections:* Generates a sub-menu that includes a shortcut to each configured network interface or dialup connection on the system.

Table 9.2   Windows 2000 Advanced Boot Options

Start Menu Option	Description
Safe Mode	Loads the minimum device drivers and system services needed to start the system. Does not load programs located in the Startup program group.
Safe Mode with Networking	Similar to standard Safe Mode; however, essential services and drivers needed to get the system on the network are loaded.
Safe Mode with Command Prompt	Similar to standard Safe Mode, but boots the machine to a command prompt rather than the GUI shell.
Enable Boot Logging	Creates a log file, NTBTLOG.TXT in the %SystemRoot% folder, during normal startup, which logs the name and the load status of all drivers as they are loaded into memory.
Enable VGA Mode	Bypasses advanced video drivers and loads only basic VGA. In the event of a corrupted or incorrect video driver, this allows the system to be booted and the situation corrected.
Last Known Good Configuration	Reverts to the last successfully started system configuration. (Discussed in the previous section.)
Directory Services Restore Mode	This option only appears on Windows 2000 domain controllers. Displays system information such as the number of processors, amount of main memory, Service Pack status, and build number during startup.
Debugging Mode	Starts Windows 2000 in kernel debug mode, which allows a debugger to break into the kernel for troubleshooting and system analysis.
Boot Normally	Starts Windows 2000, loading all normal startup files and registry values.

If WIN2K won't boot normally, the Advanced Boot Options offer a number of different ways in which it might be loaded.

Figure 9.3 WIN2K allows the user to customize the Start menu in a number of different ways.

- *Expand Printers:* Generates a sub-menu that includes a shortcut to each installed printer on the system.
- *Scroll Programs Menu:* Determines whether the Programs section of the Start menu will be displayed in multiple columns or provide a scrolling action when there are too many items to display in a single column on the screen.

ADMIN TOOLS

Most of the changes made to Admin Tools (**Figure 9.4**) are additions of new elements. Many of these new items are the result of changes in the WIN2K architecture, such as the inclusion of Active Directory. Some of the changes involve renaming familiar faces from NT. Admin Tools changes present in WIN2K include the following:

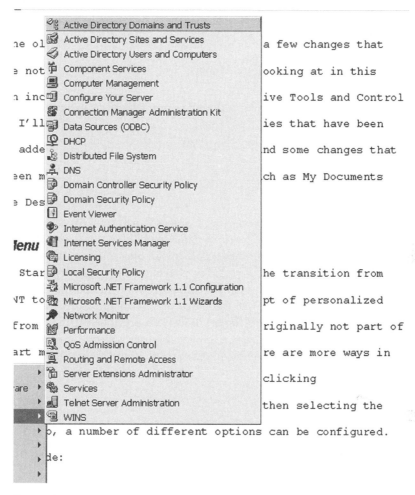

ne ol ...a few changes that

e not ...ooking at in this

n inc ...ive Tools and Control

I'll ...ies that have been

adde ...nd some changes that

een m ...ch as My Documents

e Des

enu

Star ...he transition from

VT to ...pt of personalized

from ...riginally not part of

art m ...re are more ways in

are ...clicking

...then selecting the

..., a number of different options can be configured.

...de:

Figure 9.4 WIN2K sports a new collection of Admin Tools to aid the administrator.

- *Active Directory Domains and Trusts.* Replaces Server Manager and adds several new features.
- *Active Directory Sites and Services.* Administers the virtual network topology, including various locations, installed authentication servers, and replication services.
- *Active Directory Users and Computers.* Replaces Account Manager for Domains in NT.
- *Component Services.* Provides a model for building applications that makes use of blocks of existing code, rather than assembling programs one line at a time.

- *Computer Management:* Assembles the applets used for monitoring or administering local system resources, including Event Viewer, Performance Monitor, Disk Manager, and others.
- *Domain Controller Security Policy:* Manage Security Policies of the network domain specifically managed by the local server.
- *Domain Security Policy:* Allows local domain administration, including user rights and audit policies.
- *Local Security Policy:* Administers security on the local machine.

CONTROL PANEL

There are really only two drastic changes to the Control Panel. One of them is that Administrative Tools can now be accessed from Control Panel in WIN2K Professional. (Although one of the Start menu options is to include these tools in the Start menu as well.)

A second change is in the structure of the System Applet. In previous Microsoft OS versions, certain network settings such as computer identification and domain membership were included in the Network applet. WIN2K migrates these two functions over to the System applet. A Hardware tab collects several different tools from previous OSs and puts them under one roof. In the Hardware tab of the System applet, the user will find a shortcut to the Add/Remove Hardware Wizard, a Driver Signing applet, a shortcut to Device Manager, and a wizard for managing hardware profiles.

WIN2K UTILITIES

The first thing I'm going to do in this section is revisit an old friend from WIN9x: the Backup utility. In the WIN2K Backup utility, the user gets all of the same functionality of the WIN9x version, and then some. The most prominent difference is that this utility now supports scheduled unattended backups of system and user data (**Figure 9.5**). Users can now schedule nightly backups, weekly backups, and one-time backups to occur at a time that is convenient. As long as they make sure that a usable tape is in the drive, the backup will occur. Users can also specify whether to perform a full, incremental, differential, or daily backup.

Another nifty little tool included by Microsoft is the Microsoft Management Console (MMC). Even though you may not have been aware of it at the time, as I was discussing certain Admin Tools, I was discussing applets generated by MMC. Microsoft provided users with the ability to create their own custom Admin Tools through MMC (**Figure 9.6**). Each one of the tools available, either through the Start menu or through Control Panel, is available as a *snap-in*. The user opens MMC, elects to create a new console and adds whatever snap-ins he or she desires. Once that console has been saved under a unique name, it will appear in the collection of Admin Tools.

BUZZ WORDS ⎯⎯⎯⎯⎯⎯

Snap-in: An applet that can be added to customized consoles in Microsoft Management Console.

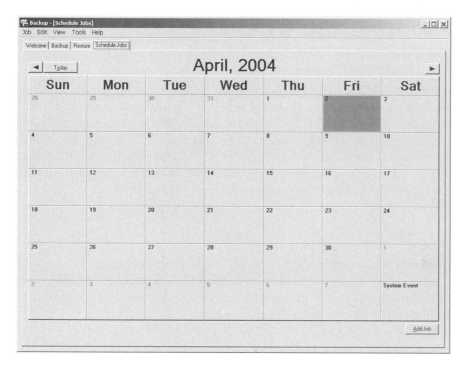

Figure 9.5
The WIN2K Backup utility adds the ability to schedule unattended backups to its arsenal.

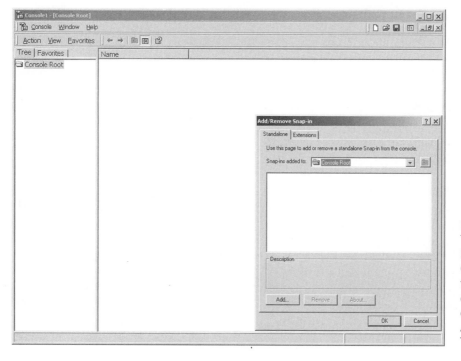

Figure 9.6
The Microsoft Management Console allows the user to create customized Administrative Tools.

Troubleshooting the WIN2K Boot Process

Because the boot process of WIN2K is so complex, when things go wrong, it can sometimes be difficult to figure out what went wrong. Fortunately WIN2K provides a number of different tools for troubleshooting this process. One of these is the BSOD, which I discussed in Chapter Eight. There are no notable differences between the blue screen of WIN2K and that of NT. Some other tools that are available include Last Known Good, Safe Mode, the System File Checker, the Recovery Console, and the Emergency Repair Diskette. Each one of these tools offers a different way into the system in the event of failure.

Last Known Good

This is a failsafe method that allows the user to boot the machine in the event that, during the previous session, a new device driver is installed that renders the computer unbootable, or an existing driver is somehow corrupted. By pressing F8 during Step 2, a menu of advanced boot options appears (**Figure 9.7**).

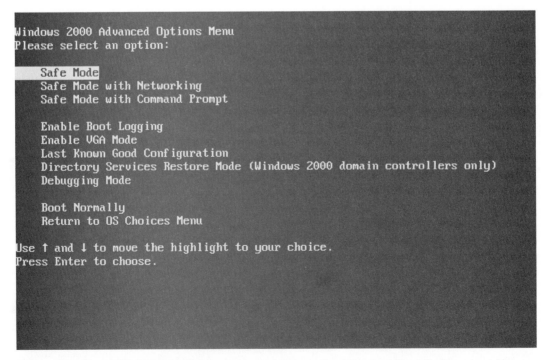

```
Windows 2000 Advanced Options Menu
Please select an option:

   Safe Mode
   Safe Mode with Networking
   Safe Mode with Command Prompt

   Enable Boot Logging
   Enable VGA Mode
   Last Known Good Configuration
   Directory Services Restore Mode (Windows 2000 domain controllers only)
   Debugging Mode

   Boot Normally
   Return to OS Choices Menu

Use ↑ and ↓ to move the highlight to your choice.
Press Enter to choose.
```

Figure 9.7 Press F8 during the boot process to bring up the Advanced Boot Options. Last Known Good forces the system to boot to the last configuration that successfully booted to a logon prompt.

Selecting this option forces the system to load the registry settings loaded in the Control Set identified by the registry as being the Last Known Good. This is in contrast with a normal boot, which loads device information collected by NTDETECT.COM. Since the LastKnownGood control set was created before the user installed the bad driver, your system makes no attempt to load the offending driver. The system starts normally.

SAFE MODE

Safe Mode is a boot option that had been a part of WIN9x, which was dropped in WINNT. When Last Known Good fails, usually because the problem wasn't detected until a successful attempt at a user logon, then Safe Mode becomes your new best friend. As mentioned in Table 9.2, Safe Mode loads only a minimal set of drivers. For example, unless you choose Safe Mode with Networking, device drivers for the NIC and all networking protocols and services are not loaded. Advanced graphics drivers are not loaded, but rather WIN2K loads using the standard VGA driver. Sound card drivers, drivers for CD-RWs, tape drives, Zip drives, and such do not load.

The one time that Safe Mode may not work is when the system employs a third-party disk drive controller not supported internally by WIN2K, which requires an advanced driver. This can result in the BSOD informing you that a valid boot device was not found.

If Windows 2000 boots successfully in Safe Mode, the problem is generally a corrupted device driver or a hardware conflict. Once you're booted into Safe Mode, you can open the Event Viewer and search the System log for any critical errors. If this fails, it's time for some trial and error. Open the Device Manager and disable every device that requires a third-party driver. Reboot the machine in Normal mode.

If the machine boots properly, enable one of the devices that you disabled and reboot. Repeat this process, enabling one device at a time, until you find the device that's causing the problem.

COMPUTER MANAGER

The Computer Manager is a management console that provides access to a great number of local system functions. This applet can be accessed by clicking Start→Administrative Tools→Computer Management. This will bring up the screen shown in **Figure 9.8**.

From this console, anyone with administrative privileges can work with system tools and all storage devices on the system, as well as manage all running services and applications. Everything that is accomplished in here is discussed in more detail in other sections of this chapter. However, this is a centralized point from which it all can be launched.

THE SYSTEM FILE CHECKER

If checking the devices doesn't cure the problem, you can try to use the System File Checker (SFC) to test the integrity of your critical system files. SFC is a command-line utility that checks the version of all files and ensures that the files are the correct size (to eliminate the possibility of file corruption.) **Figure 9.9** shows the different triggers available for SFC.

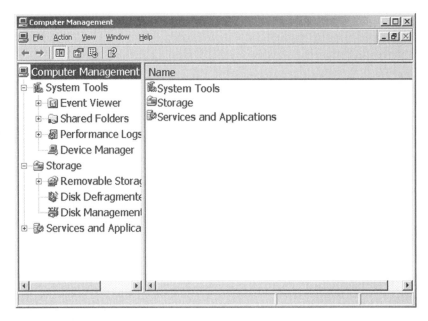

Figure 9.8 The Windows 2000 Computer Manager

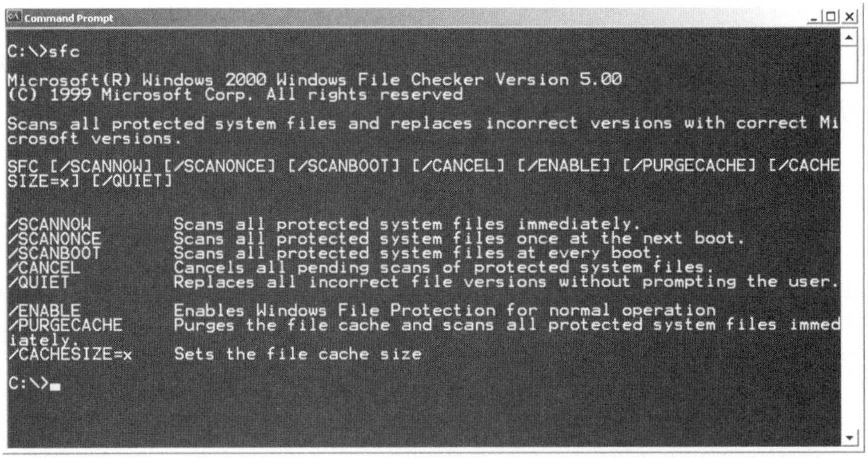

Figure 9.9 There are a number of different options for running SFC.

To run SFC, go to a command prompt and enter the command **SFC /SCANNOW**. This performs a real-time check of the files. If the utility finds any anomalies, it will replace the offending file with a new copy (this may require having a copy of all installed Service Packs as well as the WIN2K installation CD). In addition to real-time files comparison, SFC offers a few other options that can be engaged with command-line switches. **Table 9.3** lists the switches, along with a brief description of what each switch does.

Table 9.3   Options for Running System File Checker

Trigger	Description
/scannow	Scans all protected system files and replaces incorrect versions or corrupted files with official Microsoft versions. This command scans the DLLCache folder and replaces any offending files with the most recent versions. This requires access to the Windows installation source files and also the installed Service Pack files. You will be prompted for the location of these files during the scan operation.
/scanonce	Scans all protected system files once at the next boot. Requires access to the Windows installation source files along with any Service Packs.
/scanboot	Scans all protected system files each time the system is started. This requires local access to the Windows installation source files.
/cancel	Cancels all pending scans of system files.
/enable	Enables Windows File Protection (WFP) during normal operation.
/purgecache	Purges the file cache and scans all of the protected system files immediately. This command requires access to the Windows installation source files. This command is required after you run the /cachesize=x command.
/cachesize=x	Sets the file cache size in megabytes. This command requires a reboot followed by a /purgecache command to adjust the size of the on-disk cache.

There are a number of command-line triggers useful when running SFC.

Recovery Console

The Recovery Console is a tool that is a bit more advanced than the average technician will use. It's more of a tool for the systems administrator. As such, it is beyond the scope of this book to attempt a complete discussion here. Briefly, the Recovery Console is a utility that allows access to the entire system from a command prompt. The Recovery Console can be used in place of SFC for replacing corrupted or incorrect versions of files when the system won't boot to Windows. The utility can also be used to repair logical damage to the hard disk. However, Recovery Console is one of those options that do not get installed by default. Before it becomes available to the user it must have been previously installed. The only other way to access it is through the Windows 2000 installation routine. After Recovery Console has been loaded and is up and running, there are a number of command-prompt utilities that weren't available before:

chkdsk /f: Allows the user to correct most common hard-disk problems. This includes file system errors and moving data from bad sectors to good ones.

Fixmbr: A utility that attempts to repair the master boot record.

Fixboot: A utility that will attempt to repair the hard disk's boot sector.

Fdisk: A disk partitioning utility designed specifically for the different FAT file systems. It does not enable creating NTFS partitions, but it can remove them.

Format: A utility for performing a high-level format onto a disk drive.

Emergency Repair Disk

In Chapter Six, The World of NT, I introduced the concept of the ERD. I mentioned that this diskette could be created during the installation procedure, but that it was better to wait until the system was fully configured. This diskette contains a backup copy of the BOOT.INI file along with several critical registry keys. However, every time changes are made to system configuration or user accounts, the ERD must be updated, or it is useless.

In order to make use of the ERD, the user boots the system either to the WIN2K installation CD or to the installation floppies. There will come a point at which Setup asks whether you want to set up Windows 2000 or repair an existing installation. Select the repair option and have the ERD ready. As the repair process begins, the user is asked whether the system should perform a fast repair or a manual repair.

A fast repair automatically updates some key system files, the registry, the boot sector, and the startup environment. Unless you're a very astute user and know exactly what went wrong with the system, this is the appropriate choice.

If you are that astute user, a manual repair allows you to specify what changes to make. This prevents you from having to overwrite anything you don't have to. These options include the following:

- *Inspect registry files.* Choosing this option displays a screen that lists the registry hives. Users can choose the hives they wish to load. Under Inspect registry files, there is also the option to restore user accounts.

- *Restore user accounts.* The Setup program transfers the Security and SAM files from the Emergency Repair Disk to the registry. At this point, the files become registry hives. Since this is a nonreversible procedure, users will be required to confirm that they want to proceed.

- *Inspect startup environment.* This option checks the NT system's boot files. If it finds a problem with any of these files, the corrupted files will be replaced with one from the NT Setup disk.

- *Verify Windows NT system files.* This procedure runs an error-checking algorithm called checksum against each of the installation files. If checksum does not get back the expected value from any given file, or if a file cannot be located, NT replaces it with a file from the installation disks or CD-ROM.

- *Inspect boot sector.* If the user selects this option, the MBR will be examined for errors. Critical boot files, including NTLDR, BOOT.INI, and NTDETECT.EXE, are re-created.

Chapter Summary

After reading this chapter, you should be able to see the differences and the similarities between WIN2K and WINNT. WIN2K was just the next step along the evolutionary chain of Microsoft OSs. I discussed some of the changes that occurred in WIN2K as they involve the boot process, as well as some changes to the user interface.

Some of the more useful changes are in the methods by which WIN2K is, in a way, self-healing. Proper use of the tools provided by the OS can keep a system running longer and more stably without a constant need to rebuild the system from scratch every six months.

BRAIN DRAIN

1. Describe the ways the four WIN2K versions differ. Include in your discussion such details as min/max memory support and how many CPUs each one will support.

2. Describe the process of creating boot diskettes for WIN2K. What are two major differences between that process and the process WINNT uses?

3. What is the function of Last Known Good? Explain why the user logon process is important concerning whether Last Known Good will work or not.

4. List some changes that were made in the user interface between WIN9x, WINNT, and WIN2K.

5. How does Safe Mode differ from Safe Mode with Networking Support?

THE 64K$ QUESTIONS

1. Windows 2000 Professional requires a minimum of _____ RAM in order to work.
   a. 32MB
   b. 64MB
   c. 128MB
   d. 256MB

2. Windows 2000 Professional supports up to _____ RAM.
   a. 2GB
   b. 4GB
   c. 8GB
   d. 32GB

3. Windows 2000 Server requires a minimum of _____ RAM in order to work.
   a. 32MB
   b. 64MB
   c. 128MB
   d. 256MB

4. Windows 2000 Server supports up to _____ RAM.
   a. 2GB
   b. 4GB
   c. 8GB
   d. 64GB

5. Windows 2000 Datacenter requires a minimum of _____ RAM in order to work.
   a. 32MB
   b. 64MB
   c. 128MB
   d. 256MB

6. Windows 2000 Datacenter supports up to _____ RAM.
   a. 2GB
   b. 4GB
   c. 8GB
   d. 64GB

7. Only the Server versions of WIN2K support EFS.
   a. True
   b. False

8. The WIN2K Service that identifies corrupted system files and replaces them with good copies is _____.
   a. Windows File Protection
   b. Windows Security Model

c. File Synchronization Manager

d. Recovery Console

9. WIN2K Advanced Server supports up to _____ processors.

   a. 2

   b. 4

   c. 8

   d. 32

10. WIN2K Datacenter supports up to _____ processors.

   a. 2

   b. 4

   c. 8

   d. 32

11. The WIN2K floppy disk setup procedure involves _____ diskettes.

   a. 3

   b. 4

   c. 5

   d. There is no option for installing from floppies.

12. WIN2K boot disks can be created by _____.

   a. Running the MAKEBOOT utility from a command prompt

   b. Clicking the Add/Remove Programs icon in Control Panel and selecting the Add/Remove Windows Components tab

   c. Typing **WINNT /OX** at a command prompt.

   d. WIN2K won't boot from floppy diskettes.

13. Which of the following two items are required in order to install WIN2K from a remote network location?

   a. A distribution server

   b. A PXE-compliant boot diskette

c. A copy of Microsoft's MSDN Network Installation CD

d. It can't be done.

14. Which of the following does not support an upgrade path to WIN2K Professional?

   a. Windows 95 (any release)

   b. Windows 98 (any release)

   c. WFW 3.11

   d. NT 4.0 Workstation

15. Which of the following does not support an upgrade path to WIN2K Server?

   a. NT Server 3.51

   b. NT Server 4.0

   c. NT Server 4.0 Enterprise Edition

   d. NT Server 4.0 Terminal Server Edition

16. From which Microsoft products can an administrator upgrade his or her servers to WIN2K Datacenter?

   a. NT Server 3.51

   b. NT Server 4.0

   c. NT Server 4.0 Enterprise Edition

   d. Datacenter does not provide an upgrade path.

17. At what point does the WIN2K boot process write final information to the LastKnownGood section of the registry?

   a. Immediately prior to displaying the BSOD

   b. Immediately prior to displaying the user logon screen

   c. The instant the user hits enter after providing his/her credentials

   d. As soon as LSASS attempts to verify the user's credentials

18. A user can create personalized Admin Tools in WIN2K using the _____ utility.

    a. Microsoft Management Console

    b. Customize Taskbar

    c. Control Panel→Create New

    d. This can't be done.

19. You've just attempted to boot the system using Safe Mode, and you get a BSOD informing you that a valid boot partition could not be found by the system. This most likely means that _____.

    a. The hard disk MBR is corrupted

    b. The controller has failed

    c. BOOT.INI can't be read

    d. The system uses a third-party hard disk controller not supported internally by WIN2K

20. You have just completed repairing a WIN2K installation using the ERD. Only now, two new users you added last week no longer have accounts on the system. What went wrong?

    a. The new user accounts were not registered in Active Directory.

    b. You did. You didn't update the ERD after adding the accounts.

    c. Nothing. User accounts are not a function of ERD.

    d. You forgot to select the "Include Active Directory Information" when starting the recovery process.

TRICKY TERMINOLOGY

Control set: A collection of registry settings that defines the system configuration for Windows during the boot process.

Distribution server: A centralized storage location for the installation files of operating systems or applications.

Report phase: A part of the WIN2K installation procedure that seeks out and logs programs and device drivers that are likely to cause problems.

Snap-in: An applet that can be added to customized consoles in Microsoft Management Console.

ACRONYM ALERT

ADSI: Active Directory Service Interface

EFS: Encrypting File System

IIS: Internet Information Services

IPSEC: Internet Protocol Security

LDAP: Lightweight Directory Access Protocol

MAPI: Messaging Applications Programming Interface

MMC: Microsoft Management Console

NLB: Network Load Balancing

PAE: Physical Address Extension

PKI: Public Key Infrastructure

PXE: Preboot Execution Environment

RIS: Remote Installation Services

SCTS: Security Configuration Tool Set

SFC: System File Checker

VPN: Virtual Private Network

WDM: Windows Driver Model

WMI: Windows Management Instrumentation

WSH: Windows Script Host

CHAPTER 10

WIN2K SYSTEM ADMINISTRATION

Managing systems becomes a bit easier in WIN2K because of the introduction of Active Directory. As I said in Chapter Nine, An Introduction to Windows 2000, Active Directory is the Microsoft implementation of the Lightweight Directory Access Protocol (LDAP). Much of this chapter is going to involve an examination of Active Directory.

In the second half of the chapter, I'll take a look at device installation and hard disk management in WIN2K. The evolution of NTFS to Version 5 added some very interesting features and opened up new possibilities for the system administrator in terms of both security and resource management.

A+ Operating System Technologies Exam Objectives

CompTIA objectives covered in this chapter include the following:

1.1   Identify the major desktop components and interfaces and their functions. Differentiate the characteristics of Windows 9x/Me, Windows NT 4.0 Workstation, Windows 2000 Professional, and Windows XP.

1.2   Identify the names, locations, purposes, and contents of major system files.

1.4   Identify basic concepts and procedures for creating, viewing, and managing disks, directories, and files. This includes procedures for changing file attributes and the ramifications of those changes (for example, security issues).

2.4   Identify procedures for installing/adding a device, including loading, adding, and configuring device drivers and required software.

AN OVERVIEW OF ACTIVE DIRECTORY

In the days when most computer systems were stand-alone devices, there was no need for anything as sophisticated as directory services. All necessary resources could be found locally.

Today's world has increasingly become a networked world, and the networks become more complex each day. For the average user, finding resources on the network could be a real challenge, were it not for the assistance of directory services. Active Directory provides these services to the Microsoft environment.

Just what is Active Directory?

With Active Directory, information about network-based resources, including applications, files, printers, and even other people on the network, can be accessed from a unified interface. Active Directory also ensures that there is a consistent method for naming, accessing, and managing these resources.

In a way, you could compare Active Directory to the telephone book, only it's easier to browse and, in a sense, it's interactive. Through Active Directory, the user can browse network resources as easily as one finds a file or printer on a local computer using the My Computer applet.

All of this information is stored in a relational database that can be accessed through a variety of different applications. Other devices on the network can also use this information to enforce permissions and privileges, and it can be used by applications such as Microsoft's System Management Server. Active Directory makes it easier for an administrator to manage the network's infrastructure as well.

Active Directory Structure

Active Directory treats each resource on the network as though it was an *object*. This includes printers, workstations, servers, files, directories, and even the users. As insensitive as it may sound, to Microsoft the person using the computer is no more than an object. In order to facilitate management of these objects, they are put into *containers*. So if you want a comparison that might be more familiar, if you were examining just the file system on a computer, individual files would be considered objects, and the folders in which those files are stored would be containers.

These containers are organized into a hierarchical format. Containers can contain other containers; they can contain objects; or they can contain both, in the same way that a folder can have either subfolders or files. **Figure 10.1** illustrates how Active Directory might organize a very small network.

As detailed as this seems, it gets even better. The individual objects can be assigned a large number of different attributes. For example, a user object can be described by the user's full name, a variety of different numbers, including a Social Security number, various telephone numbers, or an ID number. Security settings can be applied, or a home address can be added. And then all of this information is collected into an encrypted relational

Buzz Words

Object: In reference to the OS, an object is any single resource on the system and/or network, including files, users, or devices.

Container: A collection of objects on the system or network that have been gathered together into a single administrative unit.

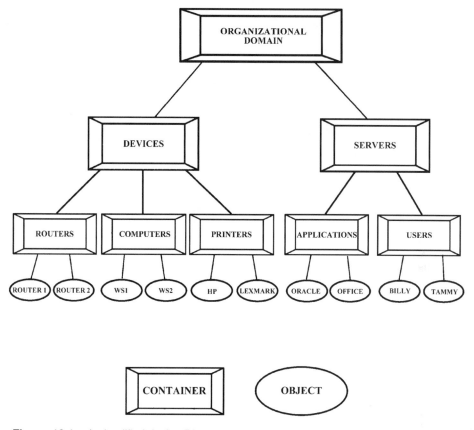

Figure 10.1   A simplified Active Directory organization

database and managed by the administrator as needed. **Figure 10.2** shows just a fraction of the different attributes that can be collected within a single user account.

MANAGING ACTIVE DIRECTORY

In Chapter Nine I described how someone could make use of Microsoft Management Console to create customized Admin Tools. Microsoft also uses MMC to facilitate the administration of Active Directory. The administrator can perform specific functions with the ease of a point and click interface using three predefined consoles:

- Active Directory Users and Computers
- Active Directory Sites and Services
- Active Directory Domains and Trusts

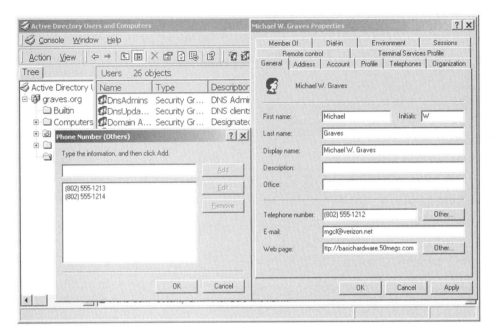

Figure 10.2 Each one of the tabs you see for this user account has several different fields that contain information. The user's entire profile is stored in Active Directory as part of the object.

There are others as well. However, a complete description of all of Active Directory's capabilities is far beyond the scope of this book.

ACTIVE DIRECTORY USERS AND COMPUTERS

WIN2K was designed to be a multi-user environment. This is true of both the Server versions as well as WIN2K Professional. An additional requirement for the server versions is to be able to manage the different computers on the network. This is the function of Active Directory Users and Computers (**Figure 10.3**). Through this console, the administrator can add new users and manage existing accounts. Also, as new computers are added to the network, this console can be used to administer computer accounts.

ACTIVE DIRECTORY SITES AND SERVICES

The server versions of WIN2K are capable of managing a number of different physical networks as well as logical subnets. And unlike WINNT, there are no longer primary and backup domain controllers. If a server has been designated as a domain controller, then it is active. It can service logon and subsequent authentication requests, and it can act as a repository for new information added by administrators. Active Directory Sites and Services (**Figure 10.4**) ensures that managing the different servers does not become an overly complex procedure.

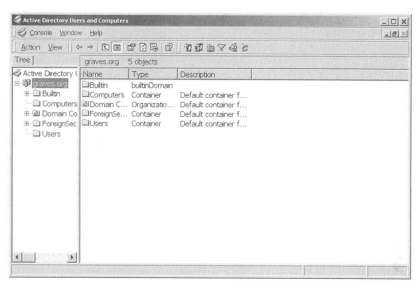

Figure 10.3   The Active Directory Users and Computers console

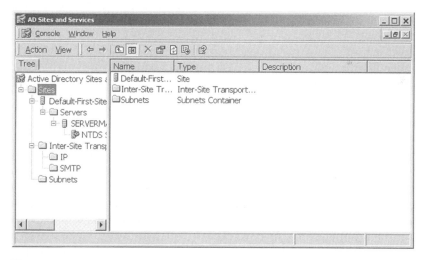

Figure 10.4   The Active Directory Sites and Services console

WIN2K designates the local network as well-connected computers. In a well-connected network, or local area network (LAN), authentication is easily managed by the local servers. However, on a wide area network (WAN) a number of different networks might be distributed around the entire globe. The Sites portion of this console allows the administrator to manage parts of the network that are not physically accessible.

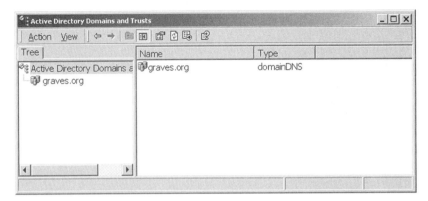

Figure 10.5   The Active Directory Domains and Trusts console

Active Directory Domains and Trusts

I've discussed in previous sections of this book how Microsoft networks can consist of several domains interconnected through trusts. If a network consists of more than one domain, the Active Directory Domains and Trusts console (**Figure 10.5**) allows an administrator with the appropriate permissions to create and manage trusts across the network. This would include the ability to manage other domains, if the correct permissions exist for the administrator.

When discussing WINNT, I pointed out that trusts in NT are non-transitive. To review, that means that if I establish a trust between Domain A and Domain B, and then I establish another between Domain B and Domain C, a trust between Domain A and Domain C is **not** automatically created. Trusts in WIN2K are transitive. The trust between Domain A and Domain C **would** be created automatically.

Device Installation in WIN2K

Adding PnP to WIN2K's arsenal of tools was supposed to make adding new hardware foolproof and trouble-free. For the most part, it has done just that. It features an Add/Remove Hardware Wizard that automatically runs when new hardware is detected and supports hot-pluggable devices in both USB and FireWire. One new feature Microsoft added threw a small wrench into the works, but as long as you know how to deal with it, it won't cause major headaches. That little wrench is called driver signing. First, I'll discuss some minor differences in the Add/Remove Hardware Wizard, and then I'll take a quick look at driver signing.

Add/Remove Hardware Wizard

There are two changes that occurred in the transition of PnP and the Add/Remove Hardware Wizard from WIN9x to WIN2K (**Figure 10.6**) that make installing new hardware substantially easier. The most obvious (aside from the name change, that is) is that the driver database of

Figure 10.6   The Add/Remove Hardware wizard in Windows 2000

WIN2K is dramatically larger. Far more devices are automatically recognized and installed without the need for external driver sources than was ever possible in any of the WIN9x versions.

The second major change is in how PnP actually works. In the old WIN9x versions, PnP was based on a technology known as the Advanced Power Management Basic Input Output Services (APM BIOS). Industry veterans who were around when WIN95 was first released can tell you basically that this technology worked so well that PnP was more frequently called "plug and pray" than it was by its correct name. Some devices, notably network cards and graphics adapters, hardly ever installed correctly the first time and had to be force-fed.

WIN2K incorporates a more up-to-date technology known as the Advanced Configuration and Power Interface (ACPI). This is an industry standard initiative that defines the interface between the system board and the system BIOS. The result is a far more stable approach to PnP.

When a new device is installed in the system, WIN2K will automatically detect its presence. Devices that are installed internally, requiring the system to be shut down, will be detected on the next boot. Hot-pluggable devices, such as USB or FireWire, can be added on the fly, and the Add New Hardware Wizard will start automatically.

If the device is one of the many that are supported by the internal database of WIN2K drivers, the user won't even have to supply a driver disk. This database is located in a hidden directory called INF. If WIN2K cannot find an appropriate driver in the INF directory, it will then prompt the user to insert a disk.

Unlike previous versions of Windows OS, WIN2K adds a new trick. Drivers can be obtained over the Internet through the Windows Update functionality. If this option is selected, the wizard will first check the disk drives or preselected locations. Assuming the driver is not found in one of these locations, Windows will automatically connect to the Internet and log on to Microsoft's Windows Update site to search for drivers.

Driver Signing

In Chapter Nine, when I was listing off all of the new features added to WIN2K, support for digital signatures was one of these new features. A *digital signature* is an encrypted piece of data that is added to a file to ensure that the file is the correct file. In the case of driver signing, the signature does not actually become a part of the file. This data is included in a catalogue (CAT) file, and this CAT file is subsequently referenced in the INF file that is generated.

In order for a device driver to receive a digital signature, the company that writes the driver must submit the software to Microsoft. Microsoft engineers will then submit this driver to very thorough testing in their Windows Hardware Quality Lab (WHQL). After the driver has passed these tests, it will receive the digital signature and be an official digitally signed driver. Any updates or revisions to this file cannot carry the digital signature until Microsoft has subjected the revised files to the same testing procedures.

There are three different security settings that can be assigned for installing new hardware, based on these digital signatures:

- *Ignore:* Any driver can be installed, whether it carries a digital signature or not.
- *Warn:* If a driver does not carry a digital signature, the user will be notified that this is the case and will be presented with the option of halting the installation or continuing.
- *Block:* If a driver does not carry a digital signature, it cannot be installed without changing this setting.

To adjust these settings, click Start→Setting→Control Panel and then double-click the System icon. Under the Hardware tab, click the Driver Signing button. It should look something like the illustration in **Figure 10.7**.

By default, the intermediate setting of Warn is selected. I would advise that unless you have overpowering reasons for doing so, you not change this. Many companies elect not to submit their driver files to Microsoft for testing. They have this strange notion that they know as much about writing drivers for their hardware as Microsoft and elect not to pay the associated fees. Not being signed by Microsoft is not an automatic indication that the driver either will not work or will somehow corrupt the system.

Disk Management in WIN2K

The inclusion of NTFS, Version 5 in WIN2K added a number of different options for disk management that were never available in previous versions of Windows operating systems. There were actually dozens of changes made, but there are five that I intend to discuss here:

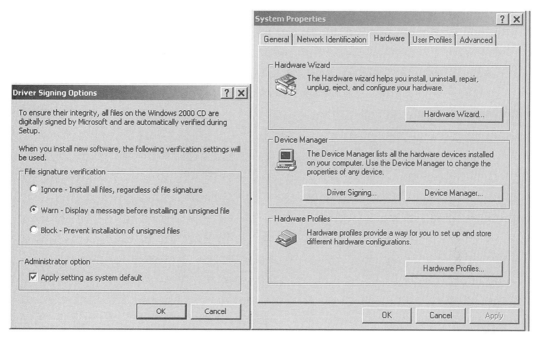

Figure 10.7   Driver Signing in Windows 2000

- EFS
- Selective file compression
- Disk quotas
- Selective file/folder compression
- Volume junction points

THE ENCRYPTING FILE SYSTEM

The Encrypting File System (EFS) allows a user to protect sensitive data in files by scrambling them in such a way that nobody else can read them. It depends on public and private key encryption and a technology called the CryptoAPI. Unlike encryption methods that work on top of the file system, EFS is an integral part of the file system. This makes EFS easier to manage and transparent to the file owner and to any applications that require access to the data.

In order to enable EFS, the user right-clicks the file or folder that is to be encrypted in Windows Explorer and selects Properties. On the General tab, there is a button labeled Advanced. When the user clicks this button, he or she will get a screen similar to the one in **Figure 10.8**. Click the checkbox next to the phrase "Encrypt contents to secure data."

When a user enables EFS, the OS generates a private key. The private key consists of a data set associated with the user's account that determines precisely how data will be scrambled and

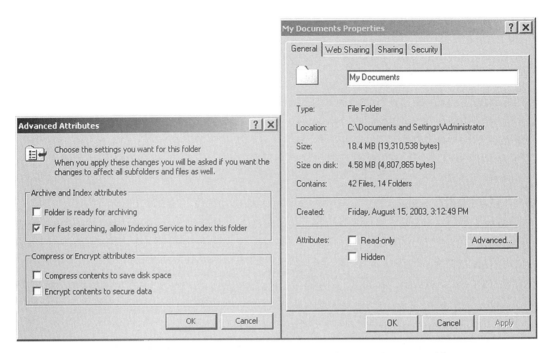

Figure 10.8 EFS is one of the Advanced file properties of a file stored on a partition formatted to NTFS.

how to put that scrambled data back into its correct form when needed. The user can be selective about the files or folders that need to be encrypted. It is not an all-or-nothing option.

For each file that is encrypted, Windows assigns a randomly generated encryption key that becomes part of that file's attributes. When the user goes to open the file, the user's private key calls up the file's encryption key. The file's encryption key will only respond to the user's private key or to a public key generated by an authorized recovery agent. A recovery agent is any user account that has been given the privilege of being a recovery agent. Having the file's encryption key respond to a recovery agent is the fail-safe that allows the user to recover data in the event that the private key is lost, or in the event that a rogue employee encrypts all the data on a machine before an unexpected departure.

So how can a recovery key get lost if it's nothing more than a piece of data stored on the system? There are two ways this can happen. If the OS is reinstalled, the key will be lost, and if the user account is deleted and recreated, the key will be lost.

Since the private key is associated with the user's account, it is possible for multiple users on the same system to protect their data. When users log on, their accounts cannot open the encrypted files of other users.

Encryption and decryption are done on the fly, without any need for user intervention. The only cost for this added security is a very slight performance hit. Opening and closing files can take longer, but on a fast system, the difference is rarely noticeable.

FILE COMPRESSION

File compression has been a part of Microsoft OSs since the days of MS-DOS. Prior to the release of NTFS5, however, it's always been an all-or-none type of thing. You either compressed the entire hard drive, or you didn't. Also, file compression techniques took a substantial toll on system performance.

With NTFS5, individual files and folders can be compressed on the fly. If a user has a very large directory of graphics or music files taking up a big chunk of hard disk real estate, compressing that folder can free up a drive space that can be used for other functions.

As with EFS, file or folder compression is one of the advanced properties. Refer back to Figure 10.8. You will see another checkbox labeled "Compress contents to save disk space." By checking this option, the contents of the file or folder will be compressed for storage but can be uncompressed and used as needed. Unless your system is exceedingly slow, the performance penalty is so minimal as to be almost unnoticeable.

DISK QUOTAS

One of the features most enthusiastically embraced by network administrators is disk quotas. On a busy network, disk storage has always been at a premium. No matter how many disk drives you install, or how big those drives are, they always manage to fill up. There are users collecting high-resolution graphics and never deleting them when no longer needed. Other users think the server is their own private jukebox and fill it up with music files. When Internet access is available on every desktop in the enterprise, users can quickly consume vast amounts of storage space with downloaded graphics, MP3s, and other downloaded files. Usually, it's only a few people causing problems, but that doesn't prevent the problem from becoming severe.

Disk quotas allow the administrator to limit the amount of storage space an individual can use. Disk quotas can be enforced on a per-user, per-partition, or per-volume basis. It doesn't work on a folder level. What this means is that the administrator can configure individual partitions or even spanned volumes independently of one another. If quotas are applied on a partition level, each partition can be configured differently even if those partitions are part of the same physical hard disk.

As a user approaches his or her allocated limit of storage space, WIN2K will warn that user that the end is near. If the administrator chooses to configure it this way, users will not be allowed to exceed their assigned storage. If each user is allowed 400MB of space, that user won't be allowed to use 401MB just because one file is going to take him or her over the limit. In order to copy that file, some disk space must be cleared up. Disk quotas don't take compression into consideration either. The system uses a file's uncompressed size when calculating user's storage consumption. This little fact has resulted in a great number of irate users. Also, file ownership is what the system uses to track disk use. If one user creates a file and another user adds to it, charges against the storage limits are applied to the creator of the file, and not the one who changed it.

Disk quotas are a function of a NTFS hard disk's properties. In order to enable disk quotas, right-click the drive letter for the selection partition or disk and select Properties. Click the

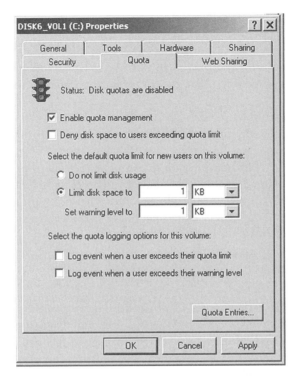

Figure 10.9 Enabling disk quotas in WIN2K

Quota tab, and you'll get the screen shown in **Figure 10.9**. Click the box labeled "Enable quota management." For strict enforcement of the quotas, also check the box labeled "Deny disk space to users exceeding quota limit." If you enable quotas, but choose not to check the latter box, an administrator can track disk usage by individual users without limiting user storage capabilities. This can be useful for a couple of reasons.

Primarily it's useful for determining who the disk hogs are. Perhaps you can convince them to limit usage without enforcing a company-wide policy. It can also be used to determine whether it's time to enforce disk quotas. There is also a commercial use for this function. If your company charges for storage, this is a method of monitoring how much storage space a particular user is consuming, and subsequently how much to charge that user for the service.

If an administrator chooses to enforce storage limitations, there are some options to configure. First, the storage limitations need to be established. How much storage space do your users need in order to properly do their jobs? The default setting applies the same quota to each user on the system who uses that volume for storage. I'll get to setting individual user quotas in a minute.

The next thing to configure is the warning limit. This is the amount of storage consumption that will trigger an alert to users that they are approaching their limit. If you want to get really

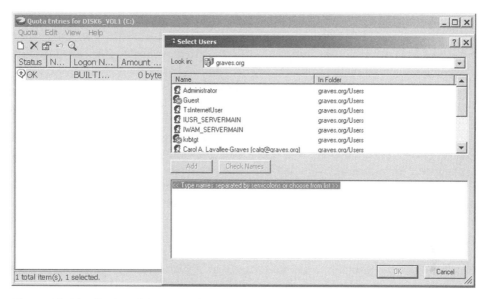

Figure 10.10   Setting disk quotas for individual users

annoying, you can do one of two things. Either set the warning limit to 1MB so that warnings start getting issued every time users save a new file to the partition. Or set it 1MB beneath the actual limit so that they get warned and cut off at the same time. On the other hand, if you want to be fair, set it at a value somewhere around 75 percent of allocated space so that there is time for users to do some house cleaning before they run out of space.

Not all users necessarily have the same storage requirements, though. Your graphics designer or in-house digital photographer is going to require a whole lot more space than a part-time receptionist. This is where individual quotas come in handy. In order to assign individual quotas, click the button labeled "Quota Entries." On the screen that follows, click Quota, and then New Quota Entry. This will bring up the screen in **Figure 10.10**. Now you can browse the individual users on the system or network and do one of two things.

By clicking the button marked "Do not limit disk usage," that user is excused from disk quota limitations on that particular volume. The other option is to set a disk quota specific to that user, along with an appropriate warning level. This setting will override general disk quota settings.

VOLUME JUNCTION POINTS

Volume Junction Points are a rarely used feature of NTFS5. But when this feature is needed, it is one that is greatly appreciated. All previous Microsoft OSs have been limited in the number of physical disks that can be installed on the system by the number of letters in the alphabet.

Since A and B are typically reserved for floppy disk drives, that allowed only twenty-four drive letters for hard disks, CD-ROM drives, CD burners, Zip drives, and so on and so forth.

For the vast majority of users, twenty-four drive letters was more than enough. For huge network storage systems containing seventy-two CD-ROM drives or seventy-two hard disks, it could be a bit of a problem. To accommodate these devices, another OS, such as UNIX, had to be selected.

Volume Junction Points (or Volume Mount Points, as they're also called) allows the user to get around the alphabet limitation. Drives no longer need to be Drive C: or Drive D:. They can now be Drive Oracle or Drive WINNT. Also, they can be physical or logical drives. So network mapped drives can be expanded beyond the alphabet as well.

The way it works is that a folder is created on the root partition with the name of the drive. The only thing contained in this folder is a pointer to the physical location of the drive or partition. There are three utilities provided by Microsoft for creating and managing junction points:

- *LINKD.EXE*: Grafts the target folder into an NTFS folder, displays the target of the junction point, and can be used to delete targets that were originally created by LINKD.EXE.
- *MOUNTVOL.EXE*: Mounts the root folder of the local volume and displays targets of junction points used to mount other volumes. It also lists all local volumes that are available for use by the system and can be used to delete volumes that were created by MOUNTVOL.EXE.
- *DELRP.EXE*: Deletes junction points.

THE WIN2K DISK MANAGEMENT CONSOLE

In WINNT, managing the disks and partitions in the system is the function of the Disk Administrator. In WIN2K these responsibilities have been absorbed into the Computer Management MMC under the Storage folder. **Figure 10.11** shows the MMC opened to Disk Management. With Disk Management, you can create volumes, format volumes with file systems, initialize disks, and create fault-tolerant disk systems. Under WIN2K disk administration, there are a few new tricks the administrator can perform, including the following:

- Create Dynamic Disks
- Manage local drives, or even remote network drives
- Mount drives

Since these are new concepts to WIN2K, they deserve a closer look. I'm going to start with Dynamic Disks, because the Dynamic Disk is what makes a lot of WIN2K's disk management functions possible.

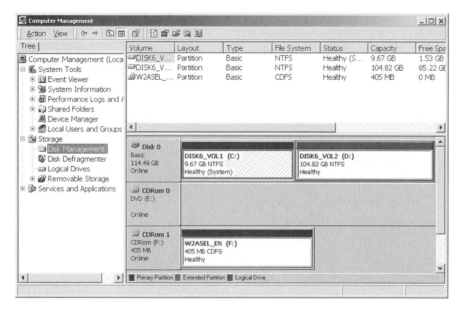

Figure 10.11   The Disk Management MMC

DYNAMIC DISKS

Under WIN2K there are two basic types of physical disk: basic and dynamic. A *basic disk* is any physical disk in the system that can be recognized, but that has not been converted to a dynamic disk. Basic disks adhere to the partition-oriented scheme of file structure typical to previous Microsoft operating systems. When Windows 2000 is first installed, the default configuration for all disks is that of a basic disk.

BUZZ WORDS

Basic disk: A disk that has been configured to conform to the legacy partition-oriented approach to file systems.

Dynamic disk: A disk that has been configured for a file system based on volumes rather than partitions.

Only basic disks are capable of the following functions:

- Creation or deletion of primary and/or extended partitions
- Creation or deletion of logical drives
- Formatting a partition
- Deletion of volume sets, stripe sets, mirror sets, and stripe sets with parity
- Breaking a mirror from a mirror set

Microsoft provides a wizard for upgrading a basic disk to a dynamic disk. A *dynamic disk* is one that is organized into volumes rather than partitions. Once created, a dynamic disk cannot be accessed directly by legacy OSs such as MS-DOS or WIN9x. They are, however, available over the network. Basic and dynamic disks can be used simultaneously on the same computer system, but you cannot mix disk types in a volume set that utilizes multiple physical disks.

Once a disk has been converted over to a dynamic disk, the following functions become available that are possible only on dynamic disks:

- Create and delete simple or spanned volumes, stripe sets, and mirrored or RAID 5 volumes
- Extend volumes
- Break a mirrored volume
- Split a volume into two volumes
- Repair mirrored or RAID 5 volumes
- Reactivate a missing or offline disk
- Revert to a basic disk

Some functions can be performed whether the disk is basic or dynamic:

- View disk properties
- View volume and partition properties
- Manage drive letter assignments for disk volumes or partitions, including CD-ROM devices
- Manage file and folder sharing and establish security for a volume or partition
- Upgrade to a dynamic disk

It should be noted that it is not possible to use dynamic disks on a portable computer. There are also a couple of other limitations that dynamic disks impose. For example, WIN2K cannot be installed onto a existing dynamic volume that was created from unallocated space. The setup program requires information that is supplied by the partition tables. Since unallocated space contains no partition tables, Setup will crash and burn.

REMOTE ADMINISTRATION

With Windows 2000 it becomes possible for the administrator to manage disks that are connected to remote computers. For this to happen the person attempting to manage the volume must have administrative privileges on the remote computer. In addition, the host and the remote computer must either be members of the same domain or a trust must have been established between the domains. To do this, however, you need to make a couple of minor changes to Disk Management. This is another place where MMC comes in handy.

Start MMC (click Start→Run and then type **MMC**). This opens the Microsoft Management console that I discussed earlier in the chapter. On the console menu, select Add/Remove Snap-in. In the window that appears will be a button labeled Add. Scroll down until you see

Disk Management and click Add. The default choice is to manage the local system only. Click Another Computer and either browse to the computer you want to manage, or type in the UNC name for that computer if you already know it. Click Finish, and you now have a console for managing that computer.

CHAPTER SUMMARY

As you can see, WIN2K provides the user and/or administrator with a whole new collection of tools for managing the computing environment. This chapter only touched on some of the major issues.

A key concept introduced in this chapter was NTFS5. Without this new file system, the majority of the other subjects discussed can't exist. Another major topic was Active Directory. Before attempting the exam, make sure you understand the material presented here. Also, the tools described in this chapter are essential for the exam and are useful in real life.

BRAIN DRAIN

1. Which of the topics discussed in this chapter aren't possible without the introduction of NTFS5?

2. Define Active Directory. On what industry standard protocol does Active Directory depend for its services?

3. Describe three MMC consoles that assist the administrator in managing Active Directory components.

4. Discuss Driver Signing and why this tool can protect unwary users.

5. What are some of the major differences between basic and dynamic disks?

THE 64K$ QUESTIONS

1. Which of the following is Active Directory not capable of managing?
   a. Users
   b. Remote Domains
   c. Other Domain Controllers
   d. System Accounts
   e. It manages all of the above.

2. A specific user on the network would be considered by Active Directory to be a(n) _____.
   a. Account
   b. Object
   c. Container
   d. Branch

3. Active Directory is an implementation of the _____ protocol.
   a. DAP
   b. ADS
   c. NetBEUI
   d. LDAP

4. Which of the following is not a predefined MMC console for managing Active Directory?
   a. Active Directory Accounts and Security
   b. Active Directory Users and Computers

c. Active Directory Sites and Services

d. Active Directory Domains and Trusts

5. Information about a remote server would be found in _____.

a. Active Directory Accounts and Security

b. Active Directory Users and Computers

c. Active Directory Sites and Services

d. Active Directory Domains and Trusts

6. WIN2K trusts are considered to be _____.

a. Non-transitive

b. Transparent

c. Bi-directional

d. Transitive

7. New hardware can be configured in the _____ wizard.

a. Add New Hardware

b. Plug 'n Play console

c. Add/Remove Hardware

d. Device Manager

8. The technology that is used by the version of PnP incorporated into WIN2K is called _____.

a. APM BIOS

b. PNPBIOS

c. ACPI

d. Active Scan

9. When a digital signature is added to a device driver, that information is stored in the _____ file.

a. INF

b. VXD

c. DRV

d. CAT

10. Selective encoding and subsequent on-the-fly decoding of data on a WIN2K FAT32 drive is made possible by _____.

a. NTFS 4.51

b. ASPICrypt Technology

c. EFS

d. It isn't possible.

11. Decoding of files encrypted by a disgruntled employee is made possible by way of the _____.

a. EFS Recovery Agent

b. The administrator's Private Key

c. Use of any administrator account

d. It's not possible.

12. Selective File Compression can be accomplished by anyone with _____.

a. Administrative privileges

b. Server Manager privileges

c. Any user can apply compression to any file he or she owns.

d. Any user can apply compression to any file he or she can access.

13. If Disk Quotas have been enabled on a server, the user can double his or her storage capacity by using compression.

a. True

b. False

14. If Disk Quotas have been enabled, the administrator must enforce a maximum disk allocation and a warning level.

a. True

b. False

15. In WIN2K, there is a limit of _____ disk volumes on a system.

    a. 16

    b. 24

    c. 256

    d. There is no limit.

16. You have a disk quota set for 500MB for all users on a system. A new user comes aboard who requires 2GB of storage space. In order to give this person the needed space you must _____.

    a. Change the global allocation to 2GB

    b. Assign the new user Server Manager privileges

    c. Click Quota Entries in the Quota Manager and highlight the new user, assigning the extra space

    d. Place that user's account onto a different volume

17. Which of the following cannot be done on a dynamic disk?

    a. Create extended volumes

    b. Create junction points

    c. Create partitions

    d. You can do anything on a dynamic disk.

18. If you want to _____, you must have a basic disk.

    a. Create a junction point

    b. Create an active partition

    c. Span two volumes

    d. Create a RAID 5 array

19. Managing disks in WIN2K is done in the _____ console.

    a. Disk Management

    b. Disk Administrator

    c. System Applet

    d. System Management

20. Once you've opened the appropriate utility for managing disks in WIN2K, you can manage the disks on a remote device.

    a. True

    b. False

TRICKY TERMINOLOGY

Basic disk: A disk that has been configured to conform to the legacy partition-oriented approach to file systems.

Container: A collection of objects on the system or network that have been gathered together into a single administrative unit.

Digital signature: An encrypted piece of data added to a file to guarantee its authenticity.

Dynamic disk: A disk that has been configured for a file system based on volumes rather than partitions.

Object: In reference to the OS, an object is any single resource on the system and/or network, including files, users, or devices.

ACRONYM ALERT

ACPI: Advanced Configuration and Power Interface. An upgrade to the PnP functionality of Windows.

APM BIOS: Advanced Power Management Basic Input Output Services

CAT: Catalog File. A compressed file in Windows that contains driver signing information.

EFS: Encrypting File System. A functionality of the NTFS 5 file system that allows individual files or directories to be encrypted on the fly.

LAN: Local Area Network

LDAP: Lightweight Directory Access Protocol. A protocol that allows network resources to be browsed in a manner similar to local disk drives.

WAN: Wide Area Network

WHQL: Windows Hardware Quality Lab. A division of Microsoft that tests hardware and driver functionality in the Windows OS. There are some who might say this is an oxymoron.

CHAPTER 11

INTRODUCING XP

Windows XP was released in October of 2001 as a result of Microsoft's resolve to move desktop computers into a truly 32-bit world. There was a great deal of brouhaha surrounding this release. Microsoft even posted a large and very detailed page on its Web site outlining dozens of "new features" in XP.

In truth, XP is a slightly improved version of WIN2K with a few added features and a facelift. The vast majority of the new features listed on Microsoft's site had already existed in WIN2K. There were a number of features that were tweaked a bit, but the majority were familiar friends who'd had cosmetic surgery. There are, however, a few brand new features in XP worth discussing. And since there was a major change in the interface, I'll spend some time on that as well.

A+ OPERATING SYSTEM TECHNOLOGIES EXAM OBJECTIVES

CompTIA objectives covered in this chapter include the following:

1.1   Identify the major desktop components and interfaces and their functions. Differentiate the characteristics of Windows 9x/Me, Windows NT 4.0 Workstation, Windows 2000 Professional, and Windows XP.

2.3   Identify the basic system boot sequences and boot methods, including the steps to create an emergency boot disk with utilities installed for Windows 9x/Me, Windows NT 4.0 Workstation, Windows 2000 Professional, and Windows XP.

2.4   Identify procedures for installing/adding a device, including loading, adding, and configuring device drivers and required software.

THE WINDOWS XP VERSIONS

Initially XP was released in three versions, with an intent that a server version would follow. However, Microsoft's .NET technology superceded XP and, until the release of Windows 2003 Server, was the only alternative to WIN2K server versions for an NOS in the Microsoft world.

A little later, two modified versions of XP were released. To summarize, the five versions of XP are listed here:

- XP Home Edition
- XP Professional Edition
- XP Tablet PC Edition
- XP Media Center Edition
- XP 64-bit Edition

XP HOME EDITION

As its name implies, this is the OS Microsoft targets as the single stand-alone PC that gets used mostly for games and a few productivity applications. Although it can be networked, it cannot be made to join a domain. Therefore, it is not suitable for the corporate environment. A small peer-to-peer network is possible.

Think of XP Home Edition as a replacement for WIN9x users. XP Home does not support SMP. If installed onto a system with multiple processors, the extra processors will not be recognized or used.

XP PROFESSIONAL EDITION

For users who took advantage of the features of WINNT Workstation or WIN2K Professional, and for computers that exist in a network domain, XP Professional is the appropriate choice. XP Professional also integrates a number of additional security measures not present in Home Edition, including the following:

- *EFS*: Discussed in Chapter Ten, WIN2K System Administration.
- *Remote Desktop*: Allows a computer to be used from anywhere on the network.
- *Offline File and Folder Synchronization*: Files that are normally stored on the network can be downloaded and subsequently used offline. Changes can then be synchronized with the network version. Offline folders can be encrypted for security.
- *Windows Management Instrumentation*: Allows remote monitoring and management of networked systems.
- *Dual Processor Support*
- *Active Directory Support*: Allows the computer to be joined to a domain.

Minimum requirements for XP Home and Professional are listed in **Table 11.1**.

> **EXAM NOTE:** Note that with XP, it is possible to be asked for both absolute minimum hardware requirements as well as minimum recommended requirements. Make sure that you know both.

Table 11.1 Minimum Requirements for Installing XP Home
or Professional Edition

Resource	Min.	Recommended
CPU	300MHz PII	500MHz PIII
RAM	128MB	256MB+
Disk Space	1.5GB	N/A
Video	800x600 SVGA	N/A
Other Media	CD-ROM or compatible device	

Remember, the minimum requirements are not the same as the recommended
requirements.

XP TABLET PC EDITION

Microsoft was quick to recognize the popularity of the new tablet PCs. These are devices that combine many of the features of a laptop computer with the features most desirable in a hand-held device. Instead of using a physical keyboard, a user inputs information either through an optional detachable keyboard, or simply by jotting it directly on the screen. The OS uses hand-writing recognition technology to convert the user's scribbles into data the tablet PC can use.

Most Microsoft Office applications can be run on this OS, with a few minor caveats. For one, as of this writing, Word and Outlook don't support handwriting recognition technology. And if you choose to send your handwritten messages by email, they can be sent only as GIF image files. This might cause issues for users who block email messages containing attachments from unfamiliar sources.

XP 64-BIT EDITION

Obviously a major difference found in this version is the fact that it supports 64-bit micropro-cessors. However, the advantages reach farther than that. The 64-bit address spaces allow it to address up to 16GB of physical RAM and up to 8 *terabytes* of virtual RAM. This allows applications to work with incredibly large data sets without excessive paging calls slowing the system. In terms of user operability, the OS is similar to XP Professional Edition.

AN OVERVIEW OF XP FEATURES

As I mentioned in the introduction to this chapter, many of the so-called new features of XP are actually features of WIN2K that received a facelift before being migrated over. For the most part, XP has the same basic engine as WIN2K and offers the same features. There are a few brand new embellishments as well. First, I'll examine some of the migrated features, and then I'll go over some new additions.

> **Exam Note:** Be able to distinguish between features that are new to XP and those that were brought over from other OSs. Also make sure that you know from which OS a migrated feature originated.

Migrated Features

Many of the features of WIN2K were inserted into XP with absolutely no changes made. Microsoft figured those features worked well enough. Some features were redesigned for better functionality. Among the changed features are the following:

- Encrypting File System (EFS)
- System Restore
- Network Installation
- Dynamic Update
- Group Policy Management

EFS

Although EFS isn't new to XP, it provides a major improvement over WIN2K's rendition. In XP, EFS has been enabled with multiuser support.

WIN2K users could encrypt their files, but once encrypted those files could not be accessed by other users. This was not very conducive to group efforts. If a file had to be accessed by several users, the security of encryption was not an option that could be employed. With XP Professional, a file can be encrypted and accessed by a group of users.

System Restore

Technically speaking, WIN2K did not have a System Restore utility. This is something borrowed from WINMe. With WIN2K, if a new driver or application is installed that prevents the system from working properly, the only options are to use Last Known Good or the ERD.

With System Restore, if a system running XP fails to boot normally, or is functioning erratically, the user can "go back in time" to a system configuration that existed before the offending changes were made. It does so by using *restore points*. A restore point is a copy of critical system files and registry entries that were in use before a system change occurred. When a restore point is created, copies of critical system files are made and stored in a hidden directory. The restore point points to that directory, and when called upon, uses those files to copy over the files that aren't working correctly in the target directory.

System Restore automatically creates a restore point every twenty-four hours, if this feature is enabled. It also allows the user to manually establish a restore point. You can store up to three weeks worth of past restore points. The number of restore

> **Buzz Words**
>
> **Restore point:** A copy of system files and registry entries that were in place at the time a major system change was introduced.

points you can save depends on how much disk space you allocate to restore points. This can be up to 12 percent of available disk space.

NETWORK INSTALLATION

Network installation has been an option in Microsoft OSs for the past several versions. XP improves on this by enhancing the security of the process. Using a utility called SysPrep, the administrator can install the OS on a number of machines simultaneously over the network using an image file. This image file can include configuration settings and applications as well as the basic installation of the OS. This can be used in conjunction with Dynamic Update to make rollouts of multiple machines faster and more efficient.

DYNAMIC UPDATE

In Chapter Ten, I discussed how Windows Update could keep the system more secure by ensuring that the most recent service packs and file versions were installed on the computer. Dynamic Update takes this process to the next level. With Dynamic Update, the system automatically logs onto Microsoft's Updates page as soon as the OS is installed and immediately downloads new files and service packs. It can then be left running in the background. On a scheduled basis, it will check with Microsoft, and if there are new files, these files will be downloaded. Of course, this is only done with the user's permission. Dynamic Update can be disabled at any time, and any downloads can be refused or aborted if already in progress.

GROUP POLICY MANAGEMENT

To review, the ability to administer group policies was introduced in WINNT. Group policies allow the administrator to establish a predefined set of rules and to enforce those rules for everyone who uses the system. Group policies can also be used across the network.

XP improves on this feature in two ways. First off, there are more than a hundred new policies the administrator can enforce. So if you think your network administrator was hard-core before, wait until he or she gets a hold of this! The other new feature that has been welcomed by the IT industry with enthusiasm is a feature called Resultant Set of Policy (RSoP).

RSoP is a feature that lets the administrator create a new policy and try it out on a small group of guinea pigs before enforcing on every system. This way the ramifications of a new policy can be examined before an overly restrictive policy plays havoc on the network. After the policy has been fully tested and approved, it can then be globally applied.

COMPLETELY NEW FEATURES IN XP

Although XP is primarily WIN2K with a coat of whitewash, it is not without some completely new features. Some of these enhance performance; some enhance stability. Among the totally new features that I will discuss are the following:

- Side-by-side DLL support
- Integrated CDR/CD-RW write capabilities

- Remote Desktop
- ClearType
- Network Location Awareness
- Device Driver Rollback
- Product Activation

Side-By-Side DLL Support

With all previous versions of Windows, there could be only a single instance of any given system file. Critical files, such as DLLs, often make a difference as to whether a program runs properly or crashes. Old DLLs were overwritten by newer versions. Older programs that used a particular DLL had no choice but to use the newer version. The vast majority of the time this wasn't a problem. Side-by-side DLL support allows Windows to keep both versions on the system and run them simultaneously.

Integrated CDR/CD-RW Write Capabilities

In order to get a CDR or CD-RW to work on older versions of Windows, a third-party application needed to be installed. With XP, the device becomes another removable media device. Files can be added to the device in a simple drag and drop operation. For more sophisticated CD production, a third-party utility might still be eminently more usable by a large number of users.

Remote Desktop

In the past, there has been a fairly strong market for programs that allowed a user on the go to connect up to his or her home or office computer and run it from a laptop or other remote computer. After all, users are more familiar with their own setup than they are a computer they've never seen. Remote Desktop is a feature that makes use of the Remote Desktop Protocol (RDP) to allow this to happen. Once logged on, the local computer displays the desktop and allows browsing of all the resources stored on the remote computer.

ClearType

Almost anyone who looks at an XP desktop for the first time remarks on how much sharper and cleaner the display looks. It's almost like buying a new monitor. ClearType is a technology that allows the graphics adapter to display screens that triple the horizontal resolution of text. This doesn't work with graphical images, and it is software driven.

> **Exam Note:** It would be a very good idea to know the functionality of both ClearType technology and Network Location Awareness (NLA).

NETWORK LOCATION AWARENESS

Network Location Awareness is a feature built into Microsoft that allows a computer to be a member of several different networks, and yet always know what to do, regardless of which network it is on at the moment. Different situations that would result in a multinetworked computer could include a portable system that moves from office to office. Or it could be a home- or office-based computer that maintains simultaneous connections between two different networks. For example, a home-networked computer that has a VPN established with the corporate offices over dialup would be a member of two different networks at the same time.

NLA can automatically detect logical network interface conditions and properly associate them with the physical attributes of the system. Logical information would come in two forms. Logical Network Identity, as the name implies, identifies which network the system is trying to join. In descending order, NLA uses the network's domain name, static information read from the registry, or finally the subnet of the network. The other form of logical network information is the Logical Network Interface. Each physical interface, including NICs and modems, and each logical interface, such as a RAS connection, is assigned an AdapterName value. The IP Helper API is a piece of software located in Windows that automatically configures each logical interface, binding the configuration to the AdapterName.

DEVICE DRIVER ROLLBACK

Have you ever downloaded a new driver for your computer, installed it, and then had the entire system go down in flames because the driver didn't work right? This can happen from a corrupted download or simply because the wrong driver was downloaded by accident and was not compatible with the device or the OS. Of course, this doesn't always result in system failure. More often than not, you simply can't get the device to work no matter how hard you try.

Device Driver Rollback copies all files related to a specific driver to another location. If the new driver turns out to be a disaster, it is a simple matter of reinstalling the older driver until it can be determined what the problem with the new driver is.

PRODUCT ACTIVATION

Product activation is a feature that really doesn't help the user all that much. It's present simply so that the same OS cannot be installed on more than one computer. This prevents software piracy from occurring on such a regular basis. With product activation, there are two processes involved in proving ownership of a license to run the OS. During installation, the user will be prompted to enter a product key. This is a long series of letters and numbers that is virtually impossible to type without mistake. When the product key is properly inserted, the OS installs.

BUZZ WORDS ————

Product activation: A newer technology that requires the end user to physically activate the product through a database managed by the product's manufacturer. This prevents the product from being installed on multiple machines.

Product activation is a separate process and is usually run concurrently with product registration. To the beginner, it may appear that these two processes are one and the same, but they are not. Product activation is mandatory and must be done within thirty days of installation, or the OS will stop functioning (except for the activation feature). Product activation collects no personal information to be transmitted to Microsoft's site. During installation a unique number called the Installation ID is generated. When users activate their software, the Installation ID and the product key are transmitted to Microsoft. This information is stored in a database. An attempt to install the OS using the same product key will fail.

Product registration is *not* required. Product registration will register you in Microsoft's database of users. However, to get the limited product support Microsoft offers, it should be done. You will also automatically be notified whenever new product updates are available.

WINDOWS XP INSTALLATION AND BOOT PROCESS

For almost every part of the XP installation process and boot sequence I can say, "See WIN2K." The differences are very few. But there are differences. Much of the reason for these differences is Microsoft's new product activation feature, which is something that cannot be turned off.

INSTALLATION DIFFERENCES

Installing XP looks, feels, and smells no different than installing WIN2K. You will go through the same basic steps. If using the upgrade version, you will still have the option of doing an upgrade or a clean install. As with WIN2K, unless there is an overpowering reason for performing an upgrade, the clean install is the way to go. If you choose to perform a clean install from an upgrade CD, make sure you have a CD for a qualifying OS at hand. During setup from the upgrade, there is a point where it will check for a specific file on the CD and compare its attributes and file size to some predefined values.

One major difference becomes evident when the installation is completed. If there is an Internet connection present and available, Setup automatically prompts you to connect to the Microsoft Activation server and activate your software. You will have the option of doing this by telephone, but the Internet activation is faster and simpler.

THE XP BOOT PROCESS

The XP boot process is virtually identical to WIN2K up to the point where NTLDR loads. As with WIN2K, the boot process is broken into stages. The XP stages are

- Initial Boot Loader
- Operating System Selection
- Hardware Detection
- Configuration Selection

INITIAL BOOT LOADER

During this stage, NTLDR switches the CPU from real mode to protected mode. From this point, memory will be read in 32-bit format. Also, the paging services are started, and the Windows Paging file is loaded. Based on the file system that was detected when the MBR was read, the correct file system drivers are loaded at this point. Then NTLDR moves into the next stage.

OPERATING SYSTEM SELECTION

Assuming that XP is the only OS loaded on this system, this is a very short phase. In the event of a multiboot system, it can become a bit more complex. NTLDR locates and loads the BOOT.INI file. The operating system options are displayed on the screen with the default OS highlighted for the number of seconds defined in the **TIMEOUT=** line of BOOT.INI. When a selection has been made, either automatically by the OS or manually by the user, the steps taken by NTLDR are identical to the WIN2K process. One difference in XP is that, if BOOT.INI cannot be located, NTLDR will attempt to load XP from the first partition of the first physical disk defined in the BIOS. If XP was installed onto that partition, then XP can load without the services of BOOT.INI.

It is also during this phase that NTLDR provides the <F8> option for loading the Advanced Boot options. These are identical to the Advanced Boot options of WIN2K and will not be discussed again here.

HARDWARE DETECTION

This is another phase that is identical to WIN2K. NTLDR locates and loads the file NTDETECT.COM. NTDETECT.COM scans the system for any hardware installed on the system and generates a list. NTDETECT.COM loads this list into memory, and NTLDR will later use it to generate the HKEY_LOCAL_MACHINE\HARDWARE hive of the registry.

CONFIGURATION SELECTION

This is another stage that is incredibly short if only a single hardware profile has been configured onto the system. If multiple profiles are configured, then the user will be shown a list of available profiles and have thirty seconds to make a selection before the default profile is loaded.

THE XP LOAD PROCESS

Now that the computer system is ready, the OS can complete the process of initialization. The first step of the load process is kernel load. The user can tell when kernel load had begun. This is when the screen clears and the progression of white markers starts marching across the bottom of the screen. While this is happening, NTLDR is finding and loading HAL.DLL. This loads the hardware abstraction layer that provides the barrier between the OS or applications running on the OS and the physical hardware. Next NTLDR loads the boot device drivers and relinquishes control of the load process to NTOSKRNL.EXE.

Next comes kernel initialization. Kernel initialization can be broken down into two sub-phases. During the first sub-phase, physical interrupts are completely disabled. After this, the second sub-phase begins to load the Executive services in this order:

- Object Manager
- Executive
- Microkernel
- Security Reference Monitor
- Memory Manager
- Cache Manager
- LPCS
- I/O Manager
- Process Manager

The I/O Manager can now assume the responsibility of locating and loading the various device drivers and all the files associated with those drivers. Should any driver fail to properly initialize, the OS will do one of two things. If the CPU can recover from the failure, it will reboot the system and attempt to load using Last Known Good. If it cannot, the adored BSOD will appear, and the user will be forced to manually reboot.

Next the Session Manager subsystem loads. This is the part of the XP kernel that allows the multiuser environment that has made XP so popular. It is *not* here, however that user logon occurs. The next file to load is WIN32K.SYS. This is the XP graphics subsystem. Any services that have been configured either by the user or by the system to be AUTO-START services will now load as well.

Now WINLOGON.EXE loads as an XP system service. The first thing WINLOGON.EXE does is locate and load LSASS.EXE. Here is where XP Pro and XP Home differ. With Pro, the network logon screen will appear. If Home Edition is installed, the pretty little screen with icons for the various users will be displayed. With Pro, the user types in his or her credentials and LSASS.EXE compares them to the information stored in SAM. This security is not enforced in Home Edition. Users have the option of securing their accounts with passwords or not. If password security is not selected, simply clicking the icon will load the user profile.

When the logon has been deemed successful by WINLOGON.EXE, Last Known Good information is written to the registry. Users are logged into their profiles, and the XP Load process is completed.

THE XP INTERFACE

Superficially, XP has undergone what appears to be a complete transformation. To the experienced Windows user, it can be a little intimidating at first. The Start button and taskbar don't look the same. When you open the Start menu for the first time, it's almost like entering a whole new world. Power users and technicians are presented with a completely different approach to the Control Panel.

If you really don't want to learn a whole new interface, don't panic. It's possible to select options that present the older WIN2K menus. Of course, rehashing old stuff doesn't make for a good book, so in this section, I'm going to take the updated Start menu and Control Panel apart and show you how they've changed in XP.

THE START MENU

The Start menu (**Figure 11.1**) in XP was redesigned from the ground up in a manner intended to make it easier to reach the most recently accessed programs without having to sift through rarely used applications. This is similar to the personalized menus in WIN2K, but takes a more sophisticated approach. In addition, commonly accessed system functions, such as the Control Panel and My Computer, have been more conspicuously placed.

EXAM NOTE: As far as XP is concerned, the majority of exam questions are likely to center on the Start menu and Control Panel. Read the following sections carefully.

The XP Start menu is divided into two sections. The programs list can be found on the left side. The programs list has actually been divided into three sections. The first section (located at the top) is called the *pinned list.* The pinned list is similar to the Favorites list in other

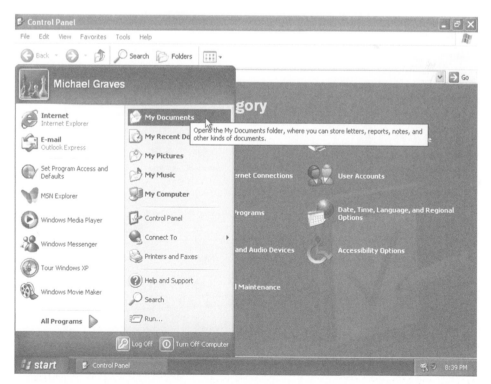

Figure 11.1   The XP Start menu in all its glory

Windows OSs and applications such as Internet Explorer. A user can place shortcuts to applications that are used day in and day out in this section. Default shortcuts that appear in the pinned list include the user's Web browser of choice and email client.

Any program can be added to the pinned list. Simply right-click the item in any Explorer window.

Buzz Words ───────────

Pinned list: A list of shortcuts to applications that are used on a regular basis.

In the popup menu that appears (**Figure 11.2**), click Pin to Start Menu. Another way an item can be added is by dragging and dropping it to the Start button or the Start menu. If a user no longer wants an item to be a part of the pinned list, it can be removed from this list by right-clicking it and clicking Unpin from Start Menu or Remove from This List. If a user is not happy with the order in which the items appear on this list, he or she can rearrange them simply by dragging and dropping items to the preferred position.

Beneath the pinned list is the Most Frequently Used (MFU) list. There is a separator line that divides the two sections. Windows keeps track of how often programs are used and displays the ones used most frequently on top, while programs that are rarely used appear on the bottom. A program that is no longer wanted on the list can be removed by right-clicking the shortcut and then clicking Remove from This List. One thing that might irk a meticulously organized user is the fact that items in this list cannot be manually arranged.

Figure 11.2 Adding a program to the pinned list is as easy as a couple of mouse clicks.

Beneath the MFU list is another horizontal line, and beneath that line is the All Programs option. Clicking that option will open a list of all applications installed on the system.

The section of the Start menu on the right-hand side provides links to user folders, such as My Documents, My Pictures, and My Music, and to frequently accessed system areas such as My Computer, Search, and Control Panel.

The Start menu that appears is specific to the profile that is selected at startup. If a user chooses to configure his or her menu differently, that is easily done. By right-clicking the Start button or by right-clicking any empty area within the Start menu, a user can make changes to the way the Start menu appears. This includes selecting the "Classic" Windows menu. This choice will make the start menu look and feel like the WIN2K menu. A user's changes will be evident only when that user is logged on. They will not affect other users on the system.

THE CONTROL PANEL

For the vast majority of users, the change in XP that gave them the most pause was Control Panel (**Figure 11.3**). Microsoft's approach to system management was so drastically changed

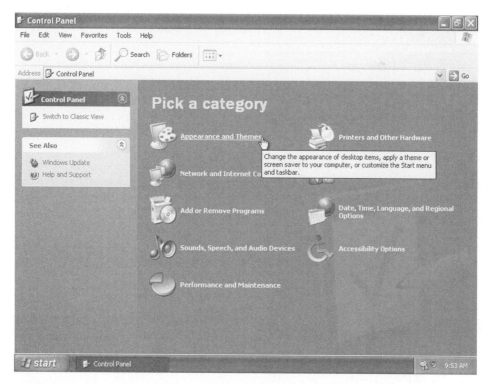

Figure 11.3 The XP Control Panel has been subdivided into several sections for better organization.

that even veteran technicians found themselves lost at first. However, once people got used to the new approach, most began to appreciate the change. The new Control Panel divides the different applets into specific categories, rather than piling them all into a single screen, arranged in alphabetical order. The categories include the following:

- Appearance and Themes
- Network and Internet Connections
- Add or Remove Programs
- Sounds, Speech, and Audio Devices
- Performance and Maintenance
- Printers and Other Hardware
- User Accounts
- Date, Time, Language, and Regional Options
- Accessibility Options

In each section, the user will be presented with shortcuts to specific tasks and shortcuts to Control Panel applets. This is handy because the user need not navigate through a number of different folders and/or menu items to get to a commonly used task such as adjusting screen resolution.

> **EXAM NOTE:** The key to the following sections is not so much to remember where all the shortcuts to the tasks are as it is to learn the shortcuts to Control Panel applets. Make sure you know where each Control Panel applet can be found in the various sections. CompTIA is more interested in the applets.

APPEARANCE AND THEMES

Appearance and Themes (**Figure 11.4**) is the collection of utilities that allows the user to configure how the desktop and applications appear to the eye. Features like colors, fonts, background pictures, and so forth are selected here. There are four tasks that can be performed here:

- *Change the computer's theme.* This option allows the user to choose between a variety of different preconfigured themes. A theme basically consists of colors and fonts that have been selected to work well together, as well as a default screen saver and background picture.
- *Change the desktop background.* This brings up a large selection of different choices of desktop patterns or photographs. Users can also select from custom designed bitmaps of their own choosing.

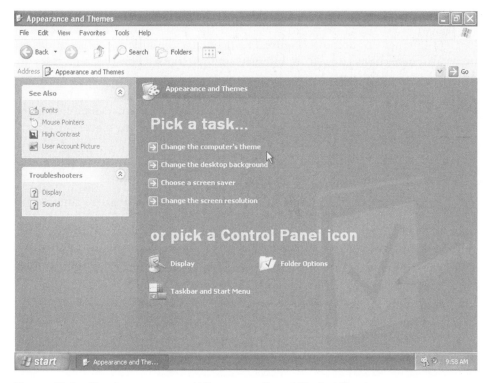

Figure 11.4   The Appearance and Themes section of Control Panel

■ *Choose a screen saver.* When a screen saver is selected, after a predesignated amount of time the image displayed on the screen when the user last left it is blanked out and the selected screensaver image appears on the screen in its place, randomly moving from position to position. The prevents a phenomenon called monitor burn-in.

■ *Change the screen resolution.* At the risk of sounding overly technical, this is where the user goes to change the dots per inch that the graphics adapter will use to create the images on the screen.

There are three Control Panel applets that have shortcuts in this section. Since these work exactly the same way they did in WIN2K and were described in detail in earlier chapters, they will not be described again here.

■ Display

■ Task Bar and Start Menu

■ Folder Options

NETWORK AND INTERNET CONNECTIONS

Network and Internet Connections (**Figure 11.5**) contains the various configurations for both local network connections as well as Internet configurations. The different tasks that are available include the following:

- *Set up or change your Internet connection:* A new Internet account can be configured here, or changes in the configuration of an existing account can be made.
- *Create a connection to the network at your workplace:* This is a more user-friendly way of telling users that they will be creating a virtual private network (VPN). A VPN is a secure connection to a remote LAN over the Internet.
- *Set up or change your home or small office network:* LAN settings are adjusted here.

There are also two Control Panel applets located in this section:

- Internet Options
- Network Connections

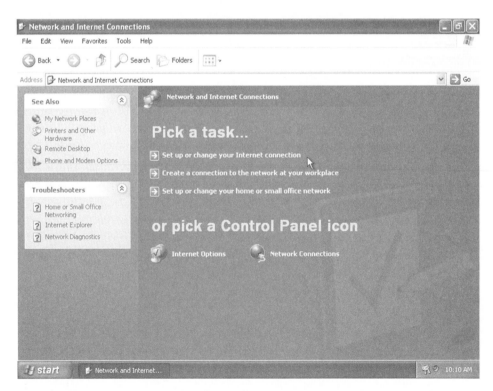

Figure 11.5 Network and Internet Connections

ADD/REMOVE PROGRAMS

The Add/Remove Programs (**Figure 11.6**) function of XP really isn't all that much different than in WIN2K. The real difference is that Microsoft brought all the functions out front where the user can see them. There are four functions available here.

- *Change or Remove Programs*: Any time the user wants to uninstall a program, Add/Remove Change or Remove is the correct procedure. It is very rare that any changes can be made to a program once installed.

- *Add New Programs*: Allows the user to install new applications from CD or floppy disk, over the network, or from a Microsoft Update over the Internet.

- *Add/Remove Windows Components*: During a typical installation, there is a large number of features available to the user that do not get installed by default. Other features may have been added that are not useful. This utility allows the user to take out unused features and add those that were not originally installed. The original installation CD will be required for adding features.

- *Set Program Access and Defaults*: This is where users can select their preferences for the default program to open different file types and to select default email clients and Web browsers.

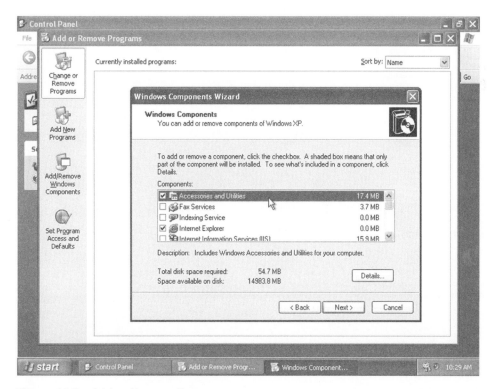

Figure 11.6   Add or Remove Programs

SOUNDS, SPEECH, AND AUDIO DEVICES

Windows XP is designed to be a multimedia OS. As such, it can be configured to play sounds to alert the user to specific events. It can also talk to you! Of course, for that to happen, the computer's hardware has to support these functions and be properly configured. The Sounds, Speech, and Audio Devices screen (**Figure 11.7**) is where the user makes all that happen.

There are three tasks and two Control Panel applets accessible from this section. The tasks, which are all self-explanatory, include the following:

- Adjust the system volume
- Change the sound scheme
- Change the speaker settings

The Control Panel applets are

- *Sounds and Audio Devices*: Hardware configuration and driver options for the audio portion of multimedia
- *Speech*: Allows the user to select the voice that will issue from the computer and how quickly the voice will speak if the Text to Speech function is enabled and selected.

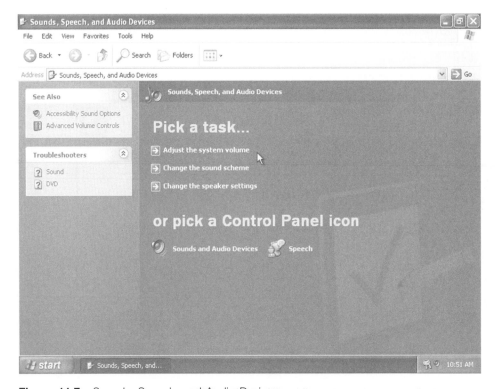

Figure 11.7   Sounds, Speech, and Audio Devices

PERFORMANCE AND MAINTENANCE

The Performance and Maintenance section (**Figure 11.8**) is one of the busiest of Control Panel's sublevels. In this grouping there are five different tasks and four different Control Panel applets available. The tasks include the following:

- *See basic information about your computer*. This function simply lists the configuration of the system. No changes can be made.
- *Adjust visual effects*. Here, the user can adjust a large number of different settings such as fading menus, animated windows, shadows, and various other items that make Windows more or less pretty.
- *Free up space on your hard disk*. This is a maintenance utility that looks for duplicate files, temporary files, temporary Internet files, and files in the Recycle Bin that can be safely deleted.
- *Back up your data*. This is a shortcut to the Windows Backup utility. This is very similar to the utility described in Chapter Ten, WIN2K System Administration.
- *Rearrange items on your hard drive to make programs run faster:* This is a shortcut to the Defrag utility.

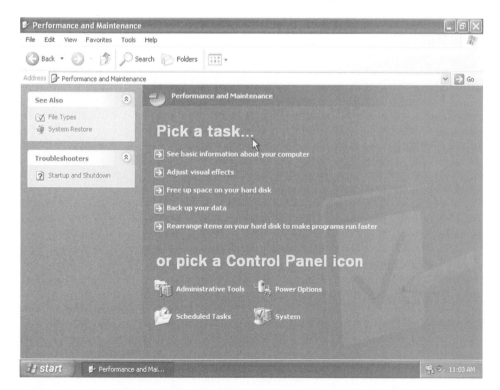

Figure 11.8 The Performance and Maintenance window

There are four Control Panel applets located here:

- Administrative Tools
- Scheduled Tasks
- Power Options
- System

PRINTERS AND OTHER HARDWARE

The place to configure graphical devices, such as printers, fax devices, digital cameras, and scanners, as well as other input devices, including the mouse, modem, and keyboard, is the Printers and Other Hardware section (**Figure 11.9**). There are two tasks and six Control Panel applets available from this screen.

The tasks include the following:

- *View installed printers or fax printers.* Allows the user to check the status and/or properties of a specific device already installed on the system.
- *Add a printer.* Allows the user to install a new device.

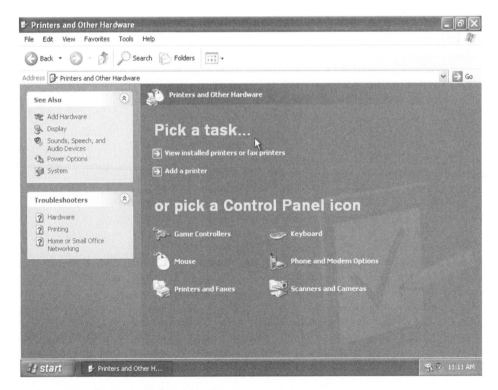

Figure 11.9 Printers and Other Hardware

The Control Panel applets found here include:

- Game Controllers
- Mouse
- Printers and Faxes
- Keyboard
- Phone and Modem Options
- Scanners and Cameras

USER ACCOUNTS

If a new user needs to be added to the system, an old user removed, or the security settings of an account changed, the User Accounts window (**Figure 11.10**) is the place to be. This is one Control Panel section that does not have a shortcut to a specific Control Panel applet. There are three basic tasks that have shortcuts here:

- *Change an account*: Personal information about users can be edited, and security settings can be modified to existing accounts. There are shortcuts at the bottom of the screen

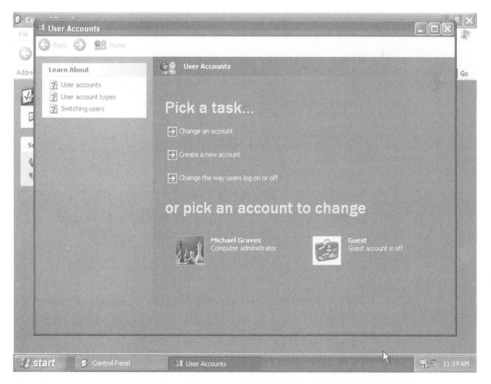

Figure 11.10 User Accounts

to go directly to existing user accounts. You must be logged on to an account with full administrative features to use this function.

■ *Create a new account:* Self-explanatory, I hope.

■ *Change the way users log on or off:* The basic Welcome screen of XP Home edition can be used in place of the network logon screen if security is not an issue. Fast User Switching allows one user to log off and another to log on without closing programs.

DATE, TIME, LANGUAGE, AND REGIONAL OPTIONS

Most of these adjustments should be self-explanatory, although the regional options might not be familiar to all. The Date, Time, Language, and Regional Options screen (**Figure 11.11**) allows users to adjust the real time clock and calendar however they see fit. Languages other than the English language are available as well. The regional options allows users to select the symbols used for currency, and set other configurations, such as how the time and date are displayed, based on local custom. There are three tasks that can be accessed from here:

■ Change the date and time

■ Change the format of numbers, dates, and times

■ Add other languages

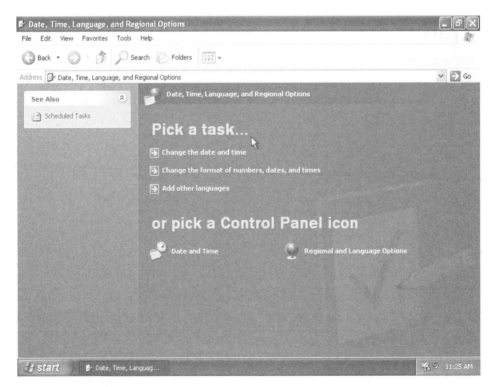

Figure 11.11 Date, Time, Language, and Regional Options

There are two Control Panel applets that can be accessed:

■ Date and Time
■ Regional and Language Options

ACCESSIBILITY OPTIONS

The final category in the Control Panel collection is the area where Accessibility Options are adjusted (**Figure 11.12**). Windows XP enables people with impaired hearing to replace the sound effects with visual effects. Likewise, people with eyesight problems can use audible menus and enhanced contrast screens. There are two tasks available here:

■ Adjust the contrast for text and colors on your screen
■ Configure Windows to work for your vision, hearing, and mobility needs

The one Control Panel applet located here is Accessibility Options.

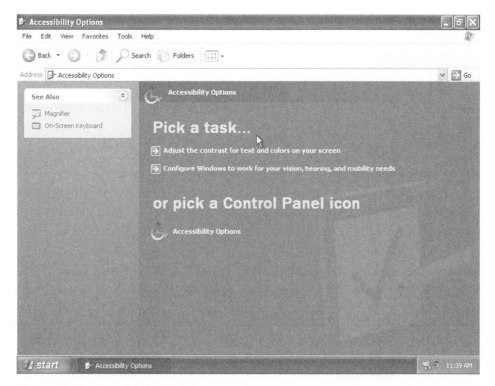

Figure 11.12 Accessibility Options

Chapter Summary

Although XP is touted as the latest and greatest of Microsoft's desktop OSs, in reality, it's nothing more than an old engine mounted into a fancy new body. A few tweaks here and there give it a bit more speed and stability. A few new toys make it more attractive to the users. But under the pretty new skin, it's not that much different from WIN2K.

Important differences to remember, though, are the subdivision of the Control Panel and the Layout of the Start menu. In addition, remember that XP now offers drag-and-drop functionality for CD-RWs.

Brain Drain

1. List the various versions of Windows XP that are available, and discuss how they differ from one another.

2. What are some features that migrated over to XP from Windows 2000 but that offer enhanced functionality in XP?

3. List some features that are brand new to XP. Discuss how they improve the product.

4. Discuss the new layout of the Start menu and how it can improve usability of the OS.

5. How is Control Panel different between XP and WIN2K?

The 64K$ Questions

1. Two of the limitations of Home Edition are that _____.
   a. It only supports one CPU
   b. It doesn't offer EFS
   c. It only supports five users per system
   d. It cannot join a domain

2. The only networking capability offered by XP Home is Internet connectivity.

   a. True
   b. False

3. XP Home requires a minimum of _____ RAM in order to run.
   a. 64MB
   b. 128MB
   c. 256MB
   d. None of the above

4. XP Professional requires a minimum of _____ RAM in order to run.
   a. 64MB
   b. 128MB
   c. 256MB
   d. None of the above

5. The absolute minimum CPU required by either Home or Professional is a _____.
   a. 266MHz PII
   b. 300MHz PII
   c. 300MHz PIII
   d. 500MHz PIII

6. XP Professional supports a maximum of _____ CPUs on a system.
   a. 1
   b. 2
   c. 4
   d. 8

7. The feature that was added to EFS that makes it different between XP and WIN2K is _____.
   a. The administrator can decrypt files
   b. A public key that will open the files is deposited in a hidden read-only directory
   c. Files can be encrypted for use by entire groups instead of only individuals
   d. There is no difference.

8. System Restore is a function that migrated over to XP from _____.
   a. WIN98SE
   b. WINMe
   c. WIN2K SP3
   d. It's a new feature.

9. Which of the following is not a new feature to XP?
   a. Group Policy Management
   b. Side-by-side DLL support
   c. ClearType
   d. Device Driver Rollback

10. You must register XP within thirty days, or it will lose functionality.
    a. True
    b. False

11. You can take over control of another user's system to help with a problem because of a protocol known as _____.
    a. Remote Systems Management Protocol
    b. Systems Management Services Protocol
    c. Remote Desktop Protocol
    d. Long Distance Management Protocol

12. ClearType works by _____.
    a. Improving the vertical resolution of text
    b. Improving the horizontal resolution of text
    c. Improving both the horizontal and vertical resolution of text
    d. Redefining the screen font used by text

13. XP offers two methods of recovering from an improperly installed device driver. What are these two methods?
    a. Auto-recovery
    b. Driver Signing
    c. Device Driver Rollback
    d. System Restore

14. The following information is transmitted to Microsoft when you activate XP.
    a. Name, address, and email address
    b. CPU serial number
    c. The file allocation tables on your hard drive
    d. The Installation ID

15. The Start menu in XP is divided into _____ sections.
    a. 1
    b. 2
    c. 3
    d. 4

16. The one section of the XP Start menu that cannot be edited by the user is _____.
    a. The pinned list
    b. The MFU
    c. All Programs
    d. The user can modify all sections of the Start menu

17. If you need to check the settings of your sound card's device driver, you would find them in the _____ section of Control Panel. (Choose all that apply.)

    a. Sounds, Speech, and Audio Devices

    b. Performance and Maintenance

    c. Printers and Other Hardware

    d. Accessibility Options

18. A digital camera can be managed from the _____ section of Control Panel.

    a. Sounds, Speech, and Audio Devices

    b. Performance and Maintenance

    c. Printers and Other Hardware

    d. Accessibility Options

19. Which of the following is not an adjustment a user can make in Accessibility Options?

    a. Screen contrast

    b. Speech options

    c. Text size

    d. Mouse cursor trails

20. Into how many different sections has Control Panel been divided in XP?

    a. 6

    b. 7

    c. 8

    d. 9

TRICKY TERMINOLOGY

Pinned list: A list of shortcuts to applications that are used on a regular basis.

Product activation: A newer technology that requires the end user to physically activate the product through a database managed by the product's manufacturer. This prevents the product from being installed on multiple machines.

Restore point: A copy of system files and registry entries that were in place at the time a major system change was introduced.

ACRONYM ALERT

MFU: Most Frequently Used. The portion of the XP Start menu that displays applications that have been opened over a predefined period of time, in the order which they were opened. Apps are displayed from most recently used to least recently.

NLA: Network Location Awareness. A feature in XP that automatically configures a computer system to the network or subnet to which the device is attached.

RDP: Remote Desktop Protocol. A protocol that allows remote administration of another computer over the network.

RSoP: Resultant Set of Policy. A feature in XP that allows the administrator to test the results of a new policy on a select group of guinea pigs before inflicting it on the entire network.

CHAPTER 12

INTRODUCING LINUX

Up until this point, you were probably thinking that this book was going to be exclusively about Microsoft operating systems. Admittedly the book is weighted heavily toward Microsoft. There are two reasons for this, and neither of them relate to quality, whether it be the quality of Microsoft products or the quality of competing products.

The biggest reason in my own mind for writing the book in this fashion is that it is intended to be a training guide to the CompTIA A+ Certification exam. And although CompTIA is vendor neutral in practically every other exam it administers, the most recent versions of the OS exam exclusively target Microsoft products.

The second reason is that the vast majority of computer systems the technician will see are powered by Microsoft products. The bundling agreements computer manufacturers have with Microsoft only serve to increase this percentage.

However, in this chapter, I'm going to point out another very viable option that's available. I won't be going into quite the detail in this chapter as I did in previous chapters, because you won't be tested on any of the material in this chapter. Therefore, if your class is targeted exclusively for the A+ Exam, you can safely skip this chapter. This chapter can be considered optional reading. In addition, note that there will be no exercises or questions at the end of this chapter.

A HISTORY AND OVERVIEW OF LINUX

Linux is an operating system that, in a way, stumbled clumsily into glory. What started out as a college student's hobby has gradually evolved into one of the few industry standard OSs that competes openly and directly with Microsoft while still operating on the same hardware platform. Although the Macintosh system competes with Microsoft, it requires completely different hardware to run.

THE HISTORY OF LINUX

Many articles and books openly state that Linux is an offshoot of another operating system called UNIX. In so much as many of the technical features, including how it handles hardware interrupts, how addressing is accomplished in the applications, and so on, are similar, this is true. However, to state that Linux was derived from UNIX suggests that much of the same code was used. That is entirely untrue.

The UNIX OS first began development in Bell Labs back in 1971. Throughout the 1970s, UNIX code was provided to a number of different organizations. Many of these organizations reworked the OS to their own specifications, and as a result, before the decade of the 1980s began, there were a number of different varieties of UNIX.

The concept of open source development is credited to a man by the name of Richard Stallman. In 1985, he published an article entitled "The GNU Manifesto." The acronym was actually a tongue-in-cheek name that meant "GNU is Not UNIX." Since part of the acronym when spelled out is the acronym itself, it technically cannot exist. In this manifesto, Mr. Stallman presented the idea that software as fundamental as an operating system should belong to the public and not a large self-serving corporation. He proposed that open source software be developed that carried an anticopyright. By this, he meant that no single individual or organization would be allowed to place a copyright on open source software.

In 1987, Professor Andrew Tannenbaum developed an OS that he intended to be freely distributed. It was nearly a direct clone of UNIX that he called Minix. A college student by the name of Linus Torvalds got interested in Minix and decided to create his own version. This version was released in 1991 as Linux 0.01 and carried with it an official GNU Public License. He called his license copyleft, another term originated with tongue firmly in cheek. As he said, it is the opposite of a copyright, in that nobody gets to own it. Everybody owns it. He issued a public appeal for top-level programmers to lend a hand in making Linux a sufficiently viable product to compete with the big wigs like Microsoft and UNIX.

The response was far greater than he could have possibly imagined. By 1994, more than a hundred thousand programmers had contributed code. And as it turned out, Torvalds' free software proved to be a commercial success as well. Since Linux, in its earlier incarnations, was anything *but* user friendly, a number of companies sprang up that made available assembled distributions. As I shall point out in the next section, the Linux OS can be a bit complex to install. A distribution contains not only the OS kernel files, but a large collection of device drivers, user interfaces, and applications to go along with the OS. Current companies that provide Linux distributions include the following, in alphabetical order:

- Debian
- Gentoo
- Inspire
- Knoppix
- Lycoris
- Mandrake
- Red Hat (Fedora)
- Slackware
- SuSE
- Xandros

Although there may be others, these were the distributions I could find at the time of this writing. If I've left anybody out, it was unintentional, and I apologize.

An Overview of Linux

One of the first things a Microsoft veteran needs to learn when trying to migrate to Linux is that it isn't Microsoft. Many things are done differently, and how some things are done is version specific. So for the next few pages, I'm going to go over some of the key issues in dealing with Linux. Some of the things I'll discuss include distribution packages, version numbering, the Linux File System, and installing packages.

DISTRIBUTION PACKAGES

As I indicated earlier in the chapter, Linux is designed to be a free OS. Yet, if you walk into any software store and most office supply stores, you see boxes advertising Linux ranging from twenty bucks on up. How is this free?

The idea of the distribution package is actually quite simple. Linux is not as easy to install and configure from scratch as is a more commercially recognizable product such as Windows. Various companies make their money by assembling packages that include the OS kernel along with a huge collection of installation packages. An installation package is an installable program that performs some specific functions. Device drivers and applications all ship as installation packages.

Different vendors have taken different approaches to developing their installation packages. For example, Red Hat favors the Red Hat Package Management (RPM) technology. Under Red Hat, an RPM is nearly as easy to install as any application that installs under Windows. Tarballs are favored by many other vendors. A tarball is a single compressed file that contains the installation package with its file system hierarchy intact. A decompression program, such as GZIP, is used to decompress the package. Tarballs can be a bit more intimidating for the beginner in that they are generally installed from a command prompt.

When you select a Linux distribution package, you are not paying for the software. Every single file (except help files and product documentation) can be obtained for free over the Internet. What you are purchasing is a collection of files and utilities that have been extensively tested and are known to work together. You are purchasing extended documentation, and in many cases, you are purchasing support from the vendor. If you are technically astute and have no need for documentation or support, there is no need to pay for a distribution package.

VERSION NUMBERING IN LINUX

This part of understanding Linux is enough to drive even the seasoned veteran over the edge. This is primarily because one distribution vendor's version has no relationship whatsoever with the version numbers used by other vendors. Therefore, it is not possible to take the version number from a Red Hat distribution and make a direct comparison to a Debian distribution. Some assumptions can be made, however.

The Linux kernel version will remain constant, regardless of the distribution or vendor. For example, as of this writing, Mandrake Linux has a version 9.0 out. It uses the Linux kernel version 2.4.19. Therefore, it is safe to assume that any other distribution by another vendor that uses that same kernel will offer the same capabilities. The various vendors, conversely, may include completely different collections of installation packages.

A kernel version will consist of three numbers, separated by dots. The first two numbers indicate the version of that file. The third number indicates the most recent OS patch updates. In the previous example, 2.4 is the version of the kernel, and 19 indicates that it is the nineteenth applied patch. A key thing to remember is that the second number will tell you whether the version you are running is a stable version or a developmental version. All stable versions carry an even number in the second position, while a version still under development will have an odd number. No distribution package sold over the counter should ever have an odd number in the second position.

THE LINUX FILE SYSTEM

For someone whose familiarity with OSs has exclusively been Microsoft products, the Linux file system can be very difficult to understand. In fact, this subject is of such great importance that I have a dedicated section to the file system later in this chapter. I wanted to include a brief note in this section, however, that the differences are so great that if you create a dual-boot system, Linux files and Microsoft files will not even be visible to the other OS.

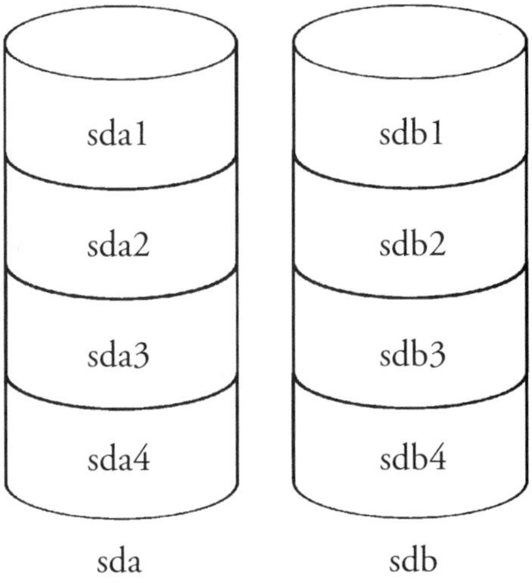

The Linux file system is derived (like the majority of other Linux technology) from UNIX. As such, the method by which data is stored and the path naming conventions are different from Windows. Linux uses ARC conventions (which were discussed in Chapter Seven, Windows NT Architecture). Although Microsoft products are able to use ARC paths, ARC is not the default method used by Microsoft.

Unlike FAT or NTFS, the hard disks in the computer are not assigned drive letters. They are given names. The first drive in the system is a, the second b, and so on and so forth. But that letter is not the entirety of the drive name. A SCSI drive is sd, and an IDE drive is hd. So the first physical SCSI hard disk is sda. A second SCSI drive would be sdb. And that's still not all. Linux is going to divide the drive into multiple partitions with each partition getting a number, starting with 1. So the first partition in the primary SCSI drive is sda1; the second partition is sda2. Get the idea? **Figure 12.1** is an attempt to illustrate this concept.

Also, file names are case-sensitive. NOVEL.doc is not the same filename as novel.doc. Early Linux versions supported file names of up to 128 characters, including the three-character extension. More recent versions allow for file names up to 256 characters. As I said, there will be a more detailed discussion of the file system later in this chapter.

Figure 12.1 Linux divides the drive into multiple partitions. The first partition in the primary SCSI drive is sda1, the second partition is sda2.

LINUX DESKTOP OR LINUX SERVER?

As Linux has emerged over the years, it has become increasingly clear that, at its core, Linux has the potential to be a very powerful server application. Since it supports very large address spaces and multiple CPUs, many consider it to be the perfect platform for a Web Server.

Conversely, those very same features make it an ideal platform for building a powerful desktop. Today's business and graphics applications are requiring vastly increased CPU horsepower and eat up memory in megabytes. The fact that Linux has historically managed memory more efficiently than Microsoft OSs has always made it popular, but a lack of applications has turned many potential users away. These days a plethora of very powerful applications and suites are available for the Linux user. That excuse is no longer viable.

LINUX ON THE DESKTOP

In the past two or three years, Linux has made some remarkable gains on both Microsoft and Apple in terms of the number of desktop computers equipped with its OS. Although public awareness undoubtedly has a great deal of responsibility for this increase in market share, simple usability accounts for even more. Linux has made some remarkable gains in both the friendliness of the desktop environment and in terms of the number of applications available to the end user.

THE LINUX DESKTOP ENVIRONMENT

In its early years, Linux was a purely command-line interface. That was the key limitation that prevented it from becoming a mainstream OS. With this in mind, Linux developers starting pursuing a graphical point-and-click environment that would make former Windows users feel more at home. Two desktop environments for Linux have taken center stage: KDE and GNOME. Both of these options provide the user with a desktop environment, file manager, a set of applications ranging from simple games to integrated Web browsers to full-fledged office productivity suites, a number of administration tools, and a set of libraries and tools that help programmers develop applications for the respective platform.

Although it's true that neither of these desktop environments offer the polish and glitter of XP, what they lack in looks they make up for in stability. A Linux desktop doesn't think twice about running twenty-four hours a day, seven days a week without requiring a restart. Application protection at the CPU level assures the end user that even if a Linux app does crash and burn, the system can remain running and stable.

AVAILABILITY OF APPLICATIONS

In answer to early complaints that Linux lacked an array of user applications, a number of developers stepped up to the table. Sun developed a suite called Star Office (current version as of this writing is 6.0). While not free, this suite still costs only a fraction of Microsoft Office. It offers a word processor, a spreadsheet program, a presentation graphics application, and a database application. All applications offer file filters so that files created by Star Office can be shared with Microsoft Office users.

Perhaps more appealing is an offering by OpenOffice.ORG. It offers all the same functionality of Star Office as well as a powerful drawing program. On top of that, it's free! In addition, OpenOffice.ORG has versions of its product that will run on Windows and the Mac OS platforms. (Much of this book has been prepared in OpenOffice applications. Just don't tell my editors. They think I'm using "the real thing.")

Digital photographers have long eschewed Linux for its lack of any professional level photo-editing software. Justification for this complaint came to an abrupt end with the release of The GIMP. GIMP doesn't mean it's disabled. The acronym stands for Gnu Image Manipulation Program. Its features and interface compare favorably to that really popular and powerful commercial program I'm supposed to be using to create the images in this book.

One of the biggest fears the habitual Windows user has about Linux is that it is too difficult to learn. This is a holdover from the old days when Linux *was* too difficult for the average user to pick up. Both KDE and GNOME insist that their Linux release offers an easy migration path for Windows users. In truth, neither one is identical to Windows in either look or feel. However, either one can be configured to offer a similar computing environment to that of Windows.

THE LINUX SERVER

The same Linux that makes such an inviting desktop environment is an equally inviting server application, with a few slight modifications and a different collection of installation packages. As with the desktop systems, anything you need to configure a fully functional enterprise server can be downloaded for free over the Internet. On the other hand, the reasonable cost of a tested installation package certainly has its allure. All of the Linux distributors mentioned earlier in the chapter offer installation packages for Linux servers.

The beauty of Linux is that a core OS can be had that runs on Intel, Power PC, or even mainframe computers. Linux users were able to take advantage of 64-bit microprocessors long before the "big boys" had anything similar to offer. Recent extensions developed by SuSE, in conjunction with Siemans AG, allow for Linux to address up to 4GB of RAM on Intel-based machines.

As a result, a Linux box is more than capable of handling the requirements of an enterprise level mail server or file server. It has long been a favorite environment for Web servers. And recent extensions that support clustering have now made it attractive to administrators responsible for large databases that see heavy traffic as well.

THE LINUX FILE SYSTEM

If you are reading this book specifically for the purpose of preparing for the A+ Core Exam, it is unlikely that you will get any questions relating to this file system. Still, there are a lot of computers out there in the real world that make use of the Linux operating system, and unless you know the basics of the file system you're going to flounder like a duck on an oil slick.

The Linux File System is virtually identical to that of the UNIX File System (UFS). It uses a tree structure in which all directories stem out from the Root, and subdirectories can stem out from other directories. If this sounds similar to the structure used by Microsoft OSs, it should. In fact, I think it's safe to say that other OSs emulated UNIX in this manner.

There are differences in how to interpret the Linux directory tree. The root directory is represented by a single /. Beneath the root are several subdirectories. The most common subdirectories seen on a Linux system are as follows:

- */bin:* Commands and directories needed by the user
- */dev:* Files used to represent specific devices, either installed on the system or remotely connected
- */etc:* Commands and utilities used for system administration
- */lib:* Libraries used by various programs or programming languages
- */tmp:* Temporary files
- */usr:* Subdivided into subdirectories; these include the games that ship with the OS and the home directory for each user created on the system
- */Kernel File:* Home of the operating system files

UFS breaks the hard drive down into *blocks*. Depending on the version being used, blocks will consist of one, two, or four sectors. Data is stored in the blocks.

The file system can be broken down into four distinct components, the boot block, the super block, the i-node list, and the data blocks. The boot block contains the information needed to initialize the operating system from a cold start. The super block defines the state of the file system. This would include such information as how many files are already stored, how much available space remains on the device, and permissions associated with the device. The i-node list, usually simply referred to as the i-list, keeps track of the locations of individual files stored on the device. And, as you might imagine, the data blocks are where the data is actually stored.

By default Linux is a network operating system. As such, it must support the ability to service multiple users at once. One of the methods it uses to accomplish this is to assign users their own home directory in the /usr directory. When users log on to the system, they are automatically directed to their home directory. Linux uses a different method of accessing files than the file systems I discussed earlier in the book. Instead of a file system table that maps out specific FAUs on the hard drive, Linux provides a unique file system for each user. Another file system is opened called the root file system.

The i-list keeps track of the file systems that are mounted at any given time. The i-list is nothing more than a fixed memory location that contains a list of entries for each file system mounted. For each file system, an i-node is generated. It is the i-node that contains the information used by UFS to locate files on the physical storage device. Each i-node can contain up to ten pointers. A *pointer* is a line of code that maps to a specific block. Each i-node can also contain one indirect pointer, one double-indirect pointer, and one triple-indirect pointer. An indirect pointer maps points to a cluster of pointers.

BUZZ WORDS

Block: The number of sectors on a hard drive that UFS uses as the smallest recognizable data unit.

Pointer: A line of code used by UFS to map a cluster used by a specific file.

The ten pointers of an i-node can basically define a 5KB file. For a file larger than 5KB, an indirect pointer maps to a storage block that stores a table of additional block pointers. If an earlier version of Linux is installed, a block points to a single sector of 512 bytes. A pointer uses 4 bytes. Therefore, a table could contain 128 pointers. A 1024-byte block could contain 256 pointers, and a 2048-byte block could contain 512. For the purposes of this discussion, I will stick to the 512-byte block. An indirect pointer adds 128 pointers per block, which would allow the system to manage a 64KB file.

After file size exceeds 64KB, a double-indirect pointer will be employed. A double-indirect pointer maintains a table of locations to up to 128 indirect pointers. Since an indirect pointer can map up to 64KB of storage space, a double-indirect pointer would map up to 128 × 64KB, or 8MB.

For files larger than 8MB, the system needs to make use of the services of the triple-indirect pointer. The triple-indirect pointer maps to 128 double-indirect pointers. This allows the UFS to support files up to a gigabyte in size.

As I mentioned earlier, the more recent versions of Linux make use of 2KB blocks. This means each block can contain up to 512 pointers. As a result, UFS can theoretically support up to 64GB files. However, a field contained in the i-node that defines file size is only 4 bytes long. This imposes a 4GB limitation on file size.

Other information stored in each i-node includes the following:

- *File Owner ID*: A number generated by the OS that is used by the security file to identify the specific user on the system who created the file.

- *Group ID*: This identifies a group of users that can be granted specific levels of access by the owner.

- *File type*: Files can be listed as any one of several file types:
    - *Regular file*: A conventional data file.
    - *D file (Directory file)*: A file that contains file names and their associated i-node numbers.
    - *L file (Symbolic link file)*: A file that contains the path information needed to access a file.
    - *C file (Character special file)*: A file that is intended to be accessed one character at a time. The file associated to your keyboard would be an example of a character file.
    - *B file (Block special file)*: A file that is accessed a block at a time. The file associated to your monitor is an example of a block special file.
    - *P file (Pipe file)*: A file associated to a device that streams data into a system, such as a modem or network card. This type of file is usually required by any device that needs to buffer data.

- *File access permissions*: There are three kinds of access, and three types of permissions:
    - *User access* is automatically granted to the person who owns the file. This is generally the creator, unless someone with administrative privileges has taken ownership.
    - *Group access* is restricted access granted to any member of a specified group.

- *Other access* consists of whatever level of access has been granted to anyone not recognized by user or group access lists.
- *Read access* allows a user to inspect the data stored in the file, but that user can make no changes or delete the file.
- *Write access* allows the user to make changes the file.
- *Execute access* allows the user to run any executable code contained within the file.

An i-node can also keep track of various access times:

- *File access time.* This indicates when the file data last opened by the system. Events that will change this value include:
  - Displaying the contents of the file
  - Copying the file to a new location or file system
  - Editing the file
- Events that will not change this value include:
  - Moving the file to another directory in the current file system
  - Using redirection to append data to an existing file
- *File modification time.* This indicates when data contained within the file was last changed. Events that will affect this value include the following:
  - Creating the file initializes the value
  - Editing a file and saving it will update this value
  - Overwriting the file with new data will update this value
  - Appending data to an existing file will update this value
- *I-node modification time.* This value shows when information in the i-node was last changed. Events that alter this value include:
  - Creating additional hard links to the file
  - Changes in file size

THE FUTURE OF LINUX

Will all these good things going for it, one would think that Linux would be the wave of the future. You can get it free if you want. Even if you need lots of handholding and personal attention along with a foolproof installation package, it's still a quarter of the price of commercial OSs. Every day seems to see more and more powerful commercial and personal applications emerge onto the marketplace that are either free or so darned cheap they may as well be free. So why is Linux showing up on fewer than 15 percent of desktops worldwide?

Much of this has to do with perception and awareness. Most individuals purchase their PCs at the local electronics store or over the Internet, and they come bundled with Windows.

Therefore, people perceive Windows as being free. Few people are aware that the OEM version of XP added between sixty and a hundred bucks to the cost of their PC, depending on which version of XP is installed on the machine and what kind of deal the manufacturer was able to cut with Microsoft.

Many corporations and institutions use Windows for the very same reason. It came bundled with the 1500 PCs they bought from Gateway or Dell or Compaq or whomever. Even those who do have the option of purchasing computers without a bundled OS feel that the lack of support available for Linux makes it a second-rate choice. Others feel that employee productivity would suffer if the workers came from Microsoft home environments to a Linux workplace. And they're probably right.

Still, signs on the horizon suggest that times may be changing. IBM, HP, Dell, and many other PC manufacturers are starting to include Linux bundles as an option with their computers. IBM has been particularly aggressive in their push toward Linux. So much so that in 2003, Santa Cruz Operations (SCO) sued IBM for a billion dollars.

It claims that IBM shared trade secrets relating to the UNIX OS with the freeware community in an effort to accelerate the already rapid growth of Linux. In its suit, SCO also claims that in migrating its systems over to Linux, IBM is severely undercutting SCO's ability to do business. Naturally, IBM denies the allegations and contends that SCO is simply attempting to retard the growth of Linux, and at the same time collecting a large chunk of cash to help bail it out of severe financial difficulties.

Whoever comes out on top in this battle may, to some extent, control the destiny of Linux in the corporate market. If it turns out that IBM is right and that there is no foundation for SCO's complaint, then Linux has a bright future. Conversely, if the computer giant winds up shelling out a cool billion dollars in damages, many other computer manufacturers are going to be wary of risking a similar lawsuit. The possibility exists that some companies already bundling Linux with their systems may curtail the practice or stop all together. We can only wait and see.

CHAPTER SUMMARY

Hopefully, this chapter made it clear that Microsoft isn't the only kid on the block. It's merely the biggest one with the most clout. Linux is a very stable OS with a lot of strong features. Each year sees more applications emerge for the business community and creative individuals alike.

I would like to think that reading this chapter at least gave you the urge to try Linux. If this is true, then I highly recommend that you log onto www.linux.org and begin your study. It might open up a whole new way of living for you.

CHAPTER 13

NETWORKING COMPUTERS

Although it is unlikely that any reasonable employer will ever ask a PC technician to take over the network engineer's job for any length of time, in this day and age it's essential that any person working in IT have some basic networking knowledge. Here I will take you through the steps of getting a computer to join either a workgroup or a domain, using WIN9x or WIN2K/XP. In the second half of the chapter, I'll go over a few basic troubleshooting techniques.

A+ OPERATING SYSTEM TECHNOLOGIES EXAM OBJECTIVES

CompTIA objectives covered in this chapter include the following:

4.1 Identify the networking capabilities of Windows including procedures for connecting to the network.

4.2 Identify concepts and capabilities relating to the Internet and basic procedures for setting up a system for Internet access.

WORKGROUPS AND DOMAINS

In the Windows environment, there are really only two models of network in use today. These are the workgroup model and the domain model. For the most part, the workgroup is used in smaller peer-to-peer (P2P) networks, and the domain is the model used by client/server networks.

By definition, a *workgroup* is any group of users and/or computers that share a common task over a network. The devices/users are set up in such a way that they are able to share files, exchange messages, and share peripheral devices. In the workgroup, each device and/or user is independently managed.

The *domain* is a bit more sophisticated. A domain consists of all users, devices, and other resources that are under the administrative control of a single entity. In the case of Microsoft networking, this control entity is the domain controller.

Although it is common to see the term workgroup used almost synonymously with the P2P network, this is not necessarily a correct assumption. It is true that the P2P network can only handle workgroup computing. However, it is possible (and relatively common) to configure workgroups within a domain.

NETWORKING IN WIN98

In today's world of the Internet, networking can mean different things to different people. To the network administrator, it means the LAN. The Internet is merely another resource to access, and to many administrators it poses a security risk. To the small office or home user, the Internet may be the

---

BUZZ WORDS

Workgroup: A collection of independently managed users and/or devices on a network that are configured to share files and devices.

Domain: A collection of users, devices, and other resources that are under the control of a single management entity.

Network client: A piece of software running on a computer that provides network access for the computer and all applications running on that computer.

---

only networking that is ever used. The basic definition of a network is two or more computers (or other devices) configured to communicate with one another. By that definition, a computer hooked up to the Internet is networked. Therefore, this section and the one that follows dealing with WIN2K/XP will be divided into two parts. The first will cover basic networking, and the second section will talk about Internet connectivity.

CONFIGURING NETWORKING IN WIN9X

There are two ways to get to the Network Applet in WIN9x. You can click Start→Settings→Control Panel. When Control Panel opens, double-click the Network icon. The other way is to right-click the Network Neighborhood icon on the desktop and then select Properties. Either way will bring up a screen similar to the one shown in **Figure 13.1**. You'll notice that there are three different tabs available in the WIN98 screen shown here.

THE CONFIGURATION TAB

In this tab, there are four different configurations that can be managed. These configurations are the type of client that the computer will use, the network adapter, the protocol of choice, and the services that will be installed.

The Client In the OS, the *network client* is a piece of software that provides access to the network for the computer and all applications running on that computer. It is *not* the end user. The network client is not only specific to the OS running on the local computer, it is also specific to the NOS running on the server on a client/server network. Therefore, if a Novell server manages your network, then each workstation must be configured with a Novell client.

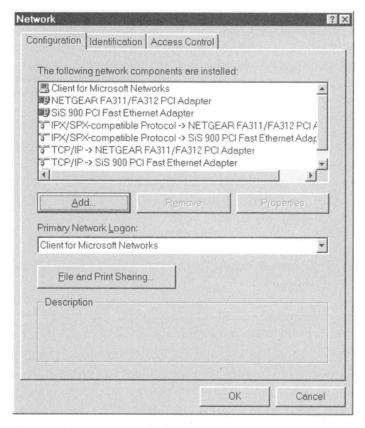

Figure 13.1 The WIN98 Network applet

If your network features both Novell and Windows servers, then in order to access all parts of the network, each workstation must be configured with a client for each NOS.

In the old days of 16-bit computing, this was sometimes a bit of a problem. Most OSs only allowed a single 16-bit client to exist on the computer at any given time. With 32-bit clients (which are about all that are ever used in modern networks), there is no issue with running multiple clients.

To select a client in WIN9x, click the Add button, double-click Client on the window that pops up, and then make your selection. WIN9x offers clients for Banyan Vines, Microsoft, and Novell networks. Banyan became obsolete in 1999, when the company changed its name to ePresence and announced that it would concentrate on Internet services from that point forward. All Banyan Vines products were discontinued.

In Microsoft, the user has the choice of Client for Microsoft Networks, Client for Novell Networks, and Microsoft Family Logon. There are two clients offered for Novell. One is the Novell NetWare Workstation Shell 3.x [NETX], and the other is the Novell NetWare Workstation Shell 4.0 and above [VLM].

Adapter Selecting this option will basically invoke an Add/Remove Hardware screen that prompts the user to select the proper network adapter. In the old days, when WIN9x was relatively inept at recognizing NICs, this function was needed with some frequency. The PnP version of WIN2K was significantly more efficient, and it was better to let PnP handle the installation process except in those cases where the card was simply not recognized.

One of the adapters listed under this tab is the MS Loopback Adapter. This is a virtual device that fools the computer into thinking there is a NIC installed when, in fact, there is none. Other virtual adapters available include the Microsoft Dial-up adapter, which treats a modem as if it were a NIC. There is also the Microsoft PPP over ATM adapter. This allows the use of the Point to Point Protocol (PPP) across a network using Asynchronous Transfer Mode (ATM). PPP allows direct virtual connections to be made between hosts over the Internet. ATM is a high-speed serial connection protocol used in networking. For more information on these protocols and others, see *The Complete Guide to Networking and Network+*, by this same author.

> **BUZZ WORDS**
>
> **Protocol:** An application running on a computer that ensures that the computer will speak the same language and follow the same rules as the computers with which it communicates.
>
> **Service:** A networking function of the OS, such as file sharing, that can be turned on and off as needed.

Protocols A *protocol* is sort of like the language that a computer speaks. But it isn't just language that is involved. Just like when a person visits a foreign country, it's important to know the social rules that control that society it's necessary for two computers to follow the same rules. A basic truth is that for two different computer systems to talk to one another, both must be running identical protocols, and those protocols must be configured properly. Microsoft provides support for three different networking protocols. These are NetBIOS Extended User Interface (NetBEUI), Internetwork Packet Exchange/Sequenced Packed Exchange (IPX/SPX), and Transmission Control Protocol/Internet Protocol (TCP/IP).

Just configuring the machine to work with all protocols is not a shortcut to success. In fact, such a practice can cause serious performance issues, not only for the host computer, but across the network as well. When a computer is asked to take part in communications over the network, information is broken down into small chunks of data called packets. These packets vary in size based on the protocol being used. Your computer will try each protocol configured, in the order in which it was installed, until it finds a protocol that works. And it will do this for each communications session that is initiated. Pick a protocol and stick with it. Since this is the world of the Internet, chances are extremely good you will be picking TCP/IP. Later in this chapter, I will provide a detailed discussion for configuring and troubleshooting TCP/IP.

Services A network *service* is a specific function of the NOS that can be turned on or turned off at will. A basic host OS such as WIN98 is relatively limited in the services that are available. In fact, there are only three. These are File and Printer Sharing for Microsoft Networks, File and Printer Sharing for Novell Networks, and Service for Netware Directory Services.

Regardless of the type of NOS used by the network servers, if local files and printers on the host are to be shared, the appropriate File and Printer Sharing service must be installed. Otherwise sharing will not be an option. Obviously, for networks powered by Novell servers, you will pick the Novell version, and vice versa.

An additional service needed by Novell networks is the Services for NetWare Directory Services. This allows the local OS to interface with Novell's Directory Services (NDS). NDS is a function provided by Novell servers that allows a user to browse the entire network as if it were a part of the user's local machine.

THE IDENTIFICATION TAB

This very simple screen (**Figure 13.2**) seems to cause more network issues than anything so simple should be allowed to cause. There are only three fields here that contain information, and one of them is optional!

Two fields that must be filled out in order for the network to properly function are Computer name and Workgroup. On any given network, there may *not* be two computers or other devices

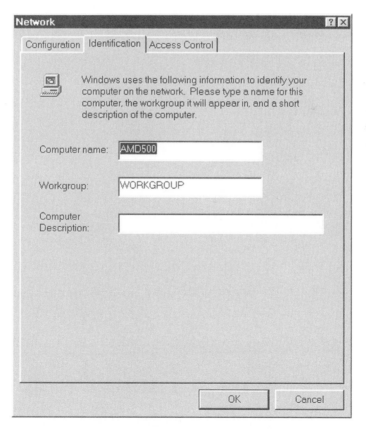

Figure 13.2   The Identification tab of the Network applet

that share the same name. If an administrator inadvertently gives two devices the same name, the first to log on will have no difficulty. The second device will not be able to log on, though.

For two devices on a workgroup to talk to one another, they must be members of the same workgroup. For example, in Figure 13.2, the computer is named AMD500 and the workgroup is simply named Workgroup. That's because Workgroup is the default name.

If I have two dozen computers on the same physical network, and half of them are assigned to the SALES workgroup while the other have are assigned to ADMIN, then all the SALES members can talk to one another. Likewise all the ADMIN computers will communicate. But SALES will not be able to communicate with ADMIN.

The third field is optional. This is the Computer Description field. Here the administrator can enter a brief line telling what that computer's function is, its location, or any other pertinent information.

THE ACCESS CONTROL TAB

The Access Control tab (**Figure 13.3**) defines how resources on the local system will be secured. The two options are share-level access control and user-level access control. Having discussed

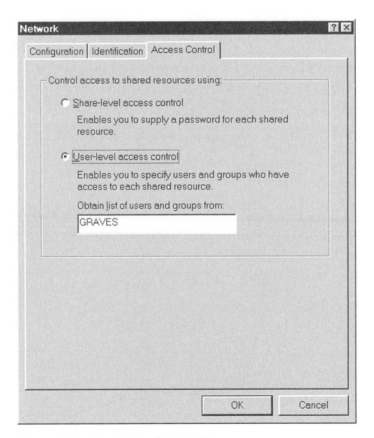

Figure 13.3 The Access Control tab

share-level versus user-level access control in Chapter Seven, I don't seen any cause to go over that material again. Suffice it to say that this is where the selection is made.

SHARING RESOURCES IN WIN9X

There's no point in setting up a network if there's nothing on the network for users to share. For resources to be made available to the network, File and Print Sharing Services must be installed and configured, as I pointed out in the previous section. After this has been accomplished, sharing resources is actually a simple matter. The two most common devices to be shared are file locations and printers. Keep in mind, though, it also possible to share out a resource such as an external disk drive and/or CD-ROM drive (either internal or external).

SHARING DRIVES, FILES, AND FOLDERS

The easiest way to share out a file or folder in WIN9x is by way of Windows Explorer (**Figure 13.4**). Explorer can be accessed in one of two ways. The easiest way is to right-click the Start button and select Explore from the menu that appears. Some people find it annoying that using this

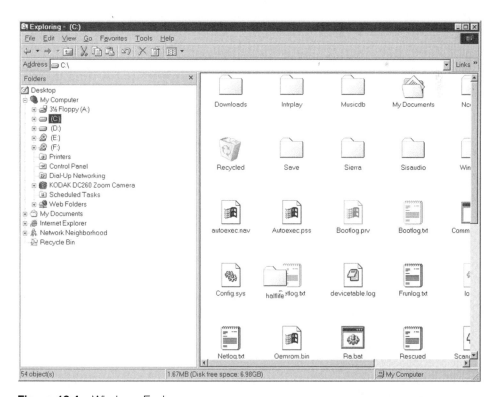

Figure 13.4   Windows Explorer

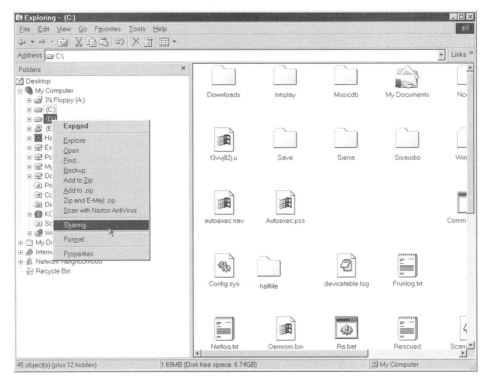

Figure 13.5 The Folder Properties window contains a Sharing tab.

method opens the Windows directory in Explorer and places them in the Start Menu folder. To avoid this inconvenience, simply click Start→Programs→Windows Explorer. You can easily create a shortcut to Explorer by right-clicking Windows Explorer in the Start menu and selecting Create Shortcut. Drag and drop the new Start Menu entry, now entitled Windows Explorer (2) to the desktop. Rename it if you so desire.

Once in Explorer, right-click the drive, file, or folder you want to share, as shown in **Figure 13.5**. This brings up the Folder Properties windows, with the Sharing tab opened. (Note that the Folder Properties windows will be named after the folder for which the properties are being viewed.)

When the Shared as button is clicked, the fields for Share Name, Comment, and Name appear (see **Figure 13.6**). By default, the share name will be the name of the folder (or device) as seen by Windows whenever possible. However, in WIN98, share names are limited to twelve characters. Therefore, long file or folder names will be truncated to that number. You can name the share anything you wish as long as you stick to names that are twelve characters or less, that is, if you have to worry about compatibility with WIN98 machines. This does not affect the name of the local file or folder, but merely how remote users see it. Therefore, in Figure 13.6, where I shared out the D drive, I chose to use a share name of SERVERD. On the local machine, this share will still be Drive D:, but when remote users browse to it over the network, they will see it as SERVERD.

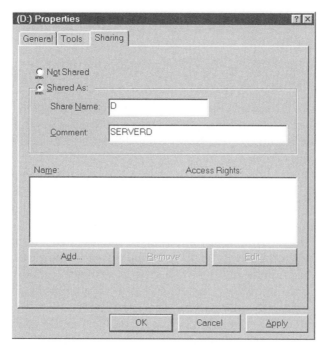

Figure 13.6   Sharing a folder in WIN98

In this window, you will also have the option of adding users and selecting their permissions. If share-level access has been selected, the options are limited. You can only select the option to use or not to use a password on the resource. If you choose to password-protect the folder, you will have the additional option of selecting whether or not to use separate passwords for full permissions and read-only permissions. With user-level security checked, you can open the list of users and groups from the domain controller and pick and choose from there.

SHARING PRINTERS IN WIN9x

Sharing printers is only slightly different than sharing folders in WIN9x. For one thing, if File and Printer Sharing is installed and configured to include printers at the time a printer is first installed, then the process is simple. The installation wizard asks whether you wish to share the printer. You select Yes and either accept the prompted share name or fill in a name of your choice (under twelve characters, once again).

If File and Printer Sharing is installed and configured after a printer has already been installed, it can be shared out over the network in a manner similar to what I discussed in Folder sharing. Open My Computer and double-click Printers. You can also get to the Printer applet through Start→Settings→Printers or Start→Settings→Control Panel, and double-clicking the Printers icon. There are a lot of ways to get to this one.

After you get there, right-click the printer you want to share. From there, the process is identical to that of sharing a folder.

DIAL-UP NETWORKING IN WIN9X

As much as we'd like to imagine that the 56K modem is a thing of the past, the fact of the matter is, it's still alive and well. It's especially prevalent in rural areas where broadband has not yet reached. Therefore, setting up Dial-Up Networking (DUN) is still a task that every technician is likely to face at some time or the other.

The first thing you need to do is make sure the modem is properly installed and functioning. That's a hardware issue and details pertaining to hardware resources and device drivers are discussed in *The A+ Guide to PC Hardware Maintenance and Repair*. This discussion assumes the hardware end has already been taken care of.

In WIN9x versions, DUN is located in the My Computer folder on the desktop. Double-clicking the My Computer icon will bring up a window similar to the one shown in **Figure 13.7**. The number and variety of icons you seen in that window will vary based on the configuration of the computer. When you double-click the Dial-up Networking icon, it launches the Welcome to Dial-Up Networking wizard (**Figure 13.8**).

The first thing the wizard is going to do is ask you to name the connection and to select the device with which you want the connection to be made (**Figure 13.9**). On the outset, this may seem a bit superfluous. However, keep in mind that it is quite possible to install multiple modems in a computer system and that each modem can be dedicated to a specific function. These functions can include more than one DUN connection, with a dedicated modem for each connection and/or a modem dedicated to fax functionality. Naturally, for multiple modems to be of any benefit, each must have a dedicated telephone line.

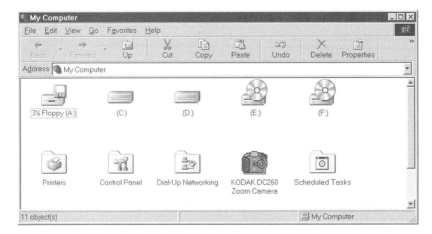

Figure 13.7 The My Computer window in WIN98

Figure 13.8   The Welcome to Dial-Up Networking wizard in WIN98

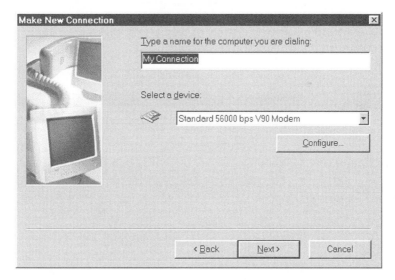

Figure 13.9   Step one is to name the connection and select a device for dialing out.

In the next screen (**Figure 13.10**), there is a field for filling in the area code, along with a second field for the telephone number of the target connection. The third field on this screen is for the country or region from which you will be dialing. By default, the region that you selected during the installation of Windows will appear in that field. It is something you can change if necessary.

That's the last thing you need to do. The next screen, entitled Make New Connection (**Figure 13.11**), is the final screen in this process. Click Finish, and DUN is configured.

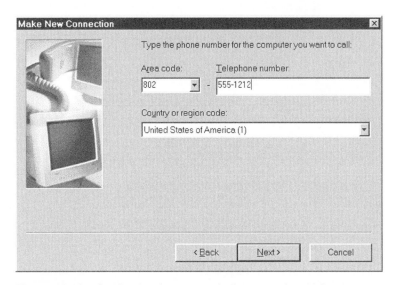

Figure 13.10   Configuring the target telephone number and country/region code

Figure 13.11   Finalizing your DUN connection

MANAGING INTERNET CONNECTIONS IN WIN9X

Since the entire reason for the existence of an extremely large percentage of personal computers in this world is to provide users with Internet access, it would be obvious that this is something with the technician should be familiar. In WIN9x, connecting to the Internet can be done in a variety of ways. The two most common are through a modem interface and through the LAN. Therefore, those are the two connections I'll discuss.

CONNECTING TO THE INTERNET BY MODEM

Once again, the following discussion assumes the modem is already configured and working in the target computer. If you have all the information you need, all you're doing is creating a new DUN connection, as discussed in the previous step. It's as simple as that. However, there is a second way to invoke the Wizard when the requested DUN is specifically for an Internet connection.

Open Control Panel by clicking Start→Settings→Control Panel and then double-click the Internet Options icon. The window that opens will have several tabs at the top. Click the Connections tab to open the window shown in **Figure 13.12**.

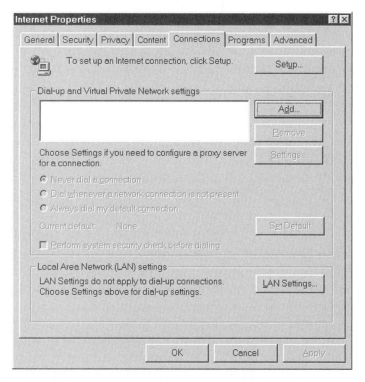

Figure 13.12   The Internet Properties window

Click the Add button, and the DUN wizard will start. From there, it is just like the steps described in the previous section.

On a WIN98SE system, it is possible to share this Internet Connection with other computers on the network that are also using WIN98SE (or later). With Internet Connection Sharing (ICS), the computer directly connected to the Internet (called the Connection Sharing computer), dolls out private IP addresses and name resolution services for the other computers on the home network. Then, the other computers on your network can access the Internet through the Connection Sharing computer using private IP addressing translation.

It stands to reason that, for this to work, each computer must be equipped with a NIC and a LAN configured and successfully running. The Connection Sharing computer can be hooked up to the Internet by way of Modem, Integrated Services Digital Network (ISDN), or Digital Subscriber Line (DSL). The latter two are high-speed connection options for the Internet.

ICS is not something that installs by default onto a WIN98 computer. It must be added unless the user performed a custom install at the time the OS was installed and configured. In order to add ICS, open Control Panel as before and click Add/Remove Programs. Click the Windows Setup tab, as shown in **Figure 13.13**, and scroll down to Internet Tools.

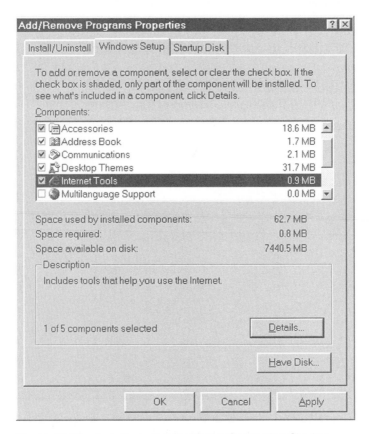

Figure 13.13 In order to install Internet Connection Sharing, you need to access the Add Windows Components wizard.

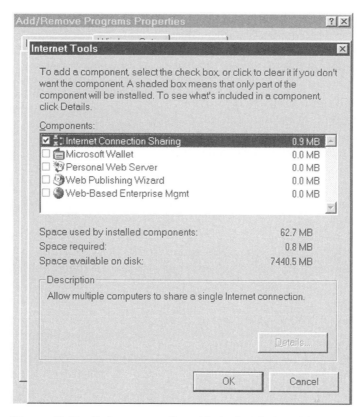

Figure 13.14   Before proceeding with the installation of Internet Tools, make sure you really need everything that will be installed.

If you simply click the checkbox and proceed, you might be installing some components you neither need nor want. So before you continue, with Internet Tools highlighted, click the Details button. In **Figure 13.14**, I have deselected all but ICS. By default, if I had simply checked the box next to Internet Tools in the previous screen, all of these would be checked and installed. Since I have no need for the rest of these tools, I chose not to install them.

Click OK, and you will be prompted to insert your WIN98 CD. Insert the CD and click next. The Add/Remove Programs Wizard will copy a bunch of files to your computer and make a few changes to the registry. Once this process has been completed, the Internet Connection Sharing wizard will launch itself. The user does not need to do anything to prompt it. Read all the information on this screen and make sure you have fulfilled all the requirements before proceeding. When you're sure, click Next to move on to the next step. From that point, it's merely a matter of following the steps on the screen. Repeat the process on all client computers.

CONNECTING TO THE INTERNET BY LAN

Connection to the Internet over the LAN can either be much easier than setting up a DUN connection, or much more difficult, depending on the configuration of your network. If the computer with the primary Internet connection is a WIN98 computer with Internet Sharing enabled, you merely install Internet Connection Sharing on the other computers and run the wizard as described previously.

Another method is to install a third-party proxy application on the host computer. This turns the host into a *proxy server*. The proxy server acts as the portal to the Internet, and all the other computers on the network access the Internet through the proxy.

BUZZ WORDS

Proxy server: A machine on the network that has been configured to be the portal to the Internet, through which all other computers on the network gain access.

To configure a proxy server, open the Internet Connections applet in Control Panel and click Connections. Click LAN Settings to bring up the screen in **Figure 13.15**. Click the box under Proxy Server that is labeled Use a proxy server for your LAN. Click Advanced to bring up the screen in **Figure 13.16**. Type the IP address for the host computer in each of the Server fields. Check the instructions that come with your proxy server application for the appropriate ports to use. Many products use dedicated ports for various protocols. Click OK.

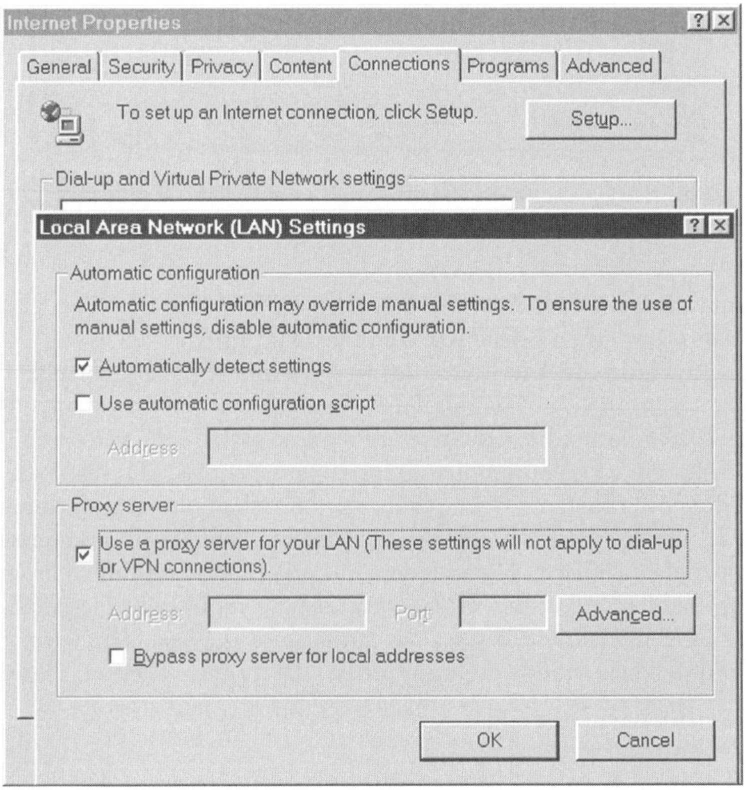

Figure 13.15 Configuring Internet LAN settings

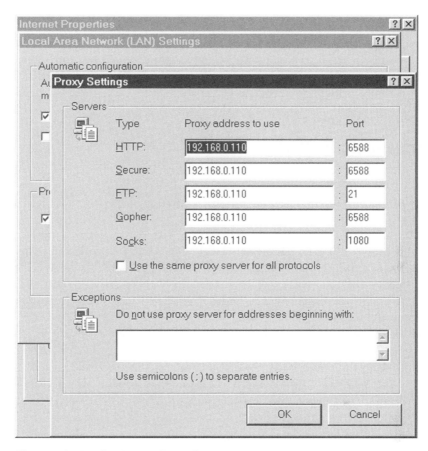

Figure 13.16   Configuring Proxy Server settings

NETWORKING IN WIN2K AND WINXP

There are really relatively few differences between WIN98 and the more recent versions of Windows in terms of networking. Most of these differences involve the location of applets and in some cases, the names of the applets. When you find where you're going, the procedures don't vary. The following list outlines various differences between the OS versions:

- *Browsing the network*: In WIN9x, the applet is called Network Neighborhood. In WIN2K and WINXP, it is My Network Places. Right-clicking the icon in any version will bring up a menu that includes an option for the Properties Screen.

- *Network identification*: In WIN9x, this is configured in the Network Properties applet, under the Identification tab. In WIN2K and WINXP, it is in the System applet under the Computer Name tab. This is also where the computer can be joined to a domain, as long as the user knows the user ID and password for an account with administrative privileges on the domain.

- *Internet sharing:* Installed by default on WIN2K and WINXP.
- *Configuring a local area connection:* In WIN98, the Network applet shows all installed connections in a single screen. To bind or unbind protocols and services from an interface, the properties of that interface must be highlighted. In WIN2K and WINXP, each interface is listed as a separate entity and can be configured independently.

CONFIGURING TCP/IP

Since TCP/IP has become the preeminent networking protocol used by network professionals throughout the world over the last couple of years, it's imperative that technicians know how to configure a computer to use TCP/IP. To configure TCP/IP, open the Network applet in WIN98 or double click the Local Area Connections icon in WIN2K or WINXP. In WIN98, highlight TCP/IP→(selected interface) and click Properties. In WIN2K or XP, open the Local Area Connection you wish to configure and, under the General tab, click Properties. Highlight Internet Protocol (TCP/IP).

TCP/IP identifies computers by an IP address. An IP address consists of a 32-bit address listed in decimal format. An example of an IP address is 192.168.0.1. As you can see, the address consists of four numbers, called *octets,* divided by periods. They are called octets because each number represents an 8-bit value. While it is beyond the scope of this book to go into IP addresses in detail, a brief overview is in order.

The IP address can be broken down into two sections. The first section identifies what network the device is on, while the second identifies the device itself. This is true whether the IP address defines a computer, a printer, or a router interface. There are five different classes of IP address. An IP address class determines how many networks can exist and how many hosts can exist on each network. Network administrators can use only three classes of IP address: Class A, Class B, and Class C.

In a Class A address, only the first octet identifies the network. All other numbers in the address point to different hosts. The first number can be any number from 1 to 127. There can be only a few Class A networks, but each one has millions of hosts.

A Class B address uses the first two octets to identify the network and the last two to identify the hosts. The first number will always be from 128 to 191. There are nearly equal numbers of Class B networks and hosts that can occupy them. I say nearly, because limitations in the first octet lower the number of available network addresses.

Class C addresses use the first three octets to identify the network, but only the last octet identifies hosts. As you might imagine, there are lots and lots of class C networks, but each one is limited to a maximum of 255 hosts.

IP addresses can be configured one of two ways. If there is a server on the network configured with the Dynamic Host Configuration Protocol (DHCP) that can dole out addresses, the simplest way is to select Obtain an IP address automatically. On boot up, the DHCP server will assign an IP address to the computer. If the administrator so desires, DHCP can also assign IP addresses to DNS servers, WINS servers, and default gateways. Don't worry at this moment what those are. I'll discuss them in a minute.

If there is no DHCP server on the network, or if the administrator simply has a reason for statically assigning IP addresses, then the box labeled Specify an IP address must be checked. At a minimum, there are two items that must be configured. The first is the actual IP address. No two computers on the network can share the same IP address. If this happens by accident, the first computer to log on has no problems. The next one is denied access.

The second item that is required by all TCP/IP configurations is the subnet mask. Earlier in this section, I pointed out that all IP addresses consist of a network address and a host address. The subnet mask defines what part of the IP address identifies the network and what part identifies the host. Your network administrator can tell you what subnet mask to use. If you happen to be setting up a small home or office network, the default subnet masks should work just fine. Default subnet masks for each class of address are as follows:

- Class A address: 255.0.0.0
- Class B address: 255.255.0.0
- Class C address: 255.255.255.0

As you can see, default subnet masks consist of all 255 and 0 numbers. The number 255 identifies the network part of the address, and the 0 identifies the host address.

Three other items that are optionally configured in TCP/IP are the gateway, the WINS server, and the DNS server. Whether you configure these depends entirely on whether or not your network uses the services. These services are described in the next couple of sections.

GATEWAY (OR DEFAULT GATEWAY)

When a computer is asked to transmit a packet of data to a remote destination, it needs to know where to send that packet. If the OS examines a packet and sees an IP address in the header of that packet, it knows exactly where to send it, right?

Well, maybe it does and maybe it doesn't. If the address in the header is an address on the local network, there is no problem. If the user is trying to send information to a remote network, though, then the OS needs to know how to find the remote network. The gateway is the IP address of a port or interface that leads to the outside world. This can be a router or a computer that has access to another NIC or to a router.

When the OS examines a packet and finds an IP address it doesn't recognize, it simply transmits that packet to the device identified by the gateway. If there is no gateway, it discards that packet and pretends it never existed.

WINS SERVERS

Older Microsoft NOSs made use of a protocol called the Windows Internet Naming Service (WINS) to translate an IP address to a computer name. Newer NOSs maintain WINS support for backward compatibility. For WINS to work, there has to be one or more servers on the network configured to act as a WINS server. For a host to make use of the service, the IP address of the WINS server must be configured in the TCP/IP properties.

DNS SERVERS

These days, most OSs use a service called Domain Name Services (DNS) for resolving host names to IP addresses. As with WINS, for DNS to work, there must be a computer on the network configured to be a DNS server. If there is a gateway configured, the DNS server can be off the local network. For example, many network administrators, and most homes and small offices, take advantage of the fact that their internet service providers (ISPs) have a minimum of two DNS servers that are far more robust and have substantially more entries than any DNS server they could ever configure. To configure a DNS server, click the DNS tab and type one or more addresses.

TCP/IP UTILITIES

One of the beauties of using TCP/IP as your default protocol lies in the number of elegant little utilities that are part of the suite. These handy little programs provide an immense amount of troubleshooting capability without spending any extra money. In addition to the ones that are part of the suite, there are huge numbers of utilities available for download on the Web that are not officially part of the suite. It is a good idea to really know your way around the TCP/IP utilities. The ones I will be covering in this chapter include three of the most useful:

- Ping
- Route
- IPCONFIG and WINIPCFG

PING

The Packet InterNet Groper, usually just called *Ping*, is one of those utilities you must have a good understanding of. It works on the basis of the Internet Control Message Protocol (ICMP), which generates and delivers error messages when and where appropriate. Ping can tell you whether or not a particular host on the network is reachable. It works by sending out a series of ECHO packets. The intended host, upon receiving the packets, will return an ECHO REPLY. If the ECHO REPLY returns successfully, Ping will calculate the total time elapsed for the round trip. The information will be returned in a screen similar to the one in **Figure 13.17**.

BUZZ WORDS

Ping: Not only is Ping an acronym, it has been universally adopted as a term that can be either a noun or a verb. As a noun it represents the packets sent when pinging another host. As a verb, it represents the process of pinging another host.

```
C:\>ping 192.168.1.1

Pinging 192.168.1.1 with 32 bytes of data:

Reply from 192.168.1.1: bytes=32 time=1ms TTL=64
Reply from 192.168.1.1: bytes=32 time<10ms TTL=64
Reply from 192.168.1.1: bytes=32 time<10ms TTL=64
Reply from 192.168.1.1: bytes=32 time<10ms TTL=64

Ping statistics for 192.168.1.1:
    Packets: Sent = 4, Received = 4, Lost = 0 (0% loss),
Approximate round trip times in milli-seconds:
    Minimum = 0ms, Maximum =  1ms, Average =  0ms

C:\>_
```

Figure 13.17   Ping provides a great deal of information.

ROUTE

The ROUTE command allows the user to add static entries to the local routing table, or it can be used to view the local routing table. These entries can include routes to networks or routes to hosts. They can also be introduced in numeric fashion or by name, if DNS is available.

When inputting a static entry using the ROUTE command, you would need to know the format of the routing tables used by the OS. By typing **route print** at the command prompt, the existing routing table will be displayed. When generating your own tables, type your entries accordingly.

BUZZ WORDS

Route: The path that data takes to move from point A to point B. It is also a TCP/IP utility that can be used to display the local router configuration on a TCP/IP-enabled device.

IPCONFIG: The TCP/IP utility that displays all TCP/IP configuration information for any given interface, or for all interfaces on a system.

IPCONFIG AND WINIPCFG

IPCONFIG is undoubtedly the most widely used of the TCP/IP utilities. This utility can return statistics on every connection configured to use TCP/IP. If a device is configured to use DHCP, a user can use IPCONFIG to release an IP address and subsequently renew it.

IPCONFIG displays information for all local TCP/IP connections, whether they be a NIC or a modem. As with the other utilities I've discussed, there are a number of triggers associated with IPCONFIG. IPCONFIG triggers vary a bit between Windows 98 and the subsequent Microsoft OSs. Therefore, I will list the triggers for both. Those for WIN98 are as follows:

/all Displays detailed report of all adapters on system.

/batch {filename} Writes a report to the file specified by filename.

/renew_all Renews the IP configuration for all adapters on the system.

/release_all Releases the IP configuration for all adapters on the system.

/renew N Renews the IP configuration for only the adapter specified in N.

/release N Releases the IP configuration for only the adapter specified in N.

The command line parameters for Windows 2000 are a bit different and there are more of them as well. They are as follows:

/all Shows complete configuration for all interfaces on system.

/release {adapter} Releases IP configuration for the adapter specified.

/renew {adapter} Renews IP configuration for the adapter specified.

/flushdns Dumps the contents of the current DNS Resolver cache.

/registerdns Refreshes all DHCP leases and reregisters DNS names.

/displaydns Displays contents of the DNS Resolver cache.

/showclassid Displays the DHCP classes allowed by the adapter.

/setclassid Modifies the DHCP class.

Windows 98 offers a graphical version of IPCONFIG that will display this information as well. This utility is called WINIPCFG. A user can access by clicking Start→Run, and typing **winipcfg** in the run field.

CHAPTER SUMMARY

In this chapter, I introduced you to some of the basic concepts of networking, along with some OS-specific tips for configuring networking and accessing the network. This is a section of the exam that gets a fair amount of exposure, so it would be a good idea to make sure you're familiar with the material in this chapter.

Network configuration is a key aspect. Make sure that you are familiar with the different protocols and services. TCP/IP is the most commonly tested protocol on the exam, so be able to configure a computer using TCP/IP. Also know how to share devices and files.

BRAIN DRAIN

1. Define a workgroup and a domain. Discuss the differences between the two.

2. Precisely what is a network client (from a software standpoint) and why is it necessary?

3. Define what a protocol is, and describe its role in networking computers.

4. Describe the process of sharing a folder in WIN98.

5. Go through the process of configuring a computer to use TCP/IP on the network.

THE 64K$ QUESTIONS

1. A collection of independently managed computers and/or devices on a network would be called a _____.
   a. Workgroup
   b. Domain
   c. Subnet
   d. Segment

2. A collection of devices on a network that are all under the control of a single administrative unit is best defined as a _____.
   a. Workgroup
   b. Domain
   c. Subnet
   d. Segment

3. The icon for browsing the network in WIN9x is called _____.
   a. My Computer
   b. My Network Places
   c. Network Neighborhood
   d. Network

4. The icon for browsing the network in WINXP is called _____.
   a. My Computer
   b. My Network Places
   c. Network Neighborhood
   d. Network

5. Which of the following protocols is the one most commonly used on the Internet?
   a. NetBEUI
   b. IPX/SPX
   c. Banyan Vines
   d. TCP/IP

6. Which of the following protocols was developed by Novell for its NOS?
   a. NetBEUI
   b. IPX/SPX
   c. Banyan Vines
   d. TCP/IP

7. Which of the following protocols was developed by Microsoft for its NOS?
   a. NetBEUI
   b. IPX/SPX
   c. Banyan Vines
   d. TCP/IP

8. File and Printer Sharing in Microsoft networking is considered a _____.
   a. Logical Adapter
   b. Service
   c. Protocol
   d. Topology

9. If a small network has several users, and each user is capable of setting up his or her own shares and assigning individual passwords for each

share, what kind of security is that network using?

a. Kerberos

b. IPSec

c. Share level

d. User level

10. If the users on a network use a single user ID and password to access all resources, what type of security is in place?

a. Kerberos

b. IPSec

c. Share level

d. User level

11. Shares on a Windows network are created in _____.

a. Internet Explorer

b. Windows Explorer

c. Network Neighborhood

d. The Network applet

12. If a computer is equipped with a 56K modem, which service must be configured in order to access the Internet?

a. RAS

b. VPN

c. DUN

d. DSL

13. Internet Connection Sharing is installed by default on WIN98 computers.

a. True

b. False

14. A computer that acts as a portal to the Internet, through which all other computers on the network gain Internet access, is called a(n) _____.

a. ISP

b. Proxy server

c. Host computer

d. DUNS server

15. Which of the two following items must be configured on every computer running TCP/IP?

a. IP address

b. DNS server address

c. Subnet mask

d. WINS server address

16. Your computer has just received a packet that contains an unfamiliar target IP address in the header. If you have a _____ properly configured, the packet can be forwarded.

a. DNS server

b. WINS server

c. Gateway

d. ARP server

17. A single number in an IP address, divided by periods, is called _____.

a. The network address

b. The primordial

c. An octet

d. The target ID

18. A Class A address uses _____ to identify the host address.

a. The first octet

b. The last octet

c. The first three octets

d. The last three octets

19. A Class A address uses _____ to identify the network address.

   a. The first octet

   b. The last octet

   c. The first three octets

   d. The last three octets

20. What is the name of the graphical utility used to view IP configuration settings in WIN98?

   a. Ping

   b. IPCONFIG

   c. MSCONFIG

   d. WINIPCFG

TRICKY TERMINOLOGY

Domain: A collection of users, devices, and other resources that are under the control of a single management entity.

IPCONFIG: The TCP/IP utility that displays all TCP/IP configuration information for any given interface, or for all interfaces on a system.

Network client: A piece of software running on a computer that provides network access for the computer and all applications running on that computer.

Octet: A decimal alliteration of a single 8-bit string of data.

Ping: Not only is Ping an acronym, it has been universally adopted as a term that can be either a noun or a verb. As a noun it represents the packets sent when pinging another host. As a verb, it represents the process of pinging another host.

Protocol: An application running on a computer that ensures that the computer will speak the same language and follow the same rules as the computers with which it communicates.

Proxy server: A machine on the network that has been configured to be the portal to the Internet, through which all other computers on the network gain access.

Route: The path that data takes to move from point A to point B. It is also a TCP/IP utility that can be used to display the local router configuration on a TCP/IP enabled device.

Service: A networking function of the OS, such as file sharing, that can be turned on and off as needed.

Share-level access: A level of security in Windows that allows users to create their own shares and set their own passwords.

User-level access: A level of security in Windows that provides users with all permitted access to network resources using a single user ID and password.

Workgroup: A collection of independently managed users and/or devices on a network that are configured to share files and devices.

ACRONYM ALERT

ATM: Asynchronous Transfer Mode

DHCP: Dynamic Host Configuration Protocol. A protocol that assigns IP addresses to client computers on the fly.

DNS: Domain Name Services. A service that resolves host name to IP address on the Internet.

DSL: Digital Subscriber Line

DUN: Dial-Up Networking. A method of connecting to a network over a modem.

ICS: Internet Connection Sharing. A service that allows multiple computers to share a single Internet access line.

IPX/SPX: Internetwork Packet Exchange/ Sequenced Packed Exchange. A Novell networking protocol.

ISDN: Integrated Services Digital Network

NetBEUI: NetBIOS Extended User Interface. A Microsoft networking protocol.

PPP: Point-to-Point Protocol

TCP/IP: Transmission Control Protocol/ Internet Protocol. The networking protocol of the Internet.

WINS: Windows Internet Naming Service. A service that resolves host name to IP address on the local network.

CHAPTER 14

Navigating the Internet

Even though this is basically a book about computer hardware, it certainly wouldn't be complete without a rundown on the Internet. Everybody uses it. In fact, everybody these days pretty much takes it for granted. It's one of those things that is just there and always was, right? However, calling the Internet just another network is like calling the space shuttle just another airplane. And as difficult as it may be to believe, the Internet hasn't always been around. Although some of us old-timers might find it difficult to believe just how long it *has* been in place.

A+ Operating System Technologies Exam Objectives

CompTIA exam objectives covered in this chapter include the following:

   4.2   Identify concepts and capabilities relating to the Internet and basic procedures for setting up a system for Internet access.

The History of the Internet

Although this may come as a disappointment to some, it is my grievous duty to report that Al Gore did not actually invent the Internet. The Internet is one of those multiheaded entities that came about as the result of the work of thousands of individuals developing protocols and hardware that would allow different systems running on different platforms to communicate. However, if you want to give any one specific individual credit for the concept, let's give it to Joseph Carl Robnett Licklider of MIT.

In 1962, he wrote a paper entitled "On-Line Man Computer Communication." In this paper, he described what he called the Galactic Network. This galactic network was composed of a worldwide conglomeration of computer systems interconnected in order to share and distribute information. Sound familiar? As the head of the Computer Research Program for the

Defense Advanced Research Projects Agency (DARPA), he was given the opportunity to put form to some of his concepts, although the work would eventually be completed by his successor, Lawrence Roberts.

Another MIT alumnus, Leonard Kleinrock, had written a paper entitled "Information Flow in Large Communication Nets," which described how information could be broken down into packets for communication over a wire. Roberts brought Kleinrock on board, and in 1965 they had their first success. They interconnected MIT's TX-2 mainframe to a Q-32 in California. To illustrate what a remarkable achievement this was for the time, the TX-2 was a computer system built by academics that used a 38-bit word and had no operating system as they are known today. Instead, programmers had to compile their own programs or data. The Q-32 was a machine custom built for the military by IBM and used a 48-bit word. The two systems made their first connection over a telephone line.

The following year, Roberts presented his plan for interconnecting a number of different computer systems scattered across the country into an integrated network. In 1969, there were a total of four computers linked together in the network now known as ARPANET. ARPANET became global in 1973 when The University College of London was successfully added to the network.

Two things happened in 1974 that provided momentum for the Internet to become the medium it is today. First and foremost was the publication of "A Protocol for Packet Network Intercommunication," by Vincent Cerf and Robert Kahn. It was in this paper that the Transmission Control Protocol was defined. The other significant event of that year was the release of the first commercial implementation of a packet-based data service. Bolt, Berenek, and Newman gave us Telenet.

Other global networks quickly began to emerge. In 1980 the Computer Science Network (CSNET) and the Because It's Time Network (BITNET) arrived. The year 1982 saw the European UNIX Network (EUNET). A major step toward interlinking all of these networks occurred in 1983 when a gateway between CSNET and ARPANET was created.

> **EXAM NOTE:** One of the occasional exam questions you might see deals with the history of the Internet. Know about ARPANET in particular.

In order to keep track of who was who in this ever-growing collection of entities, the Domain Name System (DNS) was ratified in 1984. This provided a more user-friendly way for humans to locate computers over the wire. DNS provided each entity with a host name and created the domains that identified the type of organization. At first, there were only six primary domains: education (edu), commercial (com), government (gov), military (mil), organization (org), and network (net). That has been expanded over the years.

From there, it was only a matter of time. In 1987, there were approximately 10,000 hosts on the Internet. Two years later, the number exceeded 100,000. But for most of us, the pivotal year was 1991. This was the year that the European Organization for Nuclear Research (CERN) unveiled the World Wide Web. One of their researchers, a man named Tim Berner-Lee developed a method of linking documents to one another electronically called Hypertext Markup Language (HTML).

I give you the Internet. But I didn't invent it.

FOUNDATIONS OF THE INTERNET

In the early days of development, it was apparent that the Internet was going to be a collection of internetworked networks rather than one of individual computers. A few key issues had to be resolved early on before serious development could begin. For one thing, if you wanted an organization to become a part of this global movement, you had to earn its trust. Therefore, it was decided that each network would stand alone. The process of internetworking would not require that any modifications to network structure or administration be implemented. Second, on an operational level, there would be no control of the network permitted by outside sources.

Multiple networks would be linked together by routers or gateways. These devices would not retain data after a transmission was completed. Routers had to be platform-independent.

Another key issue, after the World Wide Web was implemented, dealt with how to get individual users onto the network. The following section explains the different intermediate levels that occur from the end-user's machine up to the actual source of data being accessed by that user. The concept is illustrated in **Figure 14.1**. These intermediate levels include the following:

- User's PC
- User's datacom
- The local loop carrier
- The ISP point of presence (POP)
- User services
- ISP backbone
- Online content
- Origin of content

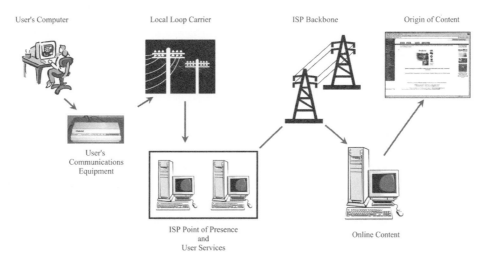

Figure 14.1   While your web browser makes it seem easy, getting online is actually a pretty complicated process.

THE USER'S PC

Of these different links, the user's PC should be the one that requires the least explanation (**Figure 14.2**). However, it should be noted that there are different hardware requirements for different applications. If you're involved in any activity requiring sound, it might be nice if you have the appropriate equipment installed. A sound card, speakers, and very likely a microphone are in order. Applications such as tele-conferencing will require this sort of setup. If you work with streaming video, an appropriate graphics adapter is in order. Obviously, you will also need some form of software interface. Most people use Web browsers such as Internet Explorer or Netscape Navigator. Other software packages that are useful include some form of FTP client, an email client, and perhaps a Telnet client.

Figure 14.2 Internet connections start with the user logging onto the Internet.

THE USER'S DATACOM

More simply put, this is the communications equipment that allows the user's PC to hook up to another PC over a communications link of some sort (**Figure 14.3**). In the old days this was a simpler matter. Everyone used modems. These days the choices include the following:

- Public Switched Telephone Network (PSTN) — Dial-up networking with a modem. ~53.3K
- Integrated Services Digital Network (ISDN) — Sometimes called digital modem. ~128K
- Digital Subscriber Line (DSL) — High-speed broadband. ~384K – 6MB
- Cable Modem — Internet over cable television services. Speed varies
- Satellite Internet — Broadband Wireless Internet. ~400K

BUZZ WORDS

Datacom: A term coined to describe any equipment used in data communications.

Figure 14.3 The user's telecommunications equipment makes the connection.

Which choice you make impacts your speed of service, as you might imagine. However, be aware that not all services are available in all areas.

THE LOCAL LOOP CARRIER

Somebody has to maintain the circuits that carry the signal between you and your service provider (**Figure 14.4**). Depending on your choice of datacom, these options include your local telephone company, cable television company, or an independent contractor. Your selection here not only impacts performance, but security as well. Some carriers are less secure than others. For example, if you use a cable modem, when you log on you become part of a local segment for the company. Any files you have shared on your computer can be browsed by others on the same segment simply by visiting Network Neighborhood. A good firewall is in order here if you have any sensitive data at all.

Other carriers, such as satellites, can be impacted by external conditions. These would include elements such as the weather, solar flares, or other conditions beyond your control. If a constant connection is critical to your organization, you should consider this before investing in the equipment needed.

BUZZ WORDS

Local loop carrier: A communications service provider. It provides the electronic link between geographically separated devices.

Figure 14.4 Your local communications services provider connects you to your ISP.

THE ISP POINT OF PRESENCE (POP)

People can't just hook themselves up to the Internet arbitrarily. They need some sort of service that provides an access point to the Internet. This provides the control necessary to prevent the presence of identical IP addresses on the Net, as well as providing a certain degree (although it's a very limited one) of security. Your Internet Service Provider (ISP) provides this function. Larger ISPs will have more than one POP. For every metropolitan area they serve, in order to provide local dial-up services, they will provide a separate POP. This POP controls your connection type and speed as well as providing user logon and authentication services.

> **EXAM NOTE:** The role of the ISP is particularly important. Some things to know about your ISP include the services they provide, such as the HyperText Transfer Protocol (HTTP), the Simple Mail Transfer Protocol (SMTP), and the Post Office Protocol (POP), as well as the fact that they host DNS servers.

The ISP also provides certain supplementary services, such as POP and SMTP services. These are the protocols for sending and receiving email. They act as your DNS server, greatly expediting your search for locations on the Internet. They also control the presence of IP addresses on the Web.

The ISP does this because when it first established its services, it obtained a block of IP addresses from an administrative organization assigned to administer IP addresses. In the old days, this was InterNIC, or the Internet's Network Information Center. It used to be the sole administrator of IP addresses and domain names. These days, it only does domain names. IP addresses are allocated by The Internet Corporation for Assigned Names and Numbers (ICANN). Any given ISP has a certain number of addresses it can hand out and no more. In order for the ISP to efficiently manage its pool of addresses, they are usually handed out by the DHCP protocol. However, dedicated links require static IP addresses. Therefore, you must use the IP address assigned to you by your ISP.

EXAM NOTE: Know who it is that assigns IP addresses and who it is that assigns domain names.

THE USER SERVICES

User services can be administered either on a local level or through your ISP. They might also be provided by a third party. Most end users depend on their ISPs for the majority of their services, but not always. These services include the following:

- Domain name services
- Email hosting services
- Web hosting
- FTP services
- Newsgroup services
- Bulletin board services

Many of these services can be quite resource intensive and require dedicated servers in order to be implemented. Therefore, many companies and organizations depend on an ISP for these services. However, in a larger organization, Internet traffic can be minimized if the services are administered locally.

THE ISP BACKBONE

ISPs are not islands alone. Many of the larger companies, such as AT&T, Sprint, PSINet, and others, maintain their own infrastructure and lease it out to smaller ISPs. The signals are routed over high-speed broadband fiber circuits maintained by the major telecommunications corporations. These would include AT&T, Sprint, MCI, and others. The different providers link their services together over banks of routers and switches.

Most major metropolitan areas have one or more Network Access Points (NAP). These provide the entry point to a large capacity circuit. This is one of those fiber circuits mentioned previously. ISPs lease fiber optics connections to link each of their POPs together. However, if that is as far as anyone went, the customers of one company would have communications with all other customers of that company if they so desired, but not with other ISPs of the world. Therefore, the various ISPs set up gateways between their networks through these NAPs.

From there, data moves over large capacity circuits to its destination NAP. Large capacity circuits range everywhere from T1 lines operating at 1.544Mb/s over the smaller connections to an OC-48 line capable of moving 2.488 gigabits of data every second. Each of the major communications carriers maintains its own backbone infrastructure. Through various international arrangements, these corporations have agreed to communicate with one another, allowing the unobstructed passage of the data moving over the lines.

ONLINE CONTENT

The material you're searching for generally resides on a Web server. Web servers are particularly potent computers running an NOS specifically designed for maintaining multiple incoming virtual connections. These operating systems include Apache, UNIX, Microsoft's Datacenter, and several others.

Web servers are likely to host hundreds or even thousands of sites on a single machine— or to be more accurate, a single cluster of machines. It is unlikely that any business seriously involved in Web hosting would entrust its future to a single box. Web sites are identified by their domain name. Any site created and published out to the Internet must be properly registered with one of the various agencies. When your computer wants to finds a specific Web site, it will make use of DNS to find it. When a specific site has been found, you will have access to any data for which you have the appropriate permissions.

ORIGIN OF CONTENT

This is the part of the chain that is providing much of the legal battleground for the Internet. The material that is actually made available for consumption constitutes *origin of content* (**Figure 14.5**). This consists of pretty much every form of medium that can be stored digitally. Hundreds of thousands of books, movies, images, musical recordings, and so on have been converted to digital format and made available to the public.

A huge stir of controversy has erupted over several issues relating to this. For one thing, how should children be protected from viewing unsuitable material? Or for that matter, is some information suitable for public distribution at all? Do we really want detailed instructions on how to make your own nuclear warhead generally available to the public? Fortunately, this book does not have to confront these issues head on.

Figure 14.5 A single Web page created by an individual or organization makes up the origin of content, which is the final data you receive.

Know your copyright laws well. The laws that protect written materials are just as valid over the Internet as they are in the public library. Just because you have the technology and the resources to copy and publish another person's creations doesn't mean you have the right.

ADMINISTERING THE INTERNET

As of 2002, a crude estimate of the Internet population was approximately a half billion people per day (**Figure 14.6**). At that time, there were a little more than 170 million Web sites competing for their attention. In order to prevent this from being total chaos, someone needs to be responsible for keeping track of things like IP addresses, domain names, security, and enforcement.

This is far too much for a single agency to keep track of. Therefore, several agencies are assigned different tasks. Domain naming and the distribution of IP addresses on a global level fall under the jurisdiction of the Internet Assigned Numbers Authority (IANA). To make things run a little more smoothly, this organization has delegated much of its responsibility to regional groups. IP addresses are managed regionally by the American Registry for Internet Numbers (ARIN), the Asia-Pacific Network Information Center (APNIC), and Réseaux IP Européens

Internet Growth

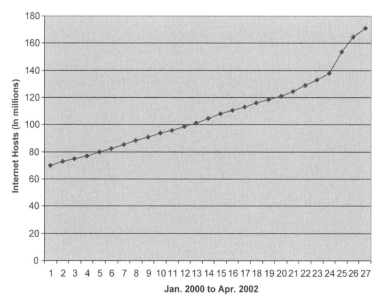

Figure 14.6   Internet growth from Jan. 2000 to Apr. 2002

(RIPE-NCC). Agencies that handle domain naming include InterNIC, RIPE-NCC, and Asia-Pacific NIC.

Even so, should you require an IP address, you would not approach any of these organizations directly. The proper procedure is to approach your ISP and make your request. It will contact an intermediate agency, known as an upstream register, in order to fill your request.

Operational control of the Internet falls under the watchful eye of the Internet Engineering Planning Group (IEPG). The American organization charged with this responsibility is the North American Network Operators Group (NANOG). It is an evolutionary offshoot of the National Science Foundation Network (NSFNET). This organization oversees the development of new Internet segments, maintains acceptable use policies, and, until it was retired in 1996, maintained the NSFNET backbone. The European entity that manages this is called EOF, and in the Asian-Pacific region, it is AP-NG.

The rash of critical viruses that erupted in 2001 brought to the spotlight another group that has been around for years. This is the Forum of Incident Response and Security Teams (FIRST). FIRST oversees a group of Computer Emergency Response Teams (CERT) in eight countries and a large number of ISPs that monitors the Internet and respond to these types of incidents. In an outbreak such as the Nimbda virus, these organizations respond quickly in an attempt to isolate the virus and stop its propagation. And then they work on finding its origin.

In addition to these organizations, there are literally hundreds of others focused on more granular issues. There are groups that oversee the development of protocols, and other groups that come up with the names for those protocols. There are legal organizations calling the shots and lobbying for or against various and sundry laws governing the Internet. There are organizations overseeing the dispersal and movement of email, newsgroups, and World Wide Web pages. It goes on and on. One organization that does a wonderful job of overseeing a large number of these groups is the Internet Society (ISOC). To get a good overview of its responsibilities and ongoing projects, visit its Web site at www.isoc.org.

CHAPTER SUMMARY

By now, I'm sure you realize that the Internet is an extremely complex entity. In some respects, it has taken on a life of its own, perpetually growing and occupying more virtual space. In this chapter, I examined a bit of the infrastructure of the Internet. Key features covered in this chapter are some of the administrative procedures involved in acquiring and maintaining an Internet presence, as well as how the millions of interconnected devices around the world make the concept of the Internet a reality.

NOTE: Since this chapter covers a topic not heavily addressed by the exam, I am intentionally including fewer practice questions.

BRAIN DRAIN

1. List the intermediate levels across which information traveling between two machines communicating over the Internet must travel.

2. Describe in as much detail as you can the structure of an ISP backbone.

3. Discuss the differences between origin of content and online content.

4. List as many organizations as you can that are involved in administering, policing, and protecting the Internet.

THE 64K$ QUESTIONS

1. Who invented the Internet?
   a. Al Gore
   b. JCR Licklider
   c. ISOC
   d. Nobody. It just grew.

2. Which of the following was the first network to span a nation?
   a. CSNET
   b. ARPANET
   c. NFSNET
   d. BITNET

3. The intermediate level that moves user data from the modem to the ISP is called _____.
   a. The user's datacom
   b. The ISP's POP
   c. User services
   d. The local loop carrier

4. The distribution of IP addresses is handled by _____.
   a. InterNIC
   b. ISOC
   c. ICAN
   d. IANA

5. The page you view when browsing the Internet is an example of _____.

   a. Online content

   b. Origin of content

   c. User services

   d. Host services

TRICKY TERMINOLOGY

Datacom: A term coined to describe any equipment used in data communications.

Local loop carrier: A communications service provider. It provides the electronic link between geographically separated devices.

Online content: The overall availability of resources across an intranet or the Internet.

ACRONYM ALERT

FIRST: Forum of Incident Response and Security Teams. An organization charged with maintaining the security of the Internet.

IANA: The Internet Assigned Numbers Authority. The organization that currently hands out IP address to those that need them.

ICANN: The Internet Corporation for Assigned Names and Numbers. One of several organizations involved in the administration of the Internet.

IEPG: The Internet Engineering and Planning Group. An organization involved in overseeing the operational control of the Internet.

InterNIC: Internet's Network Information Center. One of several organizations involved in the administration of the Internet.

ISOC: The Internet Society. The organization that oversees all the other organizations involved in managing the Internet.

ISP: Internet Service Provider. The end user's gateway to the Internet.

NAP: Network Access Point. The entry point to one of the several large capacity circuits that transport data across the Internet.

POP: Point of Presence. The physical connection supplied by an ISP that provides access to the Internet.

CHAPTER 15

TROUBLESHOOTING THE OS

Wouldn't this be a marvelous world if everything worked exactly as advertised? If cars never broke down, refrigerators only used as much electricity as a hundred-watt light bulb, and computers never crashed? I'm sorry to say, in this world, you're more like to eventually have the first two dreams come true than that last one.

Throughout this book, I've provided a number of tips and suggestions on how to keep your system running its best and how to figure out what went wrong when Windows turns your expensive toy into a doorstop. For the sake of convenience, I'm going to put it all together in a single chapter. If I repeat myself in this chapter, forgive me. Would you rather have a bit of repetition, or have to go scampering through 600 pages next time your computer acts up?

A+ OPERATING SYSTEM TECHNOLOGIES EXAM OBJECTIVES

CompTIA objectives covered in this chapter include the following:

3.1 Recognize and interpret the meaning of common error codes and startup messages from the boot sequence, and identify steps to correct the problems.

3.2 Recognize when to use common diagnostic utilities and tools. Given a diagnostic scenario involving one of these utilities or tools, select the appropriate steps needed to resolve the problem.

3.3 Recognize common operational and usability problems and determine how to resolve them.

A COLLECTION OF TROUBLESHOOTING AIDS

Every technician eventually collects his or her own little bag of tricks that is always at hand. For all of us there are some basic essentials that we just cannot live without:

- Boot disks for the various OSs
- A recovery CD for the 32-bit OSs
- A collection of diagnostic utilities
- A toolkit
- A solid knowledge of what you're doing

Hopefully, you've gotten that last one out of this book and its companion volume, *The A+ Guide to PC Hardware Maintenance and Repair*. The toolkit is something you'll need to buy, but the others are all things you can either make or download for free. Let's start with the things you can make.

Boot Disks and Recovery Disks

These are becoming less important with each new generation of PC and each new OS generation. Still, there are times they are lifesavers. When the computer absolutely will not boot to the OS and the user has critical files that were never backed up, it's important that you at least try to recover that data. Booting to a floppy (or set of floppies) is a way to get the system started.

Unfortunately, with WIN2K and XP, there isn't much you can do simply with the boot disks. That's where the recovery disks come into play. More on that in a moment. On a system running WIN9x, the file system can be accessed from the command prompt after the system has booted to the floppy. If the hard drive is still readable, it may be possible to copy that data to another hard disk.

To create a boot diskette in WIN9x, have the OS installation CD available along with a blank, formatted high-density floppy diskette. Click Start→Settings→Control Panel and then double-click Add/Remove Programs. At the top of the screen there is a tab that says Startup Disk. Click that and then click the Create Disk button. You'll be prompted for the installation CD. Once the applet reads that, it will ask you to insert the floppy diskette. If there is data on the diskette, it will be lost. If there are bad sectors on the diskette, it will be unusable. I highly recommend a brand new one.

The utility will first create a MBR on the floppy. Then it will copy a number of different files onto this diskette. It's critical to know what some of them are. The key files to be copied are listed here:

- IO.SYS: System boot file
- MSDOS.SYS: Boot option information (paths, multiboot, and so on)
- DRVSPACE.BIN: Microsoft DriveSpace compression driver
- CONFIG.SYS: Loads the device drivers
- HIMEM.SYS: Extended (XMS) Memory Manager
- COMMAND.COM: Command interpreter
- AUTOEXEC.BAT: A batch file with a number of commands that run on startup

- OAKCDROM.SYS: Generic device driver for ATAPI CD-ROM drives
- RAMDRIVE.SYS: Creates a Ramdrive during startup
- EXTRACT.EXE: File to expand the Ebd.cab file
- FDISK.EXE: Disk partition tool
- SYS.COM: System transfer tool
- FORMAT.COM: The Microsoft disk formatting utility

This diskette can start up any Intel-based PC with a 486 or greater CPU and 4MB of RAM. It doesn't matter what OS is installed on the hard disk. Remember, however, that once the machine is booted to this disk, it can only read FAT. The booted OS kernel is blind to NTFS partitions and sees them as uninitialized disks.

Therefore, on NTFS machines, it might be possible to repartition the drive using FDISK and reformat it. But it will not be possible to extract data.

WINNT DISKS

Windows NT will actually require two sets of diskettes. The first set is the installation set, consisting of three diskettes. The second is the ERD discussed in Chapter Six. The first set boots your system, while the ERD allows you to at least attempt to recover the system.

MAKING INSTALLATION DISKETTES

To do this, you will need three blank, formatted high-density diskettes. It's easiest if you do this from the command prompt or from the Start→Run command line. It really doesn't matter what OS is installed on the system. Browse to the I386 directory on the NT installation CD. Type **winnt /ox** on the command line or at the command prompt. This opens the utility that copies the necessary files to the floppies. It writes diskette number three first and then number two, and creates the bootable disk as the last one. There is a large number of files copied to these diskettes, but you really only need to remember a few from the boot diskette:

- NTLDR
- NTDETECT.COM
- BOOT.INI
- NTBOOTDD.SYS
- OSLOADER.EXE
- HAL.DLL

You can actually create a simplified boot diskette by copying just these files over to a floppy formatted in NT. That floppy will be directed to look for the NTLDR file to lead it through the boot process. You'll want to use the actual files from your working machine before it crashes. Otherwise, you'll lose your original configuration.

With WIN2K and WINXP, the procedure is similar, except you will need a total of four diskettes. Another difference is that instead of running WINNT /OX from the command line, you run a utility called MAKEBOOT. This utility is located in the BOOTDISK directory of the installation CD.

CREATING AN EMERGENCY REPAIR DISK

If a WINNT box goes down, you can utilize the ERD to boot the computer when the operating system fails to load properly. This diskette will then initiate an emergency repair process that will hopefully restore the system to its original settings. You'll be prompted to make this diskette during the Windows NT 4.0 installation. However, in order to ensure that your system configuration is up to date, the disk should be manually created after the system is properly configured and all accounts created.

To manually create an emergency repair disk, format a blank floppy disk within Windows NT. This will add the NTLDR file and the MBR to look for that file instead of conventional OS files. Next type **RDISK.EXE** at the Run line or from a command prompt. The files required to initiate and run the emergency repair process will be copied to the floppy disk. You should use the RDISK utility to update the emergency repair disk each time you make a configuration change in Windows NT 4.0. Otherwise, the ERD will restore your system to an old configuration.

WHEN THE SYSTEM FAILS TO BOOT

System boot failures generally come in one of two types. The worst-case scenario is when the system can't even find a MBR from which to boot. This generally results in one of several different errors:

- Invalid boot disk
- Inaccessible boot device (or boot device not available)
- I/O error reading Drive C:
- Missing NTLDR
- Bad or missing command interpreter

When you see any of the first three messages, all too often your first instinct is to assume your hard drive failed. Needless to say, there will be times when this is the situation. However, before replacing the drive, consider a few alternatives.

Has there been a change in the system recently that may have moved drive letters around? BOOT.INI is configured to look for a specific partition on a specific drive. If that drive letter or partition number has changed, then BOOT.INI doesn't find the boot files it needs. As far as it is concerned, the disk no longer exists. It could simply be a matter of editing BOOT.INI.

Are you using a third-party disk controller? If so, it could simply be a matter of having to reinstall the drivers. With these adapters, you can see whether the BIOS is recognizing the drives during POST. Right after the system POST and just before the MBR is loaded, you will have an opportunity to press a specific key or key sequence that will load the Setup program for the controller. While this is not always the case, generally, if the disk is visible from within the adapter's setup program, then the disk is physically working properly. That doesn't mean, however, that the OS sees it or that the MBR hasn't been corrupted by a virus.

Most anti-virus software programs come with a boot diskette for this very reason. Make sure the boot diskette has the latest signature files copied to it and boot the machine to that floppy. Let the program scan the entire system.

If all this comes up empty, it's time to pull out one of those third-party diagnostics programs to see whether the hard disk has failed. If this is the case, I certainly hope you have a recent backup. While it's possible to retrieve data from a failed hard drive, it can be quite expensive.

The messages "Missing NTLDR" or "Missing Command Interpreter" don't point to a hardware issue. They point to a corrupted OS installation. Once again, in WINNT, WIN2K, or WINXP, first check to see whether BOOT.INI is pointing to the correct drive and partition. If it's not, edit the file and away you go.

With WIN9x, it may be a simple matter of running the SYS command from the boot floppy you made earlier. Boot to the floppy, and from the command prompt, type **SYS C:**. As long as the disk is physically intact, the system will now be bootable. In the 32-bit OSs, copy NTDLR, NTDETECT.COM, and OSLOADER.EXE to the active partition to which BOOT.INI points. If this fails, it's time to pull out the ERD.

Other startup issues you may encounter might not prevent the system from booting, but they might either prevent Windows from loading or from working correctly after it loads. Some of these messages include the following:

- Error in CONFIG.SYS line XX
- HIMEM.SYS not loaded
- Missing or corrupt HIMEM.SYS
- Device/Service has failed to start

Unfortunately, with some brands of machine it's quite possible that you won't see these errors when they occur because of the splash screen. If a system is behaving erratically, freezing at some point during the boot process, or restarting after it gets to a certain point, try pressing the <Esc> key as soon as the splash screen appears. This will get rid of it, and you can watch the POST messages as they occur.

The message about an error in CONFIG.SYS is rarely as much of a problem with WIN2K or WINXP as it was with earlier versions. Since the message tells you specifically what line is causing the problem, it's easy enough to fix it. If the line was added by some device driver installation for DOS compatibility, perhaps you don't even need it. Use Notepad or the DOS Editor to add the letters **REM** in front of the line.

Life isn't that simple if HIMEM.SYS fails to load. That's the file that allows the system to use extended memory. Check the line in CONFIG.SYS that loads the driver. Examine the path listed very carefully and make sure the file is really where it's supposed to be. If not, use the EXPAND command to put a new copy into the directory. From the command prompt, change over the I386 directory on the installation CD. Type **EXPAND HIMEM.SY_ C:\%WINDIR%\SYSTEM32** (where **%WINDIR%** is the actual directory to your Windows installation).

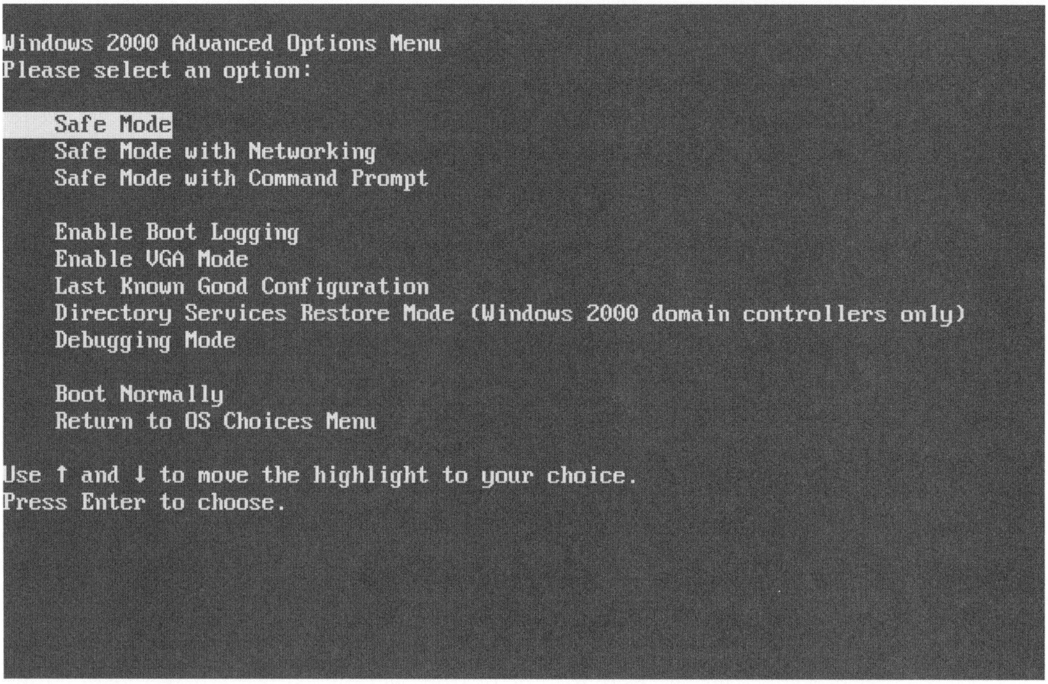

```
Windows 2000 Advanced Options Menu
Please select an option:

   Safe Mode
   Safe Mode with Networking
   Safe Mode with Command Prompt

   Enable Boot Logging
   Enable VGA Mode
   Last Known Good Configuration
   Directory Services Restore Mode (Windows 2000 domain controllers only)
   Debugging Mode

   Boot Normally
   Return to OS Choices Menu

Use ↑ and ↓ to move the highlight to your choice.
Press Enter to choose.
```

Figure 15.1 The Advanced Startup menu offers several different options for starting Windows.

In WINNT, WIN2K, and WINXP, you may get the message that a device or service has failed to start after Windows has loaded. Check Event View for little red stop signs. These indicate critical errors. By double-clicking the flagged entry, Event Viewer will tell you exactly what failed to start. In most cases, it will also tell you any other services the failed service may have required in order to run that failed to load. Virtually every message found in Event Viewer is something you can research on Microsoft's TechNet Web site for information on how to fix the problem.

ADVANCED STARTUP OPTIONS

Every version of Windows from WIN95 forward has offered the ability for the user to choose how the system is going to start. Pressing <F8> before Windows is allowed to load will bring up the advanced startup options (**Figure 15.1**). Pressing <F5> will take Windows directly into Safe Mode.

Knowing what each of these options can do for you can be valuable information. The available options are as follows:

1. Normal

2. Logged (\BOOTLOG.TXT,

3. Safe mode

4. Step-by-step confirmation

5. Command prompt only

6. Safe mode command prompt only

Normal is self-explanatory. Once in a while, after an abnormal shutdown, Windows will boot to the advanced startup options automatically. If you know there's nothing wrong, press 1 and boot to Windows.

Logged mode attempts to boot Windows normally. However, all the while that it's booting, it's recording each event that occurs during startup to a text file in the root directory called BOOTLOG.TXT. This mode of booting even records directory entries as they attempt to load. The knowledgeable user can search for entries marked LoadFail in the log and see what drivers and/or services failed.

Safe mode is the alternative boot method used most often by technicians. Someone loads a new device driver and now the system won't boot. My goodness, what can you do now? By booting into safe mode, the offending driver can be uninstalled and the correct one installed.

Step-by-step confirmation must be useful to somebody or Microsoft engineers wouldn't have bothered to include it. What it does is to allow the user to step through each line of CONFIG.SYS and AUTOEXEC.BAT and either choose to load that line or not load it. Since WIN9x pretty much ignores those two files unless a MS-DOS window is opened, this really has little effect on how Windows loads in graphical mode.

Command prompt only is just like it sounds. The machine boots to a window not a lot different from the MS-DOS of old. The OS running on the system is, in fact, MS-DOS 7.0. This method of booting was very popular among gamers who didn't want to give up their old DOS games that wouldn't run in Windows.

Safe mode command prompt only is the arena of final desperation. If the machine won't boot into safe mode successfully, the user can attempt to start the machine in safe mode command prompt. Assuming the user knows enough about the command line to do anything, perhaps the problem can be fixed. Some the things the average user can do from here are to run SCANDISK, DEFRAG, or REGEDIT, or launch a command-line antivirus application.

THIRD-PARTY DIAGNOSTICS SOFTWARE

For all the success Windows has enjoyed, one reputation that it has *never* had is that of being the most reliable OS in the world. A thriving industry has grown up around software that does nothing but fix the problems inherent in the OS. This software includes programs that scan the registry looking for obvious errors or that teach Windows to do new tricks, and general maintenance programs for Windows.

A couple of notable programs that I have grown to know and love are mentioned toward the end of this section. But before I do that, I wanted to discuss briefly how many of these programs work.

Registry tweakers, as I call them, vary in quality from pretty good to abysmal. They look at your system configuration and compare the actual configuration to what the registry thinks it is. So why would that be any different?

The registry is not a self-healing entity. As programs are added and removed, registry entries are added, but often not removed. The same is true with hardware. You may have started out with a cheap network card and a really bad sound card. Once you realized your mistake, you replaced them both. The device installations made all new registry entries for the new stuff, but didn't do anything at all about the old registry entries.

Ninety-nine times out of a hundred, that's no big deal. Once in a great while, conflicts cause the new toy to not work. Unfortunately, when you try to go back to the old device, it doesn't work any more either. Personally, I've seen that happen on two different brands of network cards and one sound card.

Registry Doctor is my personal favorite. It isn't free, but it's cheap enough it might as well be. It does a marvelous job of finding all those pesky entries that are no longer relevant to your configuration. Unused entries, even when they don't conflict, can cause your system to boot more slowly and degrade general performance as well.

FAT32 and NTFS file systems pose new problems for file recovery and disk recovery utilities. It's important that, if you need to use one of these, you use the correct version for your file system. Several different companies have come out with disk utilities.

Some commercial software packages that are particularly useful to the technician are PC Tools and Norton SystemWorks. PC Tools is a suite of hardware diagnostics utilities that rigorously test various components on the system. SystemWorks targets software related glitches. I carry a copy of each with me wherever I go.

TROUBLESHOOTING NETWORK CONNECTIONS

Here's another area where you'll spend an abundant amount of time. We live in a networked world. It used to be that home PCs didn't have networking problems. This is no longer the case. More and more homes have multiple computers and want them to share a single Internet connection. The easy solution is to set up a network. Even many single-PC households find that networking issues become commonplace once they hook up to DSL. Chapter Thirteen covered the basics of networking in a moderate amount of detail. Here, I'll discuss what you can do when things go wrong.

CONNECTIVITY ISSUES

Most novices assume that any time a computer can't see the network, that it's always an issue with the connection. True connectivity issues can be physical or logical, however. Physical issues are easier to detect. On the back of your computer, where the network cables plugs in, there will be two lights. One is an activity light, and the other is a link light. The link light only glows when there is a physical electrical connection between your NIC and whatever the other end of the cable hooks up to.

On a larger network, this is likely to be a hub or a switch. In a home network, you might be hooking directly to a DSL or cable modem. Either way, if you've got a link light, you've got a physical connection.

Logical connectivity is a different story all together. Just because the electrical path exists between one computer and the next doesn't mean that the two devices can talk.

If you don't have physical connectivity (that is, no link light), first check the cable connections. Are all cables properly seated on both ends? With RJ-45 connections, you should hear a firm *click* when the cable plugs in. If you're going wireless, you need to check and see if the signal is strong on both ends. Home wireless networks have notoriously short transmission distances.

On the RJ-45 connection, if the physical connection is secure, you might check the cable before you start fooling around with the system configuration. A good cable tester comes in handy for that, but not everybody has one of those lying around. Swap the cable out for a known good one if you can. In a larger installation, try hooking up to a different jack.

If the wiring turns out to be good, check the NIC drivers next. In Control Panel, open the System Applet and check the NIC. If there is no red X or yellow exclamation point, then Windows at least *thinks* the NIC is working properly. Open a command prompt and type **PING 127.0.0.1** and wait for a couple of seconds. If four replies come back all saying that the packet was received, then the NIC is physically doing what it's supposed to do. So now it's time to check the configuration.

On a P2P network, all computers need to be members of the same workgroup, but each one has to have a unique computer name. If you are running TCP/IP as your protocol, then the computers need to be on the same network address, but each one needs a unique host address. On a business network, there may be a DHCP server assigning addresses. Also, most DSL and cable modems act as DHCP servers. In any of these situations, IP addresses should be dynamically assigned.

It's easy enough to see what your IP address is. From a command prompt, type the command **IPCONFIG /ALL**. Note that trying this from the Start→Run command line will also work, but only if you read about a zillion words a minute. The information will appear for about a half a second and then disappear. If IPCONFIG reports an IP address of 169.*.*.*, then the NIC is configured for DHCP, but it is not seeing a DHCP server on the network.

If you're on a large network, call in the network administrator. It just became his or her job. If you're only hooked up to a cable modem, open your favorite Internet browser and type in the IP address of your modem as the Web address. That IP address should be in the documentation that came with it. If not, try either 192.168.0.1 or 192.168.1.1. Those are the most commonly used IP addresses for modems. If a logon screen for the modem setup software appears, then the NIC is working fine. The modem is the problem. Therefore, it's the responsibility of the ISP to provide the technical support.

On a P2P network, all IP addresses must be statically assigned. For a discussion on IP addresses, refer to Chapter Thirteen.

One thing that happens infrequently, but that does happen, is that the TCP/IP stack becomes corrupted. Keep in mind that a protocol is nothing more than a program running on your computer. Programs can crash or become corrupted. One sign of a corrupted TCP/IP stack is that you can successfully ping one IP address on the network, but the user at that machine can't ping you. Or vice-versa.

Rebuilding the TCP/IP stack is as simple as opening the Network applet in Control Panel, clicking the TCP/IP protocol, and then clicking Remove. Windows will ask you whether you're sure. Click Yes. If this is the only networking protocol you have installed, you will now be told that your network configuration is incomplete. Do you really wish to continue? Click Yes.

On a WIN9x box, you will have to reboot the machine. Theoretically, that isn't necessary on a WIN2K or WINXP machine. For rebuilding the TCP/IP stack, I strongly recommend you do so anyway. Once the machine has rebooted, go back into the Network applet and add TCP/IP back. You're most likely going to need your installation CD for that. Once again, even if you're not prompted to reboot once the files have all been copied, do so anyway.

CHAPTER SUMMARY

This has been only the briefest overview of basic Windows troubleshooting methods. There are a number of very complete volumes covering this subject that are available. Browsing the shelves at your local bookstore should bring up a goodly number.

What I hope you brought away from this chapter, and from previous chapters in this book, are the various resources within Windows for basic troubleshooting as well as awareness that third-party solutions exist. Do remember that this was an overview chapter and that the various chapters on each OS offered more specific detail, and for that reason, I'm not including any review questions here.

APPENDIX A

Windows Functions

Table A.1 Windows Hotkey Shortcuts

Shortcut	Action
<Alt>	Activates or deactivates the current window's menu bar.
<Delete>	Deletes selected Item(s).
Drag and Drop	Press and hold left mouse button. Slide selected object(s) over the icon that depicts the desired destination folder or device and then release.
<End>	Moves cursor to end of current line, except for Internet Explorer. In IE, moves to the bottom of the page.
<Enter>	Opens selected item or activates highlighted button.
<Esc>	Cancels current operation.
<F1>	Displays context-sensitive help for selected item.
<F2>	In IE, activates the Rename command.
<F3>	In IE, opens a file search.
<F4>	In IE, displays "My Computer" menu.
	In IE, displays "Address" history list.
<F5>	Refreshes the contents of the current window.
<F6>	Switches between active panes of current application.
<Home>	Moves cursor to beginning of line (except IE).
	In IE, moves to the top of the page.
Menu Button (▤)	Duplicates the function of the right mouse button.
<Print Screen>	Copies the current screen to clipboard as bitmap image.
Space Bar	Toggles current check box or radio button.
<Tab>	Moves between fields and/or objects of current window.
Windows Button (▣)	Open the Start menu.

(continued)

Table A.1 Windows Hot-key Shortcuts (*continued*)

Shortcut	Action
	<Ctrl> Shortcuts
<Ctrl>+A	Selects all items.
<Ctrl>+<Alt>+<Delete>	In Win98, opens Close Programs window.
	In Win2K or XP, opens Security window (allows you to lock workstation, log off, shutdown, change password, and start Task Manager).
<Ctrl>+<Backspace>	Deletes all text from the cursor to beginning of current word or punctuation mark.
<Ctrl>+C	Copies the selected item(s) to the Windows Clipboard.
<Ctrl>+Drag and Drop	Copies selected file(s) or directory(s) to target location.
<Ctrl>+<Esc>	Opens the Windows Start menu.
<Ctrl>+F	Opens a text search for current window.
<Ctrl>+<F4>	Closes active window.
<Ctrl>+G	Go to function. Allows user to move to a selected page in document.
<Ctrl>+H	In Office applications, opens a Search and Replace window.
	In IE, it opens a History bar.
<Ctrl>+<Home>	Goes to beginning of document.
<Ctrl>+<End>	Goes to end of document.
<Ctrl>+<Insert>	Copies selected item(s) to Windows Clipboard.
<Ctrl>+Left Arrow	Moves cursor to previous word in the document.
<Ctrl>+N	Opens a new file or window.
<Ctrl>+O	Starts the File→Open function.
<Ctrl>+P	Prints the contents of the current window.
<Ctrl>+Right Arrow	Moves cursor to the next word in the document.
<Ctrl>+S	Saves the current file to previous location on disk.
<Ctrl>+<Shift>+<Esc>	In WIN98, opens the Start menu. In WIN2K or XP, opens Task Manager.
<Ctrl>+V	Pastes the contents of Windows Clipboard to selected location.
<Ctrl>+X	Cuts the selected item(s) from its current location and copies it to the Windows Clipboard.
<Ctrl>+Y	Repeats the previous action.
<Ctrl>+Z	Reverses the previous action

(*continued*)

Table A.1   Windows Hotkey Shortcuts (*continued*)

Shortcut	Action
<Alt> Shortcuts	
<Alt>+<Backspace>	Reverses the previous action (similar to <Ctrl>+Z).
<Alt>+Double-click	In a document, selects entire document.
<Alt>+<Enter>	Repeats previous action.
<Alt>+<F4>	Closes the current window.
<Alt>+<Print Screen>	Copies current window to Windows Clipboard as bitmap image.
<Alt>+Space Bar	Open current Window's controls (Restore, Move, Size, Minimize, Maximize, Close).
<Alt>+<Tab>	Switches between active Applications (while holding Alt, press Tab or Shift+Tab to go to next or previous app; release Alt to restore the selected app).
<Shift> shortcuts	
<Shift>+<Alt>+<Tab>	Switches among running applications (while holding Alt, press Tab or Shift+Tab to go to next or previous app; release Alt to restore the selected app).
<Shift>+<Delete>	In Windows Explorer, deletes selected item(s) immediately and does *not* move them to the Recycle Bin.
	In other apps, cuts and moves selected items to Windows Clipboard.
<Shift>+Down	Selects all of current line. Repeating the function selects the next line.
<Shift>+Drag and Drop Selected File(s)	Moves file(s) to target folder except when target folder is Recycle Bin. When moving to Recycle Bin, it deletes the file(s) permanently.
<Shift>+<F1>+0	Displays Shortcut menu for current window (same as clicking right-mouse button).
<Shift>+<Insert>	Pastes the contents of Windows Clipboard to selected location.
<Shift>+Left	Removes the previous character from text selection.
<Shift>+<Print Screen>	Copies current window to Clipboard as bitmap image.
<Shift>+Right	Adds the current character to selected text.
<Shift>+<Tab>	Moves to previous field or control in current window.
<Shift>+Up	Removes previous line from selected text.

(*continued*)

Table A.1 Windows Hotkey Shortcuts (*concluded*)

Shortcut	Action
Windows Key Shortcuts	
⊞+<Ctrl>+F	Allows user to search for a specific computer on the network.
⊞+D	Minimizes (or restores when repeated) all open windows. (Does not work in WIN95.)
⊞+E	Launches Windows Explorer, starting with My Computer
⊞+F	Opens a Find Files window.
⊞+<F1>	Launches Windows Help.
⊞+L	Locks the computer when connected to a network domain or switches users on a computer not connected to a network domain (WINXP only).
⊞+M	Minimizes current window.
⊞+<Pause/Break>	Opens the Control Panel System Properties applet.
⊞+G	Quick-switches between users (WINXP only).
⊞+R	Opens a Run dialog box in the Start menu.
⊞+<Shift>+M	Restores all minimized windows.
⊞+<Tab>	Cycles through the buttons on the taskbar.
⊞+U	Launches the Accessibility Utility Manager (WINXP only).
⊞+V	Open voice settings (Narrator settings window must be open) (WIN2K/XP only).

Windows and Windows applications contain a large number of keyboard shortcuts called hotkeys.

Table A.2 Annotated Listing of MSCONFIG Startup Entries

Program or File Name	Description
(Default)=%SysDir%\matcher.exe	Virus removal instructions for the virus W32/Matcher@MM.
1on1mail.htm	Virus removal instructions for the virus VBS.1ON1MAIL.
3com Modem Manager or MDMMGR.EXE	Status icon for 3Com modems.
3dfx Task Manager	Configuration applet for Voodoo video cards.
3dfx Tools	Tools applet for Voodoo video cards.
3Dqtl.exe (3Dqtl.exe)	A function of Terratec128i PCI sound card drivers. This loads a sound profile at boot up, restoring volume and other audio settings to a predetermined default. (Not mandatory)
A1000 Settings Utility or CPQA1000.EXE	Compaq A1000Print Fax All-in-One copy scan printer software. Required in the Startup in order to scan, print, copy, and fax.
Access Ramp Monitor or ARMON32.EXE	A program that monitors the status of an Internet connection. (Not mandatory)
Acrobat Assistant or ACROTRAY.EXE or [ACROTRAY]	An Acrobat Reader function that converts Postscript documents to PDF. (Not mandatory)
Active CPU or ACPU.EXE or [ACTIVE CPU]	Generates a graphical representation of CPU activity. (Not mandatory)
Adaptec DirectCD or DIRECTCD.EXE	Allows a formatted CD-RW or CD-R disc to have files written directly to it from Explorer.
Adaware Bootup or AD-AWARE.EXE or [AD-AWARE 5]	Spyware removal utility. (Not mandatory)
Adobe Gamma Loader	Calibrates monitor colors more closely to print colors for Adobe applications. (Not mandatory)
AGSatellite (AGSatellite.exe)	A function of AudioGalaxy software that lets you download MP3 files from their server. (Not mandatory)
AHQTB	Audio Headquarters for a Creative Labs SoundBlaster Live! sound card. (Not mandatory)
AIM Reminder	A function of AOL's Instant Messenger service. (Not mandatory)
AIM Reminder.exe	A virus that mimics the real AIM Reminder.
Alexa	Function of Alexa Toolbar 5.0. An Internet Navigation tool that provides information about the site being viewed. (Not mandatory)

(continued)

Table A.2 Annotated Listing of MSCONFIG Startup Entries (*continued*)

Program or File Name	Description
ALOGSERV.EXE	Function of McAfee Antivirus. Logs scanning activities. (Not mandatory, and has been known to cause issues with some programs.)
AMD POWERNOW! or GEMBACK.EXE	AMD PowerNow! Utility. Maximizes battery life by decreasing CPU speed when the system is running on battery power. (Required on some laptops.)
Anti or anti.exe or [anti]	Automatically clicks AOL's idle/timer popup windows, preventing the user from being forcibly signed off.
anvshell or ANVSHELL.EXE	Puts display properties settings onto an icon in the system tray. (Not mandatory)
AOL Instant Messenger or AIM.EXE	AOL Instant Messenger. (Not mandatory).
AOLTRAY.EXE	Puts AOL icon in system tray. (Not required in startup.)
ARMON32.EXE	Monitors an Internet connection for hang-ups, connection speeds, Internet congestion, and traffic flow. (Not mandatory)
Astro or ATRO.EXE	A utility included with Quicken personal finance software. (Not mandatory)
ASUS Tweak Enable or ASTART.EXE	A utility that is placed on the system tray when the settings for certain ASUS graphics adapters have been configured beyond their normal settings. Allows other changes and/or restoring factory default settings. (Not mandatory)
ATI GART Set-up Utility	Checks the motherboard chipset and determines which drivers to install for certain ATI cards. When the drivers are installed, it should be removed.
ATI Scheduler	Function of ATI driver that remains RAM resident and automatically launches the ATI VIDEO PLAYER at time and date pre-selected by the user. Remove if not being used.
ATI Task Application	Launches display settings for ATI graphics cards. (Not mandatory)
ATI*.* (various different files)	These are associated with an ATI Rage graphics card. (Not mandatory)
AtiCwd32 or ATICWD32.EXE	ATI graphics card system tray. (Not mandatory, but useful)
ATIKEY or ATITASK.EXE or [atitask]	Shortcut to various programs, display settings, and the ATI Desktop online help system. Should not be kept in startup, but rather ran from Start menu when needed.

(*continued*)

Table A.2 Annotated Listing of MSCONFIG Startup Entries (*continued*)

Program or File Name	Description
Attune Download	Monitors PC hardware and provides a shortcut to a PC help network. Use with caution.
AttuneClientEngine or ATTUNE_CE.EXE	Provides a notification service for Attune. (Not mandatory)
AudioHQ	Desktop control panel for the Creative Labs Live card. (Not mandatory)
Aureal 3D Interactive Audio (a3dinit.exe)	3D positional sound controls for Compaq PC's with Aureal-based 3D soundcards. If removed, only standard sound can be obtained.
AutoEA or AHQRUN.EXE	A function of Creative Labs Soundblaster Live! series soundcards. Allows user to specify what audio preset to automatically associate for any audio application. (Not mandatory)
AutoUpdate or XUPDATE.EXE	Function of Mcafee Antivirus that verifies that the software is up to date. (Not mandatory. Can update manually.)
AV Console or AVCONSOL.EXE or [avconsol]	Function of Mcafee Antivirus that scans local or network drives automatically on a user-defined schedule. (Not mandatory)
BACKWEB or USERPROF.EXE	A Compaq service that automatically detects internet connection and downloads any available updates. (Not mandatory)
Battery Bar	Laptop utility that estimates remaining battery power. (Not mandatory, but useful)
BayMgr	Dell laptop utility that allows swapping a battery, DVD, or other item in an accessory bay.
BCDetect or BCDETECT.EXE	A function of Creative Labs that detects when the correct drivers are installed for the video card. It loads the BlasterControl when the drivers are detected. (Not mandatory)
BCMDMMSG or BCMDMMSG.EXE	The modem messaging applet for BCM V.90 56K modems. Required for dial-up if you have one of these modems.
BCMHal or BCMHAL9X.DLL or [bcinit]	Places Display properties for Creative Labs graphics adapters onto system tray. (Not mandatory)
BCTweak or BCTWEAK.EXE	A utility that allows the user to adjust certain settings on Creative Labs graphics adapters. (Not mandatory)

(*continued*)

Table A.2   Annotated Listing of MSCONFIG Startup Entries (*continued*)

Program or File Name	Description
BillMinder or REMIND32	A function of Quicken that reminds the user of due payments. (Not mandatory)
BitMagic or BITLOADER.EXE	A function of Bitmagic's Bitplayer that places the menu options into the toolbar. (Not mandatory)
BlackICE utility or BLACKICE.EXE	A function of Network ICE firewall that places certain menu options on the toolbar. Closing it will close the firewall. No point in removing it. It will reappear on next reboot without editing the registry.
BLSTAPP or BLSTAPP.EXE	Puts access to Creative's BlasterControl in the System Tray. (Not mandatory)
bmlic-1 or LOADER.EXE	A function of Bitmagic's Bitplayer that places certain menu items in the toolbar. Also checks for updates when Internet connection is present. (Not mandatory)
Bonzei Buddy	Talking parrot and monkey. (Neither mandatory or useful and can be quite annoying)
BMO MasterCard Wallet or EWALLET.EXE	Stores your credit card and other personal information in an encrypted file on your PC so that any talented hacker can access it. (Not mandatory)
bombshel or BOMB32.EXE	A function of McAfee Nuts & Bolts. Protects your Windows system from application failure and crashes. (Not mandatory)
BPCPOST or BPCPOST.EXE	Post-setup program for Microsoft TV Viewer. Can be removed after installation is complete.
Cal reminder shortcut	Manages the popups used by MS Works Calendar as reminders. (Not mandatory)
CallControl or FTCTRL32.EXE	A function of FaxTalk Messenger Pro that allows any TAPI-compliant application to access the modem from Windows. (Not mandatory)
Cardscan 300start or CSRESET.EXE	A function of the Cardscan 300 scanner driver that resets the scanner on startup. (Not mandatory)
CBWAttn or CBWATTN.EXE or CBWHost or CBWHOST.EXE	A function of Bitware fax software that answers incoming faxes. Not required for outgoing faxes and has known issues with Windows Power Management.
CC2KUI or COMET.EXE	A program that allows the user to change cursors on the fly. (Not mandatory)
CIJ3P2PSERVER or CIJ3P2PS.EXE	Compaq printer utility. Required for the printer to work correctly.

(*continued*)

Table A.2 Annotated Listing of MSCONFIG Startup Entries (continued)

Program or File Name	Description
CISRVR Program or CISRVR.EXE	Compaq Internet setup wizard. (Not mandatory)
CleanSweep or Smart Sweep or Internet Sweep	Function of Norton CleanSweep. Can be started manually. (Not mandatory)
Click The Button or CTB.EXE	A function of Bonzei Buddy. (Neither mandatory nor useful)
ClipMate5x or CLIPMT5X.EXE	A utility that allows the user to maintain multiple items in the Windows Clipboard. (Not mandatory, but can be useful)
Colorific Control Panel (Hgcctl95.exe)	A color-matching utility from E_Color. Ensures accurate gamma and color temperature between your monitor and other still imaging devices. (Not mandatory, but may be useful)
Compaq C3-1000 Settings Utility or cpqc31k.exe or [cpqc31k.exe]	Compaq printer utility. Required in order for the printer to work.
Compaq Internet Setup or INETWIZARD.EXE	Compaq Internet setup wizard. (Not mandatory)
Compaq Knowledge Center or SILENT.EXE & MATCLI.EXE	MATCLI.EXE is the Motive Assistant Command Line Interface that gathers system and personal information into a log file. SILENT.EXE executes matcli.exe quietly in the background. Required for accessing Compaq's Help and Support program.
Compaq Video CD Watcher	Compaq MPEG viewer. (Not mantatory)
CompaqPrinTray or PRINTRAY.EXE	Puts printer icon in toolbar. If disabled, the Control Program or Printer Driver can no longer be directly accessed from your desktop.
CompaqSystray or CPQPSCP.EXE	Compaq Systray icon. (Not mandatory)
COMSMDEXE	3Com utilities. (Not mandatory)
ConfigServices	Part of initial setup. (Not mandatory)
CONMGR.EXE	Connection Manager for Earthlink Internet Services. (Not mandatory)
Controller	Starts WinFax Pro. WinFax will not receive incoming faxes automatically unless running. (Not mandatory)
Cookie Crusher or COOKIE.EXE	A utility that gives the user control over which cookies are accepted by and stored on the system. (Not mandatory)
Cookie Pal or CPBRWTCH.EXE	A utility that gives the user control over which cookies are accepted by and stored on the system. (Not mandatory)

(continued)

Table A.2 Annotated Listing of MSCONFIG Startup Entries (*continued*)

Program or File Name	Description
Cool Desk or CDESK.EXE	A virtual desktop manager. (Not mandatory or particularly useful)
Cool Note or COOL.EXE	An electronic sticky-note program. (Not mandatory)
Corel Desktop Application Director	Function of Corel Office Suite that launches its programs from the toolbar. (Not mandatory)
Corel Registration Reminder	Function of Corel software that nags the user to register with Corel. Useful only to Corel.
CountrySelection or PCTPTT.EXE	A function of certain modem drivers. As long as the modem is installed and enabled, this feature will reappear after being disabled.
CPQA1000.EXE	Software for the Compaq A1000 print/fax/scanner. Required for this device to work.
CPQDFWAG	A utility that runs Compaq diagnostics every time the system boots. (Not mandatory)
CPQEASYACC or CPQEADM.EXE or [bttnserv]	Compaq's Easy Access button support. (Not mandatory)
CPQinet or CPQINET.EXE	A function of Compaq Easy Access Button support. Only required if EAB support is desired.
CPQInet Runtime Services	Compaq Easy Access Button support for AOL and CompuServe. (Not mandatory, and useless if you're using another ISP)
CPQINKAG.EXE	Utility for certain Compaq printers that monitors ink usage. (Not mandatory)
cpqns or CPQNPCSS.EXE	A function of Compaq.Net. Not required for those not using this service.
CPQSTUTFIX	A function of certain sound card drivers that cures problems with sound stutter. Required for those sound cards. Do not remove.
CPUFSB or CPUFSB.EXE or [cpufsb]	Utility that allows the user to adjust the motherboard's front side bus speed through the OS. **Caution:** This utility may cause your system to crash or become unstable and may also damage certain components in the system.
CQSCP2PS or CQSCP2P Server	Compaq printer utility. Required for printer to function.
CreateCD or CREATECD.EXE	A function of EZ CD Creator. (Not mandatory)

(*continued*)

Table A.2 Annotated Listing of MSCONFIG Startup Entries (*continued*)

Program or File Name	Description
Creative Lab's AudioHQ or AHQRUN.EXE or AHQTB.EXE	System tray application for SB Live! Environmental Audio Control plug-ins. (Not mandatory)
Creative Lab's Disc Detector	Auto-detects a CD-ROM, DVD-ROM, etc. (Not mandatory)
Creative Lab's Program Launcher	Adds a quick-launch bar to the top of the display and a System Tray icon. (Not mandatory)
Critical Update	Forces frequent visits to Microsoft's Web site, looking for updates. (Not mandatory and can be annoying)
CSInject.exe	A function of Norton CleanSweep (Not mandatory)
CTAVTray or CTAVTRAY.EXE	A function of Creative Labs Soundblaster Live! Soundcard driver. Plays the EAX animation on start-up and adds a System Tray icon for it. (Not mandatory)
CTFMON	Alternative Language input services for Office XP. If you want to disable this in STARTUP, then Text Services and Speech applets in the Control Panel must be disabled. (Not mandatory)
CTRegRun or CTREGRUN.EXE	A nag reminder to register a Creative Labs product. (Not mandatory and can be annoying)
CTSysVol	A function of Creative Labs sound card driver that adds volume controls to the toolbar. (Not mandatory)
Cybermedia Guard Dog or GDLAUNCH.EXE	A function of Mcafee's Internet Guard Dog Software. (Not mandatory)
CyDoor=CD_Load.exe	Spyware. Remove immediately!
Daemon or DAEMON32.EXE	Preloads game profiles for MS Sidewinder game controllers (prior to release 2.0). (Not mandatory)
datcheck or DATCHECK.EXE	Keypanic. Trojan horse that remaps the keyboard. Update your antivirus software and run again.
Dcomcnfg or DCOMCNFG.EXE	A function of Microsoft Basic. (Not mandatory)
Delay or DELAYRUN.EXE	Allows user to configure certain startup items to launch after Windows has loaded. Gives control of the computer to the user more quickly. (Not mandatory)
Description of Shortcut or EZTART.EXE	A function of Mcafee's Utilities that allows the user to customize the appearance of Windows. (Not mandatory)
DEVLDR16.EXE	A function of Creative Labs sound card drivers that provides audio support for DOS applications. (Not mandatory)

(*continued*)

Table A.2 Annotated Listing of MSCONFIG Startup Entries (*continued*)

Program or File Name	Description
DigiGuide or CLIENT.EXE	Electronic TV guide. (Not mandatory)
Digital Dashboard or DEVGULP.EXE	Control panel for a program called Digital Dashboard. (Not mandatory)
Digital River eBot or DOWNLOA~1.EXE	Utility that monitors the system and checks for updates to hardware drivers and software when an Internet connection is present. (Not mandatory)
Disc Detector or CTNOTIFY.EXE	A function of Creative Labs sound card drivers that automatically detects when a CD or DVD has been inserted into the drive. (Not mandatory)
Disknag or DISKNAG.EXE	A Dell utility that reminds the user to make backup diskettes. (Not mandatory)
DkService or DKSERVICE.EXE	A function of Executive Software's Diskeeper (a third-party disk defragmenting utility) that schedules unattended maintenance. (Not mandatory)
DMASwitch or CLDMA.EXE	A function of CyberLink PowerDVD software that allows user to toggle on/off DMA functions for CD devices. (Not mandatory)
DMISL	Desktop Management Software for Intel TokenExpress network card software. (Not mandatory)
DMISTART or WIN32SL.EXE	Dell or Intel utility that collects system information for Client Manager for remote management and/or technical support. (Not mandatory)
DNE Binding Watchdog or RUNDLL DNES.DLL or [DnDneCheckBindings]	Deterministic NDIS Extender. Part of Gilat Communications internet satellite systems. Required if you have this system.
dRMON SmartAgent or SMARTAGT.EXE	A utility that is a part of the 3COM NIC software package. (Not mandatory)
DSS	A function of Broderbund software. Sends information back to manufacturer when Internet connection is detected. (Not mandatory or useful to anyone but Broderbund)
DXM6Patch_981116 or SMARTAGT.EXE	CAB file extractor. (Not mandatory)
EACLEAN.EXE	Compaq Easy Access Button support for the keyboard. (Not mandatory)
Eapcisetup	A function of Rockwell RipTide soundcard application software. (Not mandatory)

(*continued*)

Table A.2 Annotated Listing of MSCONFIG Startup Entries (*continued*)

Program or File Name	Description
EarthLink ToolBar 5.0 or ETOOLBAR.EXE	A function of EarthLink Internet software. (Not mandatory)
eFax.com Tray Menu or HOTTRAY.EXE	Automatically launches EFAX Messenger software on startup and creates a system tray icon with menu options. (Not mandatory)
EM_EXEC or EM_EXEC.EXE	Advanced features support for a Logitech mouse. (Not mandatory, but removing it will cause certain Logitech features to become disabled.)
EncartaDictionary Quickshelf or QSHLFED.EXE	Quicklaunch for Encarta Dictionary. (Not mandatory)
ENCMON	Keeps track of the time remaining on a factory installed free trial for AT&T internet services. (Not mandatory, and totally useless if you're not using their free trial.)
ENCMONITOR or MONITOR.EXE	A Connect Direct function of the Encompass Monitor. (Not mandatory)
EnsonicMixer STARTER.EXE	A function of Ensonic sound card drivers that puts the Ensonic mixer in system tray. (Not mandatory)
EPSON Background Monitor	Monitors the status of any properly configured Epson printer. Removing does not affect the printer's ability to print. (Not mandatory)
ESSDC.EXE	A function of sound card drivers for sound cards with ESS chipset (notably Ensonic). (Not mandatory)
Etraffic or JAVARUN.EXE	Marketing software installed by a company called TopMoxie. REMOVE.
Event Reminder	A function of Dr. Watson. (Not mandatory)
EWELL.HTM	A virus. Check with your Antivirus vendor for updates and run immediately.
Explorer	System File. Must be running.
FatPipe (DHCP)	Internet connection-sharing and caching software. (Not mandatory)
FaxTalk CallControl 6.X or FTCLCTRL.EXE	A function of FaxTalk Communicator software that handles incoming and outgoing calls. (Not mandatory)
FEELitDeviceManager or FEELITDM.EXE	A function of Immersion TouchSense device drivers. Required for these devices to work.
Filterguard or FILTRGRD.EXE	A function of SOS Internet Filtering Software. Required for this software to function properly.

(*continued*)

Table A.2 Annotated Listing of MSCONFIG Startup Entries (*continued*)

Program or File Name	Description
Find Fast	Function of Microsoft Office. Indexes files for faster searches. (Not mandatory)
Fine Print Dispatcher or FPDISP3.EXE	Function of certain Compaq printer drivers. Required for printer to function properly.
Finish Installing or BBSMAR~1.EXE	A function of Bonzei Buddy that reminds the user that more files are needed to complete installation. (Not mandatory)
Fix-It Av or MEMCHECK.EXE	A function of Trend Micro's Ontrack Antivirus software. Required for software to function properly.
FlyswatDesktop or FLYDESK.EXE	A function of a program called Flyswat. (Not mandatory)
FMLITES or FMLITES.EXE	A function of some modems that puts a visual display similar to the lights of an external modem on the toolbar. (Not mandatory)
FTUNINST or FTUNINST.EXE	Fax Talk Messenger Pro uninstall program. (Not mandatory)
Gator or GATOR.EXE	A function of Gator (a form filler) software that puts menu items on the toolbar. Somewhat resource intensive. Don't use it if you don't need it. (Not mandatory)
GetRight Tray Icon or GETRIGHT.EXE	A download manager that allows the user to resume interrupted downloads and to manage multiple downloads simultaneously. The freeware version adds spyware; the paid version does not. (Not mandatory, but can be useful. Although the spyware isn't.)
Gilat SOM Enumerator or DLLHOST.EXE	A function of Gilat Communications Internet satellite systems—associated with SkyBlaster modem. Required if you have this system.
GilatFTC or FTC.EXE	A function of Gilat Communications Internet satellite systems—associated with SkyBlaster modem. Required if you have this system.
Go!Zilla Monster Downloads	Adds System Tray applet for Go!Zilla.web browser. (Not mandatory)
GuardDogEXE or GDLAUNCH.EXE	A function of Mcafee's Internet Guard Dog software. (Not mandatory)
Guardian or CMGRDIAN.EXE	A function of Mcafee's Guardian software that adds a system tray icon. (Not mandatory)

(*continued*)

Table A.2 Annotated Listing of MSCONFIG Startup Entries (continued)

Program or File Name	Description
HC Reminder or HC.EXE	Compaq software. (Not mandatory) (Note that HC.EXE can also be the HumanClick software)
help=3D	This is the VBS/Pleh@MM Virus. Check your antivirus software for updates and run immediately.
Hidserv or HIDSERV.EXE	Human Interface Device Service. Manages devices connected through the USB bus. (Not mandatory, but useful)
HIDSERV.EXE.RUN	Human Interface Device Server, it is required only if you are using USB Audio Devices. (Not mandatory)
Hotbar	Third-party utility that adds new skins for IE. (Not mandatory)
HotSync	Palm Pilot synchronization manager. (Not mandatory and should be launched manually)
HP JetDiscovery	A function of HP JetAdmin software that manages network print jobs.
HP Lamp	Utility for certain HP scanners that controls the light source. Required for these scanners to function properly.
HP ScanPicture	Adds a "Scan Picture" option to the File menu of certain applications. If disabled, the menu option will disappear, but the scanner will still function when accessed through the Start menu. (Not mandatory)
Hpha1mon or HPHA1MON.EXE	Driver for the Media Card reader for certain HP printers that support that function. Required if you wish to use that function.
hppswrsev	Utility for certain HP scanners. (Not mandatory)
hpsysdrv or SPSYSDRV.EXE	A function of the HP keyboard manager that identifies the system as being an HP. On some models, deselecting this function can prevent the system from booting.
HPSCANMonitor or HPSJVXD.EXE	HP scanning software that redirects scanned images from the scanner to the application. Required for the scanner to work properly.
Hpscanpatch or HPSCANFIX.EXE	A driver patch for certain HP scanners. Required for the scanner to work properly.

(continued)

Table A.2 Annotated Listing of MSCONFIG Startup Entries (*continued*)

Program or File Name	Description
HumanClick or HC.EXE	A program called HumanClick that allows the user to communicate with visitors on a Web site and to monitor the visitor's activities. (Not mandatory) (Note that HC.EXE can also be the HC Reminder)
HWinst	Gilat rescue (Satellite system restore) For Gilat Communications Internet satellite systems. Required if you have this system. If removed, can cause the system to become unstable and crash unexpectedly.
ICONFIG.EXE or [iconfig]	A function of the Superdisk driver. Required for the device to work properly.
ICQ NetDetect Agent	Periodically checks for Internet connectivity. If found, automatically launches ICQ. (Not mandatory and can be quite annoying)
ICSMGR	Monitors DNS and DHCP requests for Internet Connection Sharing (ICS). Required if ICS is installed.
Image & Restore or IMAGE32.EXE	A function of McAfee Nuts & Bolts. Allows a drive to be recovered after an accidental erasure or formatting. (Not mandatory, but extremely useful when you need it!)
Imesh Auto Update or WISEUPDT.EXE	Checks for downloadable Imesh updates every time an Internet connection is established. Cannot be removed in msconfig. It puts back the checkmark after you try to remove it.
Imesh or IMESHCLIENT.EXE	Utility that allows user to download files from several targets simultaneously. (Not mandatory)
Incontrol Desktop MGR or DMHKEY.EXE	A function of Intouch Control software that adds an extra tab in the Display properties for the Diamond Multimedia video card extra settings. (Not mandatory)
Instant Access	A function of TextBridge Pro OCR software. (Not mandatory)
IntelProcNumUtility	Disables CPU ID. (Not mandatory)
internat or INTERNAT.EXE	Allows user to toggle between installed keyboard languages. (Not mandatory). NOTE: Can also be added by a virus called Netsnake. If languages were not installed, update antivirus software and run immediately!
Introduction-Registration	PC introduction & registration for Compaq computers. Should run only once. Remove if it remains after initial use.

(*continued*)

Table A.2 Annotated Listing of MSCONFIG Startup Entries (*continued*)

Program or File Name	Description
Iomega Disk Icons	Iomega Zip Tools application. Changes the icon and description associated with an Iomega Zip drive from a generic icon to an Iomega Zip drive icon. (Not mandatory, nor is it useful)
Iomega QuickSync 3 or quicksync3.exe or [quicksync3]	A program used with Iomega drives, QuickSync 3 is intended to protect the user from data loss. (Not mandatory)
Iomega Startup Options or IMGSTART.EXE	Adds right-click context menu selections for a Zip drive. (Not mandatory, but useful)
Iomega Watch	Iomega Zip Tools application. Causes your Zip drive to spin down when not in use and prompts the user for a password when trying to access a write-protected disk. (Not mandatory, but useful)
IOMON98.EXE	A function of PCCILIN Antivirus software that performs real-time virus checks. (Not mandatory, but userful)
IPinst	Gilat rescue (Satellite system restore) For Gilat Communications Internet satellite systems. Required if you have this system. If removed, can cause the system to become unstable and crash unexpectedly.
IrMon	Required when an infrared wireless device is installed.
isdbdc or ISDBDC.EXE	A function of the Compaq dial-up networking wizard. (Not mandatory)
K6CPU.EXE	Identifies and authenticates AMD K6 CPU. (Not mandatory)
Kagou	The KAK virus. Update antivirus software and run immediately.
KAK.HTA	The KAK virus. Update antivirus software and run immediately.
KAK.HTML	The KAK virus. Update antivirus software and run immediately.
Kernel16	The SUB Seven Trojan Virus. Update antivirus software and run immediately.
kernel32=kern32.exe	The W32/Badtrans@MM Virus. Update antivirus software and run immediately.
Keyboard Manager or MMKEYBD.EXE	A function of the keyboard driver for certain HP keyboards. (Not mandatory)

(*continued*)

Table A.2 Annotated Listing of MSCONFIG Startup Entries (*continued*)

Program or File Name	Description
Launchboard or LNCHBRD.EXE	A program that allows the user to customize the keyboard to launch programs or Web sites. (Not mandatory)
Lexmark PrinTray or PRINTRAY.EXE	A Lexmark Printer icon. (Not required)
Lexstart or LEXSTART.EXE	Command interpreter for Lexmark printers. Has been known to induce dial-up networking to connect to the Internet. (Not mandatory)
LIU	A function of Logitech Quick Cam driver. (Not mandatory)
Load = OCRAWARE.EXE	A function of OmniPage Limited Edition that allows the user to scan directly into most word processor applications. (Not mandatory)
Load WebCheck or LOADWC.EXE	Program that manages adding, removing, and updating subscriptions. (Not mandatory)
Loadblackd or BLACKD.EXE	A function of BlackICE Defender, an intrusion detection product. Required if you want to use the product.
LoadPowerProfile	Only required if you are using Windows Power Management through Control Panel. If so, there will be two instances. One is loaded by Machine Run and the other by Machines Services. Do not uncheck one unless you uncheck both. (Not mandatory unless Power Management is enabled.)
LOADQM	MSN Explorer Query Manager (Not mandatory)
Loadqm	Loads the MSN Explorer Query Manager. (Not mandatory)
Logitech ImageWare Control Center	Function of Logitech Pagescan scanner driver. (Not mandatory)
Logitech Wakeup or LGWAKEUP.EXE	Function of Logitech autofeed scanners. Detects insertion of paper into scanner and launches scanner software. (Not mandatory, but useful)
Lotus Organizer Easy Clip	Function of Lotus Organizer. Collects information from sources such as email to create an Organizer address, appointment, task, or Notepad page. (Not mandatory)
Lotus Quick Start	Control pad for Lotus SmartSuite. (Not mandatory)
Lotus Suite Start	Start icons for Lotus SmartSuite that appear on the taskbar when you start Windows. Removing this item can result in error messages and prevent SmartSuite from working properly.

(*continued*)

Table A.2 Annotated Listing of MSCONFIG Startup Entries (*continued*)

Program or File Name	Description
LS120 Superdisk	Disk Caching utility for LS-120. (Not mandatory)
LVComs or LVCOMS.EXE	Function of the Logitech QuickCam driver. (Not mandatory)
Lwinst Run Profiler or LWTEST.EXE or LWEMON.EXE	Function of the Logitech Wingman joystick driver. (Not mandatory)
LXSUPMON (LXSUPMON.EXE)	Function of Lexmark Printer driver. (Not mandatory)
Machine Debug Manager or mdm	Part of Visual Studio 6.0. This is required only if a second machine is used to debug programs under development on current computer. (Not mandatory)
MapNDrive or MAPNDRIVE.EXE	A third-party scripting tool that manages mapped network drive. Needed if installed.
Matrox Powerdesk	A function of Matrox graphics card drivers that allows users to adjust display settings on the fly. (Not mandatory)
McAfee Guardian or CMGRDIAN.EXE	A function of McAfee Uninstaller software. Automatically identifies and removes the unnecessary files that remain after a program is removed. (Not mandatory).
McAfee Image or IMAGE32.EXE	A function of McAfee Image that creates an image snapshot of the critical sectors on your hard drive. In the event these sectors become corrupted, Image uses the snapshot to restore data. (Not mandatory)
McAfee VirusScan Registration	Function of McAfee VirusScan that nags the user to register the product. (Not mandatory)
McAfee Wingauge	A McAfee utility that monitors system performance. (Not mandatory)
McAfeeVirusScanService or AVSYNMGR.EXE	A function of McAfee VirusScan version 5.x that runs all the functions under within a single environment. (Not mandatory, but useful)
McAfeeWEbScanX or WEBSCANX.EXE or [Webscanx]	A McAfee utility that monitors Internet activity for possibly harmful events. (Not mandatory, but useful)
MDAC_RUNONCE or RUNONCE.EXE	Microsoft Data Access Components Run Once Wrapper. This is required for Microsoft Data Access Components. Run Once refers to once per session and, therefore, appears any time an MDAC app is running.
MediaRing Talk or MRTALK.EXE	Voice recognition software. Resource intensive. Remove if not needed.

(continued)

Table A.2   Annotated Listing of MSCONFIG Startup Entries (*continued*)

Program or File Name	Description
Memturbo	A shareware program that monitors memory usage and dumps code no longer in use. (Not mandatory)
MGAVRTCL.EXE or MGAVRTCL.EXE	A function McAfee Antivirus. Required for real-time virus scanning.
Microangelo Desktop	Preloads certain files critical to MicroAngelo 5.0 to facilitate faster loading. (Not mandatory)
Microsoft Critical Update	Detects and installs critical updates from the Microsoft site when an Internet connection is present. (Not mandatory)
Microsoft Find Fast	A service of Microsoft Office. Indexes files on your hard drive for faster search. (Not mandatory)
Microsoft Greetings Reminders	Reminder of special events like birthdays. (Not mandatory).
Microsoft Office Startup	Preloads certain .DLL files to speed up the launch of Microsoft Office. Also places icon in System Tray. (Not mandatory)
Microsoft Sidewinder Game Controller Software	Preloads profiles for games. (Not mandatory)
Microsoft Webserver	Personal Web server program. (Not mandatory)
Microsoft Works Calendar	MS Works program provides notifications when dates on the MS Works calendar are reached. (Not mandatory)
Microsoft Works Calendar Reminders	MS Works calendar reminder. (Not mandatory)
Microsoft Works Portfolio, WorksFUD, Microsoft Update Detection, Cal reminder shortcut	These are used by Works 2001. Check for updates and announce reminders that were configured in Works programs. (Not mandatory)
Microsoft Works update Detection	Detects and installs MS Works updates from the Microsoft site. (Not mandatory)
MINIFERT.EXE	Electronic distribution software bundled with certain Compaq computers. (Not mandatory)
Minilog or MINILOG.EXE	A function of ZoneAlarm firewall software that maintains the event log. Required for software to function properly.
Mirabilis ICQ	Automatically runs up ICQ when Internet connection is detected. (Not mandatory)
Mixghost	Management utility for Altec Lansing speakers. (Not mandatory)

(continued)

Table A.2   Annotated Listing of MSCONFIG Startup Entries (*continued*)

Program or File Name	Description
mmtray	Places a Music Box Jukebox icon in the system tray. (Not mandatory)
MoneyAgent or MONEY EXPRESS.EXE	Function of Microsoft Money. (Not mandatory)
MOSEARCH	Similar to Find Fast feature in Office 2000. Uses the Indexing Services in Office XP to create a catalog of Office files on your computer's hard disk. (Not mandatory)
MotiveMonitor (motmon.exe)	A function of HP Instant Support that watches for errors and collects information useful for resolution through the Internet and email. (Not mandatory, but useful)
Mount Safe & Sound	A function of McAfee VirusScan version 5.x. that creates back-up sets of critical files in a separate area of a hard drive. (Not mandatory)
MS Money Startup	Launches Microsoft Money. (Not mandatory)
MSKernel32 or WINDOWS\SYSTEM\MSKernel32.vbs	The LOVE-LETTER-FOR-YOU virus. Update antivirus software and run immediately.
MSMSGS or MSMSGS.EXE or MSN Messenger	MSN Instant Messenger Service. (Not mandatory)
MSNQuickView	MSN Toolbar that launches at startup.
Mstask	A Microsoft scheduling agent that can be configured to run several applications at specified times. (Not mandatory)
MSUser32 or WINDOWS\SYSTEM\MSUser32.vbs	The LOOK.VBS virus. Update antivirus software and run immediately.
NAV defalert	Norton Antivirus Definitions Alert. A function of Norton Antivirus that warns the user when AV signature files are outdated. (Not mandatory, but useful)
Nav_setup or NAV_SE~1.EXE	McAfee Installation Wizard. Indicates that software installation was not completed. Run Setup program again or remove.
Ndetect	Automatically detects Internet connection and launches ICQ. (Not mandatory)
NeoPlanet or NEO.EXE	Starts Neoplanet web browser automatically when in the startup and creates a system tray icon that allows the user to access it's options. (Not mandatory)
Netsonic or WEBMAIN.EXE	Internet caching program. (Not mandatory)

(*continued*)

Table A.2 Annotated Listing of MSCONFIG Startup Entries (*continued*)

Program or File Name	Description
Netword Agent NWANT33.EXE	Internet browsing utility that allows single-word Web searches. (Not mandatory)
NETWORK.VBS	NETWORK.VBS virus. Update antivirus software and run immediately.
NetworkSetup or DLINK.EXE	A DLink driver utility that provides shortcuts to DLink Web sites. (Not mandatory)
Netzero or NZSTART.EXE	Automatically launches Netzero ISP software at bootup. (Not mandatory)
NetZip Smart Downloader	A download utility that adds Pause, Resume, and Reconnect to your downloads. (Not mandatory)
Norton AutoProtect	Norton Antivirus program. Scans for viruses when you open a program or file. (Not mandatory, but userful)
Norton Crashguard Monitor	Function of Norton Utilities that keeps renegade applications from crashing system. Causes instability with WINMe. (Not mandatory)
Norton Email Protect	Function of Norton Antivirus that sets up a proxy server to isolate the main system from email-borne viruses. (Not mandatory)
Norton System Doctor	Norton program that monitors system configuration and alerts the user when the configuration changes in ways that may cause problems. (Not mandatory)
NovastorSchedulerd	A function of NovaStor NovaBACKUP Software. Required for unattended scheduled backups.
NPROTECT	A function of Norton Utilities. Protects files in Recycle Bin. (Not mandatory)
nscheck or NSCHECK.EXE	Internet caching software. Has been known to cause problems with certain ISPs. (Not mandatory)
oadaemon or OADAEMON.EXE or [oadaemon]	Function of the Compaq C3-1000 printer. Required for printer to function properly.
OEMCLEANUP or OEM_RESET.EXE	Resets OEM installation settings at each bootup. Useful if you want all computers in an organization to be consistent. (Not mandatory)
Office Startup or OSA.EXE	Preloads certain files for quicker launching of Office applications. (Not mandatory)
Onflow or UNISTALL ONFLOW.EXE	Onflow is software that places advertising banners in certain types of software. This program can be run to remove it. (Not mandatory)

(*continued*)

Table A.2 Annotated Listing of MSCONFIG Startup Entries (*continued*)

Program or File Name	Description
Operator	Function of Media Pilot software. Locks port open. (Not mandatory)
Pagekeeper Jobs	Function of Pagekeeper scanner software that manages documents. (Not mandatory)
Password Pal or PASSPAL.EXE	A utility that stores all passwords associated to a specific user in encrypted form. (Not mandatory)
PC Health or PCHSCHD.EXE	WINMe only. Required for the System Restore utility to function properly in Windows Me. The program takes a snapshot of the registry and places the information into data archive.
PCTVOICE or PCTVOICE.EXE	PCTVoice is a program used by certain modems for video conferencing. (Not mandatory)
Pe2ckfnt SE or CHKFONT.EXE	A function of Ulead Photo Express that confirms whether or not fonts are installed properly on a computer. (Not mandatory)
Photo Express Calender Checker SE	A function of Ulead Photo Express that configures Weekly/Monthly/Yearly calendars as wallpaper. (Not mandatory)
PiDunHk or PIDUNHK.EXE	A function of Prodigy Internet services. (Not mandatory)
PiStartup or PISTARTUP.EXE	A function of Prodigy Internet services. (Not mandatory)
Pointer POINT32.EXE	Function of the Microsoft Intellipoint mouse software. If not loaded, then the wheel may not work in certain applications. (Not mandatory, but useful)
Power Meter	Utility on Dell laptop for battery strength and AC power source for batteries. It can be manually launched when it is needed.
Power Panel plus or PANPLUS.EXE or [Panplus]	A function of PowerPanel Plus™ software (included with CyberPower's Power99 and Power2000 models of UPS). Monitors condition and charge of UPS and performs automatic shutdown of system in the event of power failure. Required for full functionality.
Power Reg Scheduler	Software registration reminder. (Not mandatory)
pp5300USB	A function of Paperport software that monitors the status of a Visioneer OneTouch 5300 scanner. (Not mandatory)
Primax 3D Mouse	Driver support for Primax Mouse. (Not mandatory)
PROMON.EXE	Part of Intel NIC diagnostics. (Not mandatory)

(*continued*)

Table A.2 Annotated Listing of MSCONFIG Startup Entries (*continued*)

Program or File Name	Description
Prpcui	Dell utility that manages Intel's Speed-Step functions. (Not mandatory)
Ptsnoop.exe	A function of several modem drivers that monitors the COM port. Will automatically reset itself as long as the modem is enabled.
Q shlf or Quick Shelf or ENCICONS.EXE or [qshlfed]	Launches Encarta dictionary program. (Not mandatory)
Qagent	Quicken Download Manager (also known as Qagent). When the Quicken Download Manager option is enabled, it takes advantage of unused bandwidth on an Internet connection to download current financial information any time your computer is connected to the Internet. (Not mandatory)
QBCD autorun	Automatically launches Quickbooks. (Not mandatory)
QD FastAndSafe	Function of Norton Cleansweep. Deletes unnecessary files. Best if run manually. (Not mandatory)
QuickenSEMessage	A messaging option for Quicken software. (Not mandatory)
QuickShelf 99	Places an icon in the system tray for launching Microsoft Bookshelf. (Not mandatory)
RamBooster or RAMBOOSTER.EXE	A utility that monitors memory usage and dumps unnecessary code. (Not mandatory)
Rave 2 or RAVE.EXE	A Windows application that allows voice communication over an Internet connection. (Not mandatory)
Real Jukebox Systray	Function of Real Jukebox software. Allows user to launch Real Jukebox by double-clicking the icon in the system tray and periodically checks for an Internet connection in order to download updates. (Not mandatory)
RealTray REALPLAY.EXE	Function of Real Audio software. Allows user to launch Real Jukebox by double-clicking the icon in the system tray and periodically checks for an Internet connection in order to download updates. (Not mandatory)
Refresh	A function of Iomega Zip drives. (Not mandatory)
Register Drop Handler	A utility for managing images created by digital cameras or scanners. (Not mandatory)
Regtrk	A function of Norton Utilities that monitors changes to the registry. (Not mandatory, but useful)

(*continued*)

Table A.2 Annotated Listing of MSCONFIG Startup Entries (*continued*)

Program or File Name	Description
Reminder	Bill payment reminder function of MS Money. (Not mandatory)
Reminder-cpqXXXXX or REMIND32.EXE	Reminder to register a Compaq printer. (Not mandatory)
RFTray	Launches the Reality Fusion GameCam Video Interaction Technology Software that ships with the Logitech QuickCam (and other) PC Video Cameras. (Not mandatory)
Ring Central Fax	Utility for allowing PC to answer faxes. (Not mandatory)
rnaapp	Application required by dial-up networking. It loads when a connection is initiated.
Run = (WINDOWS\SYSTEM\list.vbs)	The LIST.VBS virus. Update antivirus software and run immediately.
RUN=	Identifies a specific program to be run during startup. A large number of RUN= statements that are not followed by a specific command may indicate a virus infection.
RUN= (TEMP\LIST.VBS)	The LIST.VBS virus. Update antivirus software and run immediately.
RUN=HPFSCHED	Nags user to register HP printer or scanner. (Not mandatory and can be annoying)
RUNDLL32.EXE	Runs individual routines that have been packaged into a .DLL file. (Not mandatory)
SA3DSRV	Windows 3D sound extension added by Aureal 3D sound cards. (Not mandatory)
SAFEINST.EXE	A utility from Imation that is part of the LS120 Superdisk setup. It checks the parallel port chipset for compatibility. No longer required once software is installed and drive is working.
Savenow or SAVENOW.EXE	A spyware utility that transmits user information to specified locations on the Internet. REMOVE.
SCANREG	Makes a copy of the Windows Registry after attempted startup. Designates whether startup was successful or not. Useful for backing up in the event of a corrupted Registry. Does not remain in memory after the backup has been generated. WHILE NOT MANDATORY, REGISTRY BACKUPS WILL NOT BE GENERATED IF REMOVED. DO NOT REMOVE!

(continued)

Table A.2 Annotated Listing of MSCONFIG Startup Entries (*continued*)

Program or File Name	Description
ScanRegistry (WINDOWS\list.vbs)	The LIST.VBS virus. Update antivirus software and run immediately.
ScanRegistry or SCANREGW.EXE	This is the legitimate Registry scanning utility which must be run at startup. Without it, backup copies of the registry are not completed.
Scheduling Agent	Function of Task Scheduler that automates scheduled events. (Not mandatory if scheduled events are not used)
Service Connection or SCCENTER.EXE	A utility installed by Backweb software for monitoring the connection status. (Not mandatory)
ShockmachineReminder or SMREMINDER.EXE	A utility installed by Shockwave software that monitors the Shockwave Web site for software updates and new content. (Not mandatory)
SHPC32	A function of a Compaq printer driver. Required for the printer to work properly.
SKA.EXE=SKA.EXE	The Happy99.Worm. Not likely to be seen now. If found, run antivirus software immediately.
Sm56acl	System tray icon added by SM56 Modems driver installation. (Not mandatory)
SMS Client Service	Starts the Microsoft Systems Management Server client software. You can remove it, but you might get fired.
SMS Win9x Message Agent	Systems Management Server utility that directs messages to a specific server.
Snsicon or SNSICON.EXE	A utility installed by Second Nature Software, a program that changes background wallpaper based on a preconfigured schedule. Only required if you want the wallpaper to change.
Sonic A3D Control or VRTXCTRL.EXE	Management software for Sonic A3D sound cards. (Not mandatory)
SpeedRacer	A utility installed by Creative Labs sound card software. (Not mandatory).
Spinner Plus or SPINNER.EXE	A utility that provides access to Web-based music broadcasts. (Not mandatory)
SS Runner V3.0 or RUNNER.EXE	Synthesoft screensaver software that creates a system tray icon which enables the screensaver and also from which you can access its option menus. (Not mandatory)

(*continued*)

Table A.2 Annotated Listing of MSCONFIG Startup Entries (*continued*)

Program or File Name	Description
Sspdsrv or SSDPSRV.EXE	WINMe. Plug and Play function that provides Simple Service Discovery Protocol (SSDP) and General Event Notification Architecture (GENA) support.
Startacc or STARTACC.EXE	Internet caching software. Part of Webroot Accelerate 2000. (Not mandatory)
Startup	A function of Iomega Zip drive software. (Not mandatory)
Startupmonitor	A freeware tool that adds itself to your startup menu so that it can warn you whenever another program tries the same stunt.
State Manager or StateMgr or STATEMGR.EXE	WINMe only. Takes a snapshot of the registry and places the information into data archive. Required for Restore functionality. Do not remove.
Still imageMonitor or STIMON.EXE	A utility that moderates transfer of data between USB still image devices and the application. Consists of two modules, Event Monitor and Control Center. Event Monitor detects events from connected USB scanning devices while Control Center determines how to react to these incoming events. (Not mandatory, but is included with certain HP scanners. If included, then it must be running for your scanning software to work properly.)
Sxgdsenu or SXGDSENU.EXE	On some laptop computers, it is installed to manage sleep or hibernation functions of power management. If your laptop installed it, then you need it.
SymTray - Norton SystemWorks	Collects all Norton SystemWorks system tray icons together into a single icon. (Not mandatory)
SynTPEnh or SYNTPENH.EXE and SynTPLpr or SYNTPLPR.EXE	On some laptop computers, it is installed to manage the touchpad. If your laptop installed it, then you need it.
Sysdoc or SYSDOC32.EXE	Automatic startup for Norton System Doctor. Best if run manually. (Not mandatory)
System DLF or CPQDIAGA.EXE	A Compaq diagnostic utility, which allows the user to view information about your computer's hardware and software configuration. (Not mandatory)
SystemBackup = C:\WINDOWS\MTX_.EXE	The W95.MTX virus/worm. Obsolete, but occasionally reappears. Run antivirus software immediately.
SystemTray or SYSTRAY.EXE	Windows System Tray. This is the system utility that manages all this mess I'm discussing here. Required.

(*continued*)

Table A.2 Annotated Listing of MSCONFIG Startup Entries (*continued*)

Program or File Name	Description
SystemWizard Sniffer	A hardware/software diagnostics utility from SystemSoft. (Not mandatory)
SYSTRAY	Manages the Start button and taskbar region of the screen. No point in removing it. It'll just come back.
T4UMHF5=C:\WINDOWS\ TEMP\T4UMHF5.VBS	The VBS/Anjulie@MM virus. Update antivirus software and run immediately.
Taskbar Display Controls	Appears if the graphics card driver inserts Display Settings icon in the System Tray. (Not mandatory)
TaskMonitor or TASKMON.EXE	Microsoft utility that monitors program usage. (Not mandatory)
TCAUTIEXE or TCAUDIAG	A diagnostics utility for 3com NICs. Monitors status of network connection. (Not mandatory)
Time Sync Add Client	For Palm Pilots and PDA's, needed in the startup in order for those devices to function properly
Timemanager.exe	A utility that monitors how much actual time is spent on any given activity. (Not mandatory)
Tips	Popup pointers for an Intellipoint mouse. (Not mandatory)
Touch Manager	A keyboard utility. (Not mandatory)
Tour or WINCOOL.EXE	WINMe. A popup that nags at the user to watch the Windows Millennium Interactive Video Sampler. (Not mandatory and quite annoying)
Tray Temperature or WEATHERBUG.EXE or [Weatherbug]	A utility that links to the Weatherbug Web site and provides up-to-the-minute weather forecasts. (Not mandatory)
Trayzip or TRAYZIP.EXE	A Zip compression utility that creates a system tray icon. (Not mandatory)
Trickler or FSG.EXE	A spyware program that collects information from the computer and transmits it to a preconfigured Internet location. REMOVE.
TrueVector or VSMON.EXE	A function of ZoneAlarm firewall software. Required for the software to work properly.
TVWakeup	Function of Microsoft Web TV that provides controls on the taskbar. (Not mandatory)
TweakDUN	A utility that finetunes certain Windows settings in order to maximum efficiency of bandwidth usage on a dial-up networking connection. (Not mandatory, but useful)

(*continued*)

Table A.2   Annotated Listing of MSCONFIG Startup Entries (*continued*)

Program or File Name	Description
TweakUI	TweakUI is a program available from Microsoft's Web site that allows a user to adjust many features not otherwise adjustable. Most options require the program to load at startup in order to effect the changes. When TweakUI is used to enter a network password, it will be listed twice. If you remove one, you should remove both. (Not mandatory)
USB Hub Keyboard Patch or SKBPATCH.EXE	WIN95. USB Driver update that extends support to USB keyboards. Required for WIN95 users wanting to use a USB keyboard.
USBMMKBD	Utility that provides USB keyboard support. Required on most systems using USB keyboards.
User32DLL (WINDOWS\User32DLL.vbs)	The LOOK.vbs virus. Update antivirus software and run immediately.
Usrobotics online registration	Registration nag for owners of US Robotics products. (Not mandatory and quite annoying)
VidSvr	TV guide for WEBTV users. (Not mandatory)
VirusScan Console	A function of McAfee VirusScan (through version 4.x) used for scheduling unattended virus scans. Not required if you don't perform regularly scheduled scans.
VirusScan System Scan	A function of McAfee VirusScan (through version 4.x). Known to interfere with certain programs. Scan files manually. (Not mandatory)
VirusScan System Tray	A function of McAfee VirusScan (through version 4.x). Runs if you have any of the VirusScan options running.
Vistascan or VISTASCAN.EXE	Function of VistaScan scanner software. Click this icon and a menu opens. (Not mandatory)
Voodoo2 or 3DFXV2PS.DLL	Function of the Voodoo 2 graphics adapters. Restores Voodoo 2 registry settings that can't be retained normally. Required for 3dfx/Voodoo2 owners.
VortexTray	System tray application for Aureal Vortex-based soundcards. (Not mandatory)
VoyetraTray	Function of Turtle Beach Montego II (and other) sound card drivers. Provides Control Group for the sound functions/associated with AudioStation 3 and 32. (Not mandatory)
VS_STAT.EXE; VSECOMR.EXE; VSHWIN32.EXE; VSSTAT.EXE	Part of McAfee Antivirus program. Required for automated scanning of files and for scheduled system scans.

(*continued*)

Table A.2 Annotated Listing of MSCONFIG Startup Entries (*continued*)

Program or File Name	Description
Vshield	A function of McAfee Antivirus that scans new files as they are added. Not required if manual scans of downloads and disk contents are faithfully done. (Not mandatory, but quite useful)
Vshwin32EXE or VSHWIN32.EXE	A 32-bit function of McAfee Antivirus that scans new files as they are added. Not required if manual scans of downloads and disk contents are faithfully done. (Not mandatory, but quite useful)
VsStatEXE or VSSTAT.EXE	A function of McAfee Antivirus that logs files coming in and actions taken by McAfee on those files. (Not mandatory, but useful)
W3kNETWORK or W3KNET.DLL	A function of advertising-supported software that automatically downloads ads to the users' computers whenever the associated software is run. Quite annoying, but generally required for the associated software to run properly.
Washer or WASHER.EXE	The Windows utility that automatically cleans your browser's cache, cookies, history, mail trash, etc., based on whatever schedule the user has configured in the Clear History function of Internet Options. (Not mandatory, but quite useful)
washindex	A function Webroot Windows Washer, a third-party utility that deletes unnecessary duplicate and temporary files. You can remove it, but as long as the software is installed, it'll just come back.
Watchdog Program or WATCHDOG.EXE	Third-party utility that monitors ISP/dial-up connection. (Not mandatory)
Waterfall Pro 2.99 or WFP.EXE or [wfp]	Waterfall Pro is a utility that monitors CPU temperature and slows CPU speed if it gets too warm. (Not mandatory)
Wcmdmgr.exe	A function of WildTangent software that periodically contacts WildTangent servers to see whether an update is available. (Not mandatory)
Web outfitter tray or STTRAY.EXE	Automatically launches Intel's Web Outfitter software at startup and creates a system tray icon for the option menus.
WebHancer Agent or WHAGENT.EXE	System Tray for Webhancer software, a web caching utility. (Not mandatory and extremely resource intensive)

(*continued*)

Table A.2 Annotated Listing of MSCONFIG Startup Entries (*continued*)

Program or File Name	Description
Webshots	A utility that automatically downloads screensavers from the Webshots Web site. Useful only if you have Webshots updating your wallpaper on a daily basis.
WhenUstart.exe or WHENU.EXE	An on-line shopping service that automatically launches each time you run Windows. (Not mandatory or useful)
Win32DLL =WINDOWS\Win32DLL.vbs	The LOVE-LETTER-FOR-YOU.TXT.VBS virus. Update antvirus software and run immediately.
WinampAgent or WINAMPA.EXE	Launches a system tray icon for Winamp Player software. (Not mandatory)
WIN-BUGSFIX	LOVE-LETTER-FOR-YOU.TXT.vbs virus removal instructions
WINDLL.EXE	The GirlFriend 1.35 virus. Mostly obsolete but still pops up from time to time. Collects user ID and password information and transmits it to a preconfigured Internet location. Run antivirus software immediately.
Windows Eyes	A utility for blind computer users that replaces common computer responses with speech. (Not mandatory, but useful to those who need it)
Windows=c:\msdos98.exe	The MINE.EXE virus. Update antivirus software and run immediately.
WinFAT32=WinFAT32.EXE	The VBS.Loveletter virus. Update antivirus software and run immediately.
Winkey	Freeware program that allows user to custom-configure Windows hot keys.
WINMGMT.EXE	Enterprise Management software that runs from administrator's machine. Should be removed from client machines.
winmodem or WINMODEM.EXE	Utility installed by a number of software modems. (Not mandatory, but can be useful)
WinPoET or WinPPPoverEthernet.exe or [WinPPPoverEthernet]	Provides end users with authenticated access to high-speed broadband networks using the Microsoft dial-up interface. (Not mandatory)
WKCALREM	Yet another Microsoft Works Calendar reminder. (Not mandatory)
WKDETECT	Automatically looks for updates for Microsoft Works when Internet connection is present. (Not mandatory and can be annoying)

(*continued*)

Table A.2 Annotated Listing of MSCONFIG Startup Entries (*concluded*)

Program or File Name	Description
WKFUD.EXE	Microsoft marketing drivel. (Not mandatory or useful)
Yahoo Pager or YPAGER.EXE	A function of Yahoo! Messenger that allows the user to send instant messages. (Not mandatory)
zBrowser Launcher or COMMANDR.EXE or ITOUCH.EXE	Function of Logitech keyboard software that creates a system tray icon which the can access the menu options. From here, the user can program certain keys on Logitech keyboards. (Not mandatory)
ZipDisk Icons	Related to the Zip drive. (Not mandatory)
ZoneAlarm (zonealarm.exe) Uses 7% resources	Launches ZoneAlarm at startup and creates a system tray icon from which you can access the menu options. Required for ZoneAlarm to function properly.

While not a complete listing (I'm not sure that would be possible), these are some of the more commonly seen entries to the Startup options in MSCONFIG.

GLOSSARY

8.3 naming convention: A file-naming scheme used by earlier file systems that permitted file names of up to eight characters, plus an extension of up to three characters.

Active Desktop: A method of configuring the Windows desktop to behave as if it is a Web page, allowing single-click activation of icons and other Web-like features.

Active partition: A primary partition on a hard disk drive that has been identified in the MBR as being the bootable partition.

Allocation scan: A BIOS routine that reassigns resources to Plug 'n Play devices installed on a computer system.

Asymmetric multiprocessing: A method by which an operating system makes use of more than one processor, loading OS code onto one processor and application code and user data onto all others.

Attribute: A property assigned to a file or directory on the system that defines certain characteristics of that file.

Basic disk: A disk that has been configured to conform to the legacy partition-oriented approach to file systems.

BIOS extension: A string of code that interfaces the operating system to the BIOS interrupts.

Burn-in: The tendency for a CRT monitor to permanently etch an image onto the inner surface of the tube if the image stays on the screen for too long a period.

Cabinet file: A compressed file that holds a large number of smaller files that can be uncompressed and installed as needed.

Clean install: The fresh installation of an OS over a newly partitioned and formatted hard disk.

Client: A piece of software running from within an OS that allows the device to connect to a network.

Cluster: Another term for the file allocation unit (FAU).

Container: A collection of objects on the system or network that have been gathered together into a single administrative unit.

Control set: A collection of registry settings that defines the system configuration for Windows during the boot process.

Conventional memory: The first megabyte of RAM, divided into 640K for running programs and 384K reserved for system use.

Cooperative multitasking: The ability of an OS to simultaneously run more than one program, placing responsibility on the application for relinquishing control of the system.

Crash dump: A direct copy of the entire contents of system RAM copied to a file on the hard disk.

Credentials: Information provided by the user, including but not restricted to the User ID and password, that grants that user access to a system or network.

Datacom: A term coined to describe any equipment used in data communications.

Digital signature: An encrypted piece of data added to a file to guarantee its authenticity.

Directory: A container node of a file system that can contain other directories or files.

Disk duplexing: Exactly duplicating the data on a system on two different drives, each hanging off of a separate controller.

Disk mirroring: Exactly duplicating the data on a system on two different drives hanging off of a single controller.

Disk slack: The amount of disk storage that is wasted by null files and/or small files stored on the hard disk.

Distribution server: A centralized storage location for the installation files of operating systems or applications.

Domain: A collection of all resources and users that fall under the control of a single administrative unit. In the case of Windows NT, the administrative unit would be the PDC.

Dynamic disk: A disk that has been configured for a file system based on volumes rather than partitions.

Enhanced mode: An operational mode specific to Windows that took advantage of advanced functions available in the 80386 microprocessor, including the ability to use virtual memory and to function in virtual real mode.

Executive Services: The layer of the operating system responsible for running commands.

Expanded memory: Memory beyond conventional memory that is under the direct management of a paging frame and a expanded memory manager.

Extended memory: All memory installed on a system above the 1MB of conventional memory.

Extended partition: Also called a logical disk drive, this is a partition contained within a primary partition.

File: A collection of data that is intended to stay together.

Font: The size and characteristics (such as bold or italic) of a particular typeface.

Hard fault: A situation in which data sought by the CPU was neither in memory nor in the paging file. As a result, a new hard disk search must be initiated.

High memory: The first 64K of memory beyond the 1MB of conventional memory, usually used as a paging file for access into extended memory.

I/O address: A location in memory that identifies where data from a specific device will be stored as it moves from either the application or the CPU to the device, and vice versa.

Icon: A small picture linked to an application shortcut.

Interrupt: On a software level, it is a string of code that is called in order to perform a specific function. The BIOS uses software interrupts to manage hardware. On a hardware level, it is an electrical signal that notifies the CPU that a device needs to open communications (or vice versa).

IPCONFIG: The TCP/IP utility that displays all TCP/IP configuration information for any given interface, or for all interfaces on a system.

Journaling: A process used by certain OSs and applications by which any changes made to the basic infrastructure or code are recorded in a log prior to being enforced.

Kernel Mode: An operational mode for an OS that manages system functions.

Lazy writing: A disk-caching scheme that allows the OS to perform write operations to a disk at a time when the controller and disk aren't involved with read operations.

Library: In programming, a collection of subroutines that are required by several or all applications running on a computer. By storing this code in a single file, it does not need to be duplicated many times over.

Local loop carrier: A communications service provider. It provides the electronic link between geographically separated devices.

Logical partition: A pointer on a hard disk that identifies itself as a partition on the local drive, but in reality points to a partition on a remote disk.

Memory pool: The total address space available to an OS and the applications running on top of it.

Metafile: A related string of streaming data that contains the information that is used to implement the file system structure. Also, a metafile is a structured graphical file, also containing streaming data.

Mirrored volume: A single logical drive that is made of two disks, both of which contain identical data.

Multitasking: The ability of an OS to simultaneously run more than one program at once.

Native File Encryption: A technology introduced into the NTFS file system that allows files and directories to be selectively scrambled for local storage.

Network client: A piece of software running on a computer that provides network access for the computer and all applications running on that computer.

Node: Any one of several addressable types of allocated space on a hard disk that can contain the data that makes up a file.

Object: In reference to the OS, an object is any single resource on the system and/or network, including files, users, or devices.

Object counter: In Performance Monitor, it is the specific property or variable for which data is being collected.

Octet: A decimal alliteration of a single 8-bit string of data.

Online content: The overall availability of resources across an intranet or the Internet.

Operating System: A program running on a computer system that manages all of the services required by applications that are to run on the system and interfaces with the hardware.

Page fault: A noncritical error state that occurs when the OS looks for data in the paging file and fails to locate it.

Page frame: 64KB of high memory that is used for moving data down from addresses above 1MB into the 640K used by DOS programs.

Page read/write: When physical RAM in a system becomes full, data will be temporarily stored in a file called the paging file. A Page Read is a read operation from this file, while a Page Write is when data is moved from RAM to the paging file.

Parity block: A mathematical image of data that can be used to reconstruct that data in the event it is lost.

Permissions: The degrees of access a particular user has been granted to a specific resource on the network.

Ping: Not only is Ping an acronym, it has been universally adopted as a term that can be either a noun or a verb. As a noun it represents the packets sent when pinging another host. As a verb, it represents the process of pinging another host.

Pinned list: A list of shortcuts to applications that are used on a regular basis.

Pre-emptive multitasking: A way to manage multiple applications on a computer system that puts the responsibility for releasing system resources onto the OS.

Primary partition: Any one of four partitions on a hard disk drive that is defined in the MBR and can be converted into a bootable partition.

Priority boosting: A process by which the privilege level of a thread of code is promoted to a higher level in order to enhance its chances at the CPU.

Privilege level: A level of protection and priority that certain lines of code running within an OS have over other lines of code.

Privileges: The rights a particular user has been granted to perform specific functions or tasks on a system or the network in general.

Processor ring: Another term for privilege level.

Product activation: A newer technology that requires the end user to physically activate the product through a database managed by the product's manufacturer. This prevents the product from being installed on multiple machines.

Profile: Various settings and preferences specific to a particular user or piece of hardware on a system.

Promiscuous mode: An operating mode for any network interface in which all incoming packets will be accepted, even if they are not intended for that specific interface.

Protocol: An application running on a computer that ensures that the computer will speak the same language and follow the same rules as the computers with which it communicates.

Proxy server: A machine on the network that has been configured to be the portal to the Internet, through which all other computers on the network gain access.

Real mode: An operational mode for either a CPU or an OS in which only one application can be present on the system at once and only 1MB of RAM can be addressed by that application.

Real time OS: An OS designed to be able to perform specific functions at the precise time at which those functions are needed.

Recognition scan: A BIOS routine that polls each device installed on a computer system to see whether that device is Plug 'n Play, and if so, what resources it currently claims.

Redirector: An OS function (usually running within a client) that intercepts hardware and software calls that are intended for remote devices and points them in the right direction.

Registry: In Windows, it is a relational database that contains all system and application settings and/or parameters.

Report phase: A part of the WIN2K installation procedure that seeks out and logs programs and device drivers that are likely to cause problems.

Resident command: In an OS, it is any command that is an integral part of the command interpreter and does not require an external executable program.

Restore point: A copy of system files and registry entries that were in place at the time a major system change was introduced.

Root directory: The volume description, in which all other directories and files will be stored.

Route: The path that data takes to move from point A to point B. It is also a TCP/IP utility that can be used to display the local router configuration on a TCP/IP enabled device.

Sector: The smallest data storage unit recognized by a disk on a hard drive. On magnetic media, the sector is consistently 512 bytes. It can vary for other types of optical media.

Security descriptor: A token attached to a resource that defines security attributes assigned to that resource.

Service: A networking function of the OS, such as file sharing, that can be turned on and off as needed.

Share level security: A method of protecting resources on the network that involves applying the security attributes, such as password protection, to the object itself. As such, each secured object on the system may have a unique password.

Share-level access: A level of security in Windows that allows users to create their own shares and set their own passwords.

Snap-in: An applet that can be added to customized consoles in Microsoft Management Console.

Snapshot: In reference to an OS, it is a small binary file that contains information useful in replicating the organization and structure of an application or configuration.

Soft fault: The data requested by the CPU is in memory, but not part of the current working set of data. As a result, a new memory search must be initiated.

Spanned volume: A larger logical drive that is created by combining space located on two different partitions or disks.

Standard mode: An operational mode specific to Windows in which the OS could access expanded memory beyond 1MB and could task switch multiple applications.

Stop code: A number assigned to a particular catastrophic event, along with certain parameters that further define the event.

Striped volume: A logical drive that is created by storing data in chunks that are distributed among multiple physical drives.

Subdirectory: Any directory that exists beneath another directory.

Supervisory mode: A process by which an OS runs code at the highest possible privilege level.

Switch: In reference to an OS, it is an additional parameter added to the end of a command that defines advanced functions for that command to perform. The switch turns a specific function on or off.

Symmetric multiprocessing: A method by which an operating system makes use of more than one processor, distributing all code equally across all available processors.

SYSINIT: A subroutine of IO.SYS that seeks out and runs MSDOS.SYS during the MS-DOS boot process.

System call: A request for a service not directly provided by the application.

System object: On a system in general, it is any hardware or software entity to which specific properties can be assigned. In Performance Monitor, it is a category of events that can be monitored.

System Virtual Machine: An environment in Windows that emulates a complete computer system and houses all of the critical processes and functions of the OS.

Task scheduler: A system file that determines how long a particular application can retain control of system resources.

Task switching: The ability of an OS to close a program, run another, and then return to the same point in the program previously closed.

Thunking: A Microsoft process of translating 16-bit commands and data into a 32-bit format, and vice versa.

Transient command: A command that is issued and run from an external source.

Trigger: Another name for a switch.

Trojan horse: A malicious program designed to mimic another commonly recognized program that is, in fact, performing some other action in the background without the knowledge or consent of the user.

Typeface: The basic shape that letters and numbers of a particular character set will assume.

Upgrade: The replacement of an older OS with a newer, migrating as many settings and applications as possible.

User level security: A method of securing resources on a system or network that involves assigning the security attributes to an account provided to the user. Once the user has logged on, access to resources is provided based on the permissions assigned to the account.

User mode: An operational mode for an OS that manages applications and security functions.

User-level access: A level of security in Windows that provides users with all permitted access to network resources using a single user ID and password.

Virtual machine: An environment set up in system memory that emulates all functions of a working computer, providing the illusion that a program is the only code running on a computer system.

Volume set: A single logical disk drive that is created when multiple partitions or physical disks are combined.

Volume: A single managed unit of storage on a computer system. This can be a single hard disk, if that disk has been formatted to only one partition, or it can be an individual partition on a disk.

Wild card: A character that instructs a command to replace that character with any other character or collection of characters it finds in its place.

Workgroup: A collection of independently managed users and/or devices on a network that are configured to share files and devices.

GLOSSARY OF ACRONYMS

ACE: Access Control Entity. An individual entry of the ACL defining a specific object and its security attributes.

ACL: Access Control List. A data token attached to the descriptor of a specific object on the network that defines what users and/or groups are allowed to access that object and what degree of access they are allowed.

ACPI: Advanced Configuration and Power Interface. An upgrade to the PnP functionality of Windows.

ADSI: Active Directory Service Interface

AFS: Automatic File Compression. A technology built into NTFS that allows files and directories to be compressed and uncompressed on the fly.

API: Application Programming Interface. A collection of files used by Microsoft OSs that maintains and translates the basic command set required by all devices of a particular type.

APM BIOS: Advanced Power Management Basic Input Output Services

ARC: Advanced RISC Computing

ASMP: Asymmetric Multiprocessing. The ability of an OS to use more than one processor, where the OS code runs on one processor and all other application code and user data is distributed across the remaining processors.

ATAPI: Advanced Technology Application Programming Interface. The API that controls IDE devices.

ATM: Asynchronous Transfer Mode

BDC: Backup Domain Controller. Any server on an NT domain that houses a copy of the security database that is periodically updated by the PDC.

BIOS: Basic Input Output Services. The instruction set on a computer system that provides the startup code along with a number of routines that provide command support for the hardware installed on the system.

BSOD: Blue Screen of Death. The last message NT (and later Microsoft OSs) manages to choke out in its dying breath.

CAB: Cabinet. A compressed file that houses a number of smaller files that can be independently extracted as needed.

CAL: Client Access License. A license granting one user permission to access a system or network.

CAT: Catalog File. A compressed file in Windows that contains driver signing information.

CDFS: CD-ROM File System

COMDEX: Computer Dealer Exposition. An annual trade show for businesses in the computer industry.

CPL: Current Privilege Level. The level of priority at which code is running on machines. It is the method by which processor rings are defined.

CUI: Common User Interface. A feature of many OSs that dictates how certain functions related to user interaction with the programs are handled, ensuring that all applications have a similar look, feel, and function.

DAC: Discretionary Access Control. A feature written into the NTFS file system that allows an administrator to apply security on a file or directory level.

DDE: Dynamic Data Exchange. A technology for exchanging data between two autonomous programs running on a single computer.

DEC: Digital Equipment Corporation

DHCP: Dynamic Host Configuration Protocol. A protocol that assigns IP addresses to client computers on the fly.

DLL: Dynamically Linked Library. A file that contains a collection of subroutines that can be called on the fly by any application running on the system that requires the services it provides and then can be flushed from memory when its task is finished.

DMA: Direct Memory Access. A technique by which a large amount of data is moved directly from an application or device to memory, without constant intervention from the CPU.

DNS: Domain Name Services. A service that resolves host name to IP address on the Internet.

DSL: Digital Subscriber Line

DUN: Dial-Up Networking. A method of connecting to a network over a modem.

EFS: Encrypting File System. A functionality of the NTFS 5 file system that allows individual files or directories to be encrypted on the fly.

ERD: Emergency Repair Diskette. A floppy diskette that holds system configuration and account information for a machine running NT (or later) operating systems.

FAT: File Allocation Table

FILO: First In, Last Out

FIRST: Forum of Incident Response and Security Teams. An organization charged with maintaining the security of the Internet.

HCL: Hardware Compatibility List. A list of devices that have been approved by an OS manufacturer for use with a specific product.

IANA: The Internet Assigned Numbers Authority. The organization that currently hands out IP address to those that need them.

ICANN: The Internet Corporation for Assigned Names and Numbers. One of several organizations involved in the administration of the Internet.

ICS: Internet Connection Sharing. A service that allows multiple computers to share a single Internet access line.

ICS: Internet Connection Sharing. A service that allows multiple computers to simultaneously use a single hookup to the Internet.

IEPG: The Internet Engineering and Planning Group. An organization involved in overseeing the operational control of the Internet.

IFS: Installable File System. A feature in WIN9x and later OSs that allows network redirectors and third-party file systems to be installed as needed.

IIS: Internet Information Services

InterNIC: Internet's Network Information Center. One of several organizations involved in the administration of the Internet.

IPSEC: Internet Protocol Security

IPX/SPX: Internetwork Packet Exchange/ Sequenced Packet Exchange. A Novell networking protocol.

ISDN: Integrated Services Digital Network

ISOC: The Internet Society. The organization that oversees all the other organizations involved in managing the Internet.

ISP: Internet Service Provider. The end user's gateway to the Internet.

LAN: Local Area Network

LDAP: Lightweight Directory Access Protocol. A protocol that allows network resources to be browsed in a manner similar to local disk drives.

LSA: Local Security Authority. A Microsoft service that authenticates users' rights.

LSA: Local Security Authority. An NT service that manages the logon process and all subsequent access to system or network resources.

MAPI: Messaging Applications Programming Interface

MBR: Master Boot Record. Information contained on the first one or two sectors of a hard disk that contain code that initializes the file system, defines disks and partitions, and provides a pointer to the OS.

MFU: Most Frequently Used. The portion of the XP Start menu that displays applications that have been opened over a predefined period of time, in the order which they were opened. Apps are displayed from most recently used to least recently.

MIDI: Musical Instrument Device Interface. A connector for hooking up computerized musical instruments to a computer system.

MMC: Microsoft Management Console

MS-DOS: Microsoft Disk Operating System

NAP: Network Access Point. The entry point to one of the several large capacity circuits that transport data across the Internet.

NetBEUI: NetBIOS Extended User Interface. A Microsoft networking protocol.

NIC: Network Interface Card

NLA: Network Location Awareness. A feature in XP that automatically configures a computer system to the network or subnet to which the device is attached.

NLB: Network Load Balancing

NMI: Non-Maskable Interrupt. Any software or hardware induced interrupt that requires instantaneous attention from the CPU.

NTWS: NT Workstation

OLE: Object Linking and Embedding. A technology that allows an object to be created in one application and imported into a second application; should the properties of the object ever change in the first, it is automatically updated in the second.

PAE: Physical Address Extension

PCMCIA: Personal Computer Memory Card International Association

PDC: Primary Domain Controller. The server in an NT domain that houses the master security database.

PIF: Program Information File. A small descriptor file that tells Windows how a specific DOS application is going to behave.

PKI: Public Key Infrastructure

PM: Program Manager. A file and application management utility provided in Windows 3.x products.

PM: Program Manager. An applet in WIN3.x that acted as a DOS shell for file and program management functions.

PnP: Plug 'n Play. An Intel/Microsoft technology that allows the computer system and OS to automatically detect and configure certain settings for PnP compatible hardware.

POP: Point of Presence. The physical connection supplied by an ISP that provides access to the Internet.

POSIX: Portable Operating System Interface

PPP: Point-to-Point Protocol

PROM: Programmable Read-Only Memory. A chip that contains permanently embedded code.

PXE: Preboot Execution Environment

QDOS: Quick and Dirty Operating System

RAID: Redundant Array of Independent Disks

RAS: Remote Access Services. An NT service that allows a direct dial-up connection from a remote computer to access the host system.

RDP: Remote Desktop Protocol. A protocol that allows remote administration of another computer over the network.

RIS: Remote Installation Services

RSoP: Resultant Set of Policy. A feature in XP that allows the administrator to test the results of a new policy on a select group of guinea pigs before inflicting it on the entire network.

SAM: Security Account Manager. An encrypted file stored within the registry of NT that hold the security attributes for all user and group accounts.

SCTS: Security Configuration Tool Set

SDK: Software Development Kit. A collection of utilities and programs provided by an OS manufacturer that makes the development of applications to run on its OS much easier.

SFC: System File Checker

SFP: System File Protection. A Windows utility that prevents critical OS files from being deleted or overwritten, and if they are, can replace them on the fly.

SID: Security Identifier. A unique number generated and assigned to an object on the system or network that allows LSA to manage the security for that object.

SMP: Symmetric Multiprocessing. The ability of an OS to run OS or application code equally distributed across all available CPUs.

SRM: Security Reference Monitor. An NT service that compares a user's access token to the ACL and either allows or denies access to a specific resource accordingly.

TCP/IP: Transmission Control Protocol/Internet Protocol. The networking protocol of the Internet.

TSR: Terminate and Stay Resident. Any program that is launched, performs a task, but then remains in memory in case its services are required again.

UMB: Upper Memory Block. A segment of memory created by an extended memory manager in the address range between 640K and 1MB of conventional memory.

UPNP: Universal Plug 'n Play. Revised PnP standards that are constantly monitored and updated by the UPNP Forum.

VDD: Virtual Device Driver. A piece of software running within an OS that emulates a hardware device driver.

VFAT: Virtual File Allocation Table. A software driver that emulates the file allocation tables stored on a hard disk and prevents applications from making direct calls to the hardware.

VMM: Virtual Machine Manager and Virtual Memory Manager. The first is a piece of software running within an OS that creates, maintains, and breaks down in memory an environment that emulates an actual computer. The second is a piece of software running within an OS that creates and manages the swap file on a hard drive.

VMS: Virtual Memory System. An OS written by DEC.

VPN: Virtual Private Network

WAN: Wide Area Network

WDM: Windows Driver Model

WHQL: Windows Hardware Quality Lab. A division of Microsoft that tests hardware and driver functionality in the Windows OS. There are some who might say this is an oxymoron.

WINS: Windows Internet Naming Service. A service that resolves host name to IP address on the local network.

WMI: Windows Management Instrumentation

WSH: Windows Script Host

Answers to Odd-Numbered Chapter Exercises

Chapter 1

Brain Drain

1. List the five primary functions of the OS as they relate to the hardware and applications on the system.

> The OS handles the file system and directs applications to the correct locations for files in mass storage. It handles processor management and manages threads of code from the OS or apps that need to be run. Memory management ensures that data required by the CPU makes it into RAM in a timely manner and that the data can be found. Device control ensures that all applications have access to all the system devices as needed. And security ensures that data is kept safe from corruption or theft.

3. How do LFNs work in FAT32? In your discussion, include FAT entry requirements and backward compatibility.

> Up to 255 characters is allowed, including the extension. Each FAT entry must define whether a cluster is used, whether it is the last cluster in the file, and if it is not, where the next cluster is to be found. A truncated 8.3 file name is generated using the first six characters of the file name, a tilde, and the number 1. The next file name with the same first six characters is named 2, then 3, then 4. After that, random names are generated.

5. Discuss some of the additional features that distinguish NTFS 5.0 from NTFS 4.0.

> NTFS 5.0 added disk quotas, selective file encryption, and selective file compression.

THE 64K$ QUESTIONS

1. Which of the following is not a function of the OS?
   b. BIOS control

3. What was the largest partition allowed by FAT16?
   c. 2GB

5. What is the NTFS structure that houses the database that maintains file locations and attributes?
   b. VFAT

7. Native File Encryption is a function of _____.
   d. NFTS 5.0

9. A part of the hard disk treated as if it were physical memory is called _____.
   d. All of the above

11. Which of the following is not an example of an OS?
    a. MS Word

13. Your IT director asks you to copy the file IO.SYS from your hard disk to a floppy. You can't because _____.
    b. It is a hidden file.

15. An FAU on a 2GB partition located on a FAT32 drive takes up _____ of space.
    a. 4KB

17. You have a 1.5GB partition on a FAT16 drive. You copy 10,000 files to the drive that are an average of 1000 bytes long. How much free space will you need on your drive to accomplish this?
    d. 320MB

19. Two features offered by NTFS 5 that didn't appear on NTFS 4 are _____ and _____.
    b. Selective file compression
    AND
    d. Disk quotas

CHAPTER 2

BRAIN DRAIN

1. Review the various versions of MS-DOS and come up with the following answers:
   a. What was the first version of DOS that supported 1.44MB floppy diskettes?
      Answer: DOS 3.3

b. What versions supported the first hard drive?

Answer: DOS 2.0

c. What year did MS-DOS provide the first support for memory beyond 1MB?

Answer: DOS 5.0

3. Now describe the software boot process in detail, specifically using MS-DOS as the OS being booted.

As the MBR is being read, a pointer directs the boot process to the first line of code. In MS-DOS, the first thing to run is IO.SYS. IO.SYS locates and loads (but does not run) lines in CONFIG.SYS. It then locates and runs MSDOS.SYS. MSDOS.SYS executes the commands in CONFIG.SYS, and then loads AUTOEXEC.BAT. It then locates and runs COMMAND.COM. COMMAND.COM runs AUTOEXEC.BAT, and the system is running.

5. Define the function and purpose of AUTOEXEC.BAT and discuss some of the commands that might be used in that file.

AUTOEXEC.BAT runs commands and loads programs that are designed to stay RAM resident while the system is running. This can include any executable file on the system. Internal commands include PATH, PROMPT, SET, CLS, and others.

THE 64K$ QUESTIONS

1. What is the file loaded on the ROM BIOS chip that locates the MBR and turns the boot process over to the OS?

d. Bootstrap Loader

3. Which DOS file is credited with being the kernel?

d. MSDOS.SYS

5. How much conventional memory was available to a program running in MS-DOS?

a. <640K (Don't forget that certain device drivers and core OS files had to be loaded into conventional memory.)

7. The function of DOS that provides a roadmap that leads to a specific file on a drive is known as the _____.

b. Path

9. A variable applied to a specific command that instructs that command to perform in a particular manner is known as a _____.

d. Trigger

11. If you wanted to erase an entire directory, along with all of its subdirectories and all the files contained within, which command would you use?

d. DELTREE

13. Which of the following is the correct syntax for a STACKS command?

    d. STACKS=9,256

15. You've added a new device to your system. Which of the following must you do in order to make the device work properly under DOS?

    c. Add a DEVICE= statement to CONFIG.SYS to load the driver file.

17. By default, DOS will keep _____ file handles active at once.

    b. 8

19. Which of the following prompts is the result of PROMPT PG?

    c. C:\DOS>

CHAPTER 3

BRAIN DRAIN

1. Several times in this chapter, it was pointed out that Windows 3.x products were not true OSs. Explain why this is so.

    WIN3.x cannot load itself without MS-DOS being present.

3. Discuss the concept of the virtual machine. Why is it that several virtual machines can be running on a single computer at any given time?

    The virtual machine assures the application running within that it is the only application running on the system. It keeps other applications from stepping on its memory addresses and from accessing the CPU while it is present.

5. How do virtual device drivers differ from a "real" device driver?

    A virtual device is a collection of software files that intercepts hardware calls. The virtual device is what actually communicates with the hardware.

THE 64K$ QUESTIONS

1. Steve Jobs named the LISA after _____.

    d. His secretary.

3. Which of the following features of the 80386 microprocessor did Windows 3.x exclusively take advantage of when running in 386 Enhanced mode?

    c. Virtual real mode

5. Windows 3.x versions all use _____ in order to give the user the sense that multiple programs are running at the same time.

    b. Cooperative multitasking

7. Applications in Windows 3.x all run in _____.

    c. Ring 3

9. Which operational mode of Windows took advantage of memory beyond 1MB, but could not address virtual memory?

    b. Standard mode

11. Which operational mode of Windows did legacy DOS applications run in?

    a. Real mode

13. Which of the following Windows functions allowed memory beyond 1MB to be utilized?

    a. EMM386.EXE

15. Which Windows feature allows the user to move data seamlessly from one application to another on the fly?

    d. DDE

17. What is the default size of a typical UMB?

    a. 8K

19. What was the typical extension for a virtual device driver in Windows 3.x?

    c. VDD

CHAPTER 4

BRAIN DRAIN

1. Discuss the differences between cooperative multitasking and pre-emptive multitasking.

    Cooperative multitasking allows the application to dictate whether or not to give up system resources, while pre-emptive multitasking gives that control to the OS. In cooperative multitasking, a renegade app can make the system appear to be hung.

3. Draw a rough diagram of how the WIN9x Virtual Machine Manager handles difference applications, including legacy DOS apps, WIN3.x apps, and WIN9x apps.

    Diagrams will vary somewhat, but all should have each WIN9x app in its own VM with unlimited resources, each DOS app in its own VM with 1MB of RAM allocated, and all WIN3.x apps in a single machine.

5. Discuss how WINMe was responsible for a number of gray hairs in the heads of technicians worldwide.

    While it had the look and feel of WIN98, it was actually a 32-bit app. It provided only limited support for 16-bit drivers and apps.

THE 64K$ QUESTIONS

1. WIN95 was originally intended for release in the year _____.
   d. 1992

3. WIN95 required, at the minimum _____.
   d. A 20MHz 386DX processor

5. WIN95 required, at the minimum _____.
   c. VGA

7. Which of the following was not a requirement for full PnP functionality?
   b. A PnP Device Driver

9. Which protocol was incorporated into WIN95 for the first time in Microsoft's history?
   d. TCP/IP

11. WIN95 did not incorporate any version of MS-DOS into its structure.
    b. False

13. A 16-bit mouse driver would interface with _____.
    c. GDI.DLL

15. Multiple networking clients on a single computer were made possible by the addition of _____.
    c. The Installable File System

17. What version of WIN9x was the first to provide support for USB?
    b. WIN95 SR2

19. What version of WIN9x was the first to provide support for DirectX?
    d. Windows 98SE

CHAPTER 5

BRAIN DRAIN

1. Discuss the differences between a clean install and an upgrade. While you're at it, discuss the pros and cons of each type of installation.

   A clean install involves partitioning and formatting the hard drive from scratch and installing a brand new OS. The upgrade takes an existing OS and migrates all the old settings into the new OS. This is good in that the user gets a familiar look and feel. It's bad in that any flaws in the old installation show up in the new one.

3. Now discuss the different setup phases for Windows 98 and how they differ from Windows 95.

    Phase 1: Preparing to Run Windows 98 Setup. Some preliminary files are copied to temporary hidden directories. On an upgrade, these files are PRECOPY1.CAB and PRECOPY2.CAB. On a clean install, it is simply MINI.CAB.

    Phase 2: Collecting Information About Your Computer. The user reads the license agreement and selects a directory into which Windows will be installed. The user is given the opportunity to create a startup diskette.

    Phase 3: Copying Windows 98 Files to Your Computer. This phase copies the Windows 98 files to your computer.

    Phase 4: Restarting Your Computer. During this first restart, Setup collects the information it extracted from CONFIG.SYS and AUTOEXEC.BAT and integrates those settings into the registry. Devices known to cause issues are REM'ed out.

    Phase 5: Setting up Hardware and Finalizing Settings. PnP does its thing, device drivers are installed, and any networking settings that were selected are burned into the registry. You now have a WIN98 computer. Congratulations, I think.

5. How did Microsoft take the mouse from a cute little toy to a powerful tool with the release of Windows 95?

    Popup menus were added that can be brought up with the click of the right mouse button. This makes it significantly easier to navigate Windows.

THE 64K$ QUESTIONS

1. During an upgrade, Windows 95 could extract information about programs installed over WIN3.x by opening and reading the _____.

    c.   Group files

3. Which of the following is not a setup phase for WIN95?

    d.   Hardware setup

5. How does Windows Setup remove AUTOEXEC.BAT or CONFIG.SYS lines that may cause problems during an upgrade?

    b.   It places a REM statement in front of the offending command.

7. In order to bring up Display Properties, the user can _____.

    a.   Right-click the Desktop and click Properties
    OR
    d.   Click Start→Settings→Control Panel→Display Properties

9. Control Panel can be accessed from which two of the following places?

    a.   My Computer

OR
d. The Start menu

11. You've just installed a new sound card, and it places a handy little applet somewhere on your computer that allows you to adjust volume without constantly reaching up to the speakers. Where is the icon for that program most likely to be placed?

    d. On the Toolbar

13. Windows applications are consistent amongst themselves because of a feature built into Windows called the _____.

    b. CUI

15. Which Control Panel applet allows the user to turn off Daylight Savings Time?

    d. Time/Date

17. What are two methods of mapping a folder on the network server to your local machine to appear as though it were a local drive?

    a. In the folders pane, right-click the remote resource and select Map Network Drive AND

    d. Click Tools→Map Network Drive

19. Which of the following shortcuts selects all text in an open document?

    c. <Ctrl>+A

CHAPTER 6

BRAIN DRAIN

1. Discuss the differences between symmetric and asymmetric multiprocessing. Why is one more efficient than the other?

    With asymmetric multiprocessing, one processor handles OS and system, while the other processor crunches data and applications files. With symmetric multiprocessing, all processors are sharing tasks equally. With asymmetric, one processor might be running full tilt while the other is virtually idle.

3. Discuss some of the security enhancements Microsoft incorporated into NT.

    Resources can be individually secured, with different users having different levels of access, or no access at all. Also, the ability to perform certain tasks on the machine and/or network can be managed.

5. List the different domain models supported by NT and describe the differences.

    Single Domain: One PDC controls all accounts. Multiple BDCs can assist with logon authentication.

Single Master Domain: One PDC controls all user accounts, but other resource domains may control non-user objects on the network, such as a large database.

Multiple Master Domain: Several single domains have been collected into a large network. Trusts determine how much access each domain has with the others.

Compete Trust: It's a multiple master domain in which every domain trusts every other domain explicitly.

THE 64K$ QUESTIONS

1. The first version of an NT product was demonstrated in _____.
   b. 1991

3. The NT feature that provided security on a file or folder level was called _____.
   d. NTFS

5. NT 4.0 Server, Enterprise Edition can support up to _____ processors.
   c. 8MB

7. NT 4.0 Server requires a minimum of _____ RAM in order to run on a RISC machine.
   c. 16MB

9. In an NT domain the machine that maintains a copy of the security database that is updated periodically is called a _____.
   b. Backup Domain Controller

11. In order to get to the logon screen in Windows NT 4.0 (any version), you must first _____.
   c. Press <Ctrl>+<Alt>+<Delete>

13. You have created a new file on the system and assigned one password on the file that allows the users who access it full control, and another password that only lets them read the file. This is an example of _____.
   c. Share level security

15. In order to tighten up security on your network, your administrator has divided the network into two separate domains. One of these domains is where all the users log on and the other hosts the company's database servers. This is an example of _____ .
   b. The Single Master Domain

17. In order to install NT onto a machine, it is best to start with a freshly prepared hard disk on which no partitions have been defined. This allows NT to prepare the drives using its own utility.
   b. False

19. The licensing mode is selecting during the phase of the installation.

   b. Text

CHAPTER 7

BRAIN DRAIN

1. Discuss several ways that the NT boot process differs from that WIN9x.

   First of all, the MBR doesn't point to the first line of OS code. It points to a Boot Loader file that allows the user to select what OS will be run. Also, unless a file called NTLDR is located on the root partition, NT won't boot. Toward the end of the boot process, before the user can log on, he or she must press <Ctrl>+<Alt>+<Delete> to bring up the logon screen.

3. What are the two operating modes of NT? Discuss them in as much detail as you can muster.

   Kernel mode and user mode. Kernel mode is where the OS kernel files and executive services all run. These all run in privileged mode. The user mode processes are the OS processes that intercept requests from the user or applications. These run in nonprivileged mode.

5. Discuss memory management in NT and how the concept of virtual memory is critical to the OS.

   Since there is only so much physical memory available to NT, the OS makes use of physical hard drive space as virtual memory. When a thread becomes inactive for a period of time, it will be moved over to virtual memory to make space for a process that needs to be moved to physical memory. Once that process is needed again, the procedure is reversed.

THE 64K$ QUESTIONS

1. Which of the following files is not a part of the NT boot process?

   a. WIN.COM

3. What file system is not supported by NT?

   d. FAT32

5. Which of the following is not a phase of the NT load process?

   d. File System Initialization

7. Kernel Mode services run at processor _____.

   a. Ring 0

9. The Executive Services run at _____.

   a. Ring 0

11. Unix applications running in the NT environment are known as _____ apps.

    a. POSIX

13. Threads of code that are time sensitive can be assured of getting first crack at the processor because they will be given a priority _____.

    d. Between 16 and 31

15. On a system with 128MB of installed RAM, an application in NT will be assigned an address space equal to _____.

    d. 2GB

17. If a computer has been configured to divide all data equally between two or more hard drives, with no allowance for data recovery, this computer has been configured for _____.

    a. RAID 0

19. If you want to see what IRQs are being used by your system under NT, you would use _____.

    d. NT Diagnostics

CHAPTER 8

BRAIN DRAIN

1. What are some of the different actions that are taken by Dr. Watson when there is an application error on the system? How are they useful to the user?

   It generates a log file in which it stores information specific to the crash. Next it will create a crash dump file, which consists of all the information that was stored in RAM at the time of the failure. The end user might find the log file useful in determining what failed and when. The crash dump is useful only to Microsoft programmers and their accountants.

3. You suspect that CPU performance has become a serious bottleneck in the system. How can you use Performance Monitor to back up your suspicions?

   By logging the percentage of time the CPU is being utilized by both system processes and user processes, the administrator can not only see how often the CPU is maxed out, but at what times of the day saturation occurs.

5. Discuss as many of the Administrative tools as you can think of. Point out how they are useful to the system administrator.

   At a minimum, the student should mention User Manager (for creating and maintaining user accounts), Disk Administrator (for managing mass storage),

Event Viewer (for troubleshooting system errors), Network Monitor (for monitoring network traffic), and Remote Access Admin (for creating and managing network access over a modem).

THE 64K$ QUESTIONS

1. A crash dump is _____.
   c. A byte-by-byte copy of all information stored in RAM to the hard drive that occurs after a fatal system error

3. When a fatal system error does occur, NT will copy all the information in RAM to a file. By default that file is stored in the _____ directory.
   c. %windir%

5. The individual variables that can be watched by Performance Monitor are called _____.
   d. Objects

7. Page faults/sec is a variable that measures _____.
   a. How many times the CPU requests data that does not exist in RAM

9. Network Monitor automatically loads when you install NT for the first time.
   b. False

11. Of these sections, _____ of them might be useful to the average technician.
   b. Two

13. Which of the following Administrative tools will be found in NT Server, but not on NT Workstation?
   b. Network Client Administrator

15. RAS is a service that exists on Server versions of NT only.
   b. False

17. Which two of the following tasks can be accomplished from the boot diskette created by Network Client Administrator?
   b. Install an OS onto a workstation remotely
   AND
   c. Install a client onto a workstation remotely

19. The Policy Editor is where the administrator would go in order to enable auditing.
   b. False

CHAPTER 9

BRAIN DRAIN

1. Describe the ways the four WIN2K versions differ. Include in your discussion such details as min/max memory support and how many CPUs each one will support.

Version	RAM (min/rec/max)	CPU (min/# supported)	HDD Requirements
Professional	64MB/4GB	P166/2	650MB for installation/2GB minimum recommended
Server	128MB/256MB/4GB	P166/4	1GB
Advanced Server	128MB/256MB/8GB	P166/8	1GB
Datacenter	256MB/512MB/64GB	PIII Xeon/16 (32 via OEM)	2GB

3. What is the function of Last Known Good? Explain why the user logon process is important concerning whether Last Known Good will work or not.

   The Last Known Good points to the registry entries that were valid the last time the system successfully booted as far as the user logon. If the failure occurred after user logon was complete, Last Known Good is useless.

5. How does Safe Mode differ from Safe Mode with Networking Support?

   Safe Mode with Networking Support loads the device drivers for the NIC and all network configuration settings.

THE 64K$ QUESTIONS

1. Windows 2000 Professional requires a minimum of _____ RAM in order to work.
   b. 64MB

3. Windows 2000 Server requires a minimum of _____ RAM in order to work.
   c. 128MB

5. Windows 2000 Datacenter requires a minimum of _____ RAM in order to work.
   d. 256MB

7. Only the Server versions of WIN2K support EFS.
   b. False

9. WIN2K Advanced Server supports up to _____ processors.

   c. 8

11. The WIN2K floppy disk setup procedure involves _____ diskettes.

    b. 4

13. Which of the following two items are required in order to install WIN2K from a remote network location?

    a. A distribution server
    AND
    b. A PXE-compliant boot diskette

15. Which of the following does NOT support an upgrade path to WIN2K Server?

    a. NT Server 3.51

17. At what point does the WIN2K boot process write final information to the LastKnownGood section of the registry?

    c. The instant the user hits enter after providing his/her credentials.

19. You've just attempted to boot the system using Safe Mode, and you get a BSOD informing you that a valid boot partition could not be found by the system. This most likely means that _____.

    d. The system uses a third-party hard disk controller not supported internally by WIN2K

CHAPTER 10

BRAIN DRAIN

1. Which of the topics discussed in this chapter aren't possible without the introduction of NTFS5?

   EFS and disk quotas

3. Describe three MMC consoles that assist the administrator in managing Active Directory components.

   Active Directory Sites and Services. Allows the administrator to control the services that are running and to manage the network topology.

   Active Directory Users and Computers. Allows the administrator to create and manage accounts for devices, individual users, and groups on the network.

   Active Directory Domains and Trusts. This is where administrators manage local and remote domains and create or break down the trusts between domains.

5. What are some of the major differences between basic and dynamic disks?

   A dynamic disk can be used to create disk arrays, it can host pointers to remote disks, and it can support drives beyond the letter Z.

THE 64K$ QUESTIONS

1. Which of the following is Active Directory not capable of managing?
   e. It manages all of the above.

3. Active Directory is an implementation of the _____ protocol.
   d. LDAP

5. Information about a remote server would be found in _____.
   c. Active Directory Sites and Services

7. New hardware can be configured in the _____ wizard.
   a. Add/Remove New Hardware

9. When a digital signature is added to a device driver, that information is stored in the _____ file.
   d. CAT

11. Decoding of files encrypted by a disgruntled employee is made possible by way of the _____.
    a. EFS Recovery Agent

13. If disk quotas have been enabled on a server, the user can double his or her storage capacity by using compression.
    b. False

15. In WIN2K, there is a limit to _____ disk volumes on a system.
    d. There is no limit

17. Which of the following cannot be done on a dynamic disk?
    c. Create partitions

19. Managing disks in WIN2K is done in the _____ console.
    b. Disk Administrator

CHAPTER 11

BRAIN DRAIN

1. List the various versions of Windows XP that are available, and discuss how they differ from one another.

   XP Home Edition: Cannot be joined to a Domain

   XP Professional Edition: Workstation computer that can be joined to a domain

   XP Tablet PC Edition: Specific to Tablet PCs

XP Media Center Edition: Adds functionality specific to computer-based electronic entertainment

XP 64-bit Edition: Designed specifically for 64-bit microprocessors

3. List some features that are brand new to XP. Discuss how they improve the product.

Side-by-side DLL support: Older DLLs can run when required by legacy devices

Integrated CDR/CD-RW write capabilities: A third party utility is no longer required (but you'll certainly WANT one!)

Remote Desktop: Allows the user to access a PC from far away, and yet have the local desktop look, feel, and smell like the remote one

ClearType: Improves desktop resolution

Network Location Awareness: If a system is moved to another part of the network, it can automatically configure itself

Device Driver Rollback: If a new driver corrupts the system, it is an easy task to revert to the older driver

Product Activation: This is an advantage?

5. How is Control Panel different between XP and WIN2K?

It is divided into categories. Each category contains shortcuts to the applets relevant to that category as well as frequently accessed tasks from those applets.

THE 64K$ QUESTIONS

1. Two of the limitations of Home Edition is that _____.
   a. It only supports one CPU
   AND
   d. It cannot join a domain

3. XP Home requires a minimum of _____ RAM in order to run.
   b. 128MB

5. The absolute minimum CPU required by either Home or Professional is a _____.
   b. 300MHz PII

7. The feature that was added to EFS that makes it different between XP and WIN2K is _____.
   c. Files can be encrypted for use by entire groups instead of only individuals

9. Which of the following is not a new feature to XP?
   a. Group Policy Management

11. You can take over control of another user's system and help with a problem because of a protocol known as _____.

    c. Remote Desktop Protocol

13. XP offers two methods of recovering from an improperly installed device driver. What are these two methods?

    c. Device Driver Rollback
    AND
    d. System Restore

15. The Start menu in XP is divided into _____ sections.

    b. 2

17. If you need to check the settings of your sound card's device driver, you would find them in the _____ section of Control Panel. (Choose all that apply.)

    a. Sounds, Speech, and Audio Devices

19. Which of the following is not an adjustment a user can make in Accessibility Options?

    d. Mouse cursor trails

CHAPTER 12

There are no exercises in Chapter Twelve.

CHAPTER 13

BRAIN DRAIN

1. Define a workgroup and a domain. Discuss the differences between the two.

    A workgroup consists of a group of computers and other devices that are interconnected for a singular purpose within the network. P2P networks are always workgroups. A domain is any collection of users, computers, and devices that are under the control of the same administrative unit and are managed by the same security database.

3. Define what a protocol is, and describe its role in networking computers.

    A protocol is a piece of software that ensures that all devices on the network are speaking the same digital language and are following the same sets of rules.

5. Go through the process of configuring a computer to use TCP/IP on the network.

    Open the Network applet in Control Panel (or right-click Network Neighborhood or My Network Places and select Properties). Highlight the TCP/IP properties for the interface you wish to configure. If you have a DHCP server on the network, click the box next to Obtain an IP address automatically. When statically assigning IP addresses, click Specify an IP address. Type in the IP address you want this machine to use and the correct subnet mask. This is the minimum TCP/IP configuration. Advanced settings can include the IP address for a DNS server, a WINS server, and a gateway, if one exists.

THE 64K$ QUESTIONS

1. A collection of independently managed computers and/or devices on a network would be called a _____.

   a. Workgroup

3. The icon for browsing the network in WIN9x is called _____.

   c. Network Neighborhood

5. Which of the following protocols is the one most commonly used on the Internet?

   d. TCP/IP

7. Which of the following protocols was developed by Microsoft for its NOS?

   a. NetBEUI

9. If a small network has several users, and each user is capable of setting up his or her own shares and assigning individual passwords for each share, what kind of security is that network using?

   c. Share level

11. Shares on a Windows network are created in _____.

    b. Windows Explorer

13. Internet Connection Sharing is installed by default on WIN98 computers.

    b. False

15. Which of the two following items must be configured on every computer running TCP/IP?

    a. IP address
    AND
    c. Subnet mask

17. A single number in an IP address, divided by periods, is called _____.

    c. An octet

19. A Class A address uses _____ to identify the network address.

    a. The first octet

CHAPTER 14

BRAIN DRAIN

1. List the intermediate levels across which information traveling between two machines communicating over the Internet must travel.

    User's PC
    User's datacom
    The local loop carrier
    The ISP point of presence
    User services
    ISP backbone
    Online content
    Origin of content

3. Discuss the differences between origin of content and online content.

    Online content refers to the overall availability of information on a network or across the Internet. Origin of content is a specific URL or Web page.

THE 64K$ QUESTIONS

1. Who invented the Internet?

    Hopefully, you didn't take this question seriously. If you answered at all, b. Licklidder is the most appropriate choice, unless you happen to be a member of DNC.

3. The intermediate level that moves user data from the modem to the ISP is called _____.

    d. The local loop carrier

5. The page you view when browsing the Internet is an example of _____.
    b. Origin of content

CHAPTER 15

There are no exercises in Chapter Fifteen.

COMMONLY USED FILE EXTENSIONS

First off, let me say that there is *no way* I intend to provide an exhaustive list of file extensions. Such a list would easily fill a book this size if I tried to describe not only every extension in use, but every way in which any given extension is used. The same collection of letters may represent half a dozen or more different file types.

What I've done here is put together a relatively comprehensive list that shows the extensions used by the majority of programming languages in use as well as those used by popular applications. There are many extensions I've missed. Some I left out simply because a program is now obsolete or is targeted to a very exclusive audience. There are no doubt others that are commonly used that I simply missed. I'm a human being. It happens. So if you have a file you're trying to identify, hopefully this list will be of help.

A List of File Extensions

Extension	Description
A02	OzWin CompuServe E-mail/Forum Access SYSOP File, Archive Section
A03	OzWin CompuServe E-mail/Forum Access SYSOP File, Archive Section
A04	OzWin CompuServe E-mail/Forum Access SYSOP File, Archive Section
A05	OzWin CompuServe E-mail/Forum Access SYSOP File, Archive Section
A06	OzWin CompuServe E-mail/Forum Access SYSOP File, Archive Section
A07	OzWin CompuServe E-mail/Forum Access SYSOP File, Archive Section
A08	OzWin CompuServe E-mail/Forum Access SYSOP File, Archive Section

Extension	Description
A09	OzWin CompuServe E-mail/Forum Access SYSOP File, Archive Section
A10	OzWin CompuServe E-mail/Forum Access SYSOP File
A11	AIM Graphic
A2A	APLASCII EISPACK
A31	Authorware Ver. 3.x Library
A3D	Amapi 3D Modeling (Eovia)
A3K	Yamaha A3000 Sampler File
A3L	Authorware Ver. 3.x Library
A3M	Unpackaged Authorware File
A41	Authorware Ver. 4.x Library
A4L	Authorware Ver. 4.x Library
A4M	Unpackaged Authorware MacIntosh File

(continued)

Extension	Description
A4P	Authorware File without Runtime
A4W	Unpackaged Authorware Windows File
A65	Macromedia Authorware v6.5
A6P	Authorware Application (Macromedia, Inc.)
A86	A86 Assembler Source Code
AA	Audio Book
AA	PROGNOSIS Automated Analyst Document File
AAA	Sybase SQLAnywhere Temp File
AAB	Authorware Binary (Macromedia)
AAC	MPEG-2 Advanced Audio Coding File
AAF	Advanced Authoring Format File
AAM	Authorware Shocked File (Map) (Macromedia)
AAO	America's Army Map
AAP	Apollo Advanced Playlist
AAPKG	ArchestrA IDE Package (Invensys)
AAS	Authorware Shocked Packet (Segment) (Macromedia)
AAS	Movie Clip; Autodesk Animation Setup; used by Compton's Reference Collection
AAS	Audible Words File (Audible, Inc.)
AAT	Arcinfo Line Data Attribute Data
AB	Applix Builder
AB$	AutoCAD Spooled Plot
AB3	PhotoImpact Album File
ABA	Palm Address Book File (Palm)
ABAP	ABAP Source Code (SAP AG)
ABC	ABC Programming Language and ACT! E-mail Address Book File
ABD	AmBiz Bonus Calculator Data File
ABI	AOL 6 Organizer
ABK	CorelDraw AutoBackup and HP-95LX Appointment Book File
ABM	HitPlayer Audio Album File
ABR	Photoshop Brush
ABU	ACT! E-mail Address Book File
ABW	AbiWord Document File
ABX	WordPerfect Address Book File
ABY	AOL
AC3	AC3 Audio File Format
ACA	Agent Character (Microsoft)
ACAD	AutoCAD Database
ACB	AOL Cab Launcher and Photoshop Color Book
ACD	Agent Character Definition (Microsoft)
ACF	Agent Character (Microsoft)
ACF	DB/TextWorks Database Access Control File and Photoshop Custom Filter

Extension	Description
ACG	Agent Preview and Age of Wonders Saved Game
ACGI	AppleSearch CGI Interface
ACL	Access Control List
ACM	Windows System File
ACO	Photoshop Color Swatch File
ACT	FoxPro Documenting Wizard Action Diagram and Photoshop Color Table
ACW	Accessibility Wizard Settings
AD2	Compressed Voice File
AD3	Compressed Voice File
ADA	Advanced Digital Audio Compressed Audio
ADB	ACT! Activity Data File
ADD	PageMaker
ADE	Access Project Extension
ADF	Adapter Description File and Admin Config File
ADI	AutoCAD Plotter File
ADM	After Dark Screen Saver Module
ADN	Access Blank Project Template
ADO	Photoshop Duotone Options
ADP	Access Project
ADP	AOLserver Dynamic Page and FaxWorks Modem Setup File
ADR	Address Book
ADS	ADS Applications File
ADT	AutoCAD Audit Report and ACT! Document Template
AG	Lotus Agenda Application
AG4	Access G4 File
AHP	AutoCAD Help
AHQ	AudioHQ Plug-in Module
AHS	Photoshop Halftone Screens
AHTM	HTML File
AHTML	HTML File
AI	Corel Trace Drawing
AIF	Audio Interchange File
AIFC	Audio Interchange File
AIFF	Audio Interchange File
AIM	Instant Messenger
AIML	Artificial Intelligence Markup Language
AIP	Illustrator Plug-in
AIR	Flight Simulator Aircraft Performance Info File
AJL	ARCserve Backup Journal File (Computer Associates)
AKF	Acrobat Key File
AL	Oracle File
ALBM	HP Photosmart Photo Printing Album
ALC	Norton Internet Security Ad Server File

(continued)

Extension	Description
ALF	LANDesk Client Manager Configuration File
ALL	WordPerfect Printer Info
ALM	Alpha Five Database Information File (Alpha Software)
ALR	VirusScan Alert File
ALT	WordPerfect Menu File
ALV	Photoshop Levels
ALX	ActiveX Layout File and Alpha V Library Index
AME	ACT! E-mail System Library
AMF	Advanced Module Format Music
AMP	Photoshop Arbitrary Map Settings
AMS	Photoshop Monitor Setup
ANI	Windows Animated Cursor
ANS	Word Text and Layout
AOB	DVD Audio File
AOL	AOL
AOM	Download Manager Online Manager Shortcut
AOT	Novell snAppShot Application Binary Object Template File
APC	Lotus Printer Driver Characters
APD	Lotus Printer Driver
APD	PageMaker Printer Description
APE	Winamp Plug-ins AVS File
APF	Acrobat Profile File and Lotus Printer Driver Fonts
API	Application Program Interface and Acrobat Plug-in
APM	Aldus Placeable Metafiles
APP	dBASE Application Object File
APR	ArcView Project File
APS	Visual C++ File
APX	C++ Appexpert Database
AQL	AOL Windows DLL
AR	Javasoft JRE 1.3 Library File
ARA	ATI Radeon Video Driver
ARG	AutoCAD Profile Export
ARI	Compressed Archive
ARJ	Compressed Archive
ARL	AOL Organizer
ARLOLD	AOL 6 Organizer
ARQ	Compressed Archive
ART	Used by a variety of different companies for graphics files
ARV	AutoRoute User Information
ARX	AutoCAD Runtime Extension and ARX Compressed Archive
ARX	ARX Compressed Archive
ARY	Compaq SmartStart Scripting Toolkit File

Extension	Description
AS	Macromedia Flash Action Script
AS4	AS/400 Client Access
ASA	Active Server Document
ASC	ASCII Text
ASD	Word Automatic Backup
ASF	Lotus Screen Font
ASHX	ASP.NET Web Handler File
ASI	Assembler Include
ASIC	ASIC Language Source Code
ASL	Photoshop Layer Style
ASO	Assembler Object
ASP	Active Server Page, Photoshop File Index, and Photoshop Separation Setup
ASPHTML	ASP HTML
ASPX	ASP.NET Source File
ASR	Photoshop Scratch Area
AST	Photoshop Separation Tables
ASV	Photoshop Selective Color
ASX	ActiveSite Extension (Jonathon Rossi)
AT	Rescue Disk file
ATF	Photoshop Transfer Function
ATN	Photoshop Action File
ATX	A ZIP-formatted Compressed Archive
ATX	Alphasoft Trueterm 2001 Dictionaries
AT_	Audio Utility Winatb Compressed File
AU	uLaw/AU Audio File
AU3	AutoIt Ver. 3 Script
AUD	Winamp Media File
AUT	Authentication File
AUTOCONF	UNIX File
AVA	Photoshop Variations File
AVB	Inoculan Anti-Virus Virus Infected File
AVC	Kaspersky Antivirus Toolkit File
AVD	DOS7 File and Avery Label Pro Data File
AVG	AVG Virus Information Database
AVI	Audio Video Interleave File
AVS	Animation
AVS	Winamp Advanced Visualization Studio
AVX	ArcView Extension File
AWD	Award BIOS
AWE	Acrobat Bookmark XML File
AWP	MS Fax Key Viewer
AWR	Ad-aware Reference File
AWW	Office Write Document
AWX	DirectX 8.1
AX	MPEG-4 DVD Filter
AXD	Actrix Technical 2000
AXE	Paradigm C++ Integrated Debugger File and AutoRoute Export File
AXG	AutoRoute Trip File
AXS	HTML; ActiveX Script

(continued)

Extension	Description
AXT	Photoshop Replace Color/Color Range
AZ	WinDVD File
AZM	CP/M Disk Fix File
B	BASIC Language Source
B!K	Flight Simulator Scenery File
B4S	Winamp 3+ Playlist
B5I	IsoBuster CD/DVD Image File
B5T	IsoBuster Description File for a CD-Image
B64	Base 64 MIME-encoded File
BA$	MS Compressed BAS Decompress with UNPACK.EXE
BAC	Backup
BACKUP	Ad-aware Reference File
BAD	Oracle bad File
BAG	AOL 6 Organizer
BAG	Instant Messenger
BAK	Backup
BAL	BAL Borland Programming Language Source
BAN	Creatacard Banner Project
BAR	dBASE Application Generator Horizontal Menu Object
BAS	BASIC Source Code
BAT	Batch File
BBM	Deluxe Paint Image File
BBS	Bulletin Board System Text
BCB3	BC3
BCC	C++ File/Makefile
BCD	Turbo Pascal DOS File
BCH	dBASE Application Generator Batch Process Object
BCK	Backup
BCM	Compaq Easy Access Keyboard Driver
BCO	Bitstream Fontware
BCP	C++ Makefile
BCS	Windows95 Browse Information
BCT	Business Card Designer Template
BCW	C++ Version 4.5 Environment Settings
BDB	Works Database File
BDE	Borland Database Engine
BDF	Backup To CD-RW Backup Definition File and UNIX Font File
BDX	JavaBib Index File
BEN	Syssoft Sandra File
BER	German Bericht Report File
BEX	Pretty Good Privacy (PGP) Binary Extracted Public Key
BEXPK	Pretty Good Privacy (PGP) Binary Extracted Public Key
BEZ	Bezier Surface File and Bitstream Fontware

Extension	Description
BFC	Windows 95 Briefcase File
BFF	AIX Backup File Format
BFM	UNIX Font Metrics File
BFX	BitFax Document
BG	Lotus Agenda File
BGI	Borland Graphic Interface
BGL	Babylon Glossary File
BGT	Quicken 2002 Internet Common File
BHF	pcAnywhere Host File
BHI	Partminer Lib file
BHL	Partminer Lib file
BHTML	BabuHTML Embedded Software File
BHX	BinHex Compressed File ASCII Archive
BI	Binary File
BIB	Bibliography
BIC	Civilization III Scenario
BIF	GroupWise Initialization File
BIG	Chinese Text
BIG5	Chinese Text
BIL	ArcView Image File
BIN	Binary File, CDR-Win CD Image File, Linux Executable and AVG Antivirus Update File
BIP	ArcView Image File
BIX	Civilization III Scenario
BK	Backup
BK!	Backup
BK$	Backup
BK1	Bach Preludes and Fugues MIDI akmi Source, Book 1
BK1	Backup
BK2	Backup
BK3	Backup
BK4	Backup
BK5	Backup
BK6	Backup
BK7	Backup
BK8	Backup
BK9	Backup
BKF	Windows XP Backup Utility
BKG	Background File
BKP	Backup
BKS	Works Spreadsheet Backup and Windows 2000 Scheduled Backup File
BLA	Black Color Separation
BLB	ACT! Database File
BLC	BIACORE Instruments and BIAlite Project
BLD	ACT!
BLF	Beast 2.02 Trojan File
BLG	Windows Binary Performance Log
BLK	WordPerfect Temporary File

(continued)

Extension	Description
BLL	VBS/European-A Worm
BLR	BIACORE Instruments and BIAlite Project
BLS	BIACORE Instruments and BIAlite Project
BLT	Wordperfect for DOS
BLZ	Serial Number File
BM	X Windows System Bitmap
BMF	Corel Flow Image File
BML	Alpha Five Image Library File
BMM	Tacmi Pixia Palette File
BMP	Windows Bitmap Graphics
BMP24	Bitmap Graphic
BMT	Ami Pro Button Image and Alpha Five Image Library File
BMX	Alpha Five Image Library File
BMZ	Compressed BMP File
BN	AdLib Instrument Bank
BND	Flight Simulator Panels File
BNK	AdLib Instrument Bank
BOE	Outlook Express Backup File
BOF	IBM Voice Type Language Task Enroll File
BOI	Botje Bot-file (TNHteam)
BOL	Booasm Compressed Archive Library
BOM	Bill of Materials File
BONK	BONK Lossless/Lossy Audio Compressor
BOO	Compressed Archive File
BOOK	FrameMaker Book
BORLAND	C Makefile
BOX	Notes (and others) Mailbox
BOZ	BZIP Over ZIP Compressed File Archive
BP	Binary Picture TIFF Bitmap
BPG	Borland Project Group
BPI	IBM Voice Type languages Newuser File
BPK	C++ Builder Package File
BPL	AutoCAD R2000 Batch Plot List and Winamp Playlist File
BPP	Clarion for Windows Backup Application
BPP	MUSICMATCH Burner Plus Project
BPR	C++ Builder 6 Project
BPS	Works Document
BPT	Corel Bitmap Master File
BPW	ArcView World File for BIP or BMP Images
BRI	Basic Rate Interface File
BRS	Corel Painter Brush File
BRU	Photoline4 Brushes File
BRX	Multimedia Browsing Index
BS2	Basic Stamp 2 Code File
BSA	BSARC Compressed Archive

Extension	Description
BSB	MapInfo Sea Chart
BSN	MIDI File
BSP	Various Game Maps
BSQ	ArcView Image File and Oracle Control File
BSV	BASIC Bsave Graphics
BSY	FTN Soft Busy Flag
BS_	Bookshelf Find Menu Shell Extension
BTOA	Binary-to-ASCII Format
BTR	Btrieve Database File
BTR	FrontPage Binary-Tree Index
BTX	DB/TextWorks Database Term and Word Indexes
BU	Pegasus Mail Temporary File
BUD	Quicken Backup
BUF	WinXL File
BUFR	Binary Universal Form for the Representation
BUFR	Meteorological Data
BUG	Bug (Problem) File
BUGS	Generally Bugs File
BUNDLE	iMovie 3 Plug-in Bundle
BUP	Backup DVD Info File
BUY	Movie Data File
BV1	WordPerfect Overflow File
BV2	WordPerfect Overflow File
BV3	WordPerfect Overflow File
BV4	WordPerfect Overflow File
BV5	WordPerfect Overflow File
BV6	WordPerfect Overflow File
BV7	WordPerfect Overflow File
BV8	WordPerfect Overflow File
BV9	WordPerfect Overflow File
BVC	IBM Voice Type Language Newuser File
BVH	Biovision Motion File
BVI	IBM Voice Type Language Newuser File
BVL	Micrografx Picture Publisher 8 Textures File
BVS	BVS Solitaire Collection
BW	Silicon Graphics Raw Black and White Bitmap
BW1	Byteworx FMEA_ FMEA Database
BWA	BlindWrite CD Image
BWB	Visual Baler Spreadsheet File
BWC	BeadWizard Color Palette
BWP	Book Writer Project
BWR	Kermit Beware Bug List
BWS	BlindWrite
BWT	BlindWrite CD Image File and CD Mage TOC File
BWZ	Winlmage Batch Configuration File
BXP	BootXP File

(continued)

Extension	Description
BYU	Movie File
BZ	Bzip UNIX Compressed File
BZ1	WinTOTAL Automatic Backup
BZ2	Bzip 2 UNIX Compressed File
BZA	BZA Compressed Archive
BZF	Textures and Other Information
B~K	Backup
C	C/C++ Program File and Unix Compact File Archive
C#=	C#
C++	C++ Source Code
C—	Sphinx C— Source
C00	Ventura Print File
C2D	WinOnCD CD Image
C2I	Driver File
C2X	WinonCD File
C3D	Micrografx
C4	Joint Engineering Data Management (JEDMICS) DoD Engineering Data Format
C4D	Cinema 4D
C64	Commodore 64 Game ROM
C86	Computer Innovation C86 C Program
CA	Telnet Server Initial Cache Data File
CA0	Installer Packed and Split File
CA1	Delphi Install Disk11 File
CA2	Delphi Install Disk12 File
CA3	Delphi Install Disk9 File
CA4	Delphi Install Disk10 File
CA5	Delphi Install Disk11 File
CAB	Cabinet File
CAC	dBASE IV Executable File
CAD	Softdesk Drafix CAD File and QuickCAD Drawing
CAF	Southern Company Terrestrial Data Acq
CAG	Clip Gallery Catalog File
CAL	Cakewalk Application Language Script
CAL	Calendar File and SuperCalc Worksheet
CAP	Various Capture Files and Compressed Music Files
CAPS	Visimetrics Digital CCTV Recording
CAR	Card format file for various programs
CAS	Comma-delimited ASCII File
CAT	Catalog File
CAZ	Computer Associates Archive
CA_	Cakepro Compressed Audio File
CB	Brief Macro Source Code
CBD	System DLL Catroot File
CBF	Calendar Builder Saved Calendar
CBF	Infinity Game Engine Archive of Resources
CBH	ChessBase Chess Database File

Extension	Description
CBI	IBM Mainframe Column Binary Formatted File
CBK	System DLL Catroot File
CBL	COBOL Program
CBM	Fuzzy Bitmap and Xlib Compiled Bitmap
CBP	CD Box Labeler Pro
CBS	Computer Based Training
CBT	Computer Based Training
CBV	ChessBase Archive File
CBW	Cardbox Workspace
CBX	Rational XDE
CBZ	CDisplay ZIP Archived Comic Book File
CC	C++ Program File
CC5	Calendar Creator 5.x 6.x File
CCA	CC:Mail Archive File
CCAD	ClarisCAD data
CCB	Visual Basic Animated Button Configuration
CCC	WordPerfect Office Calendar File
CCD	Vector CAD Program File
CCE	Calendar Creator 2 Event File
CCH	Corel Chart
CCH	PhotoModeler
CCI	CCITT Group 3 and Group 4 Encoding
CCITT	CCITT Group 3 and Group 4 Encoding
CCJ	Crossword Compiler Compiled Crossword Applet
CCK	Corel Clipart Format
CCL	Intalk Communication Command Language
CCM	CC:Mail Mailbox
CCN	IMSI Multimedia Fusion Express File
CCO	CyberChat Data File
CCP	C Converter Profiles
CCR	Internet Chat Room Shortcut
CCRF	Calcomp Raster Bitmap
CCS	CCS-lib File
CCT	Macromedia Director Shockwave Cast
CCX	Corel Compressed Exchange File and CorelDraw File
CC_	Audio Utility Midimach Compressed File
CDA	CD Audio Track Shortcut
CDAT	Internet Security and Acceleration (ISA) Server Cache File
CDB	Clipboard File and Turbo C Database
CDBK	SPSS Database File
CDC	Nero Burning ROM CD Cover File and Claris Draw Document
CDF	ASCII Format Describing VRML Worlds and Comma Delimited Format
CDI	Phillips Compact Disk Interactive Format

(continued)

Extension	Description
CDL	CADKEY Advanced Design Language (CADL)
CDM	Compressed Music Format and Novell NetWare Disk Drivers
CDQ	CD Indexer
CDR	Corel Vector Graphic Drawing and generic sound file
CDT	Corel Draw Template
CDW	CADKEY Organized Dialog File
CDX	Active Server Document, FoxPro Index and Corel Draw Compressed Document
CE3	Calendar Creator 3.x 4.x Event List
CEL	Audition Loop File
CEM	Computer Graphics Metafile
CEO	Extension associated with Winevar Worm
CER	Internet Security Certificate File
CEV	LOUT Character Encoding File
CF	Sendmail Configuration File
CF1	Common File Format 1
CF2	Common File Format 2
CF4	Catfish File Manager Support File
CFB	Inmos Binary Configuration File
CFC	Cold Fusion File
CFD	CryptoForge Document (Ranquel Technologies)
CFE	CryptoForge Encrypted File (Ranquel Technologies)
CFF	Common File Format
CFG	Configuration File
CFL	Corel Flowchart File
CFM	Cold Fusion Template File and Corel FontMaster
CFO	Turbo C
CFR	IBM Configurator Report
CFT	Flow Chart; Corel Flow Template
CFW	ChemFinder Form
CFX	Creative DSP File
CG	Norton Crashguard File
CG3	Dungeons & Dragons Character File
CGA	CGA Resolution BMP Bitmap
CGM	Computer Graphics Metafile
CHA	Character Data
CHF	pcAnywhere Remote Control File
CHG	Quicken On-line Data File
CHH	C++ Header
CHI	Help File Index
CHJ	Help Composer Project
CHK	CHKDSK/SCANDISK Output and WordPerfect Temporary File
CHL	Configuration History Log
CHM	HTML Help Compiled Help File

Extension	Description
CHP	Ventura Publisher Chapter
CHQ	Help Combined Full-text Search File
CHR	Character or Font File
CHS	Corel WP Chart Style
CHT	Harvard Graphics Vector File
CHW	HTML Help General Index Funtionally comparable to .GID.
CHZ	ChArc Compressed File Archive
CIF	Chip Layout Information and Easy CD Creator Image File
CIK	Corel Graphics Ver. 10 Custom Dual Tone File
CIL	Clip Gallery Download Package
CIM	CompuApps Drive Backup Image
CIX	TCU Turbo C Utilities Database Index
CKB	C++ Keyboard Mapping File
CKD	CADKEY Design File
CKT	CADKEY Template File
CL	Generic LISP Source Code
CL3	Bruker Aspect NMR Data File
CL3	Easy CD Creator Layout File
CL4	Easy CD Creator Layout File
CL5	Easy CD Creator Layout File
CLA	Java Class File
CLASS	Java Class File
CLB	Corel Library
CLC	Corel Catalog
CLD	CA Clipper Debugger Configuration File
CLF	ListPro File
CLG	Disk Catalog Database
CLK	Corel R.A.V.E. Animation File
CLM	Micrografx Picture Publisher 7 Macro
CLN	Backup Configuration File
CLP	Windows Clipboard/Picture
CLS	Class Definitions for Various Programming Languages
CLW	Visual C++ Class Wizard File
CLX	Acrobat
CLY	Corel Graphics Ver.10 Custom Layouts File and ACT! Layout
CLY	ACT! Layout (Best Software CRM Division)
CMB	Xtree for Windows Button Bar
CMD	Command File for Windows NT, CPM and OS2 Plus dBASE II Program File
CMF	Corel Metafile
CMP	Address Document and JPEG Bitmap
CMR	MediaPlayer Movie
CMT	Corel Draw
CMU	CMU Window Manager Bitmap
CMV	Corel Move Animation
CMW	Custom Maintenance Wizard File

(continued)

Extension	Description
CMX	Presentation Exchange Image or Generic Patchfile
CMYK	Raw Cyan, Magenta, Yellow, and Black Samples
CNF	Configuration File
CNM	Windows Application Menu Options and Setup File
CNR	Pegasus Mail Mail Message in Systemwide Folder
CNS	Windows2000 Client Connection Manager Export File
CNT	Help File Contents
CNV	WordPerfect Temporary File
CNV	DB2 Conversion File
CNX	Rational XDE
CN_	Regeditx File
CO	Cult3D ActiveX Player Application
CO$	MS Compressed COM Decompress with UNPACK.EXE.
COB	COBOL Program File
COD	C Compiler Output and Character Set Code File
COL	HTML Help Collection File
COM	Command
CONSOLE	WinNT Console File
COV	Fax Cover Page
CPD	Corel PrintOffice File
CPE	Fax Cover Sheet
CPF	Complete Fax File
CPH	Corel PrintHouse Image
CPI	Windows or DOS International Code Page
CPL	Corel Color Palette and Windows Control Panel Extension
CPL	Windows Control Panel Extension
CPO	Corel Print House File
CPP	C++ Builder 6 and C++ Source Code File
CPR	Corel Presents Presentation
CPS	Color Postscript File, Antivirus Checksum, PC Tools Backup
CPT	Corel Photo-Paint Image and dBASE Encryted Memo
CPX	Control Panel Applet
CRC	JPEG Sheriff CRC Info File
CRD	Windows Cardfile
CRF	Database Cross-Reference File
CRP	Corel Presents Run-Time Presentation, dBASE Encrypted Database and dBASE Custom Report
CRS	WordPerfect 5.1 for Windows File Conversion Resource

Extension	Description
CRS	Dance With Intensity
CRT	Certificate File
CRV	Corel Graphics Ver. 10 Custom Gradients File
CSA	Comma Deliminated Text
CSB	Corel Photo-Paint Script
CSD	Bitstream Fontware
CSH	Photoshop Custom Shape
CSL	AOL Modem Script
CSM	C++ Symbol File or C++ Compiled Header
CSP	AudioZip Encoded Audio
CSQ	Foxpro Query
CSS	Hypertext Cascading Style Sheet
CST	Macromedia Director Cast File
CSV	Comma-Separated Variables
CSW	WordPerfect Setup Info File
CTB	AutoCAD Color-dependent Plot Style Table
CTC	PC Installer Control
CTD	Cardtable File
CTF	Calculator Text Format or Compressed TIFF File
CTL	Setup Information or User Control File
CTR	Counter file and Corel40 Trace File
CTS	ABC Programming Language Permanent Location Contents
CTT	MSN Messenger Saved Contact List
CTX	Chinese Character Input File and Compressed Text
CUR	Windows Cursor
CUS	AutoCAD Custom Dictionary
CV	Corel Versions Archive
CVA	Compaq Diagnostics
CVB	Borland BDE File
CVF	Compressed Volume File
CVP	WinFax Cover Page (Symantec)
CVS	Sound File
CVT	dBASE Converted Database Backup
CWK	Claris Works Data
CWL	ClarisWorks Library
CWS	Claris Works Template
CW_	Corel Graphics Ver. 10 Workspace
CXE	Common XML Envelope
CXT	Macromedia Director Protected Cast File
CXX	Visual C++ Source Code File
CYA	Cyan Color Separation
C~G	Windows 3.x System File
D	D Programming Language Source Code File

(continued)

Extension	Description
D00	AdLib Format File and Blaster Master Pro File
D11	Macro Mania Data File
D2V	DVD Ripper File
D30	Driver
D32	Lotus Visualisation File
D3D	Various 3D Graphics Files
D3T	Doom Texture
DA0	Windows Registry Backup
DA1	Registry Backup
DAC	Sound File
DAF	Download Accelerator
DAL	SpeedBit Download Accelerator Plus DAP List
DAN	ATI Radeon Video Driver
DAO	Windows Registry Backup
DAP	Access Data Access Page
DAS	Download Accelerator File List
DAT	Commonly Used Extension for Data Files
DAX	Daxaif Compressed Audio
DAY	Journal
DAZ	Poser 3D File
DB	Commonly used extension for database files
DB$	dBASE Temporary File
DB0	dBASE Initialization File
DB1	Adressmn
DB2	dBASE II
DB3	dBASE III File
DB4	dBASE 4 Data
DBA	Commonly Used Extension for Data Files
DBB	ANSYS Database Backup
DBC	Visual Foxpro Database Container
DBD	Oracle Record Type
DBE	Database Engine File
DBF	Commonly Used Extension for Database Files
DBG	Commonly Used Extension for Debug Files
DBI	Borland Database Explorer Information
DBK	dBASE Database Backup
DBL	Windows XP Product Activation File
DBM	Cold Fusion Template
DBO	dBASE IV Compiled Program File
DBP	Visual Studio .NET Database Project
DBQ	AutoCAD DB Query
DBR	DB/TextWorks Database
DBS	Commonly Used Extension for Database Files
DBT	Commonly used extension for database text or database template files
DBV	Abacus Law Ver. 10 Data

Extension	Description
DBW	DataBoss Database File
DBX	Database Index and Outlook Express E-mail Folder
DB_	CAD File
DC	DesignCAD CAD File
DC$	Ntgraph Visual C Wizard File
DC+	DataCAD Plus Drawing
DC2	DesignCAD CAD File
DC5	DataCAD Drawing File
DCA	Visual Basic X DateBook File
DCA	DCA Archiver Compressed Archive
DCD	FORTRAN Data File
DCD	INMOS Transputer Development System Occam Object Code
DCE	AutoCAD R2000 Dialog Error Log
DCF	Commonly Used Extension for Database Configuration Files and Disk Image Files
DCL	AutoCAD Dialog Control Language Description
DCM	Sound
DCP	Delphi Compiled Packages
DCR	Kodak Digital Camera Raw Image File
DCS	Color Separated EPS Format, Bitmap Graphic and Desktop Color Separation FIle
DCT	Dictionary
DCU	Delphi Compiled Unit
DCV	DriveCrypt Volume
DCW	Draft Choice for Windows
DCX	DesignCAD and PC Paintbrush File Extension
DDB	Commonly Used Extension for Database Files
DDD	Acrobat Distiller
DDE	Dynamic Data Exchange
DDF	Btrieve Data Dictionary File
DDI	Disk Doubler Image
DDL	SQL Data Definition Language File
DDM	Alpha Five Table Objects
DDP	Delphi 6 File
DDP	Inor DSoft Software File
DDR	FileMaker Pro Database Design Report
DDS	Photoshop Compressed Textures and DirectDraw Surface
DDV	Xbase Dbfast Example Ivadbsp File
DDW	CSPro File
DDX	Alpha Five Dictionary Index File
DEB	DOS Debug Script
DEC	DEC DX, WPS Plus Document and Decoded File
DEF	Definition File
DEL	Deleted Data List

(continued)

Extension	Description
DEM	Delphi Edit Mask
DEO	Creator Simulator Compiled Module
DEP	Visual Basic Setup Wizard Dependency
DEPLOY	DeployMaster Setup Script
DES	Description Text and Quickbooks Forms Template
DET	ACT! Saved E-mail File
DEV	Device Driver
DEX	Excel File
DEX	WinGlucofacts File
DEZ	DES Encrypted Zip File
DF	Data File
DFL	Signature Default Program Settings
DFM	C++ Builder 6 Form
DFN	Definition File
DFP	Digital Fusion Plug-in
DFS	AutoCAD Utility Defaults
DFT	WaveMaker File
DFX	AutoCAD 3D Vector Graphics and Micrografix Designer Effects
DGC	TurboTax
DGF	Acrobat
DGK	Delcam Powershape/Powermill
DGL	DynaGeo License File
DGM	Freelance Diagram
DGN	ArcView Design Drawing File
DGR	Fax Page
DHE	Visual Basic Dialog Box Help Editor Document
DHF	Help Maker File
DIC	Dictionary
DID	Acrobat Distiller
DIF	Data Interchange Format
DIL	Delphi File
DIM	AutoCAD Dimension File
DIR	Directory Indicator
DIS	Corel Draw Thesaurus
DIT	Windows2000 Active Directory Schema
DIVX	Movie Encoded with DivX-codec
DIZ	Description In Zip File
DKZ	Description In Zip File
DL	Masked .DLL File
DLD	Lotus File
DLE	Macromedia Designer 3D Translator File
DLF	Belkin Router Firmware Update
DLG	C++ Dialogue Script
DLI	Beast 2.02 Trojan File
DLK	INMOS Transputer Development System Occam Compiler Link Info
DLL	Dynamic Link Library
DLM	ASCII Delimited File, FileMake Pro Data File and Dynamic Link Module

Extension	Description
DLO	3ds max Plug-in
DLS	dataLive Database Engine File
DLV	CATIA Export File
DLW	DALiM LiTHO Line Work Bitmap
DLZ	Compressed Data File
DL_	Compressed DLL File
DM	Borland dBASE
DMA	Direct Memory Access Programming File
DMD	Corel Data Modeling Desktop
DME	Medical Manager DML System Data Merge
DMF	Windows Disk Map File
DML	Medical Manager DML System Script
DMP	Screen or Memory Dump
DMT	Delphi Menu Template
DMV	Acrobat Catalog and MPEG-1 File
DMY	Container File
DNC	Compressed Dictionary File
DOB	Visual Basic User Document Form File
DOC	Document File
DOCHTML	Word HTML Document
DOCMHTML	Word HTML Document
DOF	Delphi Option File
DOK	German or Dutch Text
DOL	D-PAS Portfolio Manager Flexible Benchmarking Analysis File
DON	Textur Editor File
DOS	DOS 7 System Files; Win 95 Boot up in DOS
DOT	Word Document Template
DOTHTML	Word HTML Document Template
DOV	Temporary File
DOX	MultiMate Document and General Extension for Text Documents
DP	Text
DPA	Archive
DPB	ProWORX Nxt Descriptor Pointer File
DPC	Delphi Package Collection File
DPD	ABC Programming Language Dyadic Predicate
DPF	Dynamic Process Format Database
DPJ	Delphi Project
DPK	Deleted Package, Windows Applications Manager
DPL	Delphi Package Library
DPMI	DOS Protected-Mode Interface Programming
DPO	Delphi Object Repository
DPP	Serif DrawPlus Drawing
DPQ	PCX Format
DPR	C++ /Delphi Default Project

(continued)

Extension	Description
DPS	DivX XP Skin
DPT	Desktop DNA Template and Publish It! Data File
DPT	Publish-It! Publication File
DPX	Animation
DQC	CP/M Disk Information File
DQY	Excel ODBC Query File
DR$	Modem Bitware Fax Disk2 File
DR9	Directory File
DRA	Dragon Naturally Speaking
DRC	Delphi Compiled Resource File
DRF	Photoline Drawing Filter
DRML	Protected Digital Content
DRS	BMP Bitmap
DRV	Device Driver
DRW	Commonly Used Extension for Drawing Programs
DRX	Photoshop Tutorial
DS	TWAIN Data Source
DSC	Description File
DSD	Document Structure Definition File
DSES	Diagnosis Session
DSF	Micrografx Designer
DSK	Commonly Used Extension for Disk Image Files
DSM	Delphi Symbol Module
DSN	ODBC Data Source
DSP	Developer Studio Project
DSQ	Corel QUERY File
DSR	Visual Basic Active Designer File and WordPerfect Driver
DSS	Digital Speech Standard File
DST	C++/Delphi Desktop Settings
DSW	C++ Desktop Settings and Visual Studio Workspace
DSX	Visual Basic Active Designer Binary File
DSY	PC Draft Symbol Library
DSZ	Win Help Related File
DT	DAT Backup
DTA	Data
DTC	Windows Applog Journal
DTE	Win Applog File
DTEA	Diagnosis Template Archive
DTF	Exchange Header File
DTG	Windows Applog File
DTH	Windows Applog File
DTI	Delphi or C++ Design Time Information and Windows Applog File
DTJ	Windows Applog File
DTL	Windows Applog File
DTP	Common Extension for Desktop Publishing Data Files

Extension	Description
DTQ	Database Tools Query
DTR	DTREG Project File
DTS	Digital Surround Audio File Format
DTX	E-Book File
DUN	Dial-Up Networking Export File
DUP	Duplicate Backup
DUT	Dutch Text File
DV	Digital Video File
DVB	AutoCAD VBA Source Code
DVC	Lotus 1-2-3 File
DVD	Animation
DVM	DVM Movie File Format
DVP	AutoCAD Device Parameter
DVR	Device Driver
DW2	DesignCAD Drawing File
DWG	AutoCAD Drawing Database
DWL	AutoCAD Drawing Database File Locking Information
DWS	AutoCAD Standarization
DWT	AutoCAD Template/Prototype and FrontPage Dynamic Web Template
DWV	WAV
DWZ	Compressed AutoCAD Drawing File
DX	Document Imaging File
DXB	AutoCAD Drawing Exchange Format
DXF	AutoCAD Drawing Interchange Format
DXP	Dynamic XML Page
DXR	Acrobat
DXX	AutoCAD Drawing Interchange Attribute File
DYN	Lotus 1-2-3 File
DZ	Dzip Compressed File
DZS	Character File
D~L	Creative DLL Copy
D~V	Windows 3.x System File
E2	Thinkdesign CAD Design
E2P	PonyProg Device File
E3	Thinkdesign CAD Design
E32	Inno Setup 1.3 File
E3D	Instant3D Project
E3D	Macromedia Extreme3D Object
E48	Emu48 HP48 Emulator File
E78	IBM 3270 Terminal Emulator Screen Layout Definition
E99	Steuer99 Daten File
EA3	Fifa 2001 Environment Data
EAC	EmEditor Auto Completion File
EAF	MicroEmacs Abbreviation File Format
EAR	Java Enterprise Application Packaging Unit
EAZ	Express Assist File
EBA	Mobile Phone Data Manager

(continued)

Extension	Description
EBF	Pocket PC Windows CE Form File
EBK	EARS Database Backup
EBK	eBook
EBO	Reader Ebook Format
EBP	Pocket PC Windows CE Project File
EBS	Windows XP Scanner File
EBX	Electronic Book Exchange
ECA	electroCAD File
ECF	Micrografx Media Manager
ECR	Ecrypt E-mail File
ECS	Encrypted Compressed GIS Software Geographic Shape File
ECW	Enhanced Compressed Wavelet
ECW	Ensoniq Waveset Format
ED	EasyDraw CAD File
EDA	Ensoniq ASR Disk Image
EDB	ACT! E-mail Data File and Exchange Server Property Store
EDD	FrameMaker Element Definition Document
EDE	Ensoniq EPS Disk Image
EDK	Ensoniq KT Disk Image
EDL	Edit Decision List
EDM	CAD Contouring Parameter Data File
EDM	Eclipse Data Module (Active Media)
EDML	Dreamweaver MX Extension File
EDN	Acrobat Document
EDQ	Ensoniq SQ1/SQ2/KS32 Disk Image
EDT	External Editor Definition
EDV	Ensoniq VFX-SD Disk Image
EDX	Editor Dictionary
EEB	WordPerfect Equation Editor Button Bar
EFA	Ensoniq ASR File
EFD	EARS Filter Definition
EFE	Ensoniq EPS File
EFK	Ensoniq KT File
EFP	Exchange Forms Designer Template
EFQ	Ensoniq SQ1/SQ2/KS32 File
EFS	Ensoniq SQ80 File
EFV	Ensoniq VFX-SD File
EGA	Enhanced Graphics Adapter Graphics Data
EGS	GIS Software Encrypted Grid Shape File
EID	IBM ViaVoice Vocabulary File
ELD	EARS Label Definition
ELF	Electronic Application Form File
ELG	EARS Log
ELH	Electronic Application Help File
ELI	ELI Compressed File Archive
ELL	ATI Radeon Video Driver
ELM	FrontPage Theme-Pack File
ELOG	McAffee Firewall Log

Extension	Description
ELT	Event List Text
EMAIL	Outlook Express Mail Message
EMB	ABT Extended Module
EMD	Micrografx System4 Media Manager File
EMF	Extended (Enhanced) Windows Metafile Format
EML	Outlook Express Electronic Mail
EMP	E-Music File Format
EMU	Emulation
EMX	MS-DOS Extender file
EMZ	Windows Compressed Enhanced Metafile
ENC	UUENCODE Encoded File
END	Corel Draw Arrow Definition
ENG	Dictionary and English Documentation
ENL	Endnote Library File
ENT	SGML Entities, Character Mapping
ENU	ATI Radeon Video Driver
ENV	Envelope or Environment
EPA	Award BIOS Logo
EPD	EARS Printer Definition
EPDF	Encapsulated Portable Document Format
EPI	Encapsulated PostScript Interchange Format
EPJ	Java-clients File
EPL	Encirq \PL Programming Language Source File
EPS	Encapsulated PostScript
EPS2	Level II Encapsulated PostScript
EPS3	Level III Encapsulated PostScript
EPSF	Encapsulated PostScript
EPSI	Encapsulated PostScript Interchange Format
EPSON	Epson Printer Graphics File
EPT	Encapsulated PostScript Interchange TIFF Preview
EQF	Winamp2/Winamp3 Equalizer Settings File
EQL	DART Pro 98 Fabric Equalization Presets
EQN	Equation
EQU	Assembly Language Equates
EQW	SPEFO Stellar Spectra Analysis File
ERM	Bitmap Graphic
ERR	Error Log
ERS	Earth Resource Mapping Satellite Image Header
ER_	Winhelp Compressed File
ES	EasySIGN Drawing Sheet
ESL	Visual FoxPro Distributable Support Library

(continued)

Extension	Description
ESO	FoxPro
ESP	Ventura File
ESPS	ESPS Audio File
ESR	4D Database Windows Procedure
EST	Streets & Trips 2001 Trip File
ET2	Electronic Tax Return Security File
ETF	Enriched Text File
ETH	HP Internet Advisor Capture File
ETL	Windows2000 Trace Log
EUC	Japanese
EUI	Ensoniq EPS Family Compacted Disk Image
EV2	Java File
EVP	Sound Envelope
EVT	Commonly used extension for event logs or event files
EWD	Express Publisher for Windows Document
EWL	Encarta Document
EX	Symantec Ghost Template File
EX$	MS Compressed EXE Decompress with UNPACK.EXE.
EX1	Renamed .EXE File
EXB	Flash Image File
EXC	Word Exclusion Dictionary
EXD	Control Information Cache
EXE	Executable File
EXO	System File
EXP	Viscal C++ Export File
EXR	OpenEXR Bitmap
EXT	E-mail Text Attachment
EXU	Euphoria File
EXW	Euphoria File
EX^	Norton Live Update File
EX_	Compressed EXE File
EZM	Text File
EZP	Edify Electronic Workforce Backup Utility
F	Compressed Archive File and FORTRAN Source Code
F01	Perfect Fax Document
F06	DOS 6-pixel Screen Font
F07	DOS 7-pixel Screen Font
F08	DOS 8-pixel Screen Font
F09	DOS 9-pixel Screen Font
F10	DOS 10-pixel Screen Font
F11	DOS 11-pixel Screen Font
F12	DOS 12-pixel Screen Font
F13	DOS 13-pixel Screen Font
F14	DOS 14-pixel Screen Font
F15	DOS 15-pixel Screen Font
F16	DOS 16-pixel Screen Font

Extension	Description
F2	Flash Bios File
F2F	File to File
F3	Flash Bios File
F32	Raw 32-bit IEEE Floating Point Values
F6	Fonts File
F64	Raw 64-bit IEEE Floating Point Values
F7	Fonts File
F77	FORTRAN 77 Program
F8	Fonts File
F90	FORTRAN Program
F96	Frecom FAX96 Document
FAD	Data File
FAQ	Frequently Asked Questions
FAQT	FAQTool XML Contents File
FAS	AutoCAD Fast-load Auto LISP
FAV	Outlook Bar Shortcuts
FAX	Fax File
FBM	Fuzzy Bitmap
FBN	ArcView Spatial Index File For Read-Only Datasets
FBS	File Burner Skin
FBX	3D Data Exchange Format
FC$	Basic Realizer Disk1 L File
FC2	Curious Labs Poser Face File
FCB	FAAST Builder File
FCD	FastCAD/EasyCAD Output and Virtual CD-ROM
FCF	HP-95LX Filer Configuration File
FCG	Mystic Photo Format
FCT	Foxpro Catalog
FCW	FastCAD File
FCX	Vax VMS Compressed File
FD	FORTRAN Declarations
FDB	FoxPro Database
FDC	Sniffer Capture File
FDE	Fade-It for AOL
FDF	Acrobat Portable Document Input Form and Format Definition File
FDL	Paradox
FDM	Floppy Disk Manager File
FEB	WordPerfect Figure Editor Button Bar
FEC	U.S. Federal Campaign Expense Submission File
FF	AGFA CompuGraphics Outline Font Description
FFA	Fast Find Status File
FFD	Flash Filer
FFE	DirectInput Force Feedback Effect
FFL	Fast Find Document List
FFP	Corel Graphics10 Custom File
FFT	DisplayWrite Document
FFX	Fast Find Index

(continued)

Extension	Description
FGX	Formula Graphics Project File
FGZ	Formula Graphics Standalone Presentation Archive
FH10	Freehand Ver. 10 File
FH11	FreehandMX Ver. 11 File
FH3	Freehand Ver. 3 Drawing
FH4	Freehand Ver. 4 Drawing
FH5	Freehand 5
FH6	Freehand 6
FH7	Freehand 7
FH8	Freehand 8
FH9	Freehand 9
FHC	Freehand
FHD	PCL Tool Form File
FHTML	HTML File
FI	Bitstream Intellifont
FIC	Windev Database System
FID	Bruker Aspect NMR Data File
FIDX	Fiasco Database Index
FIF	Font Information File
FIG	XFIG Graphic File
FIL	ACL For Windows Data, dBASE Files List Object and WordPerfect Overlay
FIN	ATI Radeon Video Driver
FIO	ULead Viewer Support File
FIP	FingerPost Information Processor File
FIT	Windows NT File Index Table
FIX	Generic Patch File
FIXED	DLL Backup Root File
FKY	Foxpro Macro
FL	Floating Format Sound
FLA	Flash Movie Authoring File and Free Lossless Audio Codec
FLASK	FlasKMPEG Language Definition File
FLC	Corel Show
FLD	VersaPro Folder Contents
FLE	Scanner Settings File
FLF	Corel Paradox Form and ASCII Editor Font File
FLF	ASCII Editor Font File
FLL	Foxpro Library
FLM	AutoCAD/Auto Shade Film and FoxPro Library
FLM	FoxPro Library
FLP	Corel Flow Project Flow Chart and Floppy Disk Image File
FLR	Live3D File
FLS	ArcView Windows Help Supporting File
FLT	Common extension for filter file
FLV	Flash Video File
FM	FileMaker Pro Spreadsheet

Extension	Description
FM1	Lotus 1-2-3 Release 2.x Spreadsheet File
FM2	Maestro Mama Demo File
FMB	Oracle Binary Form Source Code
FMD	Open Access File
FMK	FaxMaker File
FML	Oracle Mirror List
FMO	dBASE Ordered Format
FMP	AutoCAD Font Map and FileMaker Pro Document
FMS	Lotus 1-2-3 Impress Add-in
FMT	Commonly Used Extension for Format File
FMV	Frame Vector Metafile
FMX	Oracle Executable Form
FND	Explorer Saved Search
FNG	Font Navigator Group File
FNT	Font File
FO1	Turbo C Font
FO2	Turbo C Font
FOG	Fontographer Font
FOL	pfs:First Choice Database File
FOLDER	Mail Folder
FON	Font File
FOR	FORTRAN Source
FOT	Installed TrueType Font
FP	FileMaker Pro File
FP3	FileMaker Pro 3.0 File
FP5	FileMaker Pro Database
FP7	FileMaker Pro Ver. 7 Database Document
FPC	FoxPro Catalog File
FPHTML	FrontPage HTML Document
FPM	FoxPro Startup File
FPT	FileMaker Pro File Database Memo and FoxPro Memo Field
FPW	FoxPro Configuration
FPWEB	FrontPage Disk Based Web
FPX	Compiled FoxPro Program and FlashPix Bitmap
FQF	FlashFXP Queue File
FQY	FLAMES (FLARE) Command File
FR3	dBASE IV Renamed dBASEIII+ Form
FRA	FrameViewer File
FRE	Creative Digital Blaster Digital VCR File
FRF	FontMonger Font
FRG	dBASE IV Uncompiled Report
FRM	Commonly used extension for Form Files and dBASE IV Report File
FRO	dBASE IV Compiled Report
FRP	Fractal Explorer Palette

(continued)

Extension	Description
FRS	Corel Painter Pattern, Selection or Texture File
FRT	FoxPro Report File
FRX	FoxPro Report File
FRZ	FormFlow File
FS5	Flight Simulator Scenery File
FS6	Flight Simulator Panels File
FSG	IBM Voice Type Language Map File
FSI	FileSplit and Borland Paradox Form File
FSP	Floating Point Data Files
FSS	Iomega Backup File Selection Set
FST	dbFast Linkable Program
FSX	Lotus 1-2-3 Data
FT	Lotus Notes Full Text Index
FT5	FH5 File
FT7	Macromedia Freehand Drawing
FT8	Macromedia Freehand Drawing
FT9	Macromedia Freehand Drawing
FTB	Roots3 Index File
FTBL	PIPE-FLO Professional Fluid Data Table (Engineered Software)
FTC	FluxTime Clip (pCode Software)
FTG	Windows Help Full-text Search Group File
FTM	MicroGrafx Font
FTP	FTP Configuration Information
FTS	Borland BDE File
FW	Framework Database
FW2	Framework II File
FW3	Framework III File
FW4	Framework IV File
FWB	FileWrangler Data File Backup
FWEB	Fortran WEB
FWF	Xwave FWF File
FWI	PhotoSmart 850 Digital Camera Firmware Update
FWL	FileWrangler EXE Library
FWP	Worms Armageddon Fiddler Weapons Module
FWS	FileWrangler Data File for File Splitting Configuration
FX	WordPerfect Office Template File
FX2	WordPerfect Office Calendar File
FXD	FoxPro FoxDoc Support and WINFAX Sent Document
FXM	WinFax Fax
FXM	Fuxoft AY Music Chip Language
FXO	Fax Image Document
FXP	FoxPro Compiled Source
FXR	WinFax Received Document
FXS	WinFax Fax Transmit Graphic
FZF	FontZip Font Packer

Extension	Description
FZP	Fargo Primera Color Printer Dye Sub Support File
FZX	CP/M Fix File
G	Applause Data Chart and Paradox File
G4	Access
GAL	Commonly Used Extension for Image Galleries
GAM	Commonly used extension for saved game files
GAML	Generalized Analytical Markup Language
GANI	Graal Game Animation
GAP	Electrical Generation Analysis and Planification
GAS	Intelligence Tracking System Data File
GAU	Flight Simulator Gauge
GB$	BASIC VB Beispiel Kartei File
GBA	Grablt Batch Files
GBF	InteGrade Pro Gradebook File
GBL	Visual Basic Global Definition
GBR	GIMP Brush File
GBT	Photoshop
GBX	Gerber File
GC	Sierra Print Artist Greeting Card
GCA	G Compression Archiver Compressed File
GCD	Generic CADD Drawing
GCF	WinXComp Grouped Compressed File
GCM	Group Mail CMessage Store File and GeoConcept Map File
GCP	Ground Control Point File
GCR	Visual EPR COSEUL.EXE Output
GD2	GDLib Image
GDB	ACT! Group Data File
GDB	Group Mail File
GDF	GEOS Dictionary
GDG	ReliaSoft RG
GDM	Bells, Whistles, and Sound Boards Module
GDR	SymbianOS Bitmap Font File
GDS	Chip Layout Information and Image File
GED	Micrografx Simply 3D Geometry
GEF	Graphics Exchange Format
GEM	Digital Research GEM Paint
GEN	dBASE Application Generator Compiled Template
GER	German Text/HTML Info File
GEX	GEcho Configuration File
GF	METAFONT Generic Font File
GFA	Bitmap Graphic
GFB	GIFBlast Compressed GIF Image
GFM	Computer Graphics Meta-file

(continued)

Extension	Description
GFW	ArcView World File for GIF Image and BASIC GFA File
GGP	GemCom Graphic Format
GHO	Symantec Ghost Disk Image File
GHS	Symantec Ghost Disk Image Span File
GID	Windows Help Index File
GIF	Graphic Interchange Format
GIFF	Graphic Interchange Format
GIG	Sound File
GKH	Ensoniq EPS Family Disk Image
GKS	Graphics Kernel System
GLD	Glide File
GLUT	OpenGL Glut-3.6 File
GLUT2	OpenGL Glut-3.6 File
GLUT3	OpenGL Glut-3.6 File
GLY	Word Glossary
GLY	ACT! Layout
GM	Autologic Bitmap
GM0	S.A.P.S.—Sharp Advanced Presentation Software Professional
GMB	GoldMine Business Contact Management Backup Data
GML	NetRemote XML-based Configuration File
GMM	Group Mail Message Log File
GMP	Group Mail List Information File
GMS	Corel Global Macro File
GMX	Group Mail Message File
GNT	Micro Focus Generated COBOL Code
GNX	Genigraphics Graphics Link Presentation
GO	CompuServe
GOBJ	Geoworks Object Code
GOC	Geoworks GOC Source Code
GOE	McIDAS System Satellite Image Data
GOES	McIDAS System Satellite Image Data
GOH	Geoworks GOC Header
GP4	CCITT Group 4 File
GPH	Lotus 1-2-3 Graph
GPI	Bitware Fax File
GPX	BASIS File
GQ	Epson Printer Page Description Language
GQA	BI/Query Data Model Admin Layer
GQL	BI/Query Data Model
GQU	BI/Query Data Model User Layer
GR	XGMML (eXtensible Graph Markup and Modeling Language) File
GR2	Windows 3.0 Screen Driver
GR3	Windows 3.0 Screen Grabber
GR4	Pathloss Network File Sharing File
GRA	OpenGL Object
GRADS	Metafile

Extension	Description
GRAY	Raw Gray Samples
GRB	MS-DOS Shell Monitor and Gridded Binary
GRD	Photoshop Gradient File
GREY	RAW RGB 24-bit Graphic
GRF	Graph Plus Drawing
GRIB	Gridded Binary
GRP	Windows Program Manager Group and ACT! Group Data File
GRY	RAW RGB 24-bit Graphic
GRZ	GRZip Compressed Archive
GSD	Professional Draw Vector Graphics
GSM	Raw GSM 6.10 Audio Stream
GTH	Domino.Doc
GTO	Quicken On-line File
GWI	Groupwise File
GZ	Gzip Compressed Archive and GIMP Image File
GZA	GZA Compressed Archive
GZIP	Gzip Compressed Archive
H	ADS Include File and Header
H++	C++ Header File
H—	Sphinx C—Header File
H16	VC98 Include 16-bit File
HA	Compressed Archive
HAM	Image File and Novell Netware Disk Drivers
HAZ	Flight Simulator Texture File
HC	Header File
HCL	Handwritten Claims Log
HCM	IBM HCM Configuration
HCR	Half-fold Card File
HCSP	Content Server Web Page
HCT	Symantec Anti-Virus Live Update File
HCX	Harvard Graphics Chart XL Chart
HDAT	Objective Analysis Package Data File
HDB	Nero and ACT! History File
HDF	Help Development Kit Help File and Hierarchical Data Format File
HDM	Handheld Markup Language File
HDML	Handheld Markup Language File
HDMP	WinXP Trouble Report
HDO	Helpdesk-One File
HDR	ArcInfo Binary and Commonly Used Extension for Header Files
HDS	Hierarchical Data System
HDW	Harvard Graphics Draw Vector Graphics
HDX	Help Index
HEP	Novell NetWare Help Librarian Data File
HER	Grafic GIF File
HEX	Hex Dump
HFI	HP Font Info

(continued)

Extension	Description
HFX	Harvard Graphics F/X File
HGL	HP Graphics Language (Plotter File)
HH	C++ Header
HHC	HTML Help Table of Contents
HHH	Power C Precompiled Header
HHK	HTML Help Index
HHL	Visual Basic File
HHP	HTML Help Project
HHS	HTML Help Samples
HHTML	Realmedia Adstream HTML File
HIF	Quicken On-line File
HIPS	Bitmap Graphic
HIR	Hidden Icon Resource
HIS	Commonly Used Extension for History Files
HIX	System SYSUTIL File
HK5	ACT! Database File
HKC	HTML-KIT Auto Complete Short-cuts
HL$	Compressed DOS Help File
HLB	VAX Help Library
HLF	BASIC QuickBAS QuickB01 File
HLM	Winhelp Vbhilfe File
HLN	Microstation Hidden Line File
HLP	Help File
HLX	Visual C++ Syntax Coloring Instructions
HLZ	Multi-Edit Packed Help File
HM	Windows Help Context IDs used by MAKEHM.EXE.
HM2	Help & Manual Help File Project
HM3	Help & Manual Help File Project (ver 3)
HMF	HOOPS Metafile
HMS	MS SMS Inventory File
HM~	Help&Manual Backup Help File Project
HNC	CNC Program File Heidenhain Dialog
HP	HP Graphics Language (Plotter)
HP$	NTgraph Visual C Wizzard File
HP-	HP Distribution Binary File
HP-UX	HP-UNIX File
HP8	HP NewWave Write ASCII Roman8 Character Set
HPF	PageMaker HP LaserJet Font
HPG	HP Graphics Language (Plotter)
HPGL	HP Graphics Language (Plotter)
HPH	Designer Graphics System2 File
HPJ	Help Project File
HPJ	Visual Basic Help Project
HPK	Compressed Archive
HPL	HP Graphics File
HPLJ	Hewlett-Packerd LaserJet Vector Image
HPP	C++ Program Header
HPPCL	Hewlett-Packard Printer Control Language Vector Image

Extension	Description
HPUX	HP-UNIX File
HPW	CompuServe Home Page Wizard
HP_	Winhelp Compressed File
HP~	V-help File
HQP	CP/M Disc Utility Information
HQX	Macintosh BinHex 4 Compressed Archive
HR2	Curious Labs Poser Hair File
HRH	C++ and Resources Common Header
HRU	HRU Bitmap
HSI	HSI JPEG Bitmap
HSK	Nimbus 7 SAMS Data File
HSS	Photoshop Hue/Saturation Information
HST	Commonly used extension for History Files
HT3	HTML File
HTA	Hypertext Application
HTC	HTML Component
HTF	HTF Sounding File and Virtual HyperText Font
HTI	Win Help Related File
HTM	Hypertext Markup Language
HTML	Hypertext Markup Language
HTMLS	Secure HTML File
HTR	HTML-like script
HTT	Microsoft Hypertext Template
HTX	Extended Hypertext Template
HTZ	HTML Editor Archive
HWL	Corel Shared Writing Tools 9.0 File
HX	THOR Database Cross-reference Hash File
HXC	Help 2 Project/Collection File
HXI	Help 2 Compiled Help File
HXK	Help TOC/Index File
HXK	Help 2 Keyword Index
HXM	Descent2 HAM File
HXM	Procomm Plus Alternate Protocol Selection Menu for All Users
HXS	Help 2 Compiled Help File
HXT	Help TOC/Index File
HXX	C++ Header
HX_	C Poet Compressed Disk1 File
HYC	WordPerfect Hyphenation File
HYD	WordPerfect for Windows Hyphenation Dictionary
HYP	Hypertext File and Hyphenation FIle
HZ	Chinese Text
H_	Winhelp Compressed File
H__	C++ Header Seldom used C++ Header (same as H++ and H)
I	C++ Preprocessor Intermediate File
I0	Winter Windows Scheduler File

(continued)

Extension	Description
I00	Winphone Phonebook
I16	Nokia Phone Logo File
I2S	Invision for mIRC Settings
IAF	Outlook Express, Outlook 97 and 2000 E-mail Account Settings
IBA	IBasic Source Code File and Type of Image File
IBD	Windows Installer File
IBF	Instant Backup
IBG	NASA PDS Graphic Format
IBK	Sound Blaster Instrument Bank
IBS	i2 iBase File
IC1	Imagic Bitmap Graphic
IC2	IMagic Bitmap Graphic
IC3	IMagic Bitmap Graphic
ICA	Citrix Independent Computer Architecture File
ICB	Image Capture Board
ICC	ICC Profile Format File
ICL	Icon Library File
ICM	Image Color Matching Profile File
ICMP	Internet Control Message Protocol
ICN	AT&T Graphic Format
ICO	Icon File
ICS	Outlook Calendar File
ICT	TIFF and ISO Image Related File
ICW	MS Internet Explorer Internet Connect Wizard
ID	Lotus Notes ID File and MS Data Map
IDAPI	Integrated Database Application Programming Interface
IDB	Delphi Pascal Object File
IDC	Internet Database Connector Document and SQL Connector File
IDD	MIDI Instrument Definition
IDE	C++ Project
IDF	Identification File and MIDI Instruments Definition File
IDIF	Netscape Saved Address Book
IDL	Visual C++ Interface Definition File
IDM	Ulead Photo Express Messages File
IDQ	Internet Data Query File and SQL Query
IDT	Identification File and Windows Installer File
IDW	IntelliDraw Vector Graphic
IDX	Index
IDY	Debug Information File and Index File
IE1-3	Internet Explorer 3 Address Book
IE3	Internet Explorer 3 File
IEE-695	IEEE 695 Information
IEF	Image File

Extension	Description
IFF	Bitmap Graphic and Simple Musical Score
IFO	Information File
IFS	IconForge Image EXE Library and Installable File System
IFX	Fax File
IGF	Vector Graphic
IGN	ICQ Igonre List
IGS	CAD Overlay
IHT	Intranet Connector Script File
IHTML	Inline HyperText Markup Language
II	GCC Preprocessed C++ Source Code
IIF	QuickBooks Import/Export Interchange File
III	Intel IPhone Compatible File
IKO	Windows Icon Resource
IL	Icon Library
ILM	Iomega Zip Drive Speed Configuration File
ILS	Internet Security And Acceleration Server Summary
ILSR	Iomega Reader
IMA	WinImage File
IMF	MIDI Music File
IMG	Commonly Used Extension for an Image File or for a Disk Image File
IMI	Turbo Pascal DOS File
IMJ	JFIF File with a Microsoft Windows BMP Header
IML	ACT! Internet Mail Message File
IMP	FileMaker Database Translation Filter and DVD File
IMS	Music File
IMV	Yahoo Instant Messenger IMVironment
IMZ	Compressed Floppy Image
IN	Input File
IN0	INI Backup
IN1	INI Backup
INA	DOS File
INC	Commonly Used Extension for Include Files
IND	dBASE IV and Windows Shared Database File
INDEX	Index File
INDIGO	Indigo Graphics Format
INF	Information File
INI	Initialization/Configuration File
INL	Visual C++ Inline Function File
INP	Oracle Source Code
INS	Instrument Music File and Internet Communication Settings
INST	Object Oriented Graphics Library

(continued)

Extension	Description
INT	Foxpro Code Page
INV	Windows Update file, Invoice File and Inventory File
INX	Foxpro Foxbase Index
IN_	Setup Information
IOCA	Image Object Content Architecture (IOCA) Graphics File
IP	Files serving the Internet Protocol
IPF	SMS Installer Script
IPJ	Inventor Project
IPK	internet Package Archive
IPL	Corel Pantone Spot Reference Palette
IPP	Help & Manual Proprietary Image
IPR	IntelliJ Project XML File
IPZ	ICQ Skin
IQ	IBM Query File
IQF	Integra 3.0 Query File
IQI	IBM Query
IQR	IBM Query
IQS	AmeriCalc Security File
IQT	IBM Query
IQU	AmeriCalc Update
IQY	Excel Web Query and Internet Inquiry File
IRC	IRCAM Format Sound
IRIS	Silicon Graphics RGB
IRS	WordPerfect Resource File
IRX	IBM Mainframe Rule File
ISH	Compressed Archive File
ISO	ISO-9660 CD Disc Image
ISP	IIS Internet Service Provider Settings
ISR	Uninstaller Text File
ISU	Easy CD Creator 4 Uninstall File
ITG	Intergraph Format
ITM	Item or Article or Zone
ITX	Texture File
IVI	MSDN InfoViewer 5.0 Topic
IVT	MSDN InfoViewer 5.0 Information Title
IW	IBM Updater File
IWA	IBM Writing Assistant Text
IWP	Wang Text File
IWR	i-write 2.0 File
IWR_BAK	i-write 2.0 Backup File
IX	FrameMaker Index File and WordPerfect Office Template File
IX2	WordPerfect Office Template File or WP Calendar File
IXA	Ulead Image File
IXC	Index+ for Windows Code Definition File
IXF	Index+ for Windows Form Definition File
IXL	DB/TextWorks Database Indexed List

Extension	Description
IXP	ISIPublisher Publication Information Export (Image Solutions, Inc.)
IXR	Index+ for Windows Report Definition File
IXS	ArcView Geocoding Index For Read-Write Shapefiles (ESRI)
IXT	ISIPublisher Publication Template (Image Solutions, Inc.)
IXX	C++ Include File
IZD	Intrexx Application Export Format
IZT	IZL Binary Token
IZX	Intermezzon Designer E-Learning Published File (Intermezzon Learning Systems AB)
I_I	Eru/erd File
J	JPEG / JFIF Image, Java Source Code and JAR Compressed File
J2K	JPEG-2000 JP2 File
JA	IBM Tools Updater File
JAD	Java Application Descriptor File
JAG	Jaguar Server File
JAM	E-mail
JAR	Java Archive
JAS	Paint Shop Pro Compressed Graphic
JASC	JAS Compressed Graphic
JAV	Java Source Code
JAVA	Java Source Code
JBF	Paint Shop Pro Browser Cache
JBR	Paint Shop Pro Brush
JBS	DesignArt
JBX	Project Scheduler File
JCF	JAWS for Windows Configuration File
JCL	Job Control Language IBM
JCM	Java Commerce Message Commerce Message
JCS	Flashget Script HTML Table
JED	JEDEC Programming Specification
JFF	JPEG Image
JFI	JPEG/JIFF Image
JFIF	JPEG/JIFF Image
JGD	Paint Shop Pro Gradient
JIF	JPEG/JIFF Image
JIS	Japanese Industrial Standard Text File
JJ	JavaCC File
JJC	Canvas Compressed Audio File
JLA	VisualPro BMP Image
JLS	JPEG-LS File
JMD	Paint Shop Pro Image Map Settings
JMF	Java Multimedia File
JMH	JPEG File Interchange Format
JMM	Digital Camera Video Clip

(continued)

Extension	Description
JMP	SAS JMP Discovery Chart-to-Statistics File
JNC	Communication Log File
JNG	JPEG Network Graphic Bitmap
JNK	Junk
JNLP	Java Web Start
JNT	Windows XP Tablet PC Edition Journal
JOB	Job File
JOR	SQL Server Journal File
JOY	Joystick Calibration File
JP2	JPEG-2000 JP2 File
JPC	JPEG-2000 Code Stream Bitmap and Japan Picture Format
JPE	JPEG/JIFF Image
JPEG	JPEG/JIFF Image
JPG	JPEG/JIFF Image
JPR	Oracle JDeveloper Model JProject
JPS	Stereo Image
JPX	JPEG-2000 JP2 File
JRC	Jrchive Compressed Archive
JS	JavaScript Source Code
JSD	Join-Split File
JSE	JScript Encoded Script File
JSF	Macromedia Fireworks Batch Script
JSL	Paint Shop Pro Shapes File
JSP	Java Server Page
JSP10	Java Server Page
JSV	Java Structure Viewer
JSV	VXML JavaServer Page
JSW	WML JavaServer Page
JTF	JPEG Tagged Interchange Format Image
JTIF	JPEG Tagged Interchange Format Image
JTK	Java ToolKit File
JTP	Windows XP Tablet PC Edition Journal
JW	Q & A Write for Windows 3.0
JWL	Easy CD Creator's CD Label
JXX	C++ Header File
JZZ	Jazz Spreadsheet
K	Desktop Color Separation Specification Black Layer
K01	Clarion DOS Database Key File
K02	Clarion DOS Database Key File
K03	Clarion DOS Database Key File
K04	Clarion DOS Database Key File
K05	Clarion DOS Database Key File
K06	Clarion DOS Database Key File
K07	Clarion DOS Database Key File
K08	Clarion DOS Database Key File
K09	Clarion DOS Database Key File
K1S	Wave Glib19 File

Extension	Description
K25	Kodak DC25 Digital Camera File
K3D	3DS Macro Language Description
K7	DCMO6 Emulator Tape Image
KAR	FOX+ 2.0
KB	C++ Keyboard Script
KBD	Keyboard Script File Layout
KBM	Reflection Keyboard Script File Layout
KBM	Scala Keyboard Mapping
KDC	Kodak Photo-Enhancer/Photogen File
KDK	Kodak Proprietary Decimated TIFF Format
KDO	Kudo Picture Browser
KE$	Modem Bitware Fax Disk2 File
KED	KEDIT Profile and Macro File
KEN	Player CDcheck Compressed File
KEP	Turbo Pascal DOS TP19 Compressed Kepler File
KEY	Keyboard Definition File
KFX	2D Graphic
KGB	Z80 Spectrum Emulator Snap/File Formats
KGP	Image
KIC	Kodak Image Compression File
KID	Tonline Bsw4 Install Mdmimp File
KIF	AutoCAD Key Index
KIZ	Kodak Digital Postcard File and UU Encoded File
KMA	Kodak Memory Album
KNN	Clarion for Windows Database Key
KNO	Personal Knowbase Data
KNW	Known Problems
KOD	Code
KOE	Turbo Pascal DOS File
KOR	Korean Text File
KPL	Kazaa Playlist
KPS	IBM KIPS Bitmap
KS	Works Sheet
KSH	UNIX Shell Script
KST	Olivetti Olitext Plus Script File
KTP	Clarion for Windows Temporary Key File
KTT	KeyText Data File
KVT	BASIC QuickBAS QuickB03 File
KW$	NTgraph Visual C Wizzard File
KWB	KeyWord Braille File
KWD	Keyword
KWF	Delphi Pascal Chart
KXS	Kexis Lossless Compressed Audio
KYB	Keyboard Layout
KYE	Kye Game Data
KYF	Visual-Voice Mouth Movement File
KYS	Photoshop CS Keyboard Shortcut
KZP	Kazoo3D or KazooStudio KazooPicture

(continued)

Extension	Description
L95	Library File
LAA	LucasArts AdLib Audio File Format
LAB	Mailing Labels
LAD	Daylon Leveller Animation Data
LAM	Netscape Media Player Streaming Audio Metafile
LAN	Novell NetWare LAN Drivers
LBA	Liberty BASIC File
LBG	dBASE IV Label Generator
LBI	Dreamweaver Library File
LBL	Label
LBO	dBASE IV Ordered Labels
LBR	Compressed Archive File
LBT	Foxpro Label Memo
LBX	Foxpro Label
LCF	Linker Control File
LCH	IBM Works for OS/2 Chart
LCK	Lock File
LCL	FTP Software Data
LCN	WordPerfect Dictionary File
LCS	ACT! History File
LD1	dBASE Overlay File
LDB	Access Lock File
LDF	SQL Server Transaction Log File
LDI	LDIF File
LDIF	LDAP Data Interchange Format
LDIF	LDIF File
LDL	Corel Paradox Delivered Library
LDR	Symantec Ghost Template File
LDS	Corel40 Programs Data File
LE$	BASIC VB
LES	Lesson File
LET	Letter
LEX	Lexicon (Dictionary) and Lexmark Printer Installation File
LE_	BASIC VB Compressed Disk1 File
LF	SoftwareKey License File
LFA	LifeForm File
LFD	LucasArts Games Resource
LFF	LucasFilm Format
LFL	LucasFilm Library
LFM	LifeForm File
LFP	LifeForm File
LFQ	LeechFTP Queue File
LG	Logo Procedure Definition
LGA	Windows Applog File
LGC	Windows Application Log
LGD	Windows Application Log
LGE	Windows Application Log
LGF	Windows Application Log
LGG	Windows Application Log
LGH	Windows Application Log

Extension	Description
LGI	Windows Application Log
LGJ	Windows Application Log
LGK	Windows Application Log
LGL	Windows Application Log
LGM	Windows Application Log
LGN	Windows Application Log
LGO	Windows Logo Driver
LGP	Windows Application Log
LGQ	Windows Application Log
LGR	Windows Application Log
LGS	Windows Application Log
LGZ	Windows Application Log
LHA	Compressed Archive File
LHZ	LHA Compressed Archive File
LI$	MS Compressed Library
LIA	P-CAD Schematic Library
LIB	Library File
LIC	License File
LID	WinDVD File
LIF	Compressed Archive File
LIM	Limit Compressed Archive
LIN	AutoCAD Linetype Definition
LIS	Compiler Listing File
LIT	Reader eBook File
LIVEREG	Symantec Norton Anti-Virus Update Session
LIVESUBSCRIBE	Symantec Norton Anti-Virus Update Catalog
LIVEUPDATE	Norton Anti-Virus Update Settings File (Symantec)
LJ	HP LaserJet Graphic Bitmap
LKO	Outlook Express Linked Object
LKS	WinAmp Links File
LLD	Links Language Data File
LM8	Picture File
LMA	Netscape Packetized Audio
LNG	Commonly used extension for Language Files
LNK	Windows Shortcut File
LNM	WordPerfect SGML Alias
LOC	Localisation String Resource Header File
LOD	Load File
LOG	Log File
LPK	License Package
LQT	Winamp File
LRF	C/C++ Linker Response File
LRG	Macromedia XRes Multi-resolution Bitmap
LRM	Encarta Class Server Learning Resource
LRP	IBM Works for OS/2 Report
LRS	Language Resource File
LS1	Winhelp Source File

(continued)

Extension	Description
LSF	Libronix DLS Resource
LSI	Corel Layout Specification Instance SGML
LSL	Corel Paradox Saved Library
LSL	Lotus Script Library
LSN	Works File
LST	List or Spooler File
LSZ	WinFax
LTM	Lotus Form
LTR	Letter
LTT	HP Library and Tape Tools Log File
LUN	DB-MAIN Project File
LVP	Lucent Voice Player
LWD	LotusWorks Text Document
LWP	Wordpro 96/97 Document (Lotus)
LYR	Song Lyric File
LZD	Binary Difference File
LZH	Compressed Archive File
LZO	Izop Compressed Archive
LZS	Compressed Archive File
LZS	LARC Compressed File Archive
LZX	Compressed File
M	Desktop Color Separation Specification Magenta Layer and Objective C Source
M12	S-BASIC File
M1A	MPEG-1 Audiostream
M1S	MPEG Media File
M1V	MPEG-1 Video File
M2A	MPEG-2 Audio
M2P	MPEG-2 Program Stream Format File
M2S	MPEG-2 Audio and Video
M2V	MPEG-2 Video Only File
M3A	MPEG Archive Enhanced .M3U Playlist File
M3D	Corel Motion 3D Animation
M3U	MP3 Playlist File
M3URL	MP3 Playlist File
M4	Meta4 Source Code
M4A	MPEG-4 Audio Layer
M68	Turbo Pascal DOS File
MA3	Harvard Graphics Macro
MAB	Mozilla Personal Address Book or Collected Address Book B
MAC	Macro and Access Shortcut
MAD	Access Module Shortcut
MAF	Access
MAG	Access Diagram Shortcut and Magenta Color Separation
MAI	MS Mail Message
MAILHOST	E-mail Server Preferences File
MAILVIEW	MSN Mail

Extension	Description
MAK	Visual Basic Ver. 3.0 Project and Visual C++ Project
MAKI	Winamp3 Compiled Script
MAN	Windows 2000 Mandatory User Profile
MAP	Color Palette and Common Extension Used for Map Files
MAPIMAIL	Outlook Express Mail File
MAPIMAIL	Sendto File
MAPISEND	MAPISEND File
MAPLET	Maplet Design File
MAQ	Access Query Shortcut
MAR	Access Report Shortcut and Bibliographic Data Format
MAS	Access Stored Procedures
MAT	Access Table Shortcut
MAV	Access View Shortcut
MAW	Access Data Access Page
MB	Paradox Memo Holder
MBD	Multimedia Builder MP3 Authoring File
MBF	Money Backup File
MBG	MS Mail Mailbag
MBK	dBASE IV Multiple Index Backup
MBS	Mailbag Assistant Script
MBX	Database Index and Mailbox Message File
MC6	C File/Makefile
MCC	Microsoft Network Shortcut
MCF	Master Command File and Media Container Format
MCI	Media Control Interface Command Set
MCL	Macro Command Language
MCM	Enable Macro
MCP	Master Compiler Profile
MCQ	McAfee Quarantined File
MCR	CuteFTP Script
MCX	Graphic File
MD5	MD5 Checksum File
MD8	CDrom Database File
MDA	Access Add-in
MDB	Access Application or Database
MDE	Office File
MDF	Menu Definition File and SQL Master Database File
MDHTML	Access HTML File
MDI	MIDI-sequention Sound and Office Document Imaging File
MDMP	Win XP Trouble Report
MDN	Access Blank Database Template
MDO	Internet Information Server Configuration Backup
MDP	Visual C++ MAK File and Visual J++ Project Workspace

(continued)

Extension	Description
MDS	Directx Mid2stream File
MDT	Access Add-in Data
MDW	Access Workgroup Information
MDX	Borland Database Engine Index
MDZ	Access Wizard Template
MEB	WordPerfect Macro Editor Bottom Overflow File
MED	WordPerfect Macro Editor Delete Save
MEM	FoxPro Memory Variable Save File
MEN	Menu
MEQ	WordPerfect Macro Editor Print Queue
MER	WordPerfect Macro Editor Resident Area and Data Interchange Format
MES	Message File
MET	Presentation Manager Meta File
MEU	DOS Shell Menus
MEX	WordPerfect Macro Editor Expound File
MF	MetaFont Text File
MFD	Adobe Multiple Master Font Metrics Directory File
MFF	MIDI File Format
MFM	DMP Music Format
MGC	Clipart Collection Catalog
MGF	Image File and Micrografx Font
MGR	MGR Bitmap
MGX	Micrografx Picture Publisher Clipart
MHG	Multimedia File
MHT	MHTML Document
MHTM	MHTML Document
MHTML	MHTML Document
MI	Miscellaneous
MIB	Management Information Base File
MIF	FrameMaker Interchange Format and MIDI Instrument File
MIP	Paint Shop Pro Multiple Image Print File
MIPSEL	Mips File
MIX	Multi-layer Picture File and Windows Sound Mix
ML	ML language Source Code File
MLB	FoxPro for Macintosh Library
MLI	AutoCAD Material-Library File
MLM	Novel Groupwise E-mail File
MLN	AutoCAD Multiline Definition
MMB	Oracle Forms Menu Binary Source Code
MMC	Media Catalog
MME	Multi-Purpose Internet Mail Extensions (MIME) File
MMF	Mail File
MML	Mail Meta Language
MMM	Multimedia Movie
MMP	MS Music Producer

Extension	Description
MMS	JPEG-6b File
MMW	Media Content
MMX	Oracle Forms Compiled Menu
MN1	Money Ver 1 Data File
MN2	Money Ver 2 Data File
MN3	Money Ver 3 Data File
MN4	Money Database
MN4	Money Ver 4 Data File
MN5	Money Ver 5 Data File
MN6	Money Ver 6 Data File
MN7	Money Ver 7 Data File
MN8	Money Ver 8 Data File
MN9	Money Ver 9 Data File
MNC	AutoCAD Compiled Menu
MND	AutoCAD Menu Program
MNF	Saved MSN Search
MNR	AutoCAD Compiled Menu
MNS	AutoCAD ASCII Menu
MNT	Foxpro Menu Memo
MNU	AutoCAD Menu Template or FoxPro Menu
MOD	Digital Music Sound Clip and Commonly Used Extension for a Modeling File
MOF	MSinfo
MOI	French Text File
MOM	CDrom Runtime Database File
MOO	QuickTime Movie Clip
MOOV	QuickTime Movie
MOS	System DOS 6.2 File
MOV	Movie File
MOZ	Netscape Temp File
MP+	MPEG Plus Audio File
MP1	MPEG Audio Stream, Layer I
MP2	MPEG Audio Stream, Layer II
MP2S	Max Payne 2 Saved Game (Rockstar Games)
MP2S	MPEG-2 Video
MP2V	MPEG Audio Stream, Layer II
MP3	MPEG Audio Stream, Layer III
MP3PRO	mp3PRO Enhanced MP3 File
MP4	MPEG-4 Video File
MPA	MPEG Audio Stream, Layer I, II, or III
MPD	Windows Mini-port Driver
MPE	MPEG Movie Clip
MPEG	MPEG Movie
MPG	MPEG Animation
MPG4	MPEG-4 Media File
MPGA	Mpeg-1 Layer3 Audio Stream
MPKG	Meta Package File
MPM	MPEG Movie
MPP	CAD Drawing File

(continued)

Extension	Description	Extension	Description
MPR	FileMaker Spelling Dictionary	MXT	C Data
MPS	MPEG-1 Audio and Video File	MYD	MySQL Database
MPT	Multipage TIFF Bitmap	MYDOCS	MyDocs Drop Target
MPV	MPEG-1 Video File	MYI	MySQL Database Index
MPV2	MPEG Audio Stream, Layer II	NA2	Netscape Communicator Address Book
MPX	Foxpro Compiler Menu	NAB	Netscape Communicator or Novell
MRB	C++ Multiple Resolution Bitmap Graphic		Groupwise Address Book
MRC	Bibliographic Data Format	NAI	WinINSTALL File
MRG	Merge File	NAM	Office Name File
MRI	MRI Scan	NAP	NAP Metafile Vector Image
MRK	Markup File	NAPLPS	North American Presentation Layer
MRS	WordPerfect Macro Resource File		Protocol Syntax = Vector image
MS	Checksum File for Anti-Virus	NAS	NASTRAN File
MSC	C Makefile and Microsoft Management	NAV	Microsoft Network Component
	Console Snap-in File	NB	Mathematica Notebook
MSD	Microsoft Diagnostic Utility Report	NCD	Norton Change Directory
MSF	Multiple Sequence File	NCF	Lotus Notes Internal Clipboard and
MSG	Message File		NetWare Command File
MSI	Windows Installer File	NCH	Outlook Express Folder File
MSM	Windows Installer Merge Module	NCS	Netscape Conference Call File
MSN	Microsoft Network Document	NCT	Nero Cover Designer Template
MSO	FrontPage File	NDB	ACT! Notes Data File
MSP	Windows Installer Patch	NDF	SQL Server Secondary Data File
MSPX	XML-based Web Page	NDL	Lotus Notes
MSQ	MIDI File	NED	MSN Application Extension
MSR	OzWin CompuServe E-mail/Forum	NEF	Nikon Digital SLR Cameras Raw
	Access SYSOP File		Graphic File Format
MSS	Manuscript Text File	NET	Network Configuration
MST	Test Document	NEW	New Information
MSW	Word Text File	NEWS	News Bitmap Image
MSWMM	Windows Movie Maker Project	NFL	AutoCAD Multiline Filter List
MTT	Messenger Saved Contact File	NFO	System Info File
MTW	Minitab Data File	NG	Norton Guide Online Documentation
MTX	Adobe Atmosphere File and Marked	NHF	Nero HFS-CD Compilation
	Text Source File	NHV	Nero Burning ROM HFS CD
MT_	Encore Compressed Audio File	NIB	Corel Graphics10 Photopoint File
MUD	ACT! Database File	NIF	Network Initialization File
MUI	Configuration Resource File	NIP	Network Interface Plug-in
MUS	Music File	NK2	Outlook AutoComplete File
MVA	Setup Program Archive	NL	Norton Desktop Icon Library
MVB	Manual Storage Format and Multimedia	NLB	Oracle 7 Data
	Viewer File	NLD	ATI Radeon Video Driver
MVD	MicroDVD DVD Movie	NLU	Norton Live Update E-Mail Trigger File
MVF	AutoCAD / AutoFlix Stop Frame File	NMD	Nero Burning ROM miniDVD
MVI	AutoCAD Movie Command	NOR	ATI Radeon Video Driver
MVP	MediaView Project	NOT	Acrobat Spelling File and Notation File
MVX	Mixer File	NPI	dBASE Application Generator Source
MWP	Lotus Wordpro 97 Smartmaster File	NPM	Corel Graphics Ver 10 Draw Media
MX3	MP3 Encoded File		Lines File
MXE	Quatro Pro Startup Macro	NPS	Lotus Agenda File
MXI	Macromedia Extension Information	NPS	NeroMix
MXP	Macromedia Extension Manager	NR3	Nero MP3 CD-ROM Compilation

(continued)

Extension	Description
NR4	Nero Burning ROM
NRA	Nero Audio-CD Compilation
NRB	Nero CD-ROM Boot Compilation
NRC	Nero UDF/ISO CD-ROM Compilation
NRD	Nero DVD Compilation
NRE	Nero CD Extra Compilation
NRG	Nero CD-Image File and Norton Registration Entries
NRH	Nero Hybrid CD-ROM Compilation
NRI	Nero ISO CD-ROM Compilation
NRM	Nero Mixed-Mode-CD Compilation
NRS	Nero Burning ROM CD Boot
NRU	Nero UDF/ISO CD-ROM Compilation
NRV	Nero Video-CD Compilation
NRW	Nero WMA CD-ROM Compilation
NS2	Lotus Notes 2 Database
NS3	Lotus Notes Database
NS4	Lotus Notes Database
NS5	Lotus Notes Domino File
NSC	Windows Media Station File
NSD	Norton System Doctor Sensors Configuration
NSD	Nero Burning ROM Super Video CD
NSF	Lotus Notes Database
NSF	NES Sound File
NSG	Lotus Notes
NSH	Lotus Notes Database (Older Form)
NSV	Winamp3 Video Format File
NSX	Apollo Database Engine Index
NT	Windows NT Startup File
NTF	Notes Database Template
NTS	Norton Tutorial
NTX	Clipper Index
NU4	Norton Utilities DLL Root File
NU6	Norton Utilities System DLL File
NUM	DOS 7 File
NW3	Netware.3x File
NW4	Netware.4x File
NWS	Outlook Express News File
NZL	Corel Painter Nozzle File
O	Object File
O$$	Output File
OAB	Outlook Address Book
OAF	ETH Oberon Applet File
OB$	Compressed OBJ
OBD	Office Binder Template
OBJ	Object File
OBR	C++ Object Browser Data File
OBS	ObjectScript Script
OBT	Office Binder Template
OBV	ObjectScript Visual Interface
OBZ	Office Binder Wizard

Extension	Description
OCA	OLE Custom Control Library Information
OCF	Object Craft File
OCM	Netscape Communicator Aim File
OCP	Advanced Art Studio
OD1	Omnis5 Database File
OD2	Omnis5 Database File
OD3	Omnis5 Database File
OD4	Omnis5 Database File
OD5	Omnis5 Database File
OD6	Omnis5 Database File
OD7	Omnis5 Database File
OD8	Omnis5 Database File
OD9	Omnis5 Database File
ODB	ArcView Object Database ASCII File
ODC	Office Data Connection
ODE	Office Object Data Embedding File
ODIF	Open Document Interchange Format
ODL	Object Definition Language
ODL	Visual C++ Type Library Source
ODS	Outlook Express Mailbox
OEB	Outlook Express Backup Wizard
OEM	OEM Data Used During Device Install
OFC	Open Financial Connectivity File
OFD	ObjectView Form Defintion
OFM	PostScript Font Description File
OFT	Outlook Item Template
OGX	C++ Component Gallery Exported Classes and Resources
OHP	DOS 7 File
OLB	MS Project Object Library
OLD	Old Version
OLE	Object Linking and Embedding (OLE) Object
OLK	MS Mail Mailbag Lock
OLK	Outlook Address Book
OLN	Visual C++ Outline Examples
OLT	Visual C++ Outline Examples
OMO	Oracle Media Objects File
OND	Lotus Notes-related File
OP	Rescue Disk File
OPC	Office Upgrade Control File
OPS	Office Profile Settings File
OPX	OPL Extension DLL
OQY	Excel OLAP Query File
OR2	Lotus Organizer 2 File
OR3	Lotus Organizer 97 File
OR4	Lotus Organizer File
OR5	Lotus Organizer File
OR6	IBM Organizer Data File
ORA	Oracle 7 Configuration
ORC	MIDI File and Oracle Scripting File
ORF	Olympus Digital Camera Raw Image File

(continued)

Extension	Description
ORG	Lotus Organiser File
ORI	Original
ORIG	Gen Original File
OSF	Distribution Bin File
OSS	Office Saved Search
OST	Exchange or Outlook Offline File
OTF	Open Type Font Format
OTM	Outlook VBA Module
OUT	Outlines or Output File
OVL	Program File - Overlay
OVR	Program File - Overlay
OYZ	Lotus Approach Alternate dBASE Index
P	PASCAL Program File
P01	Toast CD Image
P01	Parity Volume Set
P02	Parity Volume Set
P03	Parity Volume Set
P04	Parity Volume Set
P05	Parity Volume Set
P06	Parity Volume Set
P07	Parity Volume Set
P08	Parity Volume Set
P09	Parity Volume Set
P1	MicroImages Print Driver File
P10	Certificate Request
P12	Personal Information Exchange File
P3E	PC-Doctor File
P3I	PC-Doctor File
P3P	Platform for Privacy Preferences
P56	Patch
P64	H.261 Encoded Video File
P65	PageMaker Version 6.5 File
PA3	Turbo Pascal DOS File
PA4	Turbo Pascal DOS File
PA5	Turbo Pascal DOS File
PAB	Personal Address Book (Microsoft)
PAC	Windows Applications Manager Added or Changed Package
PAD	Scanner Output
PAE	PowerArchiver 20002 Encrypted Archive
PAF	Ensoniq PARIS Audio Format and Personal Ancestral File
PAG	Visual Basic Property Page File
PAK	Compressed Archive File
PAL	Color Palette File, Personal Ancestral File and Compressed File Format
PAM	Tonline Ob4hbci Smartupdate File
PAN	CorelDraw Printer-Specific File
PAP	Corel Painter Pattern, Selection or Texture File
PAQ	HP System Recovery File

Extension	Description
PAR	Commonly Used Extension for Parameter Files and Windows 3.x Swap File
PAR2	Parity Archive Volume Set
PAS	C++, Pascal and Delphi Source Code File
PAT	Commonly used extension for both Pattern Files and Patch Files
PATCH	General Patch File
PATTERN	Photoline5 Defaults File
PAU	OzWin CompuServe E-mail/Forum Access Paused Message
PAV	Panda Antivirus File
PB	WinFax Pro Phone Book
PB1	First Publisher Document
PB2	STABCAL (Stability Calculation for Aqueous Systems) File
PBA	PowerBASIC Source Code
PBB	MS Mail Address Information File
PBD	Faxit Phone Book, PowerBuilder Dynamic Library and Graphic Format
PBF	Portable Bitmap Format File and PBook E-book Format
PBH	PowerBASIC Help File
PBI	AXIALIS image JPEG JFIF and PowerBASIC Include File
PBK	Phonebook
PBL	PowerBASIC and PowerBuilder Library File
PBM	UNIX Portable Bitmap Graphic
PBMV	Portable Bitmap File
PBN	Portable Bridge Notation
PBO	Profiler Binary Output
PBP	Perl Builder File
PBQ	Audio
PBR	PowerBuilder Resource File
PBS	PowerArchiver Backup Script
PBT	Profiler Binary Table
PBV	Paint Shop Pro Bevel Preset
PBX	Outlook Express Message Folder
PC	PC-specific Text File and Oracle Pro-C Source Code
PC2	AutoCAD R14 Plotter Configuration
PC3	AutoCAD R2000 Plotter Configuration
PC8	ASCII Text IBM-8
PCA	PCAnywhere Registry Backup
PCB	Broderbund Print Shop Business Card
PCB	Ivex Winboard Design File, PrintShop Business Card and PC Doctor File
PCC	PC Checkup System Information and PC Paintbrush Image File
PCD	Images CD Creator Corel Adaptec

(continued)

Extension	Description
PCDS	Photo-CD Image
PCE	Borland Package Collection Editor File, Mail Signature and PC Doctor FIle
PCF	Profiler Command File and Unix Font File
PCF	Cisco VPN Client Configuration
PCG	Photo CD Graphic File
PCH	C PreCompiled Header and Patch File
PCI	PC-Doctor File and Windows PCI Miniport File
PCK	Package and Turbo Pascal Pick File
PCL	HP Printer Control Language
PCM	LaserJet Printer Cartridge Metric and Sound File
PCN	Paint Shop Pro Contour Preset
PCP	AutoCAD R13 and Prior Plotter Configuration, PC Paint Bitmap and Symantec Live Update Package
PCR	PCMark Benchmark File
PCT	Commonly Used Extensions for Various Graphics Files
PCW	PC Write Text File
PCX	PC Paintbrush Bitmap Graphic
PD	Paradox Table
PDA	Print Shop Bitmap Graphic
PDB	Photo Deluxe Image and Visual C++ Program Database File
PDBX	Insight II X-PLOR Coordinate File
PDD	PhotoDeluxe Image
PDF	Acrobat Portable Document Format and ArcView Preferences Definition File
PDG	PrintShop Deluxe File
PDL	C++ Project Description Language, Print Shop Project and Programmable Driver Language
PDM	Sybase Power Designer File
PDN	Plan de Negocio
PDO	Access Package Deployment Script
PDP	Broderbund Print Shop Deluxe File and Photoshop PDF Format
PDR	Port Driver
PDS	Print Shop Graphic and Source Code File
PDV	Paintbrush Printer Driver
PDW	Professional Draw Document
PDX	Acrobat Catalog Index and PageMaker Printer Description
PDZ	GZipped Brookhaven Protein Databank File
PD_	Visc15 Images Setup File
PE	Portable Executable File

Extension	Description
PEB	WordPerfect Program Editor Bottom Overflow File
PEBPRJ	PEBundle File
PED	WordPerfect Program Editor Delete Save
PEM	Audio Module and WordPerfect Program Editor Macro
PEP	TurboProject Project File
PEQ	WordPerfect Program Editor Print Queue File
PER	WordPerfect Program Editor Resident Area
PERL	Perl Source File
PES	WordPerfect Program Editor Work Space File
PET	WordPerfect Program Editor Top Overflow File
PEW	IAR Embedded Workbench
PEX	Proboard Executable Program
PF	Archive and Monitor or Printer Profile File
PFA	PostScript Font
PFB	PostScript Type 1 Font
PFC	First Choice Text File
PFE	Programmers File Editor
PFK	XTree Programmable Function Keys
PFR	Paint Shop Pro Frame
PFS	First Publisher ART File and PFS Data File
PFX	Personal Information Exchange File
PF_	Encore Compressed Audio File
PGA	IBM Professional Graphics Adapter Image
PGC	Compressed Portfolio Graphic
PGD	Pretty Good Privacy Virtual Disk File
PGE	Solitaire Peg Back
PGF	PGC Portfolio Graphics Compressed Bitmap
PGL	HP Plotter Language
PGM	Portable Graymap Graphic
PGN	Portable Game Notation
PGP	Program Parameter and Pretty Good Privacy
PGR	Pretty Good Privacy PGP Groups
PGS	Commonly used extension for a Page File
PGX	Visual Basic Binary Property Page File
PG_	Improve Compressed Audio File
PH	PERL Header
PHB	Arcsoft PhotoBase and TreeView File
PHD	PC Help Desk File
PHL	Database Configuration File

(continued)

Extension	Description
PHM	DN—Lync Phone Book
PHN	Commonly used extension for a Phonebook File
PHP	Picture It! Publishing Project File
PHT	Partial Hypertext File
PHTM	PHP Script
PHTML	web-iPerl Document
PH_	C Poet Compressed Disk1 File
PI	Extension Associated with W32.Sobig.D@mm Worm
PI$	MS Compressed PIF
PIC	Commonly used extension for a Picture file
PICIO	Pixar Picture
PICON	Personal Icon
PICS	PICT Drawing Sequence
PID	UNIX Process ID File
PIF	GDF Format Vector Image and Windows Program Information File
PIM	Personal Information Manager File
PIP	JPEG,JPG,JPE, JFIF,PJPEG Compressed Bitmap Picture
PIPL	Photoshop 5.0 SDK Samplecode Colorpicker File
PIX	Commonly used extension for Picture Files
PIXAR	Pixar Picture
PI_	Compressed PIC or PIF File
PJ	PaintJet PCL Bitmap
PJG	Photo Assistant Image
PJL	ProCite Term Lists and Journal Title Lists
PJP	JPEG Image
PJPEG	JPEG Image
PJT	Foxpro Project Memo
PJX	Foxpro Project Index
PJXL	PaintJet XL PCL Bitmap
PK	Audition Graphical Waveform
PKA	Compressed Archive File
PKB	Oracle Package Body
PKD	Turbo Pascal DOS Compressed Batch File
PKD	PowerKaraoke Project File (PAW)
PKG	Commonly Used Extension for Package Files
PKO	PublicKey Security Object
PKP	MS Development Common IDE Pakage Project File
PKPAK	Archive
PKR	Pretty Good Privacy Public Keyring
PKS	Oracle Package Specification

Extension	Description
PL	Harvard Graphics Palette and PERL Program File
PL3	Harvard Graphics Chart Palette
PLB	Commonly used extension for Library Files
PLC	Lotus Add-in
PLD	PhotoDeluxe PhotoLine Image Document
PLEX	Visual Perl File
PLF	InterVideo WinDVD Playlist File
PLH	Paint Shop Pro Light Preset
PLI	Oracle 7 Data Description
PLIST	Property List XML File
PLJ	PlayJ Music Format
PLK	ATI Radeon Video Driver
PLN	ArchiCAD Project and WordPerfect Spreadsheet File
PLOT	UNIX Plot Format
PLR	Player File
PLS	Commonly used extension for a Playlist File
PLT	AutoCAD Plot drawing, HP Graphics Language and Palette File
PLX	Executable Perl Script
PLY	Harvard Graphics Spotlight Presentation Screen
PLZ	Lotus Freelance Presentation
PM	Perl Module and PageMaker Document
PM3	PageMaker Version 3 Document
PM4	PageMaker Version 4 Document
PM5	PageMaker Version 5 Document
PM6	PageMaker Version 6 Document
PMA	Windows Performance Monitor File
PMB	Bitmap Image
PMC	Windows Performance Monitor File
PMD	PageMaker
PMF	ArcReader GIS Mapping
PMG	Paint Magic
PML	NT4 Performance Monitor Log File and PageMaker Library
PMO	Print Master Gold Text
PMP	AutoCAD R2000 Plotter Model Parameters
PMR	Windows Performance Monitor File
PMT	PageMaker Template
PMW	Windows Performance Monitor File
PN3	Harvard Graphics Printer Driver
PNF	Portable Network Graphics Frame Bitmap and Windows Precompiled Setup Information
PNG	Portable (Public) Network Graphic
PNL	Panel File

(continued)

Extension	Description
PNQ	ICQ Instant Message File
PNT	ARC Format Vector Point Data
POD	Text
POL	Windows Policy File
POP	dBASE Popup Menu
POR	Corel Painter Portfolio File
POT	PowerPoint Template
POTHTML	Powerpoint HTML Template
PP4	Picture Publisher
PP5	Picture Publisher
PPA	PowerPoint Add-in
PPB	WordPerfect Print Preview Button Bar
PPC	Roxio Easy CD Creator File
PPD	PostScript Printer Description
PPF	Paint Shop Pro Soft Plastic Preset File and Micrografx Picture Publisher File
PPG	PowerPoint Presentation
PPI	PowerPoint Graphics File
PPK	PPK Archive
PPL	Harvard Graphics Polaroid Palette Plus ColorKey Driver
PPP	Point to Point Protocol
PPS	PowerPoint Slideshow
PPT	PowerPoint Presentation
PPTHTML	Powerpoint HTML Document
PPW	Micrografx Picture Publisher Wizard
PPX	Serif PagePlus Publication
PPZ	PowerPoint Packaged Presentation
PQ	PageMaker Default Printer Style
PQB	PowerQuest Batch File
PQF	Corel Presentations File
PQG	Rescue ME/OS2/DOS File
PQI	PowerQuest Drive Imaging Software
PQW	Corel Presentations 9 Runtime
PQX	Power Quest Drive Image Index
PR2	dBASE IV Printer Driver
PR3	dBASE IV PostScript Printer Driver
PR4	Harvard Graphics Presentation
PRC	Corel Presentation
PRE	Freelance Presentation
PRF	Commonly Used Extension for Preference Files and Profile Files
PRG	Program File
PRH	Cold Fusion Studio 3.1 Project
PRJ	Project File
PRL	Perl Script
PRM	Parameter File
PRN	Commonly used extension for Printer Definition or Printer Driver Files
PRO	PROLOG Program File
PRP	InstantDB Database File
PRR	Perfect Resume Data

Extension	Description
PRS	Printer Resource File, dBASE Procedure and Harvard Graphics Presentation
PRT	Commonly used extension for Printer Information or Driver File and Presentations Template
PRV	Previous Version
PRX	Foxpro Compiler Program
PRZ	Freelance Graphics 97 File
PR_	Compressed Project File
PS	PostScript and Works File
PS1	PostScript File
PS2	Level II PostScript File
PS3	Level III PostScript File
PSA	Photoshop Album Photo Album File
PSB	Paint Shop Pro Sunburst Preset and Project Scheduler Configuration File
PSC	Paint Shop Pro Sculpture Preset
PSD	Photoshop Format
PSF	PostScript Support File and PhotoStudio Graphic
PSH	Lexmark Firmware Flash File
PSI	Psion A-law Audio (Psion PLC)
PSID	PostScript Image Data
PSM	Turbo Pascal Symbol Table
PSN	Post-it Software Notes
PSP	Paint Shop Pro Image
PSP	Project Scheduler Planning File
PSQ	Postscript Graphic
PSR	PowerSoft Report and Project Scheduler Resource File
PST	Commonly used extension for Preset Files and for Post Office Box Files
PSW	Windows Password File and Print Shop Deluxe Ver. 6 File
PT	Kodak Precision Color Management System
PT3	PageMaker Version 3 Document Template and Harvard Graphics Device Driver
PT4	PageMaker Version 4 Document Template
PT4	ProtoTRAK Design Control File (Southwestern Industries, Inc.)
PT5	PageMaker Version 5 Document Template
PT6	PageMaker Version 6 Document Template
PTB	Peachtree Complete Accounting Backup Data File
PTC	ABBYY Finereader 5.0 Pro
PTDB	Peachtree Accounting Database
PTE	Picture to EXE Project

(continued)

Extension	Description
PTE	Pop!site
PTI	IBM Configurator Configuration
PTN	CADKEY Pattern File
PTP	ACT! Modem Sync File
PTX	Paint Shop Pro Texture Preset
PUB	Pretty Good Privacy Public Key Ring
PUT	PUT Compressed File Archive
PVD	Install-It Script
PVG	Encarta World Atlas Pushpins
PVK	MS Development Common IDE Resources File
PVL	Instalit Library
PVR	PVR-CONV
PW	Professional Write Text File
PWA	Password Agent File
PWK	Password Keeper File
PWL	Windows Password List
PWP	Professional WritePlus Document
PWT	AutoCAD Publish-to-Web Template
PWZ	PowerPoint Wizard
PXI	Associated with a Trojan
PXN	Twain32 File
PXP	3D Studio Process File
PXR	Pixar Picture
PXW	Twain32 File
PY	Oracle Batch Procedure
PYC	Python Compiler Script
PYD	Python Dynamic Module
PYO	Python Optimized Code
PYW	Python Script
PZ	PNG Compressed File
PZA	MGI PhotoSuite II/III/4 Album File
PZC	GraphPad Prism Script
PZP	MGI PhotoSuite II/III/4 Project File
PZS	MGI PhotoSuite II/III/4 Slide Show File
Q	Win95 Fax Queue
Q00	Quicken 2000 File
Q01	Quicken 2001 File
Q1	Winamp Equalizer Settings
Q1A	QuickClean Restore Point
Q3D	Quickdraw 3D File
Q3O	Quick3D Model
Q4Q	Solar Cell Photoshop/Paint Shop Pro Plug-In
Q5Q	SuperBladePro Preset
Q5R	Melancholytron Photoshop/Paint Shop Pro Plug-In
Q7Q	India Ink Photoshop/Paint Shop Pro Plug-In
Q8R	Flood Photoshop/Paint Shop Pro Plug-In
Q98	Quicken 98 File

Extension	Description
Q99	Quicken 99 File
Q9Q	BladePro Graphic Plug-in File
Q9R	Glitterato Photoshop/Paint Shop Pro Plug-In
Q9S	Mr. Contrast Photoshop/Paint Shop Pro Plug-In
QAB	SYBYL Binary Field Files
QAD	PF QuickArt Document
QAG	Norton Desktop Quick Access Group
QAP	Omnis Quartz Application File
QAX	ExpressTracker Data File
QB	Tony Hawk's Pro Skater Script
QB1	Quicken File
QBA	QuickBooks Accountant's Copy File
QBB	QuickBooks Backup File
QBD	Keyboard Layout
QBE	Database Saved Query
QBF	QuickBASIC Font File
QBI	Quickbooks Crash Roll Back File
QBL	Business Lawyer Document
QBO	dBASE IV Ordered Query
QBS	Quick Basic Program File
QBW	QuickBooks Primary Data File
QBX	Intuit de Online File
QCC	QC-CALC File
QCH	Quicken for DOS ver 2 Data File
QCK	Quick Charts File and QuickCard File
QCS	CADQC Standard File
QCT	Memory-Map File
QD3	QuickDraw 3D Metafile
QD3D	QuickDraw 3D Metafile
QDB	Quicken Data File Backup
QDF	Quicken for Windows Data File
QDI	Quicken Data File
QDK	Quarterdeck QEMM File
QDP	MPQDraft Plug-in
QDT	QuarkXpress Dictionary File and Quicken Data File
QEF	Excel Query
QEL	Quicken Electronic Library File
QEM	Expense Report
QEP	IRMA Wordstation for Windows
QEX	Expensible Data File
QFC	Quick File Collection Archive
QFI	Quicken 2002 File
QFX	Quicken Transfer File
QIC	Backup Set
QIF	Quicken Interchange Format
QIX	Quicken for DOS ver 2 Data File
QL$	MS Compressed QLB
QLB	C and QuickBasic-DOS and Visual Basic Quick Library

(continued)

Extension	Description
QLC	PostScript Help File and Type Manager ATM Type 1 Font Script
QLP	QuickLink Printer Driver
QMD	Quicken for Windows ver 5,6 Data File
QME	Win3 Quicken Windows File
QMF	Lotus Approach Database Query
QML	Quicken for DOS ver 2 Data File
QMR	OzWin CompuServe E-mail/Forum Access Quickscan History
QMT	Quicken Memory List
QN2	QuickNote File
QNA	High ASCII Quake Name Maker
QNX	Quicken Indexes
QPB	Quicken Payroll File
QPD	Win3 Quicken Windows File
QPH	Quicken Price History File
QPI	Win3 Quicken File
QPR	FoxPro Relational Query
QPS	Quattro Pro Software Application File
QPW	Quattro Pro Project File
QPX	FoxPro Ordered Query
QR2	Delphi Database Quick Report File
QRD	BI/Query Query Result
QRS	WordPerfect Equation Editor
QRT	QRT Ray Tracing Graphic
QRY	Query
QSA	Encrypted QSA Specifications Database Export File
QSD	Quicken for Windows Data File
QSF	Micrografx QuickSilver Compressed Internet Live Graphic
QST	Ami Pro QuickStart Tutorial Image
QTC	QuickTime Ver 2.0+ Windows CODEC
QTE	Questionnaire Specification Language File
QTF	Qtracker Filter
QTI	QuickTime Image
QTIF	QuickTime Image
QTK	Apple Quicktake
QTL	QuickTime Movie
QTM	QuickTime Movie
QTP	QuickTime Preferences
QTPF	QuickTime PreFlight Text
QTPP	Qtracker Program Package
QTR	QuickTime Resource File
QTS	QuickTime System File
QTSK	Qtracker Skin
QTV	QuickTime Virtual Reality Movie
QTVR	QuickTime VR
QTW	QText File
QTX	Quicken Data File and QuickTime Ver 3/4 Windows CODEC

Extension	Description
QUE	Task Scheduler Queue Object
QUP	QuickTime Update Package
QW	Symantec Q&A Write Program File
QW5	Quicken 5 File
QW6	Quicken 6 File
QWB	Money Quotes WriteBack Import File
QWK	QWK Reader Message
QXB	QuarkXpress Books File
QXD	QuarkXpress Document
QXL	QuarkXpress Element Library
QXP	QuarkXpress Project
QXT	QuarkXpress Template File
R	Paradox File
R00	WinRAR Split Compressed Archive
R01	WinRAR Split Compressed Archive
R02	WinRAR Split Compressed Archive
R03	WinRAR Split Compressed Archive
R04	WinRAR Split Compressed Archive
R05	WinRAR Split Compressed Archive
R06	WinRAR Split Compressed Archive
R07	WinRAR Split Compressed Archive
R08	WinRAR Split Compressed Archive
R09	WinRAR Split Compressed Archive
R1M	RealOne Metadata Package
R3D	Realsoft 3D Image
R8	RAW Graphic File
R8L	LaserJet Landscape Font
R8P	Intellifont PCL 4 Bitmap Font File
R8P	LaserJet Portrait Font
RA	RealMedia Streaming Media
RA	Remote Access Data File
RAD	Reality AdLib Tracker 2-op FM Music
RAM	RealMedia Metafile
RAP	Rapidocs Document
RAR	WinRAR Compressed Archive
RAS	Commonly used extension for Raster File
RAT	Rating System File
RAW	RAW RGB 24-bit Graphic and Raw Signed PCM Data
RAX	RealMedia Streaming File
RB0	Anti-Virus Backup
RB1	Anti-Virus Backup and R:Base Data
RB2	Anti-Virus Backup and R:Base Data
RB3	Anti-Virus Backup and R:Base Data
RB4	Anti-Virus Backup and R:Base Data
RB5	Anti-Virus Backup
RB6	Anti-Virus Backup
RB7	Anti-Virus Backup
RB8	Anti-Virus Backup
RB9	Anti-Virus Backup
RBB	Top Secret Crypto Gold File

(continued)

Extension	Description
RBF	Oracle Backup File and R:Base Data
RBF	Rollback File
RBH	RoboHelp Configuration
RBN	Real Sound File
RBO	Sometimes associated with the Magistr.B Worm
RBPM	Portable Bitmap
RBS	Rollback Script
RBX	XStream Multimedia Simulation Format
RBZ	Rail Baron Player Saved Game
RC	C++ Resource Compiler Script File and Resource Script
RC2	Developer Studio Non-editable Resources
RCD	PC Anywhere Recorded Session File
RCG	Netscape Newsgroup File
RCV	Resource Compiler; Resource Script
RC_	Winhelp Compressed File
RD	Philips Raw Data
RD3	CorelDream 3D
RDA	Oracle Storage Area File
RDB	Oracle Database Root File and Netscape Communicator Aim File
RDF	Oracle Report Binary Source
RDI	Device-Independent Bitmap
RDL	Paradox
RDO	Oracle Redo Log File
RDP	Remote Desktop Connection
README	Documentation File
REC	ARCSERVE Archivation Protocol and Commonly Used Extension for Recorded Macros
REF	Reference
REG	Registration Data
REL	ACT! Alarm Data File and Norton Internet Security 2001 Log File
REM	Annotation and ACT! Database Maintenance File
REN	Renamed File
REP	Report File
REQ	Request
RES	Resource
REV	FrameMaker Document and Revised File
REX	Oracle Report Definition
REZ	Resource File
RF	FrameMaker Document
RFG	RFG Integrator System Database
RFM	Rich Music Format
RFR	Photoshop Frame Filter File
RG	Bitmap Graphic
RGB	RGB Bitmap

Extension	Description
RGE	R.A.G.E. Driver
RH	C++ Resource Header File
RI	Lotus 1-2-3 File
RIF	Raster Image File Format
RIP	Remote Imaging Protocol and Notes Error File
RJS	RealJukebox Skin
RL4	Bitmap Graphic
RL8	Bitmap Graphic
RLB	Harvard Graphics
RLC	Run Length RLC Bitmap
RLE	Run Length Encoded Bitmap
RLL	SQL Server Resource Library
RMF	Acrobat Rights Management Document
RMI	MIDI File
RMJ	RealJukebox Media
RMS	RealMedia Secure Media File
RND	Pretty Good Privacy (PGP) Random Seed (PGP Corporation)
RNX	RealPlayer File
ROB	Microsoft Art Gallery File
ROL	AdLib Visual Composer Music File
ROM	Read Only Memory Image
ROY	TrueType
RPBM	Portable Image
RPF	AutoCAD Raster-pattern Fill Definition
RPG	RPG Programming Language
RPGM	Portable Greyscale
RPL	Replica Text File and Reply Message
RPM	RealMedia Player Plug-in
RPS	Borland Translation Repository
RPT	Report
RPV	Real Player Visualization File
RPX	Oracle Visual Information Retrieval Raw Pixel Format File
RQY	Excel OLE DB Query File
RRF	Musicmatch Jukebox File
RSA	PKCS7 Signature, MD5 + RSA
RSC	Resource File
RSG	EPOC Compiled Resource Header
RSL	PageMaker File, Paradox 7 Report and PC Tools Resources Library
RSML	Real Player File
RSP	Commonly used extension for a Response File
RSS	Rich Site Summary File
RS_	ArcView Image File
RT	Rich Text
RTC	Rescue Me File
RTF	Rich Text Format File
RTH	ANSYS Results
RTK	Run Time Library

(continued)

Extension	Description
RTP	Patch File and TurboTax Update File
RTS	RealAudio RTSL Document
RTX	Rich Text Document
RT_	Winhelp Compressed File
RU	Javasoft JRE 1.3 Library File
RUJ	Oracle Recovery-Unit Journal
RUL	Rule Repository
RUN	PC Tools Script Tools Program
RUS	Russian Text
RV	RealVideo Clip
RVML	Rich Vector Markup Language
RVW	Review
RWG	Random Word Generator
RWP	IBM Configurator Report
RWS	C++ Resource Workshop Symbol File
RWX	Netscape Live 3D
RWZ	Outlook Rules Wizard File
RX	DOS 7 File
RXC	Easy CD Creator Drag to Disk File
RXD	Reflex Database
RXF	Recipe Exchange Format
RXH	Reflex Database Help File
RXN	MDL Rxn File
RXP	Easy CD & DVD Creator 6 Playlist
RXR	Reflex Database Report
RXS	Reflex Database Screen Driver and AudioCentral Roxio Markup Sound
S	Source Code
S$$	Temporary Sort File
S01	WordPerfect Distribution File
S02	WordPerfect Distribution File
S03	WordPerfect Distribution File
S11	Sealed MPEG-1 Video
S14	Sealed MPEG-4 Video
S16	Sigames File
S17	SubSeven Saved Settings File
S19	Motorola Assembly-Language Program ASCII-HEX Data File
S1A	Sealed Acrobat Document
S1E	Sealed Excel Worksheet
S1G	Sealed GIF Image
S1H	Sealed HTML Document
S1J	Sealed JPEG Image
S1M	Sealed MP3 Audio
S1N	Sealed PNG Graphic
S1P	Sealed PowerPoint Presentation
S1Q	Sealed QuickTime Movie
S1W	Sealed Word Document
S3D	Micrografx Simply 3D Project
S7P	SubSeven Trojan File
S??	RAR Compressed File
SAK	Software Administration Kit

Extension	Description
SAL	Database Program; SQL Application Language
SAM	Ami Pro Document and Office 97 File Converter
SAS	VMS SAS Source Code
SAT	Surprise! AdLib Tracker
SAV	Saved File
SBC	SBC Compressed Archive
SBI	Selfboot Inducer and Sound Blaster Instrument File
SBK	Creative Labs SB AWE 32
SBL	Softbridge Basic Language
SBP	Superbase DML Program
SC	Framework Screen Driver
SC$	Modem Bitware Fax Disk1 File
SC2	Schedule+ File
SC3	dBASE Screen Mask File
SCA	Norton Anti-Virus File
SCB	System Cleaner
SCF	Windows Explorer Command
SCH	Schedule+ File
SCI	System Configuration Information
SCM	ICQ Sound Compressed Sound Scheme
SCN	Compressed Screen Format
SCP	Dial-Up Networking Script
SCR	Screen Font or Screen Dump and Windows Screen Saver File
SCT	Foxpro Screen and Scripting Tools
SCT	Lotus Screen Capture Text
SCX	FoxPro Screen File
SD	Simple Diary
SD2	Base SAS Database
SDA	OpenOffice.org Drawing and Star Office Drawing
SDB	Simply Accounting File and Windows Compatibility Solution Database
SDC	OpenOffice.org Spreadsheet and StarOffice Spreadsheet
SDD	OpenOffice.org Presentation and StarOffice Presentation
SDF	Standard Data Format and Schedule Data File
SDG	Star Office Gallery
SDI	Borland Single Document Interface and Quickbooks Data
SDK	AutoSketch Drawing
SDL	Paradox Script
SDN	Shell Archive
SDO	Sealed Word Document
SDOC	Sealed Word File

(continued)

Extension	Description
SDP	Real Player File and StarOffice Picture File
SDS	OpenOffice.org Chart and StarOffice Chart
SDT	QuickBooks Data
SDW	OpenOffice.org Text and StarOffice Text
SE1	Flight Simulator Scenery File
SEA	StuffIT Expander Archive Format
SEB	Franklin eBookMan Format
SEC	MP3 Music File
SED	Sed/unix Doc File
SEL	Paint Shop Pro Selection File
SEM	Sealed E-mail and Alpha Five Set Object File
SEP	TIFF Bitmap Separation
SEQ	Commonly Used Extension for Sequence File
SERVER	Analog File
SES	Commonly Used Extension for Session File
SET	Configuration File and Backup File Set
SEX	Alpha Five Set Index
SE_	Cakepro Compressed Audio File
SF	Signature Instructions File
SF0	Windows Sytem File Check File
SF2	Creative Labs Soundfont 2.0 Bank File
SFB	HP Soft Font
SFC	Windows System File Check File
SFF	Scene File Format
SFI	Ventura Printer Font
SFL	LaserJet Landscape Font
SFO	CuteFTP Search File
SFP	LaserJet Portrait Font
SFS	OpenOffice.org Frame and StarOffice Frame
SFX	Self-extracting Archive
SFZ	SFzip SoundFont File Archive
SGF	StarWriter Document
SGI	Sealed GIF Image
SGIF	Sealed GIF File
SGL	OpenOffice.org Master Document and StarOffice Master Document
SGM	Standard Generalized Markup Language IETF Document
SGML	Standard Generalized Markup Language IETF Document
SGT	Signature Keyboard Macro
SH	UNIX/LINUX Shell Script
SHA	CorelDRAW Shader
SHB	Windows Shortcut into a Document
SHD	Print Spooler Shadow File
SHE	Windows 95 .ShellExt

Extension	Description
SHM	WordPerfect Shell Macro
SHP	Commonly Used Extension for a Shape File
SHT	S-HTML Document
SHTM	HTML File Containing Server Side Directives
SHTML	HTML File Containing Server Side Directives
SHTML3	SHTML File
SHW	Presentation SlideShow
SIC	Quicken 2002 Order File
SIF	Windows NT Setup Information File
SIG	Signature File
SIK	Backup
SIM	Simulation
SITX	StuffIt StuffIt X Archive
SJF	Split Files Shell Extension
SJP	Sealed JPEG Image
SJPG	Sealed JPEG File
SKF	AutoSketch
SKN	Commonly Used Extension for Skin Files
SLB	AutoCAD Slide Library
SLD	AutoCAD Slide
SLG	AutoCAD Status Log
SLL	Static Link Library
SLM	Visual FoxPro
SLN	Visual Studio .NET Solution
SLT	Selection
SMD	OpenOffice.org Mail and StarOffice Mail Document
SMF	OpenOffice.org Formula and StarOffice Formula
SMI	CC:Mail Smart Icon
SML	Simple Markup Language
SMP	Ad Lib Gold Sample
SMP3	Sealed MP3 File
SMPEG	Sealed MPEG Movie
SMPG	Sealed MPG Movie
SMT	QuickBooks
SMV	Streaming Mobile Video File
SN	Serial Number File
SNC	ACT! E-mail/Folder Synchronization File
SND	Commonly Used Extension for a Sound File
SNF	UNIX Font File
SNP	Commonly Used Extension for a Snapshop File
SNX	QuickBooks Data
SOB	Visual Basic
SOM	Paradox Sort Info
SPC	Multiplan Program

(continued)

Extension	Description
SPD	Postscript Mini-driver and Harvard Graphics Bitstream Typefaces
SPDF	Sealed PDF File
SPEC	General Specification File
SPF	Setup File
SPIFF	Still Picture Interchange File Format Bitmap
SPJ	Site Publisher Project File
SPK	Acorn Spark Compressed Archive
SPL	Compressed Archive File and Printer Spool File
SPM	WordPerfect
SPN	Sealed PNG Graphic
SPNG	Sealed PNG Graphic
SPP	Sealed PowerPoint Presentation
SPPT	Sealed PowerPoint File
SPR	Foxpro Generated Screen Program
SPS	Oracle Package Specification
SPT	Split File
SPX	Foxpro Compiler Screen Program
SQB	SyQuest Backup
SQC	Structured Query Language Common Code File
SQL	Structured Query Language Data
SQW	Archive
SQZ	Compressed Archive File
SR	Netscape File
SRB	Corel ClipArt ScrapBook
SRC	Sourcecode
SREC	ASCII Load File
SRP	QuickLink Script
SRQ	Unprocessed Microsoft Server Request
SRT	DVD Subtitle File
SRV	Help Maker File
SSC	HP Library and Tape Tools Script
SSF	Enable Spreadsheet File and Sound Set File
SSL	Paradox 5 File
SSW	Sealed Flash File
SSWF	Sealed Flash File
STA	Eudora File
STB	AutoCAD R2000 Plot Style Table
STC	OpenOffice.org Spreadsheet Template
STD	OpenOffice.org Drawing Template
STF	Setup Information
STG	SNMP Traffic Grapher Network Graphic
STI	OpenOffice.org Presentation Template
STL	C++ Standard Template Library
STM	SHTML File and Sound Set File
STML	Sealed HTML File
STML	SHTML File
STR	dBASE Structure List

Extension	Description
STS	C Project Status Info
STW	OpenOffice.org Text Document Template and Staroffice Writer Template
STY	Commonly used extension for Style Files
SUB	DIVX Subtitles
SUM	Summary
SUP	Startup Screen Bitmap and Supplemental Data
SUR	Surveyor Document
SVC	Simple Visual Compiler
SVF	Simple Vector Format
SVG	Scalable Vector Graphics File
SVGZ	Compressed Scalable Vector Graphics File
SWA	Shockwave Audio File
SWB	PageMaker or Photoshop Version 7 ColorSync Component
SWFS	Dreamweaver File
SWL	Macromedia Flash Format
SWP	Swap File
SWT	Macromedia Authoring Flash File
SXC	OpenOffice.org Spreadsheet and Staroffice Spreadsheet File
SXD	OpenOffice.org Draw File
SXG	OpenOffice.org Master Document
SXI	OpenOffice.org Presentation File
SXL	Sealed Excel Worksheet
SXLS	Sealed Excel File
SXM	OpenOffice.org Math File
SXM	Sealed XML Document
SXML	Sealed XML Document
SXW	OpenOffice.org Text Document and Staroffice Writer Document
SY3	Harvard Graphics Symbol File
SYM	Commonly Used Extension for Symbol Libraries and C++ Precompiled Headers
SYN	Synonym File
SYS	System Configuration and System Device Driver
SYW	Harvard Graphics Symbol Graphic
SY_	Compressed SYS File
T	Paradox Database File
T$	Modem Bitware Fax Disk5 File
T02	TaxCut 2002 Tax Return File
T03	TaxCut 2003 Tax Return File
T2	TrueType Font
T2W	NTgraph Turbo Pascal File
T3	Tarshare File
T32	Drive Image5 File
T3D	Fifa2000 Environment Data
T44	dBASE IV Temporary File

(continued)

Extension	Description
T65	PageMaker Template
T98	Kiplinger Tax Cut File
T99	Kiplinger Tax Cut File
T??	Ingres Table/Index File
T??	RAR Compressed File
TA0	TaxACT Tax Year 2000 Form
TA1	TaxACT Tax Year 2001 Form
TA2	TaxACT Tax Year 2002 Form
TA8	TaxACT Tax Year 1998 Form
TA9	TaxACT Tax Year 1999 Form
TAB	Commonly Used Extension for a Table File
TAH	Turbo Assembler Help File
TAI	INMOS Transputer Development System Occam Analyse Info
TAL	Typed Assembly Language File
TAP	Tape File
TAR	Tape Archive File
TAT	Text File
TAX	TurboTax Tax Return
TAZ	Compressed File
TB1	Turbo C Font
TB2	Turbo C Font
TBD	MSE File and Visual Studio File
TBH	Turbo Basic Help File
TBL	Commonly used extension for Table Files
TBR	Norton Desktop Custom Toolbar
TBR	SoftQuad XMetaL Toolbar/Menu Configuration
TBS	German Word Text Elements
TBX	Project Scheduler Table
TC	Borland Configuration File
TCC	Turbo C / GCC Include Std File
TCH	Borland Help File
TCT	TurboCAD Template
TCW	TurboCAD Drawing
TCX	TurboCAD Drawing as Text
TD	Turbo Debugger for DOS Configuration File
TD2	Turbo Debugger for Win32 Configuration File
TDB	ACT! Transaction Data File
TDF	Setup Program Data and Typeface Definition File
TDO	Compressed File
TDT	ASCII Data File in CSV Format
TEL	Telnet Host File
TEM	Turbo Editor Macro Language
TEMP	Temporary File
TER	CorelFlow Line Terminator
TET	Tetris Results

Extension	Description
TEX	Text File or Texture File
TEXT	ASCII Text
TFR	IBM Client Access File Transfer
TGT	Watcom C/C++ Individual Target
TH	Javasoft JRE 1.3 Library File
THEME	Plus! Theme File
THM	Thumbnail Bitmap Image
THML	Theological HTML
THN	Graphics Workshop for Windows Thumbnail
THS	WordPerfect Thesauraus
TIF	Tagged Image Format File
TIFF	Tagged Image Format File
TIM	TIFF Image (rev 6)
TLB	Commonly Used Extension for Type Library Files
TLD	Tag Library Descriptor
TLF	Short Message Service File
TM	HP Internet Advisor Capture File
TMD	Lotus TvMap Document
TMF	WordPerfect Tagged Font Metric File
TMO	Zortech C++ Global Optimizer Output File
TMP	Temporary File/Folder
TMPL	Website META Language Template
TNC	SuperJPG ThumbNail Cache File
TNEF	Transport Neutral Encapsulation Format File
TNF	Transport Neutral Encapsulation Format File
TNL	Thumbnail
TOC	Table of Contents
TOK	C++ 4.x External Token
TP	Turbo Pascal Configuration File
TP3	Harvard Graphics Template
TPA	Corel Graphics10 Custom File
TPH	Turbo Pascal Help File
TPL	Access Workflow Designer
TPL	Commonly Used Extension for Template Files
TPM	TextPad Macro
TPP	Turbo Pascal Protected Mode Unit
TPU	Turbo Pascal Compiled Unit
TPZ	Compressed File
TQL	Tree Query Language File and SQL Server Query Analyzer Header File
TR	Turbo Debugger Session-state Settings
TR1	Novell LANalyzer Capture File
TRC	Commonly Used Extension for Debug Files
TRE	PC Tools Directory Tree
TRG	Symantec LiveUpdate File

(continued)

Extension	Description
TRI	LiveUpdate Product Update List
TRM	Terminal Settings
TRN	PageMaker and SQL Server Transaction Backup
TRU	True BASIC Source Code
TRW	Turbo Debugger Session-state Settings
TSC	Win Help Related File
TSG	Enable File
TSN	MIDI File
TSP	Windows Telephony Service Provider
TSQ	ODBC Script
TST	WordPerfect Printer Test File
TTC	TrueType Compressed Font and TrueType Font Collection
TTF	TrueType Font
TTR	TrueType Font
TT_	Compressed TTF File
TURBOC3	Turbo C Make File
TUT	Tutorial
TUW	Office File
TV	Paradox Table View Settings
TVF	dBASE Table View Settings
TVL	TurboTax
TVR	Boot File
TVS	VectorMAX Streaming Video
TVT	RealPlayer
TVVI	InterVideo WInDVR
TWE	ThinkWave Educator Data File
TX8	DOS Text File
TXE	Enriched Text File
TXF	Compressed File
TXF	Tax Exchange Format
TXR	Corel Graphics Ver 10 Custom File
TXT	Text File
TX_	Compressed TXT File
TZ	Compressed File
TZB	Compressed File
TZT	CP/M Information File
U	Subsampled Raw YUV Bitmap
U8	Raw Unsigned 8-Bit Audio Data
U96	EasyZip Temporary File
UAP	User Agent Wireless Telephony Profile
UB	Raw Unsigned Byte
UBB	BASIC UBAS File
UBD	BASIC UBAS File
UC2	Compressed File
UCN	Compressed Archive
UCS	Universal Classification Standard Database File
UDB	Works File and Windows 2000 Uniqueness Database File

Extension	Description
UDF	Excel User Defined Function and Windows NT Uniqueness Database File
UDL	Data Link
UDW	Raw Unsigned Double-Word
UE2	Encrypted Archive
UEF	Unified Emulator Format
UFA	UFA Compressed File Archive
UHA	UHARC Compressed Archive
UHS	Universal Hint System File
UI	User Interface
UKS	Works File
ULS	Internet Location Service
UMB	MemMaker Backup Archive
UMI	CDDB Database and PC Music Library in PlayCenter
UND	A86 Assembler Undefined Symbols
UNF	Btreive Unformatted File
UNQ	Fax View File
UNT	AutoCAD Unit Definition
UNX	Text File
UPD	dBASE Update File and Universal Print Driver
UPF	Universal Picture Format Bitmap
UPG	Firmware Upgrade File
UPO	dBASE Compiled Update File
UPR	FileMaker User Spelling Dictionary
UPS	Works File
UPT	Connectivity Memory Model Update Timing Input File
URI	List of Uniform Resource Identifiers
URIS	List of Uniform Resource Identifiers
URL	Internet Location
URLS	GetRight URL List
USA	Office Header File
USL	LaserJet Landscape Font
USP	LaserJet Portrait Font and PageMaker Printer Font
USR	User Database
USTAR	POSIX tar Compressed Archive
UTL	QuickBooks Data
UU	Compressed Archive File
UUD	Uudecoded
UUE	Uuencoded
UW	Raw Unsigned Word
UWL	WordPerfect User Word List (Corel)
UX	UNIX File
UZE	Ultimate Zip Compresion Agent
V	Subsampled Raw YUV Bitmap
V$$	Cheyenne/Inoculan AntiVirus Temporary File
VAF	Visual Studio Common Tools Vanalyzer Project Item

(continued)

Extension	Description
VAL	dBASE Values and Paradox Validity Checks
VAM	Visual Studio Common Tools Vanalyzer Project Item
VAP	Annotated Speech Audio
VAR	Commonly used extension for Variables File
VB	VBScript File or Any VisualBasic Source
VBA	VBase File
VBB	VirtualBoss Backup File (VirtualBoss Development Co.)
VBD	ActiveX
VBD	Visual Basic 5 Active Document
VBF	Outlook Free/Busy File
VBG	Visual Basic Group Project
VBK	VisualCADD Backup File
VBL	User Control Licensing File
VBN	Norton Corporate Anti-Virus Quarantined File
VBO	Access Package Deployment References
VBP	Visual Basic Ver. 4.0-6.0 Project
VBPROJ	Visual Studio .NET Visual Basic Project
VBPROJ. USER	Visual Studio .NET File
VBR	Remote Automation Registration Files
VBS	MPEG Movie Clip and VBScript Script File
VBS	VBScript Script File
VBW	Visual Basic Project Workplace
VBX	Visual Basic Extension
VBZ	Wizard Launch File
VCA	Visual Clip Art
VCD	VisualCADD Drawing File
VCL	Borland Visual Component Library
VCM	Visual Component File
VCP	Visual C++ Wordspace Information
VCS	vCalendar File
VCT	FoxPro Class Library
VCW	Visual C++ Workbench Information File
VCWIN32	Visual C Make File
VCX	FoxPro Class Library or Spreadsheet File
VDA	CAD File
VDB	Norton AntiVirus Update File
VDB	PC-cillin Quarantined File
VDF	Commonly Used Extension for Anti-virus Definition Files
VDM	VDM Play
VDP	Visual Studio .NET Setup and Deployment Project

Extension	Description
VDPROJ	Visual Studio .NET Setup and Deployment Project
VDX	Vector Graphic File and Virtual Device Driver
VEM	Voice E-mail File
VER	TurboTax Installed Version Record
VEW	Lotus Approach or Novel Groupwise View File
VFA	FontLab Database File
VFB	Font Description File
VFD	Virtual Floppy Drive Image
VFF	DESR VFF Greyscale Bitmap Image
VFM	Ventura Publisher Font Metrics File
VFW	Video for Windows
VGA	VGA Screen Driver
VGR	Ventura Graphic
VHD	Virtual PC File
VHDL	VHDL Design File
VH~	V-help File
VID	Media Player Video
VIR	Virus Infected File
VKL	Virtual Edit
VL	Visual Labels File
VLB	Corel Ventura Library
VLM	Novell Virtual Loadable Module
VMB	Quicken 2002 Order File
VMC	Virtual Memory Configuration
VMDC	VMware Virtual Disk File
VMDK	VMware Virtual Disk File
VME	Virtual Matrix Encryption File
VMF	FaxWorks Audio File
VNC	Virtual Network Computing
VOC	Creative Labs Sound and Other Sound Files
VOR	OpenOffice.org Template
VP	Ventura Publisher File
VPF	Vector Product Format
VPS	Visual Pinball Script
VPT	Visual Pinball Table
VRB	Dictionary File
VRF	Oracle 7 Configuration File
VRM	Quattro Pro Overlay File
VRML	Virtual Reality Modeling Language
VRO	DVD Recorder File
VRS	WordPerfect Graphics Driver
VRT	Virtual World
VRW	VREAMScript Command Language ActiveX 3D
VS	Vivid Include File
VS2	Roland-Bass Transfer File
VSB	VSampler Soundbank
VSC	VirusScan Configuration

(continued)

Extension	Description
VSD	Visio Drawing
VSH	VirusShield Configuration File
VSK	Microsoft Development Common IDE File
VSL	Visio Library
VSM	VisSim Simulation Model
VSR	Access Branded Report Format
VSS	Visio Stencil
VST	Visio Template
VSW	Visio Workspace File
VSX	XML for Visio Stencil File
VTM	Cold Fusion Studio Query
VTS	VTune Performance Monitor Project File (Intel)
VTX	XML for Visio Template File
VUE	dBASE View File and Schedule+ Configuration File
VWR	PC Tools File Viewer
VWT	MGI VideoWave Video Wave Thumbnail
VXD	Virtual Device Driver
VXML	VoiceXML Source File
VXP	VTune Performance Monitor Pack and Go File (Intel)
VXS	Voice Xpress User Profile
VXX	IOsubsys Driver File
W$	Modem Bitware Fax Disk3 File
W20	Windows 2000 Related File
W31	Windows 3.1 Startup File
W32	Win32 File
W40	Win95 Backup File
W44	dBASE Temporary File
W51	WordPerfect Ver. 5.1 Document
W60	WordPerfect Ver. 6.0 Document
W61	WordPerfect Ver. 6.1 Document
W95	Windows95-related Data File
W98	Windows98-related Data File
WAB	Outlook Address Book
WAD	Programming Library
WAL	Winamp3 Skin Format
WAP	WAVPAC Filtered .WAV File Output
WAR	Java Web Archive
WAS	Procomm Plus Script Source Code File
WAT	IBM Voice Type Language Map File
WAV	Waveform Audio
WAVE	Waveform Audio
WAX	Windows Media Audio Redirector
WA_	Doko Compressed Install File
WA~	Outlook Address Book Temporary File
WB	Dictionary Project Data File
WB1	QuattroPro for Windows
WB2	QuattroPro for Windows
WB3	QuattroPro for Windows

Extension	Description
WBD	Works Database File
WBF	Windows Batch File
WBK	Word Backup and WordPerfect Workbook
WBMP	Wireless Bitmap File Format
WCD	WordPerfect Macro Token List
WCH	Corel Office PerfectScript
WCM	Corel Presentations and WordPerfect Macro
WCP	WordPerfect Product Information
WDB	Works Database
WDL	Windows XP Watchdog Log File
WDM	Visual Interdev98 Templates Web Project Items File
WEB	Corel Xara Web Document
WEBPNP	Support for Internet Printing
WED	Windows Editor File
WFM	dBASE Form Designer Form Object
WFN	Corel Symbols and Fonts
WFO	Delphi Runimage Delphi Demos Doc Formdll DB File
WFP	Turtle Beach WaveFront Program
WFS	Windows Installation Script
WFT	WaveFront 3D Object
WFW	Pci Smc File
WFX	WinFax Data File
WG1	Lotus 1-2-3 Worksheet
WG2	Lotus 1-2-3 Worksheet
WGL	Wingate License File
WHT	NetMeeting Old Whiteboard Document
WI	Wavelet Image and All Corel Products Compressed Image
WIF	Wavelet Image File and Window Intermediate File Template
WIL	WinImage File
WIN	FoxPro/dBASE Window File and Windows Backup File
WIP	Windows Installer Project
WIZ	Word Wizard File
WK!	Lotus Spreadsheet File
WK1	1-2-3 Spreadsheet File
WK3	Lotus Spreadsheet File
WK4	Lotus Spreadsheet File
WKB	Workbook and WordPerfect and WordPerfect for Windows Document
WKQ	Quattro Spreadsheet
WKS	Lotus or Works for Windows Spreadsheet File
WKZ	Compressed Spreadsheet
WLD	Acrobat Distiller
WLG	Dr. Watson Log
WLL	Word Add-in

(continued)

Extension	Description
WLZ	WinImage File
WM	Windows Media A/V File
WM$	BASIC VB
WM2D	Working Model Motion Simulation
WM5	Dyndlg2 File
WMA	Windows Media Audio File
WMC	WordPerfect Macro
WMD	Windows Media Download File
WMDB	Media Player Ver. 9+ Library
WME	Windows Media Encoder Session Profile
WMF	Windows Metafile
WML	Wireless Markup Language File
WMP	Windows Media Player File
WMR	Windows Media Recorder Media Stream
WMS	Windows Media Skin File
WMV	Windows Media File
WMX	Audio Playlist
WMZ	Windows Media Compressed Skin File
WNF	Outline Font
WOA	Windows Swap File
WOC	Windows OrgChart Organization
WP	WordPerfect Document
WP4	WordPerfect Ver. 4 Document
WP5	WordPerfect Ver. 5.0/5.1/5.2 Document
WP6	WordPerfect Ver. 6.0/6.1 Document
WPA	ACT! Word Processor Document
WPB	openCanvas Image
WPC	Word and Write File Converter
WPD	Windows Printer Driver and ACT! Word Processor Document
WPF	WordPerfect Text File
WPG	WordPerfect/Drawperfect Graphic
WPJ	Watcom C/C++ Project
WPK	Keyboard Information File and WordPerfect Macro
WPL	PFS WinWorks Spreadsheet
WPM	WordPerfect Macro
WPP	WordPerfect Color Palette
WPS	Works Text Document
WPT	WordPerfect Template
WPW	PerfectWorks Document and WordPerfect Document
WPX	Printer Information File
WQ	Spreadsheet
WQ!	Compressed Quattro Pro Spreadsheet
WQ1	Quattro Pro Spreadsheet
WQ2	Quattro Pro Spreadsheet
WR!	Compressed Lotus Spreadsheet
WRI	Write Document
WRK	Spreadsheet File
WRML	Plain Text VRML File

Extension	Description
WRS	WordPerfect Windows Printer Driver
WS	Windows Script File and WordStar Ver. 5.0/6.0 Document
WS1	WordStar for Windows Ver. 1 Document
WS2	WordStar for Windows Ver. 2 Document
WS3	WordStar for Windows Ver. 3 Document
WS4	WordStar for Windows Ver. 4 Document
WS4D	Web Server 4D Custom Web Page
WS5	WordStar for Windows Ver. 5 Document
WS6	WordStar for Windows Ver. 6 Document
WS7	WordStar for Windows Ver. 7 Document
WSA	Animation Shop Workspace
WSC	Windows Script Component
WSD	WordStar Ver. 2000 Document
WSDL	Web Services Description Language
WSF	Windows Script File
WSH	Windows Script Host Settings File
WSI	Wise Windows Installer Project
WSP	Paint Shop Pro Workspace and Visual C++, FORTRAN Workspace Info
WST	WordStar Text File
WSX	WinMX Protocol List
WSZ	WinAmp Skin Zip File
WS_	Visc15 Adressen Setup File
WT	WildTangent Branded .X 3D Model
WT2	WordExpress Document Template
WTA	WinTune DLL
WTC	Watertec Encrypted Database (Watertite Limited)
WTD	WinTune Document
WTH	WildTangent Says Hello
WTK	WinTalk URL Address
WTR	Winter Windows Scheduler File
WTS	WION Technology Setup (WION Technology)
WTX	ASCII Text
WVE	Component of a DIVX Movie Conversion
WVL	Wavelet Compressed Bitmap
WVX	Windows Media Redirector
WVZ	Brazilian Music Format
WWB	WordPerfect Button Bar
WWD	Works Wizard File
WWF	WWF Rant Pakk Sound File
WWK	WordPerfect Keyboard Layout
WWL	Word Add-in File

(continued)

Extension	Description
WWP	Works Wizard File
WWS	Works Wizard File
WZ	WinAmp Skin
WZS	MS Word Wizard
X	Direct3D Object
X01	Paradox Secondary Index
X02	Paradox Secondary Index
X03	Paradox Secondary Index
X04	Paradox Secondary Index
X05	Paradox Secondary Index
X06	Paradox Secondary Index
X07	Paradox Secondary Index
X08	Paradox Secondary Index
X09	Paradox Secondary Index
X10	X Window Dump Bitmap
X11	X Windows System Window Dump Bitmap
X13	Hooligans
X16	Macromedia Program Extension
X32	Macromedia Program Extension
X3D	Xara 3D Project File
X3F	Sigma Camera RAW Picture File (Sigma)
X4M	TeamLinks Mail File Data
X5	Rockwell Software Logix 5 File
X64	C64 Emulator Disk Image
XA	Extended Architecture File
XAB	Mail Address Book
XAD	eXotic AdLib Format
XAR	Corel Xara Drawing
XBF	Database File
XBL	Extensible Binding Language
XBM	X Bitmap Graphic
XB~	IC File
XC	X Server Constant Screen Image Bitmap
XCF	GIMP Image File
XDB	Norton AntiVirus Update File
XDF	Extended Disk Format Image
XDK	XML Development Kit Project
XDP	UNIX File
XDS	OpenGL Performer Script
XEX	KERMIT Control File
XFD	XML Form in XFDL Format
XFDF	Acrobat Forms Document
XFM	OmniForm XML Format
XFN	Ventura Printer Font
XFR	Ventura Publisher Bitmap Editor Font File
XFX	Fax File
XG0	Database Index; Paradox Secondary Index

Extension	Description
XG1	Database Index
XG1	Techno Toys XG-909 MIDI Drum Machine File
XG2	Database Index
XG3	Database Index
XG4	Database Index
XG5	Database Index
XGO	Paradox Database-related File
XHDML	XML Version of HDML File
XHT	Extensible HyperText Markup Language File
XHTM	Extensible HyperText Markup Language File
XHTML	Extensible HyperText Markup Language File
XHTML	Libxml HTML File
XIF	Xerox Image File
XJS	WinExplorer Java Script
XJT	Compressed GIMP Image with Properties of GIMP
XJTGZ	Compressed GIMP Image with Properties of GIMP
XJTZ2	Compressed GIMP Image with Properties of GIMP
XL	Excel Spreadsheet
XLA	Excel Add-in
XLB	Excel Worksheet
XLC	Excel Chart
XLD	Excel Dialog
XLK	Excel Backup
XLL	Excel Add-in
XLM	Excel Macro
XLR	Works
XLS	Excel or Works Worksheet
XLSHTML	Excel HTML Document
XLSMHTML	Excel Archived HTML Document
XLT	Excel Template
XLTHTML	Excel HTML Template
XLV	Excel VBA
XLW	Excel Workspace
XLXML	Excel XML Worksheet
XMI	Winamp Extended MIDI File
XML	Extensible Markup Language File
XMLBACKUP	EnABLE Backup File
XMP	Graphic File
XMS	AutoCAD External Message
XMX	AutoCAD External Message Compiled File
XNK	Exchange Shortcut
XNML	NML Language Language Extension
XP	System Utility File
XPL	Music File

(continued)

Extension	Description	Extension	Description
XQT	SuperCalc Macro Sheet	YYC	Wave Sapphire Distribution File
XRF	Cross Reference	YZ	YAC Compressed Archive File
XSC	XML Schema	YZ1	DeepFreezer Compressed Archive
XSD	XML Schema	Z	UNIX Compressed Archive File
XSL	XML Stylesheet	Z0	ZoneAlarm Mailsafe Renamed .JS File
XSLT	XSL Transform File	Z01	WinZip Split Compressed Archive
XSU	Fortran Libf77 File	Z02	WinZip Split Compressed Archive
XTD	XML Type Definition	Z03	WinZip Split Compressed Archive
XTP	XTree Data File	Z04	WinZip Split Compressed Archive
XUL	XML User Interface Language	Z05	WinZip Split Compressed Archive
XVP	Xview Package File	Z1	ZoneAlarm File
XVS	Xview Scene Package File	Z2	ZoneAlarm Mailsafe
XWD	X Windows Dump	Z3	ZoneAlarm Mailsafe
XWP	Xerox Writer Text File	Z3D	Zmodeler Model File
XWS	Xara Webstyle File	Z4	ZoneAlarm Mailsafe
XX	Xxencoded File	Z5	ZoneAlarm Mailsafe
XXE	Xxencoded File	Z6	ZoneAlarm Mailsafe
XXL	Archive	Z7	ZoneAlarm Mailsafe
XXT	Extension DLL	Z8	ZoneAlarm Mailsafe
Y	Desktop Color Separation Specification Yellow Layer	Z9	ZoneAlarm Mailsafe
Y01	Paradox Secondary Index	ZABW	AbiWord Compressed Document
Y02	Paradox Secondary Index	ZAP	FileWrangler Compressed File
Y03	Paradox Secondary Index	ZBF	Z-Buffer Radiance File
Y04	Paradox Secondary Index	ZBX	Disk Volume Identification
Y05	Paradox Secondary Index	ZC	Zipkey Configuration File
Y06	Paradox Secondary Index	ZDB	EPSQ Security Officer Submission
Y07	Paradox Secondary Index	ZFD	ABC Programming Language Zeroadic Function
Y08	Paradox Secondary Index	ZFS	C++ Assembly Source
Y09	Paradox Secondary Index	ZH	Communicator Java Classes File
YBK	Encarta Yearbook	ZH_TW	Communicator Java Classes File
YBS	YBS Compressed Archive	ZIP	Compressed Archive File
YC	YAC Compressed Archive	ZKA	Quicken6 File
YEL	Yellow Color Separation	ZL	Easy CD Creator Drag to Disk File
YENC	yEnc Encoded File	ZMK	Z-Up Maker Project File
YG0	Paradox Secondary Index	ZMS	ECLIPSE Server Macro Script File
YG1	Paradox Secondary Index	ZMV	ZSNES Movie File
YG2	Paradox Secondary Index	ZOO	ZOO Compressed Archive File
YG3	Paradox Secondary Index	ZPD	ABC Programming Language Zeroadic Function
YG4	Paradox Secondary Index	ZPJ	ECLIPSE Server Project File
YGM	YahooGroupManager Ver. 1.x Database	ZPK	Z-Firm Package
YGM2	YahooGroupManager Ver. 2.x Database	ZPL	ZIG File
YGO	Paradox Database-related File	ZPW	ZippedWeb Archive
YIF	Graphic	ZS	ECLIPSE Server Script File
YMG	Yahoo! Messenger File	ZTE	E-Tabs Reader File
YNC	yEnc Encoded File	ZTL	ZBrush ZTool Native File
YPL	Yahoo! Player Playlist	ZTM	ZTreeWin Macro
YPS	Yahoo! Messenger File	ZW	Chinese Text
YPT	Cryptic File	ZWL	WinLabel Ver. 3.0 Label
YSP	Bitmap Graphic	ZZ	ZZip Compressed Archive
YUV	Color Space Pixel Format	ZZE	ASCII Encoded File Archive
YUV3	CCIR 601 2:1:1 Bitmap		

INDEX